International specification for in-service data feedback
(Part 2 / 2)

S5000F-B6865-05000-00

Issue No. 3.0

S-Series IPS specifications
Block release 2021

Publishers:

AeroSpace and Defence
Industries Association of Europe

Aerospace Industries
Association of America

Applicable to: All

S5000F-A-00-00-0000-00A-001A-A

This specification has been developed by the following organizations (in alphabetic order):

–	A2L Consultants	France
–	Airbus Defense & Space	Spain & Germany
–	Airbus Helicopters	France
–	Andromeda Systems, Inc	United States of America
–	Boeing	United States of America
–	Bundeswehr	Germany
–	Cimpa	France
–	Connectiv-IT	France
–	Dassault Aviation	France
–	ESG	Germany
–	General Electric Aviation	United States of America
–	Leonardo	Italy
–	Lockheed Martin	United States of America
–	Ministry of Defence	Netherlands
–	Ministry of Defence	United Kingdom
–	Nexter Systems	France
–	NH Industries	France
–	O'Neill Associates	United States of America
–	Rockwell Collins	United States of America
–	Rolls-Royce	United Kingdom
–	Saab	Sweden
–	Shipdex	International (based in Cyprus)

Editor:

–	O'Neil Associates	United States of America

The following people contributed to the development of this specification (in alphabetic order):

BARTER, Michael	DE DIEGO GÓMEZ, Carlos	OELGARTE, Christian
BARTLETT, Andrew	ERDL, Magnus	OLLIVIER, Guillaume
BLÁZQUEZ DE LA TORRE, Aranzazu	GARSAUD, Pascal	ORLANDINI, Serena
BOUSQUET, Etienne	GIOVANELLI, Franck	RAUST, Bernard
BRACKLOW, Dirk	HE, Edward	RIDDERBUSCH, Daniel #
BURKHARDT, Hartmut	HUGHES, Denis	ROUX, Francois-Xavier
CASETTA, Andrea	KRÄMER, Oliver ‡	SCHMEDAKE, Robert #
CHACHRA, Vijay	MALMÉN, Mikael #	SCHMIDT, Michael
CICARELLI, Gaetano	MARTÍNEZ ORTEGA, Juan José	SOIMAKALLIO, Asko
DARTAGUIETTE, Jean-Baptiste	MARTORANO, Luca	SOMOZA, Ramón *
DAY, Michael	MITJANS, Félix	VATTERONI, Marco

* = Chair   # = Former Chair/Vice-Chair   ‡ = Secretary

Copyright and user agreement

1 Copyright

2 Agreement for use of the S5000F™ suite of information

2.1 Definitions

S5000F™ suite of information means, but is not limited to:

- the International specification for in-service data feedback - S5000F
- any other software, examples or any other information under the heading "**S5000F™ suite of information**", available for download from www.S5000F.org

Copyright holder means AeroSpace and Defense Industries Association of Europe (ASD).

2.2 Notice to user

By using all or any portion of the **S5000F™ suite of information** you accept the terms and conditions of this user agreement.

This user agreement is enforceable against you and any legal entity that has obtained the **S5000F™ suite of information** or any portion thereof and on whose behalf, it is used.

2.3 License to use

If you comply with the terms of this user agreement, then the copyright holders grant to you a non-exclusive license to use the **S5000F™ suite of information.**

2.4 Intellectual property rights

S5000F™ suite of information is the intellectual property of, and is owned by, the copyright holder. Except as expressly stated herein, this user agreement does not grant you any intellectual property right in the **S5000F™ suite of information** and all rights not expressly granted are reserved by the copyright holder.

2.5 No modifications

You must not modify or adapt, in whole or in part, the **S5000F™ suite of information**. You may however add business rules or tailor it for use on a specific program.

2.6 Translation

You must not translate, in whole or in part, the **S5000F™ suite of information**, except if explicit permission is granted in writing by ASD.

2.7 No warranty

The S5000F™ suite of information is being delivered to you "as is". The copyright holder does not warrant the performance or result you may obtain by using the **S5000F™ suite of information**. The copyright holder makes no warranties, representations or indemnities, express or implied, whether by statute, common law, custom, usage or otherwise as to any matter including without limitation merchantability, integration, satisfactory quality, fitness for any particular purpose, or non-infringement of third parties' rights.

2.8 Limitation of liability

In no event will the copyright holder be liable to you for any damages, claims or costs whatsoever or any consequential, indirect or incidental damages, or any lost profits or lost savings or for any claim by a third party, even if the copyright holder has been advised of the possibility of such damages, claims, costs, lost profits or lost savings.

2.9 Indemnity

You agree to defend, indemnify, and hold harmless the copyright holder and its parents and affiliates and all of their employees, agents, directors, officers, proprietors, partners, representatives, shareholders, servants, attorneys, predecessors, successors, assigns, and those who have worked in the preparation, publication or distribution of the **S5000F™ suite of information** from and against any and all claims, proceedings, damages, injuries, liabilities, losses, costs, and expenses (including reasonable attorneys' fees and litigation expenses), relating to or arising from your use of the **S5000F™ suite of information** or any breach by you of this user agreement.

2.10 Governing law and arbitration

This user agreement will be governed by and construed in accordance with the laws of the Kingdom of Belgium.

In the event of any dispute, controversy or claim arising out of or in connection with this user agreement, or the breach, termination or invalidity thereof, the parties agree to submit the matter to settlement proceedings under the ICC (International Chamber of Commerce) ADR (Alternative Dispute Resolution) rules. If the dispute has not been settled pursuant to the said rules within 45 days following the filing of a request for ADR or within such other period as the parties may agree in writing, such dispute shall be finally settled under the rules of arbitration of the International Chamber of Commerce by three arbitrators appointed in accordance with the said rules of arbitration. All related proceedings should be at the place of the ICC in Paris, France.

The language to be used in the arbitral proceedings shall be English.

Note

The following letter from the Secretary General of ASD extends the special usage rights of this specification and has been included for information, without affecting the technical contents. The content of this letter will be included in the copyright information as part of the S-Series 2024 block release.

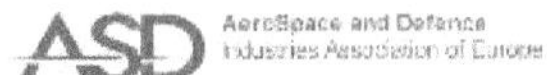

Special Usage Rights for the S-Series Specifications

To whom it may concern,

This letter seeks to clarify the special usage rights for the suite of documents known as the S-Series Specifications, for which the Aerospace and Defence Industries Association of Europe (ASD) holds the copyright and trademark.

The special usage rights are described as follows:

Permission to use or deliver training from the information contained in the S-Series Specifications, and the right to reproduce or publish the S-Series Specifications, in whole or in part, is hereby given to the following:

1. National Associations who are members of ASD and all their member companies;

2. Members of Aerospace Industries Association of America;

3. Members of the ATA e-Business Program;

4. Members of International Coordinating Council of Aerospace Industries Associations (ICCAIA) not included in categories 1 through 2 inclusively;

5. Airlines and Armed Forces that are customers of Companies included in Categories 1 through 3 inclusively;

6. Ministries of Defence of the member countries of ASD, of NATO and NATO Partners[1];

7. The Department of Defense of the USA;

8. NATO bodies, organizations & agencies;

9. Universities;

10. Technologies and Research Institutes.

Any further requirement for clarification, should in the first instance be directed to the Service Commission of the ASD.

Yours Sincerely,

Jan Pie

Secretary General of ASD

---

[1] as per: https://www.nato.int/cps/en/natohq/51288.htm);

Applicable to: All

S5000F-A-00-00-0000-00A-021A-A

Page intentionally blank.

Chapter 24.5

Data Model - Use case message diagrams

Table of contents
Page

1	Introduction	5
2	Use case messages	6
2.1	S5000F Use case UC50000 - In-service data feedback	6
2.2	S5000F Use case UC50301 - Monitor equipment performance	7
2.3	S5000F Use case UC50302 - Influence design	8
2.4	S5000F Use case UC50303 - Report trends and failures	9
2.5	S5000F Use case UC50304 - Report availability	10
2.6	S5000F Use case UC50305 - Report maintenance management and contracting for availability	11
2.7	S5000F Use case UC50306 - Assess maintainability effectiveness	12
2.8	S5000F Use case UC50307 - Report retaining performance	13
2.9	S5000F Use case UC50308 - Report mission capability	14
2.10	S5000F Use case UC50309 - Report efficiency and performance	15
2.11	S5000F Use case UC50310 - Report testability	16
2.12	S5000F Use case UC50311 - Report fault diagnostics	17
2.13	S5000F Use case UC50401 - Report manufacturer maintenance schedule	18
2.14	S5000F Use case UC50402 - Report Product user maintenance program	19
2.15	S5000F Use case UC50403 - Report maintenance performed	20
2.16	S5000F Use case UC50404 - Report Product performance	21
2.17	S5000F Use case UC50405 - Report new modifications	22
2.18	S5000F Use case UC50406 - Report technical queries	23
2.19	S5000F Use case UC50407 - Report shop findings	24
2.20	S5000F Use case UC50408 - Report structural damage	25
2.21	S5000F Use case UC50409 - Provide equipment calibration certificate	26
2.22	S5000F Use case UC50410 - Track support equipment usage	27
2.23	S5000F Use case UC50501 - Report safety issue	28
2.24	S5000F Use case UC50502 - Report safety warning	29
2.25	S5000F Use case UC50503 - Provide special safety instructions	30
2.26	S5000F Use case UC50601 - Report inventory	31
2.27	S5000F Use case UC50602 - Report shelf life	32
2.28	S5000F Use case UC50603 - Report spares and pool	33
2.29	S5000F Use case UC50604 - Report logistic response time	34
2.30	S5000F Use case UC50605 - Report facilities	35
2.31	S5000F Use case UC50606 - Plan for transport	36
2.32	S5000F Use case UC50701 - Provide Cost Breakdown Structure (CBS)	37
2.33	S5000F Use case UC50702 - Report maintenance costs	38
2.34	S5000F Use case UC50703 - Report operational costs	39
2.35	S5000F Use case UC50704 - Report modification costs	40
2.36	S5000F Use case UC50705 - Report in-service costs	41
2.37	S5000F Use case UC50801 - Evaluate maintenance actions	42
2.38	S5000F Use case UC50802 - Collect warranty costs	43
2.39	S5000F Use case UC50803 - Determine warranty misuse	44
2.40	S5000F Use case UC50804 - Identify warranty risks	45
2.41	S5000F Use case UC50805 - Improve warranty rules	46
2.42	S5000F Use case UC50901 - Record health data	47
2.43	S5000F Use case UC50902 - Report usage information	48
2.44	S5000F Use case UC50903 - Respond to usage information	49
2.45	S5000F Use case UC51001 - Perform obsolescence planning	50
2.46	S5000F Use case UC51002 - Determine obsolescence candidates	51

Applicable to: All

S5000F-A-24-05-0000-00A-040A-A

Chap 24.5

2.47	S5000F Use case UC51003 - Determine obsolescence strategy	52
2.48	S5000F Use case UC51004 - Monitor obsolescence	53
2.49	S5000F Use case UC51005 - Solve obsolescence	54
2.50	S5000F Use case UC51006 - Provide obsolescence alert	55
2.51	S5000F Use case UC51101 - Elaborate assignment proposal	56
2.52	S5000F Use case UC51102 - Cancel fleet task	57
2.53	S5000F Use case UC51103 - Modify fleet task	58
2.54	S5000F Use case UC51104 - Elaborate fleet plan	59
2.55	S5000F Use case UC51105 - Evaluate fleet task	60
2.56	S5000F Use case UC51106 - Prepare Product for fleet task	61
2.57	S5000F Use case UC51107 - Recover Product after fleet task	62
2.58	S5000F Use case UC51108 - Report fleet availability	63
2.59	S5000F Use case UC51201 - Request software feature	64
2.60	S5000F Use case UC51202 - Report software error	65
2.61	S5000F Use case UC51203 - Assess software usability	66
2.62	S5000F Use case UC51204 - Report software documentation errors	67
2.63	S5000F Use case UC51205 - Assess HW-SW interoperability	68
2.64	S5000F Use case UC51206 - Report software installation	69
2.65	S5000F Use case UC51207 - Report software configuration	70
2.66	S5000F Use case UC51208 - Assess software maturity	71
2.67	S5000F Use case UC51209 - Report help desk tickets	72
2.68	S5000F Use case UC51210 - Assess software delivery	73
2.69	S5000F Use case UC51211 - Communicate data loading	74
2.70	S5000F Use case UC51301 - Provide as-delivered configuration	75
2.71	S5000F Use case UC51302 - Provide as-allowed configuration	76
2.72	S5000F Use case UC51303 - Provide operational configuration	77
2.73	S5000F Use case UC51304 - Provide customer modification	78
2.74	S5000F Use case UC51305 - Provide as-desired configuration	79
2.75	S5000F Use case UC51401 - Provide contractual information	80
2.76	S5000F Use case UC51402 - Provide Work Breakdown Structure (WBS)	81
2.77	S5000F Use case UC51403 - Provide Cost Breakdown Structure (CBS)	82
2.78	S5000F Use case UC51404 - Provide Organizational Breakdown Structure (OBS)	83
2.79	S5000F Use case UC51405 - Provide activity planning	84
2.80	S5000F Use case UC51406 - Report Service-Level Agreement (SLA) compliance	85
2.81	S5000F Use case UC51407 - Report contract costs	86
2.82	S5000F Use case UC51408 - Provide status report	87
2.83	S5000F Use case UC51409 - Provide location information	88
2.84	S5000F Use case UC51410 - Manage service request	89
2.85	S5000F Use case UC51411 - Request resource	90
2.86	S5000F Use case UC51412 - Define security	91
2.87	S5000F Use case UC51413 - Exchange export control information	92
2.88	S5000F Use case UC51414 - Provide labor rates	93
2.89	S5000F Use case UC51415 - Provide documentation traceability	94
2.90	S5000F Use case UC51503 - Provide disposal location information	95
2.91	S5000F Use case UC51504 - Report infrastructure availability	96
2.92	S5000F Use case UC51505 - Define or update environment	97
2.93	S5000F Use case UC51506 - Reallocate fleet or Product	98
2.94	S5000F Use case UC51601 - Exchange environmental data	99
2.95	S5000F Use case UC51602 - Report environmental data to authorities	100
2.96	S5000F Use case UC51603 - Report modification impact on disposal	101
2.97	S5000F Use case UC51604 - Report valuable items from disposal	102
2.98	S5000F Use case UC51605 - Request item disposal	103
2.99	S5000F Use case UC51606 - Report Product disposal	104
2.100	S5000F Use case UC51607 - Request waste disposal	105
2.101	S5000F Use case UC51608 - Report waste disposal	106
2.102	S5000F Use case UC51609 - Report disposal costs	107
2.103	S5000F Use case UC51610 - Notify unacceptable condition disposal	108

S5000F-A-24-05-0000-00A-040A-A

Applicable to: All

Chap 24.5

2.104 S5000F Use case UC52301 - Provide project-specific values 109
2.105 S5000F Use case UC52302 - Provide non-predefined information 109

List of tables

1 References 5

List of figures

1 S5000F Use Case UC50000 - In-Service Data Feedback 6
2 S5000F Use Case UC50301 - Monitor Equipment Performance.................................... 7
3 S5000F Use Case UC50302 - Influence Design 8
4 S5000F Use Case UC50303 - Report Trends and Failures.. 9
5 S5000F Use Case UC50304 - Report Availability 10
6 S5000F Use Case UC50305 - Report Maintenance Management Availability 11
7 S5000F Use Case UC50306 - Assess Maintainability Effectiveness............................12
8 S5000F Use Case UC50307 - Report Retaining Performance 13
9 S5000F Use Case UC50308 - Report Mission Capability 14
10 S5000F Use Case UC50309 - Report Efficiency and Performance..............................15
11 S5000F Use Case UC50310 - Report Testability 16
12 S5000F Use Case UC50311 - Report Fault Diagnostics 17
13 S5000F Use Case UC50401 - Report Manufacturer Maintenance Schedule 18
14 S5000F Use Case UC50402 - Report Product User Maintenance Program 19
15 S5000F Use Case UC50403 - Report Maintenance Performed 20
16 S5000F Use Case UC50404 - Report Product Performance......................................21
17 S5000F Use Case UC50405 - Report New Modifications 22
18 S5000F Use Case UC50406 - Report Technical Queries 23
19 S5000F Use Case UC50407 - Report Shop Findings 24
20 S5000F Use Case UC50408 - Report Structural Damage...25
21 S5000F Use Case UC50409 - Provide Equipment Calibration Certificate....................26
22 S5000F Use Case UC50410 - Track Support Equipment Usage 27
23 S5000F Use Case UC50501 - Report Safety Issue 28
24 S5000F Use Case UC50502 - Report Safety Warning 29
25 S5000F Use Case UC50503 - Provide Special SafetyInstructions 30
26 S5000F Use Case UC50601 - Report Inventory 31
27 S5000F Use Case UC50602 - Report Shelf Life 32
28 S5000F Use Case UC50603 - Report Spares and Pool 33
29 S5000F Use Case UC50604 - Report Logistic Response Time 34
30 S5000F Use Case UC50605 - Report Facilities 35
31 S5000F Use Case UC50606 - Plan for Transport 36
32 S5000F Use Case UC50701 - Provide Cost Breakdown Structure (CBS) 37
33 S5000F Use Case UC50702 - Report Maintenance Costs 38
34 S5000F Use Case UC50703 - Report Operational Costs 39
35 S5000F Use Case UC50704 - Report Modification Costs 40
36 S5000F Use Case UC50705 - Report In-Service Costs 41
37 S5000F Use Case UC50801 - Evaluate Maintenance Actions 42
38 S5000F Use Case UC50802 - Collect Warranty Costs 43
39 S5000F Use Case UC50803 - Determine Warranty Misuse 44

40	S5000F Use Case UC50804 - Identify Warranty Risks	45
41	S5000F Use Case UC50805 - Improve Warranty Rules	46
42	S5000F Use Case UC50901 - Record Health Data	47
43	S5000F Use Case UC50902 - Report Usage Information	48
44	S5000F Use Case UC50903 - Respond To Usage Information	49
45	S5000F Use Case UC51001 - Perform Obsolescence Planning	50
46	S5000F Use Case UC51002 - Determine Obsolescence Candidates	51
47	S5000F Use Case UC51003 - Determine Obsolescence Strategy	52
48	S5000F Use Case UC51004 - Monitor Obsolescence	53
49	S5000F Use Case UC51005 - Solve Obsolescence	54
50	S5000F Use Case UC51006 - Provide Obsolescence Alert	55
51	S5000F Use Case UC51101 - Elaborate Assignment Proposal	56
52	S5000F Use Case UC51102 - Cancel Fleet Task	57
53	S5000F Use Case UC51103 - Modify Fleet Task	58
54	S5000F Use Case UC51104 - Elaborate Fleet Plan	59
55	S5000F Use Case UC51105 - Evaluate Fleet Task	60
56	S5000F Use Case UC51106 - Prepare Product for Fleet Task	61
57	S5000F Use Case UC51107 - Recover Product After Fleet Task	62
58	S5000F Use Case UC51108 - Report Fleet Availability	63
59	S5000F Use Case UC51201 - Request Software Feature	64
60	S5000F Use Case UC51202 - Report Software Error	65
61	S5000F Use Case UC51203 - Assess Software Usability	66
62	S5000F Use Case UC51204 - Report Software Documentation Errors	67
63	S5000F Use Case UC51205 - Assess HW-SW Interoperability	68
64	S5000F Use Case UC51206 - Report Software Installation	69
65	S5000F Use Case UC51207 - Report Software Configuration	70
66	S5000F Use Case UC51208 - Assess Software Maturity	71
67	S5000F Use Case UC51209 - Report Help Desk Tickets	72
68	S5000F Use Case UC51210 - Asssess Software Delivery	73
69	S5000F Use Case UC51211 - Communicate Data Loading	74
70	S5000F Use Case UC51301 - Provide As-Delivered Configuration	75
71	S5000F Use Case UC51302 - Provide As-Allowed Configuration	76
72	S5000F Use Case UC51303 - Provide Operational Configuration	77
73	S5000F Use Case UC51304 - Provide Customer Modification	78
74	S5000F Use Case UC51305 - Provide As-Desired Configuration	79
75	S5000F Use Case UC51401 - Provide Contractual Information	80
76	S5000F Use Case UC51402 - Provide Work Breakdown Structure (WBS)	81
77	S5000F Use Case UC51403 - Provide Cost Breakdown Structure (CBS)	82
78	S5000F Use Case UC51404 - Provide Organizational Breakdown Structure (OBS)	83
79	S5000F Use Case UC51405 - Provide Activity Planning	84
80	S5000F Use Case UC51406 - Report Service-Level Agreement (SLA) Compliance	85
81	S5000F Use Case UC51407 - Report Contract Costs	86
82	S5000F Use Case UC51408 - Provide Status Report	87
83	S5000F Use Case UC51409 - Provide Location Information	88
84	S5000F Use Case UC51410 - Manage Service Request	89
85	S5000F Use Case UC51411 - Request Resource	90
86	S5000F Use Case UC51412 - Define Security	91
87	S5000F Use Case UC51413 - Exchange Export Control Information	92

88	S5000F Use Case UC51414 - Provide Labor Rates	93
89	S5000F Use Case UC51415 - Provide Documentation Traceability	94
90	S5000F Use Case UC51503 - Provide Disposal Location Information	95
91	S5000F Use Case UC51504 - Report Infrastructure Availability	96
92	S5000F Use Case UC51505 - Define or Update Environment	97
93	S5000F Use Case UC51506 - Reallocate Fleet or Product	98
94	S5000F Use Case UC51601 - Exchange Environmental Data	99
95	S5000F Use Case UC51602 - Report Environmental Data to Authorities	100
96	S5000F Use Case UC51603 - Report Modification Impact on Disposal	101
97	S5000F Use Case UC51604 - Report Valuable Items from Disposal	102
98	S5000F Use Case UC51605 - Request Item Disposal	103
99	S5000F Use Case UC51606 - Report Product Disposal	104
100	S5000F Use Case UC51607 - Request Waste Disposal	105
101	S5000F Use Case UC51608 - Report Waste Disposal	106
102	S5000F Use Case UC51609 - Report Disposal Costs	107
103	S5000F Use Case UC51610 - Notify Unacceptable Condition Disposal	108
104	S5000F Use Case UC52301 - Provide Project-Specific Values	109
105	S5000F Use Case UC52302 - Provide Non-Predefined Information	110

References

Table 1 References

Chap No./Document No.	Title
Chap 28	Data required for the different use cases.

1 Introduction

This section describes the messages that are used for each individual S5000F use case, as described in the data model. Each use case is defined as a separate message.

The different use case messages are listed by use case number. The use case number indicates first the specification number ("5"), then uses two digits for the chapter number where it is defined (eg, "04") and two further sequential numbers that allow to differentiate them within their chapter.

The classes that are included in each use case and therefore in each message are listed in Chap 28.

Note

The classes shown in the message diagrams are only those classes being part of the use case that have an existence of their own and can therefore be sent as part of a message. Relationships and compositions of other classes are not listed, as they are wrapped in their parent class as far as the message is concerned. For this reason, the classes shown in the following diagrams may not include all classes described in Chap 28.

2 Use case messages

2.1 S5000F Use case UC50000 - In-service data feedback

In-service data feedback represents a message providing all the necessary information required for a generic use case (UC50000) that allows all S5000F information to be sent.

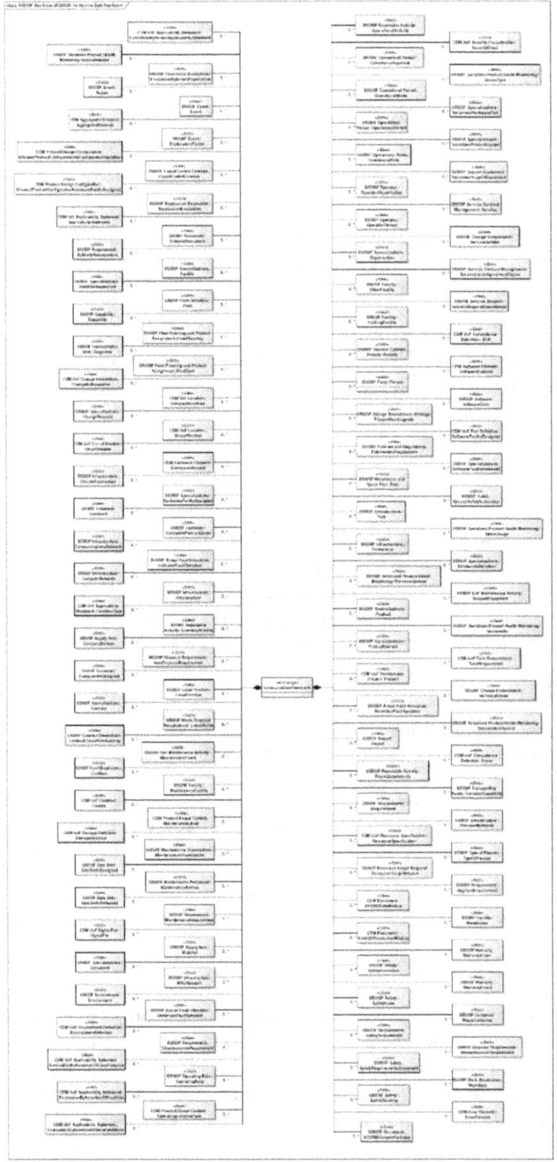

ICN-B6865-5000F24500-001-01

Fig 1 S5000F Use case UC50000 - In-service data feedback

2.2   S5000F Use case UC50301 - Monitor equipment performance

Monitor equipment performance represents a message associated with a use case (UC50301) providing the necessary information to be able to monitor the performance of an equipment.

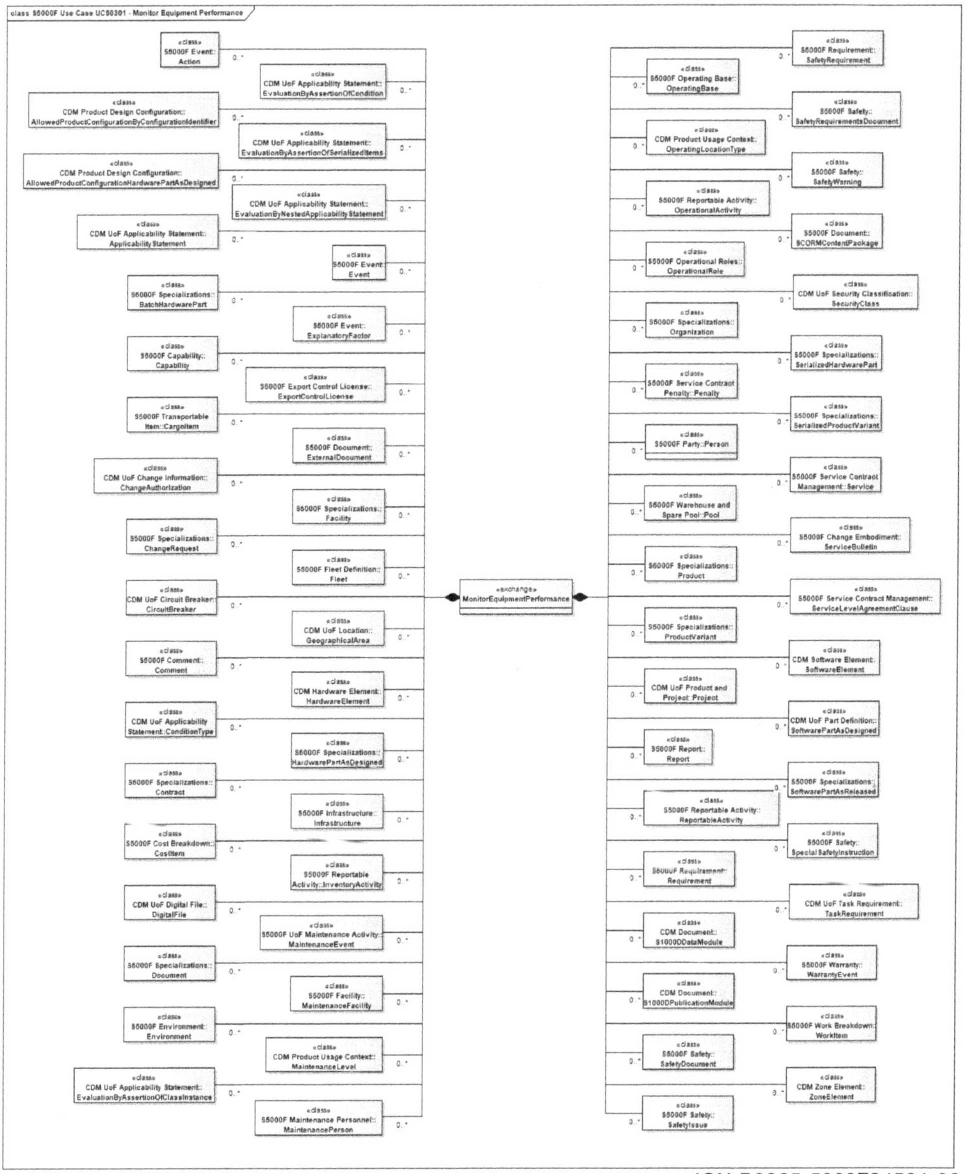

ICN-B6865-5000F24501-001-01

Fig 2 S5000F Use case UC50301 - Monitor equipment performance

2.3 S5000F Use case UC50302 - Influence design

Influence design represents a message associated with a use case (UC50302) providing the necessary information to be able to raise a change request.

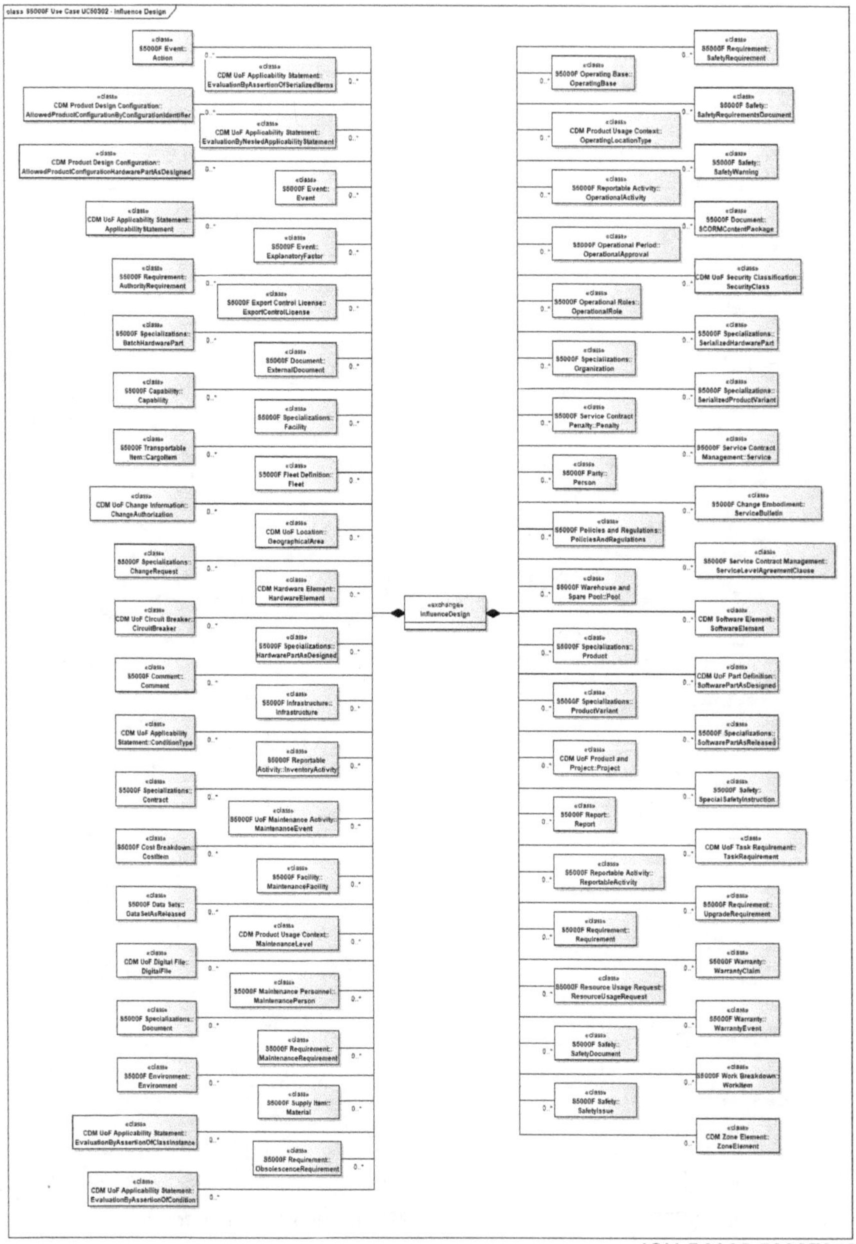

ICN-B6865-5000F24502-001-01

Fig 3 S5000F Use case UC50302 - Influence design

2.4   S5000F Use case UC50303 - Report trends and failures

Report trends and failures represents a message associated with a use case (UC50303) providing the information about failures in order to report failure trends.

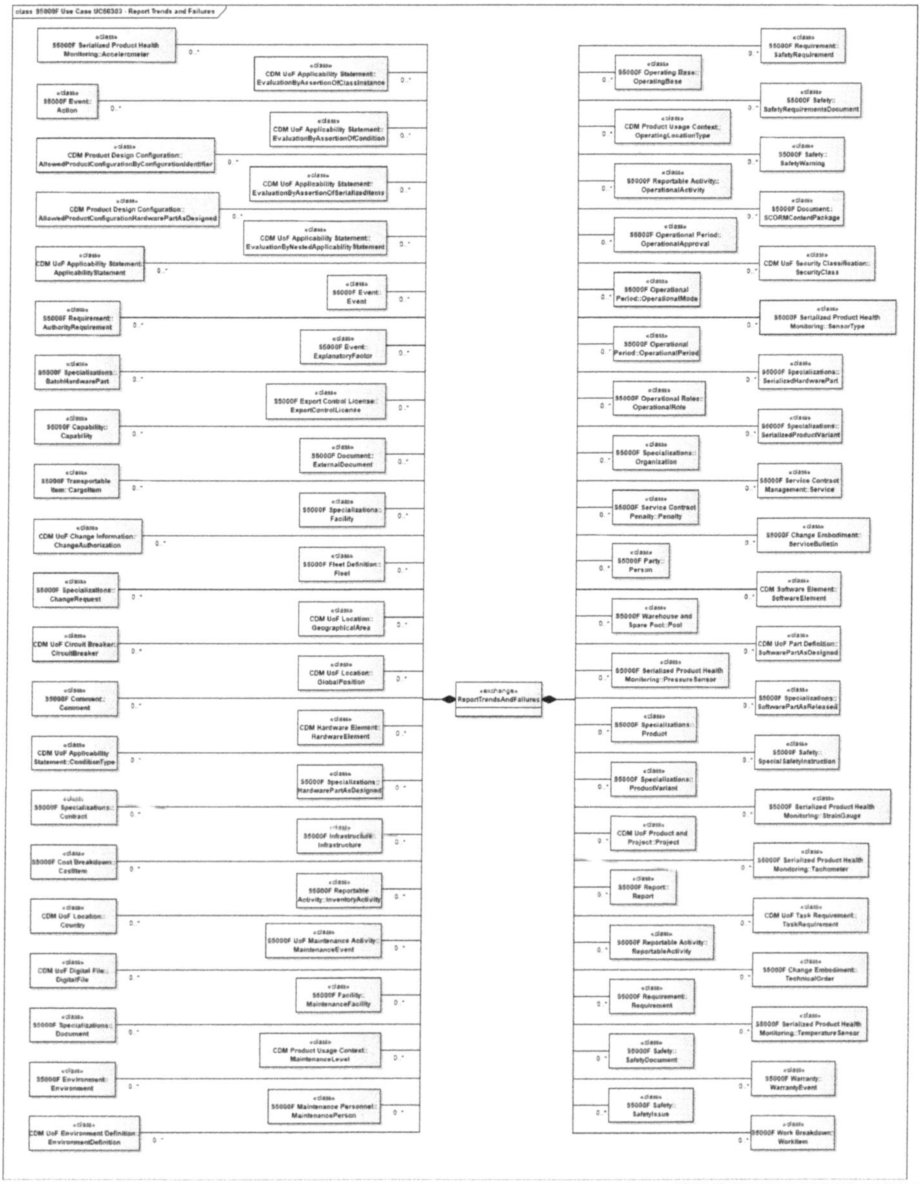

ICN-B6865-5000F24503-001-01

Fig 4 S5000F Use case UC50303 - Report trends and failures

2.5   S5000F Use case UC50304 - Report availability

Report availability represents a message associated with a use case (UC50304) allowing the availability of a serialized Product item and the root causes for non-availability to be reported.

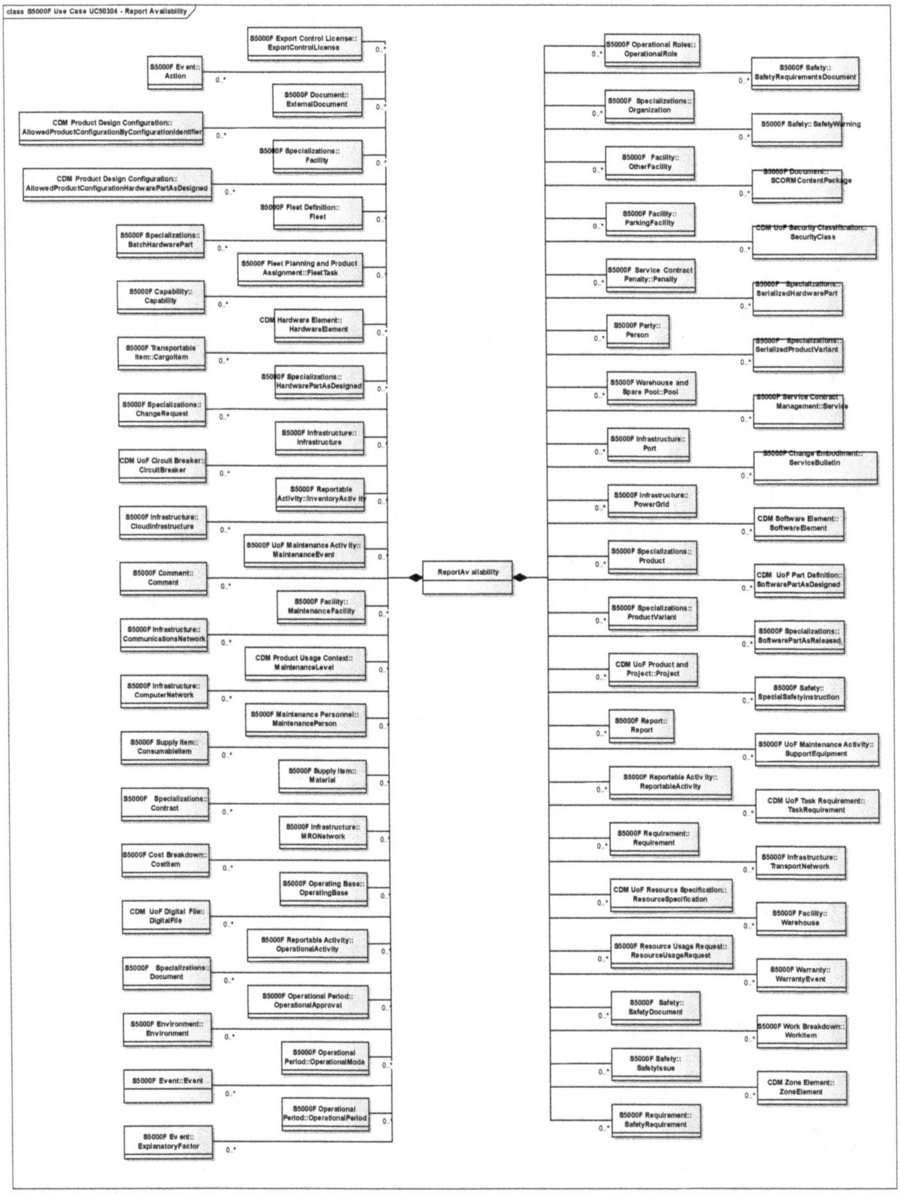

ICN-B6865-5000F24504-001-01

Fig 5 S5000F Use case UC50304 - Report availability

2.6 S5000F Use case UC50305 - Report maintenance management and contracting for availability

Report maintenance management and contracting for availability represents a message associated with a use case (UC50305) providing the necessary information to management maintenance, and contract for availability.

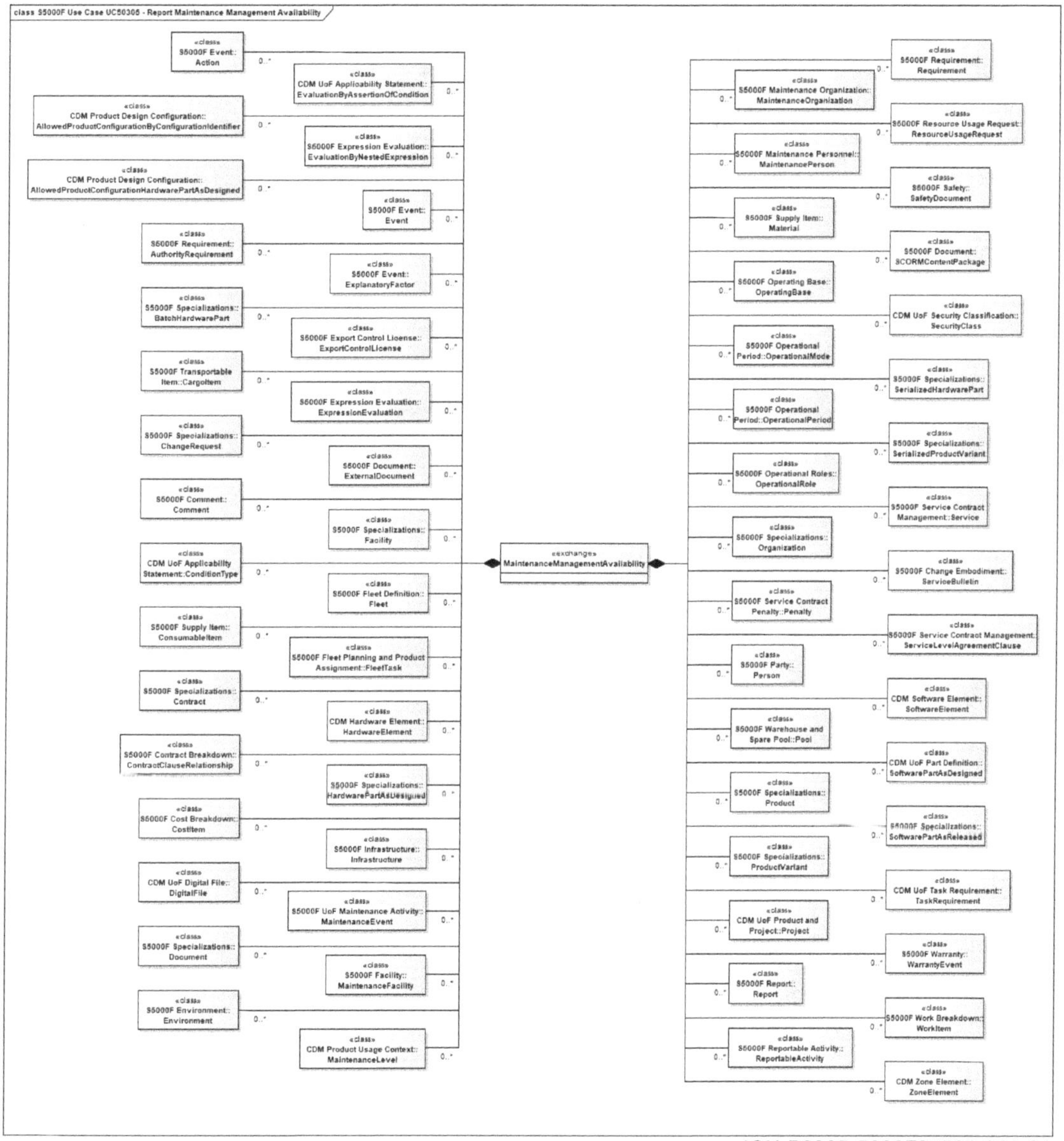

ICN-B6865-5000F24505-001-01

Fig 6 S5000F Use case UC50305 - Report maintenance management and contracting for availability

2.7   S5000F Use case UC50306 - Assess maintainability effectiveness

Assess maintainability effectiveness represents a message associated with a use case (UC50305) providing the necessary information to assess the effectiveness of maintenance.

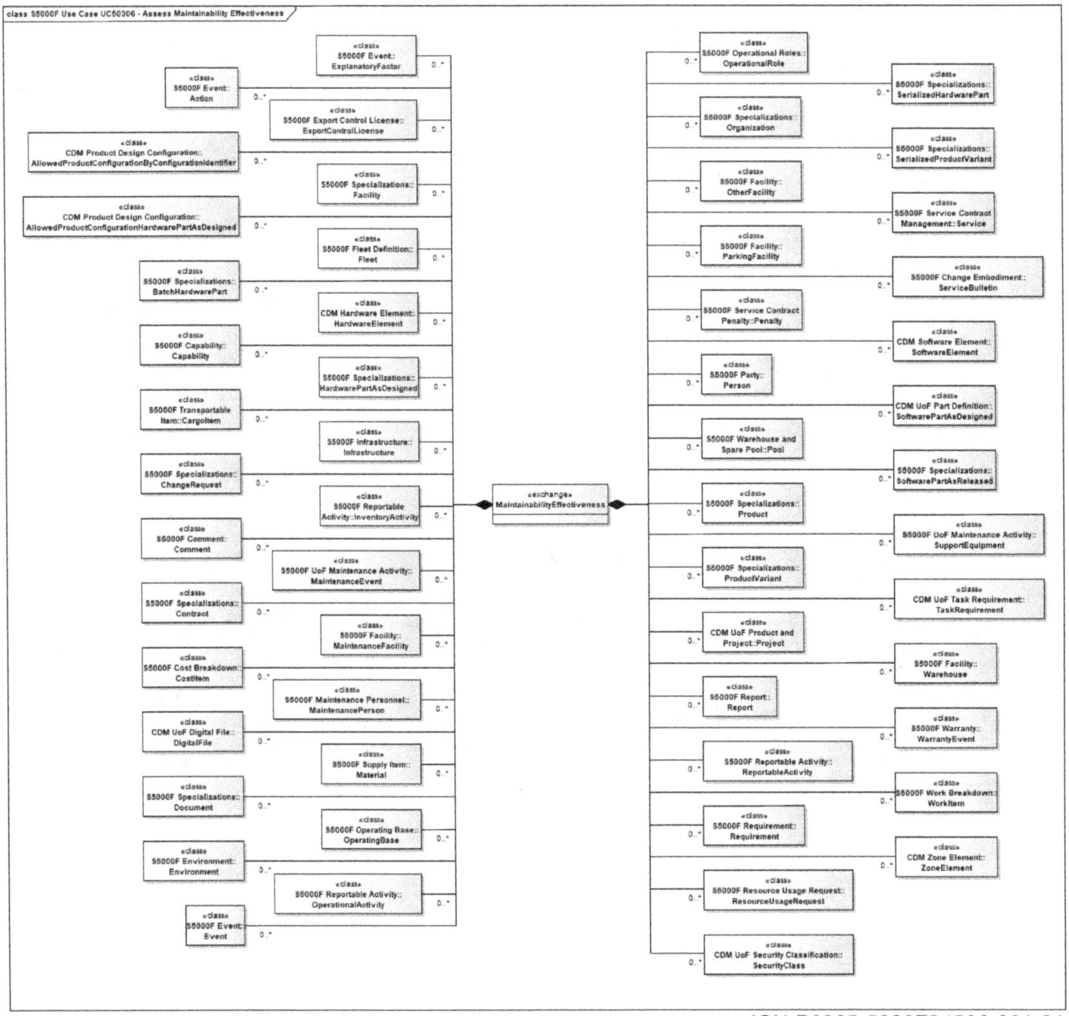

ICN-B6865-5000F24506-001-01

Fig 7 S5000F Use case UC50306 - Assess maintainability effectiveness

2.8 S5000F Use case UC50307 - Report retaining performance

Report retaining performance represents a message associated with a use case (UC50307) providing the information required to ensure that proper Product performance is maintained.

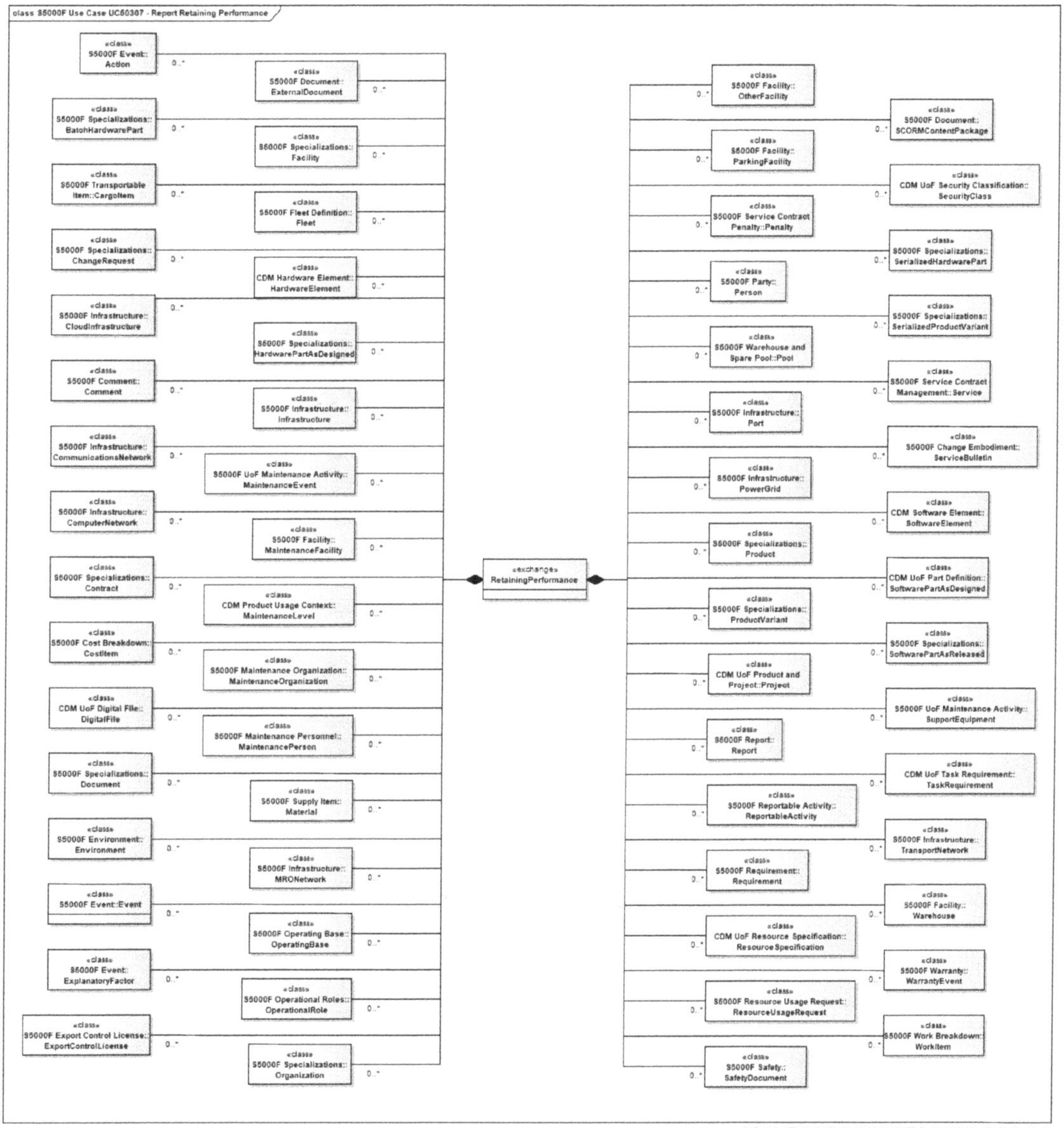

ICN-B6865-5000F24507-001-01

Fig 8 S5000F Use case UC50307 - Report retaining performance

2.9 S5000F Use case UC50308 - Report mission capability

Report mission capability represents a message associated with a use case (UC50308) providing the information required to report on whether an individual Product is or not mission cable.

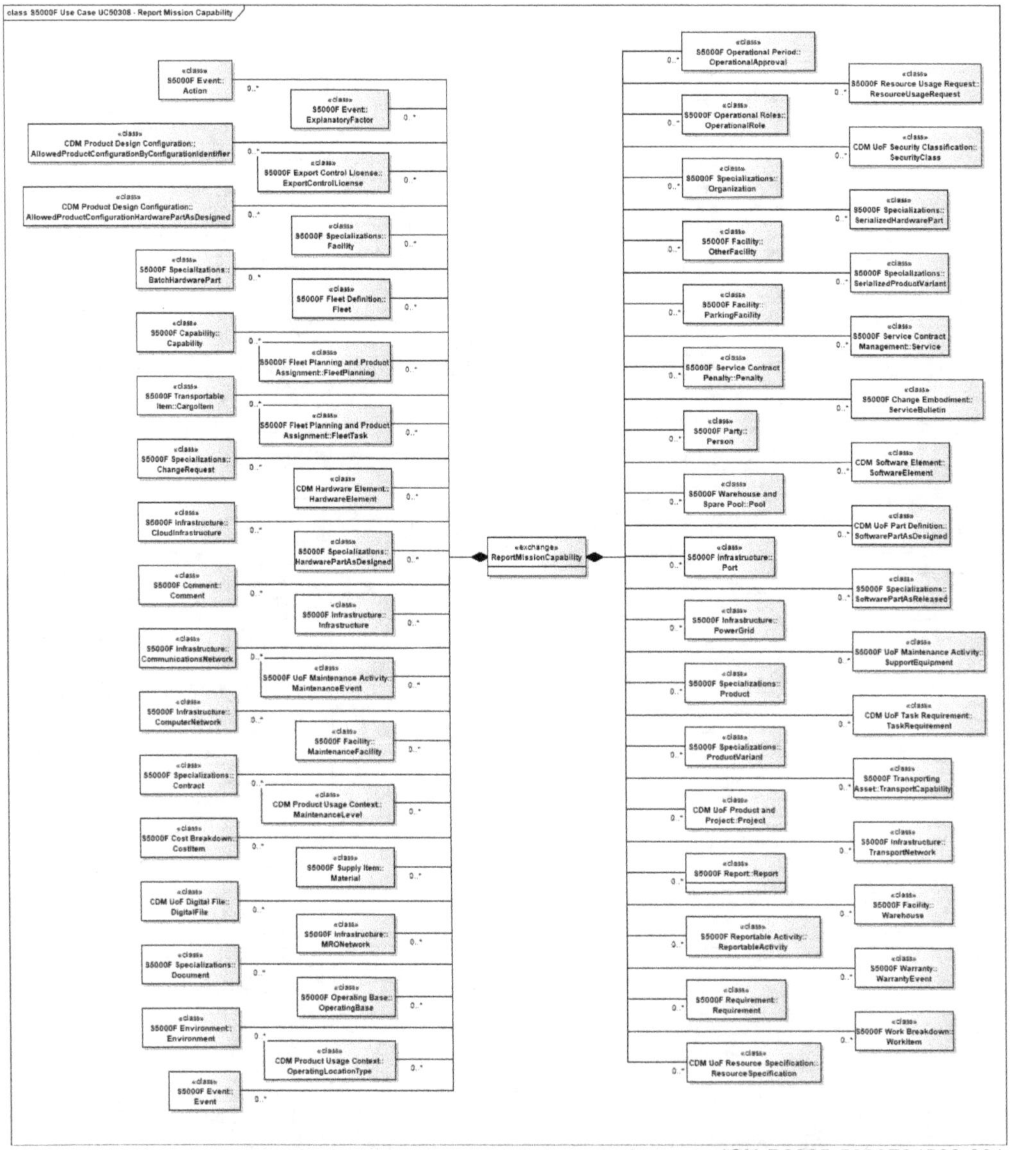

ICN-B6865-5000F24508-001-01

Fig 9 S5000F Use case UC50308 - Report mission capability

2.10   S5000F Use case UC50309 - Report efficiency and performance

Report efficiency and performance represents a message associated with a use case (UC50309) allowing efficiency and performance metrics to be reported.

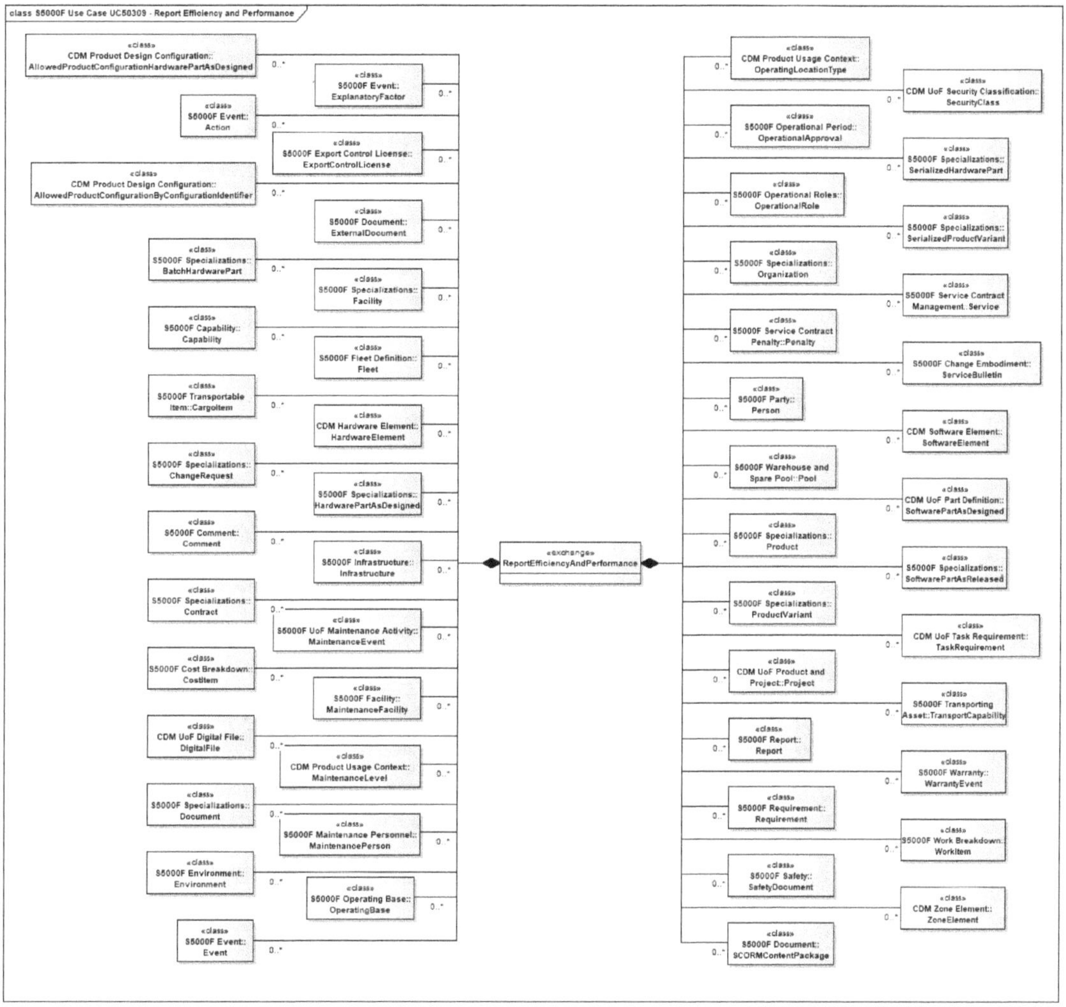

ICN-B6865-5000F24509-001-01

Fig 10 S5000F Use case UC50309 - Report efficiency and performance

2.11   S5000F Use case UC50310 - Report testability

Report testability represents a message associated with a use case (UC50310) providing the information required to assess the testability of an item.

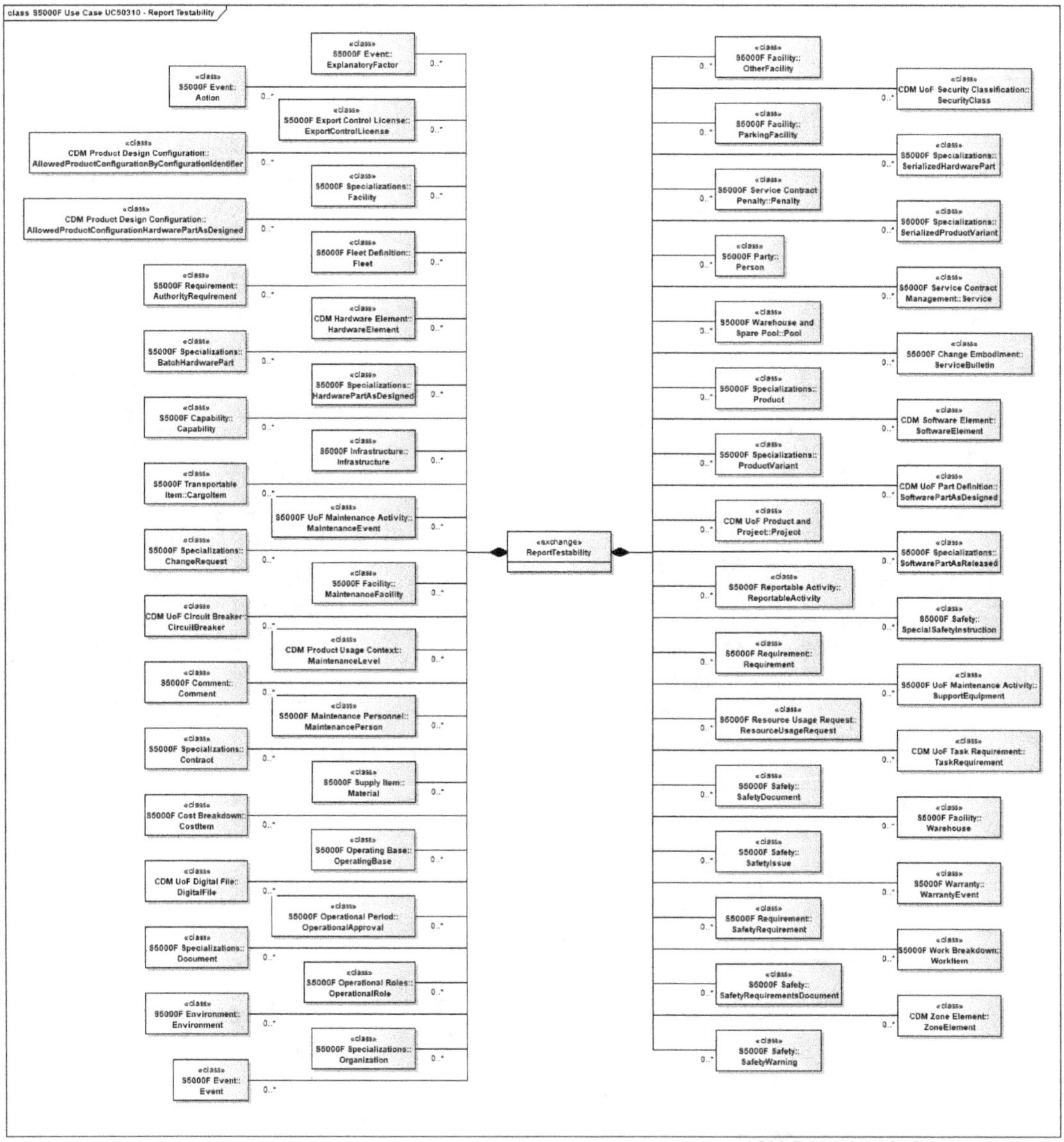

ICN-B6865-5000F24510-001-01

Fig 11 S5000F Use case UC50310 - Report testability

2.12 S5000F Use case UC50311 - Report fault diagnostics

Report fault diagnostics represents a message associated with a use case (UC50311) allowing fault diagnostics data to be provided.

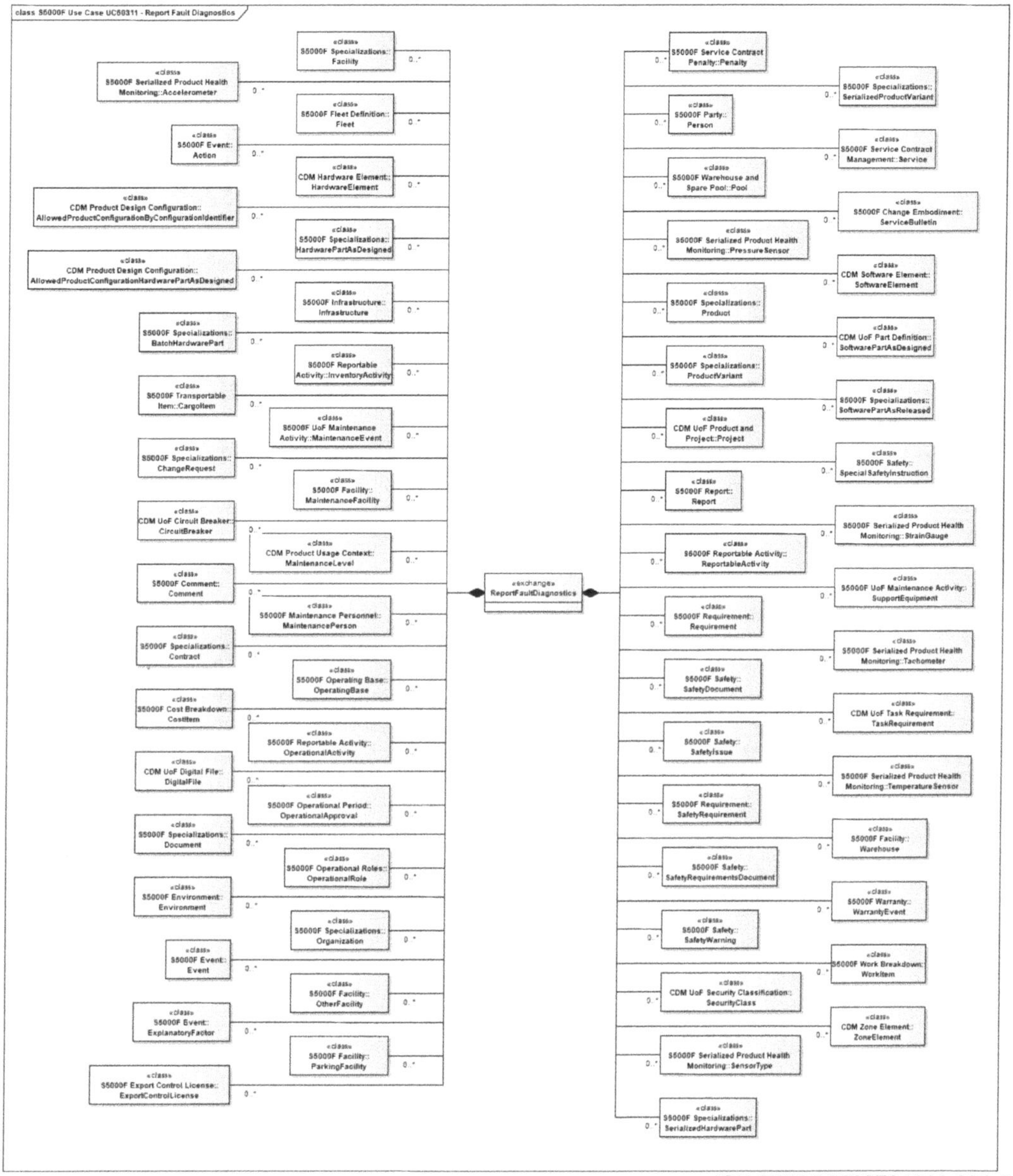

ICN-B6865-5000F24511-001-01

Fig 12 S5000F Use case UC50311 - Report fault diagnostics

2.13 S5000F Use case UC50401 - Report manufacturer maintenance schedule

Report manufacturer maintenance schedule represents a message associated with a use case (UC50401) providing the information required to report on the maintenance schedule defined by the manufacturer of a Product.

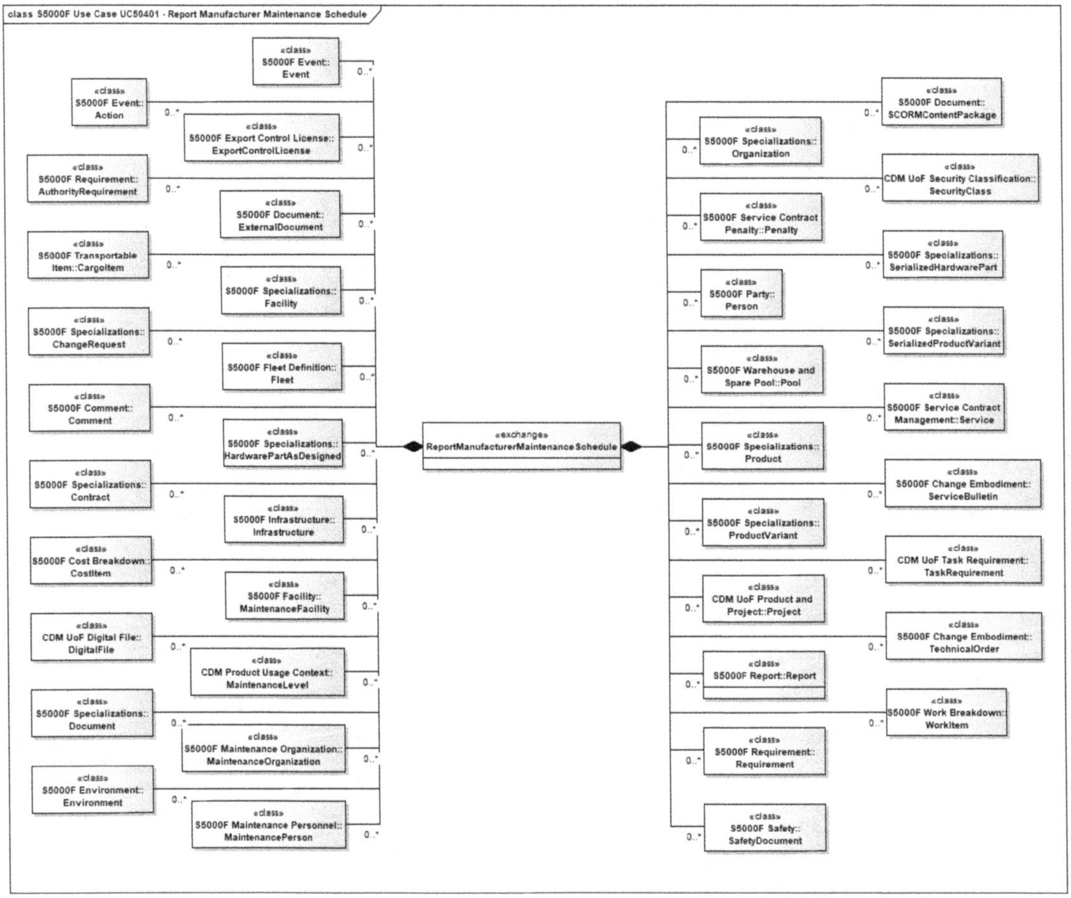

ICN-B6865-5000F24512-001-01

Fig 13 S5000F Use case UC50401 - Report manufacturer maintenance schedule

2.14 S5000F Use case UC50402 - Report Product user maintenance program

Report Product user maintenance program represents a message associated with a use case (UC50402) providing the information required to report on the maintenance program provided by the Original Equipment Manufacturer (OEM) of the Product or by the operator.

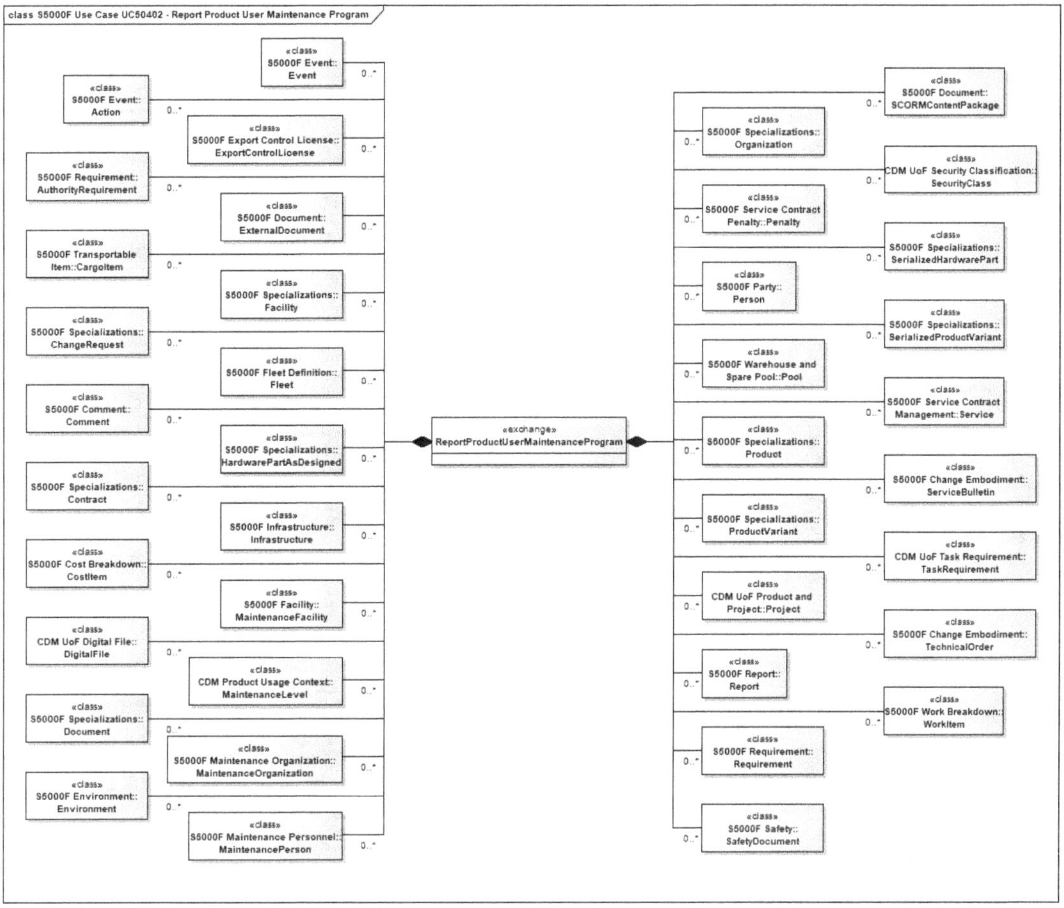

ICN-B6865-5000F24513-001-01

Fig 14 S5000F Use case UC50402 - Report Product user maintenance program

2.15 S5000F Use case UC50403 - Report maintenance performed

Report maintenance performed represents a message associated with a use case (UC50403) providing the information required to report on the maintenance that has been performed on a Product.

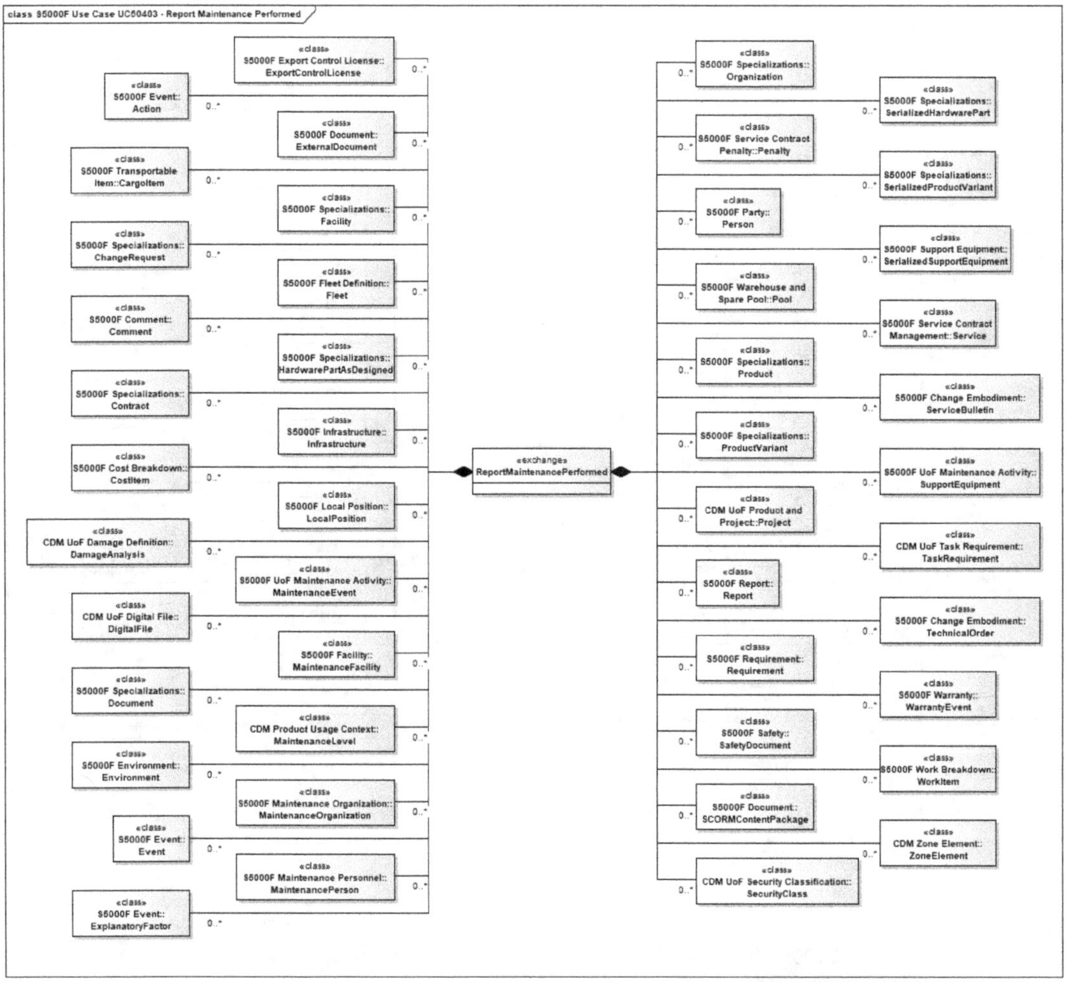

ICN-B6865-5000F24514-001-01

Fig 15 S5000F Use case UC50403 - Report maintenance performed

2.16   S5000F Use case UC50404 - Report Product performance

Report Product performance represents a message associated with a use case (UC50404) providing the information required to report on the performance of a Product.

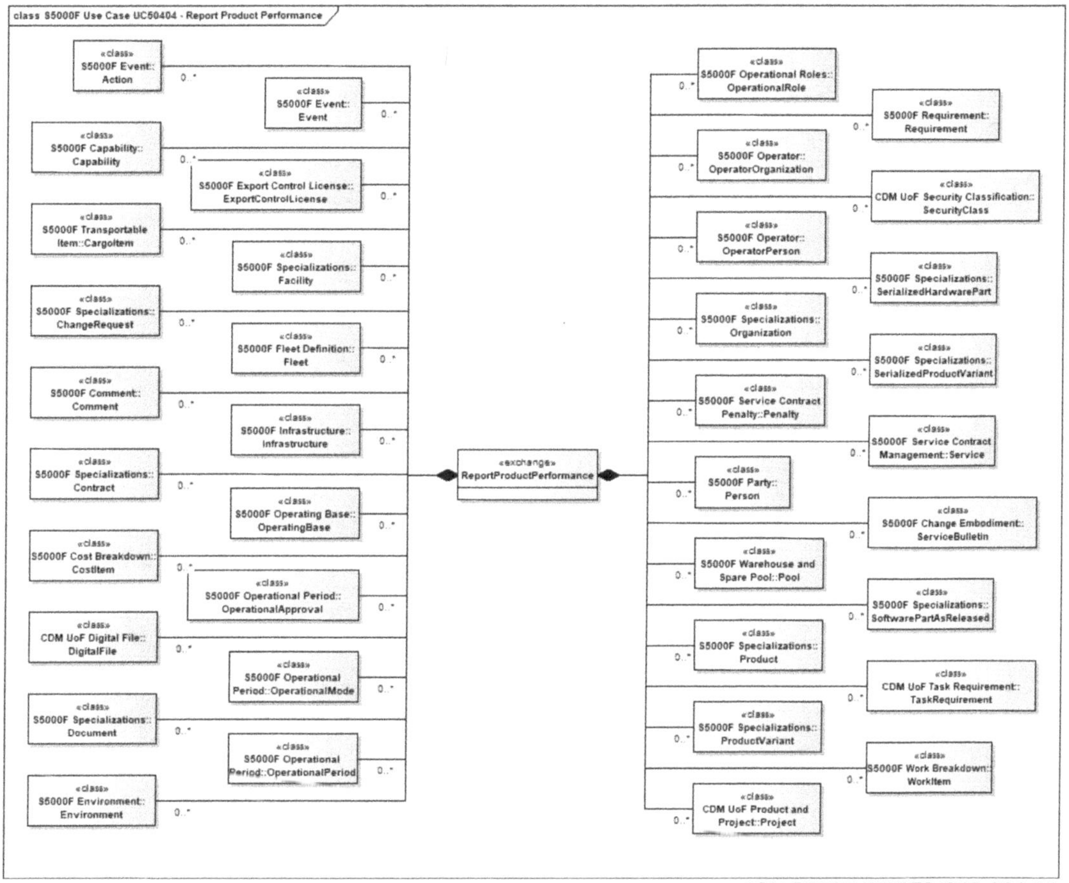

ICN-B6865-5000F24515-001-01

Fig 16 S5000F Use case UC50404 - Report Product performance

2.17   S5000F Use case UC50405 - Report new modifications

Report new modifications represents a message associated with a use case (UC50405) providing the information required to report on new modifications to the Product.

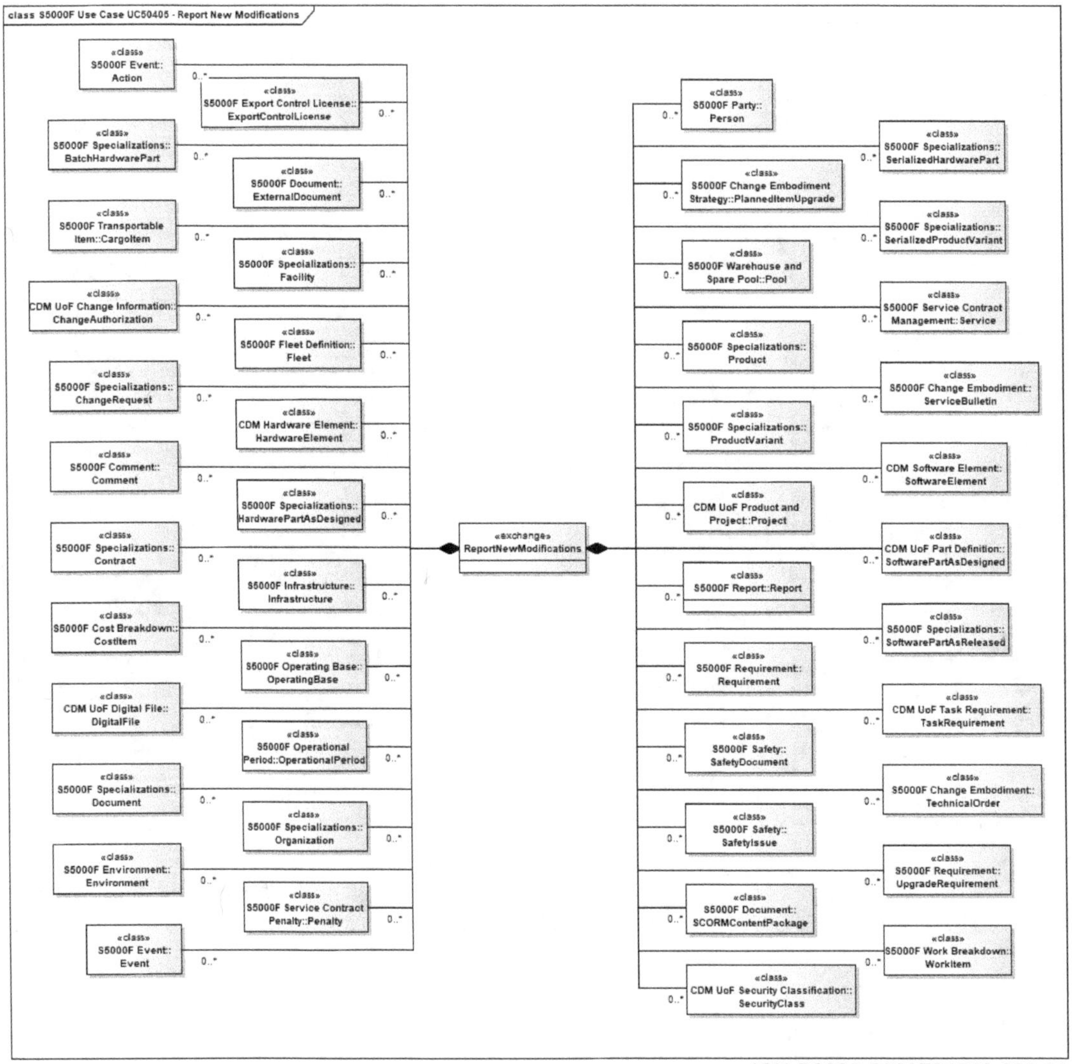

ICN-B6865-5000F24516-001-01

Fig 17 S5000F Use case UC50405 - Report new modifications

2.18 S5000F Use case UC50406 - Report technical queries

Report technical queries represents a message associated with a use case (UC50406) providing the information required to perform a technical query and receive a response.

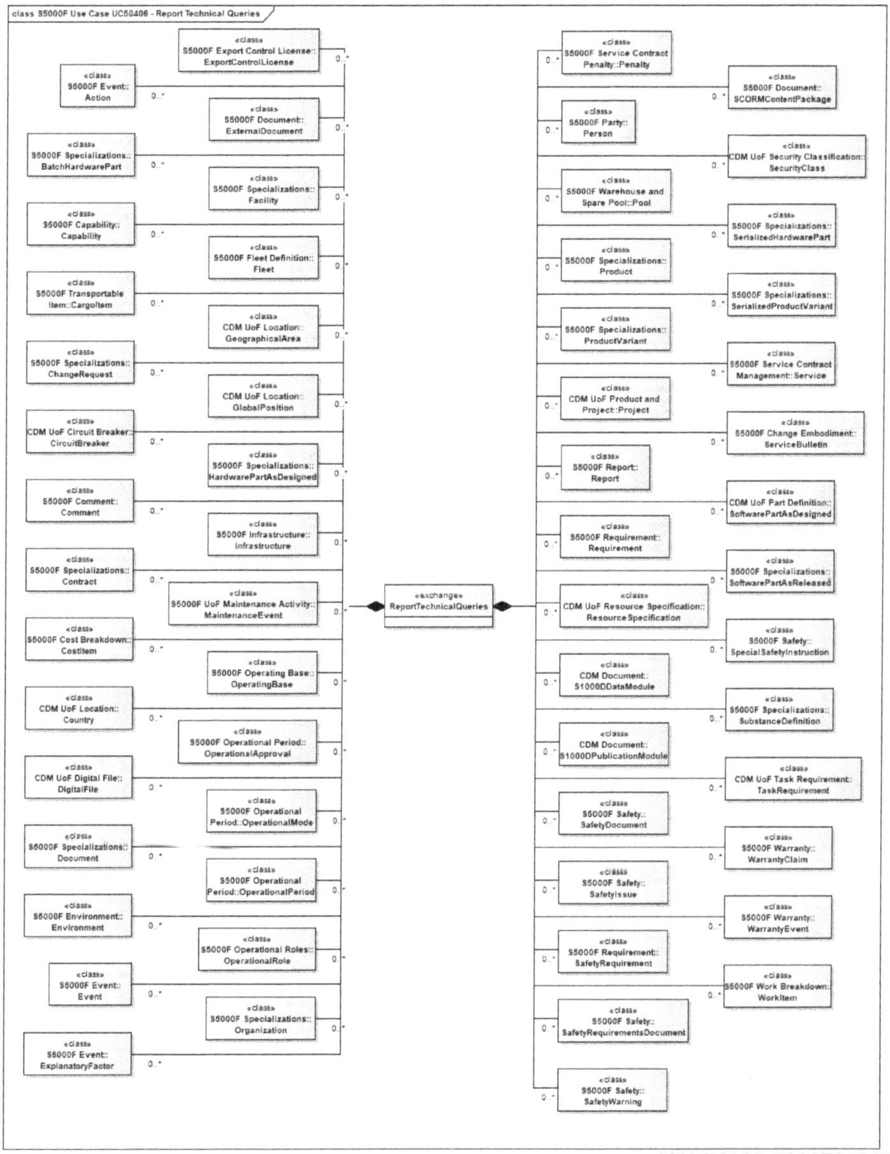

ICN-B6865-5000F24517-001-01

Fig 18 S5000F Use case UC50406 - Report technical queries

2.19   S5000F Use case UC50407 - Report shop findings

Report shop findings represents a message associated with a use case (UC50407) providing the information required to report the results from a workshop when repairing a unit that has been sent in for repair.

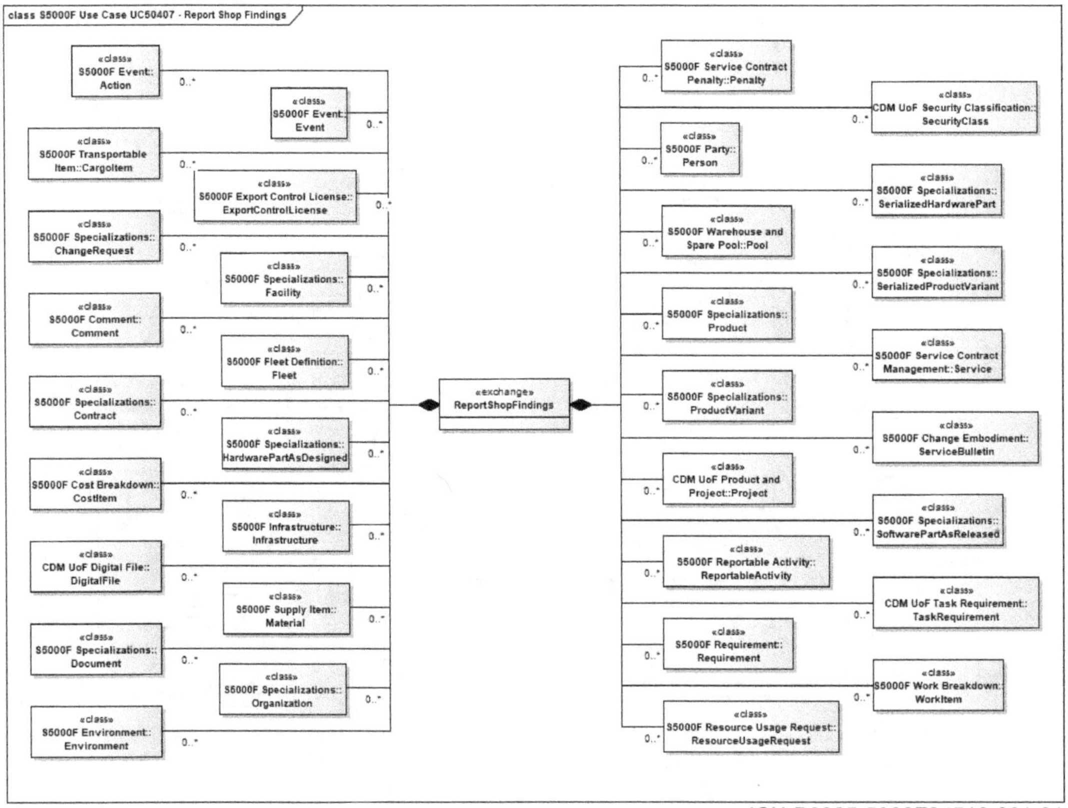

ICN-B6865-5000F24518-001-01

Fig 19 S5000F Use case UC50407 - Report shop findings

2.20 S5000F Use case UC50408 - Report structural damage

Report structural damage represents a message associated with a use case (UC50408) providing the information required to report any structural damage.

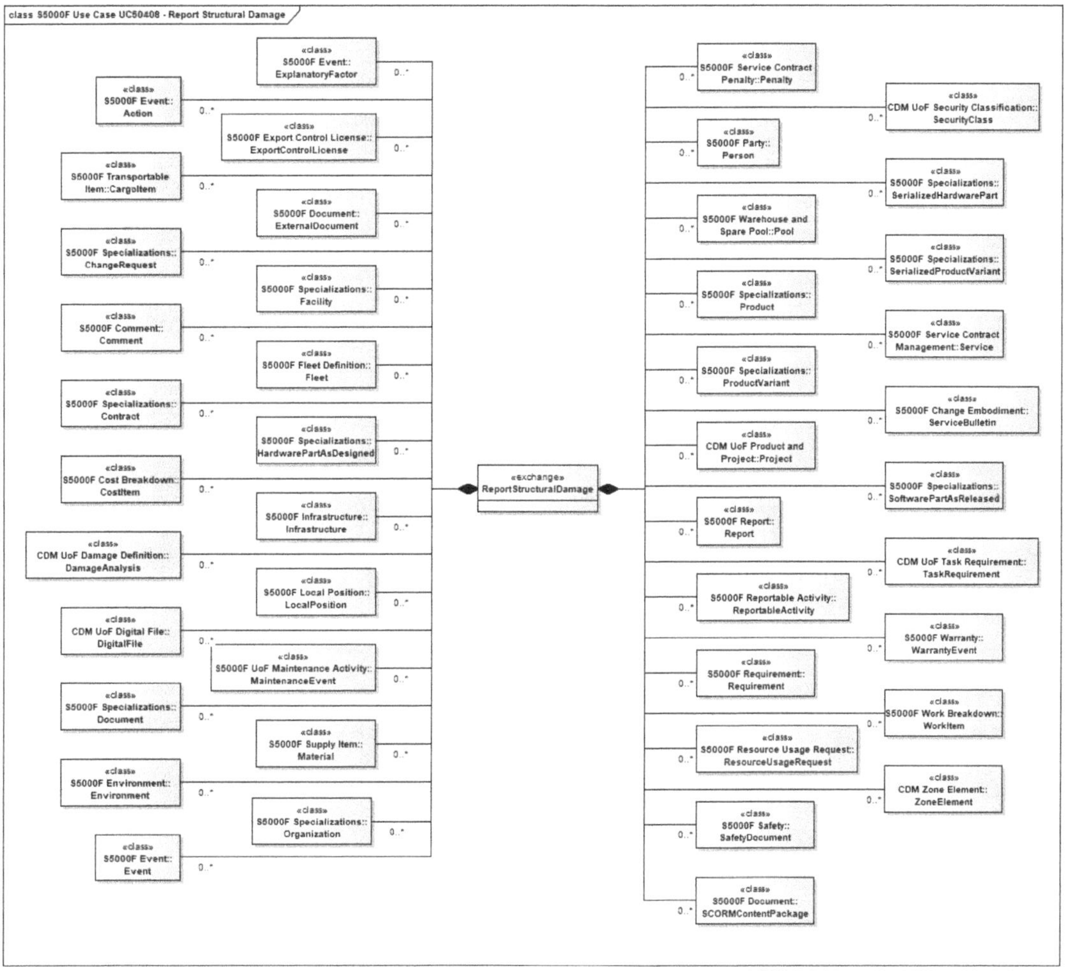

ICN-B6865-5000F24519-001-01

Fig 20 S5000F Use case UC50408 - Report structural damage

2.21   S5000F Use case UC50409 - Provide equipment calibration certificate

Provide equipment calibration certificate represents a message associated with a use case (UC50409) allowing information associated with an equipment calibration and associated certificate, to be provided.

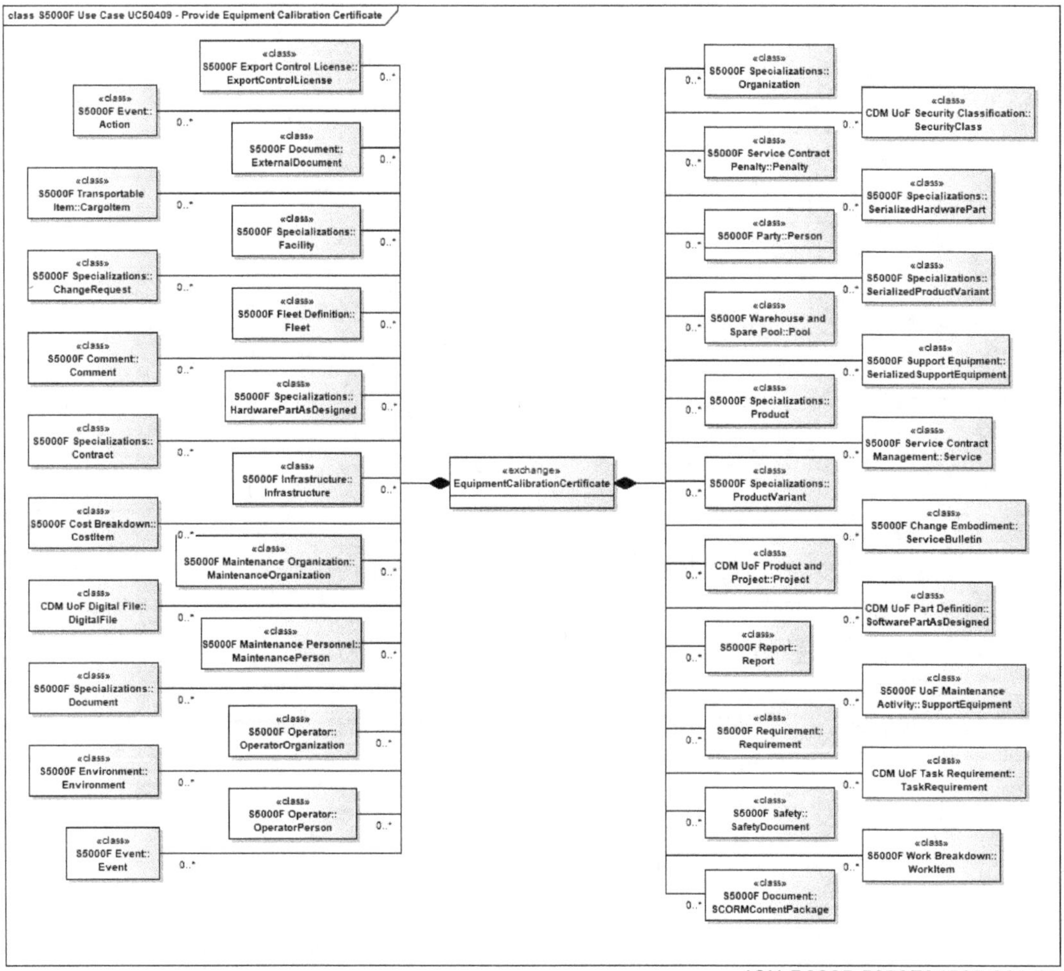

ICN-B6865-5000F24520-001-01

Fig 21 S5000F Use case UC50409 - Provide equipment calibration certificate

2.22   S5000F Use case UC50410 - Track support equipment usage

Track support equipment usage represents a message associated with a use case (UC50410) allowing the usage of a support equipment to be tracked.

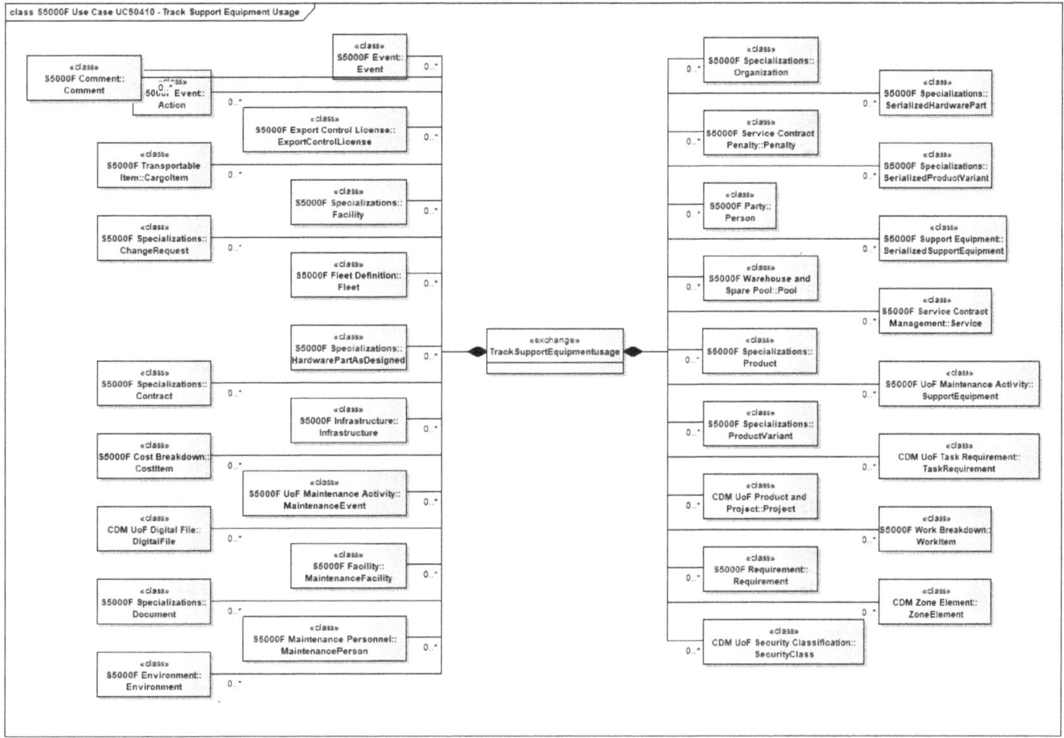

ICN-B6865-5000F24521-001-01

Fig 22 S5000F Use case UC50410 - Track support equipment usage

2.23 S5000F Use case UC50501 - Report safety issue

Report safety issue represents a message associated with a use case (UC50501) providing the information required to report an issue impacting the Product safety.

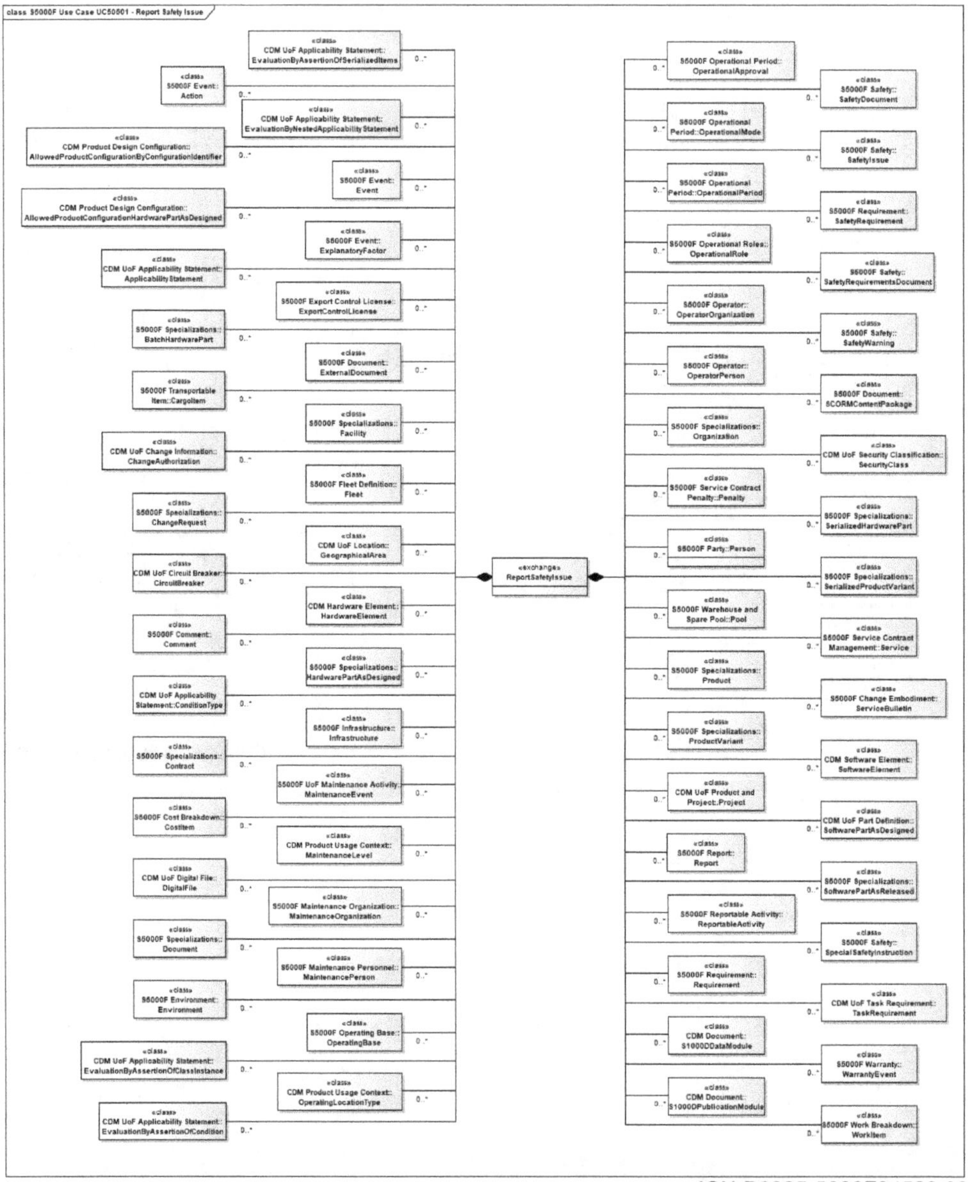

ICN-B6865-5000F24523-001-01

Fig 23 S5000F Use case UC50501 - Report safety issue

2.24   S5000F Use case UC50502 - Report safety warning

Report safety warning represents a message associated with a use case (UC50502) providing the information required to send out a safety warning to the operators of a Product.

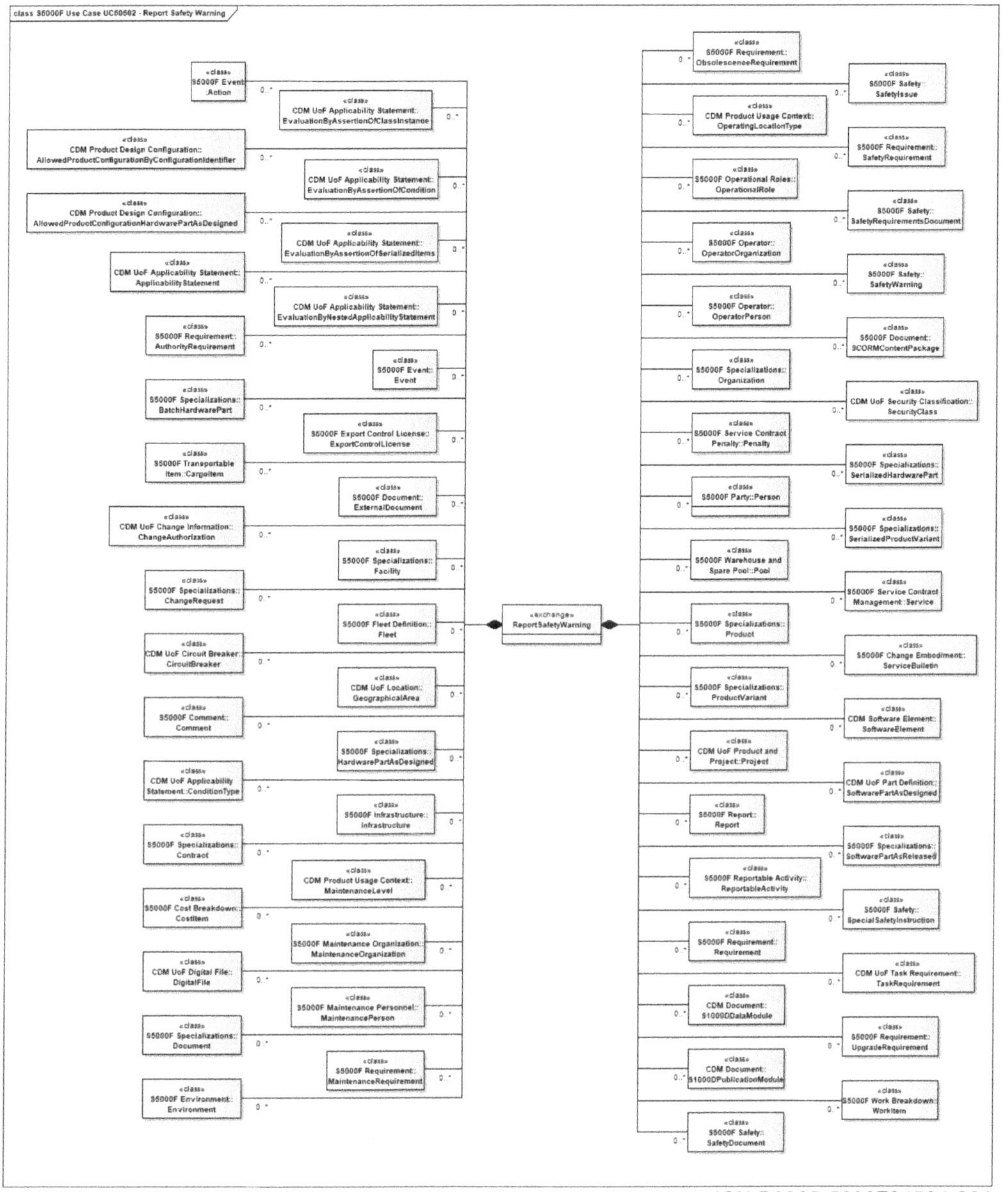

ICN-B6865-5000F24524-001-01

Fig 24 S5000F Use case UC50502 - Report safety warning

2.25 S5000F Use case UC50503 - Provide special safety instructions

Provide special safety instructions represents a message associated with a use case (UC50503) allowing special safety instructions to be transmitted to the operators of a Product, in the event of safety issues.

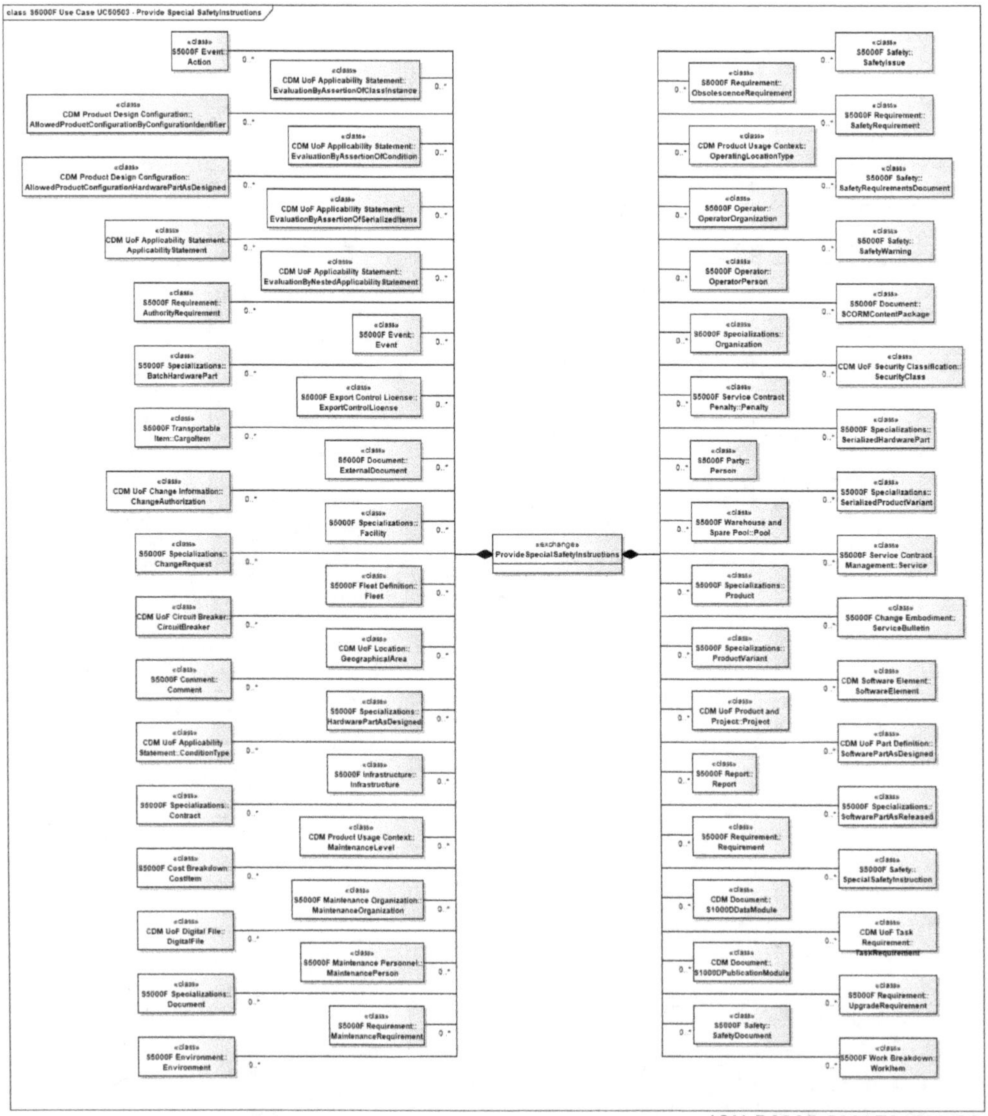

ICN-B6865-5000F24525-001-01

Fig 25 S5000F Use case UC50503 - Provide special safety instructions

2.26 S5000F Use case UC50601 - Report inventory

Report inventory represents a message associated with a use case (UC50601) that provides the inventory information for a warehouse or spares pool.

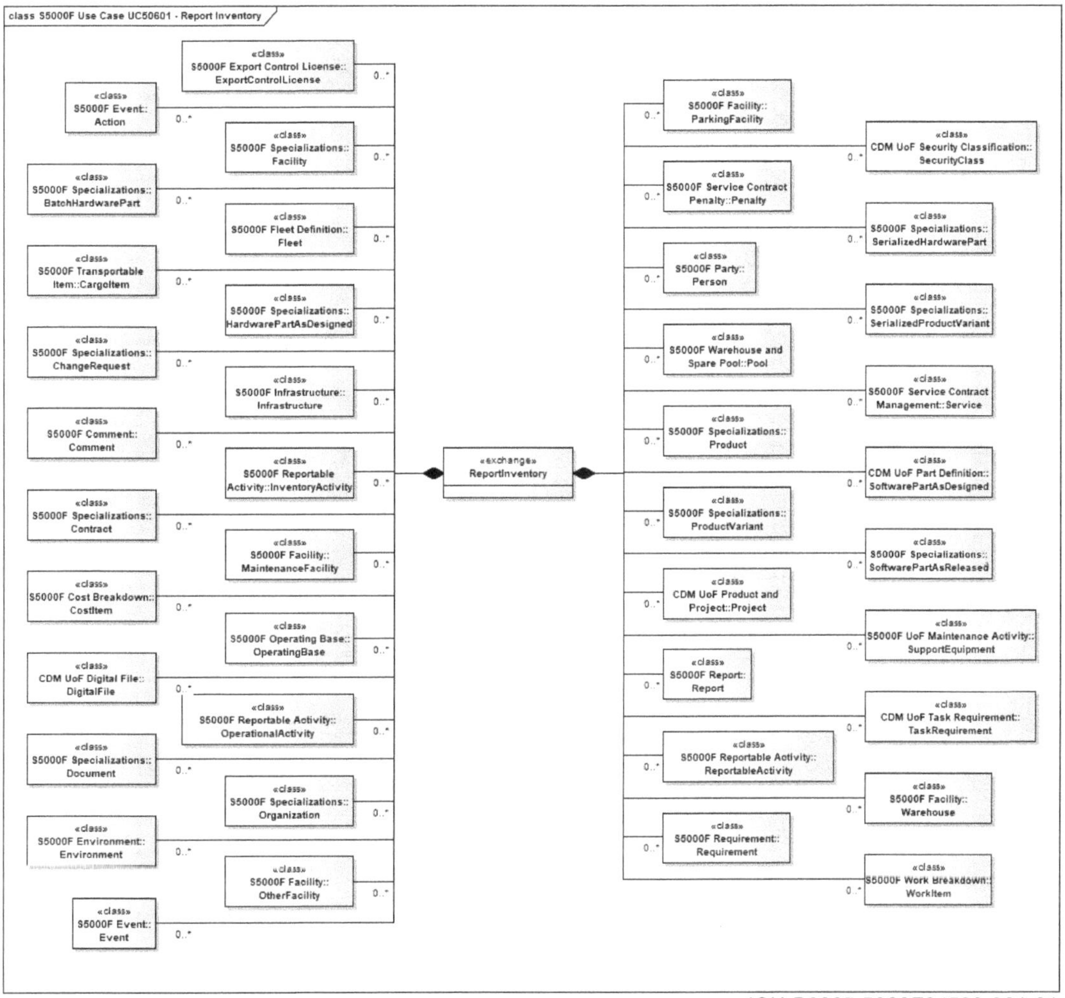

ICN-B6865-5000F24526-001-01

Fig 26 S5000F Use case UC50601 - Report inventory

2.27   S5000F Use case UC50602 - Report shelf life

Report shelf life represents a message associated with a use case (UC50602) providing the information required to report on the shelf life of parts on stock.

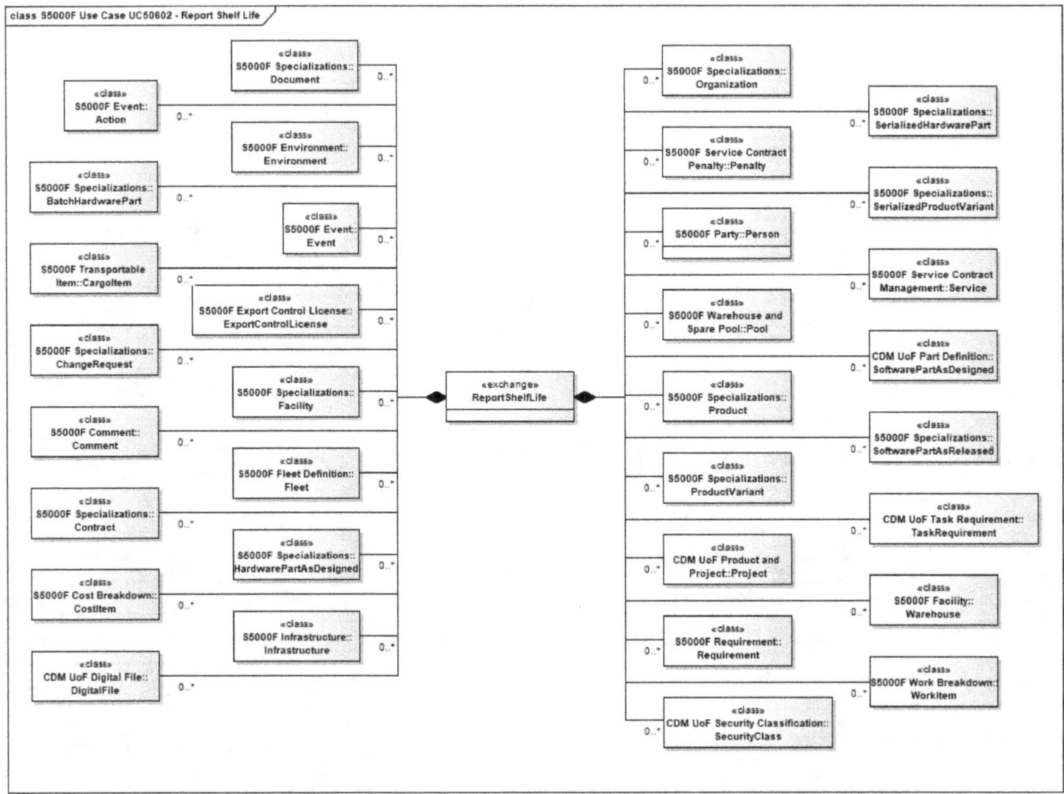

ICN-B6865-5000F24527-001-01

Fig 27 S5000F Use case UC50602 - Report shelf life

2.28 S5000F Use case UC50603 - Report spares and pool

Report spares and pool represents a message associated with a use case (UC50603) providing the information required to report on the spares available in a warehouse or spares pool.

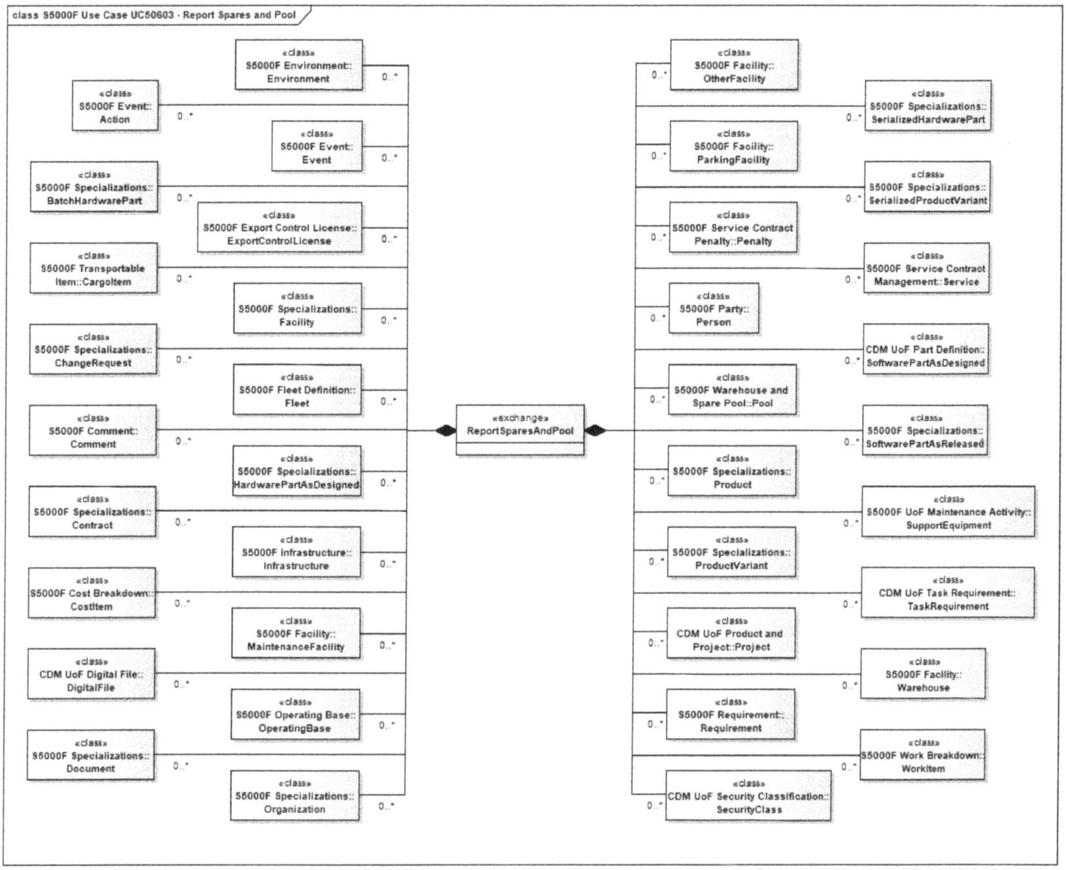

ICN-B6865-5000F24528-001-01

Fig 28 S5000F Use case UC50603 - Report spares and pool

2.29   S5000F Use case UC50604 - Report logistic response time

Report logistic response time represents a message associated with a use case (UC50604) providing the response time that is achieved when responding to a logistic request.

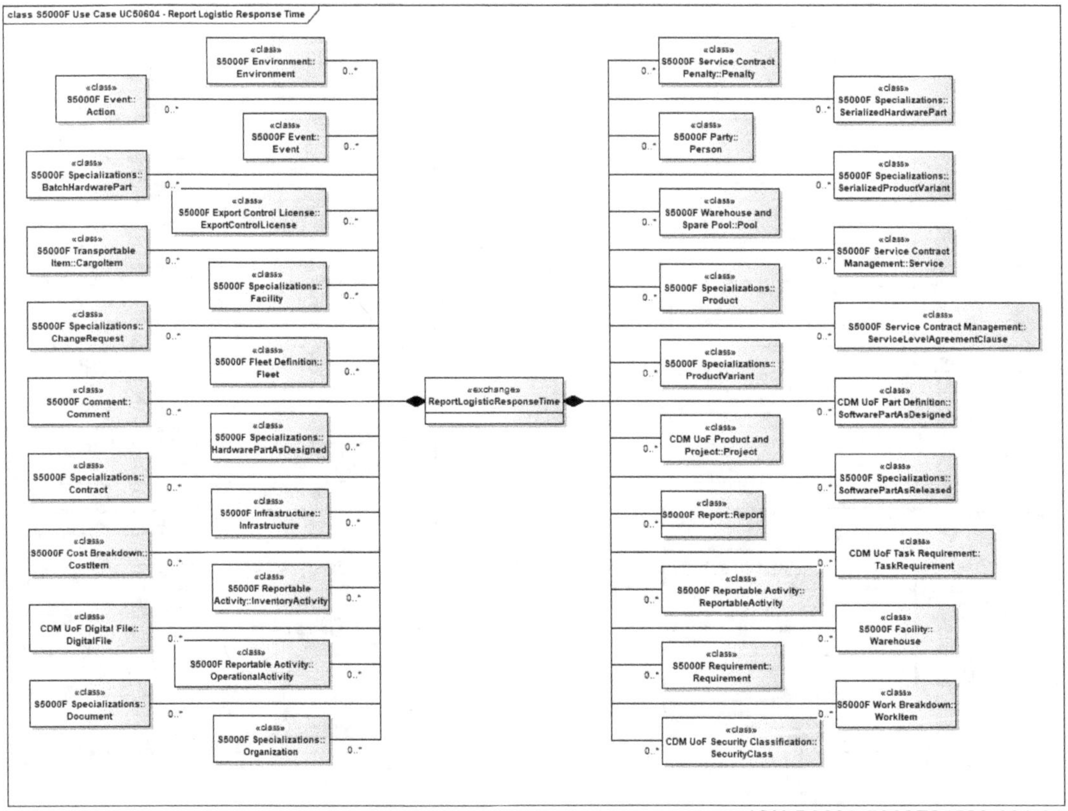

ICN-B6865-5000F24529-001-01

Fig 29 S5000F Use case UC50604 - Report logistic response time

2.30 S5000F Use case UC50605 - Report facilities

Report facilities represents a message associated with a use case (UC50605) providing information about existing facilities.

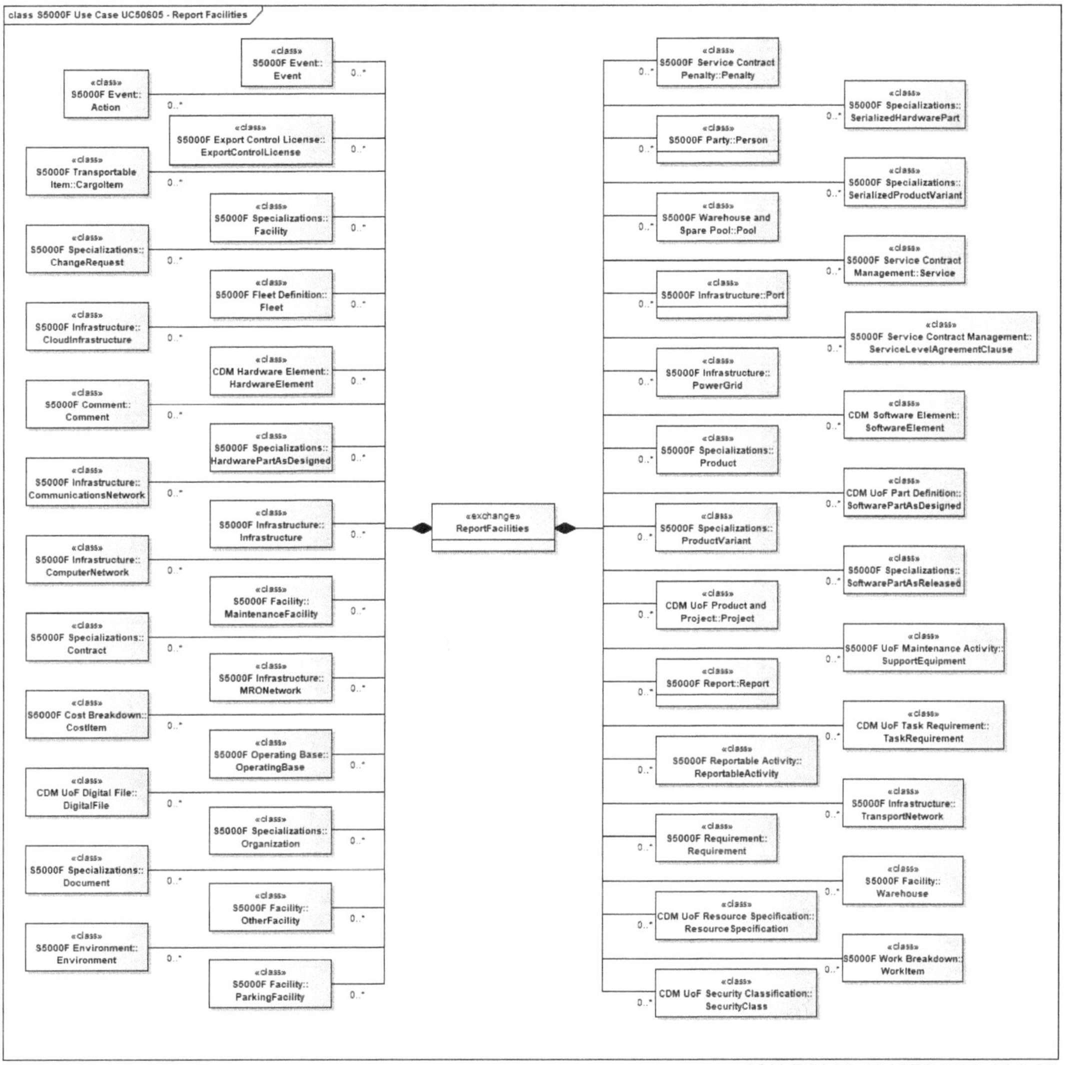

ICN-B6865-5000F24530-001-01

Fig 30 S5000F Use case UC50605 - Report facilities

2.31   S5000F Use case UC50606 - Plan for transport

Plan for transport represents a message associated with a use case (UC50606) providing the information required to plan for the transport of assets.

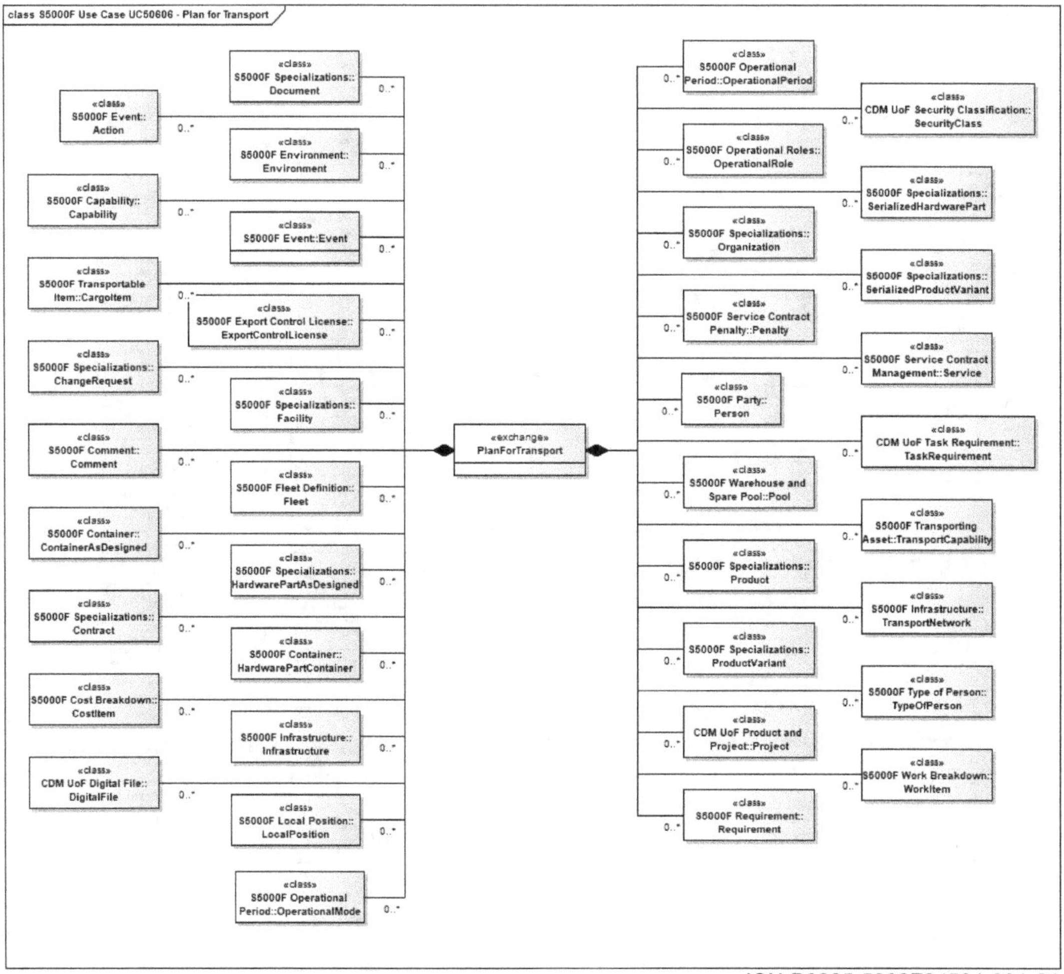

ICN-B6865-5000F24531-001-01

Fig 31 S5000F Use case UC50606 - Plan for transport

2.32   S5000F Use case UC50701 - Provide Cost Breakdown Structure (CBS)

Provide Cost Breakdown Structure (CBS) represents a message associated with a use case (UC50701) allowing a cost breakdown structure to be provided to a different party.

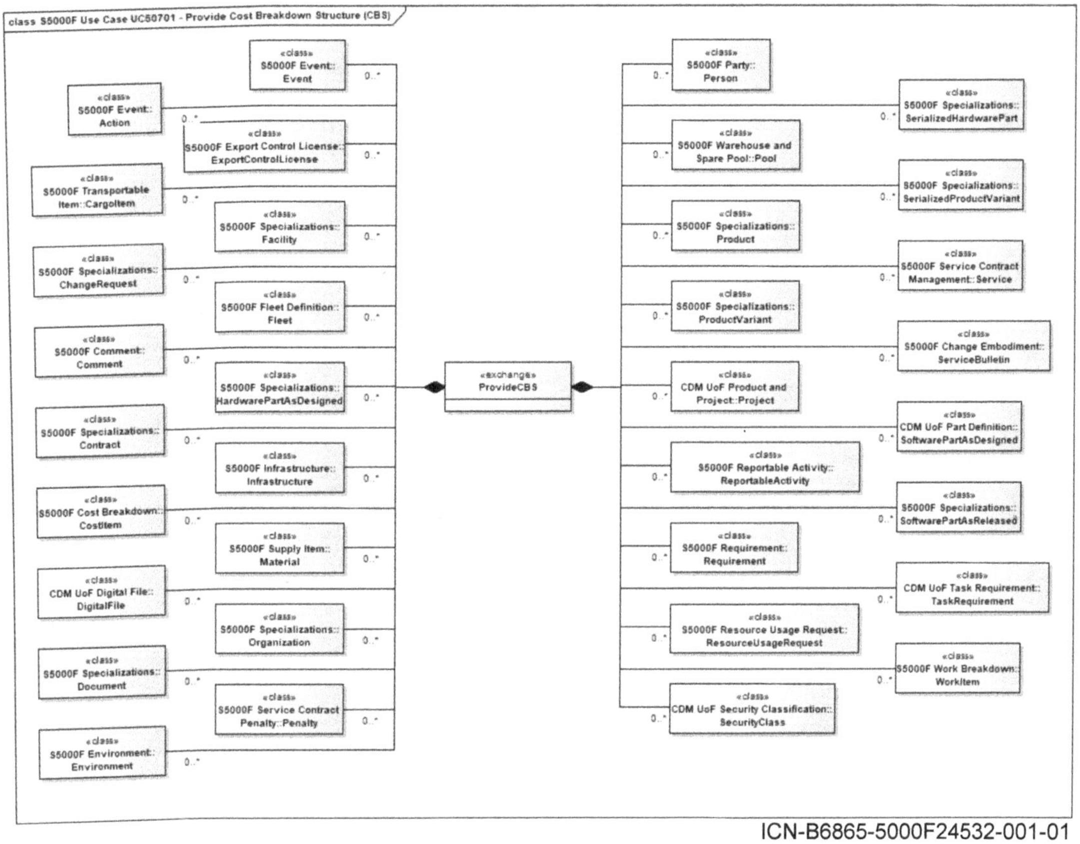

ICN-B6865-5000F24532-001-01

Fig 32 S5000F Use case UC50701 - Provide Cost Breakdown Structure (CBS)

2.33   S5000F Use case UC50702 - Report maintenance costs

Report maintenance costs represents a message associated with a use case (UC50702) providing the information required to report on the costs associated to maintenance.

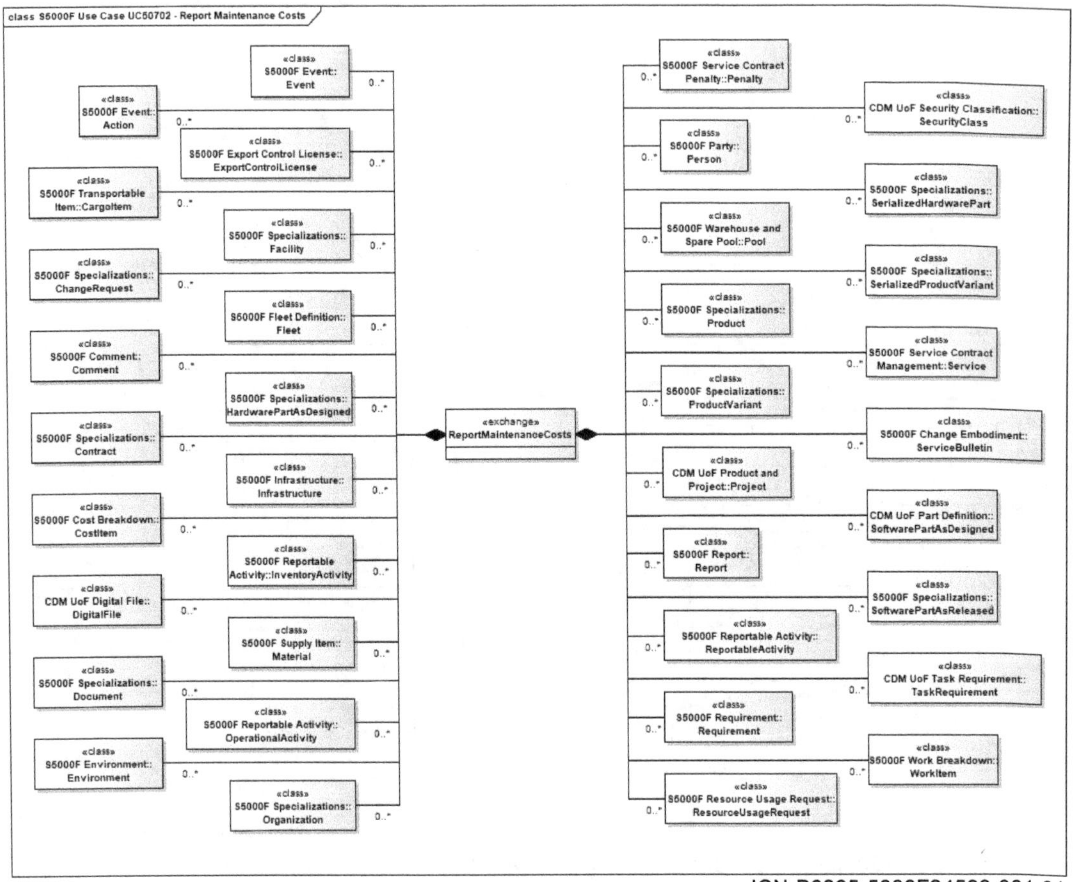

ICN-B6865-5000F24533-001-01

Fig 33 S5000F Use case UC50702 - Report maintenance costs

2.34 S5000F Use case UC50703 - Report operational costs

Report operational costs represents a message associated with a use case (UC50703) providing the information required to report on the operational costs of a Product.

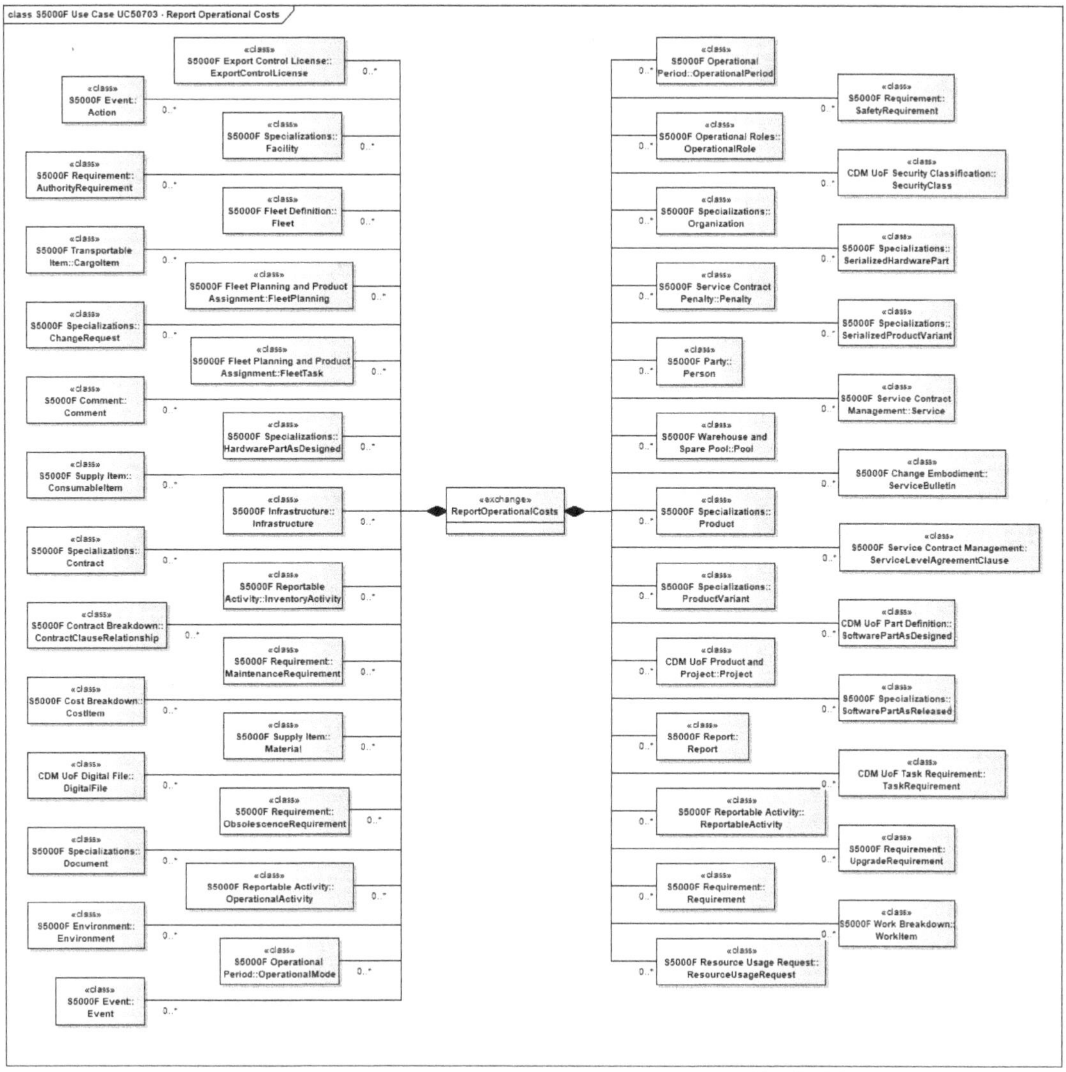

ICN-B6865-5000F24534-001-01

Fig 34 S5000F Use case UC50703 - Report operational costs

2.35 S5000F Use case UC50704 - Report modification costs

Report modification costs represents a message associated with a use case (UC50704) providing the information required to report on the cost of a modification to the Product.

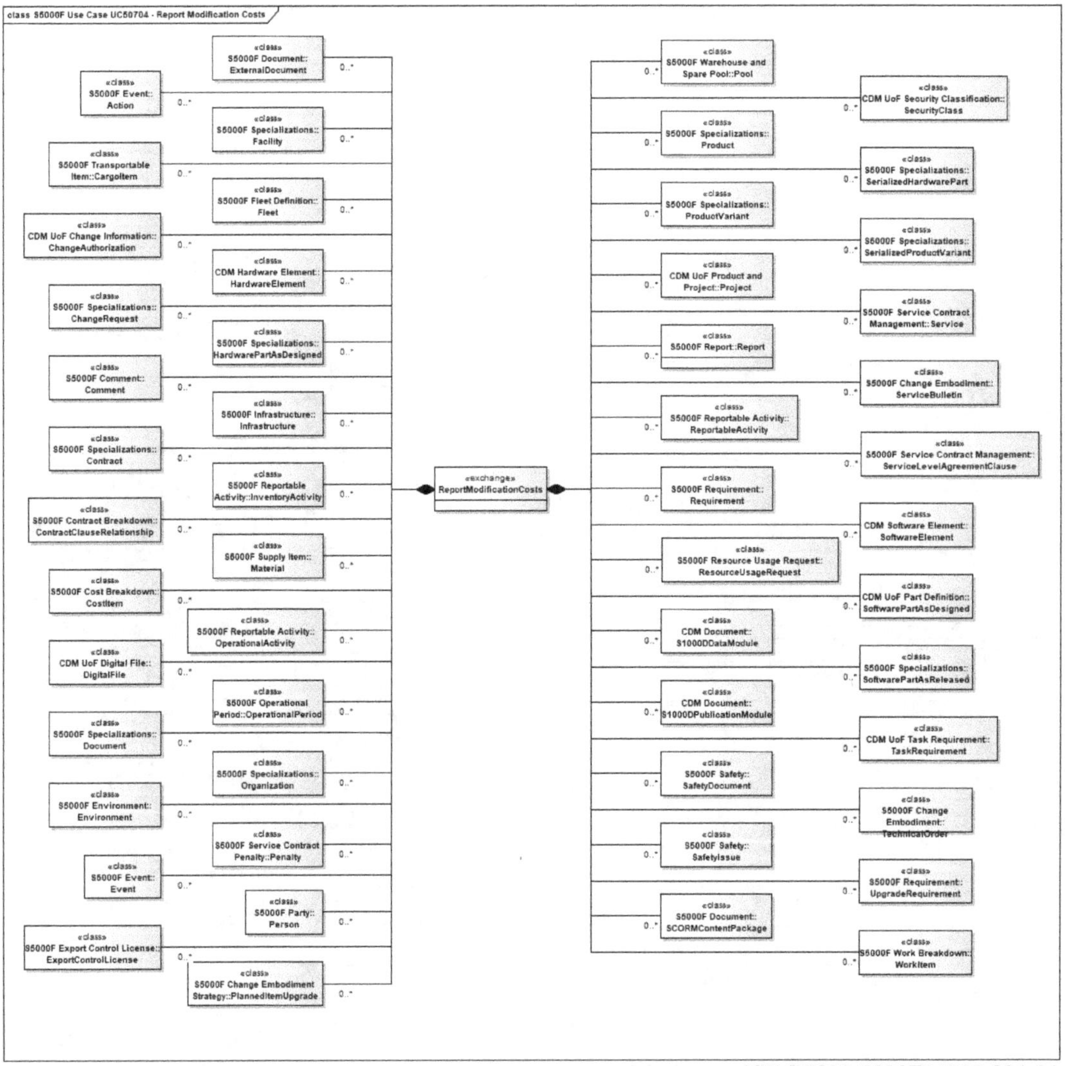

ICN-B6865-5000F24535-001-01

Fig 35 S5000F Use case UC50704 - Report modification costs

2.36   S5000F Use case UC50705 - Report in-service costs

Report in-service costs represents a message associated with a use case (UC50705) that allows costs incurred during the in-service phase to be reported.

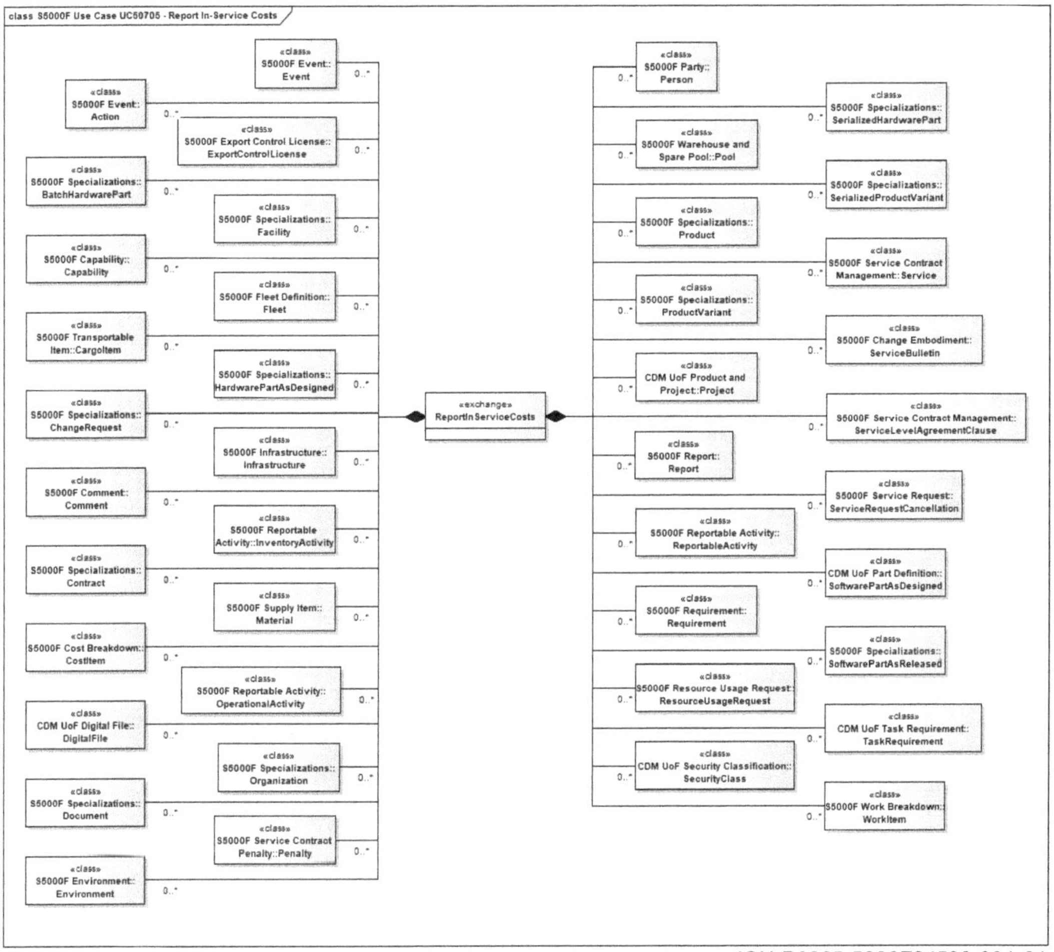

ICN-B6865-5000F24536-001-01

Fig 36 S5000F Use case UC50705 - Report in-service costs

2.37   S5000F Use case UC50801 - Evaluate maintenance actions

Evaluate maintenance actions represents a message associated with a use case (UC50801) that allows the effectivity of maintenance actions to be assessed.

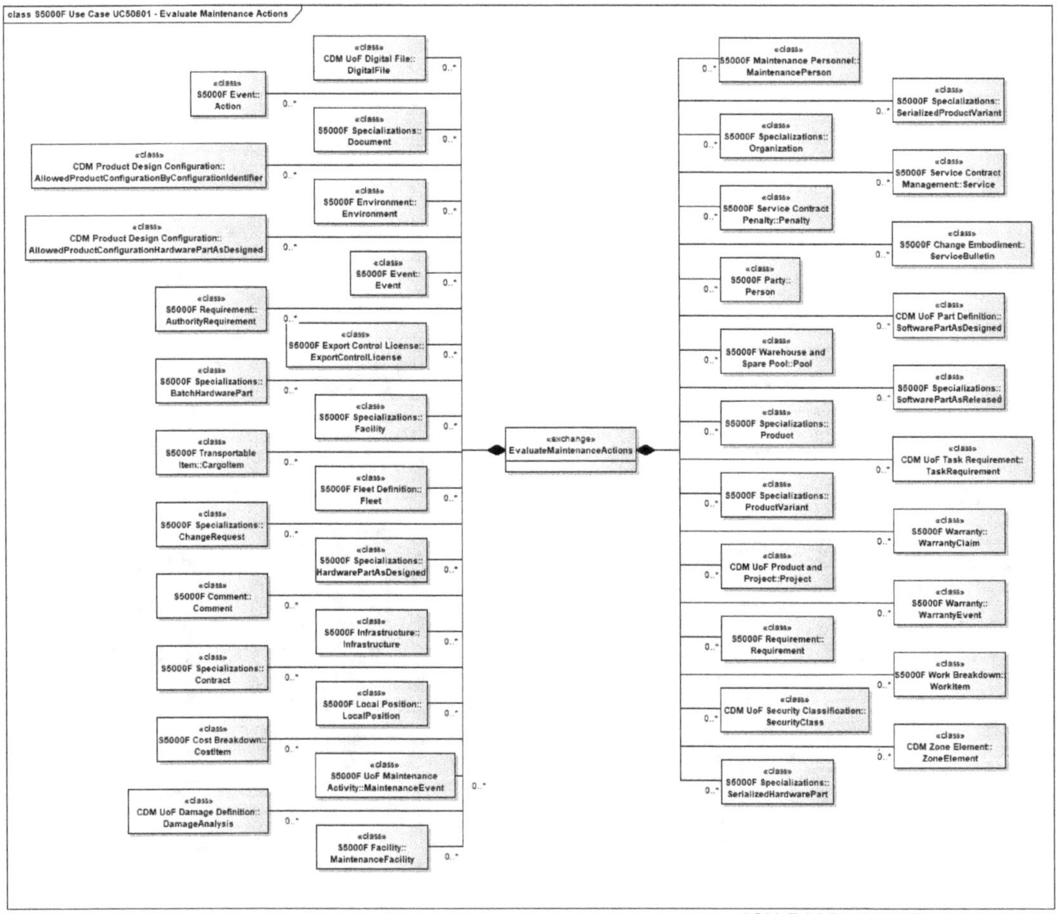

ICN-B6865-5000F24537-001-01

Fig 37 S5000F Use case UC50801 - Evaluate maintenance actions

2.38 S5000F Use case UC50802 - Collect warranty costs

Collect warranty costs represents a message associated with a use case (UC50802) providing the necessary information to compile the costs of warranty.

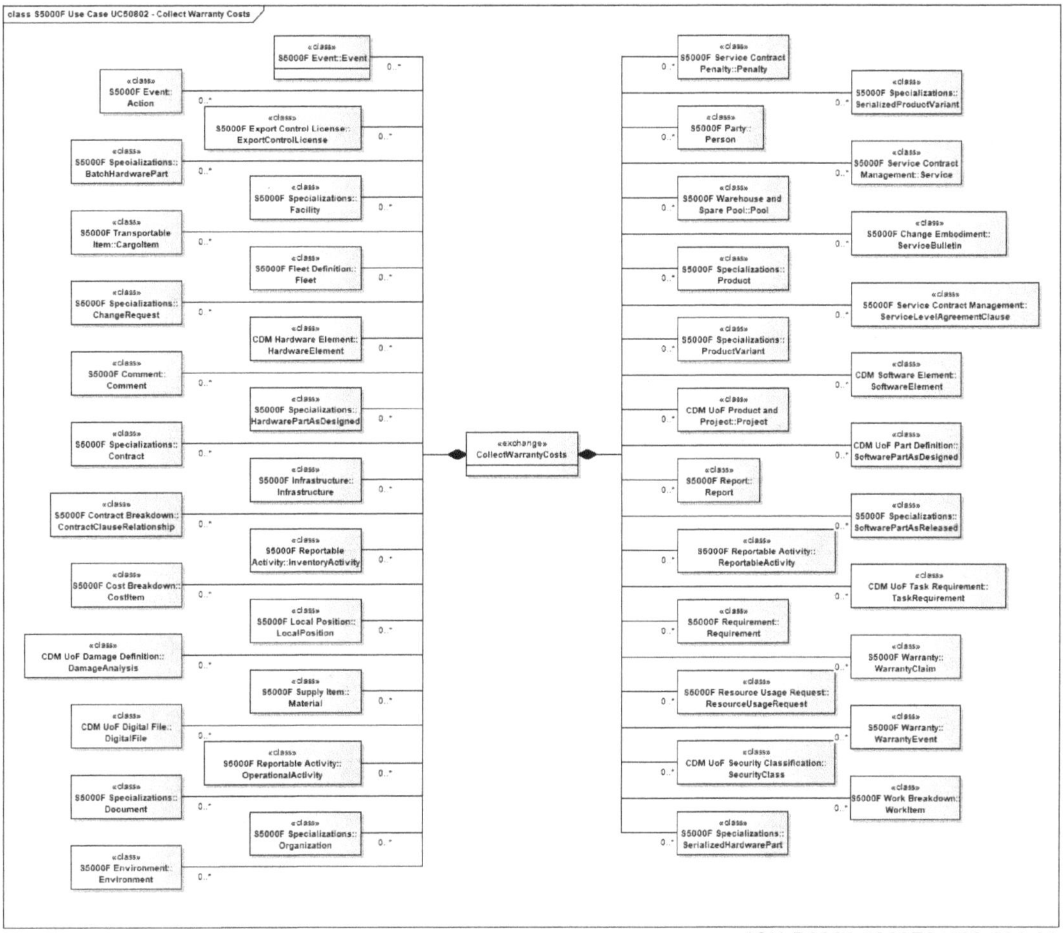

ICN-B6865-5000F24538-001-01

Fig 38 S5000F Use case UC50802 - Collect warranty costs

2.39   S5000F Use case UC50803 - Determine warranty misuse

Determine warranty misuse represents a message associated with a use case (UC50803) providing the necessary information to determine whether warranty was or not misused.

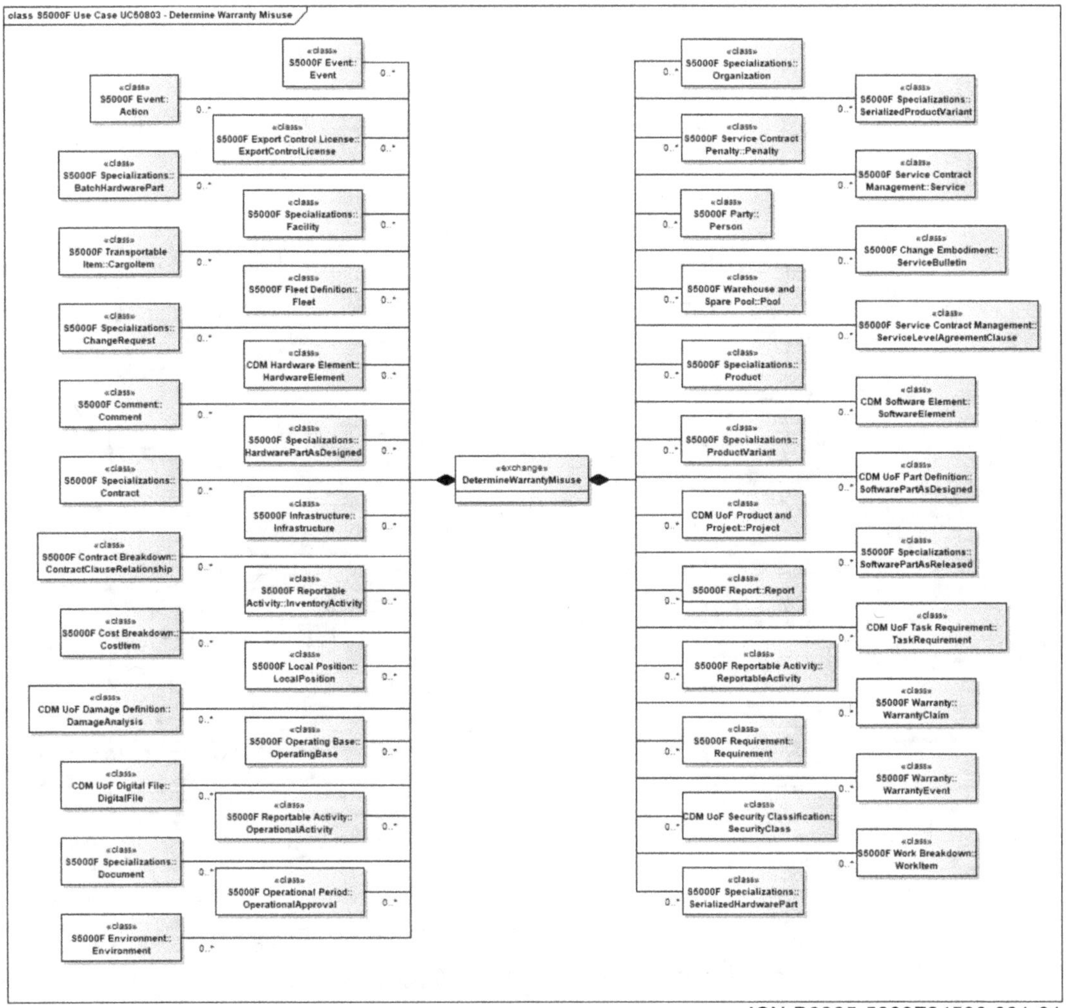

ICN-B6865-5000F24539-001-01

Fig 39 S5000F Use case UC50803 - Determine warranty misuse

S5000F Use case UC50804 - Identify warranty risks

Identify warranty risks represents a message associated with a use case (UC50804) providing the necessary information to identify potential warranty risks.

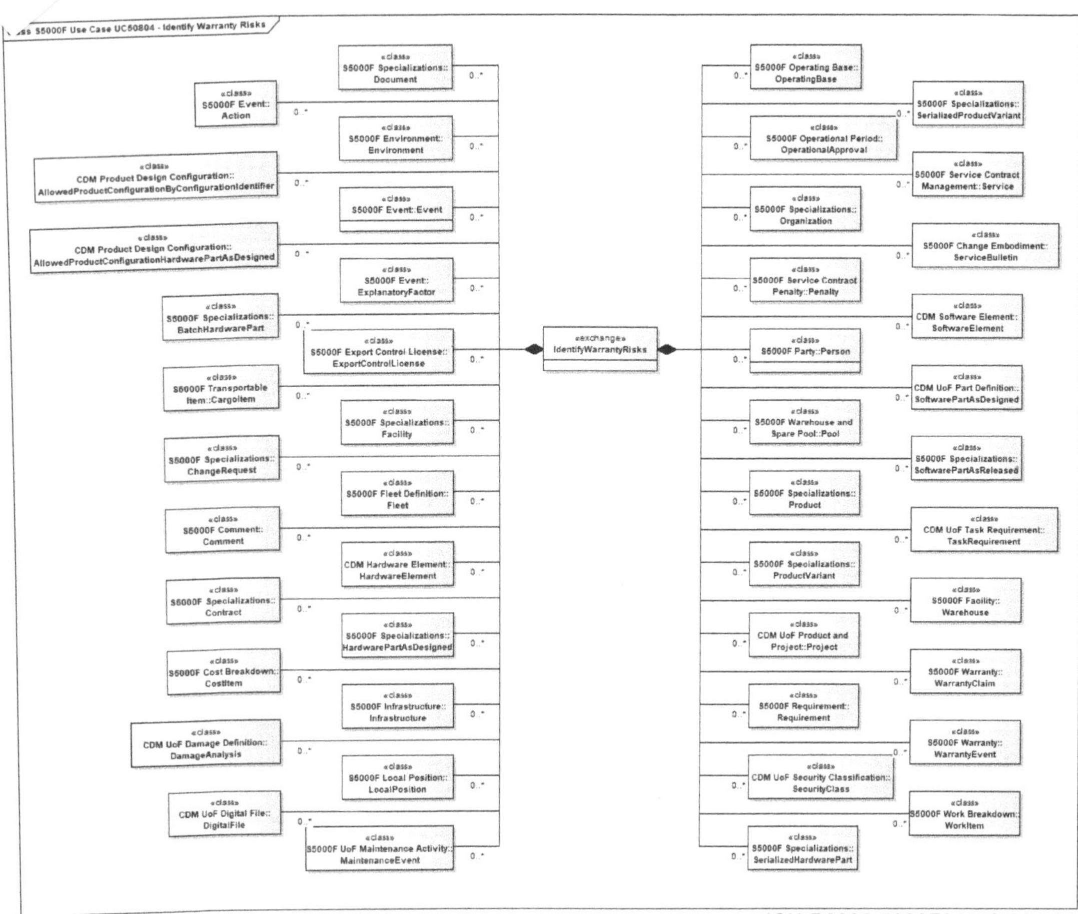

ICN-B6865-5000F24540-001-01

Fig 40 S5000F Use case UC50804 - Identify warranty risks

2.41   S5000F Use case UC50805 - Improve warranty rules

Improve warranty rules represents a message associated with a use case (UC50805) providing the necessary information to evaluate the suitability of existing warranty rules.

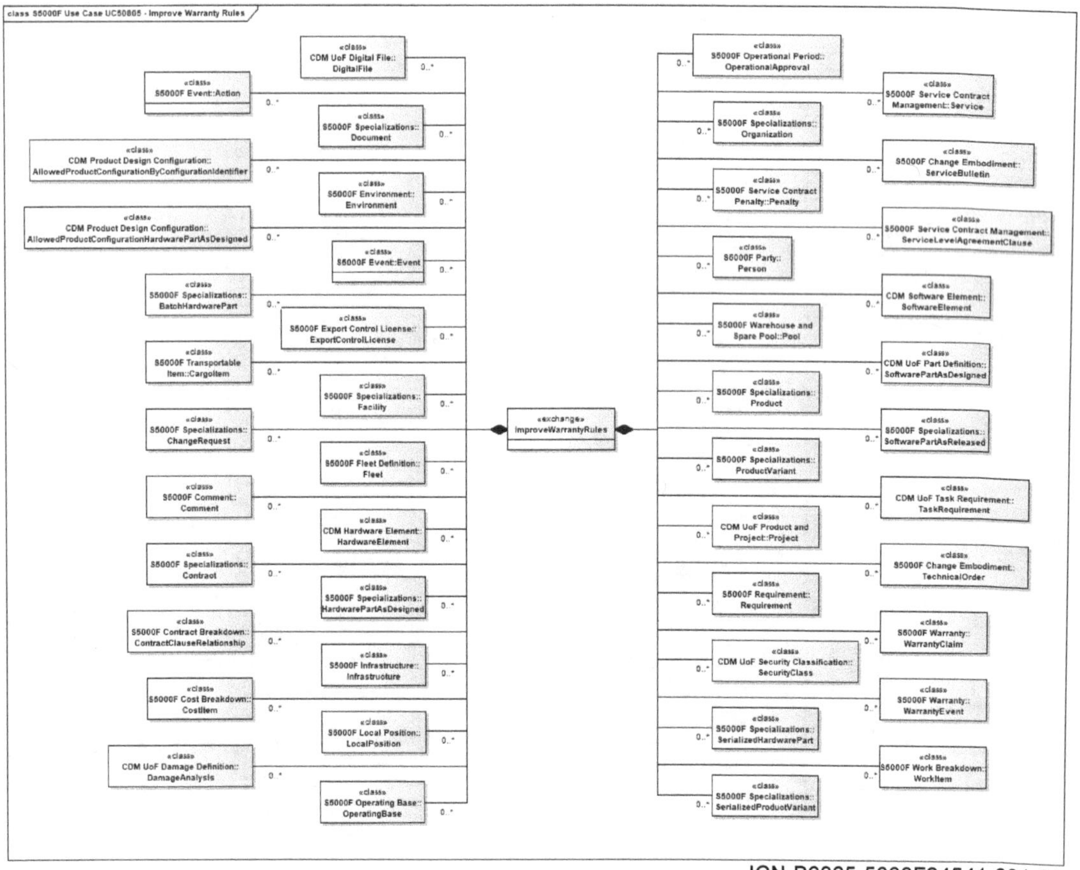

ICN-B6865-5000F24541-001-01

Fig 41 S5000F Use case UC50805 - Improve warranty rules

2.42 S5000F Use case UC50901 - Record health data

Record health data represents a message associated with a use case (UC50901) allowing health and monitoring data for a serialized Product to be transferred.

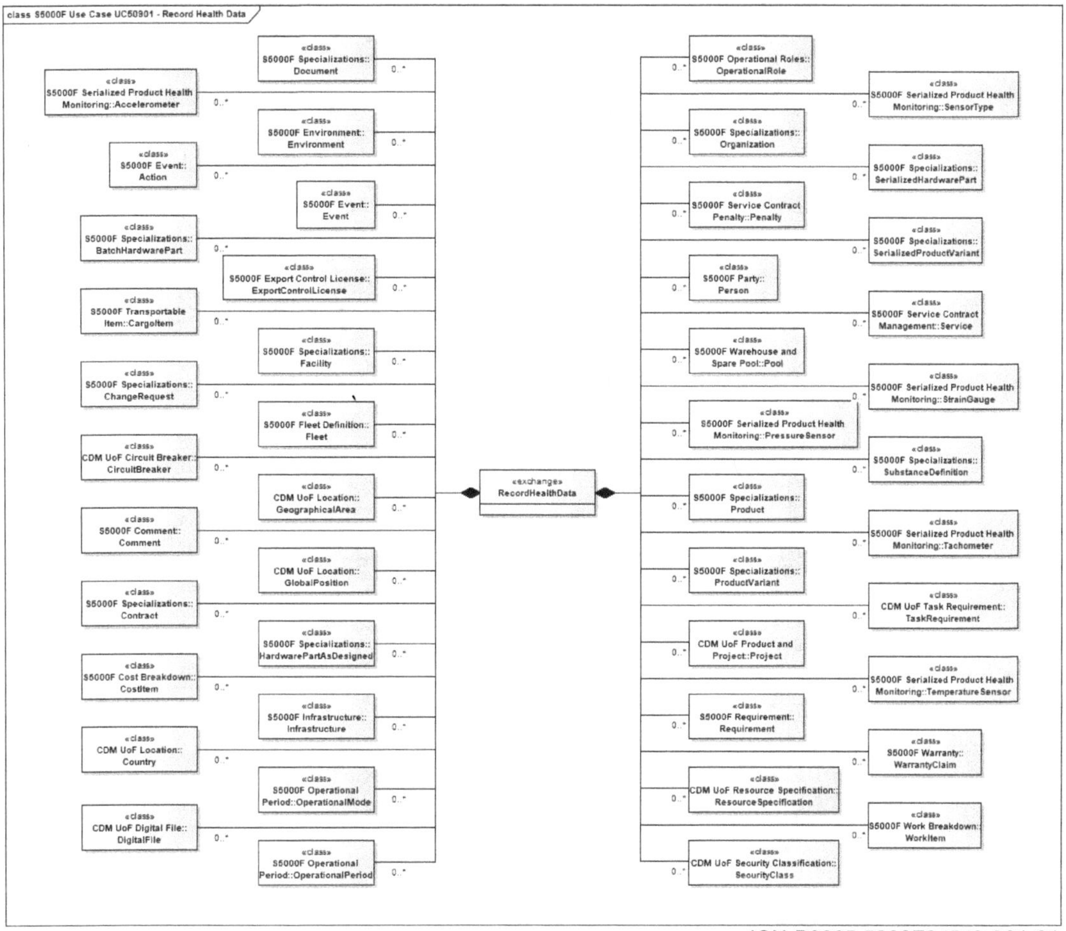

ICN-B6865-5000F24542-001-01

Fig 42 S5000F Use case UC50901 - Record health data

2.43   S5000F Use case UC50902 - Report usage information

Report usage information represents a message associated with a use case (UC50902) providing the information about a Product usage.

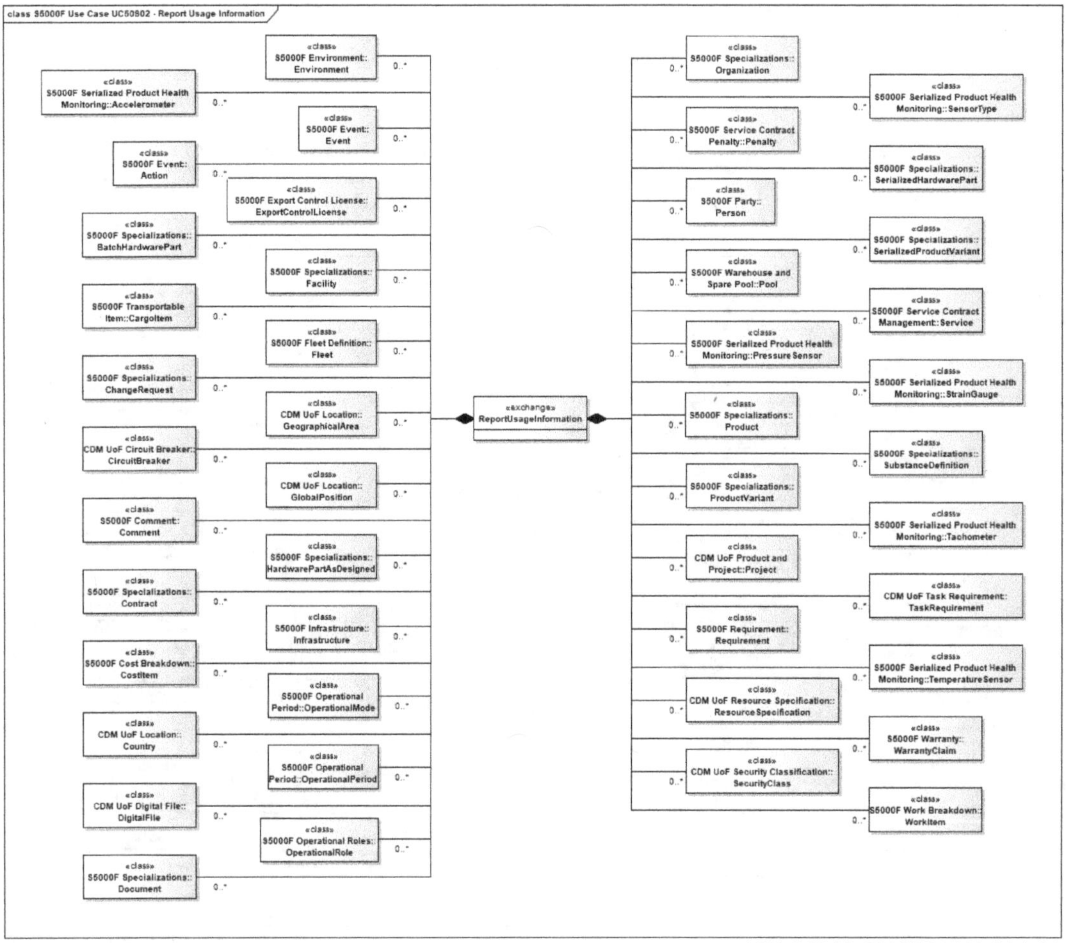

ICN-B6865-5000F24543-001-01

Fig 43 S5000F Use case UC50902 - Report usage information

2.44 S5000F Use case UC50903 - Respond to usage information

Respond to usage information represents a message associated with a use case (UC50903) providing the information required to take action after receiving usage information.

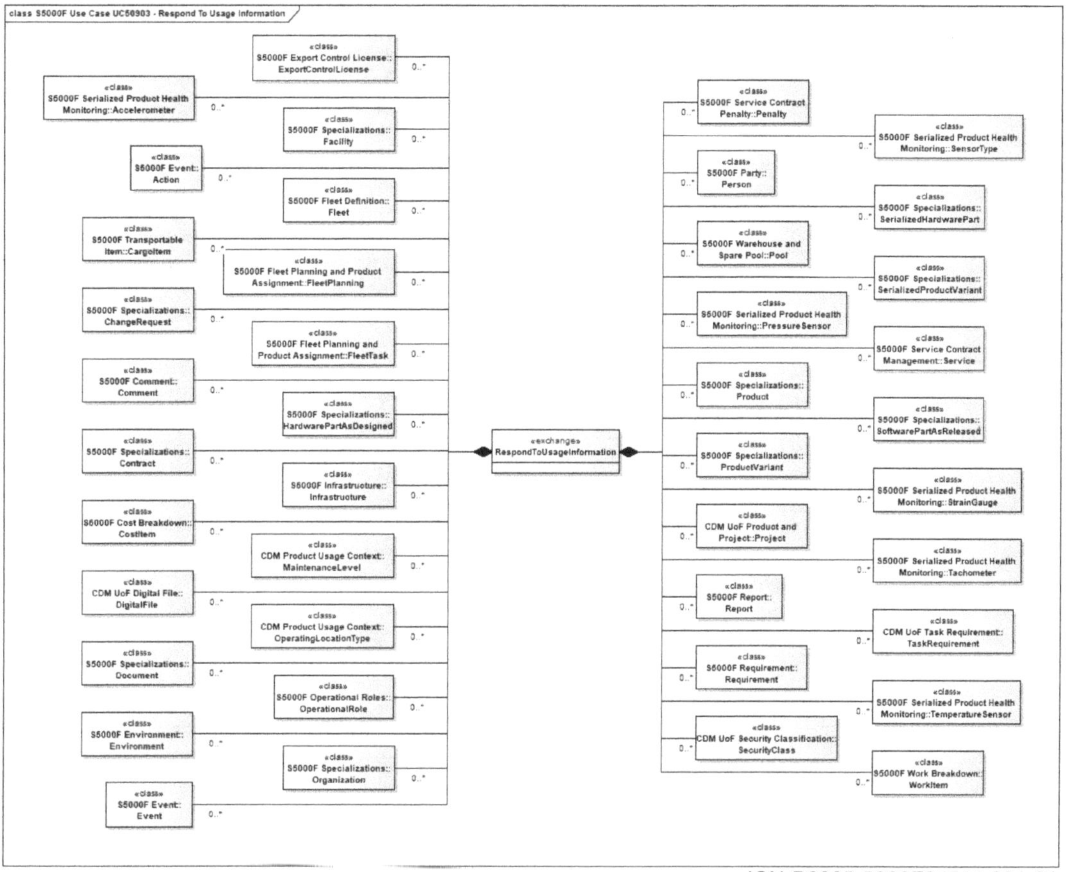

ICN-B6865-5000F-24544-001-01

Fig 44 S5000F Use case UC50903 - Respond to usage information

2.45   S5000F Use case UC51001 - Perform obsolescence planning

Perform obsolescence planning represents a message associated with a use case (UC51001) providing the necessary information to plan for the obsolescence of an item.

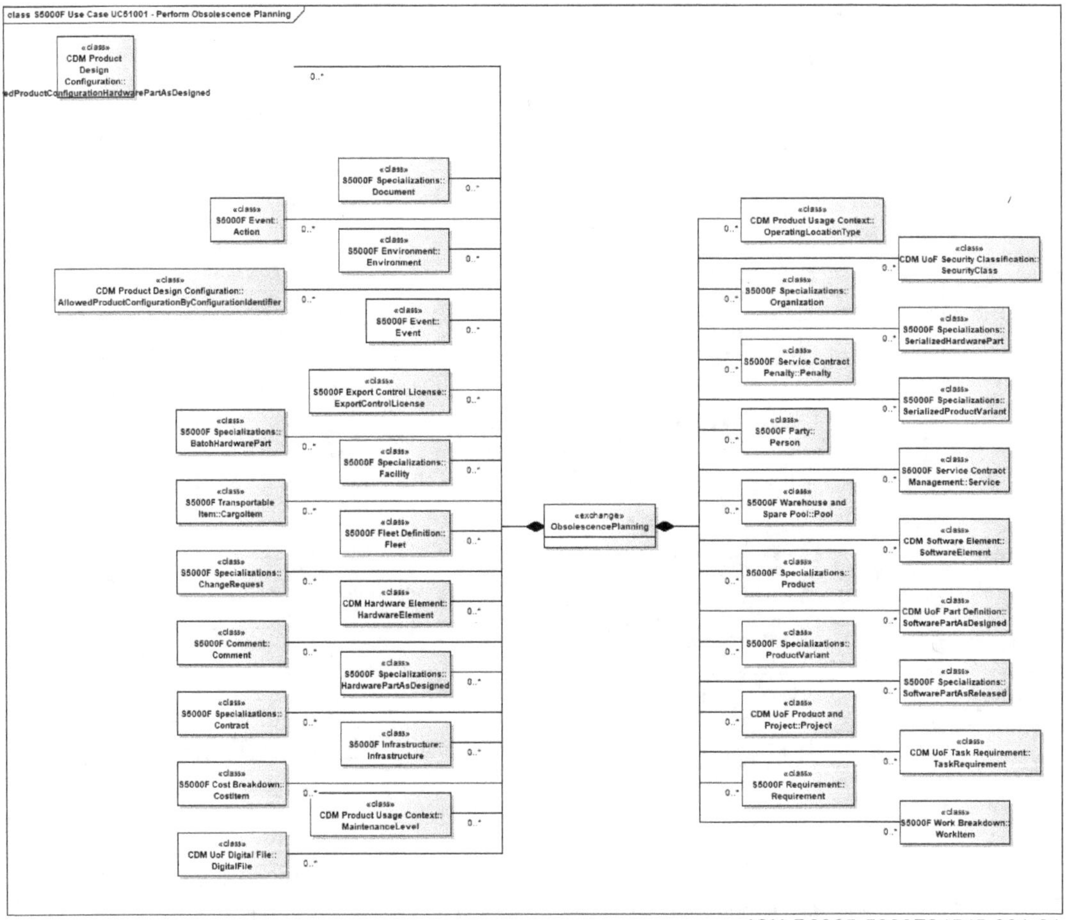

ICN-B6865-5000F24545-001-01

Fig 45 S5000F Use case UC51001 - Perform obsolescence planning

2.46 S5000F Use case UC51002 - Determine obsolescence candidates

Determine obsolescence candidates represents a message associated with a use case (UC51002) providing the necessary information to identify items that are facing potential obsolescence.

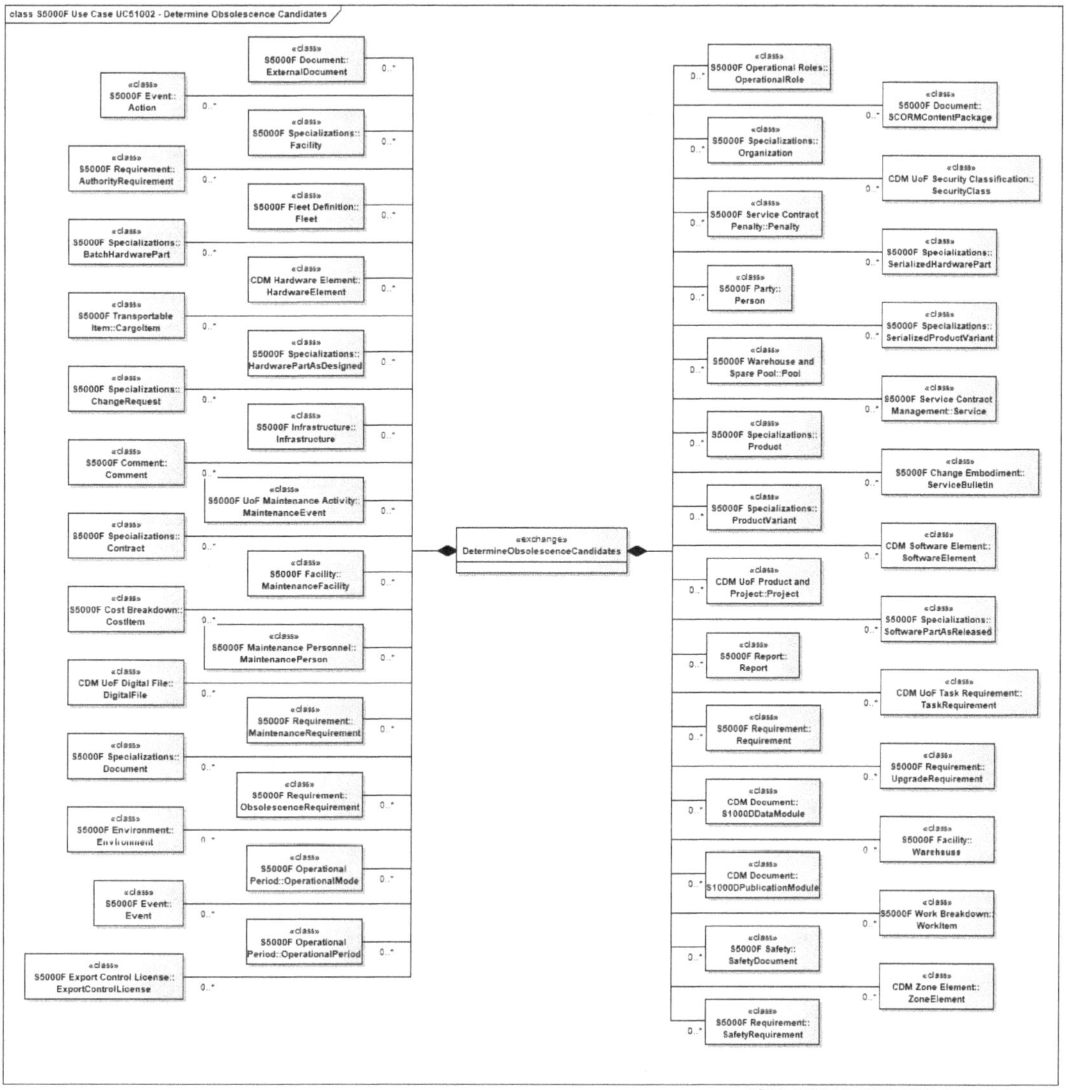

ICN-B6865-5000F24546-001-01

Fig 46 S5000F Use case UC51002 - Determine obsolescence candidates

2.47   S5000F Use case UC51003 - Determine obsolescence strategy

Determine obsolescence strategy represents a message associated with a use case (UC51003) providing the necessary information to define the strategy on handling obsolescence.

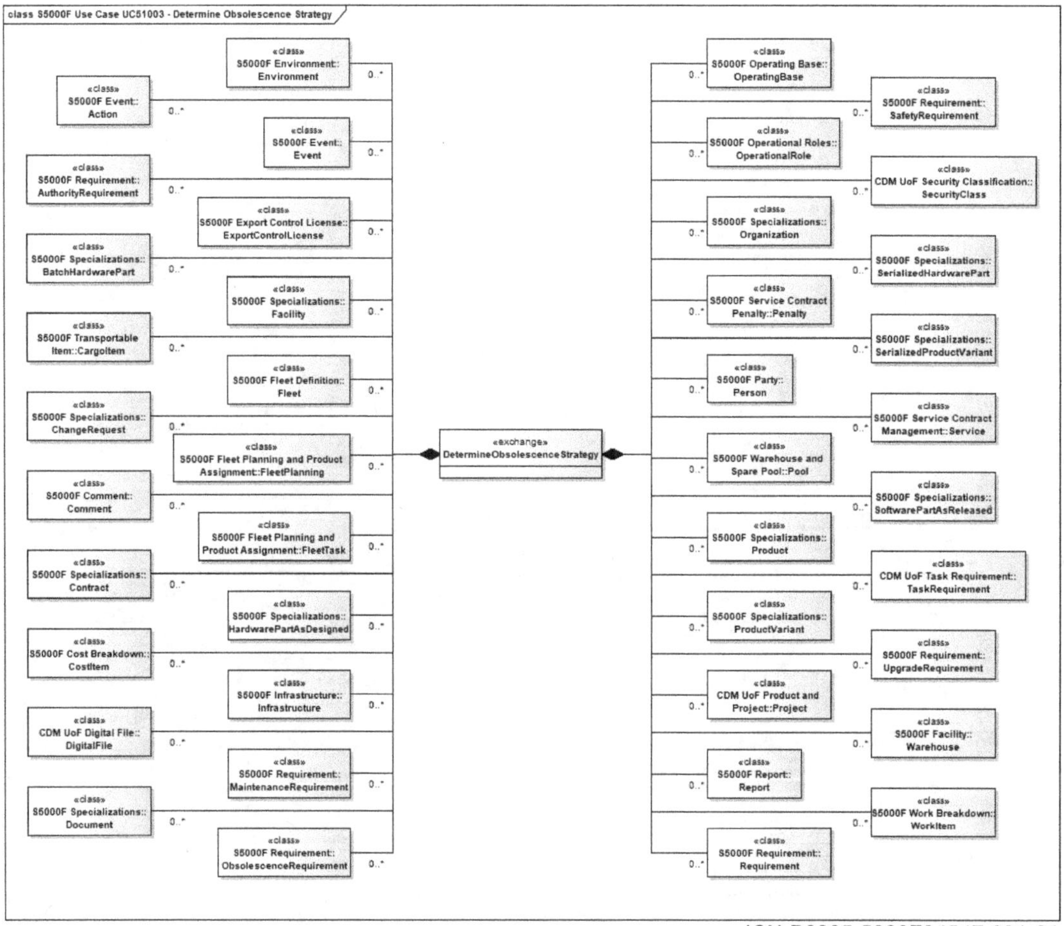

ICN-B6865-5000F24547-001-01

Fig 47 S5000F Use case UC51003 - Determine obsolescence strategy

2.48 S5000F Use case UC51004 - Monitor obsolescence

Monitor obsolescence represents a message associated with a use case (UC51004) providing the necessary information to monitor possible obsolescences and prepare for them.

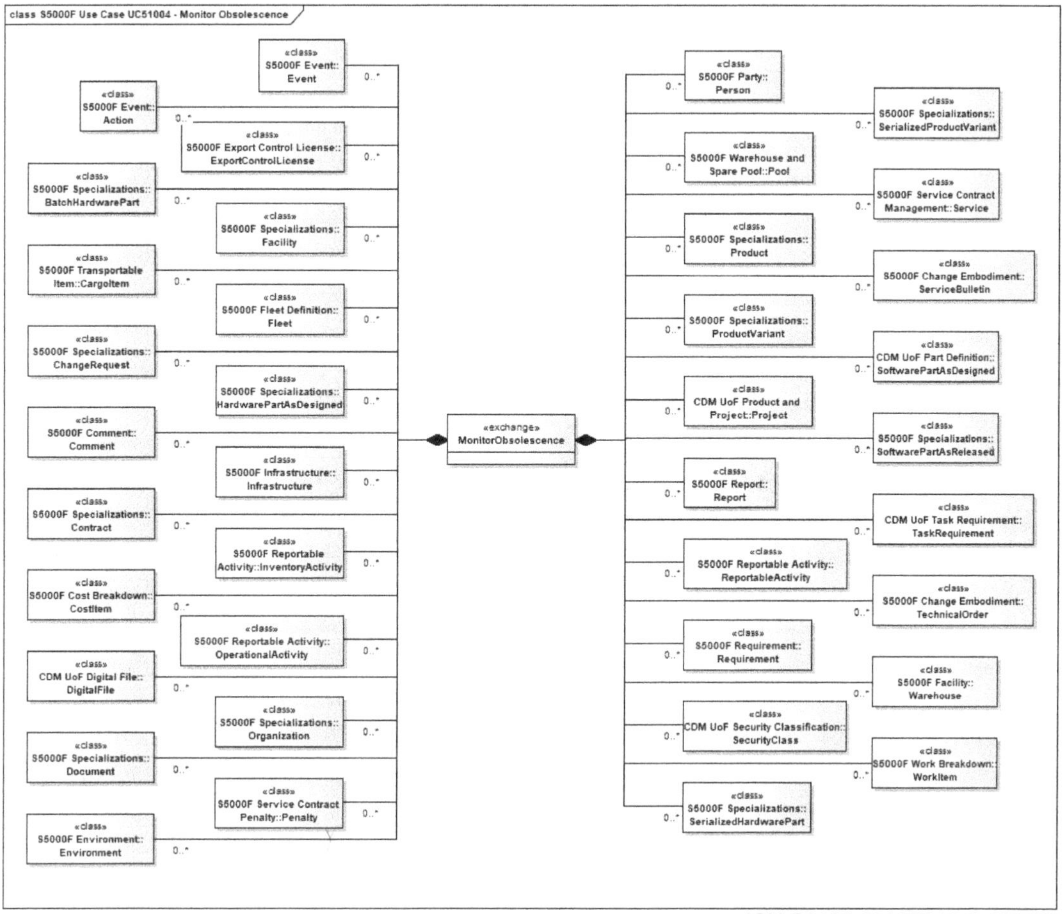

ICN-B6865-5000F24548-001-01

Fig 48 S5000F Use case UC51004 - Monitor obsolescence

2.49   S5000F Use case UC51005 - Solve obsolescence

Solve obsolescence represents a message associated with a use case (UC51005) providing the information required to solve an obsolescence.

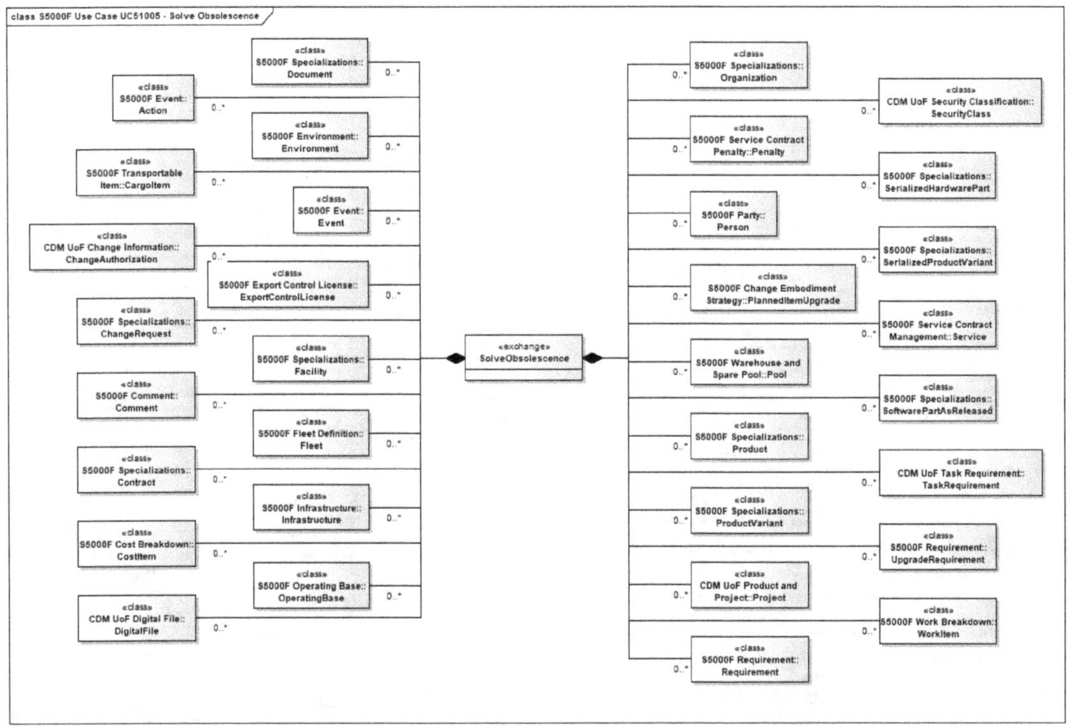

ICN-B6865-5000F24549-001-01

Fig 49 S5000F Use case UC51005 - Solve obsolescence

2.50 S5000F Use case UC51006 - Provide obsolescence alert

Provide obsolescence alert represents a message associated with a use case (UC51006) providing the capability to inform other parties about an upcoming obsolescence.

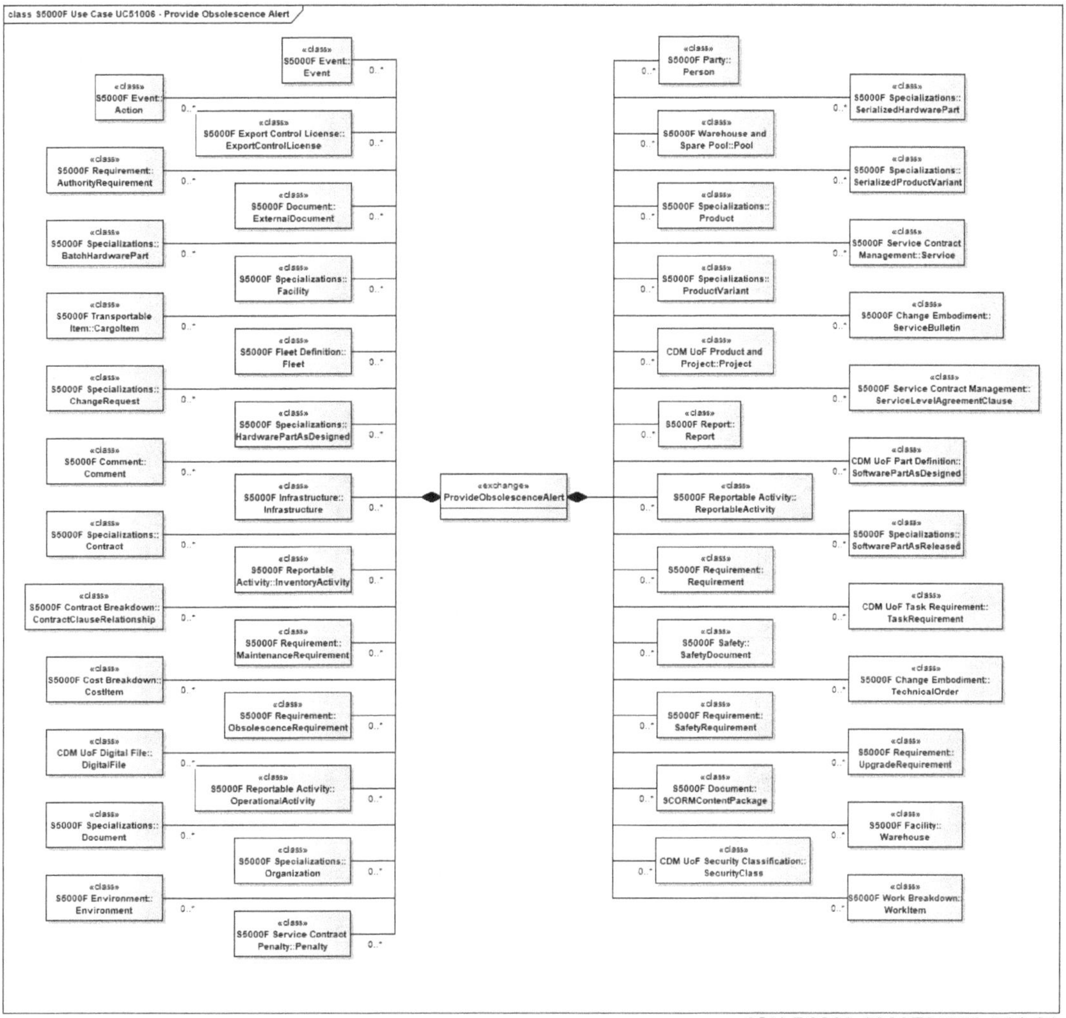

ICN-B6865-5000F24550-001-01

Fig 50 S5000F Use case UC51006 - Provide obsolescence alert

2.51   S5000F Use case UC51101 - Elaborate assignment proposal

Elaborate assignment proposal represents a message associated with a use case (UC51101) providing the necessary information to provide a proposal about how a serialized Product variant can perform a specific fleet task.

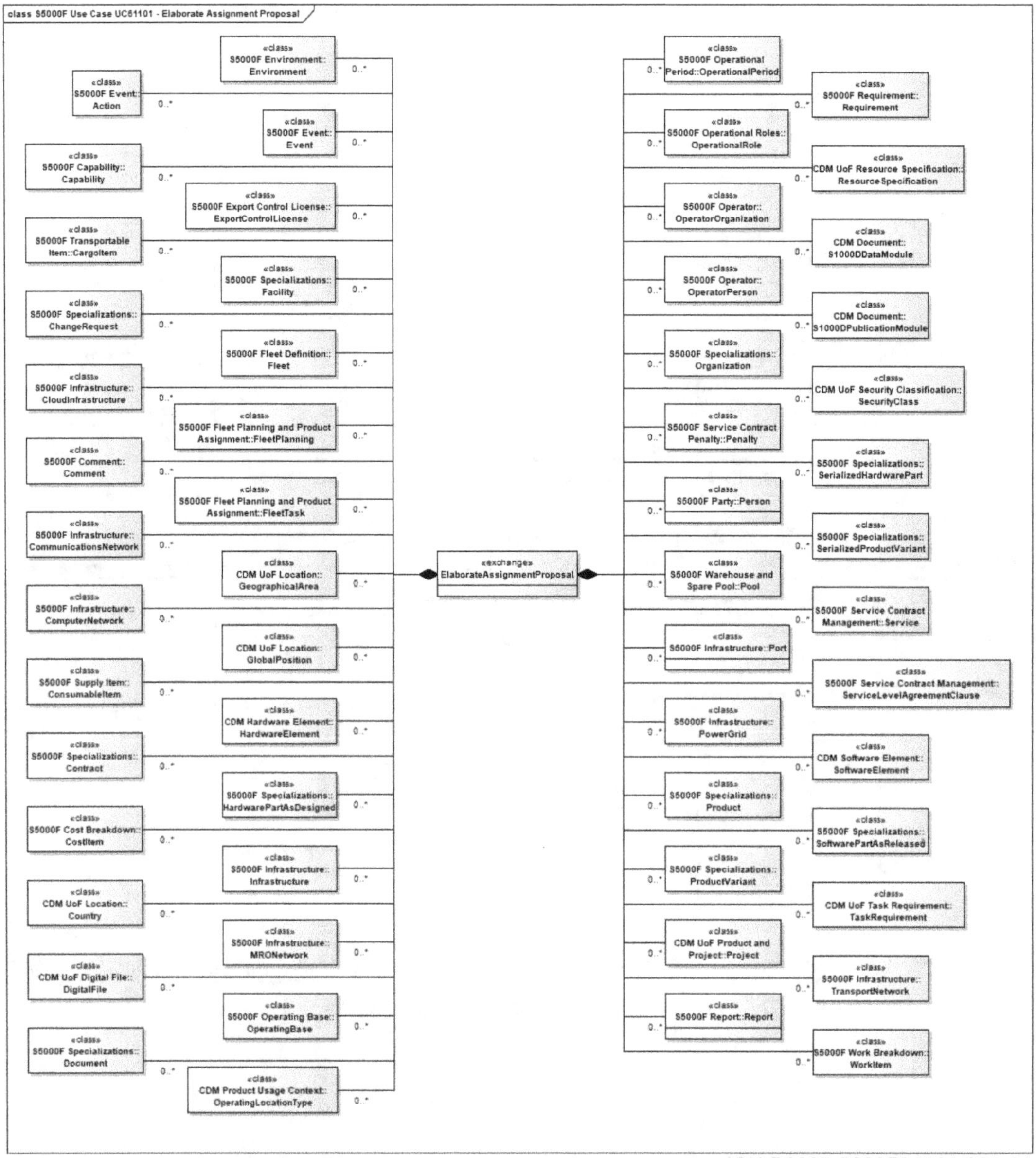

ICN-B6865-5000F24551-001-01

Fig 51 S5000F Use case UC51101 - Elaborate assignment proposal

2.52   S5000F Use case UC51102 - Cancel fleet task

Cancel fleet task represents a message associated with a use case (UC51102) providing the necessary information to cancel an ongoing or planned fleet task.

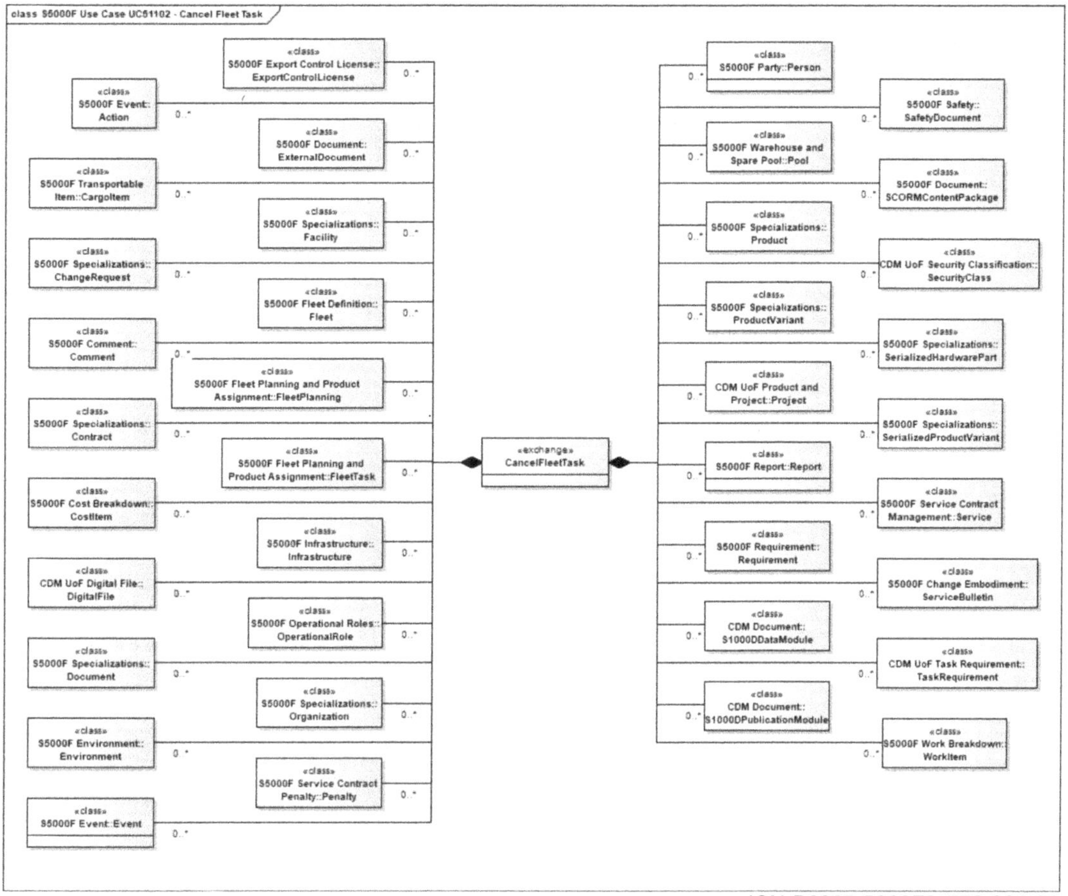

class S5000F Use Case UC51102 - Cancel Fleet Task

«class» S5000F Event::Action — 0..*
«class» S5000F Export Control License::ExportControlLicense — 0..*
«class» S5000F Document::ExternalDocument — 0..*
«class» S5000F Transportable Item::CargoItem — 0..*
«class» S5000F Specializations::Facility — 0..*
«class» S5000F Specializations::ChangeRequest — 0..*
«class» S5000F Fleet Definition::Fleet — 0..*
«class» S5000F Comment::Comment — 0..*
«class» S5000F Fleet Planning and Product Assignment::FleetPlanning — 0..*
«class» S5000F Specializations::Contract — 0..*
«class» S5000F Fleet Planning and Product Assignment::FleetTask — 0..*
«class» S5000F Cost Breakdown::CostItem — 0..*
«class» S5000F Infrastructure::Infrastructure — 0..*
«class» CDM UoF Digital File::DigitalFile — 0..*
«class» S5000F Operational Roles::OperationalRole — 0..*
«class» S5000F Specializations::Document — 0..*
«class» S5000F Specializations::Organization — 0..*
«class» S5000F Environment::Environment — 0..*
«class» S5000F Service Contract Penalty::Penalty — 0..*
«class» S5000F Event::Event — 0..*

«exchange» CancelFleetTask

«class» S5000F Party::Person — 0..*
«class» S5000F Safety::SafetyDocument — 0..*
«class» S5000F Warehouse and Spare Pool::Pool — 0..*
«class» S5000F Document::SCORMContentPackage — 0..*
«class» S5000F Specializations::Product — 0..*
«class» CDM UoF Security Classification::SecurityClass — 0..*
«class» S5000F Specializations::ProductVariant — 0..*
«class» S5000F Specializations::SerializedHardwarePart — 0..*
«class» CDM UoF Product and Project::Project — 0..*
«class» S5000F Specializations::SerializedProductVariant — 0..*
«class» S5000F Report::Report — 0..*
«class» S5000F Service Contract Management::Service — 0..*
«class» S5000F Requirement::Requirement — 0..*
«class» S5000F Change Embodiment::ServiceBulletin — 0..*
«class» CDM Document::S1000DDataModule — 0..*
«class» CDM UoF Task Requirement::TaskRequirement — 0..*
«class» CDM Document::S1000DPublicationModule — 0..*
«class» S5000F Work Breakdown::WorkItem — 0..*

ICN-B6865-5000F24552-001-01

Fig 52 S5000F Use case UC51102 - Cancel fleet task

2.53 S5000F Use case UC51103 - Modify fleet task

Modify fleet task represents a message associated with a use case (UC51103) providing the necessary information required to modify a fleet task.

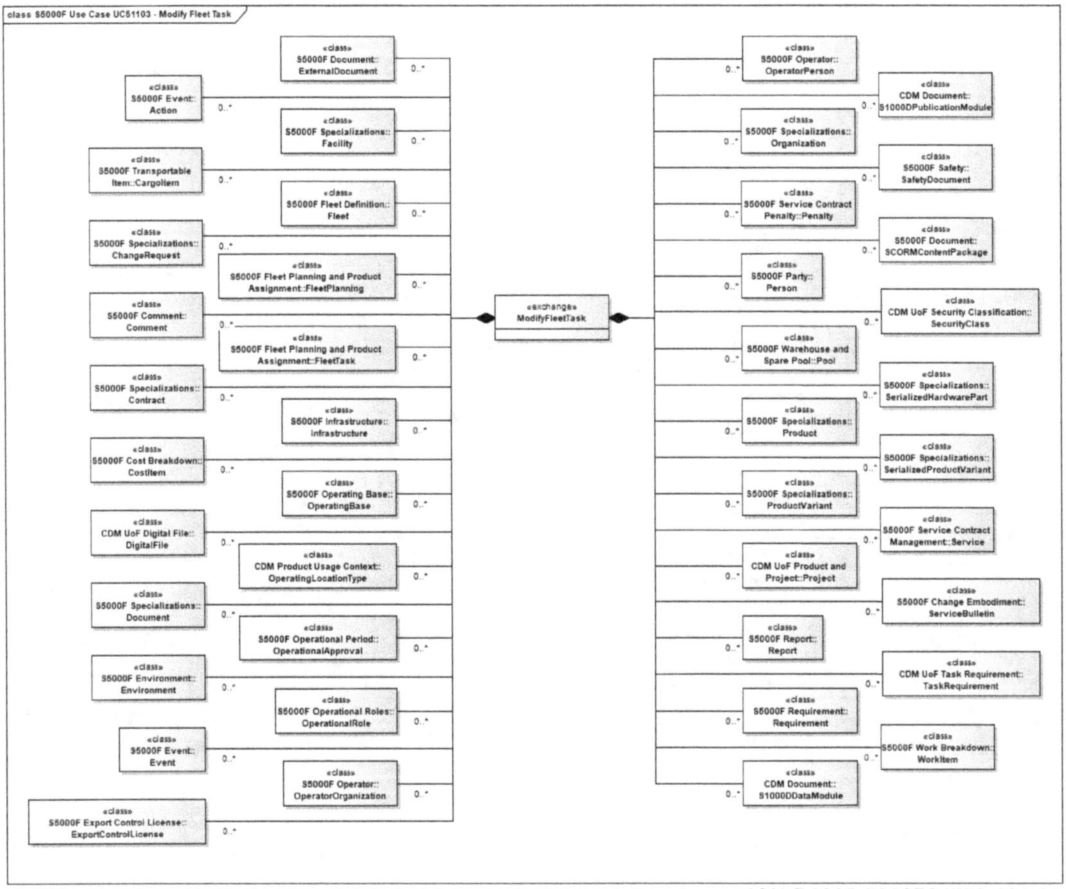

ICN-B6865-5000F24553-001-01

Fig 53 S5000F Use case UC51103 - Modify fleet task

2.54   S5000F Use case UC51104 - Elaborate fleet plan

Elaborate fleet plan represents a message associated with a use case (UC51104) providing the necessary information to elaborate a plan for effectively managing a fleet.

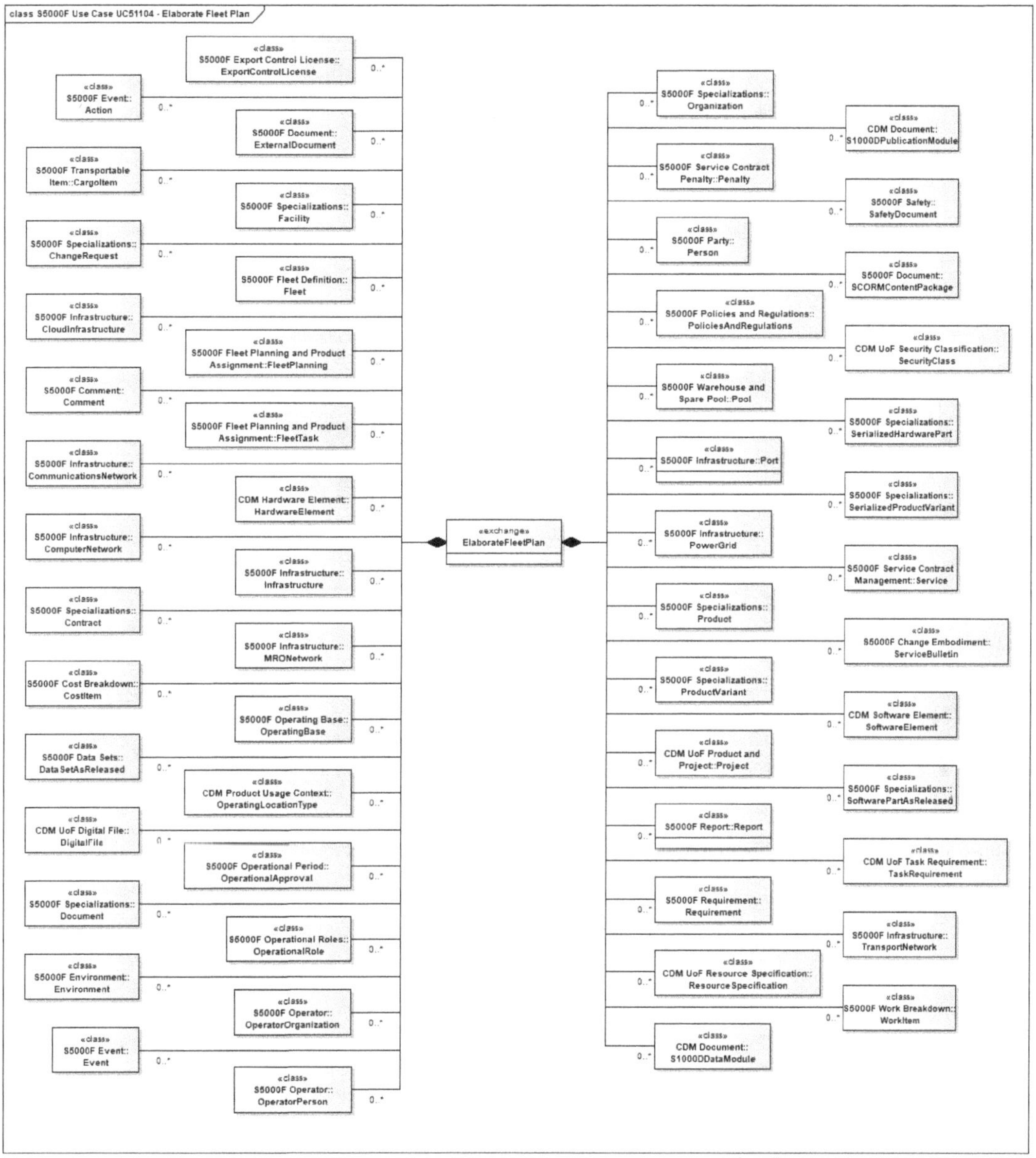

ICN-B6865-5000F24554-001-01

Fig 54 S5000F Use case UC51104 - Elaborate fleet plan

2.55 S5000F Use case UC51105 - Evaluate fleet task

Evaluate fleet task represents a message associated with a use case (UC51105) providing the necessary information to evaluate the effectiveness of a fleet task.

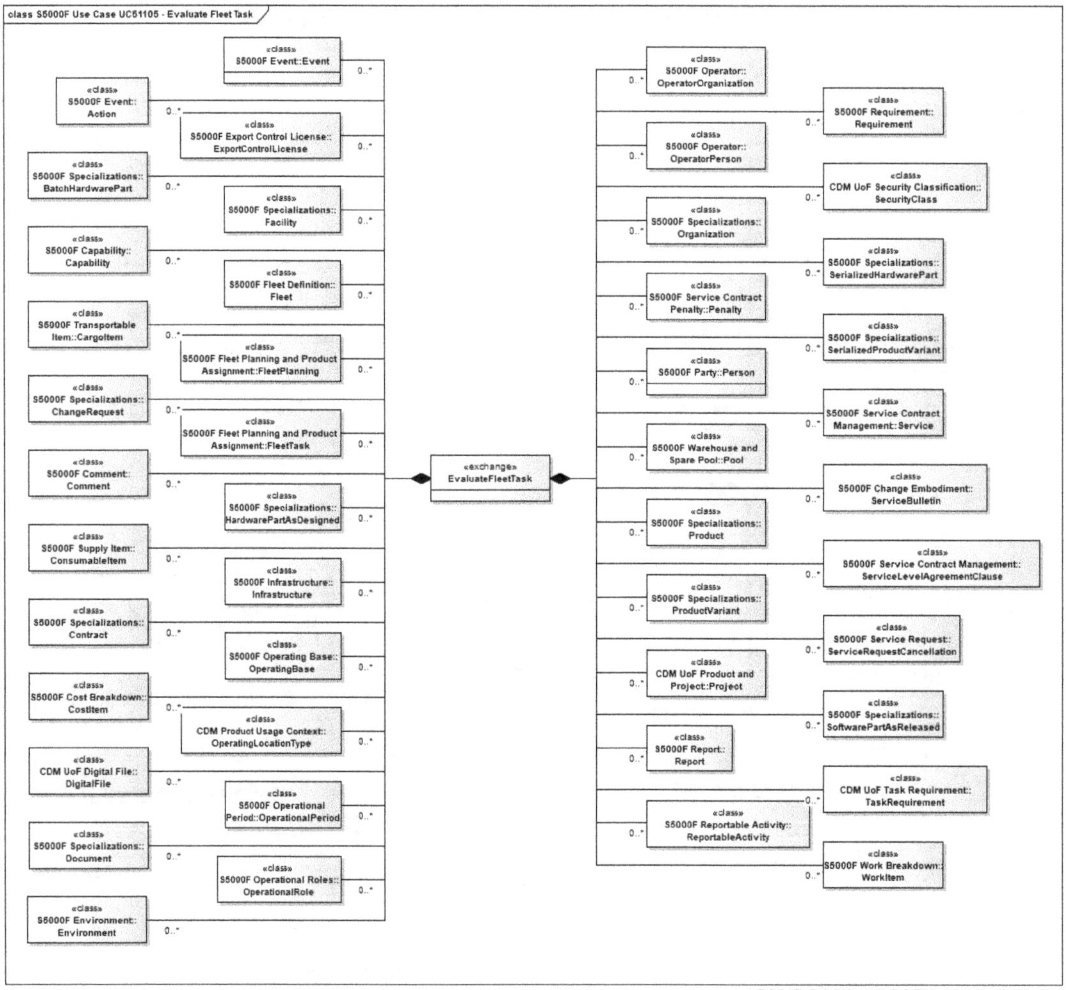

ICN-B6865-5000F24555-001-01

Fig 55 S5000F Use case UC51105 - Evaluate fleet task

2.56   S5000F Use case UC51106 - Prepare Product for fleet task

Prepare Product for fleet task represents a message associated with a use case (UC51106) allowing the information required to prepare the execution of a fleet task to be provided.

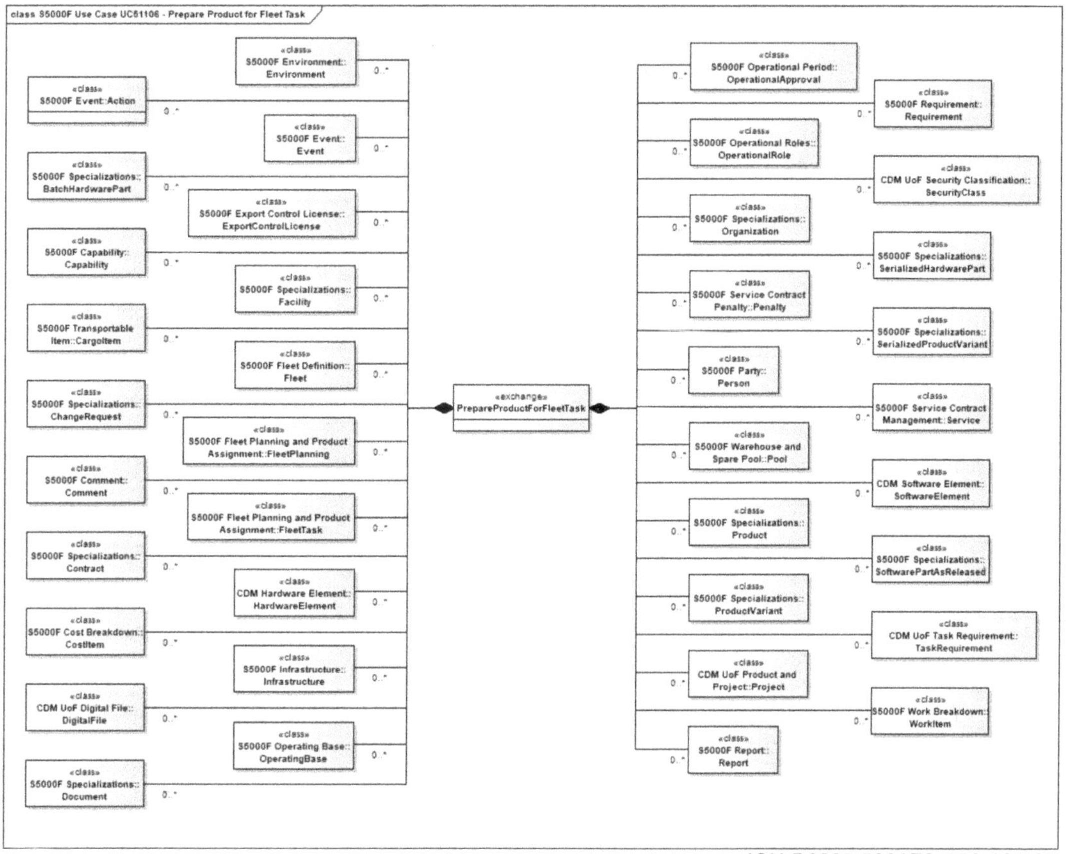

ICN-B6865-5000F24556-001-01

Fig 56 S5000F Use case UC51106 - Prepare Product for fleet task

2.57   S5000F Use case UC51107 - Recover Product after fleet task

Recover Product after fleet task represents a message associated with a use case (UC51107) allowing a record of actions taken to recover a serialized Product after executing a fleet task to be reported.

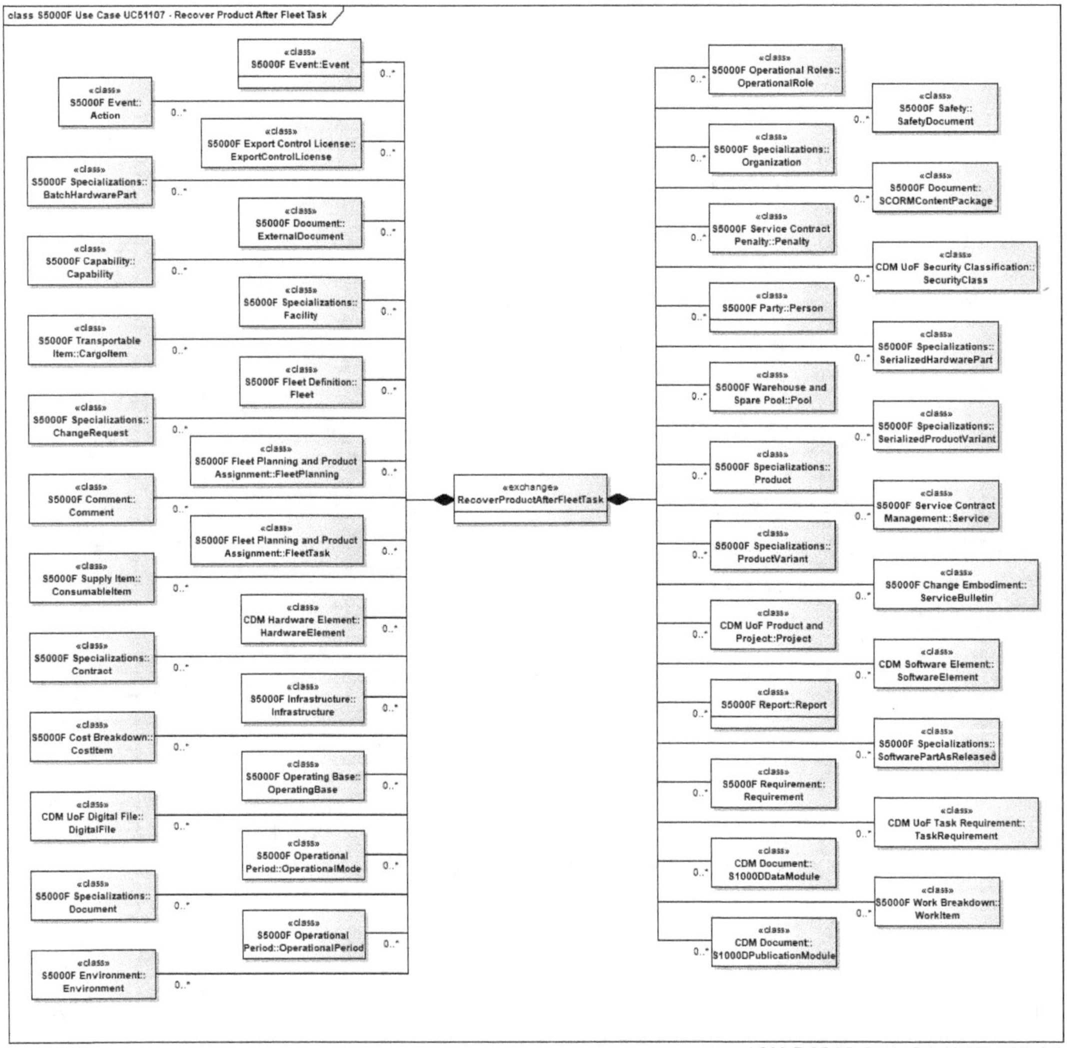

ICN-B6865-5000F24557-001-01

Fig 57 S5000F Use case UC51107 - Recover Product after fleet task

2.58   S5000F Use case UC51108 - Report fleet availability

Report fleet availability represents a message associated with a use case (UC51108) allowing to report on the availability of a Fleet or a Product variant.

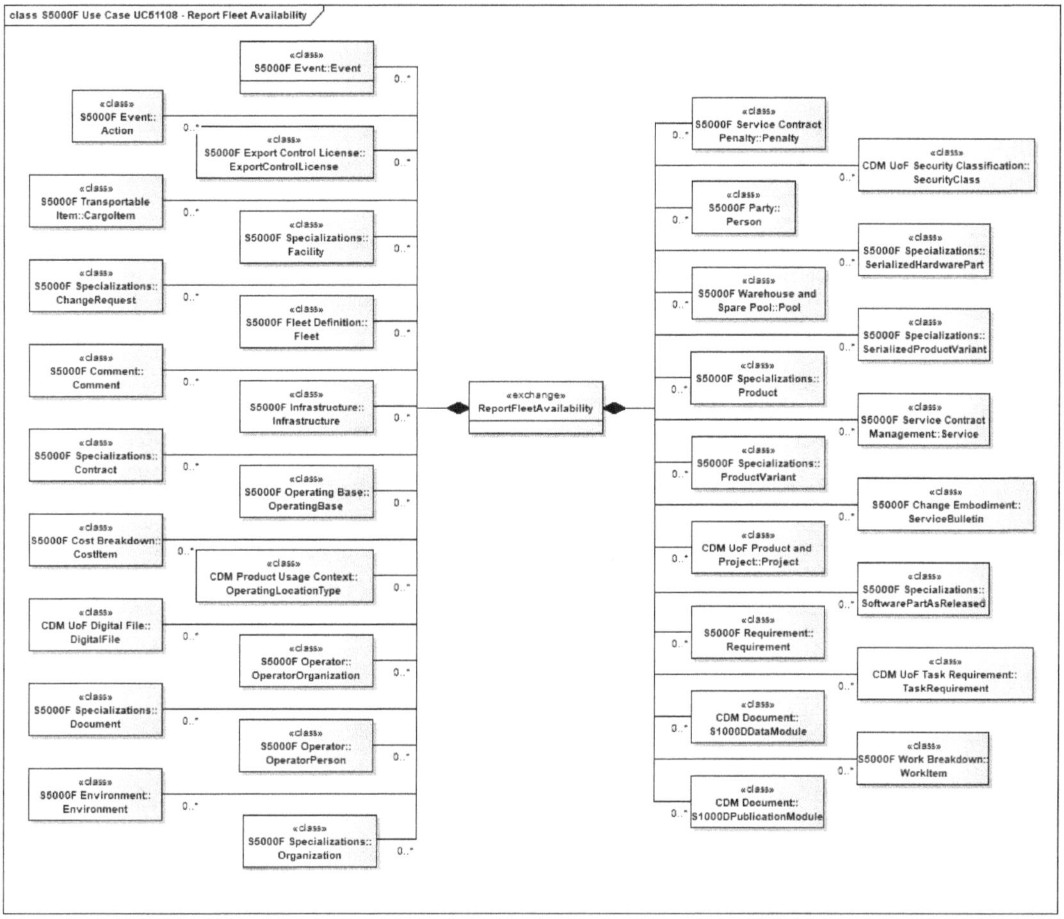

ICN-B6865-5000F24605-001-01

Fig 58 S5000F Use case UC51108 - Report fleet availability

2.59 S5000F Use case UC51201 - Request software feature

Request software feature represents a message associated with a use case (UC51201) providing the information required to request a new software feature.

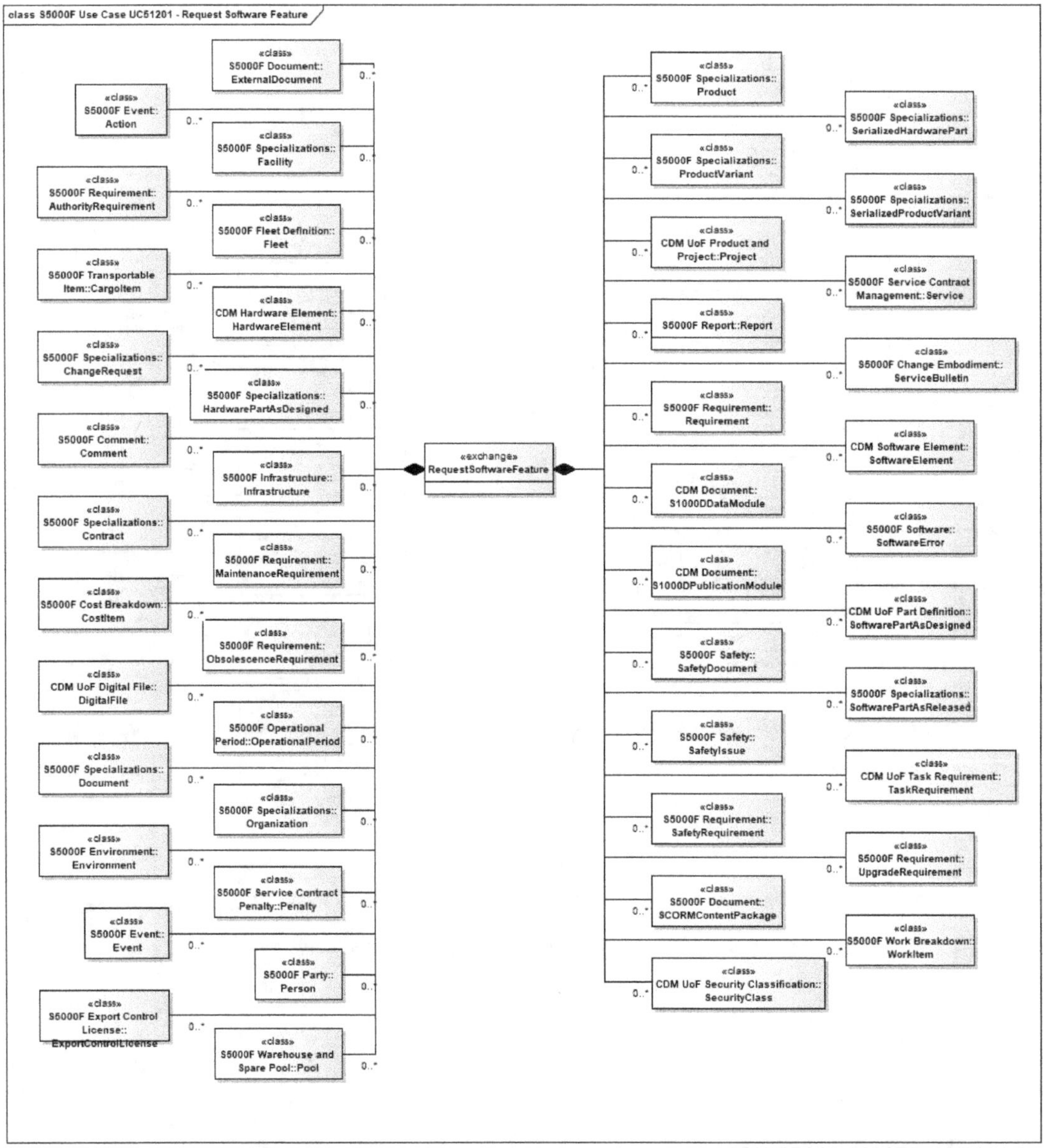

ICN-B6865-5000F24558-001-01

Fig 59 S5000F Use case UC51201 - Request software feature

2.60 S5000F Use case UC51202 - Report software error

Report software error represents a message associated with a use case (UC51202) providing the information required to report a software bug.

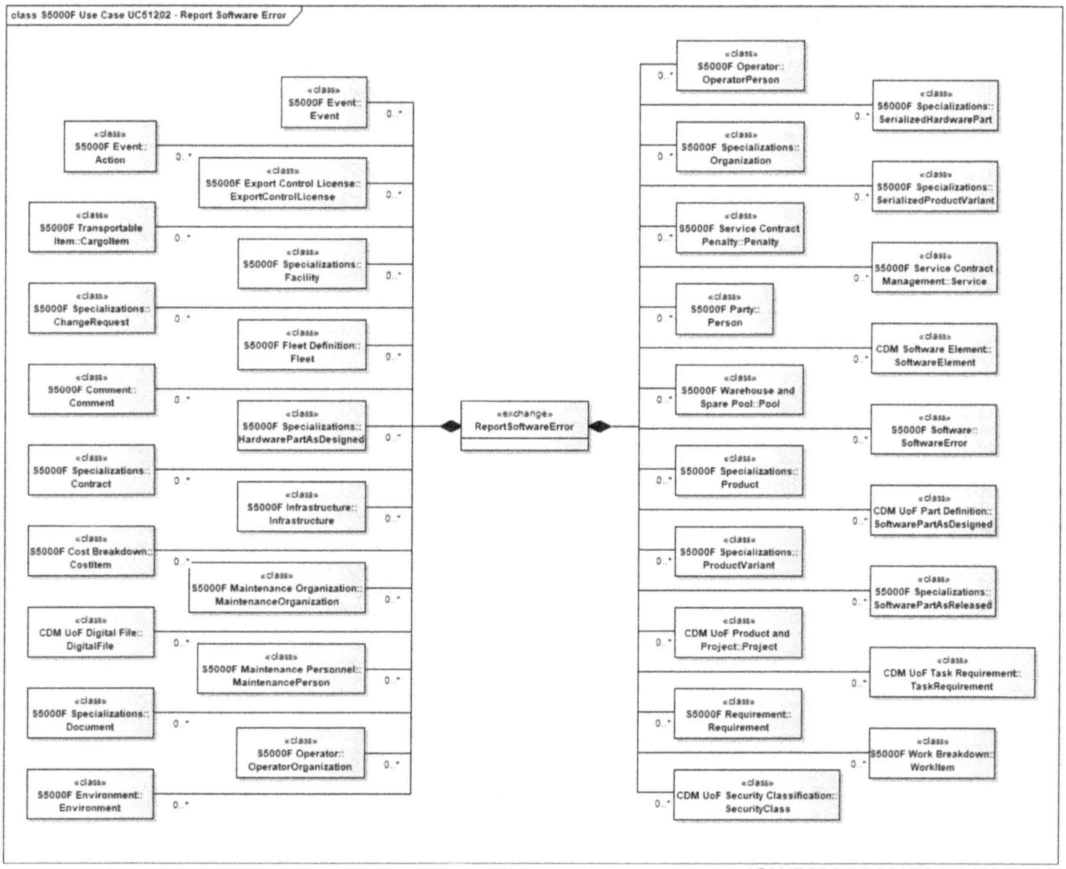

ICN-B6865-5000F24559-001-01

Fig 60 S5000F Use case UC51202 - Report software error

2.61　S5000F Use case UC51203 - Assess software usability

Assess software usability represents a message associated with a use case (UC51203) providing the necessary information to report on how usable a piece of software is.

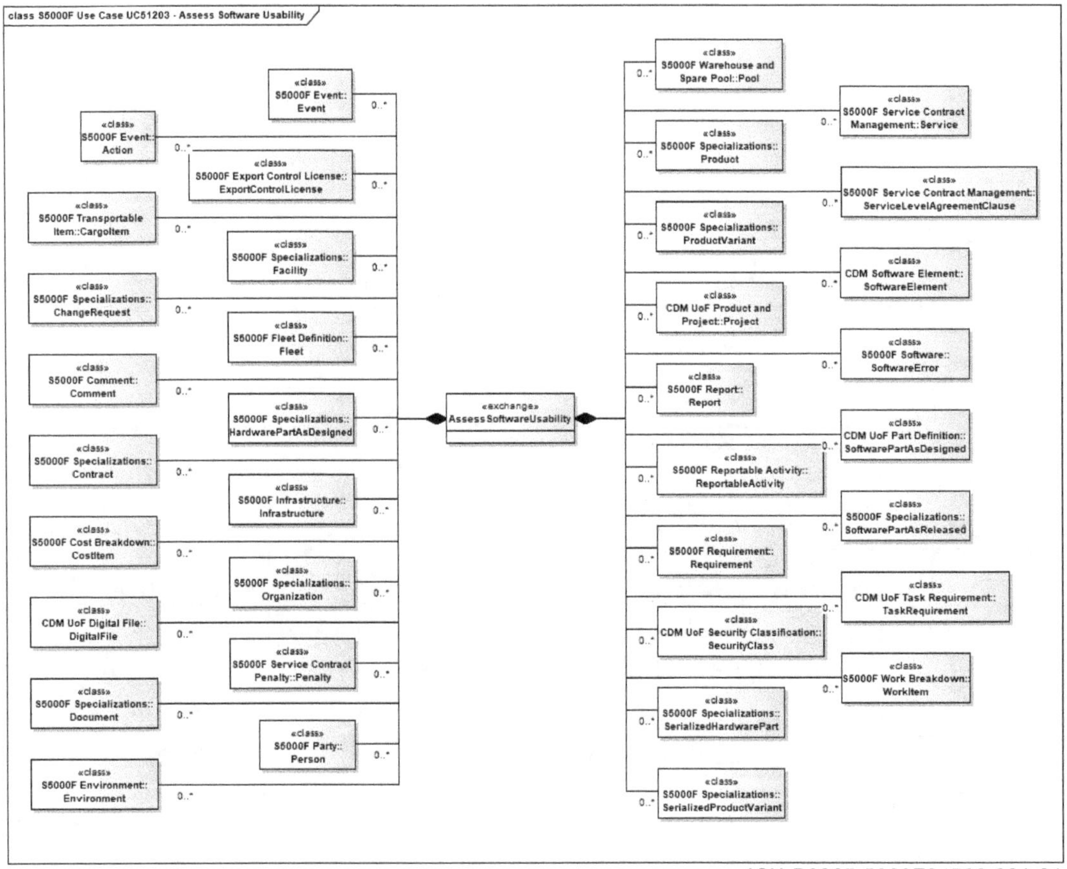

ICN-B6865-5000F24560-001-01

Fig 61 S5000F Use case UC51203 - Assess software usability

2.62   S5000F Use case UC51204 - Report software documentation errors

Report software documentation errors represents a message associated with a use case (UC50501) providing the information required to report errors in the documentation of a software item.

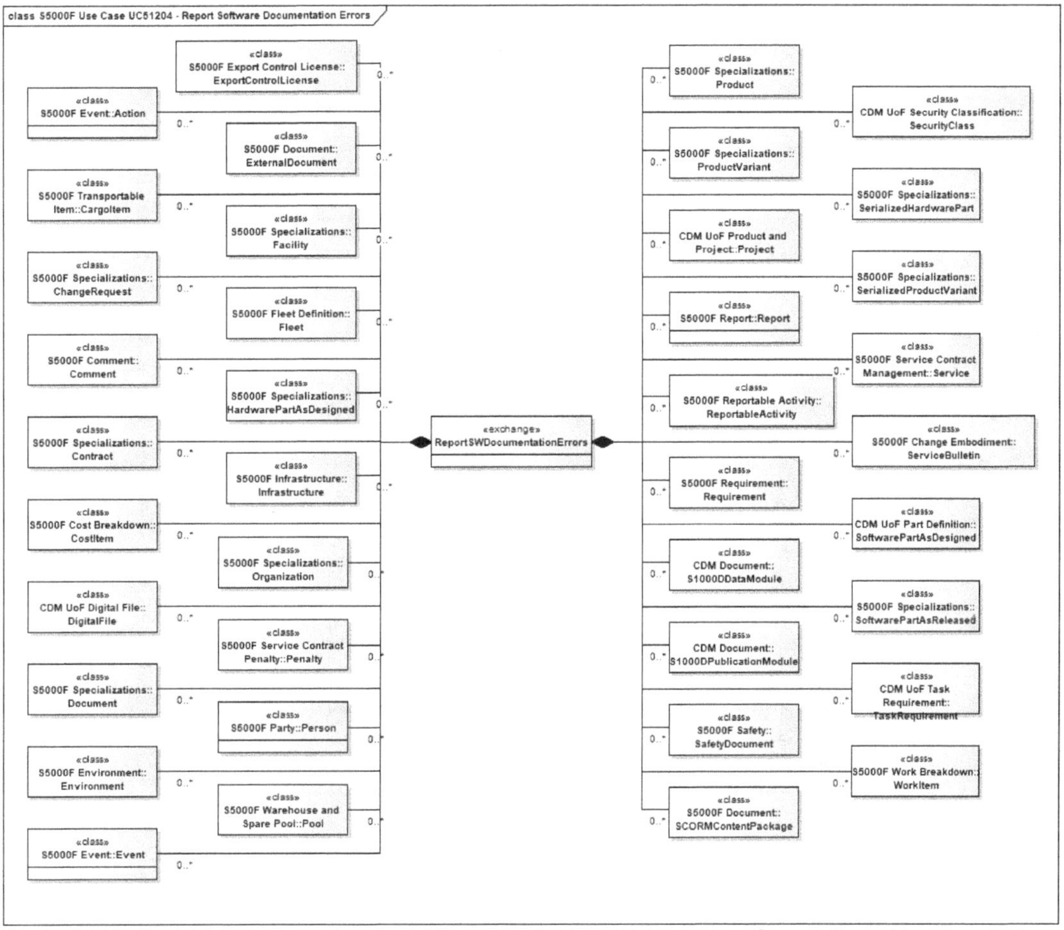

ICN-B6865-5000F24561-001-01

Fig 62 S5000F Use case UC51204 - Report software documentation errors

2.63   S5000F Use case UC51205 - Assess HW-SW interoperability

Assess HW-SW interoperability represents a message associated with a use case (UC51205) providing the necessary information to evaluate whether there are hardware-software incompatibilities.

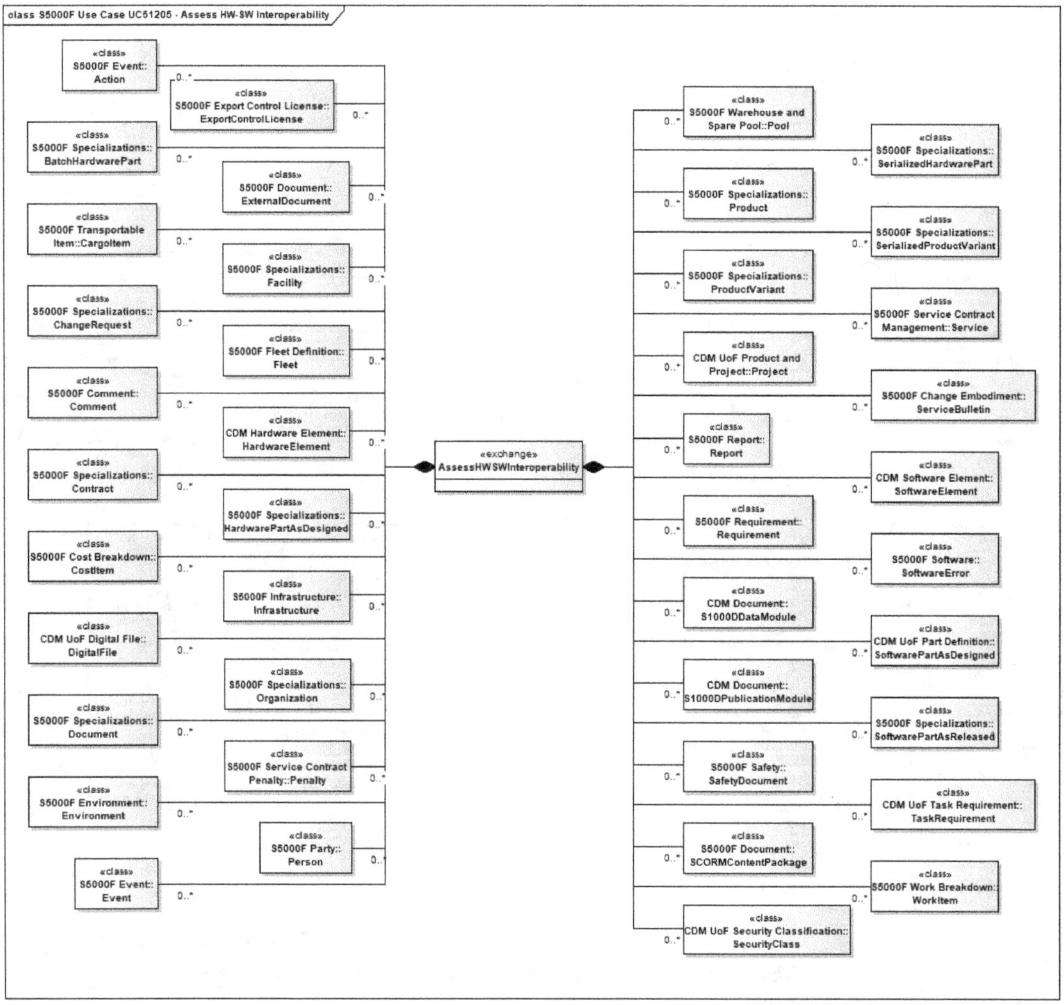

ICN-B6865-5000F24562-001-01

Fig 63 S5000F Use case UC51205 - Assess HW-SW interoperability

2.64 S5000F Use case UC51206 - Report software installation

Report software installation represents a message associated with a use case (UC51206) providing the information required to report that a piece of software has been installed on an item.

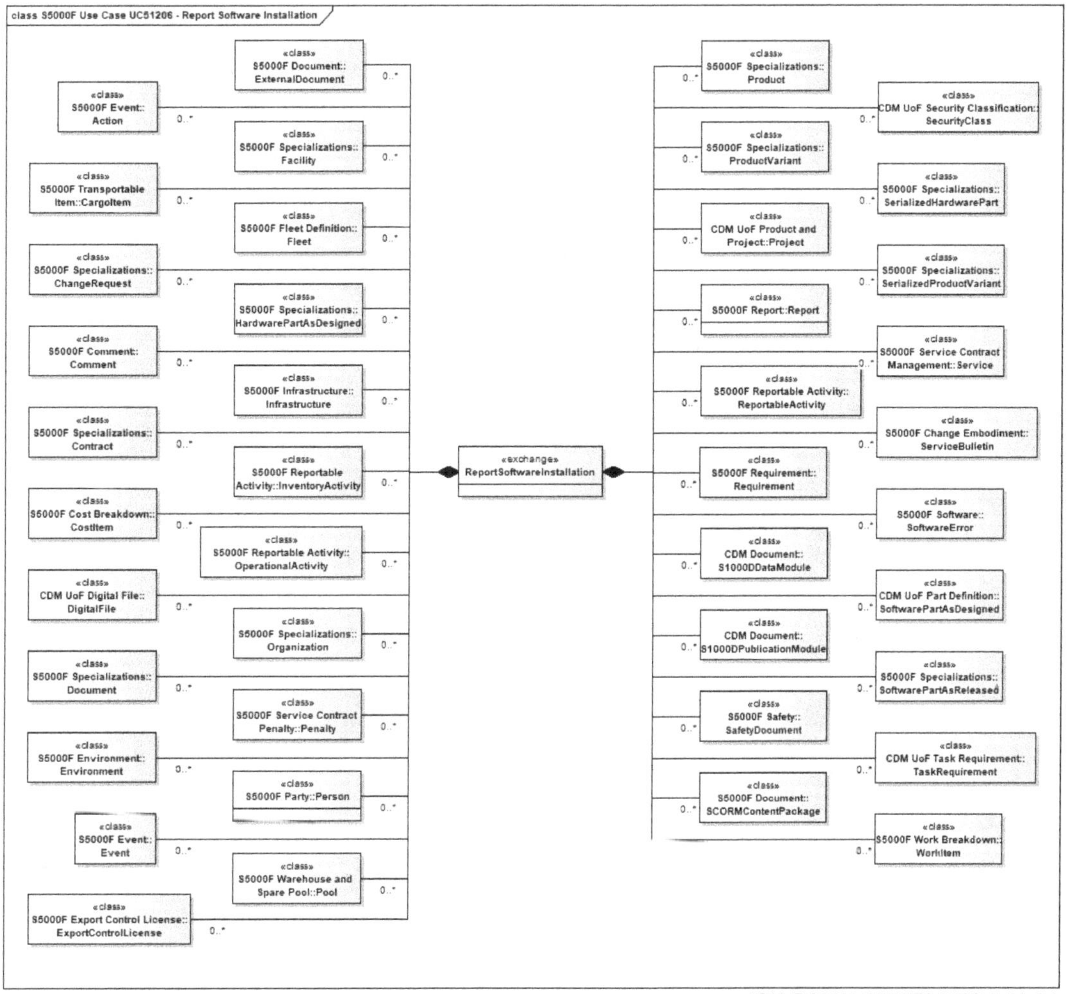

ICN-B6865-5000F24563-001-01

Fig 64 S5000F Use case UC51206 - Report software installation

2.65 S5000F Use case UC51207 - Report software configuration

Report software configuration represents a message associated with a use case (UC51207) providing the information required to report on the configuration of software.

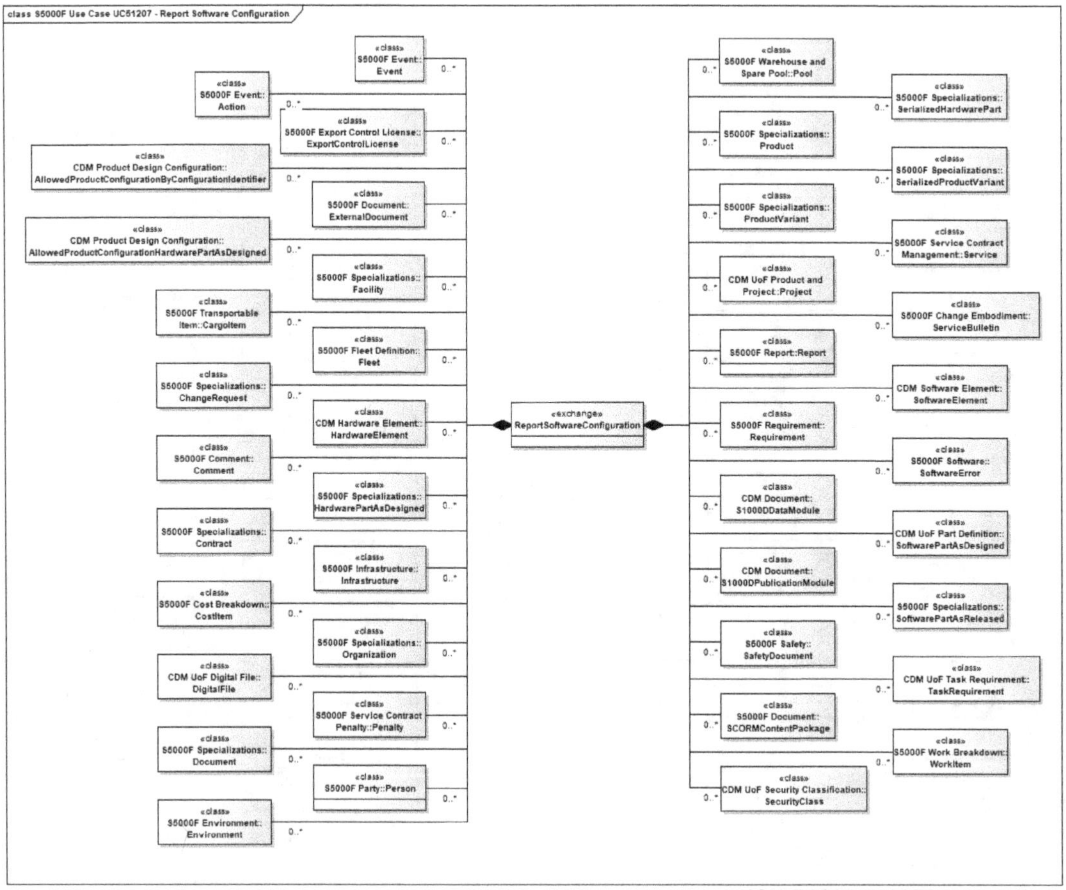

ICN-B6865-5000F24564-001-01

Fig 65 S5000F Use case UC51207 - Report software configuration

2.66   S5000F Use case UC51208 - Assess software maturity

Assess software maturity represents a message associated with a use case (UC51208) providing the necessary information to report on the maturity of a software item.

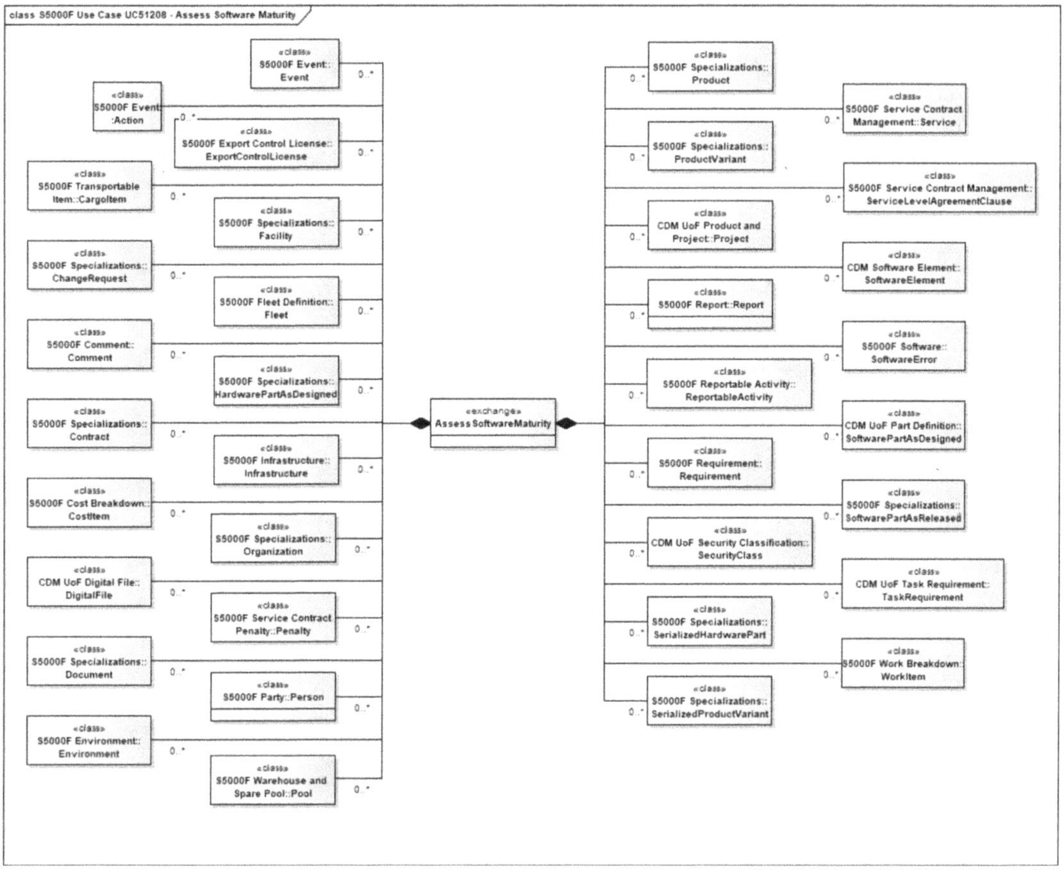

ICN-B6865-5000F24565-001-01

Fig 66 S5000F Use case UC51208 - Assess software maturity

2.67 S5000F Use case UC51209 - Report help desk tickets

Report help desk tickets represents a message associated with a use case (UC51209) allowing help desk tickets to be created.

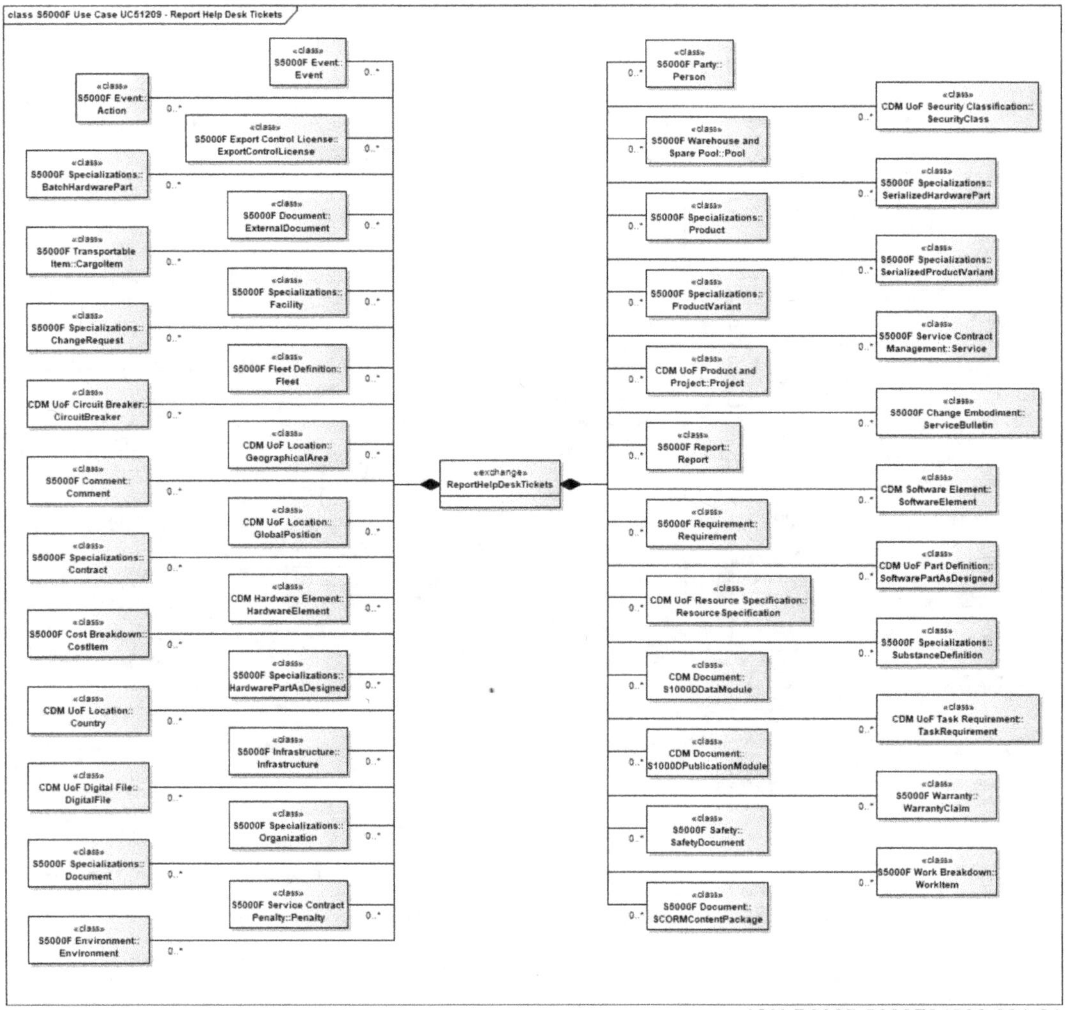

ICN-B6865-5000F24566-001-01

Fig 67 S5000F Use case UC51209 - Report help desk tickets

2.68   S5000F Use case UC51210 - Assess software delivery

Assess software delivery represents a message associated with a use case (UC51210) providing the necessary information to report on the delivery of a software item.

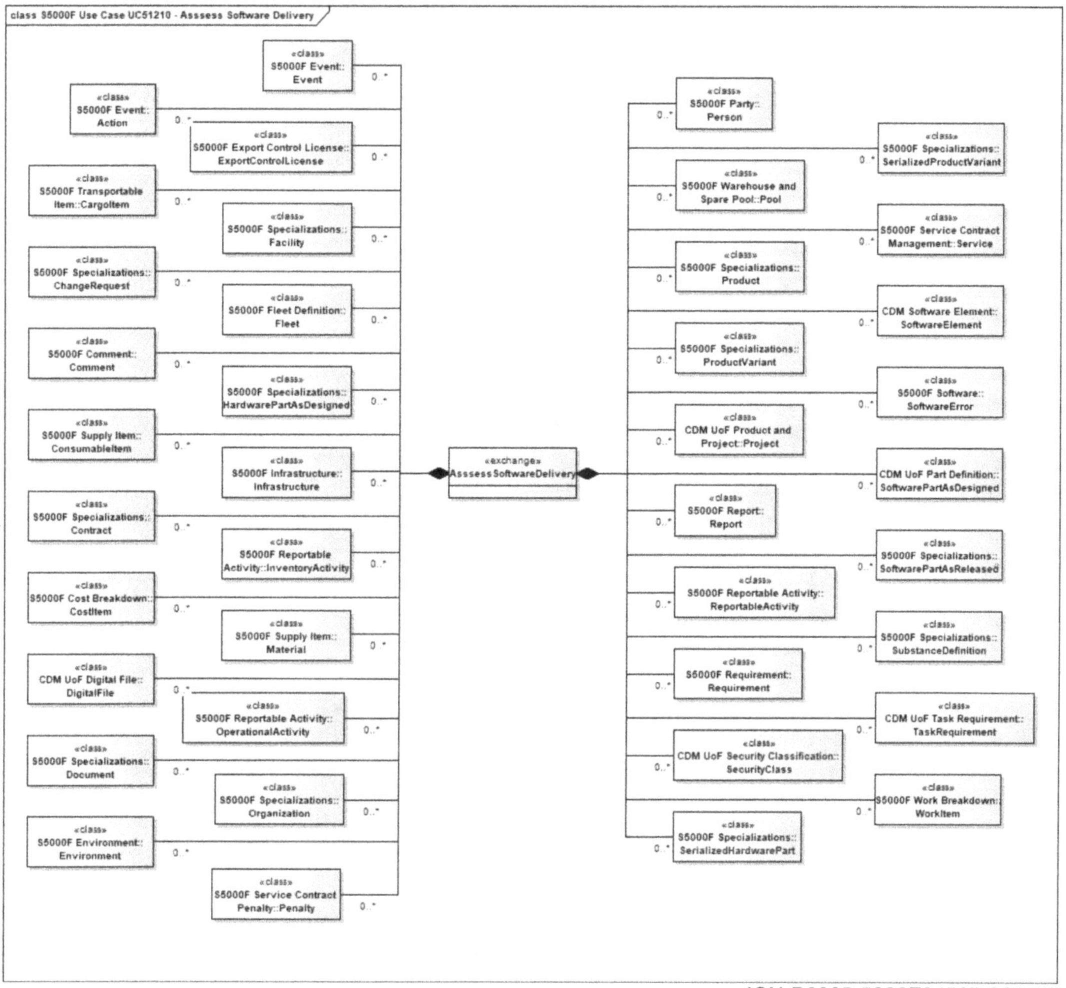

ICN-B6865-5000F24567-001-01

Fig 68 S5000F Use case UC51210 - Assess software delivery

2.69   S5000F Use case UC51211 - Communicate data loading

Communicate data loading represents a message associated with a use case (UC51211) providing the necessary information to report on the loading of a specific data set or software item.

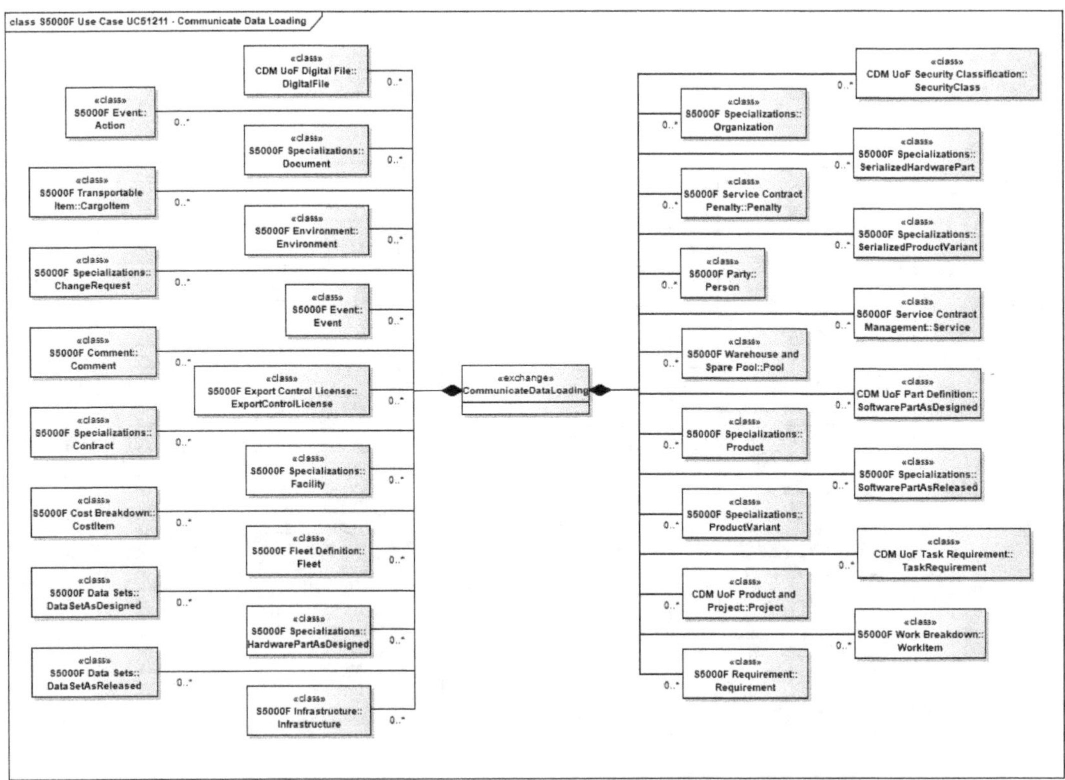

ICN-B6865-5000F24568-001-01

Fig 69 S5000F Use case UC51211 - Communicate data loading

2.70 S5000F Use case UC51301 - Provide as-delivered configuration

Provide as-delivered configuration represents a message associated with a use case (UC51301) allowing another party with the configuration information of a delivered serialized Product variant to be provided.

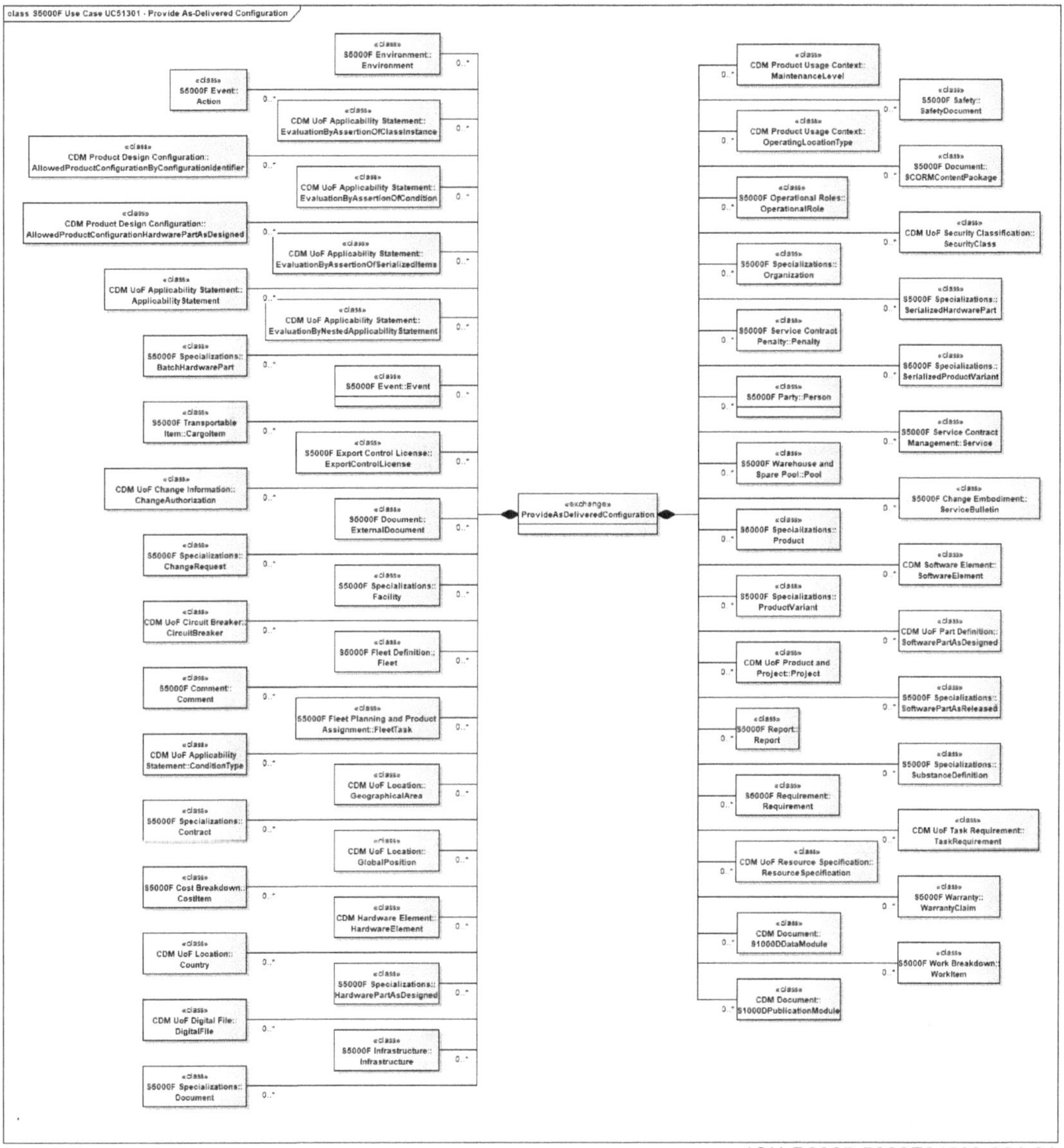

ICN-B6865-5000F24569-001-01

Fig 70 S5000F Use case UC51301 - Provide as-delivered configuration

2.71 S5000F Use case UC51302 - Provide as-allowed configuration

Provide as-allowed configuration represents a message associated with a use case (UC51302) allowing another party to be provided with the set of configurations that the serialized Product variant is allowed to have, to ensure safe operation.

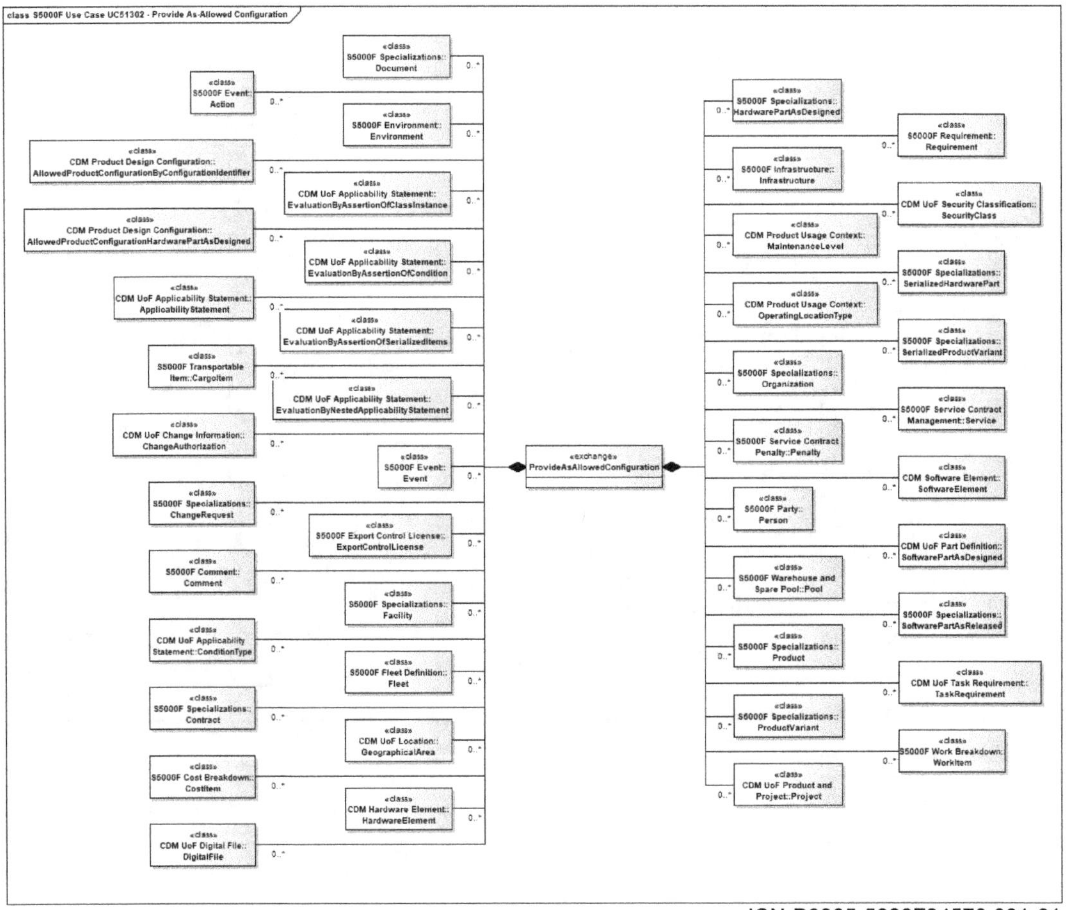

ICN-B6865-5000F24570-001-01

Fig 71 S5000F Use case UC51302 - Provide as-allowed configuration

2.72 S5000F Use case UC51303 - Provide operational configuration

Provide operational configuration represents a message associated with a use case (UC51303) allowing to provide the operational configuration of a serialized product variant at a specific moment in time.

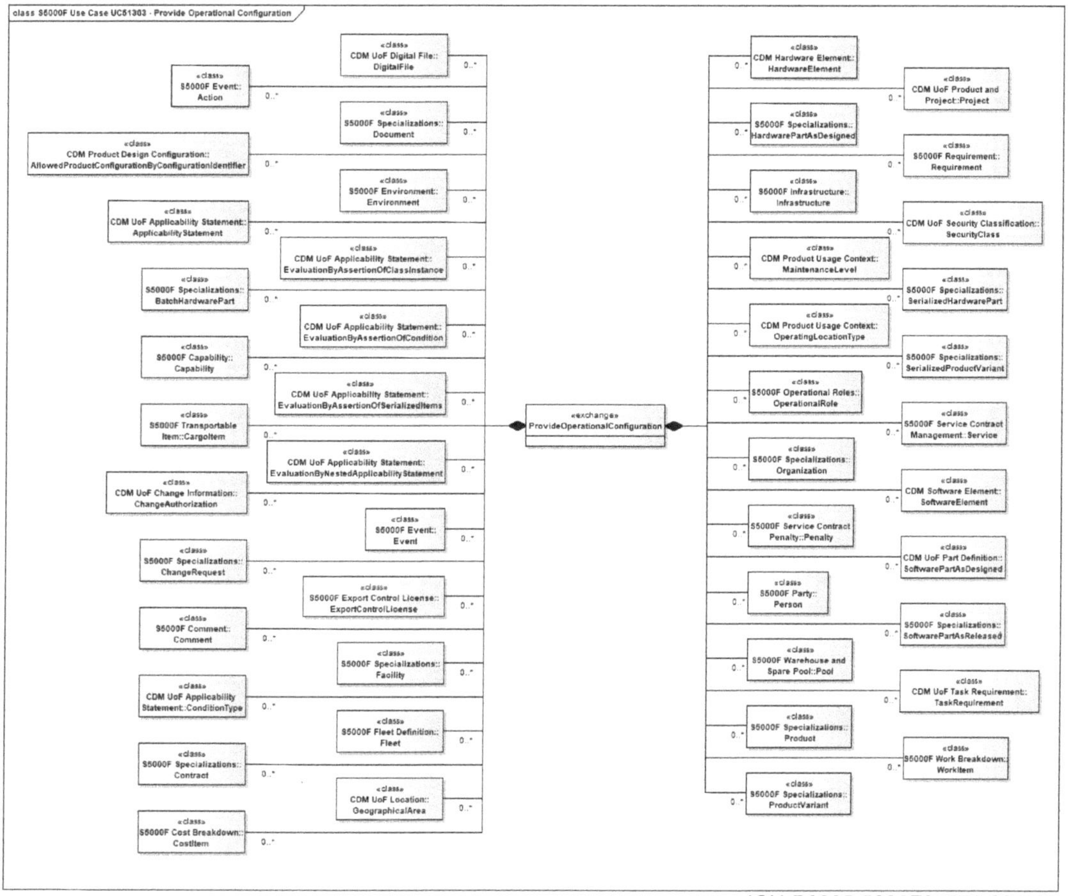

ICN-B6865-5000F24571-001-01

Fig 72 S5000F Use case UC51303 - Provide operational configuration

2.73   S5000F Use case UC51304 - Provide customer modification

Provide customer modification represents a message associated with a use case (UC51304) allowing information about a customer-driven modification to be provided.

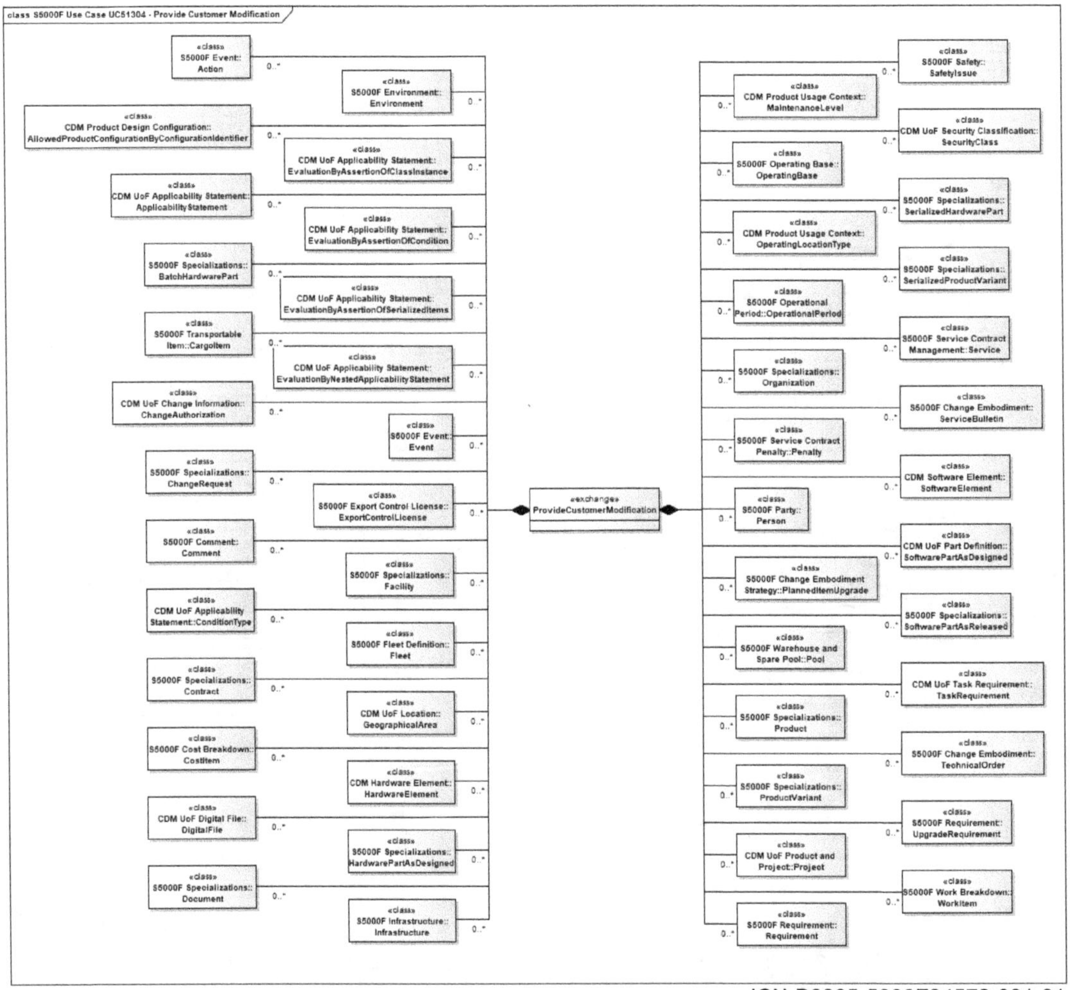

ICN-B6865-5000F24572-001-01

Fig 73 S5000F Use case UC51304 - Provide customer modification

2.74 S5000F Use case UC51305 - Provide as-desired configuration

Provide as-desired configuration represents a message associated with a use case (UC51305) allowing to ask another party for a specific (operational) configuration (eg, to perform a certain mission).

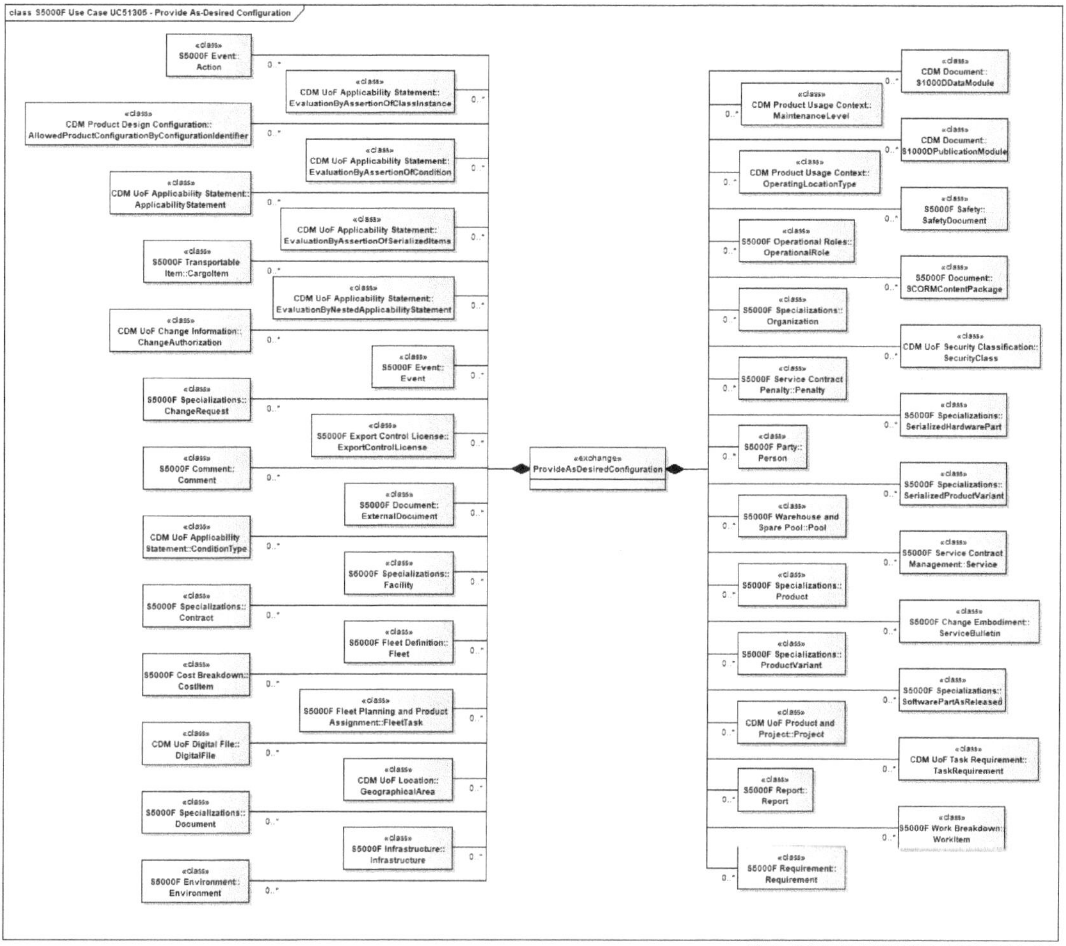

ICN-B6865-5000F24573-001-01

Fig 74 S5000F Use case UC51305 - Provide as-desired configuration

2.75 S5000F Use case UC51401 - Provide contractual information

Provide contractual information represents a message associated with a use case (UC51401) allowing information about a contract to be provided.

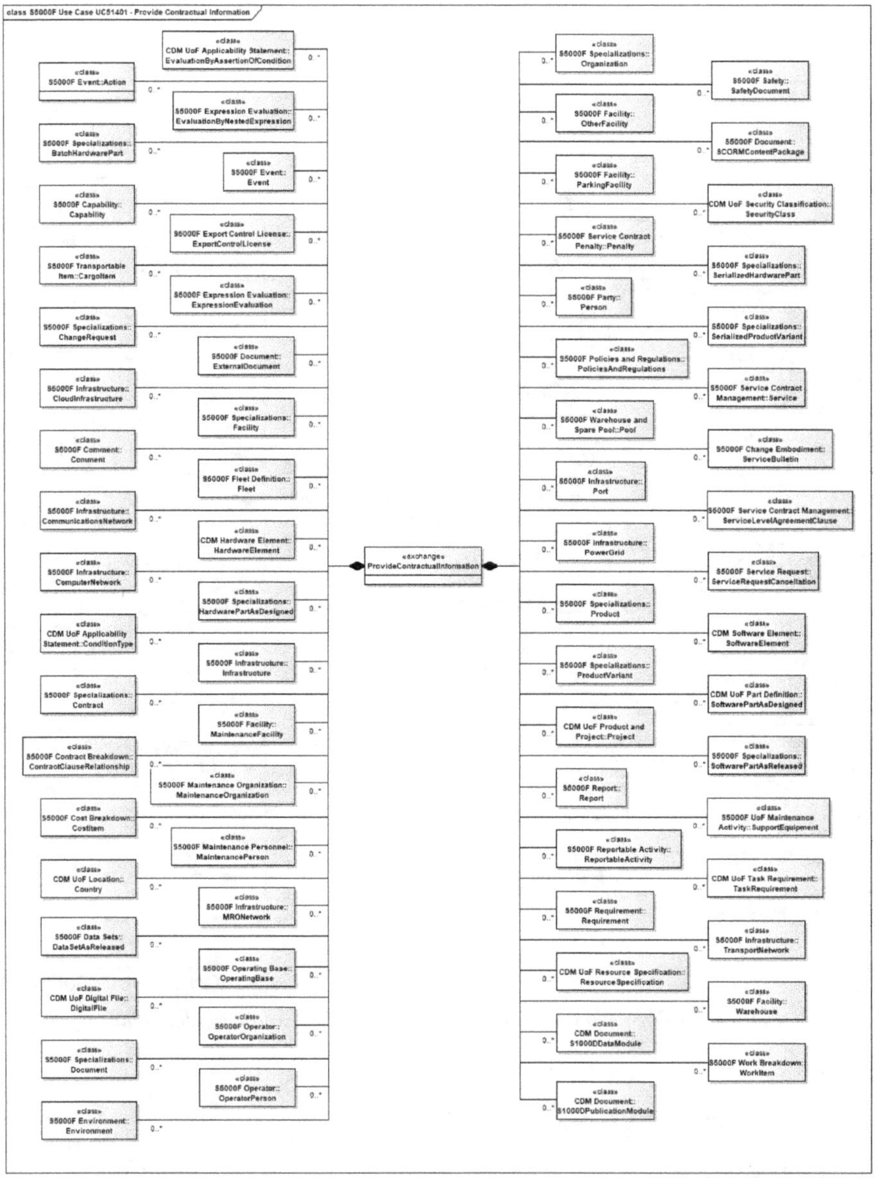

ICN-B6865-5000F24574-001-01

Fig 75 S5000F Use case UC51401 - Provide contractual information

2.76   S5000F Use case UC51402 - Provide Work Breakdown Structure (WBS)

Provide WBS represents a message associated with a use case (UC51402) that allows a WBS to be transferred.

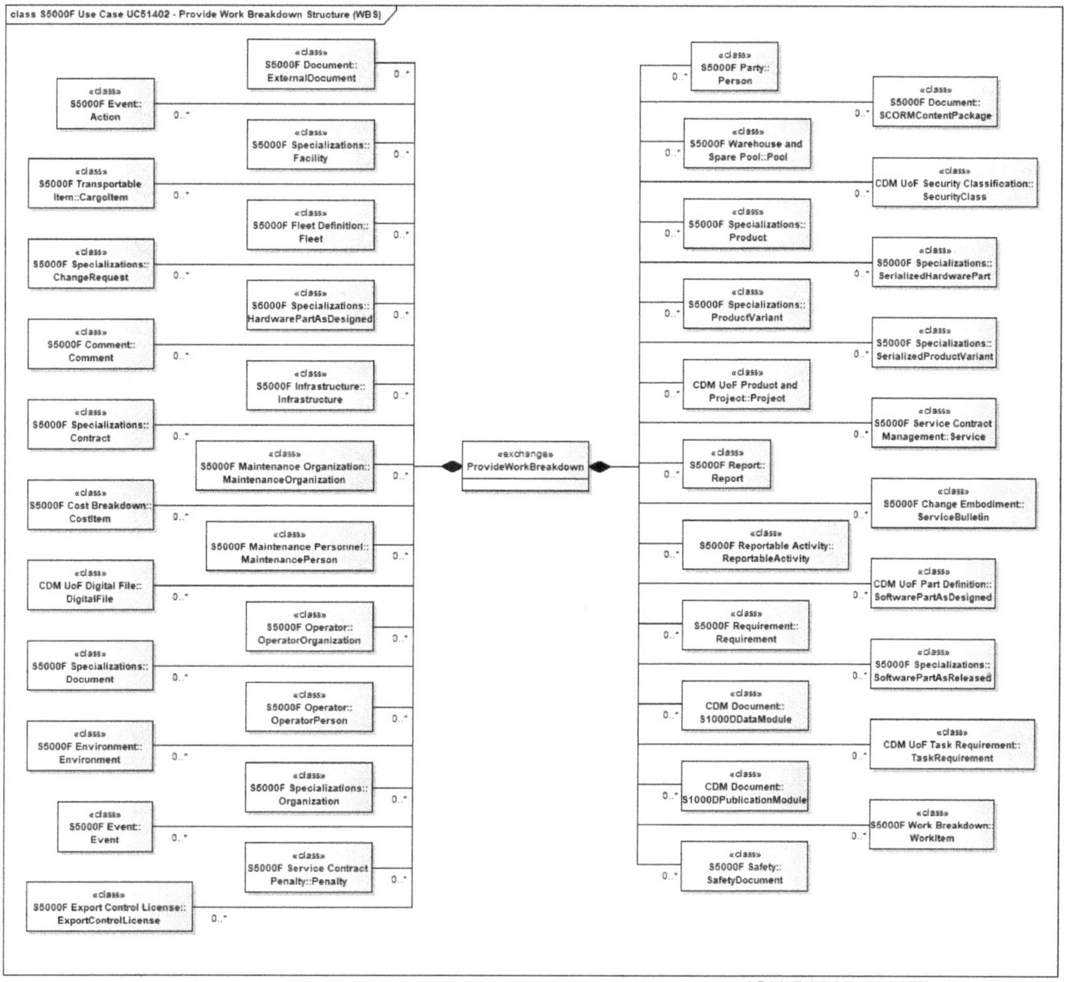

ICN-B6865-5000F24575-001-01

Fig 76 S5000F Use case UC51402 - Provide Work Breakdown Structure (WBS)

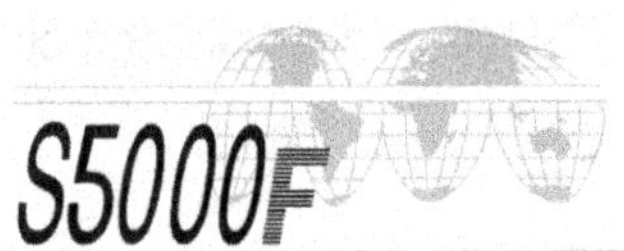

2.77 S5000F Use case UC51403 - Provide Cost Breakdown Structure (CBS)

Provide CBS represents a message associated with a use case (UC51403) that provides cost breakdown information.

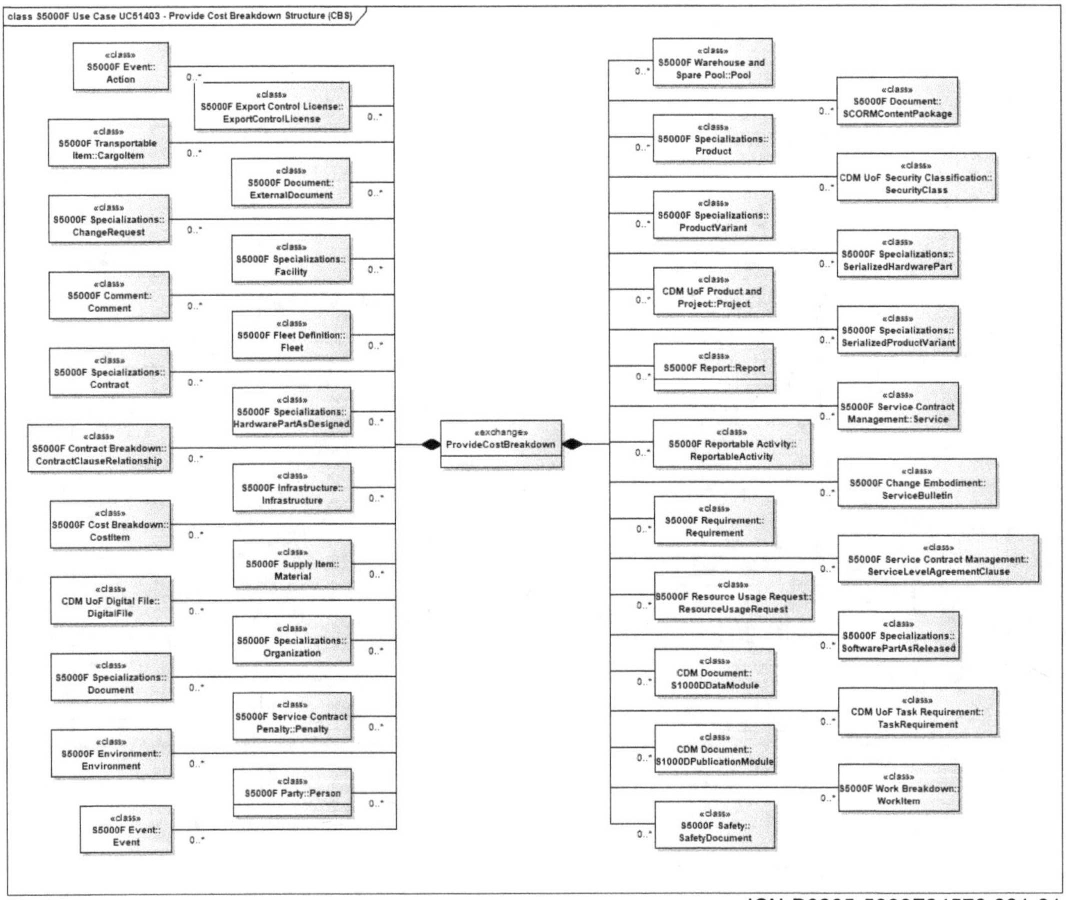

ICN-B6865-5000F24576-001-01

Fig 77 S5000F Use case UC51403 - Provide Cost Breakdown Structure (CBS)

2.78 S5000F Use case UC51404 - Provide Organizational Breakdown Structure (OBS)

Provide OBS represents a message associated with a use case (UC51404) allowing an OBS to be provided to another party.

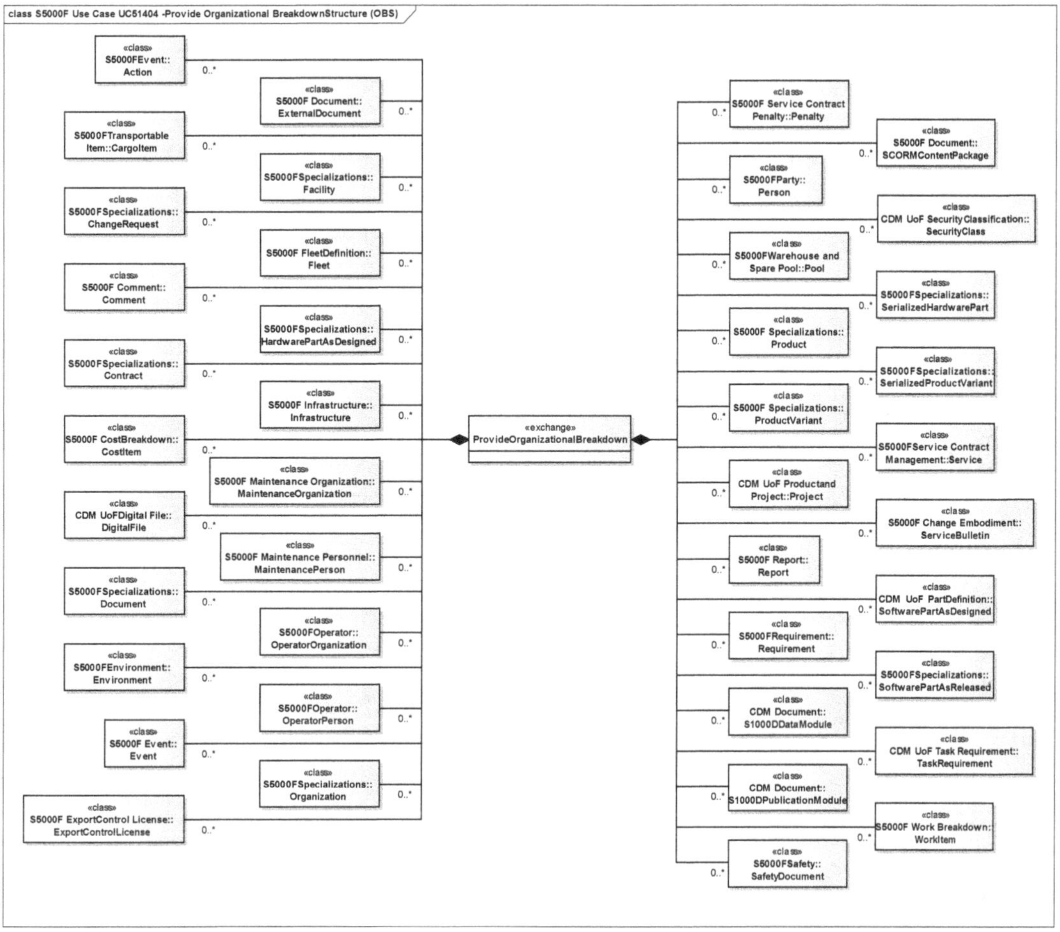

ICN-B6865-5000F24577-001-01

Fig 78 S5000F Use case UC51404 - Provide Organizational Breakdown Structure (OBS)

2.79 S5000F Use case UC51405 - Provide activity planning

Provide activity planning represents a message associated with a use case (UC51405) allowing another party to be provided with the list of planned activities.

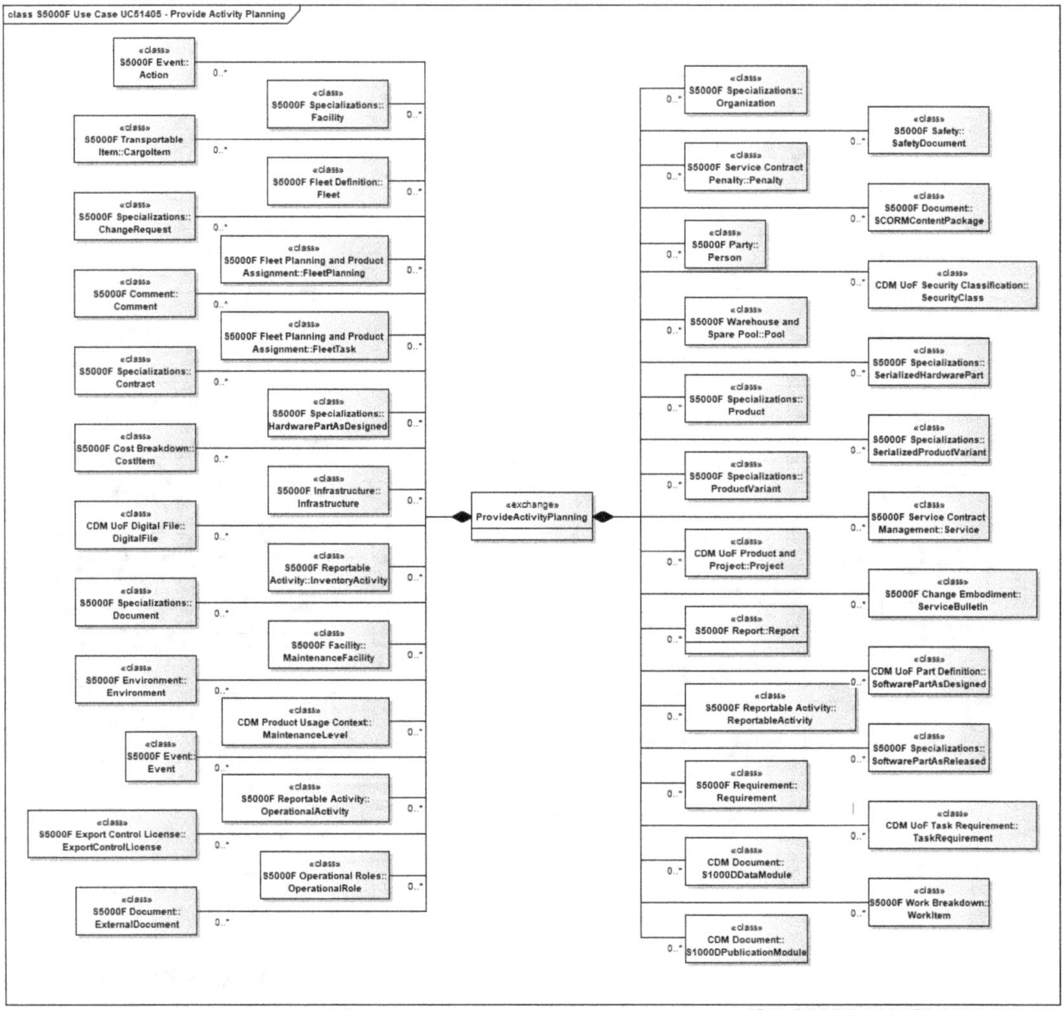

ICN-B6865-5000F24578-001-01

Fig 79 S5000F Use case UC51405 - Provide activity planning

2.80 S5000F Use case UC51406 - Report Service-Level Agreement (SLA) compliance

Report SLA compliance represents a message associated with a use case (UC51406) providing the information required to report the compliance with an SLA.

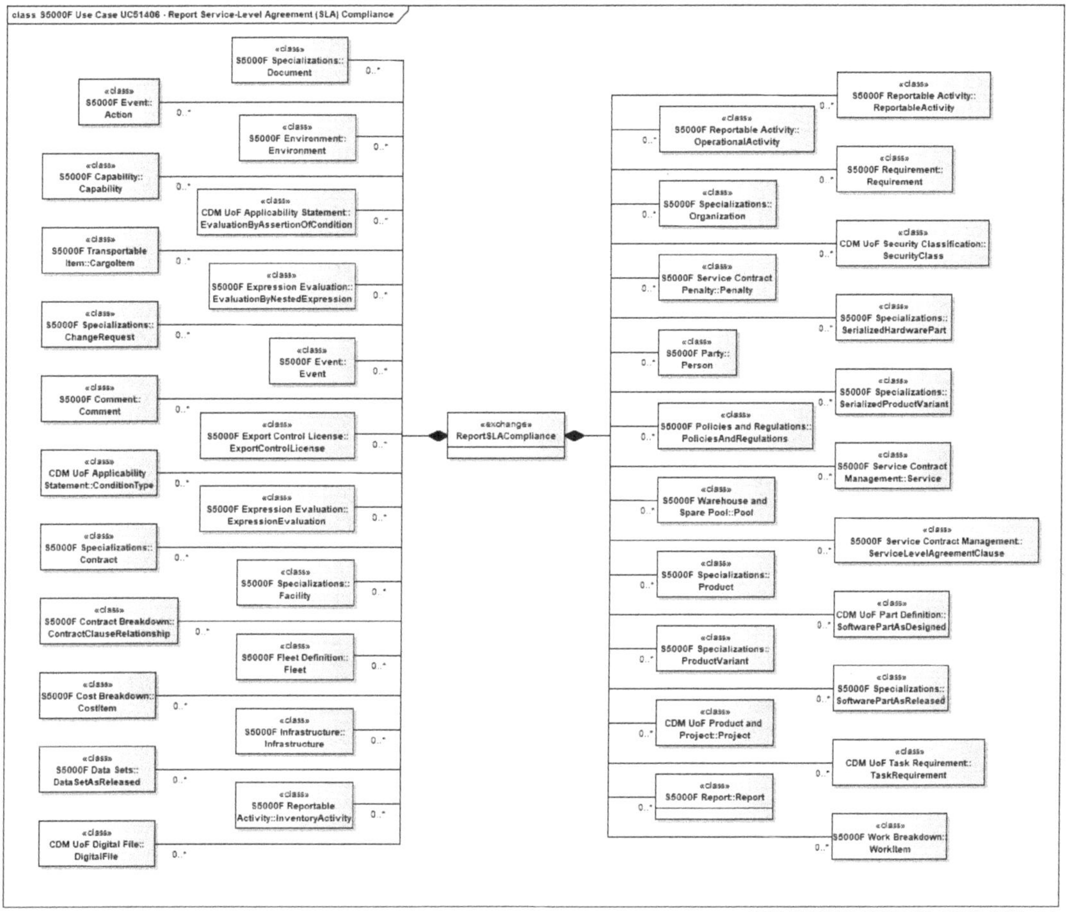

class S5000F Use Case UC51406 - Report Service-Level Agreement (SLA) Compliance

«class» S5000F Specializations::Document 0..*
«class» S5000F Event::Action 0..*
«class» S5000F Environment::Environment 0..*
«class» S5000F Capability::Capability 0..*
«class» CDM UoF Applicability Statement::EvaluationByAssertionOfCondition 0..*
«class» S5000F Transportable Item::CargoItem 0..*
«class» S5000F Expression Evaluation::EvaluationByNestedExpression 0..*
«class» S5000F Specializations::ChangeRequest 0..*
«class» S5000F Event::Event 0..*
«class» S5000F Comment::Comment 0..*
«class» S5000F Export Control License::ExportControlLicense 0..*
«class» CDM UoF Applicability Statement::ConditionType 0..*
«class» S5000F Expression Evaluation::ExpressionEvaluation 0..*
«class» S5000F Specializations::Contract 0..*
«class» S5000F Specializations::Facility 0..*
«class» S5000F Contract Breakdown::ContractClauseRelationship 0..*
«class» S5000F Fleet Definition::Fleet 0..*
«class» S5000F Cost Breakdown::CostItem 0..*
«class» S5000F Infrastructure::Infrastructure 0..*
«class» S5000F Data Sets::DataSetAsReleased 0..*
«class» S5000F Reportable Activity::InventoryActivity 0..*
«class» CDM UoF Digital File::DigitalFile 0..*

«exchange» ReportSLACompliance

«class» S5000F Reportable Activity::ReportableActivity 0..*
«class» S5000F Reportable Activity::OperationalActivity 0..*
«class» S5000F Requirement::Requirement 0..*
«class» S5000F Specializations::Organization 0..*
«class» CDM UoF Security Classification::SecurityClass 0..*
«class» S5000F Service Contract Penalty::Penalty 0..*
«class» S5000F Specializations::SerializedHardwarePart 0..*
«class» S5000F Party::Person 0..*
«class» S5000F Specializations::SerializedProductVariant 0..*
«class» S5000F Policies and Regulations::PoliciesAndRegulations 0..*
«class» S5000F Service Contract Management::Service 0..*
«class» S5000F Warehouse and Spare Pool::Pool 0..*
«class» S5000F Service Contract Management::ServiceLevelAgreementClause 0..*
«class» S5000F Specializations::Product 0..*
«class» CDM UoF Part Definition::SoftwarePartAsDesigned 0..*
«class» S5000F Specializations::ProductVariant 0..*
«class» S5000F Specializations::SoftwarePartAsReleased 0..*
«class» CDM UoF Product and Project::Project 0..*
«class» CDM UoF Task Requirement::TaskRequirement 0..*
«class» S5000F Report::Report 0..*
«class» S5000F Work Breakdown::WorkItem 0..*

ICN-B6865-5000F24579-001-01

Fig 80 S5000F Use case UC51406 - Report Service-Level Agreement (SLA) compliance

2.81   S5000F Use case UC51407 - Report contract costs

Report contract costs represents a message associated with a use case (UC51407) allowing costs incurred against a program to be reported.

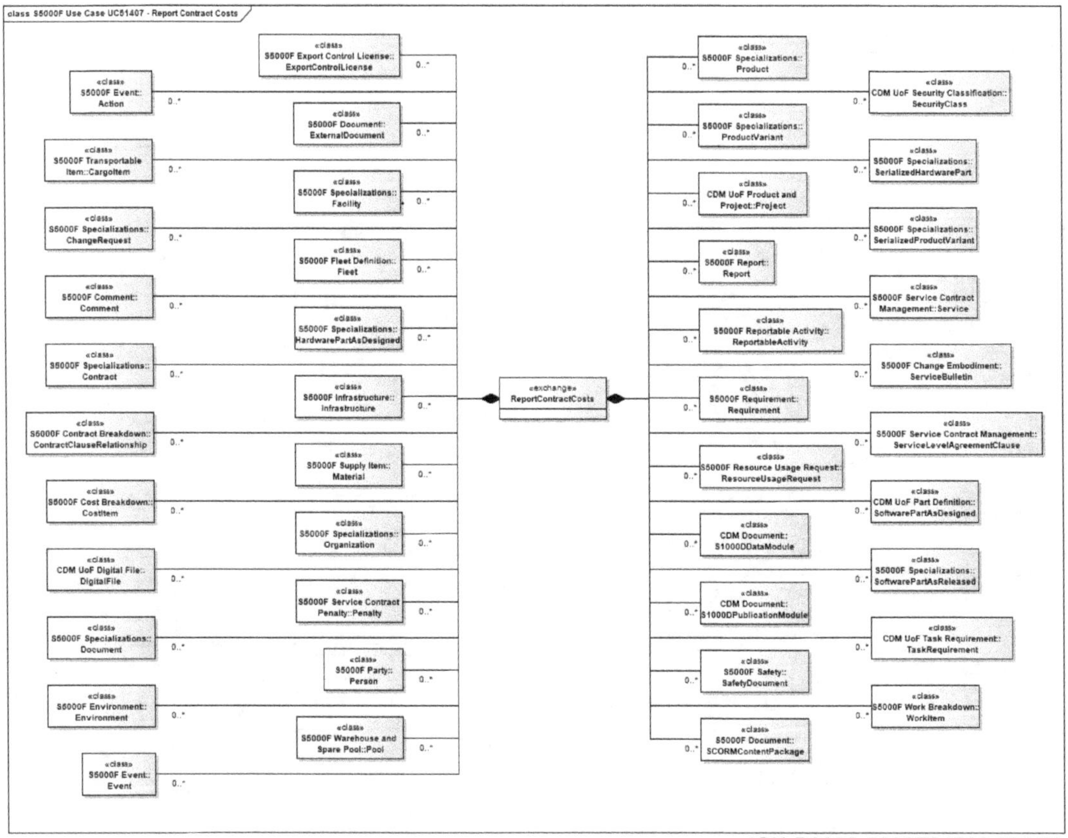

ICN-B6865-5000F24580-001-01

Fig 81 S5000F Use case UC51407 - Report contract costs

2.82   S5000F Use case UC51408 - Provide status report

Provide status report represents a message associated with a use case (UC51408) allowing a report in electronic format to be provided.

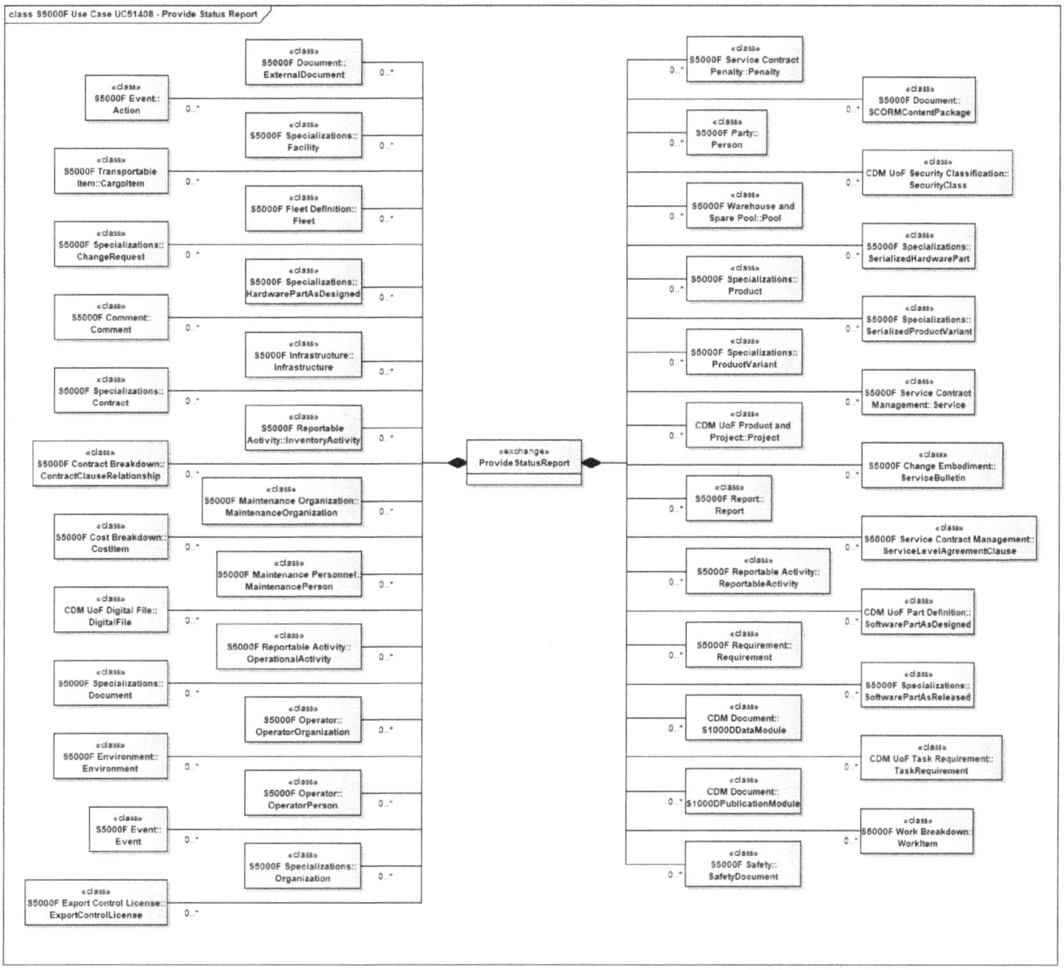

ICN-B6865-5000F24581-001-01

Fig 82 S5000F Use case UC51408 - Provide status report

2.83   S5000F Use case UC51409 - Provide location information

Provide Location Information represents a message associated with a use case (UC51409) allowing the location information of an item to be indicated.

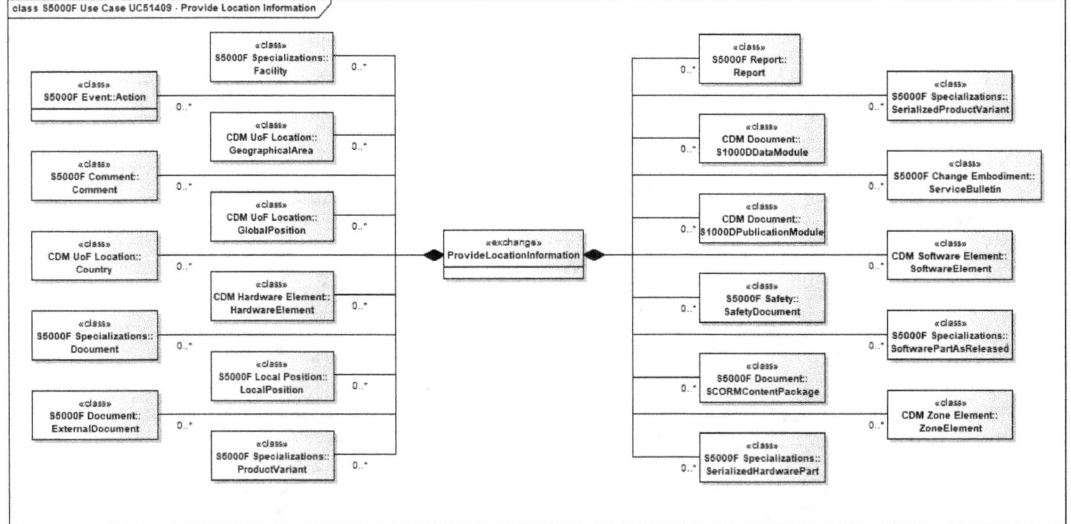

ICN-B6865-5000F24582-001-01

Fig 83 S5000F Use case UC51409 - Provide location information

2.84 S5000F Use case UC51410 - Manage service request

Manage service request represents a message associated with a use case (UC51410) providing the necessary information to address the response to a service request.

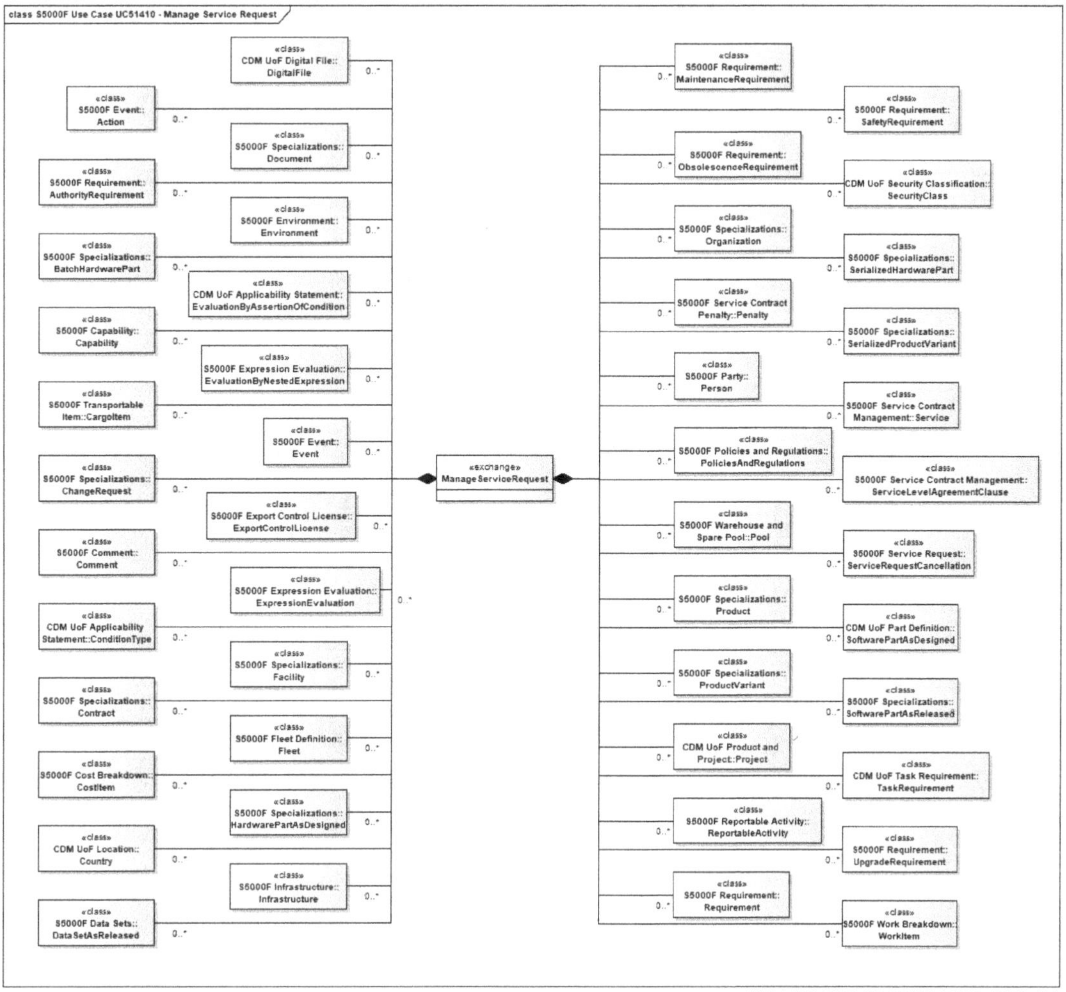

ICN-B6865-5000F24583-001-01

Fig 84 S5000F Use case UC51410 - Manage service request

2.85   S5000F Use case UC51411 - Request resource

Request resource represents a message associated with a use case (UC51411) providing the required information to request the usage of a resource.

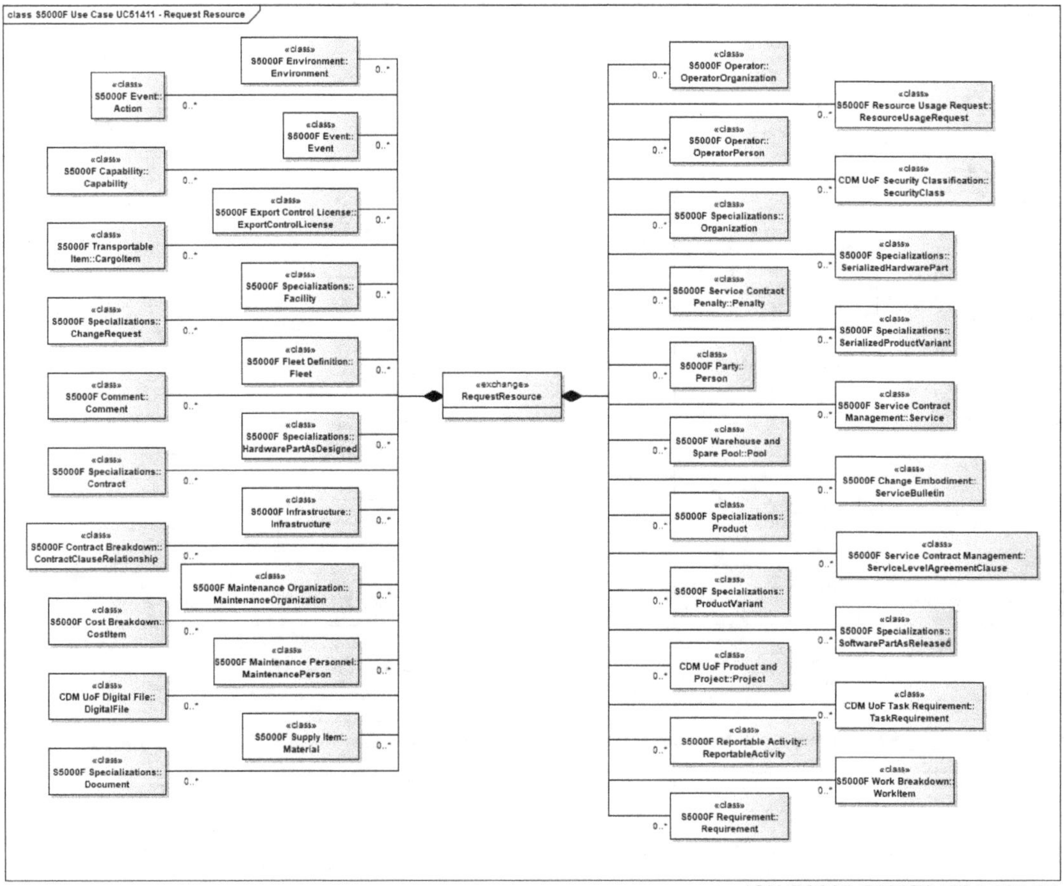

ICN-B6865-5000F24584-001-01

Fig 85 S5000F Use case UC51411 - Request resource

2.86　S5000F Use case UC51412 - Define security

Define security represents a message associated with a use case (UC51412) providing the necessary information to ensure that proper security classifications are applied to classified items.

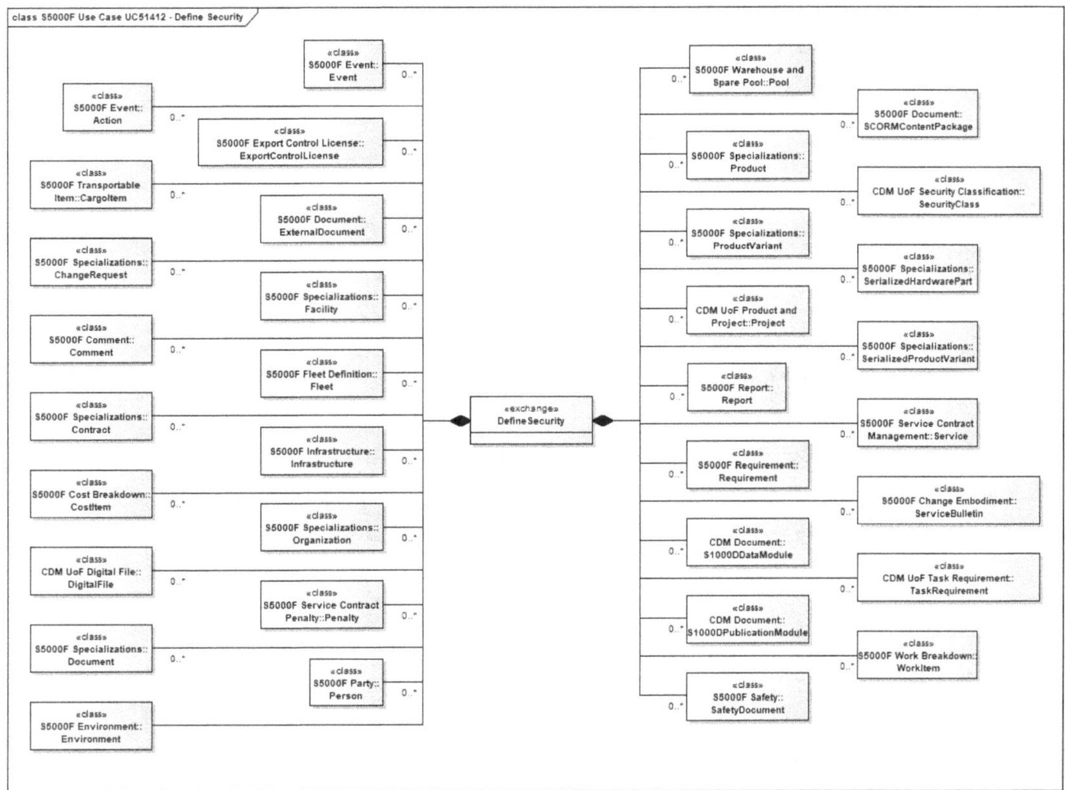

ICN-B6865-5000F24585-001-01

Fig 86 S5000F Use case UC51412 - Define security

2.87 S5000F Use case UC51413 - Exchange export control information

Exchange export control information represents a message associated with a use case (UC51413) providing the necessary information to ensure compliance with export control regulations.

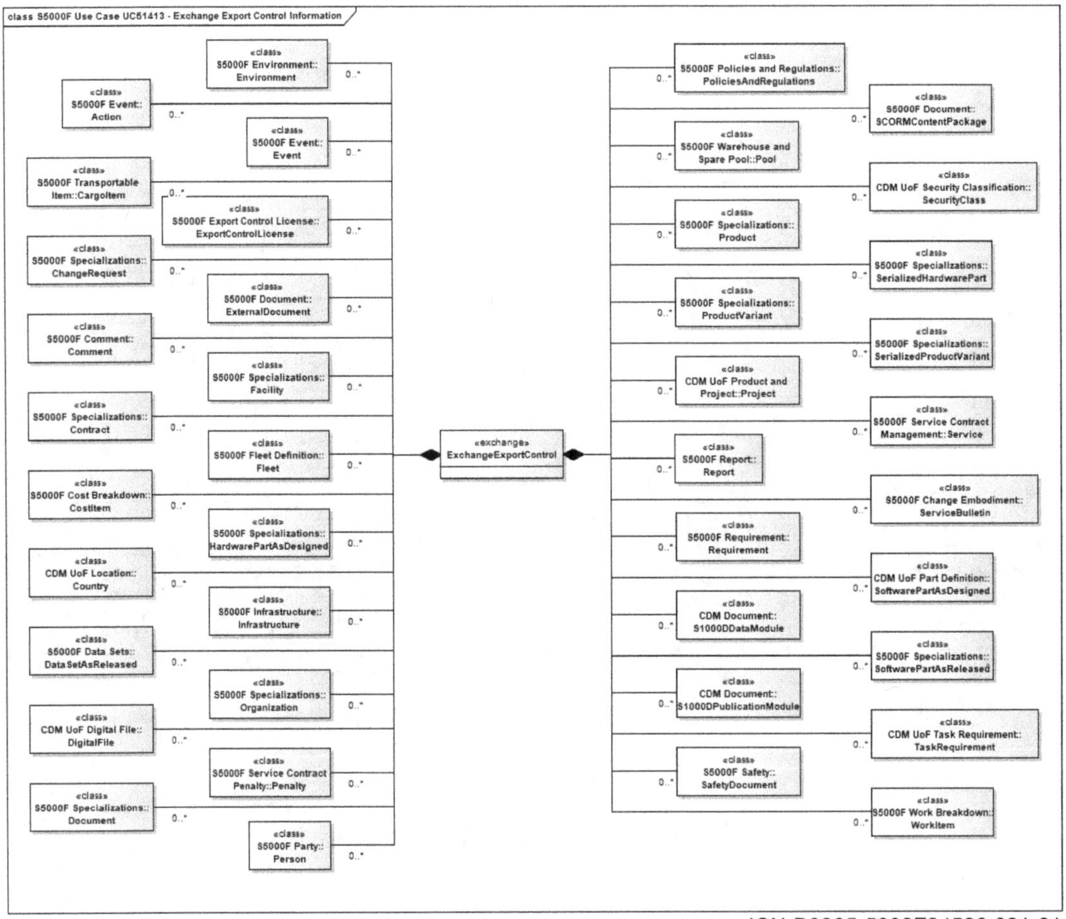

ICN-B6865-5000F24586-001-01

Fig 87 S5000F Use case UC51413 - Exchange export control information

2.88   S5000F Use case UC51414 - Provide labor rates

Provide labor rates represents a message associated with a use case (UC51414) allowing labor rates from one party to be provided to another.

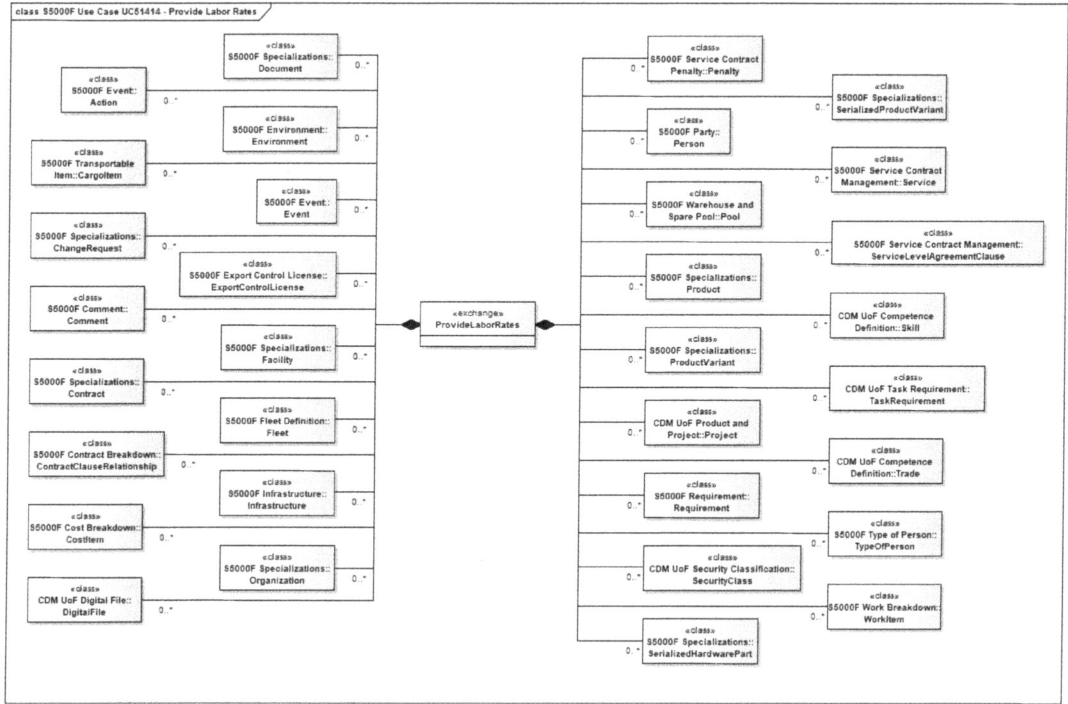

ICN-B6865-5000F24587-001-01

Fig 88 S5000F Use case UC51414 - Provide labor rates

2.89 S5000F Use case UC51415 - Provide documentation traceability

Provide documentation traceability represents a message associated with a use case (UC51415) ensuring the traceability of documentation.

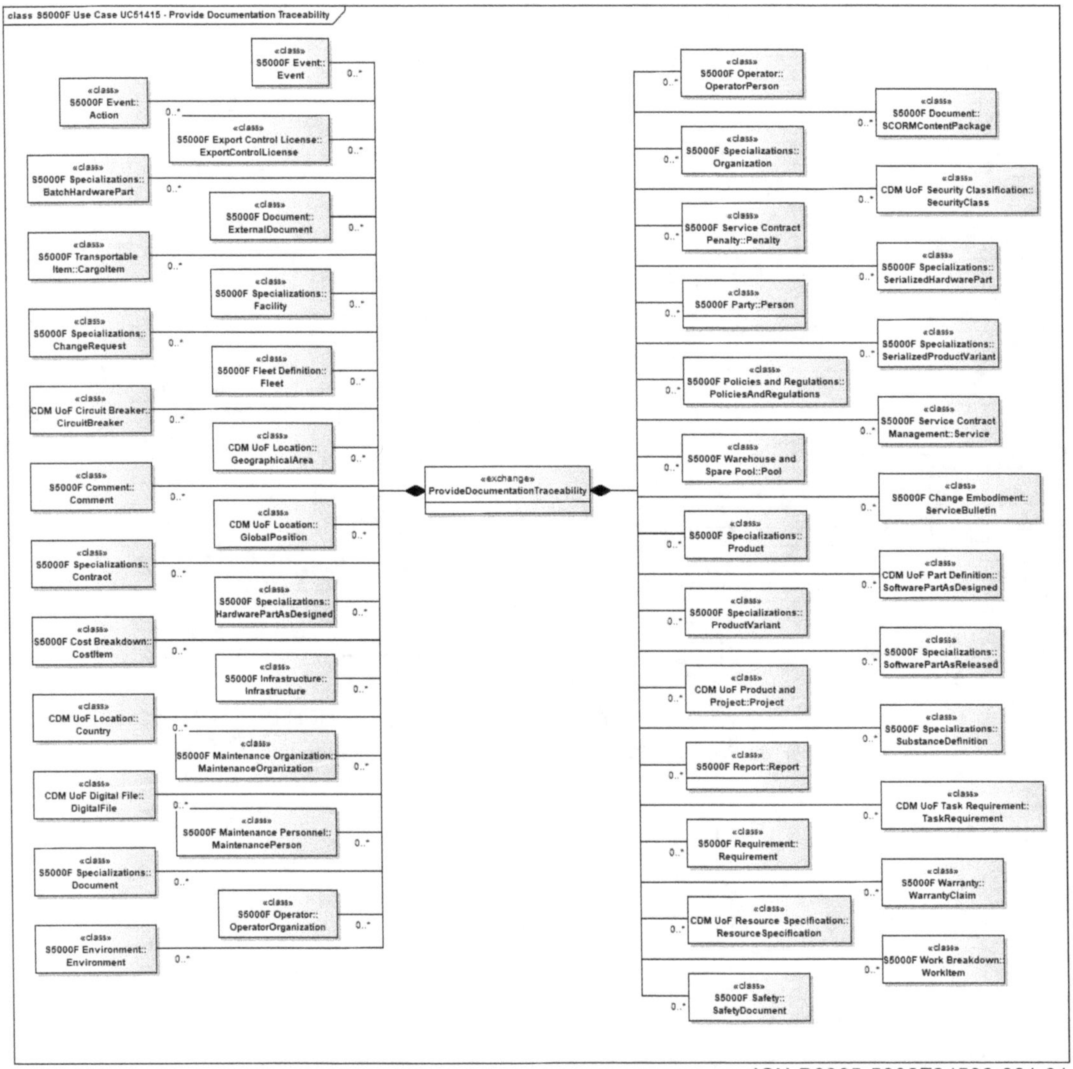

ICN-B6865-5000F24588-001-01

Fig 89 S5000F Use case UC51415 - Provide documentation traceability

2.90 S5000F Use case UC51503 - Provide disposal location information

Provide disposal location information represents a message associated with a use case (UC51503) allowing the location information of an item to be indicated.

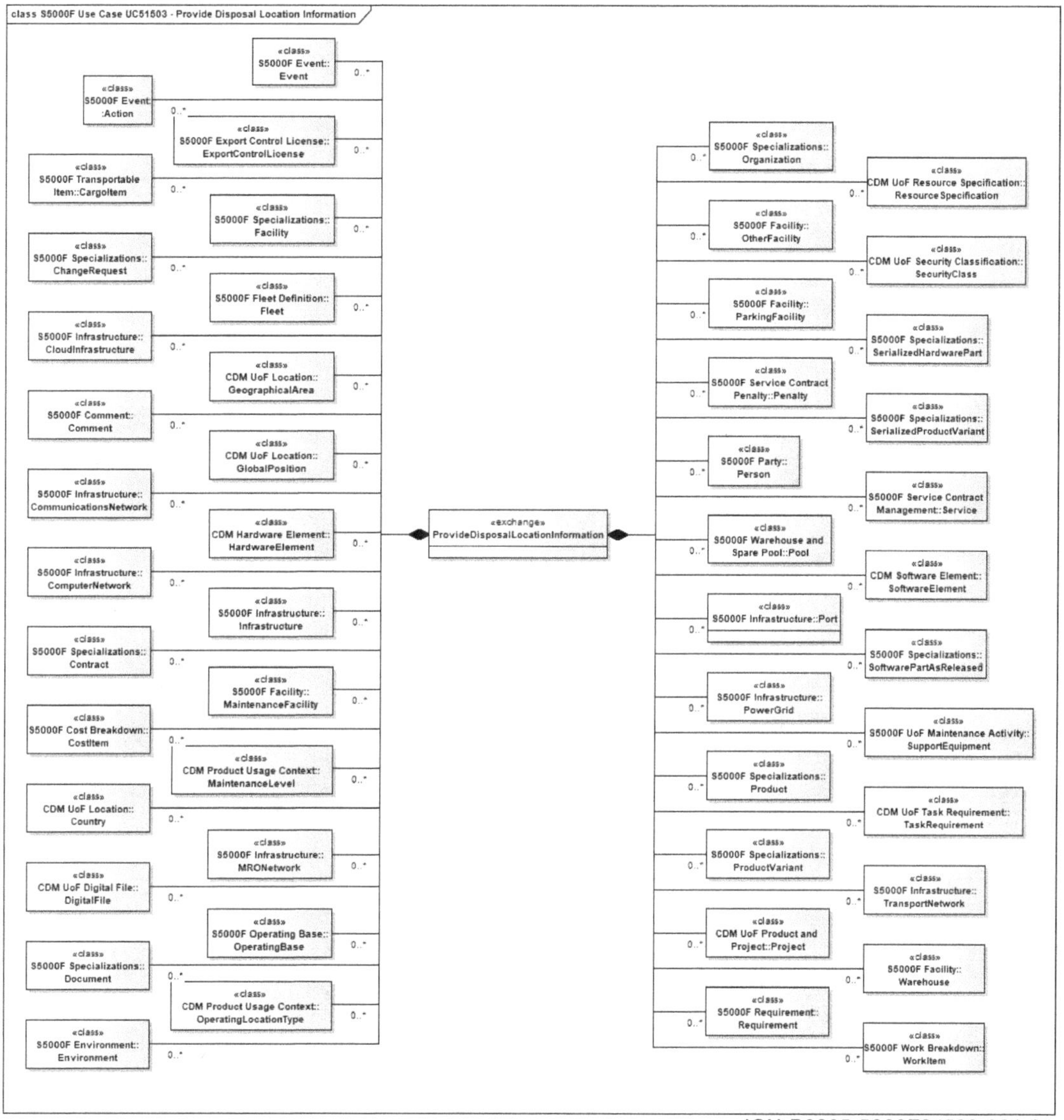

ICN-B6865-5000F24589-001-01

Fig 90 S5000F Use case UC51503 - Provide disposal location information

2.91   S5000F Use case UC51504 - Report infrastructure availability

Report infrastructure availability represents a message associated with a use case (UC51504) allowing information about the current, past and future availability of an infrastructure to be provided.

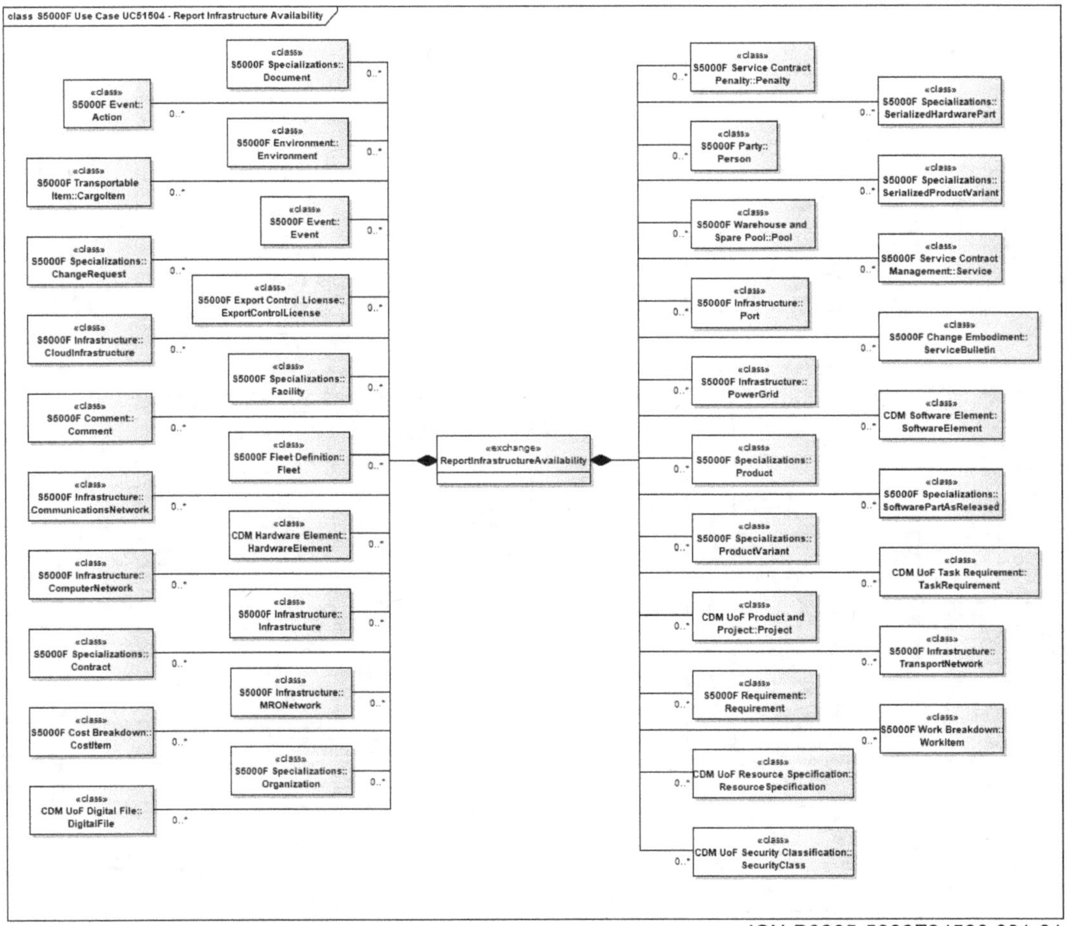

ICN-B6865-5000F24590-001-01

Fig 91 S5000F Use case UC51504 - Report infrastructure availability

2.92   S5000F Use case UC51505 - Define or update environment

Define or update environment represents a message associated with a use case (UC51505) allowing information about the environment in which the Product operates or is maintained to be defined or updated.

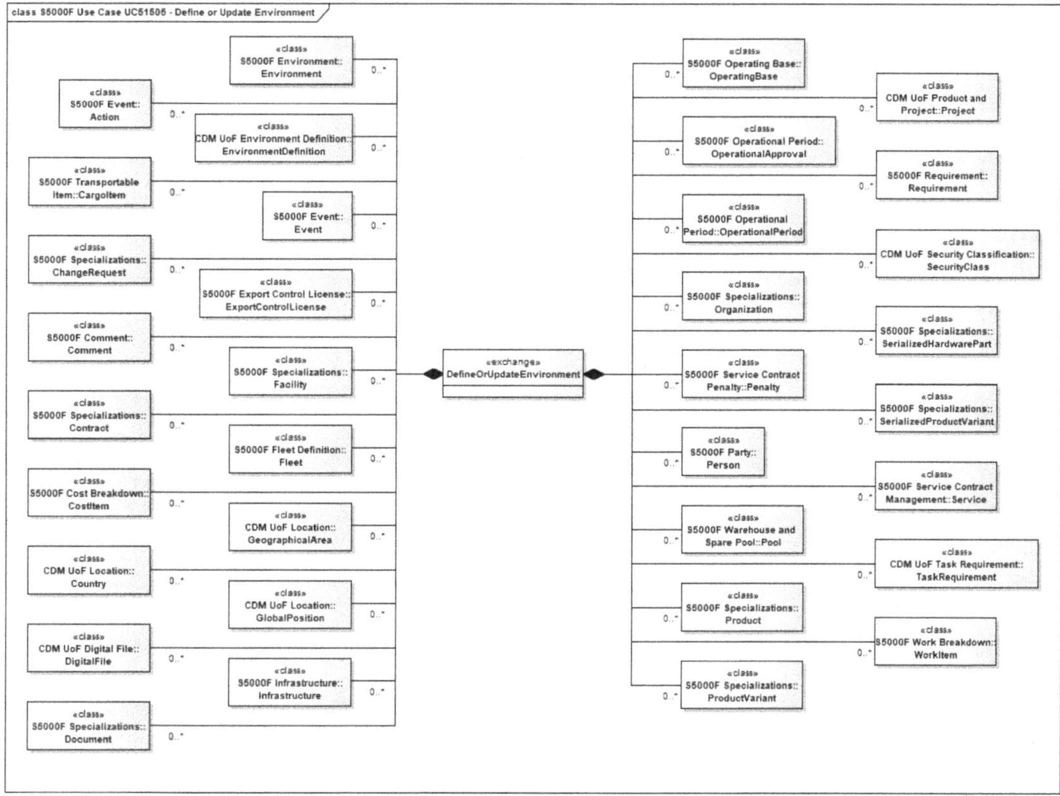

ICN-B6865-5000F24591-001-01

Fig 92 S5000F Use case UC51505 - Define or update environment

2.93   S5000F Use case UC51506 - Reallocate fleet or Product

Reallocate fleet or Product represents a message associated with a use case (UC51506) allowing to report the re(allocation) of a Fleet or Product to a different operator, owner or operating location (eg, to indicate change of ownership).

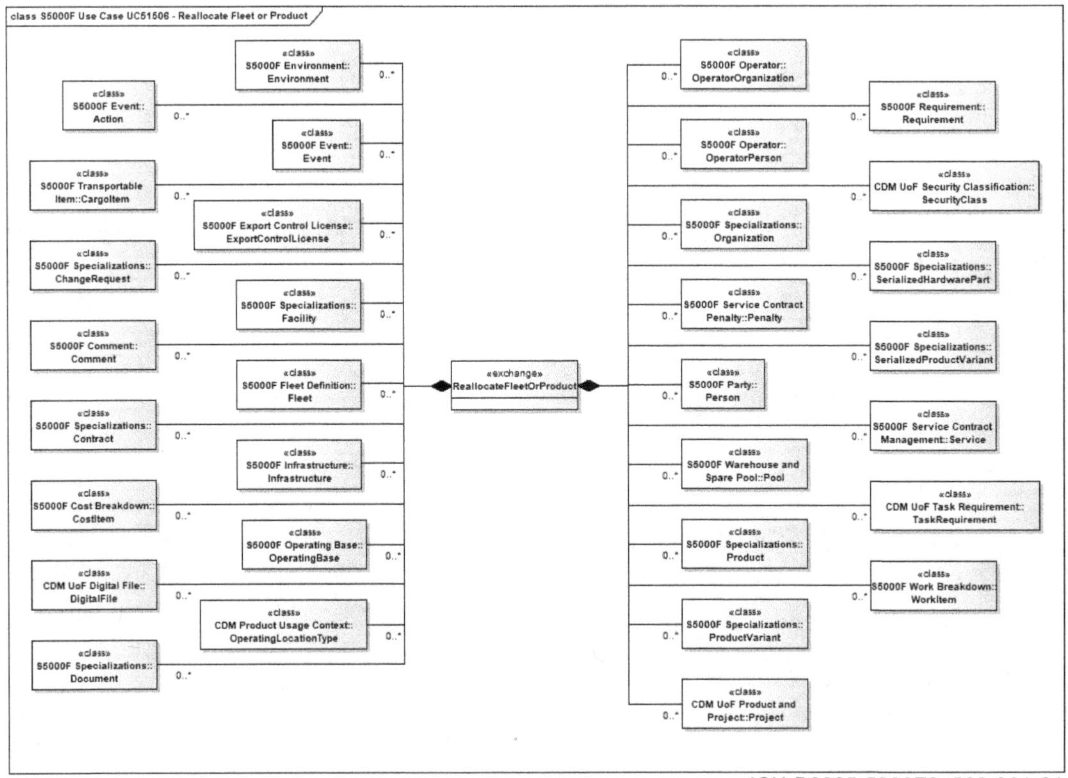

ICN-B6865-5000F24592-001-01

Fig 93 S5000F Use case UC51506 - Reallocate fleet or Product

2.94 S5000F Use case UC51601 - Exchange environmental data

Exchange environmental data represents a message associated with a use case (UC51601) allowing consumption and emission information between different parties due to Product operation to be reported.

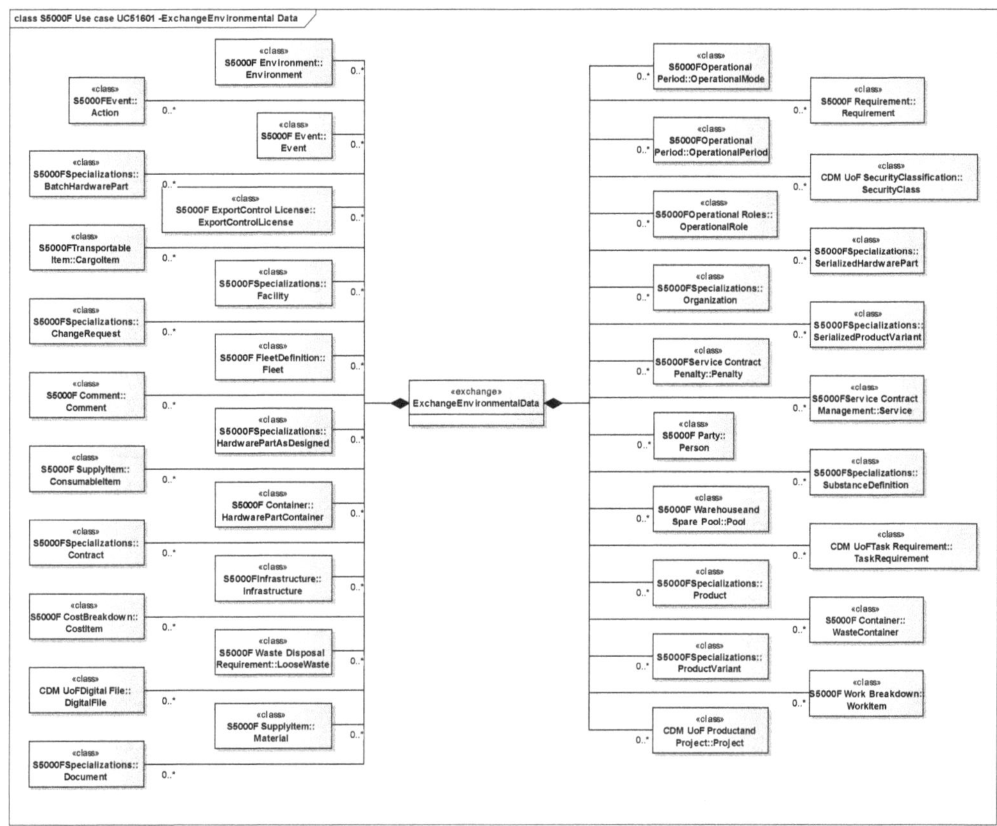

ICN-B6865-5000F24593-001-01

Fig 94 S5000F Use case UC51601 - Exchange environmental data

2.95 S5000F Use case UC51602 - Report environmental data to authorities

Report environmental data to authorities represents a message associated with a use case (UC51602) allowing consumption and emission information to be reported to the authorities, not only for the Product but also for the facilities or infrastructure required to support the Product.

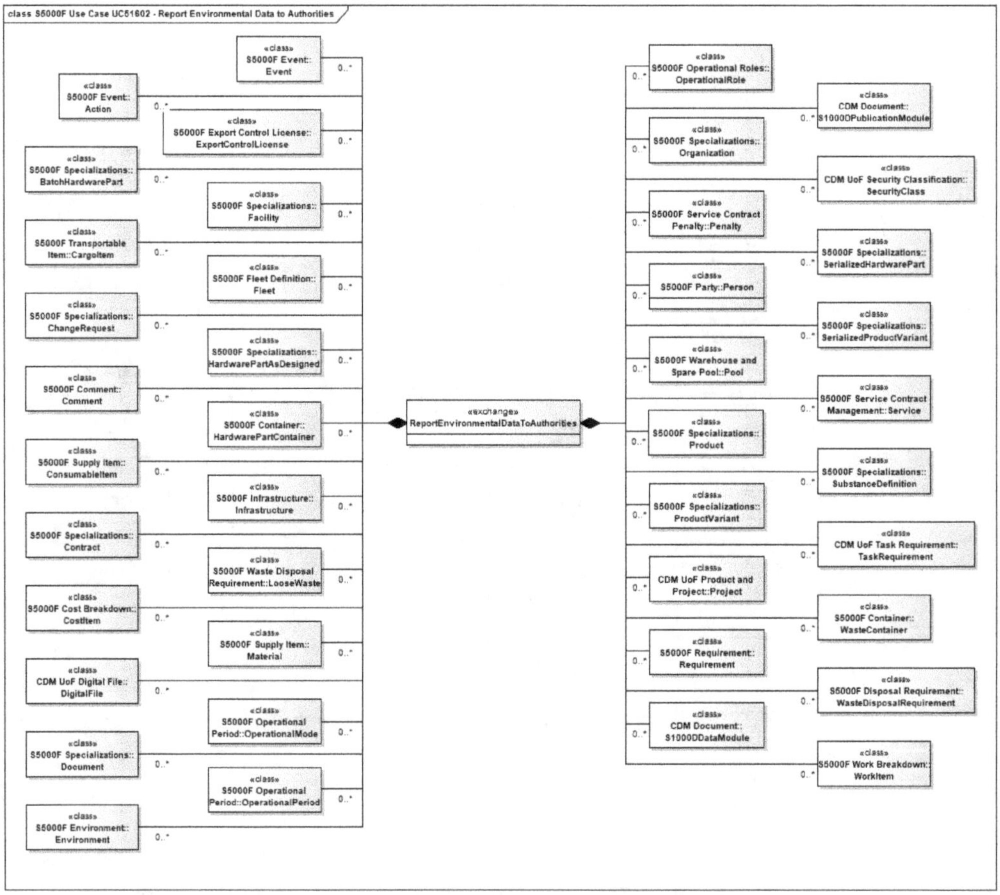

ICN-B6865-5000F24594-001-01

Fig 95 S5000F Use case UC51602 - Report environmental data to authorities

2.96 S5000F Use case UC51603 - Report modification impact on disposal

Report modification impact on disposal represents a message associated with a use case (UC51603) allowing the potential environmental and disposal impact of a Product modification to be reported.

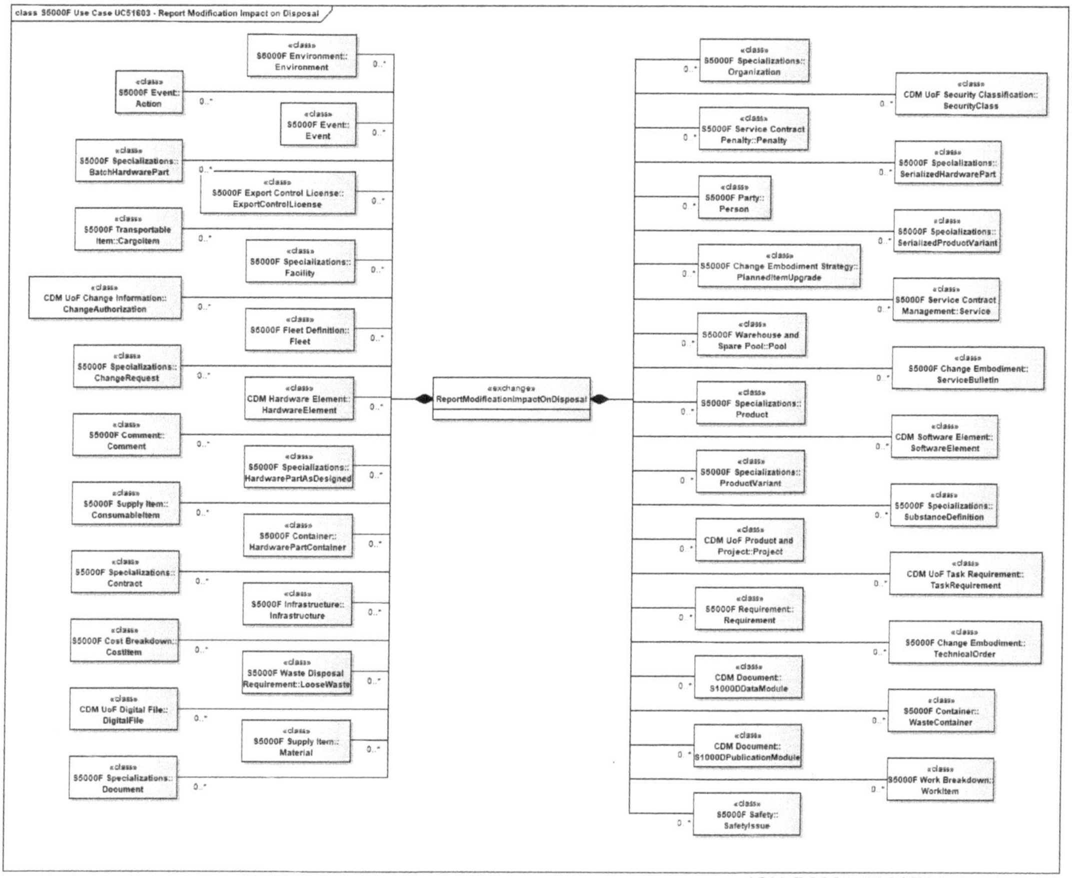

ICN-B6865-5000F24595-001-01

Fig 96 S5000F Use case UC51603 - Report modification impact on disposal

2.97   S5000F Use case UC51604 - Report valuable items from disposal

Report valuable items from disposal represents a message associated with a use case (UC51604) allowing reporting on the valuable items that have been recovered during the disposal of a serialized Product variant.

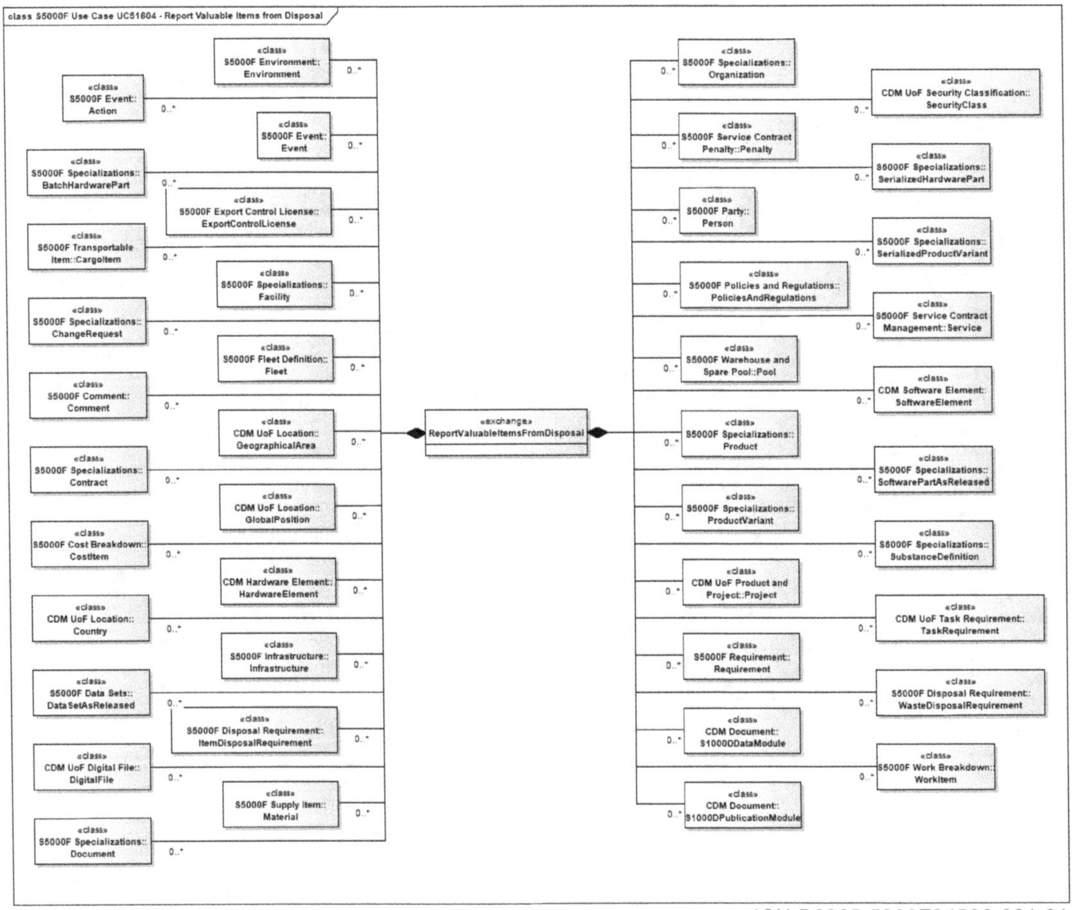

ICN-B6865-5000F24596-001-01

Fig 97 S5000F Use case UC51604 - Report valuable items from disposal

2.98　S5000F Use case UC51605 - Request item disposal

Request item disposal represents a message associated with a use case (UC51605) allowing the disposal of a Product or other end item to be requested.

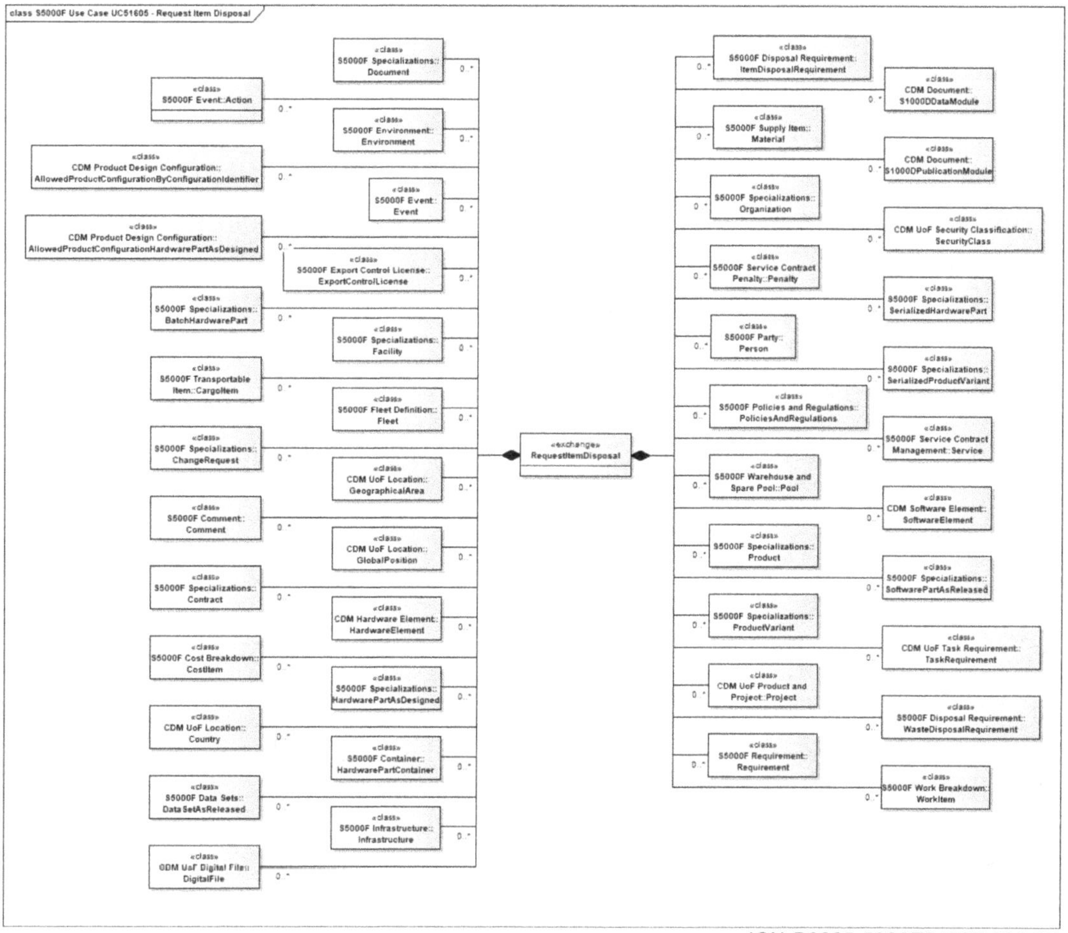

ICN-B6865-5000F24597-001-01

Fig 98 S5000F Use case UC51605 - Request item disposal

2.99   S5000F Use case UC51606 - Report Product disposal

Report Product disposal represents a message associated with a use case (UC51606) allowing information about the disposal of a Product to be reported.

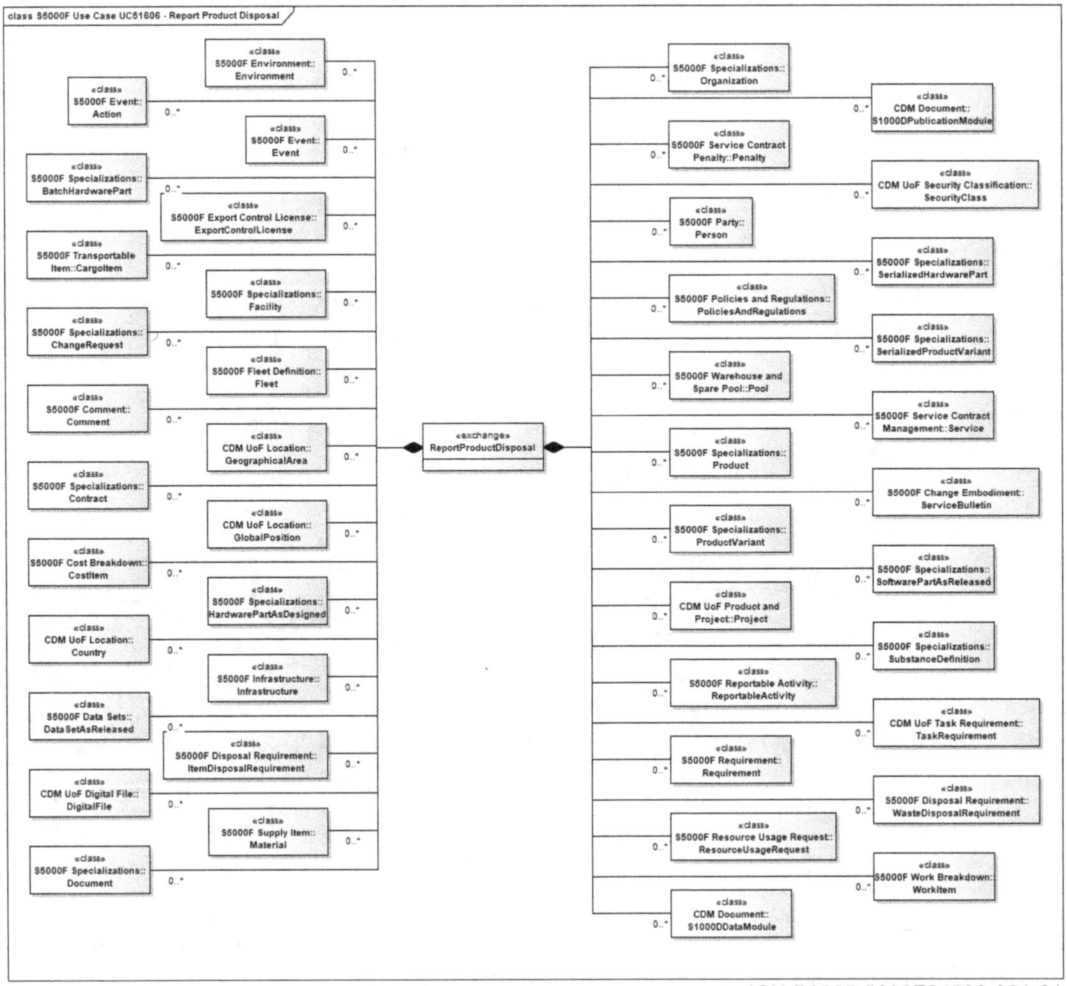

ICN-B6865-5000F24598-001-01

Fig 99 S5000F Use case UC51606 - Report Product disposal

2.100   S5000F Use case UC51607 - Request waste disposal

Request waste disposal represents a message associated with a use case (UC51607) that allows the disposal of waste or hazardous material to be requested.

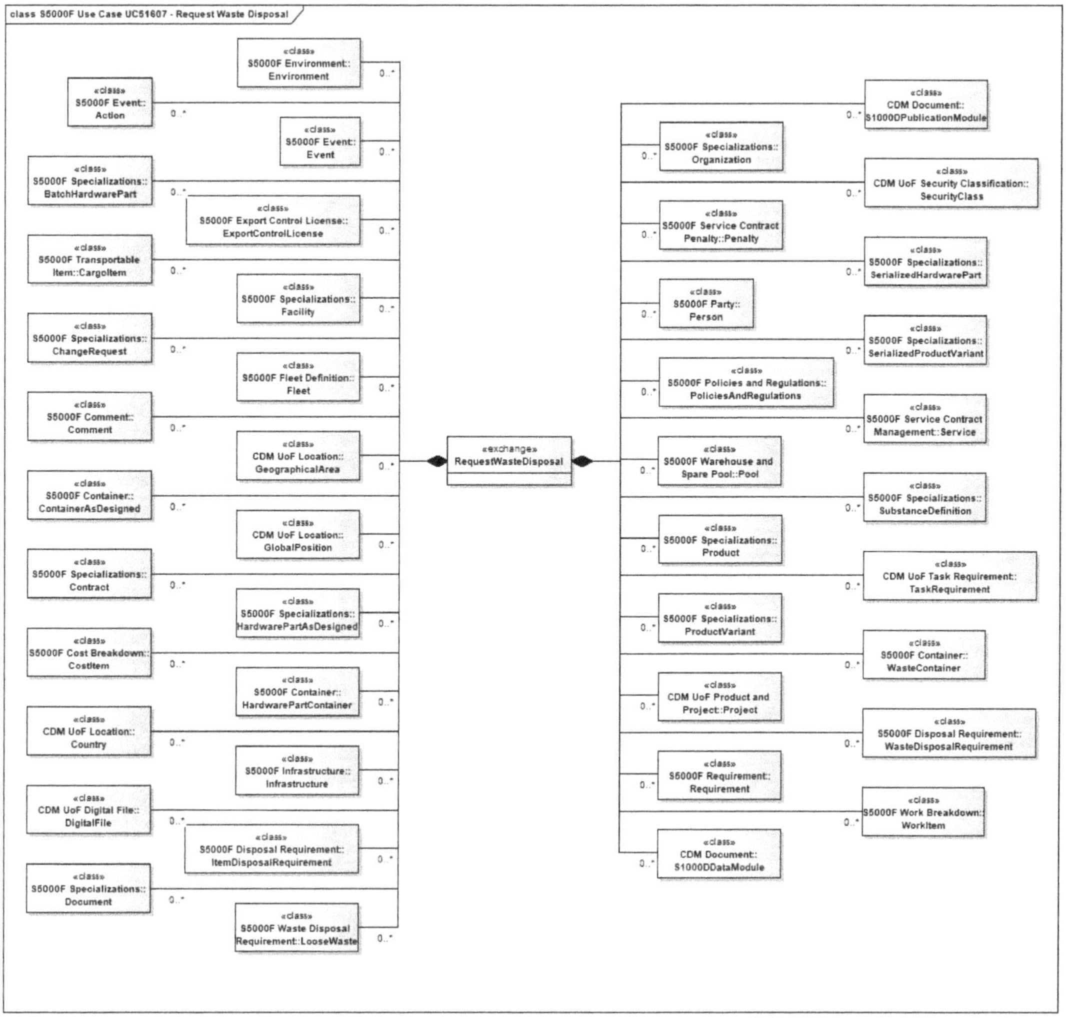

ICN-B6865-5000F24599-001-01

Fig 100 S5000F Use case UC51607 - Request waste disposal

2.101   S5000F Use case UC51608 - Report waste disposal

Report waste disposal represents a message associated with a use case (UC51608) allowing information about the disposal of waste to be reported.

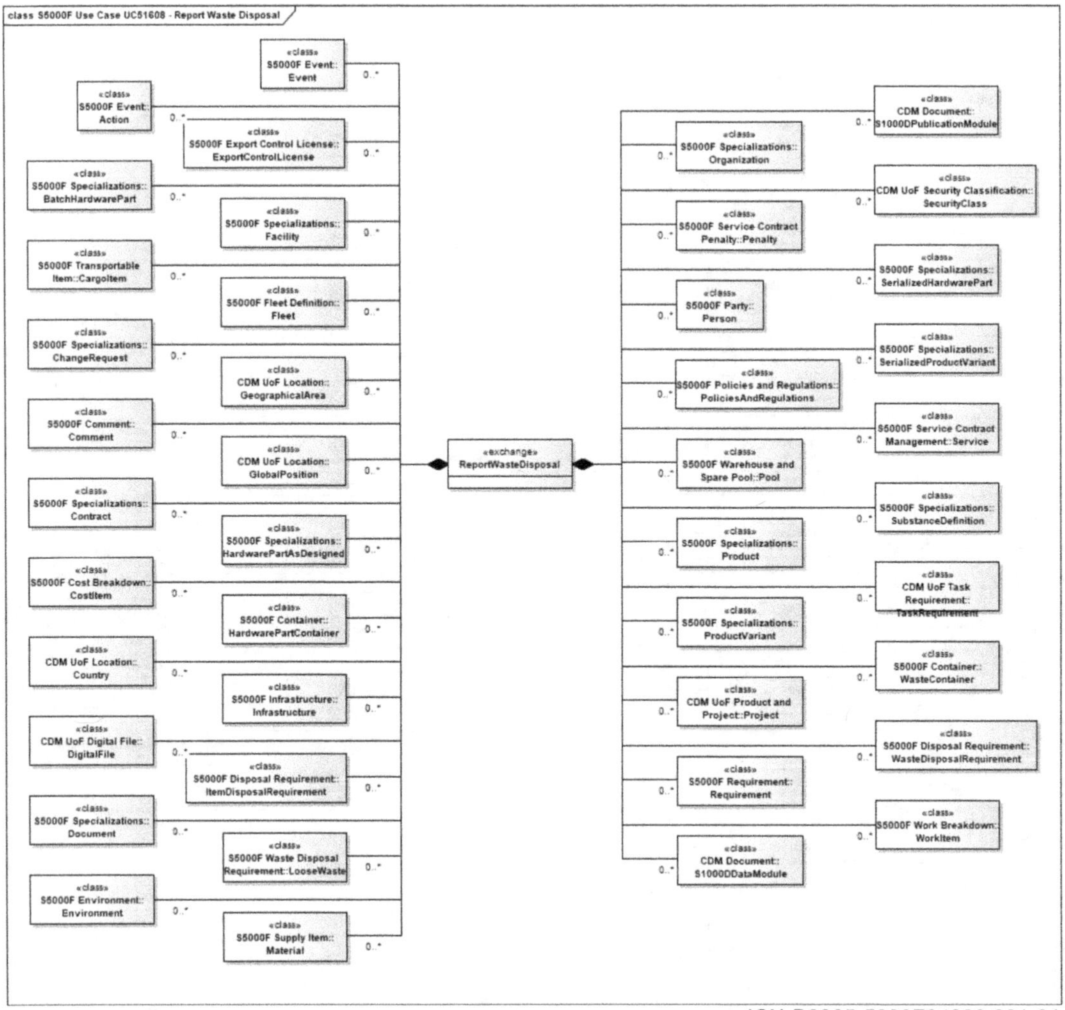

ICN-B6865-5000F24600-001-01

Fig 101 S5000F Use case UC51608 - Report waste disposal

2.102 S5000F Use case UC51609 - Report disposal costs

Report disposal costs represents a message associated with a use case (UC51609) allowing cost information about a disposal to be reported.

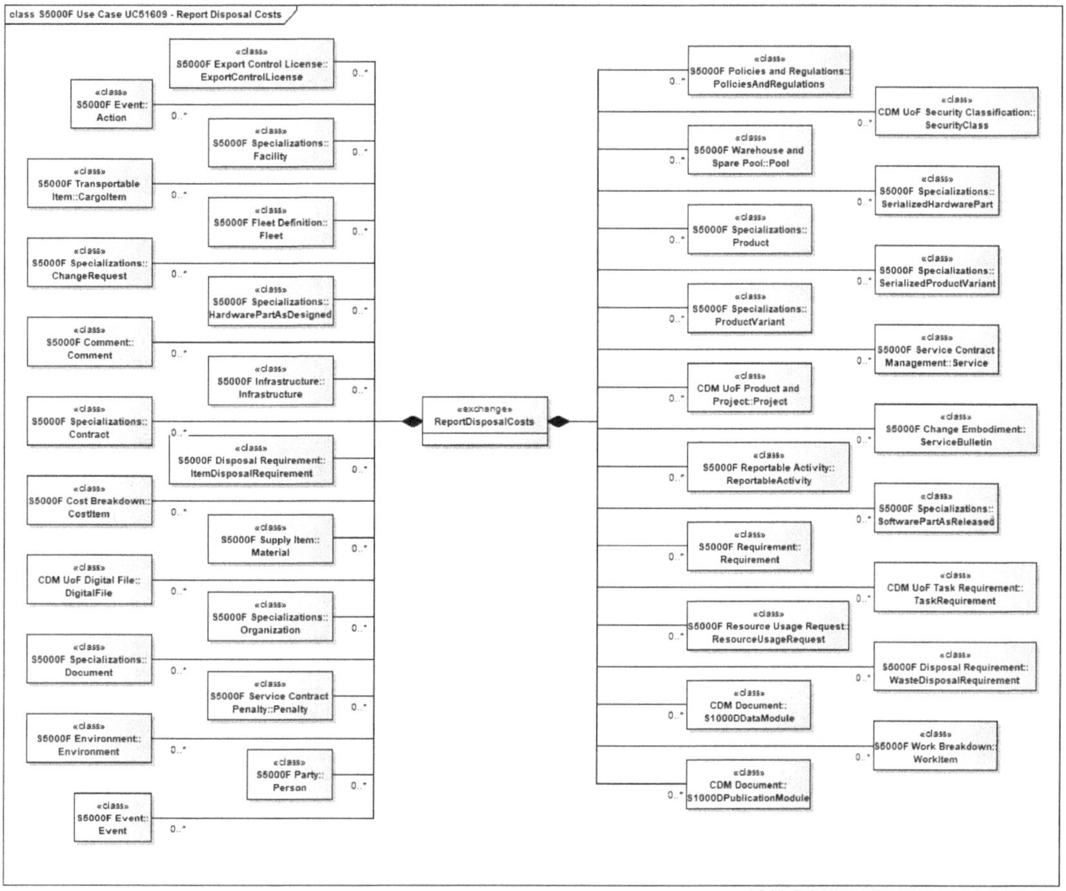

ICN-B6865-5000F24601-001-01

Fig 102 S5000F Use case UC51609 - Report disposal costs

2.103 S5000F Use case UC51610 - Notify unacceptable condition disposal

Notify unacceptable condition disposal represents a message associated with a use case (UC51610) allowing the need for disposal of an item due to unacceptable conditions, usually in the context of a Warranty claim to be reported.

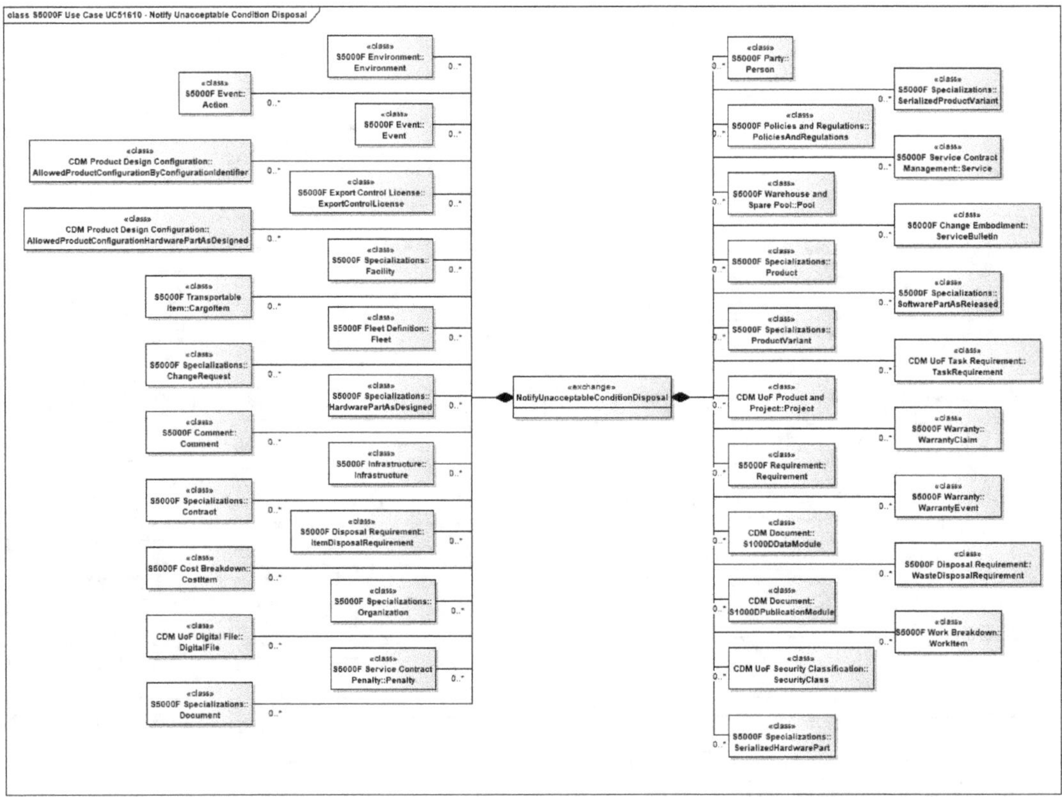

ICN-B6865-5000F24602-001-01

Fig 103 S5000F Use case UC51610 - Notify unacceptable condition disposal

2.104   S5000F Use case UC52301 - Provide project-specific values

Provide project-specific values represents a message associated with a use case (UC51501) allowing project-specific values for a specific purpose to be exchanged.

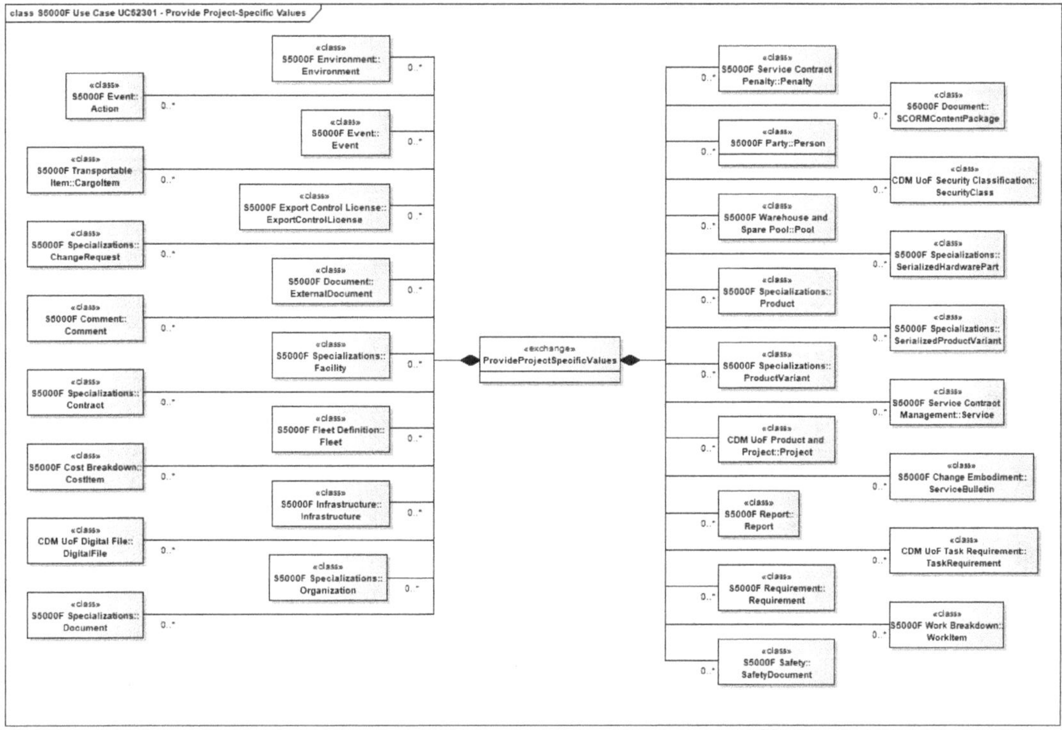

ICN-B6865-5000F24603-001-01

Fig 104 S5000F Use case UC52301 - Provide project-specific values

2.105   S5000F Use case UC52302 - Provide non-predefined information

Provide non-predefined information represents a message associated with a use case (UC51502) allowing non-structured information not contemplated by the specification itself (eg, photos, videos, built-in-test files, etc) to be transferred.

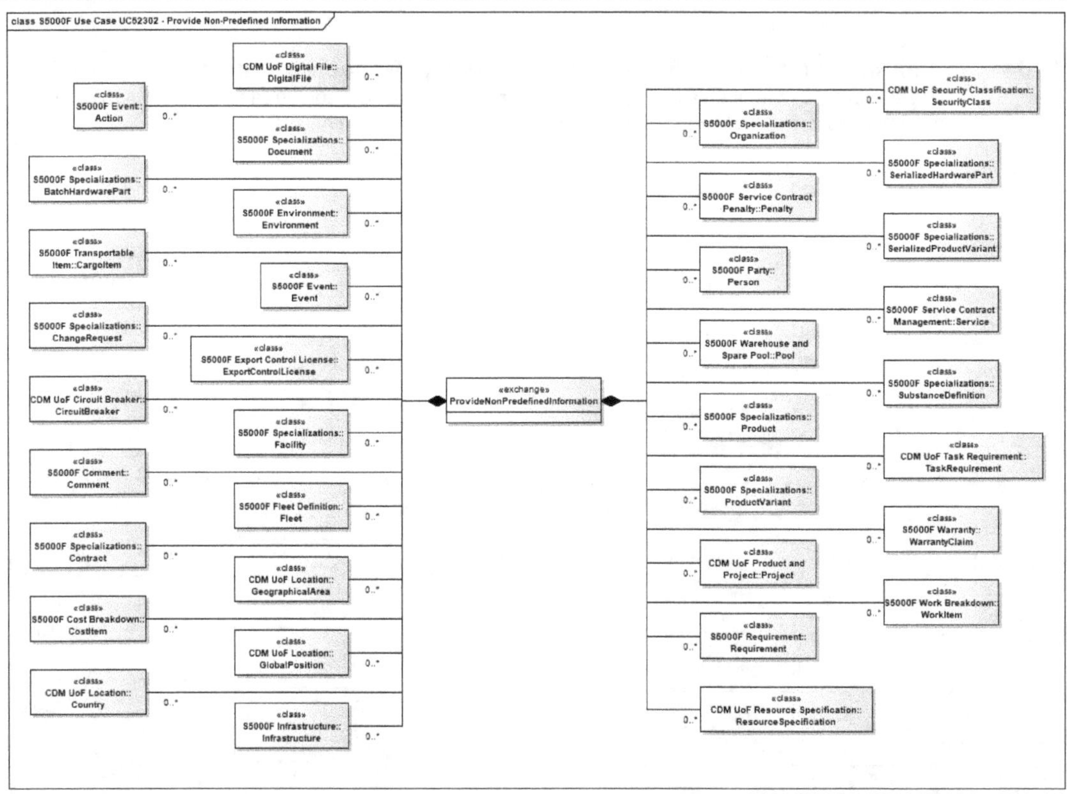

ICN-B6865-5000F24604-001-01

Fig 105 S5000F Use case UC52302 - Provide non-predefined information

Chapter 24.6

Data model - Mapping of use cases to individual UoFs

Table of contents

Page

Data model - Mapping of use cases to individual UoFs 1

References 2

1   General 2

2   Usage of UoFs for specific use cases 3

3   Mapping of use cases to UoFs 3

3.1   UoFs for reliability, availability, maintainability, capability and testability use cases 4

3.2   UoFs for maintenance analysis use cases 7

3.3   UoFs for safety analysis use cases 9

3.4   UoFs for supply support use cases 11

3.5   UoFs for LCC analysis use cases 12

3.6   UoFs for warranty analysis use cases 13

3.7   UoFs for platform usage & health monitoring use cases 14

3.8   UoFs for obsolescence management use cases 15

3.9   UoFs for integrated fleet management use cases 17

3.10   UoFs for software support cases 18

3.11   UoFs for configuration management use cases 20

3.12   UoFs for management of in-service contracts use cases 21

3.13   UoFs for In-service environment data 23

3.14   UoFs for environmental impact and disposal data 24

3.15   UoFs for non-predefined information use cases 26

List of tables

1   References 2

2   UoFs for RAMCT use cases 5

3   UoFs for maintenance analysis use cases 8

4   UoFs for safety analysis use cases 10

5   UoFs for supply support use cases 11

6   UoFs for LCC analysis use cases 12

7   UoFs for warranty analysis use cases 13

8   UoFs for platform usage and health monitoring use cases 15

9   UoFs for obsolescence management use cases 15

10   UoFs for integrated fleet management use cases 17

11   UoFs for software support use cases 19

12   UoFs for configuration management use cases 20

13   UoFs for in-service contract management use cases 22

14   UoFs for in-service environment data use cases 24

15   UoFs for product environmental and disposal data use cases 25

16   UoFs for non-predefined information use cases 26

References

Table 1 References

Chap No./Document No.	Title
Chap 3	Feedback data for the purpose of reliability, maintainability, capability and testability
Chap 4	Feedback of data for maintenance analysis
Chap 5	Feedback of safety data
Chap 6	Feedback of data for supply support
Chap 7	Feedback for Life Cycle Cost analysis
Chap 8	Feedback of data for warranty analysis
Chap 9	Feedback data for the purpose of platform health and usage monitoring
Chap 10	Feedback of data to support obsolescence management
Chap 11	Feedback of data for integrated fleet management
Chap 12	Feedback for software support
Chap 13	Feedback of configuration management data
Chap 14	Feedback of data to support the management of in-service contracts
Chap 15	Feedback of in-service environment data
Chap 16	Feedback of Product environmental and disposal data
Chap 23	Feedback of non-predefined information
Chap 24.3	Data model - Common Data Model (CDM) units of functionality
Chap 24.4	Data model - Units of functionality
Chap 27	Tailoring and contracting against S5000F

1 General

The S5000F data model has been defined on the basis of the use cases defined throughout this specification. This will ensure that when applying a specific use case, all necessary information is available so as to be able to carry out that use case.

This chapter provides a mapping of the Units of Functionality (UoF) as defined in Chap 24.3 and Chap 24.4 that are required for each individual use case.

Note
> It is important to observe that the mapping provided in this chapter is not mandatory and is just a guidance provided to assist the users in identifying the information that they could require for a specific use case.

2   Usage of UoFs for specific use cases

UoFs are snapshots of segments of the data model that cover a specific functionality. Data exchanges do not therefore have to fit exactly to a UoF. Classes that are not required can be dropped from the exchange, and related classes from a different UoF can be added to a specific use case as required.

Similarly, it is an acceptable practice to adding and/or removing UoFs to a specific use case as necessary, as is defining project-specific use cases using arbitrary UoFs, provided that the data model is not changed.

Users of the specification are invited to propose new use cases to the S5000F Steering Committee by submitting a change request at http://www.sx000i.org/CPF.

Details about how to tailor a data exchange are provided in Chap 27.

For the definition of data exchanges for specific use cases, it is advised to start by looking at the UoFs of the following corresponding functional domains, as defined in Chap 24.4:

- **Configuration** - to exchange all information related to configuration aspects, including breakdown and change management
- **Environmental impact and disposal** – to exchange information about environmental impact or product disposal.
- **Elements** - to exchange information about individual components, irrespective of whether these are hardware, software, or data
- **Environment and Infrastructure** - to provide environmental information or fixed locations that are needed or referenced in the context of Product support
- **Events and Consequences** - to document things that have happened, as well as the potential damages and failures that could have occurred due to the occurred events
- **Fleet** - to identify and manage multiple supported items as a group
- **Information** - to provide documents or supplementary data to the use case information
- **Maintenance** - to provide information about the maintenance environment and execution
- **Management** - to provide management information required to manage or control a program
- **Material** - to exchange information for supply support, obsolescence and stock management or transport planning
- **Message** - to control the actual definition of a message exchange
- **Miscellaneous** - to cover the exchange of heterogeneous aspects such as the definition of requirements, capabilities, report on availability or measurements, as well as to define complex evaluation expressions
- **Operations** - to provide feedback on the actual Product operation
- **People and Organizations** - to define and provide information about organisations and individuals, including skills and labour rates
- **Product** - to identify the usage of a Product and provide feedback about individual serialized Products
- **Regulatory** - to provide information related to legal aspects such as policies, regulations, security or export control
- **Safety** - to exchange information on Safety issues

3   Mapping of use cases to UoFs

The following tables describe the UoFs that are used for each individual use case, using the following codes:

- X - mandatory
- O - optional/recommended
- (blank) - in principle, not used

As highlighted above, this mapping is a recommendation and it can be therefore tailored for each specific project.

Note

The following UoFs are added to all use cases for documentation/classification purposes:

- CDM UoF Document
- S5000F UoF Comment
- S5000F UoF Comment Item
- S5000F UoF Project Specific Attribute Definition
- S5000F UoF Remark
- S5000F UoF Security Classification

3.1 UoFs for reliability, availability, maintainability, capability and testability use cases

The UoFs required for the different Reliability, Availability, Maintainability, Capability and Testability (RAMCT) use cases, as defined in Chap 3, are listed in Table 2. In order to avoid having to cross-check the use case numbers, a summary of each use case is provided below:

The Reliability use cases are as follows:

1 UC50301: Monitor the performance of equipment

2 UC50302: Influencing future designs

3 UC50303: Trends, Failures, Root Cause Analysis and Issue Warnings

The Availability use cases are as follows:

1 UC50304: Operations and deployment support, through-life support and equipment availability

2 UC50305: Maintenance Management and Contracting for availability

The Maintainability use cases are as follows:

1 UC50306: Maintenance Activities, Effectiveness of repairs, Specified Maintenance, predict Maintenance Periods, Products status

2 UC50307: Retaining Performance, Support manuals and Support Infrastructure

The Capability use cases are as follows:

1 UC50308: Mission capable, capability shortfalls

2 UC50309: Efficiency, Performance against specification

The Testability use cases are as follows:

1 UC503010: Can Product be tested

2 UC503011: Fault diagnosis, fault identification

Table 2 UoFs for RAMCT use cases

UoF Name	Reliability UC50301	UC50302	UC50303	Availability UC50304	UC50305	Maintainability UC50306	UC50307	Capability UC50308	UC50309	Testability UC50310	UC50311
CDM UoF Applicability Statement	X	X	X								
CDM UoF Breakdown Structure	X	X	X	O	X	X	X	O	X	X	X
CDM UoF Document	O										
CDM UoF Hardware Element	X	X	X	X	X	X	X	O	X	X	X
CDM UoF Product Design Configuration	X	X	X	O	O	X		X	X	X	X
CDM UoF Product Usage Context	X	X									
CDM UoF Software Element	X	X	O	O	X		X		X		
S5000F UoF Applicability Statement Items	X	X	X								
S5000F UoF Availability	X	X	X	X	X	X	X			X	X
S5000F UoF Breakdown Item	X	X									
S5000F UoF Capability								X	X		
S5000F UoF Comment	O	O	O	O	O	O	O	O	O	O	O
S5000F UoF Comment Item	O	O	O	O	O	O	O	O	O	O	O
S5000F UoF Contract Breakdown					X						
S5000F UoF Cost Entry		X		O	O	O	O	O		O	
S5000F UoF Document	O	O	O	O	X		X		O		
S5000F UoF Environment			O								
S5000F UoF Equipment	X	X	X		O	X	X	O	X	X	X
S5000F UoF Equipment Calibration Certificate Information										X	X
S5000F UoF Event	X	X	X	X	O	X	X	X	X	X	X
S5000F UoF Event - Event Item	X	X									
S5000F UoF Expression Evaluation					X						
S5000F UoF Facility				O		X	X	O		O	X
S5000F UoF Failure Detection and Location			X							X	
S5000F UoF Fleet Monitoring				X	X						

UoF Name	Reliability			Availability		Maintainability		Capability		Testability	
	UC50301	UC50302	UC50303	UC50304	UC50305	UC50306	UC50307	UC50308	UC50309	UC50310	UC50311
S5000F UoF Fleet Planning and Product Assignment								X			
S5000F UoF Infrastructure				O			X	O			
S5000F UoF Infrastructure Availability				X			X	O			
S5000F UoF Logbook	X	X	X	X	O	X		X	X	X	X
S5000F UoF Maintenance Activity	X	X		X	X	X			X	X	X
S5000F UoF Maintenance Activity - Maintenance Item	X	X			X	X			X	X	X
S5000F UoF Maintenance Facility Planning				X	X		X	X		O	O
S5000F UoF Maintenance Organization				X			X				
S5000F UoF Maintenance Personnel			X	O	X	X	X			O	O
S5000F UoF Maintenance Program			X		X					X	
S5000F UoF Maintenance Program Item			X		X					X	
S5000F UoF Maintenance Work Order Source			X								
S5000F UoF Measurement Point			X								
S5000F UoF Non-Availability Cause Item	X	X	X	X	X	X	X			X	X
S5000F UoF Operational Environment		X	X	X				X	X	O	X
S5000F UoF Operational Event	X	X	X	X		X	X	X	X	X	X
S5000F UoF Operational Period			O	X	X						
S5000F UoF Operational Roles	X	X	X	X		X		X	X	X	
S5000F UoF Operational Times			X	X	X			X		O	
S5000F UoF Part As Realized			X								
S5000F UoF Part Definition	X	X	X	O	X	X	X	O	X	X	X
S5000F UoF Policies and Regulations		X									
S5000F UoF Product Defined Operational Configuration		X	X	O	O	X	X	X			X
S5000F UoF Product Usage Phase		X									
S5000F UoF Project and Contract				X							

UoF Name	Reliability			Availability		Maintainability		Capability		Testability	
	UC50301	UC50302	UC50303	UC50304	UC50305	UC50306	UC50307	UC50308	UC50309	UC50310	UC50311
S5000F UoF Project Specific Attribute Definition	O	O	O	O	O	O	O	O	O	O	O
S5000F UoF Remark	O	O	O	O	O	O	O	O	O	O	O
S5000F UoF Report	O	O		O	O	X					X
S5000F UoF Report Context Item	O					X					X
S5000F UoF Reportable Activity	O	O	O	O		X					X
S5000F UoF Reportable Metric	O	O			X						
S5000F UoF Requirement		X									
S5000F UoF Safety	X	X	X	X						X	X
S5000F UoF Safety - Safety Item	X	X	X	X						X	X
S5000F UoF Security Classification	O	O	O	O	O	O	O	O	O		O
S5000F UoF Serialized Item	X	X	X	X	X	O	O	O	O	X	X
S5000F UoF Serialized Product Health Monitoring		X									X
S5000F UoF Serialized Product Variant	X		X	O	X	O	O	X	X	O	X
S5000F UoF Serialized Product Variant Configuration	X	X	X	O	O	X	X	X	X	X	X
S5000F UoF Shop Findings											X
S5000F UoF Warranty		X									

3.2 UoFs for maintenance analysis use cases

The UoFs required for the different maintenance analysis use cases, as defined in Chap 4, are those listed in UC50409: Equipment calibration certificate

1 UC50410 Track support equipment usage

Table 3. In order to avoid having to cross-check the use case numbers, a summary of each use case is provided below:

2 UC50401: Manufacturer maintenance schedule

3 UC50402: Product user maintenance program

4 UC50403: Maintenance performed

5 UC50404: Product performance

6 UC50405: New modifications for in-service Products

7 UC50406: Technical queries

8 UC50407: Component shop findings

9 UC50408: Structural damages

10 UC50409: Equipment calibration certificate

11 UC50410 Track support equipment usage

Table 3 UoFs for maintenance analysis use cases

UoFName	UC50401	UC50402	UC50403	UC50404	UC50405	UC50406	UC50407	UC50408	UC50409	UC50410
CDM UoF Digital File						X				
CDM UoF Document						X				
S5000F UoF Availability				X						
S5000F UoF Change Embodiment					X					
S5000F UoF Change Embodiment Planning					X					
S5000F UoF Change Embodiment Reporting					X					
S5000F UoF Change Embodiment Strategy					X					
S5000F UoF Change Information					X					
S5000F UoF Change Request					X					
S5000F UoF Comment	O	O	O	O	O	X	O	O	O	O
S5000F UoF Comment Item	O	O	O	O	O	X	O	O	O	O
S5000F UoF Cost Entry							X	O		
S5000F UoF Damage			X					X		
S5000F UoF Digital File - Digital File Referenced Item						X				
S5000F UoF Digital File Digital File Referencing Item						X				
S5000F UoF Document	O	O	O		O	X		O	O	
S5000F UoF Equipment			X							
S5000F UoF Equipment Calibration Certificate Information			O						X	X
S5000F UoF Event			X			X		X		
S5000F UoF Failure Detection and Location			O				O			
S5000F UoF Local Position								O		
S5000F UoF Maintenance Activity			X							X

UoFName	UC50401	UC50402	UC50403	UC50404	UC50405	UC50406	UC50407	UC50408	UC50409	UC50410
S5000F UoF Maintenance Activity - Maintenance Item			X							
S5000F UoF Maintenance Facility Planning	O	O	X							
S5000F UoF Maintenance Organization	X	X	X							
S5000F UoF Maintenance Personnel	O	O	X							
S5000F UoF Maintenance Program	X	X								
S5000F UoF Maintenance Program Item	X	X								
S5000F UoF Maintenance Work Order Source	O	O	X							
S5000F UoF Non-Availability Cause Item				X						
S5000F UoF Operating Base				X						
S5000F UoF Operational Environment				X		X				
S5000F UoF Operational Event				X		X		X		
S5000F UoF Operational Period				X		O				
S5000F UoF Operational Roles				X		X				
S5000F UoF Operator				X						
S5000F UoF Part As Realized					X	X				
S5000F UoF Part Definition									X	
S5000F UoF Party									O	
S5000F UoF Project Specific Attribute Definition	O	O	O	O	O	O	O	O	O	O
S5000F UoF Remark	O	O	O	O	O	O	O	O	O	O
S5000F UoF Safety						X				
S5000F UoF Safety - Safety Item						X				
S5000F UoF Security Classification	O	O	O	O	O	O	O	O	O	O
S5000F UoF Serialized Item			X							
S5000F UoF Shop Findings			X					X		
S5000F UoF Support Equipment			X						X	X

3.3 UoFs for safety analysis use cases

The UoFs required for the different safety use cases, as defined in Chap 5, are those listed in Table 4. In order to avoid having to cross-check the use case numbers, a summary of each use case is provided below:

1   UC50501: Report safety issue

2   UC50502: Provide operational limitations due to safety issue

3   UC50503: Provide special safety instructions

Table 4 UoFs for safety analysis use cases

UoFName	UC50501	UC50502	UC50503
CDM UoF Applicability Statement	O	X	X
CDM UoF Document	O	O	O
CDM UoF Product Design Configuration	X	X	X
CDM UoF Software Element		X	X
S5000F UoF Applicability Statement Items	O	X	X
S5000F UoF Comment	O	O	O
S5000F UoF Comment Item	O	O	O
S5000F UoF Document	O	O	O
S5000F UoF Event	X		
S5000F UoF Logbook	X		
S5000F UoF Operational Environment	X		
S5000F UoF Operational Event	O		
S5000F UoF Operational Period	X		
S5000F UoF Part As Realized	X	X	X
S5000F UoF Party	X	X	X
S5000F UoF Product Defined Operational Configuration	X	X	
S5000F UoF Project Specific Attribute Definition	O	O	O
S5000F UoF Remark	O	O	O
S5000F UoF Report	X	X	
S5000F UoF Report Context Item	X		
S5000F UoF Requirement		X	X
S5000F UoF Safety	X	X	X
S5000F UoF Safety - Safety Item	X	X	X
S5000F UoF Security Classification	O	O	O
S5000F UoF Serialized Product Variant Configuration	O		

3.4 UoFs for supply support use cases

The UoFs required for the different supply support use cases, as defined in Chap 6, are those listed in Table 5. In order to avoid having to cross-check the use case numbers, a summary of each use case is provided below:

1 UC50601: Inventory management

2 UC50602: Shelf life management

3 UC50603: Spares and SE pool management

4 UC50604: Logistic Response time

5 UC50605: Facilities management and maintenance

6 UC50606: Plan for transport

Table 5 UoFs for supply support use cases

UoFName	UC50601	UC50602	UC50603	UC50604	UC50605	UC50606
S5000F UoF Comment	O	O	O	O	O	O
S5000F UoF Comment Item	O	O	O	O	O	O
S5000F UoF Facility	O		X		X	
S5000F UoF Infrastructure					X	
S5000F UoF Infrastructure Availability					X	
S5000F UoF Operational Period						X
S5000F UoF Part As Realized		X	X			
S5000F UoF Part Definition		X				
S5000F UoF Project Specific Attribute Definition	O	O	O	O	O	O
S5000F UoF Remark	O	O	O	O	O	O
S5000F UoF Report	X			X	X	
S5000F UoF Report Context Item				X	X	
S5000F UoF Reportable Activity	X			X		
S5000F UoF Reportable Metric				X	X	
S5000F UoF Security Classification	O	O	O	O	O	O
S5000F UoF Shop Findings	X					
S5000F UoF Transport Anchoring Point						X
S5000F UoF Transportable Item						X
S5000F UoF Transporting Asset						X
S5000F UoF Warehouse and Spare Pool	X	X	X	X		

3.5 UoFs for LCC analysis use cases

The UoFs required for the different LCC use cases, as defined in Chap 7, are those listed in Table 6. In order to avoid having to cross-check the use case numbers, a summary of each use case is provided below:

1. UC50701: Provide cost breakdown structure

2. UC50702: Estimate maintenance costs

3. UC50703: Costs due to operational requirements

4. UC50704: Cost of modifications or upgrades

5. UC50705: Costs of in-service support

Table 6 UoFs for LCC analysis use cases

UoFName	UC50701	UC50702	UC50703	UC50704	UC50705
CDM UoF Document				O	
S5000F UoF Change Embodiment				O	
S5000F UoF Change Embodiment Reporting				X	
S5000F UoF Change Embodiment Strategy				O	
S5000F UoF Change Information				O	
S5000F UoF Change Request				X	
S5000F UoF Comment	O	O	O	O	O
S5000F UoF Comment Item	O	O	O	O	O
S5000F UoF Contract Breakdown			X	X	
S5000F UoF Cost Breakdown	X	X	X	X	X
S5000F UoF Cost Breakdown Context	X	X	X	X	X
S5000F UoF Cost Entry	X	X	X	X	X
S5000F UoF Document				X	
S5000F UoF Fleet Monitoring			X		
S5000F UoF Fleet Planning and Product Assignment			X		
S5000F UoF Operational Period			X		
S5000F UoF Operational Times			X		
S5000F UoF Project and Contract	O			O	X
S5000F UoF Project Specific Attribute Definition	O	O	O	O	O
S5000F UoF Remark	O	O	O	O	O
S5000F UoF Report		X	X	X	X

UoFName	UC50701	UC50702	UC50703	UC50704	UC50705
S5000F UoF Report Context Item		X	X	X	X
S5000F UoF Reportable Activity		X	X	X	X
S5000F UoF Requirement			X		
S5000F UoF Security Classification	O	O	O	O	O
S5000F UoF Service Contract Management					X
S5000F UoF Service Contract Penalty					X
S5000F UoF Service Request					X

3.6 UoFs for warranty analysis use cases

The UoFs required for the different warranty use cases, as defined in Chap 8, are those listed in Table 7. In order to avoid having to cross-check the use case numbers, a summary of each use case is provided below:

1. UC50801: Evaluate maintenance actions

2. UC50802: Collect warranty costs

3. UC50803: Determine misuse of warranty

4. UC50804: Identify items causing risk to warranty program

5. UC50805: Improve standard warranty rules and process

Table 7 UoFs for warranty analysis use cases

UoFName	UC50801	UC50802	UC50803	UC50804	UC50805
CDM UoF Product Design Configuration	X			X	X
S5000F UoF Change Embodiment Reporting					X
S5000F UoF Comment	O	O	O	O	O
S5000F UoF Comment Item	O	O	O	O	O
S5000F UoF Contract Breakdown		X	X		O
S5000F UoF Cost Breakdown		O			
S5000F UoF Cost Entry		X			
S5000F UoF Damage	X	X	X	X	X
S5000F UoF Equipment	X	X		X	X
S5000F UoF Equipment Calibration Certificate Information				X	X

UoFName	UC50801	UC50802	UC50803	UC50804	UC50805
S5000F UoF Event				X	
S5000F UoF Failure Detection and Location	O				
S5000F UoF Maintenance Activity	X				
S5000F UoF Maintenance Activity - Maintenance Item	X				
S5000F UoF Maintenance Program	X				
S5000F UoF Maintenance Program Item	X				
S5000F UoF Operational Environment			X	X	X
S5000F UoF Operational Event	X		X		
S5000F UoF Operational Times			X		
S5000F UoF Part As Realized	O		X	X	X
S5000F UoF Project and Contract		O	X		O
S5000F UoF Project Specific Attribute Definition	O	O	O	O	O
S5000F UoF Remark	O	O	O	O	O
S5000F UoF Report		X	X		
S5000F UoF Report Context Item		X			
S5000F UoF Reportable Activity		X	X		
S5000F UoF Reportable Metric		O	O		
S5000F UoF Security Classification	O	O	O	O	O
S5000F UoF Serialized Product Variant Configuration		O	O	O	X
S5000F UoF Shop Findings	X		X	X	X
S5000F UoF Warehouse and Spare Pool				X	
S5000F UoF Warranty	X	X	X	X	X

3.7 UoFs for platform usage & health monitoring use cases

The UoFs required for the different usage & health monitoring use cases, as defined in Chap 9, are those listed in Table 8. In order to avoid having to cross-check the use case numbers, a summary of each use case is provided below:

1 UC50901: Record usage and health data

2 UC50902: Report usage information

3 UC50903: Respond to usage information

Table 8 UoFs for platform usage and health monitoring use cases

UoFName	UC50901	UC50902	UC50903
CDM UoF Digital File	X	X	
CDM UoF Product Usage Context			X
S5000F UoF Comment	O	O	O
S5000F UoF Comment Item	O	O	O
S5000F UoF Digital File - Digital File Referenced Item	X	X	
S5000F UoF Digital File Digital File Referencing Item	X	X	
S5000F UoF Fleet Planning and Product Assignment			X
S5000F UoF Logbook	X	X	X
S5000F UoF Operational Period	X	X	
S5000F UoF Product Defined Operational Configuration			X
S5000F UoF Product Usage Phase		X	X
S5000F UoF Project Specific Attribute Definition	O	O	O
S5000F UoF Remark	O	O	O
S5000F UoF Security Classification	O	O	O
S5000F UoF Serialized Product Health Monitoring	X	X	X

3.8　UoFs for obsolescence management use cases

The UoFs required for the different obsolescence use cases, as defined in Chap 10, are those listed in Table 9. In order to avoid having to cross-check the use case numbers, a summary of each use case is provided below:

1　UC51001: Create basis for obsolescence management planning

2　UC51002: Determine obsolescence candidates /perform risk assessment

3　UC51003: Determine obsolescence strategy

4　UC51004: Obsolescence monitoring

5　UC51005: Solutions/proposals to solve obsolescence

6　UC51006: Provide obsolescence alert

Table 9 UoFs for obsolescence management use cases

UoFName	UC51001	UC51002	UC51003	UC51004	UC51005	UC51006
CDM UoF Document		O				

UoFName	UC51001	UC51002	UC51003	UC51004	UC51005	UC51006
CDM UoF Product Design Configuration	X					
CDM UoF Product Usage Context	X					
CDM UoF Software Element	X					
S5000F UoF Change Embodiment Planning			X		X	
S5000F UoF Change Embodiment Reporting				X		X
S5000F UoF Change Embodiment Strategy					X	
S5000F UoF Comment	O	O	O	O	O	O
S5000F UoF Comment Item	O	O	O	O	O	O
S5000F UoF Contract Breakdown						O
S5000F UoF Document		O				O
S5000F UoF Equipment			X			
S5000F UoF Fleet Planning and Product Assignment			X			
S5000F UoF Logbook		X	X	X		
S5000F UoF Maintenance Activity		X				
S5000F UoF Maintenance Activity - Maintenance Item		X				
S5000F UoF Obsolescence Management Candidates		X				X
S5000F UoF Operational Period		X				
S5000F UoF Part As Realized	X					O
S5000F UoF Project Specific Attribute Definition	O	O	O	O	O	O
S5000F UoF Remark	O	O	O	O	O	O
S5000F UoF Report				X		X
S5000F UoF Reportable Activity				X		X
S5000F UoF Reportable Metric						X
S5000F UoF Requirement		X	X			X
S5000F UoF Security Classification	O	O	O	O	O	
S5000F UoF Serialized Product Variant Configuration	X	X				
S5000F UoF Shop Findings				X		O
S5000F UoF Warehouse and Spare Pool		X	X	X		O

3.9 UoFs for integrated fleet management use cases

The UoFs required for the different integrated fleet management use cases, as defined in Chap 11, are those listed in UC51108: Report fleet availability

Table 10. In order to avoid having to cross-check the use case numbers, a summary of each use case is provided below:

1 UC51101: Assignment Proposal Elaboration

2 UC51102: Fleet task cancellation

3 UC51103: Fleet task modification

4 UC51104: Fleet availability plan elaboration

5 UC51105: Fleet Task Evaluation

6 UC51106: Product preparation for fleet task

7 UC51107: Product Recovery after fleet task

8 UC51108: Report fleet availability

Table 10 UoFs for integrated fleet management use cases

UoFName	UC51101	UC51102	UC51103	UC51104	UC51105	UC51106	UC51107	UC51108
CDM UoF Document	O	O	X	X			O	O
S5000F UoF Availability				X	X			X
S5000F UoF Comment	O	O	O	O	O	O	O	O
S5000F UoF Comment Item	O	O	O	O	O	O	O	O
S5000F UoF Document		O	O	X			O	
S5000F UoF Fleet Definition	X		X	X	X			X
S5000F UoF Fleet Monitoring	X				X		X	
S5000F UoF Fleet Planning and Product Assignment	X	X	X	X	X	X	X	
S5000F UoF Fleet Task Cancellation		X						
S5000F UoF Infrastructure	O			X				
S5000F UoF Infrastructure Availability	O		X	X				
S5000F UoF Location and Locator	X							
S5000F UoF Logbook					X			
S5000F UoF Non-Availability Cause Item				X	X			X
S5000F UoF Operating Base	X		X	X	X	X	X	
S5000F UoF Operational Environment			X	X		X		
S5000F UoF Operational Event							X	

UoFName	UC51101	UC51102	UC51103	UC51104	UC51105	UC51106	UC51107	UC51108
S5000F UoF Operational Period							O	
S5000F UoF Operational Roles	X					X	X	
S5000F UoF Policies and Regulations				X				
S5000F UoF Product Defined Operational Configuration	X							
S5000F UoF Project Specific Attribute Definition	O	O	O	O	O	O	O	O
S5000F UoF Remark	O	O	O	O	O	O	O	O
S5000F UoF Security Classification	O	O	O	O	O	O	O	O
S5000F UoF Serialized Product Variant Configuration						X	X	
S5000F UoF Service Contract Management	X				X			
S5000F UoF Service Request					O			

3.10 UoFs for software support cases

The UoFs required for the different software support use cases, as defined in Chap 12, are those listed in Table 12. In order to avoid having to cross-check the use case numbers, a summary of each use case is provided below:

1   UC51201: Request S/W feature

2   UC51202: Report S/W error

3   UC51203: Report S/W usability

4   UC51204: Report S/W documentation errors

5   UC51205v: Report Software and hardware interoperability

6   UC51206: Report S/W installation/unloading/erasure

7   UC51207: Report S/W configuration

8   UC51208: Report S/W maturity

9   UC51209: Report help desk tickets

10   UC51210: Report S/W delivery, deployment and servicing

11   UC51211: Report Data loading for software operations

Table 11 UoFs for software support use cases

UoFName	UC51201	UC51203	UC51203	UC51204	UC51205	UC51206	UC51207	UC51208	UC51209	UC51210	UC51211
CDM UoF Digital File									O		
CDM UoF Document	X			O	O	O	O		X		
CDM UoF Hardware Element					X		X		X		
CDM UoF Product Design Configuration							O				
CDM UoF Software Element	X	X	X		X		X	X	X	X	
S5000F UoF Change Request	X										
S5000F UoF Comment	O	O	O	O	O	O	O	O	X	O	O
S5000F UoF Comment Item	O	O	O	O	O	O	O	O	X	O	O
S5000F UoF Data Sets											X
S5000F UoF Digital File - Digital File Referenced Item									O		
S5000F UoF Digital File Digital File Referencing Item									O		
S5000F UoF Document	O			O	O	O	O		O		
S5000F UoF Part As Realized					X						
S5000F UoF Part Definition		O			X		X				
S5000F UoF Party		O									
S5000F UoF Project Specific Attribute Definition	O	O	O	O	O	O	O	O	O	O	O
S5000F UoF Remark	O	O	O	O	O	O	O	O	O	O	O
S5000F UoF Report			X	O		O		X		X	
S5000F UoF Report Context Item			X	O				X		X	
S5000F UoF Reportable Activity						X				X	
S5000F UoF Reportable Metric			X					X			
S5000F UoF Requirement	X										
S5000F UoF Security Classification	O	O	O	O	O	O	O	O	O	O	O
S5000F UoF Shop Findings					O						
S5000F UoF Software	X	X	X		X	X	X	X		X	
S5000F UoF Supply Item										X	

3.11 UoFs for configuration management use cases

The UoFs required for the different configuration management use cases, as defined in Chap 13, are those listed in Table 12. In order to avoid having to cross-check the use case numbers, a summary of each use case is provided below:

1 UC51301: Provide as-delivered configuration

2 UC51302: Provide as-allowed configuration

3 UC51303: Provide operational configuration

4 UC51304: Provide customer modification

5 UC51305: Provide as-desired configuration

Table 12 UoFs for configuration management use cases

UoFName	UC51301	UC51302	UC51303	UC51304	UC51305
CDM UoF Applicability Statement	X	X	X	X	X
CDM UoF Breakdown Structure	X	X			
CDM UoF Digital File	O				
CDM UoF Document	O				O
CDM UoF Hardware Element	X	X		O	
CDM UoF Product Design Configuration	X	X			
CDM UoF Software Element	X	X		O	
S5000F UoF Applicability Statement Items	X	X	X	X	X
S5000F UoF As-desired Configuration	X				X
S5000F UoF Change Embodiment				O	
S5000F UoF Change Embodiment Planning				O	
S5000F UoF Change Embodiment Reporting				O	
S5000F UoF Change Embodiment Strategy				O	
S5000F UoF Change Information	X			X	
S5000F UoF Change Request				X	
S5000F UoF Comment	O	O	O	O	O
S5000F UoF Comment Item	O	O	O	O	O
S5000F UoF Digital File - Digital File Referenced Item	O				
S5000F UoF Digital File Digital File Referencing Item	O				
S5000F UoF Document	O				O
S5000F UoF Logbook	X		X		

UoFName	UC51301	UC51302	UC51303	UC51304	UC51305
S5000F UoF Operational Roles			X		
S5000F UoF Part As Realized	X		X	X	
S5000F UoF Part Definition	X	X		O	
S5000F UoF Product Defined Operational Configuration			X		
S5000F UoF Project Specific Attribute Definition	O	O	O	O	O
S5000F UoF Remark	O	O	O	O	O
S5000F UoF Security Classification	O	O	O	O	O
S5000F UoF Serialized Product Variant Configuration	X		X		

3.12 UoFs for management of in-service contracts use cases

The UoFs required for the different management of in-service contracts use cases, as defined in Chap 14, are those listed in Table 13. In order to avoid having to cross-check the use case numbers, a summary of each use case is provided below:

1. UC51401: Provide contractual information

2. UC51402: Provide Work Breakdown Structure (WBS)

3. UC51403: Provide Cost Breakdown Structure (CBS)

4. UC51404: Provide Organisational Breakdown Structure (OBS)

5. UC51405: Provide/update activity planning

6. UC51406: Report Service Level Agreement (SLA) compliance

7. UC51407: Provide incurred contract costs

8. UC51408: Provide status report

9. UC51409: Replaced by UC51503. Refer to Para 3.13.

10. UC51410: Manage service request

11. UC51411: Request/grant/deny usage of resource

12. UC51412: Assign security classification

13. UC51413: Provide exchange export control information

14. UC51414: Provide labour rates

15. UC51415: Provide documentation traceability

Table 13 *UoFs for in-service contract management use cases*

UoFName	UC51401	UC51402	UC51403	UC51404	UC51405	UC51406	UC51407	UC51408	UC51410	UC51411	UC51412	UC51413	UC51414	UC51415
CDM UoF Digital File														O
CDM UoF Document	O	O	O	O	O		O	O			O	O		
S5000F UoF Budget			O				O		O	O				
S5000F UoF Comment	O	O	O	O	O	O	O	O	O	O	O	O	O	O
S5000F UoF Comment Item	O	O	O	O	O	O	O	O	O	O	O	O	O	O
S5000F UoF Contract Breakdown	X		O			X	X	O		O			X	
S5000F UoF Cost Breakdown	O		X				X			O				
S5000F UoF Cost Breakdown Context			X				X			O				
S5000F UoF Cost Entry			X				X			O				
S5000F UoF Digital File - Digital File Referenced Item														O
S5000F UoF Digital File Digital File Referencing Item														O
S5000F UoF Document	O	O	O	O	O		O	O			O	O		X
S5000F UoF Export Control License	O								O			X		X
S5000F UoF Export Control Requirement	O								O			X		X
S5000F UoF Expression Evaluation	X					X				O				
S5000F UoF Facility	O													
S5000F UoF Fleet Planning and Product Assignment					X									
S5000F UoF Infrastructure	O													
S5000F UoF Maintenance Facility Planning					X									
S5000F UoF Organizational Breakdown Structure	O			X	O									
S5000F UoF Party	X	X		X				O		O				O
S5000F UoF Person Competences and Labor Rates													X	

Applicable to: All

UoFName	UC51401	UC51402	UC51403	UC51404	UC51405	UC51406	UC51407	UC51408	UC51410	UC51411	UC51412	UC51413	UC51414	UC51415
S5000F UoF Policies and Regulations	X					O			X			X		
S5000F UoF Project and Contract	X	O		O			X		O					O
S5000F UoF Project Specific Attribute Definition	O	O	O	O	O	O	O	O	O	O	O	O	O	O
S5000F UoF Remark	O	O	O	O	O	O	O	O	O	O	O	O	O	O
S5000F UoF Report					X	X		X						
S5000F UoF Report Context Item					X			X						
S5000F UoF Reportable Activity					X	O		X						
S5000F UoF Reportable Metric						X		X						
S5000F UoF Requirement									O					
S5000F UoF Resource Usage Request										X				
S5000F UoF Security Classification	O	O	O	O	O	O	O	O	O	O	X	O	O	X
S5000F UoF Service Contract Management	X					X			O	O				
S5000F UoF Service Contract Penalty	X					X			O					
S5000F UoF Service Request	X								X					
S5000F UoF Work Breakdown	O	X			X		O	O						
S5000F UoF Work Breakdown Context		X			X		O	O						

3.13 UoFs for In-service environment data

The UoFs required for the different in-service environment data use cases, as defined in Chap 15, are those listed in Table 14. In order to avoid having to cross-check the use case numbers, a summary of each use case is provided below:

1　UC51501: Replaced by UC52301

2　UC51502: Replaced by UC52302

3　UC51503: Location information

4   UC51504: Infrastructure availability

5   UC51505: Environment definition of update

6   UC51506: Reallocation of fleet or product

Note

Use cases UC51501 and UC51502 were renumbered in line with their new chapter number.

Table 14 UoFs for in-service environment data use cases

UoFName	UC51503	UC51504	UC51505	UC51506
CDM UoF Product Usage Context	X			
S5000F UoF Availability		X		
S5000F UoF Comment	O	O	O	O
S5000F UoF Comment Item	O	O	O	O
S5000F UoF Environment			X	
S5000F UoF Facility	X			
S5000F UoF Fleet Definition				X
S5000F UoF Infrastructure	X	X		
S5000F UoF Infrastructure Availability		X		
S5000F UoF Location and Locator	X			
S5000F UoF Non-Availability Cause Item		X		
S5000F UoF Operating Base				X
S5000F UoF Operational Environment			O	
S5000F UoF Operator				O
S5000F UoF Project Specific Attribute Definition	O	O	O	O
S5000F UoF Remark	O	O	O	O
S5000F UoF Security Classification	O	O	O	O
S5000F UoF Serialized Item				O
S5000F UoF Serialized Product Variant				X

3.14   UoFs for environmental impact and disposal data

The UoFs required for the environmental impact and disposal data use cases, as defined in Chap 16, are those listed in Table 15. In order to avoid having to cross-check the use case numbers, a summary of each use case is provided below:

1   UC51601: Exchange environmental data

2   UC51602: Environmental data for authorities

3   UC51603: Impact of modification on environment or disposal

4   UC51604: Valuable items recovered from disposal

5   UC51605: Request disposal of item

6   UC51606: Product disposal information

7   UC51607: Request waste disposal

8   UC51608: Waste disposal information

9   UC51609: Disposal costs

10   UC51610: Notification of disposal due to unacceptable condition

Table 15 UoFs for environmental and disposal data use cases

UoFName	UC51601	UC51602	UC51603	UC51604	UC51605	UC51606	UC51607	UC51608	UC51609	UC51610
CDM UoF Document	O	O	O	X	O	X	O	O	O	O
CDM UoF Product Design Configuration					X					O
S5000F UoF Change Embodiment			X							
S5000F UoF Change Request Environmental Impact			X							
S5000F UoF Comment	O	O	O	O	O	O	O	O	O	O
S5000F UoF Comment Item	O	O	O	O	O	O	O	O	O	O
S5000F UoF Consumptions and Emissions	X	X								
S5000F UoF Contained Materials	X	X	X		X					
S5000F UoF Contained Substances	X	X	X				X	O		
S5000F UoF Container								X		
S5000F UoF Cost Breakdown									X	
S5000F UoF Cost Breakdown Context									X	
S5000F UoF Cost Entry							X		X	
S5000F UoF Disposal Requirement					X	X	X	X	X	X	O
S5000F UoF Disposal Site					X	X	X	X	X	
S5000F UoF Infrastructure Operating Period	X	X								
S5000F UoF Item Disposal Operation					X		X			
S5000F UoF Item Disposal Requirement					X	X	X			
S5000F UoF Operational Period	X	X								

UoFName	UC51601	UC51602	UC51603	UC51604	UC51605	UC51606	UC51607	UC51608	UC51609	UC51610
S5000F UoF Operational Period Items	X	X								
S5000F UoF Policies and Regulations				O	O	O				
S5000F UoF Recovered Item				X		X				
S5000F UoF Recovered Material				X		X		X		
S5000F UoF Remark	O	O	O	O	O	O	O	O	O	O
S5000F UoF Security Classification	O	O	O	O	O	O	O	O	O	O
S5000F UoF Serialized Product Variant Configuration				X	X					
S5000F UoF Unacceptable Item Condition Disposal										X
S5000F UoF Warranty										O
S5000F UoF Waste Disposal Operation		X						X		
S5000F UoF Waste Disposal Requirement							X			

3.15 UoFs for non-predefined information use cases

The UoFs required for the different non-predefined information use cases, as defined in Chap 23, are those listed in Table 16. In order to avoid having to cross-check the use case numbers, a summary of each use case is provided below:

1 UC52301: Provide project-specific values. (Previously numbered UC51501)

2 UC52302: Provide non-predefined information. (Previously numbered UC51502)

Note

Use cases UC52301 and UC52302 were renumbered because the introduction of new chapters changed the number of the chapter where they were defined, and this could be a cause of confusion.

Table 16 UoFs for non-predefined information use cases

UoFName	UC51501	UC51502
CDM UoF Digital File		X
CDM UoF Document	O	O
S5000F UoF Comment	O	O
S5000F UoF Comment Item	O	O
S5000F UoF Digital File DigitalFileReferencedItem		O

UoFName	UC51501	UC51502
S5000F UoF Digital File DigitalFileReferencingItem	-	O
S5000F UoF Export Control License	-	O
S5000F UoF Export Control Requirement	-	O
S5000F UoF Project Specific Attribute Definition		X
S5000F UoF Remark	O	O
S5000F UoF Security Classification	O	O

Page intentionally blank.

Chapter 25

Data exchange

Table of contents

Page

Data exchange 1

References 1

1   General 2
1.1   Introduction 2
1.2   Objective 2
1.3   Scope 2
1.4   Out of scope 2
1.5   Interoperability 2
2   Data exchange 2
3   Feedback to other S-Series IPS specifications 3
4   S5000F XML Schemas 3
5   Product Life Cycle Support (PLCS) 4
6   In-service information database 5
7   Data quality 6

List of tables

1   References 1

List of figures

1   Feedback to other S-Series IPS specifications 3
2   ASD XML Schema to PLCS implementation mapping 4
3   Outline of data exchange and in-service databases 5

References

Table 1 References

Chap No./Document No.	Title
Chap 24	Data Model
Chap 27	Tailoring and contracting against S5000F
Chap 28	Data required for the different use cases
S1000D	International specification for technical publications using a common source database
S3000L	International procedure specification for Logistic Support Analysis (LSA)
S3000X	Input specification for S3000L

SX000i	International guide for the use of the S-Series Integrated Product Support (IPS) specifications
SX002D	Common data model for the S-Series IPS Specifications
ISO 8000	Data Quality
ISO 10303-239 (AP239)	Product Life-Cycle Services (PLCS)

1 General

1.1 Introduction

The purpose for this chapter is to define a coherent set of guidelines for the implementation of the data exchange required for the operational and maintenance data feedback. The exchange of data for S5000F is defined using XML and XML Schemas.

The S5000F XML Schemas use the XML Schemas defined for SX002D to ensure the interoperability with the other S-Series IPS Specifications.

The S5000F XML Schemas are published separately on the S5000F website (http://www.s5000f.org).

1.2 Objective

The objective for this chapter is to describe how the S5000F SML schemas support the S5000F feedback and its interaction with other business processes.

1.3 Scope

The scope of the data exchange includes all mechanisms related to the operational and maintenance data feedback outlined in this specification, including:

- an overview of S5000F data exchange using S5000F XML Schemas
- an overview of the defined S5000F SML Schemas
- the relationship between the S5000F XML Schemas and ISO 10303-239
- recommendations regarding an in-service data repository
- recommendations regarding data quality

1.4 Out of scope

The data exchange does not cover potential the processing or cleansing of exchanged information.

1.5 Interoperability

This data exchange has considered for its development both the existing S5000F data model and the Common Data Model (CDM) that has been developed across all S-Series specifications, to ensure the interoperability of S5000F with the other S-Series specifications. Refer to SX002D.

This data exchange has also considered global policies as defined by the AIA/ASD Data Modelling and Exchange Working Group (DMEWG), to ensure the interoperability with the exchange of data with other S-Series specifications. Refer to SX000i.

2 Data exchange

Data exchange of S5000F data is performed by means of XML messages. The basic messages are defined in SX002D and replicated here in UoF Message. A message is a collection of information to be communicated from one party to another. Messages can provide new information (creation), modify existing information (update) or require deletion of existing information.

S5000F does not mandate the content of a specific message. It can be the information associated to a single class, or to multiple classes. Typically, information sets to be exchanged in one or multiple messages will include the information associated to one single use case. Information shared by multiple use cases should be sent as a separate message.

The messages to be sent, as well as their frequency and the business rules to which they should comply, must be defined during the guidance conference, as detailed in Chap 19.

It must be highlighted that the in-service feedback is not unidirectional (eg, from the operator to the OEM) but rather multi-directional, in the sense that different roles can be taken by Customer and Contractor in different contracts, and thus the data flows can change. The data formats remain the same, but the actors who provide and receive data can be different due to contractual arrangements. The responsibilities of who provides which information must be also defined as detailed in Chap 27.

Data exchanged should be logged, to provide traceability of the exchange. The data itself should be stored in an in-service data repository, as described in Para 6.

3 Feedback to other S-Series IPS specifications

S5000F does not provide a direct set of information for all other specifications. Though sharing the same common data model, some conversion could be required to feed the S5000F feedback data for the use of the individual specifications. Thus, data could be converted, filtered according to certain criteria or aggregated for their use. For example, failure data could require both filtering and aggregation to calculate the resulting in-service MTBF.

Such conversion/filtering/aggregation will be performed as defined in the corresponding input specification of the consumer specification. For example, S3000X will define how S5000F data will be used by S3000L for an in-service LSA.

Note that the individual specifications will receive only the information that is specific for them. Feedback that is common to several specifications will follow the process as defined in SX000i, typically through S3000L.

Fig 1 shows the example flow for both S3000L and S1000D.

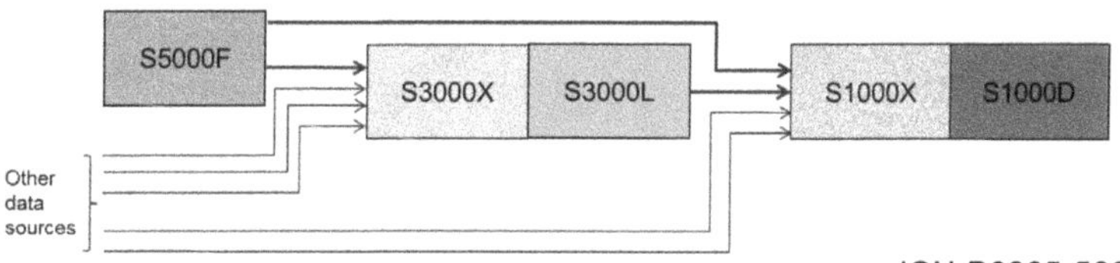

ICN-B6865-5000F1601-001-00

Fig 1 Feedback to other S-Series IPS specifications

4 S5000F XML Schemas

The S5000F XML Schemas are derived from the S5000F data model defined in Chap 24. The method of mapping the S5000F data model to the S5000F XML Schemas is performed in accordance with the XML Schema Authoring Rules defined by the DMEWG, which is common to all S-Series IPS specifications.

An added feature for the exchange of in-service data feedback data using the XML Schemas of S5000F, is the option to only exchange updates. Update messages can be sent in between complete baseline messages and can accommodate both minor and major changes to the in-service data.

This means that the receiver of in-service data does not need to analyze what actions need to be taken to update the target data set (eg, in-service database).

The XML Schema used for complete baseline messages enforce all the rules defined in the S5000F data model in order to guarantee consistency in the exchanged data set.

The XML schemas of S5000F, support all the UoFs defined in Chap 24 and all Use Cases defined throughout the whole specification.

5 Product Life Cycle Support (PLCS)

The S5000F XML Schemas will provide mappings to ISO 10303-239 PLCS (Product Life Cycle Support) edition 3, in order to support continued use of ISO 10303-239 PLCS and enable mapping of the feedback data to design information through the internal Product Life-cycle Management (PLM) systems. These mappings will be an integral part of the respective S5000F XML schemas.

Thus, organizations wishing to use PLCS instead of the defined XML schemas, will be able to implement S5000F using ISO 10303-239 edition 3.

The rationale for introducing the S5000F XML Schemas as the basis for supporting S5000F data exchanges is to allow for organizations that do not have the required PLCS skills (eg, small and medium enterprises) to still support the S5000F specified data exchanges.

In awaiting ISO 10303-239 PLCS edition 3 and its associated data exchange development environment, all future S-Series IPS specifications will follow the same XML Schema approach as described for S5000F. Fig. 2 illustrates how the S-Series IPS specification XML Schemas should be viewed in general in respect of ISO 10303-239 PLCS and OASIS PLCS PSM. Note that the mapping to OASIS PSM is not envisaged but can be handled by other organizations.

The S-Series IPS Specifications XML Schemas are targeted to support data exchange at the Business Object Model (BOM) layer. However, each XML Schema will also include the mapping details required for an unambiguous mapping of each element and attribute to PLCS in order to enable PLCS-based data exchanges and/or PLCS-based data consolidation, as well as the future integration with other ISO 10303 (STEP) based data (eg, AP233, AP242).

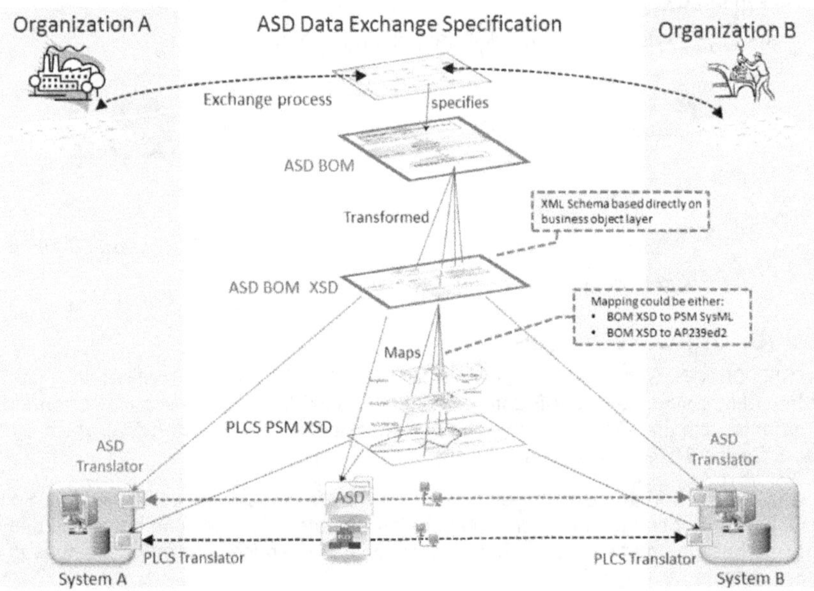

B6865-S3000L0237-001-00

Fig 2 ASD XML Schema to PLCS implementation mapping

This approach has been approved by the AIA/ASD IPS Specification Council for all S-Series IPS specifications.

6 In-service information database

It is recommended that all the information provided as part of the operational and maintenance feedback is stored in a common repository. The data model of this specification has been designed so that all data can be integrated into a single database, including project-specific information.

It is also recommended that the in-service feedback data is maintained separately from other logistic databases. The reasons for this include, but are not limited to:

1 The data received are likely to be received from multiple actors (eg, multiple OEMs or multiple customers/operators) and could require harmonization.

2 The data received will have different levels of quality and could require filtering and/or validation before it is useable.

3 The mapping of the received data always being mapped directly to other IPS databases (eg, the S3000L database) cannot be guaranteed, either because such databases do not exist at the other actor or because the actor at the other side of the exchange does not maintain the cross-referencing between the different logistic elements.

4 Each actor could have a different IT infrastructure and different applications. It is therefore advisable to have a common reference data set for all applications using in-service feedback data.

5 Having the same in-service database at both sides of the communication channel allows for proper synchronization of data, better data integration and improved data quality, easy clarification of doubts, and the dissociation of individual actor's IT systems and the way that the information is internally distributed in an organization from the actual exchange.

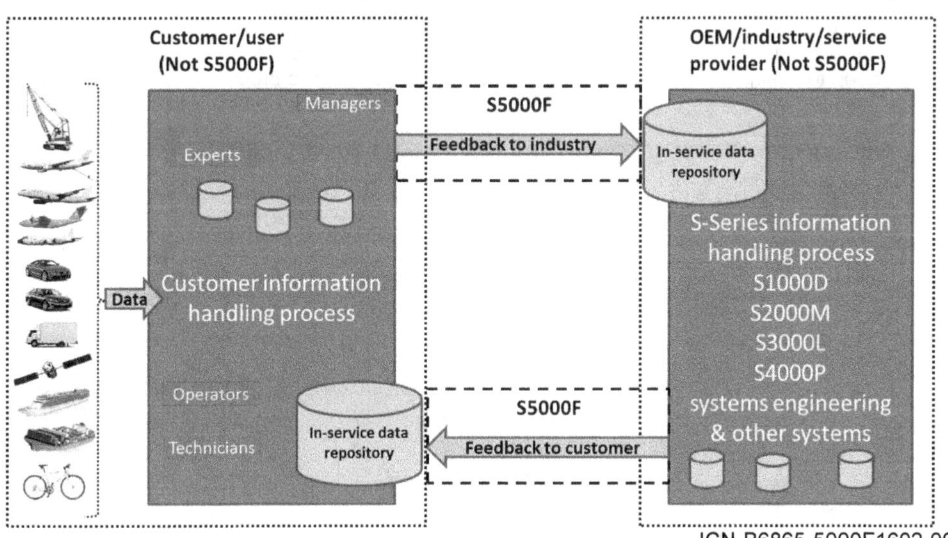

ICN-B6865-5000F1602-001-00

Fig 3 Outline of data exchange and in-service databases

It is recommended that the data exchange is performed to/from the in-service repositories, to ensure consistency of the information. These in-service repositories would integrate the

information from different IT systems and would distribute the information to other internal IT systems, ensuring the consistency of the information sent and received.

This does NOT imply that the repositories on both sides of the exchange should contain the same information, nor even have the same database structure. Indeed, the information contained at both sides of the exchange will be different, as the operator/customer will store the in-service information for different Products and the OEM/industry will store the information for different customers. The importance of these in-service repositories is to have a single version of the truth at each side, rather than trying to reconcile multiple systems across multiple organizations. While it is possible to have a specific in-service repository that is the same at both sides of the exchange, this would imply higher costs and increase systems integration complexity, as repositories would be created for each different program and/or customer.

An important benefit of a single in-service database at the customer/user side is that all operational and maintenance data associated with the Product fleet is stored in one single repository, therefore allowing to control the performance across multiple Products from different vendors and assessing improvement measures.

On the OEM/industry side the benefit of a single in-service database is to have the data from multiple customers in one single repository, therefore having a statistically significant corpus of information for statistical analysis (eg, reliability purposes) even if the number of Products purchased by individual customers is not statistically significant. It also allows comparing customer information, to identify potential issues at one particular customer if their data deviates from the general pattern.

An additional benefit to all users of an integrated in-service database is that it provides a coherent repository of information that is unlikely to be achieved by integrating a set on heterogeneous in-service tools (usually at a great expense).

However, the establishment/usage of an integrated in-service information database does not imply the usage of a single tool for the in-service activities, neither at customer/user nor OEM/industry level. The integrated in-service information database is a consolidated repository of information, which can be created by the aggregation of information from different tools. Similarly, multiple tools can access this repository for the capture of in-service data, without the need to design ad-hoc interfaces with other related tools. The process of aggregating data into this integrated in-service information database exceeds the scope of this specification.

An in-service information repository can be created using the Data Model specified in Chap 24.

7   Data quality

In-service operational and maintenance data feedback is often dirty and usually cannot be used as is without some processing. While the implementation of this specification provides the means to transfer the data in a standard way, it does not provide the means to clean the data.

This dirtiness (or inadequacy of the data) is often due to four reasons:

- the data is incomplete: It lacks attribute values, lacks certain attributes of interest or contains only aggregated data. (eg, Missing country name). Incomplete data is usually due to:
  - data values were not available when collected
  - different criteria were used between the time when data was collected and when it was analyzed
  - legacy systems did not include the necessary information, or collected it in a way that could not be properly transformed to be fed back in accordance with this specification
  - human/hardware/software problems

- the data is noisy - the information contains errors or outliers (eg, spelling, phonetic and typing errors, word transpositions, multiple values in a single free-form field). Noisy data usually is due to the following factors:

  - data collection by faulty instruments
  - data entry: human or computer errors
  - data transmission problems

  Examples: Age=-10

  Name="Jones", LastName="Mike"

  ManufacturingDate="31/12/9999"

- the data is inconsistent - the information contains discrepancies in codes and/or names (eg, synonyms and nicknames, prefix and suffix variations, abbreviations, truncation, and initials). Inconsistent and redundant data is usually due to:

  - different data sources, so non-uniform naming conventions/data codes
  - different data models across legacy applications
  - functional dependency and/or referential integrity violation in source systems
  - inadequate data conversion to the S5000F format

  Examples:

  Age = "42", Birthday="03/12/2012"

  Part number 203 Name="CAMU HW" and "CAMU H/W"

  Was rating "1,2,3", now rating is "A,B,C"

- the data is out of context - some information can be meaningless and/or be misinterpreted if it is not supplied within a specific context. Out of context data is usually due to an incomplete definition of the required data.

  Examples:

  Date and time without a time zone reference can be misinterpreted. Product

  data without customer or contract reference cannot be processed.

The greatest impact of data quality is found in the collection and preparation of the raw data. Data quality controls should be established to ensure that the data that is collected and prepared for exchange is both complete and accurate. The later quality controls are introduced in the process, the higher the impact of the lack of data quality will be.

It is emphasized that implementing S5000F does not guarantee the adequacy or quality of the data, only that it is provided in a specific format and within specific ranges. Thus, the implementation of S5000F should be accompanied by business rules that provide the means to validate the received data. Refer to Chap 27.

For example, a business rule to ensure that the date of a maintenance task cannot take place before the Product delivery or Product manufacturing date. These business rules can be used not only for validation of received data, but also for checking data quality during the collection of the data, or at least before it is provided as feedback.

The application of a data quality process standard such as the ISO 8000 is also recommended so that the quality of both the prepared and the exchanged data is enhanced.

The cleansing of received data is usually performed as part of a process called staging, where received data is validated in accordance with business rules, supplemented with additional information if required, and then stored in the in-service database, where it is also cross-referenced to other IPS elements. The description of how this cleansing and cross-referencing should be performed is outside of the scope of S5000F. However, it is recommended that a record is kept of what the cleansing entailed, for full traceability of potential data transformations.

Similarly, the specific purpose for which the data is being exchanged must be taken into consideration. The incompleteness of the data, or the fact that it is out of context, can prevent the purpose of the exchange being fulfilled. Chap 28 provides a mapping of the use cases of S5000F to the classes that these use cases require. It is recommended that this mapping is used so that data being exchanged is always complete and within context, so that it will comply with a specific business scenario.

Notwithstanding these data quality checks, which are usually carried out at the data receiving party, it is emphasized that the responsibility for providing quality data always lies on the party providing such data, and that these checks should also be performed before the data is exchanged. It is recommended that a data quality group is established by both parties, so that data quality issues can be properly reported, and appropriate measures are taken by the party generating the data to correct any data quality issues.

Chapter 26

Data element list

Table of contents

Page

Data element list 1

References 1

1   General 1

2   Classes 1

3   Data element list 85

4   Data element valid values 197

5   Valid value libraries 245

List of tables

1   References 1

2   List of classes 3

3   List of data elements 85

4   List of valid values 197

5   List of valid value libraries 245

References

Table 1 References

Chap No./Document No.	Title
Chap 24.3	Data Model - Common Data Model (CDM) units of functionality
Chap 24.4	Data Model - S5000F units of functionality
Chap 27	Tailoring and contracting against S5000F
Chap 28	Data required for the different use cases
SX001G	Glossary for the S-Series ILS specifications
SX002D	Common data model for the S-Series ILS specifications

1   General

This chapter defines all the classes, data elements (attributes) and valid values that are used in the S5000F data model, refer to Chap 24.4.

2   Classes

The full list of S5000F classes is provided in Table 2. This includes classes from SX002D used by S5000F but defined originally in SX001G. If the Unit of Functionality (UoF) is S5000F Specializations, then this class extends or restricts the class defined originally in SX002D.

Table 2 is organized alphabetically by the class name, and contains:

- class name
- class type and Stereotype (refer to Chap 24.4. on more details on class types and Stereotypes used in S5000F)
- class definition contains a textual definition
- UoF, identifies the section in Chap 24.4 where the class is defined. If the UoF name is preceded by CDM, then the UoF is originally defined in SX002D

For completeness, the classes of the UoFs used as is from SX002D are also listed in this specification, The UoFs from SX002D used by this specification are listed in Chap 24.4.

A mapping of the classes and attributes required for the individual use cases can be found in Chap 28.

Table 2 List of classes

Class name	Type	Stereotype	Definition	UoF
Accelerometer	Class	class	Accelerometer is a SensorType that measures acceleration.	S5000F Serialized Product Health Monitoring
Action	Class	class	Action is a fact or process of doing something, typically to achieve an aim.	S5000F Event
ActualEnvironment	Interface	select	ActualEnvironment is a <<select>> interface that allows to select either an actual environment or one of its revisions.	S5000F Environment
AggregatedElement	Class	class	AggregatedElement is a BreakdownElement that is a container for a collection of BreakdownElements which are grouped for an identified purpose.	CDM UoFAggregated Element
AggregatedElementRevision	Class	class	AggregatedElementRevision is a BreakdownElementRevision representing an iteration applied to an AggregatedElement.	CDM UoF Aggregated Element
AllowedProductConfiguration	Interface	extend	AllowedProductConfiguration is an <<extend>> interface that provides its associated data model to those classes that must define permitted combinations of hardware and software parts which can or must be installed in specific locations (positi **Note** An allowed product configuration can also include associated engineering instructions that must be adhered to during assembly and operation and that demonstrates that a product complies with applicable regulations. **Note** One and the same serialized product can adhere to different allowed product configurations over time. **Example** – Applicable regulations can be a type certificate.	CDM UoFProduct Design Configuration
AllowedProductConfiguration ByConfigurationIdentifier	Class	class	AllowedProductConfigurationByConfigurationIdentifi er is a <<class>> that defines an	CDM UoFProduct Design Configuration

Class name	Type	Stereotype	Definition	UoF
			`AllowedProductConfiguration` by means other than a part number.	
`AllowedProductConfiguration HardwarePartAsDesigned`	Class	class	`AllowedProductConfigurationHardwarePartAsDesigned` is a `HardwarePartAsDesigned` that is managed as an `AllowedProductConfiguration`.	CDM UoFProduct Design Configuration
`AllowedProductConfiguration Item`	Interface	select	`AllowedProductConfigurationItem` is a <<select>> interface that identifies items which can be selected as an allowed product configuration.	CDM UoFProduct Design Configuration
`AllowedProductConfiguration PhysicalData`	Class	attributeGroup	`AllowedProductConfigurationPhysicalData` is an <<attributeGroup>> that provides physical characteristics associated to an `AllowedProductConfiguration`.	S5000F Operational Roles
`AllowedProductConfiguration Role`	Class	relationship	`AllowedProductConfigurationRole` is a <<relationship>> that defines what `OperationalRoles` can be performed by a specific `AllowedProductConfiguration`.	S5000F Operational Roles
`AllowedProductOperationalCo nfigurationItem`	Interface	select	`AllowedProductOperationalConfigurationItem` is an <<interface>> that allows to define the items that can be included in the `AllowedProductConfigurationRole`.	S5000F Product Defined Operational Configuration
`AllowedRoleChange`	Class	relationship	`AllowedRoleChange` is a <<relationship>> that defines the role changes that are possible to allow a `Product` in one specific role to be configured for a different role.	S5000F Operational Roles
`AlternatePartAsDesigned`	Class	relationship	`AlternatePartAsDesigned` is a <<relationship>> that defines an alternate `PartAsDesigned` which can replace the `base PartAsDesigned` in all its usages ie, it is context independent, and is form, fit and function equivalent. **Note** A part can have one or more alternate parts. The alternate part is interchangeable with the `base` part in any/all uses.	CDM UoF Part Definition

Class name	Type	Stereotype	Definition	UoF
AnchoringPoint	Class	class	AnchoringPoint is a <<class>> representing a point where an item can be moored or tied down.	S5000F Transport Anchoring Point
ApplicabilityStatement	Class	class	ApplicabilityStatement is a <<class>> that defines the situation or situations under which related items are valid.	CDM UoF Applicability Statement
ApplicabilityStatementItem	Interface	extend	ApplicabilityStatementItem is an <<extend>> interface that provides its associated data model to those classes which can have restricted validity as defined by an associated ApplicabilityStatement.	CDM UoF Applicability Statement
Area	Class	compoundAttribute	Area is a <<class>> that represents the extent or measurement of a surface.	S-Series_Compound_Attributes_2-0_002-00
AssessHWSWInteroperability	Class	exchange	AssessHWSWInteroperability is an <<exchange>> that represents a message associated with a use case (UC51205) providing the necessary information to evaluate whether there are hardware-software incompatibilities.	S5000F Use Cases
AssessSoftwareMaturity	Class	exchange	AssessSoftwareMaturity is an <<exchange>> that represents a message associated with a use case (UC51208) providing the necessary information to report on the maturity of a software item.	S5000F Use Cases
AssessSoftwareUsability	Class	exchange	AssessSoftwareUsability is an <<exchange>> that represents a message associated with a use case (UC51203) providing the necessary information to report on how usable a piece of software is.	S5000F Use Cases
AssociatedActualEnvironment	Class	relationship	AssociatedActualEnvironment is a <<relationship>> that associates an EnvironmentItem with an ActualEnvironemnt relevant to its existence, operation and/or support during a specified period of time.	S5000F Environment
AssessSoftwareDelivery	Class	exchange	AssessSoftwareDelivery is an <<exchange>> that represents a message associated with a use case (UC51210) providing the necessary information to report on the delivery of a software item.	S5000F Use Cases
AuthorityRequirement	Class	class	AuthorityRequirement is a Requirement that has been issued by a technical or legal authority.	S5000F Requirement

Applicable to: All

DMC-S5000F-A-26-00-0000-00A-040A-A

Chap 26

2021-04-30 Page 5

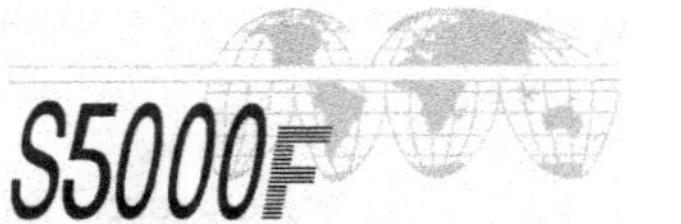

Class name	Type	Stereotype	Definition	UoF
AuthorityToOperate	Class	class	AuthorityToOperate is a <<class>> that represents a certification allowing a specific configuration of a product to be put into operation. **Note** A design change cannot be put into operation without re-certification. **Note** Type certificate for an aircraft signifies the airworthiness of its design.	CDM UoFProduct Design Configuration
AuthorizedLife	Class	compoundAttri bute	AuthorizedLife is a <<compoundAttribute>> that identifies the maximum usage limit and upon reaching this limit any further usage of the item must be re-authorized.	S-Series_Compound_Attributes_2-0_002-00
Availability	Class	class	Availability is an indication of the global availability status of an AvailabilityItem at a specific day.	S5000F Availability
AvailabilityItem	Interface	extend	AvailabilityItem is an <<extend>> interface that allows to associate an Availability to an item.	S5000F Availability
BaseObject	Class	metaclass	BaseObject is a <<class>> that represents the most elementary behaviour that is common to all S-Series classes.	S-Seri UoFes_Base_Object_Definition_2-0_003-00
BatchHardwarePart	Class	class	BatchHardwarePart is a <<class>> that represents actual physical parts which can be identified by their batch membership.	S5000F Specializations
Breakdown	Class	class	Breakdown is a <<class>> that identifies a specific partitioning of a Product to form a parent-child structure of related instances of BreakdownElement.	CDM UoF Breakdown Structure
BreakdownElement	Class	class	BreakdownElement is a <<class>> defining a partition of a Product that is used in one or many instances of Breakdown.	CDM UoF Breakdown Structure
BreakdownElementInZone	Class	relationship	BreakdownElementInZone is a <<relationship>> where a BreakdownElementInZoneItem relates to the ZoneElement where it is located.	CDM UoFZone Element

Class name	Type	Stereotype	Definition	UoF
BreakdownElementInZoneItem	Interface	extend	BreakdownElementInZoneItem is an <<extend>> interface that provides its associated data model to those classes that implement it.	CDM UoF Zone Element
BreakdownElementRevision	Class	class	BreakdownElementRevision is a <<class>> representing an iteration applied to a BreakdownElement.	CDM UoF Breakdown Structure
BreakdownElementRevisionRelationship	Class	relationship	BreakdownElementRevisionRelationship is a <<relationship>> where one BreakdownElementRevision relates to another BreakdownElement or BreakdownElementRevision.	CDM UoF Breakdown Structure
BreakdownElementRevisionRelationshipItem	Interface	select	BreakdownElementRevisionRelationshipItem is a <<select>> interface that provides the capability to be associated with a BreakdownElementRevision.	CDM UoF Breakdown Structure
BreakdownElementStructure	Class	relationship	BreakdownElementStructure is a <<relationship>> that establishes a hierarchical structure between two usages of BreakdownElement that belong to the same BreakdownRevision.	CDM UoF Breakdown Structure
BreakdownElementUsageInBreakdown	Class	class	BreakdownElementUsageInBreakdown is a <<class>> that represents a member of a BreakdownRevision. **Note** A BreakdownElementRevision can belong to multiple BreakdownRevisions.	CDM UoF Breakdown Structure
BreakdownElementUsageRelationship	Class	relationship	BreakdownElementUsageRelationship is a <<relationship>> where one usage of a BreakdownElement relates to the usage of another BreakdownElement. **Note** Both related instances of BreakdownElementUsageInBreakdown must reside within the same BreakdownRevision.	CDM UoF Breakdown Structure

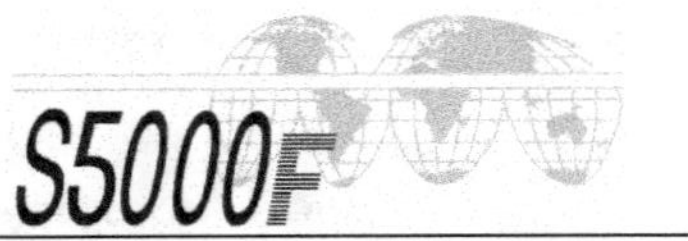

Class name	Type	Stereotype	Definition	UoF
			Example – Version C of a radio is restricted to the use of software version B in breakdown revision 2.	
BreakdownItem	Interface	extend	BreakdownItem is an <<extend>> interface that provides its associated data model to those classes that implement it.	CDM UoF Breakdown Structure
BreakdownRevision	Class	class	BreakdownRevision is a <<class>> representing an iteration applied to a Breakdown. **Note** BreakdownRevision is used to document design iterations and not breakdown variants.	CDM UoF Breakdown Structure
Budget	Class	class	Budget is a class representing a cost proposal to perform a specific service or provide a certain item.	S5000F Budget
BudgetingItem	Interface	extend	BudgetingItem is an <<extend>> interface that allows to associate Budgets to specific items.	S5000F Budget
Calibration	Class	class	Calibration is an <<attributeGroup> that provides historical data about calibration.	S5000F Equipment Calibration Certificate Information
CalibrationDocument	Class	relationship	CalibrationDocument is a <<relationship>> that associates a Calibration to a Document.	S5000F Equipment Calibration Certificate Information
CalibrationMeasurement	Class	attributeGroup	CalibrationMeasurement is a <<attributeGroup>> that provides the individual measurements performed to carry out an individual Calibration.	S5000F Equipment Calibration Certificate Information
CancelFleetTask	Class	exchange	CancelFleetTask is an <<exchange>> that represents a message associated with a use case (UC51102) providing the necessary information to cancel an ongoing or planned fleet task.	S5000F Use Cases
Capability	Class	class	Capability is a class that defines an actual ability or potential for an indicated use or deployment.	S5000F Capability

Class name	Type	Stereotype	Definition	UoF
			Note The actual Capablity can be a combination of multiple predefined `CapabilityDefinitionRevisions`.	
`CapabilityDefinition`	Class	class	`CapabilityDefinition` is a <<class>> that defines an ability. **Example** – 1 month autonomy – Air vehicle accomodation – Air-to-air refuel – Body detection – Deep water exploration – Paratroop launch – Patient transport – Small-sized ammunition resistance – Unpaved runway landing	CDM UoF Capability Definition
`CapabilityDefinitionCharact eristic`	Class	class	`CapabilityDefinitionCharacteristic` is a <<class> that specifies a measurable or observable feature which is significant for the CapabilityDefinition. **Example** – Provide pressure air up to 100 psi	CDM UoFCapability Definition
`CapabilityDefinitionItem`	Interface	extend	`CapabilityDefinitionItem` is an <<extend>> interface that provides its associated data model to those classes that can have an associated `CapabilityDefinition`.	CDM UoF Capability Definition
`CapabilityDefinitionRevisio n`	Class	class	`CapabilityDefinitionRevision` is a <<class>> representing an iteration applied to a `CapabilityDefinition`.	CDM UoFCapability Definition
`CapabilityItem`	Interface	extend	`CapabilityItem` is an <<extend>> interface that allows to assign a Capabilities to an item.	S5000F Capability
`CapabilityLimitation`	Class	class	`CapabilityLimitation` is a <<class>> that defines a limitation on the use of a specific `Capability`. **Example** – environmental restriction	S5000F Capability

Class name	Type	Stereotype	Definition	UoF
			– legal restriction – weight restriction	
CargoItem	Class	class	CargoItem is a class representing one or several items that need to be transported as part of a FleetTask. **Note** CargoItem can be used to designate several entities of a same type, such as 50 passengers for a bus, or 2 pallets to be loaded on a truck. **Note** The total dimensions of the CargoItem cannot be determined in case it consists of several items, as the final dimensions will depend on the arrangement of the different items. **Note** The total volume can be only determined by summing up the volume of the different units. **Note** The total weight of the CargoItem must be calculated by multiplying the unitary weight by the number of units. **Example** – chicken cage(s) – container(s) – pallet(s) – passenger(s) – rug (s)	S5000F Transportable Item
ChangeAuthorization	Class	class	ChangeAuthorization is a <<class>> that is the record of the permission to modify product design, its procedures and/or associated product support data.	CDM UoF Change Information
ChangeControlledItem	Interface	extend	ChangeControlledItem is an <<extend>> interface that provides its associated data model to those classes that can be affected by a ChangeAuthorization.	CDM UoF Change Information
ChangedItemAvailabilityRequirement	Class	relationship	ChangedItemAvailabilityRequirement is a <<relationship>> that defines the required availability of the	S5000F Change Embodiment Strategy

Class name	Type	Stereotype	Definition	UoF
			SerializedProductVariant or ProductVariant fleet into which the item to be upgraded has to be embodied during the Product upgrade.	
ChangeEmbodimentRequirement	Class	class	ChangeEmbodimentRequirement is a Requirement to embody an authorized modification into one or several items. **Example** - Embody change within 6 months after change approval.	S5000F Requirement
ChangeNotification	Class	relationship	ChangeNotification is a <<relationship>> that identifies an item changed due to the associated ChangeAuthorization.	CDM UoF Change Information
ChangeRequest	Class	class	ChangeRequest is a <<class>> that represents a formal proposal for a modification to a configuration item upon a given baseline.	S5000F Specializations
ChangeRequestAddedOrRemoved Material	Class	relationship	ChangeRequestAddedOrRemovedMaterial is a <<relationship>> that allows to associate to an item the material that has been added or removed as a consequence of a ChangeRequest.	S5000F Change Request Environmental Impact
ChangeRequestAddedOrRemoved Substance	Class	relationship	ChangeRequestAddedOrRemovedSubstance is a <<relationship>> that allows to associate to an item the substances that have been added or removed as a consequence of a ChangeRequest.	S5000F Change Request Environmental Impact
ChangeRequestCause	Class	relationship	ChangeRequestCause is a <<relationship>> that allows to associate the underlying cause(s) for a ChangeRequest.	S5000F Change Request
ChangeRequestConsumptionCha nge	Class	relationship	ChangeRequestConsumptionChange is a <<relationship>> that allows to associate an increase or reduction of an item consumption to the ChangeRequest that caused it.	S5000F Change Request Environmental Impact
ChangeRequestEmissionChange	Class	relationship	ChangeRequestEmissionChange is a <<relationship>> that allows to associate an increase or reduction of a substance emission to the ChangeRequest that caused it.	S5000F Change Request Environmental Impact

Class name	Type	Stereotype	Definition	UoF
ChangeRequestEnvironmentall yImpactedItem	Interface	select	ChangeRequestEnvironmentallyImpactedItem is a <<select>> interface that allows to associate materials or substances as a consequence of a ChangeRequest to teh classes implementing it.	S5000F Change Request Environmental Impact
ChangeRequestItem	Interface	select	ChangeRequestItem is a <<select>> interface that allows to associate the item to be changed to a ChangeRequest.	S5000F Change Request
ChangeRequestReasonItem	Interface	select	ChangeRequestReasonItem is a <<select>> interface that allows to associate the underlying cause for a ChangeRequest.	S5000F Change Request
Circle	Class	compoundAttri bute	Circle is a <<class>> representing a geometrical round plane figure whose boundary (the circumference) consists of points equidistant from a fixed point (the center).	S-Series_Compound_Attributes_2-0_002-00
CircuitBreaker	Class	class	CircuitBreaker is a <<class>> that represents an individual circuit breaker identified in the context of a defined Product.	CDM UoF Circuit Breaker
CircuitBreakerSetting	Class	class	CircuitBreakerSetting is a <<class>> that specifies an individual circuit breaker that must be in a specific state.	CDM UoF Task
CircuitBreakerSettings	Class	class	CircuitBreakerSettings is a <<class>> that identifies a set of circuit breakers that must be set in specific states.	CDM UoF Task
ClassInstanceAssertItem	Interface	select	ClassInstanceAssertItem is a <<select>> interface that identifies classes from which an instance can be used as the EvaluationByAssertionOfClassInstance assert item.	CDM UoF Applicability Statement
CloudInfrastructure	Class	class	CloudInfrastructure is an Infrastructure that represents a network of remote servers hosted on the Internet and used to store, manage, and process data in place of local servers or personal computers.	S5000F Infrastructure
CodeProperty	Class	compoundAttri bute	CodeProperty is a compoundAttribute representing an alphanumeric code with the classification of the assigning specification. **Example** – '.es' (IANA internet top-level domain code) – '+34' (ITU-T E.164)	S5000F Compound Attributes

Class name	Type	Stereotype	Definition	UoF
			- 'SP' (FIPS10-4)	
CollectWarrantyCosts	Class	exchange	CollectWarrantyCosts is an <<exchange>> that represents a message associated with a use case (UC50802) providing the necessary information to compile the costs of warranty.	S5000F Use Cases
Comment	Class	class	Comment is a textual statement about a related item that deals with an issue associated to that item that needs to be addressed.	S5000F Comment
CommentAction	Class	relationship	CommentAction is a <<relationship>> that allows to associate a Comment to one or several Actions performed in response to the Comment.	S5000F Comment
CommentItem	Interface	extend	CommentItem is an <<extend>> interface allowing to establish an association between an item and the comments that are associated to it.	S5000F Comment
CommentParty	Class	relationship	CommentParty is a <<relationship>> defining the association between a Comment and a Party. **Example** - Comment raised by organization XYZ.	S5000F Comment
CommentRelationship	Class	relationship	CommentRelationship is a <<relationship>> that defines the association between two different Comments.	S5000F Comment
CommunicateDataLoading	Class	exchange	CommunicateDataLoading is an <<exchange>> that represents a message associated with a use case (UC51211) providing the necessary information to report on the loading of a specific data set or software item.	S5000F Use Cases
CommunicationsNetwork	Class	class	CommunicationsNetwork is an Infrastructure that represents a number of machines, computers and communication lines that allow the communication between different parties or machines.	S5000F Infrastructure
CompetenceDefinitionItem	Interface	select	CompetenceDefinitionItem is a <<select>> interface that identifies items which define measurable or observable possession of knowledge and skills.	CDM UoF Competence Definition

Class name	Type	Stereotype	Definition	UoF
CompliesWith	Class	relationship	CompliesWith is a <<relationship>> that allows to associate an item with the PoliciesAndRegulations with which it complies.	S5000F Policies and Regulations
ComputerNetwork	Class	class	ComputerNetwork is an Infrastructure that represents a number of interconnected computers, irrespectively of their location.	S5000F Infrastructure
ConditionDefinitionItem	Interface	select	ConditionDefinitionItem is a <<select>> interface that identifies classes from which an instance can be used as the EvaluationByAssertionOfCondition assert condition.	CDM UoF Applicability Statement
ConditionInstance	Class	class	ConditionInstance is a <<class>> that defines an individual concept or object having the characteristics of a generic ConditionType. **Example** – Uniquely identified service bulletin	CDM UoF Applicability Statement
ConditionType	Class	class	ConditionType is a <<class>> that defines a concept or an object that needs to be included in applicability statements where the concept or object is not already represented in the data model. **Example** – Environmental conditions	CDM UoF Applicability Statement
ConditionTypeAssertMember	Class	class	ConditionTypeAssertMember is <<class>> that defines a member for a given ConditionType which can be mapped to a Boolean expression and be evaluated to be either TRUE or FALSE.	CDM UoF Applicability Statement
Consequence	Class	class	Consequence is a class providing information about the consequences of an Event.	S5000F Event
ConsumableItem	Class	class	ConsumableItem is a supply item that is consumed and cannot be reused. **Example** – detergent – fuel – grease	S5000F Supply Item

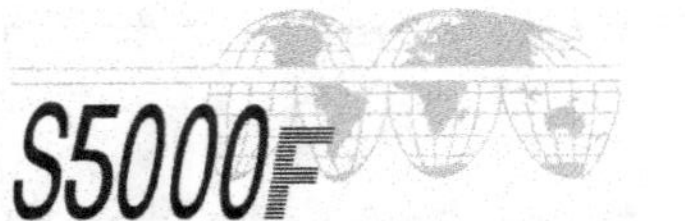

Class name	Type	Stereotype	Definition	UoF
			– oil	
`Consumption`	Class	relationship	`Consumption` is a <<relationship>> that defines the `Product`(s) that have been consumed by a `SerializedProductVariant` as part of an operational period, movement or movement leg. **Example** – fuel consumption – oil consumption	S5000F Consumptions and Emissions
`ConsumptionPeriod`	Interface	extend	`ConsumptionPeriod` is an <<extend>> interface that allows to associate the consumption of a consumable item with the period of time during which this consumption takes place..	S5000F Consumptions and Emissions
`ContainedMaterial`	Class	relationship	`ContainedMaterial` is a <<relationship>> that allows to associate an item to the amount of material that it contains.	S5000F Contained Materials
`ContainedSubstance`	Class	relationship	`ContainedSubstance` is a <<relationship>> that associates a `HardwarePartAsDesigned` with a contained `SubstanceDefinition`.	CDM UoF Part Definition
`ContainerAsDesigned`	Class	class	`ContainerAsDesigned` is a `HardwarePartAsDesigned` representing a vessel for the storage or transport of items. **Note** A `ContainerAsDesigned` can be something as simple as a bucket or cardboard box of a specific size.	S5000F Container
`ContainerPart`	Class	relationship	`ContainerPart` is a <<relationship>> that allows to associate a `HardwarePartContainer` with one or more `HardwarePartAsDesigned` that it contains.	S5000F Container
`Contract`	Class	class	`Contract` is a <<class» that represents a binding agreement between two or more parties **Example** – leasing contract – procurement contract – service contract	S5000F Specializations

Class name	Type	Stereotype	Definition	UoF
			– subcontract	
ContractClause	Class	class	ContractClause is a specific provision included in a Contract. **Note** A ContractClause allows for a finer granularity of a Contract. However, if this granularity is not available or desirable, a ContractClause can be defined which is the whole Contract. **Note** A ContractClause will address a specific aspect of the Contract between the Parties, detailing the agreement to ensure all Parties understand what is expected of the other.	S5000F Contract Breakdown
ContractClauseRelationship	Class	class	ContractClauseRelationship is a <<relationship>> that allows to associate different ContractClauses.	S5000F Contract Breakdown
ContractItem	Interface	select	ContractItem is a <<select>> interface that identifies items which can be selected for the Contract.	CDM UoF Product and Project
ContractItemDetails	Class	relationship	ContractItemDetails is a <<relationship>> that identifies an item which is the subject of the Contract.	CDM UoF Product and Project
ContractParty	Class	relationship	ContractParty is a <<relationship>> that identifies a Contract stakeholder.	CDM UoF Product and Project
ContractRelationship	Class	relationship	ContractRelationship is a <<relationship>> where one Contract relates to another Contract.	CDM UoF Product and Project
CostBreakdown	Class	class	CostBreakdown is a class used to group all the different cost concepts associated to a particular purpose.	S5000F Cost Breakdown
CostBreakdownContext	Interface	extend	CostBreakdownContext is an <<extend>> interface that allows to assign a CostBreakdown to an item.	S5000F Cost Breakdown
CostBreakdownRelationship	Class	relationship	CostBreakdownRelationship is a <<relationship>> that allows to define associations between two different CostBreakdowns.	S5000F Cost Breakdown

Class name	Type	Stereotype	Definition	UoF
CostBreakdownRevision	Class	class	CostBreakdownRevision is an iteration that is applied to a CostItem.	S5000F Cost Breakdown
CostEntry	Class	class	CostEntry is an individual expense made at a specific date for a specific amount that needs to be recorded for accounting purposes.	S5000F Cost Breakdown
CostEntryItem	Interface	select	CostEntryItem is a <<select>> interface that associates a CostEntry to the item whose cost has to be incurred.	S5000F Cost Breakdown
CostItem	Class	class	CostItem is a generic concept used to group individual expenses for accounting or program management purposes. **Note** A same CostItem can be associated to several CostBreakdownRevisions.	S5000F Cost Breakdown
CostItemRelationship	Class	relationship	CostItemRelationship is a <<relationship>> that establishes the association between two different CostItems.	S5000F Cost Breakdown
Country	Class	class	Country is a self-governing political entity, occupying a particular territory.	CDM UoF Location
Cuboid	Class	compoundAttribute	Cuboid represents a three-dimensional object where all its faces are rectangles and all angles are right angles.	S-Series_Compound_Attributes_2-0_002-00
Cylinder	Class	compoundAttribute	Cylinder represents a three-dimensional object with straight parallel sides and a circular section.	S-Series_Compound_Attributes_2-0_002-00
Damage	Class	class	Damage is a harm to an item resulting in loss of value or the impairment of usefulness.	S5000F Damage
DamageAnalysis	Class	class	DamageAnalysis is an AnalysisActivity that represents the objective for, and outcome of, a damage analysis carried out for the AnalysisCandidateItem.	CDM UoF Damage Definition
DamageAnalysisRevision	Class	class	DamageAnalysisRevision is an AnalysisActivityRevision representing an iteration applied to a DamageAnalysis.	CDM UoF Damage Definition

Class name	Type	Stereotype	Definition	UoF
DamageCharacteristic	Class	class	`DamageCharacteristic` is a `<<class>>` that allows to document the characteristics of a `Damage`.	S5000F Damage
DamageDefinition	Class	class	`DamageDefinition` is a `<<class>>` that represents a loss or reduction of functionality due to external causes or use outside specified limits.	CDM UoF Damage Definition
DamagedItem	Interface	select	`DamagedItem` is a `<<select>>` interface that allows to associate a `Damage` to the item where the `Damage` has occurred.	S5000F Damage
DataSetAsDesigned	Class	class	`DataSetAsDesigned` is a class representing a data structure.	S5000F Data Sets
DataSetAsReleased	Class	class	`DataSetAsReleased` is a class representing a set of actual data that are structured as a `DataSetAsDesigned`.	S5000F Data Sets
DataSetAssociatedWith	Class	relationship	`DataSetAssociatedWith` is a `<<relationship>>` that allows to associate a `DataSetAsDesigned` to a `PartAsDesigned`	S5000F Data Sets
DatedClassification	Class	compoundAttribute	`DatedClassification` is a `<<compoundAttribute>>` that represents a classification in conjunction with its recording date.	S-Series_Compound_Attributes_2-0_002-00
DateRange	Class	compoundAttribute	`DateRange` is a `<<compoundAttribute>>` that identifies an interval of dates. **Note** The range pattern can be open-ended.	S-Series_Compound_Attributes_2-0_002-00
DateTimeRange	Class	compoundAttribute	`DateTimeRange` is a `<<compoundAttribute>>` that identifies an interval of date and times.	S-Series_Compound_Attributes_2-0_002-00
DefineOrUpdateEnvironment	Class	exchange	`DefineOrUpdateEnvironment` is an `<<exchange>>` that represents a message associated with a use case (UC51505) allowing information about the environment in which the Product operates or is maintained to be defined or updated.	S5000F Use Cases

Class name	Type	Stereotype	Definition	UoF
DefineSecurity	Class	exchange	DefineSecurity is an <<exchange>> that represents a message associated with a use case (UC51412) providing the necessary information to ensure that proper security classifications are applied to classified items.	S5000F Use Cases
DerivedChangeRequestRequirement	Class	relationship	DerivedChangeRequestRequirement is a <<relationship>> that allows to associate a Requirement or more of them to an existing ChangeRequest.	S5000F Change Request Environmental Impact
DetectionMean	Interface	extend	DetectionMean is an <<extend>> interface that allows to associate DetectionMeanCapabilities to the elements that allowed for detection of a failure.	S5000F Failure Detection and Location
DetectionMeanCapability	Class	class	DetectionMeanCapability is a class that identifies the capability to detect a failure.	S5000F Failure Detection and Location
DetectionMechanism	Class	class	DetectionMechanism is a class that allows to define the mechanism by means of which a failure is detected.	S5000F Failure Detection and Location
Detector	Interface	select	Detector is a <<select>> interface representing the elements that can detect or have detected an anomalous behaviour (fault) in a SerializedHardwarePart.	S5000F Failure Detection and Location
DetermineObsolescenceCandidates	Class	exchange	DetermineObsolescenceCandidates is an <<exchange>> that represents a message associated with a use case (UC51002) providing the necessary information to identify items that are facing potential obsolescence.	S5000F Use Cases
DetermineObsolescenceStrategy	Class	exchange	DetermineObsolescenceStrategy is an <<exchange>> that represents a message associated with a use case (UC51003) providing the necessary information to define the strategy on handling obsolescence.	S5000F Use Cases
DetermineWarrantyMisuse	Class	exchange	DetermineWarrantyMisuse is an <<exchange>> that represents a message associated with a use case (UC50803) providing the necessary information to determine whether warranty was or not misused.	S5000F Use Cases
DigitalFile	Class	class	DigitalFile is a <<class>> that provides the identification of data stored on an electronic device that can be interpreted by a computer.	CDM UoF Digital File

Applicable to: All

Class name	Type	Stereotype	Definition	UoF
DigitalFileReference	Class	relationship	DigitalFileReference is a <<relationship>> that allows a DigitalFile to reference a DigitalFileReferencedItem.	CDM UoF Digital File
DigitalFileReferencedItem	Interface	select	DigitalFileReferencedItem is a <<select>> interface that identifies an item which in some way is associated with the content of the DigitalFile.	CDM UoF Digital File
DigitalFileReferencingItem	Interface	extend	DigitalFileReferencingItem is an <<extend>> interface that provides its associated data model to those classes that implement it.	CDM UoF Digital File
Dimensions	Class	compoundAttribute	Dimensions is a <<compoundAttribute>> that represents a set of values that define the measurable extent of a particular kind for a specific item. **Example** – area – volume	S5000F_Compound_Attributes_00 2-00
DisposalItem	Interface	select	DisposalItem is a <<select>> interface that allows to define items that require disposal.	S5000F Item Disposal Requirement
DisposalLocation	Class	relationship	DisposalLocation is a <<relationship>> that allows to associate the different locations involved in a DisposalRequirement.	S5000F Disposal Requirement
DisposalRequirement	Class	class	DisposalRequirement is a Requirement to proceed with the disposal of an item, waste or hazardous material.	S5000F Disposal Requirement
DisposalRequirementContext	Interface	select	DisposalRequirementContext is a <<select>> interface that defines the context in which the DisposalRequirement is established.	S5000F Disposal Requirement
DisposalRequiringItem	Interface	extend	DisposalRequiringItem is an <<extend>> interface that allows to associate disposal information and a disposal requirement to an item requiring disposal.	S5000F Item Disposal Requirement
DisposalSite	Interface	select	DisposalSite is a <<select>> interface that defines the involved sites during a disposal.	S5000F Disposal Site

Class name	Type	Stereotype	Definition	UoF
DisposalTransportRequiremen t	Class	relationship	DisposalTransportRequirement is a <<relationship>> that a allows to associate a DisposalRequirement with a TransportRequirement.	S5000F Disposal Requirement
Document	Class	class	Document is a <<class>> that represents a compiled set of information that serves a purpose. **Note** Document is an abstract class, ie, it must be instantiated by one of the classes implementing it. **Example** – drawing – manual – report	S5000F Specializations
DocumentCharacteristicItem	Interface	extend	DocumentCharacteristicItem is an <<extend>> interface that provides the capability to associate additional relationships to Documents and DocumentIssues..	S5000F Document
DocumentIssue	Class	class	DocumentIssue is a <<class>> that represents a specific release of a Document	S5000F Specializations
DocumentItem	Interface	select	DocumentItem is a <<select>> interface that identifies items which can be selected as Document.	CDM UoFDocument
DocumentParty	Class	relationship	DocumentParty is a <<relationship>> class that defines the association of a document with a specific Party. **Example** – approved by – prepared by – reported to	S5000F Document
DocumentReferencingItem	Interface	extend	DocumentReferencingItem is an <<extend>> interface that provides its associated data model to those classes that implement it.	CDM UoF Document

Class name	Type	Stereotype	Definition	UoF
`DownTimePeriod`	Class	class	`DownTimePeriod` is a class representing a planned or actual downtime for a `SerializedProductVariant`. **Example** – Non-working hours – Overhaul period	S5000F Change Embodiment Planning
`EffectiveOnProductConfiguration`	Class	relationship	`EffectiveOnProductConfiguration` is a <<relationship>> that identifies that a `EffectiveOnProductConfigurationItem`, included in the `Breakdown` for the overall `Product`, is effective in the associated `AllowedProductConfiguration`.	CDM UoFProduct Design Configuration
`EffectiveOnProductConfigurationItem`	Interface	extend	`EffectiveOnProductConfigurationItem` is an <<extend>> interface that provides its associated data model to those classes that can be included in one or many instances of `AllowedProductConfiguration`.	CDM UoFProduct Design Configuration
`ElaborateAssignmentProposal`	Class	exchange	`ElaborateAssignmentProposal` is an <<exchange>> that represents a message associated with a use case (UC51101) providing the necessary information to provide a proposal about how a serialized Product variant can perform a specific fleet task.	S5000F Use Cases
`ElaborateFleetPlan`	Class	exchange	`ElaborateFleetPlan` is an <<exchange>> that represents a message associated with a use case (UC51104) providing the necessary information to elaborate a plan for effectively managing a fleet.	S5000F Use Cases
`Environment`	Class	class	`Environment` is a class that represents the actual environment in which the `Product` operation or maintenance takes place.	S5000F Environment
`EnvironmentDefinition`	Class	class	`EnvironmentDefinition` is a <<class>> that specifies the circumstances, objects, events and/or conditions by which something can be surrounded and that influence the performance of an associated item.	CDM UoF Environment Definition
`EnvironmentDefinitionRevision`	Class	class	`EnvironmentDefinitionRevision` is a <<class>> representing an iteration applied to an `EnvironmentDefinition`.	CDM UoF Environment Definition

Class name	Type	Stereotype	Definition	UoF
EnvironmentItem	Interface	extend	EnvironmentItem is an <<extend>> interface that provides its associated data model to those classes that implement it.	S5000F Environment
EnvironmentRelationship	Class	relationship	EnvironmentRelationship is a <<relationship>> that allows associations between two different Environments to be defined.	S5000F Environment
EnvironmentRevision	Class	class	EnvironmentRevision is a <<class>> representing an iteration applied to an Environment. **Note** EnvironmentRevision can correspond to a combination of EnvironmentDefinitionRevisions (eg, continental and volcanic).	S5000F Environment
EquipmentCalibrationCertificate	Class	exchange	EquipmentCalibrationCertificate is an <<exchange>> that represents a message associated with a use case (UC50409) allowing information associated with an equipment calibration and associated certificate, to be provided.	S5000F Use Cases
EquipmentOperation	Class	relationship	EquipmentOperation is a <<relationship>> that defines which Party has operated a SerializedHardwarePart during a specific time period.	S5000F Equipment
EquipmentOwner	Class	relationship	EquipmentOwner is a <<relationship>> defining who and to what extent is the equipment owner during a specific period of time.	S5000F Equipment
EquipmentStatus	Class	attributeGroup	EquipmentStatus is an <<attributeGroup>> that represents the status of a SerializedHardwarePart during a specific period of time and the reason for such status.	S5000F Equipment
EvaluateFleetTask	Class	exchange	EvaluateFleetTask is an <<exchange>> that represents a message associated with a use case (UC51105) providing the necessary information to evaluate the effectiveness of a fleet task.	S5000F Use Cases
EvaluateMaintenanceActions	Class	exchange	EvaluateMaintenanceActions is an <<exchange>> that represents a message associated with a use case (UC50801) that allows the effectivity of maintenance actions to be assessed.	S5000F Use Cases

Applicable to: All

Class name	Type	Stereotype	Definition	UoF
`EvaluationByAssertionOfClassInstance`	Class	class	`EvaluationByAssertionOfClassInstance` is an `EvaluationCriteria` that identifies a class instance to be used as an assert item and be mapped to a Boolean expression which can be evaluated to be either TRUE or FALSE.	CDM UoF Applicability Statement
`EvaluationByAssertionOfCondition`	Class	class	`EvaluationByAssertionOfCondition` is an `EvaluationCriteria` that identifies a combination of a defined condition and a defined value to be used as an assert item and be mapped to a Boolean expression which can be evaluated to be either TRUE or FALSE.	CDM UoF Applicability Statement
`EvaluationByAssertionOfSerializedItems`	Class	class	`EvaluationByAssertionOfSerializedItems` is an `EvaluationCriteria` that identifies a class instance together with an associated serial number range to be used as an assert item and be mapped to a Boolean expression which can be evaluated to be either TRUE or	CDM UoF Applicability Statement
`EvaluationByNestedApplicabilityStatement`	Class	class	`EvaluationByNestedApplicabilityStatement` is an `EvaluationCriteria` that enables an `ApplicabilityStatement` to be reused as part of this `EvaluationCriteria`. **Note** This class enables the definition of nested applicability statements.	CDM UoF Applicability Statement
`EvaluationByNestedExpression`	Class	class	`EvaluationByNestedExpression` is an `EvaluationCriteria` that defines a Boolean expression between additional `EvaluationCriteria` that can be evaluated to either TRUE or FALSE.	S5000F Expression Evaluation
`EvaluationCriteria`	Class	class	`EvaluationCriteria` is a <<class>> that defines conditions that can be mapped to a Boolean expression which can be evaluated to be either TRUE or FALSE.	CDM UoF Applicability Statement

Class name	Type	Stereotype	Definition	UoF
Event	Class	class	`Event` is an important happening or occurrence at a specific point in time that requires to be documented or recorded.	S5000F Event
EventAffectedBreakdownEleme nt	Class	relationship	`EventAffectedBreakdownElement` is a <<relationship>> that allows to associate an `Event` to the `BreakdownElements` affected by it.	S5000F Event
EventExplanation	Class	relationship	`EventExplanation` is a <<relationship>> that allows to associate an `Event` to the `ExplanatoryFactors` that explain it.	S5000F Event
EventItem	Interface	select	`EventItem` is a <<select>> interface that allows to associate `Events` to items	S5000F Event
EventRelationship	Class	relationship	`EventRelationship` is a <<relationship>> describing the association between two different events.	S5000F Event
EventRelationshipItem	Class	relationship	`EventRelationshipItem` is a <<relationship>> that allows to associate an `Event` to an item.	S5000F Event
EventReporter	Class	relationship	`EventReporter` is a <<relationship>> that permits to associate an event to the `Party` that has reported that `Event`.	S5000F Event
ExchangeEnvironmentalData	Class	exchange	`ExchangeEnvironmentalData` is an <<exchange>> that represents a message associated with a use case (UC51601) allowing consumption and emission information between different parties due to `Product` operation to be reported.	S5000F Use Cases
ExchangeExportControl	Class	exchange	`ExchangeExportControl` is an <<exchange>> that represents a message associated with a use case (UC51413) providing the necessary information to ensure compliance with export control regulations.	S5000F Use Cases
ExplanatoryFactor	Class	class	`ExplanatoryFactor` is a class that provides information about the factor that caused an `Event`. **Example** – explosion – human error	S5000F Event

Class name	Type	Stereotype	Definition	UoF
			– strong lateral wind	
ExportControlledItem	Interface	select	ExportControlledItem is a <<select>> interface that defines the items that can be subject to export control.	S5000F Export Control License
ExportControlLicense	Class	class	ExportControlLicense is a <<class>> representing an authorization to one or more parties to export item(s) under the terms of an ExportControlRegulation.	S5000F Export Control License
ExportControlLicenseItem	Class	relationship	ExportControlLicenseItem is a <<relationship>> that associates an ExportControlLicense to the export-controlled items to which this license applies.	S5000F Export Control License
ExportControlParty	Class	relationship	ExportControlParty is a <<relationship>> that associates an ExportControlLicense to the parties to which it applies or that control it.	S5000F Export Control License
ExportControlRegulation	Class	class	ExportControlRegulation is a legal document that defines export control restrictions to one or several items or item categories.	S5000F Export Control Requirement
ExportControlRequirementAppliedToCountry	Class	relationship	ExportControlRequirementAppliedToCountry is a <<relationship>> that defines to which countries an ExportControlRegulation is applied.	S5000F Export Control Requirement
ExpressionEvaluation	Class	class	ExpressionEvaluation is a Boolean expression that can be evaluated to be either TRUE or FALSE.	S5000F Expression Evaluation
ExternalDocument	Class	class	ExternalDocument is a specialization of class Document, and represents all documents that do not have a specialied class.	S5000F Document
Facility	Class	class	Facility is a <<class>>that represents a physically limited infrastructure which exists, or is intended to be built or installed, and is established to serve a particular purpose.	S5000F Specializations
FacilityLocation	Class	relationship	FacilityLocation is a <<relationship>> that defines at which Location a Facility is located.	S5000F Facility

Class name	Type	Stereotype	Definition	UoF
FacilityOperator	Class	relationship	FacilityOperator is a <<relationship>> that identifies the party responsible for running the Facility **Example** – The FacilityOperator has leased the Facility from the FacilityOwner.	S5000F Specializations
FacilityOperatorItem	Interface	select	FacilityOperatorItem is a <<select>> interface that identifies classes from which an instance can be selected to be the FacilityOperator.	CDM UoF Facility
FacilityOwner	Class	relationship	FacilityOwner is a <<relationship>> that defines the total or partial ownership of a facility by a specific party during a specific period of time.	S5000F Facility
FacilityRelationship	Class	relationship	FacilityRelationship is a <<relationship>> that defines how two Facilities are related with each other.	S5000F Facility
Failure	Interface	select	Failure is a <<select>> interface that allows to identify the reason for an EquipmentFault.	S5000F Failure Detection and Location
FailureDetection	Class	relationship	FailureDetection is a <<relationship>> that allows to define which DetectionMechanism is capable of detecting a specific Failure.	S5000F Failure Detection and Location
FailureMode	Class	class	FailureMode is a <<class>> that defines a functional consequence of an unacceptable state of the FailureModeAnalysisItem. **Example** – No output from electrical circuit.	CDM UoF Failure Mode
FailureModeCause	Class	class	FailureModeCause is a <<class>> that specifies the physical or chemical process(es) that is the reason for the FailureMode.	CDM UoF Failure Mode
FailureModeEffect	Class	class	FailureModeEffect is a <<class>> that defines the consequences of an identified FailureMode on the operation, function, or status for the referred item.	CDM UoF Failure Mode

Class name	Type	Stereotype	Definition	UoF
Fault	Class	class	`Fault` represents an unidentified anomalous behavior that occurred on a specific item at a specific date.	S5000F Actual Fault Indication
FaultCause	Class	relationship	`FaultCause` is a `<<relationship>>` that allows to associate a `Fault` to its underlying cause.	S5000F Failure Detection and Location
FaultSymptom	Class	class	`FaultSymptom` is a `<<class>>` that represents an indication of the existence of a `Fault`.	S5000F Actual Fault Indication
Fleet	Class	class	`Fleet` is a `<<class>>` representing a group of `SerializedProductVariants` that move together, are engaged in the same activity, belong to a same owner or are operated by a same organization. **Note** `SerializedProductVariants` in a `Fleet` do not need to belong necessarily to a same `ProductVariant`. **Note** Though `Fleet` is typically used for vehicles, the concept can be extended, for example to group all robots in a same manufacturing line. **Example** – all aircraft of one airline (independent of type) – bicycles or cars of one hire company – individual machines of a specific part number that operate in a specific region – municipal buses of one town – warships of several countries performing joint exercises	S5000F Fleet Definition
FleetBasedAt	Class	relationship	`FleetBasedAt` is a `<<relationship>>` that indicates the location at which as `Fleet` is based at a specific point in time.	S5000F Fleet Definition
FleetManager	Interface	extend	`FleetManager` is an `<<extend>>` interface that allows to assign capabilities to the `OperatorOrganization` or `OperatorPerson` that manages a `Fleet`.	S5000F Fleet Definition

Class name	Type	Stereotype	Definition	UoF
FleetOperatedBy	Class	relationship	FleetOperatedBy is a <<relationship>> that allows to assign an Operator to a Fleet during a specific period of time.	S5000F Fleet Definition
FleetOperatesAtLocation	Class	relationship	FleetOperatesAtLocation is a <<relationship>> that indicates the location at which as Fleet operates at a specific point in time.	S5000F Fleet Definition
FleetOperator	Interface	select	FleetOperator is a <<select>> interface that allows to identify the operator of a Fleet.	S5000F Fleet Definition
FleetPlanning	Class	class	FleetPlanning is a class representing the planned usage of a fleet during a specified period of time.	S5000F Fleet Planning and Product Assignment
FleetRelationship	Class	relationship	FleetRelationship is a <<relationship>> that indicates how two Fleets are related with each other.	S5000F Fleet Definition
FleetRequirement	Class	class	FleetRequirement is a Requirement (need) that a fleet must comply with. **Example** – Two A/C in MedEvac role need to be available Monday thru Thursday.	S5000F Fleet Planning and Product Assignment
FleetTask	Class	class	FleetTask is a planned activity to be carried out by a SerializedProductVariant as part of the activities that the fleet has to perform.	S5000F Fleet Planning and Product Assignment
FleetTaskCancellationNotice	Class	class	FleetTaskCancellationNotice is a Document published by an Operator to cancel a FleetTask.	S5000F Fleet Task Cancellation
FleetTaskCargo	Class	relationship	FleetTaskCargo is a <<relationship>> that allows to associate a CargoItem to a FleetTask.	S5000F Fleet Planning and Product Assignment
FleetTaskList	Class	relationship	FleetTaskList is a <<relationship>> that defines which FleetTasks are performed by which Fleets for a specific FleetPlanning.	S5000F Fleet Planning and Product Assignment

Applicable to: All

Class name	Type	Stereotype	Definition	UoF
`GeographicalArea`	Class	class	`GeographicalArea` is a <<class>> that represents a particular extent of space.	CDM UoF Location
`GlobalPosition`	Class	class	`GlobalPosition` is a <<class>> that identifies a point in space by a set of coordinates.	CDM UoF Location
`HardwareElement`	Class	class	`HardwareElement` is a `BreakdownElement` that is realized as a `HardwarePartAsDesigned`.	CDM UoFHardware Element
`HardwareElementPartRealization`	Class	relationship	`HardwareElementPartRealization` is a <<relationship>> where a `HardwareElementRevision` relates to an instance of `HardwarePartAsDesigned` which fulfills the `HardwareElement` specification.	CDM UoFHardware Element
`HardwareElementRevision`	Class	class	`HardwareElementRevision` is a `BreakdownElementRevision` representing an iteration applied to a `HardwareElement`.	CDM UoF Hardware Element
`HardwarePartAsDesigned`	Class	class	`HardwarePartAsDesigned` is a `PartAsDesigned` that is to be realized as physical items (hardware) including non-countable material. **Example** – Examples of non-countable materials are: oil, sealant, paint.	S5000F Specializations
`HardwarePartAsDesignedCommerceData`	Class	attributeGroup	`HardwarePartAsDesignedCommerceData` is a <<class>> that documents pricing information of a part based on its units of issue. The prices are used for planning purposes on customer side and reflect initial prices, provided by provisioning.	S5000F Warehouse and Spare Pool
`HardwarePartAsDesignedDesignData`	Class	attributeGroup	`HardwarePartAsDesignedDesignData` is an <<attributeGroup>> that collects `HardwarePartAsDesigned` characteristics identified during design activities.	CDM UoF Part Definition
`HardwarePartAsDesignedSupportData`	Class	attributeGroup	`HardwarePartAsDesignedSupportData` is an <<attributeGroup>> that collects `HardwarePartAsDesigned` characteristics identified during supportability analysis activities.	CDM UoF Part Definition

Class name	Type	Stereotype	Definition	UoF
HardwarePartContainer	Class	class	HardwarePartContainer represents a container holding one or several similar HardwareParts that are not managed individually. **Example** – A box of recovered rivets during dismantling for their recycling.	S5000F Container
IdentifiedTaskRequirement	Class	relationship	IdentifiedTaskRequirement is a <<relationship>> that associates a TaskRequirement with a TaskRequirementAnalysisItem.	CDM UoF Task Requirement
IdentifyWarrantyRisks	Class	exchange	IdentifyWarrantyRisks is an <<exchange>> that represents a message associated with a use case (UC50804) providing the necessary information to identify potential warranty risks.	S5000F Use Cases
ImproveWarrantyRules	Class	exchange	ImproveWarrantyRules is an <<exchange>> that represents a message associated with a use case (UC50805) providing the necessary information to evaluate the suitability of existing warranty rules.	S5000F Use Cases
IndicatedFaultSymptom	Class	class	IndicatedFaultSymptom is a <<class>> that represents an indication of the existence of a Fault by some measuring or monitoring device.	S5000F Actual Fault Indication
InfluenceDesign	Class	exchange	InfluenceDesign is an <<exchange>> that represents a message associated with a use case (UC50302) providing the necessary information to be able to raise a change request.	S5000F Use Cases
Infrastructure	Class	class	Infrastructure is a <<class>> that represents the basic physical and organizational structures and facilities needed for the operation of an organization or Product or required for the provision of a service. **Note** An infrastructure can be located across many different locations or can even be mobile. **Example** – airport – bus service – railroad – roads	S5000F Infrastructure

Class name	Type	Stereotype	Definition	UoF
			– set of buildings	
InfrastructureAvailable	Class	relationship	InfrastructureAvailableFor is a <<relationship>> that provides the capability of associating an Infrastructure to items that can use it during a certain period.. **Note** The infrastructure availability is always for a specific item. It is possible that the Infrastructures is available for a specific Product but not for a different one at a specific moment in time (eg, due to size constraints).	S5000F Infrastructure Availability
InfrastructureCompliance	Class	relationship	InfrastructureCompliance is a <<relationship>> that documents how the InfrastructureCompliantItem fulfills requirements stated in the associated ResourceSpecification.	CDM UoF Facility
InfrastructureCompliantItem	Interface	extend	InfrastructureCompliantItem is an <<extend>> interface that provides its associated data model to those classes that implement it.	CDM UoF Facility
InfrastructureItem	Interface	extend	InfrastructureItem is an <<extend>> interface that allows to associate additional capabilities to items that can belong to an Infrastructure.	S5000F Infrastructure
InfrastructureNode	Interface	select	InfrastructureNode is a <<class>> representing one item that forms part of an Infrastructure.	S5000F Infrastructure
InfrastructureNodeAtLocation	Class	relationship	InfrastructureNodeAtLocation is a <<relationship>> that defines the Location at which an InfrastructureNode is located.	S5000F Infrastructure
InfrastructureOperatingPeriod	Class	class	InfrastructureOperatingPeriod is a <<class>> indicating a period of time during which an infrastructure has operated at total or partial capability.	S5000F Infrastructure Operating Period
InfrastructureParty	Class	relationship	InfrastructureParty is a <<relationship>> that associates a Party to an Infrastructure.	S5000F Infrastructure

Class name	Type	Stereotype	Definition	UoF
`InfrastructureRelationship`	Class	relationship	`InfrastructureRelationship` is a `<<relationship>>` that defines how two `Infrastructures` are related with each other.	S5000F Infrastructure
`InfrastructureRequiringItem`	Interface	select	`InfrastructureRequiringItem` is a `<<select>>` interface that defines items requiring an `Infrastructure`.	S5000F Infrastructure Availability
`InfrastructureRevision`	Class	class	`InfrastructureRevision` is a `<<class>>` representing an iteration applied to an `InfrastructureRevision`.	S5000F Infrastructure
`InServiceDataFeedback`	Class	exchange	`InServiceDataFeedback` is an `<<exchange>>` that represents a message providing all the necessary information required for a generic use case (UC50000) that allows all S5000F information to be sent. **Note 1** The fact that all S5000F information can be sent with this message does not imply that all information must be sent. **Note 2** A project-specific use case with only a limited subset of data can use this generic use case to send its information, instead of creating a specific one.	S5000F Use Cases
`InstallationLocation`	Class	class	`InstallationLocation` is a `<<class>>` that represents a position within the associated `SerializedProductVariant`. **Note** `InstallationLocation` is also referred to as installation slot.	CDM UoF Serialized Product Variant Configuration
`InstallationLocationDefinitionItem`	Interface	select	`InstallationLocationDefinitionItem` is a `<<select>>` interface that identifies items which can contain the basic definition for the `InstallationLocation`.	CDM UoF Serialized Product Variant Configuration
`InstalledPart`	Class	class	`InstalledPart` is a `<<class>>` that identifies a period during which a given `RealizedPart` is, or has been, installed at the `InstallationLocation`.	CDM UoF Serialized Product Variant Configuration
`InstalledPartItem`	Interface	extend	`InstalledPartItem` is an `<<extend>>` interface that provides its associated data model to those classes that implement it.	CDM UoF Serialized Product Variant Configuration

Applicable to: All

Class name	Type	Stereotype	Definition	UoF
InventoryActivity	Class	class	InventoryActivity is an Activity associated to the management of spares or warehouses-	S5000F Reportable Activity
InvolvedDisposalOrganizatio n	Class	relationship	InvolvedDisposalOrganization is a <<relationship>> that allows to document the organizations involved in a disposal.	S5000F Disposal Requirement
ItemDamage	Interface	extend	ItemDamage is an <<extend>> interface that allows to document the Damage that an item has suffered.	S5000F Damage
ItemDemilitarizationData	Class	attributeGroup	ItemDemilitarizationData is an <<attributeGroup>> that collects item characteristics that require a special handling of an item because of its military nature.	S5000F Item Disposal Requirement
ItemDisposalOperation	Class	class	ItemDisposalOperation is a <<class>> representing the action that has been taken in order to dispose of a DisposableItem.	S5000F Item Disposal Operation
ItemDisposalOperationAction	Class	relationship	ItemDisposalOperationAction is a <<relationship>> that allows to associate an ItemDisposalOperation with one or more Actions.	S5000F Item Disposal Operation
ItemDisposalRequirement	Class	class	ItemDisposalRequirement is a DisposalRequirement to proceed with the disposal of an individual item.	S5000F Disposal Requirement
ItemExportControlRegulation	Class	relationship	ItemExportControlRegulation is a <<relationship>> that allows to associate an ItemUnderExportControl with the ExportControlRegulation that governs its export,	S5000F Export Control Requirement
ItemUnderExportControl	Interface	extend	ItemUnderExportControl is an <<extend>> interface that enables to define which items are subject to export control rules.	S5000F Export Control Requirement
ItemWarranty	Class	relationship	ItemWarranty is a <<relationship>> that defines the association between a WarrantyItem and the legal justification for the warranty of the WarrantyItem, such as a contract or contract clause.	S5000F Warranty
LaborRateItem	Interface	select	LaborRateItem is a <<select>> interface that allows to associate a LaborRate to a skilled labor.	S5000F Person Competences and Labor Rates

Class name	Type	Stereotype	Definition	UoF
LaborRates	Class	relationship	LaborRates is a <<relationship>> that allows to assign labor rates to different skills, skill levels and trades.	S5000F Contract Breakdown
LegalParty	Interface	select	LegalParty is a <<select>> interface identifies entities that has legal standing in the eyes of the law.	CDM UoF Product and Project
LocalPosition	Class	class	LocalPosition is a <<class>> representing the local coordinates that uniquely identify a position within a ReferencedPositionItem.	S5000F Local Position
Location	Interface	extend	Location is an <<extend>> interface that provides its associated data model to those classes that implement it.	CDM UoF Location
LocationItem	Interface	select	LocationItem is a <<select>> interface that identifies items which can be selected to provide the definition of a geographic location.	CDM UoF Location
LocationRelationship	Class	relationship	LocationRelationship is a <<relationship>> where one LocationItem relates to another LocationItem	CDM UoF Location
Locator	Class	class	Locator is a functional area that indicates where an item is physically placed at a specific location. **Note** Contrary to Location, a Locator cannot be placed on a map and can be reassigned from one location to a different one. **Example** – Drawer or shelf in a warehouse. – Location identifier for company department. – P.O. Box	S5000F Location and Locator
LogBook	Class	class	LogBook is a class that represents a set of records called LogBookEntries that compile critical activities or events that need to be registered for a defined purpose.	S5000F Logbook
LogBookEntry	Class	class	LogBookEntry is an individual entry into a logbook, defining one critical activity or event to be included in the LogBook.	S5000F Logbook

Class name	Type	Stereotype	Definition	UoF
			Note 1 A `LogBookEntry` can be used for operation, maintenance, overhaul, etc. **Note 2** Multiple `MeasurementPoints` can be associated to a single logbook entry. **Example** – cycles – flight hours – landings – maintenance actions – operating hours – overhaul	
`LogBookEntryMeasurementPoint`	Class	class	`LogBookEntryMeasurementPoint` represents a measurement point in a `SerializedItem` corresponding to a specific `LogBookEntry`.	S5000F Logbook
`LogicalAND`	Class	class	`LogicalAND` is an `EvaluationCriteria` that defines a Boolean operation where the results of all its associated `EvaluationCriteria` must be TRUE for the result to be TRUE, otherwise the result is FALSE.	CDM UoF Applicability Statement
`LogicalNOT`	Class	class	`LogicalNOT` is an `EvaluationCriteria` that defines a Boolean operation where the result from its associated `EvaluationCriteria` must be FALSE for the result to be TRUE, otherwise the result is FALSE.	CDM UoF Applicability Statement
`LogicalOR`	Class	class	`LogicalOR` is an `EvaluationCriteria` that defines a Boolean operation where the result from at least one of its associated `EvaluationCriteria` must be TRUE for the result to be TRUE, otherwise the result is FALSE.	CDM UoF Applicability Statement
`LogicalXOR`	Class	class	`LogicalXOR` is an `EvaluationCriteria` that defines a Boolean operation where the result from one and only one of its associated	CDM UoF Applicability Statement

Class name	Type	Stereotype	Definition	UoF
			`EvaluationCriteria` must be `TRUE` for the result to be `TRUE`, otherwise the result is `FALSE`.	
`LooseWaste`	Class	class	`LooseWaste` is a <<class>> representing a certain volume of solid waste that cannot be easily transported by means of containers or is not stored in containers at the source location. **Note** Loose waste is usually loaded directly onto a truck, instead of stored in containers. **Example** – contaminated soil – waste water to be extracted from reservoir	S5000F Waste Disposal Requirement
`MaintainabilityEffectivenes`s	Class	exchange	`MaintainabilityEffectiveness` is an <<exchange>> that represents a message associated with a use case (UC50305) providing the necessary information to assess the effectiveness of maintenance.	S5000F Use Cases
`MaintenanceActivity`	Class	class	`MaintenanceActivity` is a `ReportableActivity` that is associated to a maintenance task.	S5000F Maintenance Activity
`MaintenanceActivityDocument`	Class	relationship	`MaintenanceActivityDocument` is a <<relationship>> that allows to associate documents (relating) to a `MaintenanceActivity` requiring them (related).	S5000F Maintenance Activity
`MaintenanceActivityParty`	Class	relationship	`MaintenanceActivityParty` is a <<relationship>> that allows to associate a `MaintenanceActivity` to the person who is going to carry out the `MaintenanceActivity`.	S5000F Maintenance Activity
`MaintenanceActivityPlan`	Class	attributeGroup	`MaintenanceActivityPlan` is an <<attributeGroup>> that details the information associated to the planning of a `MaintenanceActivity`.	S5000F Maintenance Activity
`MaintenanceActivityRecord`	Class	attributeGroup	`MaintenanceActivityRecord` is an <<attributeGroup>> that details the information associated to the execution of a `MaintenanceActivity`.	S5000F Maintenance Activity

Class name	Type	Stereotype	Definition	UoF
`MaintenanceEvent`	Class	class	`MaintenanceEvent` is an event that consists in the realization of one or several maintenance activities or occurs as the result of a maintenance activity.	S5000F Maintenance Activity
`MaintenanceFacility`	Class	class	`MaintenanceFacility` is a `Facility` that is mainly established for providing product support.	S5000F Facility
`MaintenanceFacilityLevel`	Class	relationship	`MaintenanceFacilityLevel` is a <<relationship> that defines the `MaintenanceLevels` of a `Facility`.	S5000F Maintenance Facility Planning
`MaintenanceFacilitySlot`	Class	class	`MaintenanceFacilitySlot` is a fixed position within a `MaintenanceFacility` in which exactly one `SerializedProductVariant` can be accommodated.	S5000F Maintenance Facility Planning
`MaintenanceFacilitySlotAcco modation`	Class	relationship	`MaintenanceFacilitySlotAccomodation` is a <<relationship>> that defines which `ProductVariants` can be accommodated in a specific `MaintenanceFacilitySlot`.	S5000F Maintenance Facility Planning
`MaintenanceFacilitySlotPlan nedUsage`	Class	relationship	`MaintenanceFacilitySlotPlannedUsage` is a <<relationship>> that indicates the planned allocation of a `MaintenanceFacilitySlot` to a specific `SerializedProductVariant`.	S5000F Maintenance Facility Planning
`MaintenanceItem`	Interface	select	`MaintenanceItem` is a <<select interface>> that allows to select an item of a specific type that can be maintained.	S5000F Maintenance Activity
`MaintenanceLevel`	Class	class	`MaintenanceLevel` is a <<class>> that represents the definition of a set of maintenance capabilities which will be made available to support a defined `Product`. **Note** `MaintenanceLevel` can be established either by a single organization or be distributed between a set of organizations.	CDM UoFProduct Usage Context
`MaintenanceLicense`	Class	class	`MaintenanceLicense` is a class representing the authorization of an authority to a `MaintenancePerson` to perform specific maintenance tasks.	S5000F Maintenance Personnel

Class name	Type	Stereotype	Definition	UoF
			Example – B1 aircraft maintenance license.	
MaintenanceManagementAvaila bility	Class	exchange	MaintenanceManagementAvailability is an <<exchange>> that represents a message associated with a use case (UC50305) providing the necessary information to management maintenance, and contract for availability.	S5000F Use Cases
MaintenanceOrganization	Class	class	MaintenanceOrganization is an organization approved to perform maintenance tasks on a specific set of Products or ProductVariants.	S5000F Maintenance Organization
MaintenanceOrganizationAppr oval	Class	relationship	MaintenanceOrganizationApproval is a <<relationship>> that identifies the authorization of an Organization to operate as a Maintenanceorganization for a specific period of time.	S5000F Maintenance Organization
MaintenancePerson	Class	class	MaintenancePerson is a person with the skills to be able to perform maintenance activities.	S5000F Maintenance Personnel
MaintenancePersonApprovedPr oduct	Class	relationship	MaintenancePersonApprovedProduct is a <<relationship>> that defines which MaintenancePersons have been approved to carry out maintenance on specific ProductVariants, possibly with a specific approval by an organization.	S5000F Maintenance Personnel
MaintenancePersonFacility	Class	relationship	MaintenancePersonFacility is a <<relationship>> that documents the MaintenanceFacility where a MaintenancePerson is working during a specific period of time.	S5000F Maintenance Personnel
MaintenanceProgram	Class	class	MaintenanceProgram is a class that represents a set of TaskRequirements that must be applied to a ProductVariant so as to maintain the ProductVariant in an operational state. **Example** – OEM maintenance program – Operator maintenance program	S5000F Maintenance Program

Class name	Type	Stereotype	Definition	UoF
`MaintenanceProgramItem`	Interface	extend	`MaintenanceProgramItem` is an <<extend>> interface that allows to associate a `MaintenanceProgram` to an item. **Example** – equipment – facility – individual aircraft – power grid – ship	S5000F Maintenance Program
`MaintenanceProgramRevision`	Class	class	`MaintenanceProgramRevision` is an iteration of a `MaintenanceProgram`.	S5000F Maintenance Program
`MaintenanceRequirement`	Class	class	`MaintenanceRequirement` is a `Requirement` to carry out one or several maintenance actions.	S5000F Requirement
`MaintenanceWorkOrderSource`	Interface	extend	`MaintenanceWorkOrderSource` is an <<extend>> interface that allows to define the sources for `WorkOrders`.	S5000F Maintenance Work Order Source
`MajorComponent`	Class	relationship	`MajorComponent` is a <<relationship>> declaring that a `SerializedHardwarePart` is of special importance within a `SerializedProductVariant` and therefore needs special tracking. **Note** A `MajorComponent` is typically an item that, though embedded in a `Product`, can be considered a `Product` of its own and can be tracked or managed separately. **Example** – engine – landing gear	S5000F Serialized Product Variant
`ManagedFleet`	Class	relationship	`ManagedFleet` is a <<relationship>> that allows to associate a `FleetManager` to the `Fleet` that it manages during a specific period of time.	S5000F Fleet Definition

Class name	Type	Stereotype	Definition	UoF
ManageServiceRequest	Class	exchange	ManageServiceRequest is an <<exchange>> that represents a message associated with a use case (UC51410) providing the necessary information to address the response to a service request.	S5000F Use Cases
Material	Class	class	Material is a solid substance that can be refined in a manufacturing process. **Example** – copper – plastic – sheet metal	S5000F Supply Item
MaterialContainingItem	Interface	extend	MaterialContainingItem is an <<extend>> interface that allows to associate materials that they contain to the items implementing it.	S5000F Contained Materials
MeasurementPoint	Class	class	MeasurementPoint is a <<class>> that represents a measured value recorded for the associated item.	CDM UoF Measurement Point
MeasurementPointItem	Interface	extend	MeasurementPointItem is an <<extend>> interface that provides its associated data model to those classes that implement it.	CDM UoF Measurement Point
Message	Class	class	Message is a <<class>> that represents the collection of information brought together by a message sender for the purpose of communicating it to another party.	CDM UoF Message
MessageContent	Class	exchange	MessageContent is a <<exchange>> definition that represents the collection of information that is the subject of the Message.	CDM UoF Message
MessageContext	Class	relationship	MessageContext is a <<relationship>> between a Message and the context for which it is being provided. **Example** – Contract – Product – Project	CDM UoF Message
MessageContextItem	Interface	select	MessageContextItem is a <<select>> interface that identifies items which can be selected as the context for a Message.	CDM UoF Message

Applicable to: All

Class name	Type	Stereotype	Definition	UoF
`MessageParty`	Class	relationship	`MessageParty` is a `<<relationship>>` between a `Message` and a stakeholder for the `Message`.	CDM UoF Message
`MessagePartyItem`	Interface	select	`MessagePartyItem` is a `<<select>>` interface that identifies items which can be selected as the party for a `Message`.	CDM UoF Message

`MessageRelationship`	Class	relationship	`MessageRelationship` is a `<<relationship>>` where one `Message` relates to another `Message`.
			
			Example
			  – One `Message` is a reply to another `Message`
			  – One `Message` is an update to another `Message`
				CDM UoF Message

`ModifyFleetTask`	Class	exchange	`ModifyFleetTask` is an `<<exchange>>` that represents a message associated with a use case (UC51103) providing the necessary information required to modify a fleet task.	S5000F Use Cases
`MonitorEquipmentPerformance`	Class	exchange	`MonitorEquipmentPerformance` is an `<<exchange>>` that represents a message associated with a use case (UC50301) providing the necessary information to be able to monitor the performance of an equipment.	S5000F Use Cases
`MonitorObsolescence`	Class	exchange	`MonitorObsolescence` is an `<<exchange>>` that represents a message associated with a use case (UC51004) providing the necessary information to monitor possible obsolescence's and prepare for them.	S5000F Use Cases
`Movement`	Class	class	`Movement` represents the act of autonomously changing the physical location or position of a `SerializedProductVariant`. **Note** The `Movement` of a `SerializedProductVariant` must be autonomous but not necessarily self-propelled. The flight of a glider and the orbiting of a satellite are considered movements. **Note** The transport of a `SerializedProductVariant` by another item cannot be considered a movement, as the `Movement` is performed by the `TransportingAsset` that transports it.	S5000F Operational Period

Class name	Type	Stereotype	Definition	UoF
			Example – Aircraft flying from Madrid to Rome. – Orbiting of a satellite – Robot moving to a different position. – Ship sailing from London to New York. – Train driving from Paris to Munich.	
MovementLeg	Class	class	MovementLeg is a class representing one of the individual displacements performed during a Movement, which will be at least one MovementLeg. **Note** A characteristic of a MovementLeg is that there is a physical Interruption of the Movement at the end of the MovementLeg, which can be followed by further MovementLeg(s) to complete the Movement. **Note** A Movement that is uninterrupted would only have one single MovementLeg. **Example** – A flight from Madrid to Singapore, stopping at Dubai, has two movement legs: Madrid-Dubai and Dubai-Singapore.	S5000F Operational Period
MovementLegDelay	Class	class	MovementLegDelay is a class representing a delay that occurred during a travelLeg.	S5000F Operational Period
MovementLegPosition	Class	relationship	MovementLegPosition is a <<relationship>> that defines at which point in space a Product was at a certain moment during a MovementLeg.	S5000F Operational Period
MRONetwork	Class	class	MRONetwork is an Infrastructure consisting of Maintenance, Repair and Overhaul (MRO) facilities. **Note** The different facilities do not need to be in a same location, but can be spread world-wide. **Example** – aircraft overhaul center	S5000F Infrastructure

Class name	Type	Stereotype	Definition	UoF
			– equipment repair shop – shipyard	
NestedAllowedProductConfiguration	Class	relationship	NestedAllowedProductConfiguration is a <<relationship>> that defines that one AllowedProductConfiguration includes a subordinate AllowedProductConfiguration.	CDM UoFProduct Design Configuration
NestedProductVariant	Class	relationship	NestedProductVariant is a <<relationship>> that defines that one ProductVariant includes a subordinate ProductVariant.	CDM UoF Product Design Configuration
NestedSerializedProductVariant	Class	relationship	NestedSerializedProductVariant is a <<relationship>> that that defines that one SerializedProductVariant includes a subordinate SerializedProductVariant.	S5000F Serialized Product Variant
NonAvailabilityAttribution	Interface	select	NonAvailabilityAttribution is a <<select>> interface that allows to associate a NonAvailability to the underlying responsible for the non-availability.	S5000F Availability
NonAvailabilityCause	Class	class	NonAvailabilityCause is a <class>> that describes why a Availability was not achieved at a certain date.	S5000F Availability
NonAvailabilityCauseItem	Interface	select	NonAvailabilityCauseItem is a <<select>> interface that allow to point out the root cause for a non-availability.	S5000F Availability
NonConformanceData	Class	attributeGroup	NonConformanceData is an <<attributeGroup>> that collects information on how the EffectiveOnProductConfigurationItem does not comply with the requirements of its usage.	CDM UoFProduct Design Configuration
NotifyUnacceptableConditionDisposal	Class	exchange	NotifyUnacceptableConditionDisposal is an <<exchange>> that represents a message associated with a use case (UC51610) allowing to report the need for disposal of an item due to unacceptable conditions, usually in the context of a Warranty claim.	S5000F Use Cases
ObservedFaultSymptom	Class	class	ObservedFaultSymptom is a <<class>> that represents an indication of the existence of a Fault by means of physical observation.	S5000F Actual Fault Indication

Class name	Type	Stereotype	Definition	UoF
ObsolescenceItem	Interface	select	ObsolescenceItem is a <<select>> interface that allows to define an item to which an ObsolescenceRequirement can apply.	S5000F Obsolescence Management Candidates
ObsolescenceParameter	Class	class	ObsolescenceParameter is a class representing a criterion that allows to evaluate whether an ObsolescenceRequirement has been met. **Example** – No longer manufactured – Older than ten years	S5000F Obsolescence Management Candidates
ObsolescencePlanning	Class	exchange	ObsolescencePlanning is an <<exchange>> that represents a message associated with a use case (UC51001) providing the necessary information to plan for the obsolescence of an item.	S5000F Use Cases
ObsolescenceRequirement	Class	class	ObsolescenceRequirement is a Requirement that indicates when an item becomes obsolete. **Example** – Seek replacement every five years or when supplier informs that item is discontinued.	S5000F Requirement
OpeningTimes	Class	attributeGroup	OpeningTimes is an <<attributeGroup>> that defines the times at which a certain address is open to the public.	S5000F Location and Locator
OperatingBase	Class	class	OperatingBase is a Facility that is mainly established for providing support for operations. **Example** – airfield – garage – harbor	S5000F Operating Base
OperatingBaseCapacity	Class	relationship	OperatingBaseCapacity is a <<relationship>> that identifies the capacity of an OperatingBase to allow the operation of a specific ProductVariant. **Example** – 2 buses	S5000F Operating Base

Class name	Type	Stereotype	Definition	UoF
			– 8 cars	
`OperatingLocationType`	Class	class	`OperatingLocationType` is a `<<class>>` that represents the definition of the nature of the environment in which a product will be operated.	CDM UoFProduct Usage Context
`OperationalActivity`	Class	class	`OperationalActivity` is an Activity associated to the operation of a SerializedProduct.	S5000F Reportable Activity
`OperationalApproval`	Class	class	`OperationalApproval` is a class that represents the authorization to a `SerializedProductVariant` for a specific mode of operation. **Example** – `Area` Navigation (RNAV) – Autonomous approach – Cargo – Extended Operations (ETOPS) – Passenger transport	S5000F Operational Period
`OperationalEvent`	Class	class	`OperationalEvent` is a class representing an `Event` during the `SerializedProductVariant` operation that can have an impact on the operation itself, on maintenance, or on safety.	S5000F Operational Event
`OperationalEventMessage`	Class	class	`OperationalEventMessage` is a message, failure code or acoustic or visual warning that occurred during an `OperationalEvent`.	S5000F Operational Event
`OperationalEventOperator`	Class	relationship	`OperationalEventOperator` is a `<<relationship>>` that allows to associate an `OperationalEvent` to the `Party` that was operating the `ProductVariant` at that moment in time.	S5000F Operational Event
`OperationalMode`	Class	class	`OperationalMode` represents the actual usage mode of a `SerializedProductVariant` during a specific `OperationalPeriod`. **Note** A same `OperationalRole` can have different `OperationalModes` associated to it (scheduled, unscheduled, passenger or cargo transport, dual/solo training, etc.)	S5000F Operational Period

Class name	Type	Stereotype	Definition	UoF
			Note Can be used to provide European Coordination Centre for Accident and Incident Reporting Systems (ECCAIRS) information. **Example** – non-scheduled international passenger transport – scheduled cargo transport	
`OperationalModeStatus`	Class	attributeGroup	`OperationalModeStatus` is an `<<attributeGroup>>` describing the mode of operation that is associated to a `LogBookEntry`. **Example** – ETOPS (for aviation) – full power	S5000F Logbook
`OperationalMoment`	Interface	extend	`OperationalMoment` is an `<<extend>>` interface that allows to associate an operational moment to other items.	S5000F Operational Period
`OperationalMomentItem`	Interface	select	`OperationalMomentItem` is a `<<select>>` interface that allows linking to a specific operational moment, such as an operating period, movement or travel leg.	S5000F Operational Period
`OperationalPeriod`	Class	class	`OperationalPeriod` is a class that defines the characteristics of a time frame during which a `SerializedProductVariant` was operated.	S5000F Operational Period
`OperationalPeriodOperator`	Class	relationship	`OperationalPeriodOperator` is a `<<relationship>>` that defines which `Party` has carried out the operation during an `OperationalPeriod`.	S5000F Operational Period
`OperationalPeriodRelationship`	Class	relationship	`OperationalPeriodRelationship` is a `<<relationship>>` that defines the association between two different `OperationalPeriods`. **Example** – after – before – simultaneous to	S5000F Operational Period

Class name	Type	Stereotype	Definition	UoF
OperationalRequirement	Class	class	OperationalRequirement is a Requirement to perform a specific operation with a Product.	S5000F Fleet Planning and Product Assignment
OperationalRequirementsPlanning	Class	relationship	OperationalRequirementsPlanning is a <<relationship>> that relates an OperationalRquirement to the FleetPlanning during one or several OperationalPeriods.	S5000F Fleet Planning and Product Assignment
OperationalRole	Class	class	OperationalRole defines the capabilities that a product must be able to provide so as to perform a specific task or mission as part of its operation.	S5000F Operational Roles
OperationalTime	Class	attributeGroup	OperationalTime is an <<attributeGroup>> that can be associated to an OperationalTimeItem.	S5000F Operational Times
OperationalTimeItem	Interface	extend	OperationalTimeItem is an <<extend>> interface that can have operational time information associated to it.	S5000F Operational Times
Operator	Interface	select	Operator is a <<select interface>> that represents the entities that operate one or several SerializedProductVariants.	S5000F Operator
OperatorOrganization	Class	class	OperatorOrganization is an Organization that operates one or several SerializedProductVariants.	S5000F Operator
OperatorPerson	Class	class	OperatorPerson is a Person that operates one or several ProductVariants. **Example** – drone pilot – truck driver	S5000F Operator
Organization	Class	class	Organization is a <<class>> that represents an administrative structure with a particular purpose belonging to a legal entity. **Example** – government department – international agency – company	S5000F Specializations

Class name	Type	Stereotype	Definition	UoF
OrganizationalBreakdownStructure	Interface	extend	OrganizationalBreakdownStructure is an <<extend>> interface that allows to relate an organizational structure to a Project or Contract.	S5000F Organizational Breakdown Structure
OrganizationalBreakdownStructureRevision	Class	class	OrganizationalBreakdownStructureRevision is an class that represents a specific revision of an organizational breakdown structure.	S5000F Organizational Breakdown Structure
OrganizationalRole	Class	relationship	OrganizationalRole is a <<relationship>> that defines the role that a Party performs within a project or contract-specific organizational structure.	S5000F Organizational Breakdown Structure
OrganizationOperationsApproval	Class	relationship	OrganizationOperationsApproval is a <<relationship>> that identifies the authorization of an OperatorOrganization to operate a specific ProductVariant by a specific Organization for a specific period of time. **Example** – Municipal authorization to operate a bus line.	S5000F Operator
OtherFacility	Class	class	OtherFacility is a Facility that has no specific classification.	S5000F Facility
ParkingFacility	Class	class	ParkingFacility is a Facility used to park SerializedProductVariants that are mobile and can move beween different Locations.	S5000F Facility
PartAction	Class	class	PartAction is an action performed on a part as a result of a MaintenanceActivity. **Example** – cleanse – erase (software or data) – install – load (software or data) – remove	S5000F Equipment

Class name	Type	Stereotype	Definition	UoF
PartAsDesigned	Class	class	`PartAsDesigned` is a `<<class>>` that represents the definitional information for an artifact fulfilling a set of requirements, which can be produced or realized.	CDM UoF Part Definition
PartAsDesignedPartsList	Class	class	`PartAsDesignedPartsList` is a `<<class>>` that represents the definitional information for the collection of `PartAsDesignedPartsListEntry` included in the `assembly` of the parent `PartAsDesigned`. **Note** `PartAsDesignedPartsList` is typically referred to as a Bill of `Material` (BOM).	CDM UoF Part Definition
PartAsDesignedPartsListEntry	Class	class	`PartAsDesignedPartsListEntry` is a `<<class>>` that represents the inclusion of a `PartAsDesigned` in a `PartAsDesignedPartsListRevision`.	CDM UoF Part Definition
PartAsDesignedPartsListRelationship	Class	relationship	`PartAsDesignedPartsListRelationship` is a `<<relationship>>` where one `PartAsDesignedPartsList` relates to another `PartAsDesignedPartsList`.	CDM UoF Part Definition
PartAsDesignedPartsListRevision	Class	class	`PartAsDesignedPartsListRevision` is a `<<class>>` representing an iteration applied to a `PartAsDesignedPartsList`.	CDM UoF Part Definition
PartInPool	Class	relationship	`PartInPool` is a `<<relationship>>` that indicates the period during which a part has been in a defined `Pool` of parts.	S5000F Warehouse and Spare Pool
PartInWarehouse	Class	relationship	`PartInWarehouse` is a `<<relationship>>` that defines the time that a `SerializedHardwarePart` has been stored in a `Warehouse`.	S5000F Warehouse and Spare Pool
PartOwner	Class	relationship	`PartOwner` is a `<<relationship>>` that allows to associate a `SerializedHardwarePart` with its owning `Party`.	S5000F Part As Realized
Party	Interface	select	`Party` is an `<<interface>>` representing an entity that is capable of signing a contract or carrying out actions by itself without being instructed to do so.	S5000F Party

Class name	Type	Stereotype	Definition	UoF
			Example – organization – person	
`PartyAddress`	Class	relationship	`PartyAddress` is a <<relationship>> that defines the association between a `Party` and an Address.	S5000F Party
`PartyContactData`	Class	attributeGroup	`PartyContactData` is an <<attributeGroup>> that provides the contact details for a `Party`.	S5000F Party
`PartyItem`	Interface	extend	`PartyItem` is an <<extend>> interface that allows to provide additional capabilities to `Organizations` and `Persons`.	S5000F Party
`PartyRelationship`	Class	relationship	`PartyRelationship` is a <<relationship>> existing between two Parties (organizations or people).	S5000F Party
`Penalty`	Class	class	`Penalty` is a <<class>> that represents a punishment imposed for breaking or not complying with a contract.	S5000F Service Contract Penalty
`PerformanceParameter`	Class	class	`PerformanceParameter` is a <<class>> that represents a metric that if changed, or not fulfilled, can have a major impact on the performance, schedule, cost and/or risk for the `PerformanceParameterItem`.	CDM UoF Performance Parameter
`PerformanceParameterItem`	Interface	extend	`PerformanceParameterItem` is an <<extend>> interface that provides its associated data model to those classes that can have an associated `PerformanceParameter`.	CDM UoF Performance Parameter
`PerformanceParameterRevisio n`	Class	class	`PerformanceParameterRevision` is a <<class>> that represents an iteration applied to a `PerformanceParameter`.	CDM UoF Performance Parameter
`PerformanceParameterValueGr oup`	Class	attributeGroup	`PerformanceParameterValueGroup` is an <<attributeGroup>> that organizes `PerformanceParameter` values for a defined purpose.	CDM UoF Performance Parameter
`Person`	Class	class	`Person` is a living human being.	S5000F Party

Class name	Type	Stereotype	Definition	UoF
PersonCompetence	Class	relationship	PersonCompetence is a <<relationship>> that defines the competences that a Person has acquired.	S5000F Person Competences and Labor Rates
PersonCompetenceItem	Interface	extend	PersonCompetenceItem is an <<extend>> interface that allows to associate a PersonCompetence to a GenericPerson. or an individual.	S5000F Person Competences and Labor Rates
PersonGroup	Class	relationship	PersonGroup is a <<relationship>> that allows to associate a Person to different types of persons.	S5000F Type of Person
PersonOperationsApproval	Class	relationship	PersonOperationsApproval is a <<relationship>> that documents the authorization by an Organization to an OperatorPerson to operate a ProductVariant during a specific period of time. **Example** – driver's license – mariner license – pilot type certificate	S5000F Operator
PlanForTransport	Class	exchange	PlanForTransport is an <<exchange>> that represents a message associated with a use case (UC50606) providing the information required to plan for the transport of assets.	S5000F Use Cases
PlannedItemUpgrade	Class	class	PlannedItemUpgrade is a <<class>> that defines the planning for the upgrade for a ChangeEmbodimentRequirement for one or several items.	S5000F Change Embodiment Strategy
PlannedPartInstallationLocation	Class	relationship	PlannedPartInstallationLocation is a <<relationship>> that allows to indicate which Part was installed or uninstalled at which location on a specific SerializedProductVariant.	S5000F Change Embodiment Planning
PlannedUpgradeTimescales	Class	class	PlannedUpgradeTimescales is a class that defines the planned periods of times during which a PlannedUpgrade will be performed on specific items.	S5000F Change Embodiment Planning

Class name	Type	Stereotype	Definition	UoF
PoliciesAndRegulations	Class	class	PoliciesAndRegulations is a Document that defines mandatory practices for a Project, Product, Contract, Service or major item requiring specific guidelines.	S5000F Policies and Regulations
PoliciesAndRegulationsCompliantItem	Interface	extend	PoliciesAndRegulationsCompliantItem is an <<extend>> interface that allows to associate an item to the PoliciesAndRegulations with which it complies	S5000F Policies and Regulations
Pool	Class	class	Pool is a set of parts that are managed as a functional group and that is shared by different Parties.	S5000F Warehouse and Spare Pool
PoolItem	Interface	select	PoolItem is a <<select>> interface that represents an item that belongs to a pool.	S5000F Warehouse and Spare Pool
PoolOwner	Class	relationship	PoolOwner is a <<relationship>> that defines the ownership ration and period of a Party over a Pool.	S5000F Warehouse and Spare Pool
PoolStockedInWareHouse	Class	relationship	PoolStockedInWareHouse is a <<relationship>> that allows to indicate the Warehouse or Warehouses where a Pool of parts is stocked.	S5000F Warehouse and Spare Pool
PoolUser	Class	relationship	PoolUser is a <<relationship>> that associates a spare Pool with the Parties that are allowed to access and use that SparePool.	S5000F Warehouse and Spare Pool
Port	Class	class	Port is an infrastructure used for the docking of ships.	S5000F Infrastructure
PositionReferencingItem	Interface	extend	PositionReferencingItem is an <<extend>> interface that allows to document the LocalPositions of an item.	S5000F Local Position
PowerGrid	Class	class	PowerGrid is an Infrastructure used to generate, transport and distribute power.	S5000F Infrastructure
PrepareProductForFleetTask	Class	exchange	PrepareProductForFleetTask is an <<exchange>> that represents a message associated with a use case (UC51106) allowing the information required to prepare the execution of a fleet task to be provided.	S5000F Use Cases

Class name	Type	Stereotype	Definition	UoF
PressureSensor	Class	class	PressureSensor is a SensorType that measures pressure.	S5000F Serialized Product Health Monitoring
PriceBreakData	Class	attributeGroup	PriceBreakData is an <<attributeGroup>> that details price information for HardwarePartAsDesignedCommerceData.	S5000F Warehouse and Spare Pool
Product	Class	class	Product is <<class>> that represents a family of items which share the same underlying design purpose. **Example** – Aegis Class Destroyer – Airbus A340 – Ford Fusion – iPhone 7 – Pegasus engine – Stryker	S5000F Specializations
ProductParameterAtOperationalEvent	Class	class	ProductParameterAtOperationalEvent provides the value of a Product parameter when an operational event occurred.	S5000F Operational Event
ProductUsagePhase	Class	class	ProductUsagePhase is a distinct period of time during which a Product, ProductVariant or SerializedProductVariant will be used in a specific way, which is different from any other ProductUsagePhase. **Example** – cruise – immersion – take-off	S5000F Product Usage Phase
ProductUsagePhaseHierarchicalRelationship	Class	relationship	ProductUsagePhaseHierarchicalRelationship is a <<relationship>> that allows to define a hierarchical association between two ProductUsagePhases.	S5000F Product Usage Phase
ProductUsagePhaseItem	Interface	extend	ProductUsagePhaseItem is an <<extend>> interface which associates a ProductUsagePhase to the item(s) that have that type of usage.	S5000F Product Usage Phase

Class name	Type	Stereotype	Definition	UoF
ProductUsagePhaseRelationship	Class	relationship	ProductUsagePhaseRelationship is a <<relationship>> that defines how two ProductUsagePhases are associated with each other.	S5000F Product Usage Phase
ProductUsagePhaseSequentialRelationship	Class	relationship	ProductUsagePhaseSequentialRelationship is a <<relationship>> that allows to define a sequential association between two ProductUsagePhases.	S5000F Product Usage Phase
ProductVariant	Class	class	ProductVariant is a <<class>> that defines a member of a Product family which is configured for a specific purpose and is made available to the market. **Note** A product variant is often known as a model. **Example** – Boeing 787-800 versus 787-900 – Ford Fusion S versus SE versus SEL	S5000F Specializations
ProductVariantMaintenance	Class	relationship	ProductVariantMaintenance is a <<relationship>> allowing to associate a MaintenanceOrganisation (relating) to the ProductVariants it can maintain (related).	S5000F Maintenance Organization
ProductVariantSupportedByPool	Class	relationship	ProductVariantSupportedByPool is a <<relationship>> that indicates that a ProductVariant is supported by a defined part Pool.	S5000F Warehouse and Spare Pool
Project	Class	class	Project is a <<class>> that represents the overall set of Integrated Product Support (IPS) activities defined for a Product. **Note** Project is often referred to as an IPS program.	CDM UoF Product and Project
ProjectContract	Class	relationship	ProjectContract is a <<relationship>> that establishes an association between a Project and a Contract.	CDM UoF Product and Project
ProjectRelationship	Class	relationship	ProjectRelationShip is a <<relationship>> that defines an association between two different Projects.	S5000F Project and Contract

Class name	Type	Stereotype	Definition	UoF
ProvideActivityPlanning	Class	exchange	ProvideActivityPlanning is an <<exchange>> that represents a message associated with a use case (UC51405) allowing another party to be provided with the list of planned activities.	S5000F Use Cases
ProvideAsAllowedConfigurati on	Class	exchange	ProvideAsAllowedConfiguration is an <<exchange>> that represents a message associated with a use case (UC51302) allowing another party to be provided with the set of configurations that the serialized Product variant is allowed to have, to ensure safe operation.	S5000F Use Cases
ProvideAsDeliveredConfigura tion	Class	exchange	ProvideAsDeliveredConfiguration is an <<exchange>> that represents a message associated with a use case (UC51301) allowing another party with the configuration information of a delivered SerializedProductVariant to be provided.	S5000F Use Cases
ProvideAsDesiredConfigurati on	Class	exchange	ProvideAsDesiredConfiguration is an <<exchange>> that represents a message associated with a use case (UC51305) allowing to ask another party for a specific (operational) configuration (eg, to perform a certain mission).	S5000F Use Cases
ProvideCBS	Class	exchange	ProvideCBS is an <<exchange>> that represents a message associated with a use case (UC50701) allowing a cost breakdown structure to be provided to a different party.	S5000F Use Cases
ProvideContractualInformati on	Class	exchange	ProvideContractualInformation is an <<exchange>> that represents a message associated with a use case (UC51401) allowing information about a contract to be provided.	S5000F Use Cases
ProvideCostBreakdown	Class	exchange	ProvideCostBreakdown is an <<exchange>> that represents a message associated with a use case (UC51403) that provides cost breakdown information.	S5000F Use Cases
ProvideCustomerModification	Class	exchange	ProvideCustomerModification is an <<exchange>> that represents a message associated with a use case (UC51304) allowing information about a customer-driven modification to be provided.	S5000F Use Cases

Class name	Type	Stereotype	Definition	UoF
ProvideDisposalLocationInformation	Class	exchange	ProvideDisposalLocationInformation is an <<exchange>> that represents a message associated with a use case (UC51503) allowing the location information of an item to be indicated. **Note** This use case has been renumbered because it has changed chapter (was formerly UC51409).	S5000F Use Cases
ProvideDocumentationTraceability	Class	exchange	ProvideDocumentationTraceability is an <<exchange>> that represents a message associated with a use case (UC51415) ensuring the traceability of documentation.	S5000F Use Cases
ProvideLaborRates	Class	exchange	ProvideLaborRates is an <<exchange>> that represents a message associated with a use case (UC51414) allowing labor rates from one party to be provided to another.	S5000F Use Cases
ProvideLocationInformation	Class	exchange	ProvideLocationInformation is an <<exchange>> that represents a message associated with a use case (UC51409) allowing the location information of an item to be indicated.	S5000F Use Cases
ProvideNonPredefinedInformation	Class	exchange	ProvideNonPredefinedInformation is an <<exchange>> that represents a message associated with a use case (UC51502) allowing non-structured information not contemplated by the specification itself (eg, photos, videos, built-in-test files, etc) to be transferred. **Note** This use case has been renumbered (was formerly UC51502).	S5000F Use Cases
ProvideObsolescenceAlert	Class	exchange	ProvideObsolescenceAlert is an <<exchange>> that represents a message associated with a use case (UC51006) providing the capability to inform other parties about an upcoming obsolescence.	S5000F Use Cases
ProvideOperationalConfiguration	Class	exchange	ProvideOperationalConfiguration is an <<exchange>> that represents a message associated with a use case (UC51303) allowing to provide the operational configuration of a serialized product variant at a specific moment in time.	S5000F Use Cases

Class name	Type	Stereotype	Definition	UoF
`ProvideOrganizationalBreakdown`	Class	exchange	`ProvideOrganizationalBreakdown` is an <<exchange>> that represents a message associated with a use case (UC51404) allowing an OBS to be provided to another party.	S5000F Use Cases
`ProvideProjectSpecificValues`	Class	exchange	`ProvideProjectSpecificValues` is an <<exchange>> that represents a message associated with a use case (UC51501) allowing project-specific values for a specific purpose to be exchanged. **Note** This use case has ben renumbered (was formerly UC51501).	S5000F Use Cases
`ProvideSpecialSafetyInstructions`	Class	exchange	`ProvideSpecialSafetyInstructions` is an <<exchange>> that represents a message associated with a use case (UC50503) allowing special safety instructions to be transmitted to the operators of a Product, in the event of safety issues.	S5000F Use Cases
`ProvideStatusReport`	Class	exchange	`ProvideStatusReport` is an <<exchange>> that represents a message associated with a use case (UC51408) allowing a report in electronic format to be provided.	S5000F Use Cases
`ProvideWorkBreakdown`	Class	exchange	`ProvideWorkBreakdown` is an <<exchange>> that represents a message associated with a use case (UC51402) that allows a WBS to be transferred.	S5000F Use Cases
`RealizedPart`	Interface	select	`RealizedPart` is a <<select>> interface that identifies which items can be used as an `InstalledPart`.	CDM UoF Serialized Product Variant Configuration
`ReallocateFleetOrProduct`	Class	exchange	`ReallocateFleetOrProduct` is an <<exchange>> that represents a message associated with a use case (UC51506) allowing to report the re(allocation) of a `Fleet` or `Product` to a different operator, owner or operating location.	S5000F Use Cases
`RecordedFaultSymptom`	Class	class	`RecordedFaultSymptom` is a <<class>> that represents an indication of the existence of a `Fault` that has been recorded by a monitoring device.	S5000F Actual Fault Indication

Class name	Type	Stereotype	Definition	UoF
`RecordHealthData`	Class	exchange	`RecordHealthData` is an `<<exchange>>` that represents a message associated with a use case (UC50901) allowing health and monitoring data for a `SerializedProductVariant` to be transferred.	S5000F Use Cases
`RecoveredItem`	Class	relationship	`RecoveredItem` is a `<<relationship>>` that allows to identify the items that have been recovered as part of an `ItemDisposalOperation`.	S5000F Recovered Item
`RecoveredMaterialOrSubstances`	Interface	select	`RecoveredMaterialOrSubstances` is a `<<select>>` interface that allows to identify the items, materials and substances that can be recovered from the waste.	S5000F Recovered Material or Substances
`RecoverProductAfterFleetTask`	Class	exchange	`RecoverProductAfterFleetTask` is an `<<exchange>>` that represents a message associated with a use case (UC51107) allowing a record of actions taken to recover a serialized Product after executing a fleet task to be reported.	S5000F Use Cases
`Rectangle`	Class	compoundAttribute	`Rectangle` is a `<<class>>` representing a geometrical plane figure with four straight sides and four right angles, especially one with unequal adjacent sides, in contrast to a square.	S5000F Compound Attributes
`ReferencedDigitalFile`	Class	relationship	`ReferencedDigitalFile` is a `<<relationship>` that allows an item to refer to a `DigitalFile`.	CDM UoF Digital File
`ReferencedDocument`	Class	relationship	`ReferencedDocument` is a `<<relationship>>` where one `DocumentReferencingItem` relates to a `DocumentItem`.	CDM UoFDocument
`ReferencedPositionItem`	Interface	select	`ReferencedPositionItem` is a `<<select>>` interface that represents the item where a `LocalPosition` is located.	S5000F Local Position
`ReleasedDataSetAssociatedWith`	Class	relationship	`ReleasedDataSetAssociatedWith` is a `<<relationship>>` that allows to associate `DataSetAsReleased` with an item.	S5000F Data Sets
`ReleasedDataSetItem`	Interface	select	`ReleasedDataSetItem` is a `<<select>>` interface that allows to associate items to a `DataSetAsReleased`.	S5000F Data Sets

Class name	Type	Stereotype	Definition	UoF
Remark	Class	attributeGroup	Remark is an <<attributeGroup>> that provides additional information about the associated item. **Note** A remark can be a personal opinion ("I prefer more onions in my soup") or it can be a technical fact ("The manufacturer recommends heating the soup to 45 degrees Celsius").	CDM UoF Remark
RemarkItem	Interface	extend	RemarkItem is an <<extend>> interface that provides its associated data model to those classes that implement it.	CDM UoF Remark
Report	Class	class	Report is a Document that provides information about the execution of certain activities or significant events that have taken place. **Note** The relationship of Report with the subject of the Report (eg, a Contract) is performed through the DocumentAssignmentItem <<interface>> that is inherited from the Document class. **Example** – cost report – progress report – technical report	S5000F Report
ReportableActivity	Class	class	ReportableActivity is an activity that is part of work item that is deemed to be of sufficient importance as to be reported. **Example** – maintenance action	S5000F Reportable Activity
ReportableItem	Interface	select	ReportableItem is a <<select interface>> representing everything that is worth reporting. **Example** – incurred cost – maintenance activity – operational event	S5000F Report

Class name	Type	Stereotype	Definition	UoF
ReportableMetric	Class	class	ReportableMetric is a measure of a specific characteristic that can evolve over time and is reported periodically for program or contract management purposes.	S5000F Reportable Metric
ReportableMetricItem	Interface	extend	ReportableMetricItem is an <<extend>> interface that allows to assign ReportableMetrics to different items.	S5000F Reportable Metric
ReportAvailability	Class	exchange	ReportAvailability is an <<exchange>> that represents a message associated with a use case (UC50304) allowing the availability of a serialized product item and the root causes for non-availability to be reported.	S5000F Use Cases
ReportContext	Class	relationship	ReportContext is a <<relationship>> that allows a Report to be associated to its context.	S5000F Report
ReportContextItem	Interface	select	ReportContextItem is a <<select>> interface that allows to indicate on which items a Report provides information.	S5000F Report
ReportContractCosts	Class	exchange	ReportContractCosts is an <<exchange>> that represents a message associated with a use case (UC51407) allowing costs incurred against a program to be reported.	S5000F Use Cases
ReportDisposalCosts	Class	exchange	ReportDisposalCosts is an <<exchange>> that represents a message associated with a use case (UC51609) allowing cost information about a disposal to be reported.	S5000F Use Cases
ReportEfficiencyAndPerformance	Class	exchange	ReportEfficiencyAndPerformance is an <<exchange>> that represents a message associated with a use case (UC50309) allowing efficiency and performance metrics to be reported.	S5000F Use Cases
ReportEnvironmentalDataToAuthorities	Class	exchange	ReportEnvironmentalDataToAuthorities is an <<exchange>> that represents a message associated with a use case (UC51602) allowing consumption and emission information to be reported to the authorities, not only for the Product but also for the facilities or infrastructure required to support the Product.	S5000F Use Cases

Class name	Type	Stereotype	Definition	UoF
ReportFacilities	Class	exchange	ReportFacilities is an <<exchange>> that represents a message associated with a use case (UC50605) providing information about existing facilities.	S5000F Use Cases
ReportFaultDiagnostics	Class	exchange	ReportFaultDiagnostics is an <<exchange>> that represents a message associated with a use case (UC50311) allowing fault diagnostics data to be provided.	S5000F Use Cases
ReportFleetAvailability	Class	exchange	ReportFleetAvailability is an <<exchange>> that represents the availability of a Fleet or a SerializedProductVariant.	S5000F Use Cases
ReportHelpDeskTickets	Class	exchange	ReportHelpDeskTickets is an <<exchange>> that represents a message associated with a use case (UC51209) allowing help desk tickets to be created.	S5000F Use Cases
ReportInfrastructureAvailability	Class	exchange	ReportInfrastructureAvailability is an <<exchange>> that represents a message associated with a use case (UC51504) allowing information about the current, past and future availability of an infrastructure to be provided.	S5000F Use Cases
ReportingParty	Interface	select	ReportingParty is a <<select>> interface that allows to define the author of a Report.	S5000F Report
ReportInServiceCosts	Class	exchange	ReportInServiceCosts is an <<exchange>> that represents a message associated with a use case (UC50705) that allows costs incurred during the in-service phase to be reported.	S5000F Use Cases
ReportInventory	Class	exchange	ReportInventory is an <<exchange>> that represents a message associated with a use case (UC50601) that provides the inventory information for a warehouse or spares pool.	S5000F Use Cases
ReportLogisticResponseTime	Class	exchange	ReportLogisticResponseTime is an <<exchange>> that represents a message associated with a use case (UC50604) providing the response time that is achieved when responding to a logistic request.	S5000F Use Cases

Class name	Type	Stereotype	Definition	UoF
ReportMaintenanceCosts	Class	exchange	ReportMaintenanceCosts is an <<exchange>> that represents a message associated with a use case (UC50702) providing the information required to report on the costs associated to maintenance.	S5000F Use Cases
ReportMaintenancePerformed	Class	exchange	ReportMaintenancePerformed is an <<exchange>> that represents a message associated with a use case (UC50403) providing the information required to report on the maintenance that has been performed on a Product.	S5000F Use Cases
ReportManufacturerMaintenanceSchedule	Class	exchange	ReportManufacturerMaintenanceSchedule is an <<exchange>> that represents a message associated with a use case (UC50401) providing the information required to report on the maintenance schedule defined by the manufacturer of a Product.	S5000F Use Cases
ReportMissionCapability	Class	exchange	ReportMissionCapability is an <<exchange>> that represents a message associated with a use case (UC50308) providing the information required to report on whether an individual Product is or not mission cable.	S5000F Use Cases
ReportModificationCosts	Class	exchange	ReportModificationCosts is an <<exchange>> that represents a message associated with a use case (UC50704) providing the information required to report on the cost of a modification to the Product.	S5000F Use Cases
ReportModificationImpactOnDisposal	Class	exchange	ReportModificationImpactOnDisposal is an <<exchange>> that represents a message associated with a use case (UC51603) allowing the potential environmental and disposal impact of a Product modification to be reported.	S5000F Use Cases
ReportNewModifications	Class	exchange	ReportNewModifications is an <<exchange>> that represents a message associated with a use case (UC50405) providing the information required to report on new modifications to the Product.	S5000F Use Cases
ReportOperationalCosts	Class	exchange	ReportOperationalCosts is an <<exchange>> that represents a message associated with a use case (UC50703) providing the information required to report on the operational costs of a Product.	S5000F Use Cases

Class name	Type	Stereotype	Definition	UoF
ReportParty	Class	relationship	ReportParty is a <<relationship>> that allows a ReportingParty to be associated to a Report.	S5000F Report
ReportProductDisposal	Class	exchange	ReportProductDisposal is an <<exchange>> that represents a message associated with a use case (UC51606) allowing information about the disposal of a Product to be reported.	S5000F Use Cases
ReportProductPerformance	Class	exchange	ReportProductPerformance is an <<exchange>> that represents a message associated with a use case (UC50404) providing the information required to report on the performance of a Product.	S5000F Use Cases
ReportProductUserMaintenanceProgram	Class	exchange	ReportProductUserMaintenanceProgram is an <<exchange>> that represents a message associated with a use case (UC50402) providing the information required to report on the maintenance program provided by the Original Equipment Manufacturer (OEM) of the Product or by the operator.	S5000F Use Cases
ReportSafetyIssue	Class	exchange	ReportSafetyIssue is an <<exchange>> that represents a message associated with a use case (UC50501) providing the information required to report an issue impacting the Product safety.	S5000F Use Cases
ReportSafetyWarning	Class	exchange	ReportSafetyWarning is an <<exchange>> that represents a message associated with a use case (UC50502) providing the information required to send out a safety warning to the operators of a Product.	S5000F Use Cases
ReportShelfLife	Class	exchange	ReportShelfLife is an <<exchange>> that represents a message associated with a use case (UC50602) providing the information required to report on the shelf life of parts on stock.	S5000F Use Cases
ReportShopFindings	Class	exchange	ReportShopFindings is an <<exchange>> that represents a message associated with a use case (UC50407) providing the information required to report the results from a workshop when repairing a unit that has been sent in for repair.	S5000F Use Cases

Class name	Type	Stereotype	Definition	UoF
ReportSLACompliance	Class	exchange	ReportSLACompliance is an <<exchange>> that represents a message associated with a use case (UC51406) providing the information required to report the compliance with an SLA.	S5000F Use Cases
ReportSoftwareConfiguration	Class	exchange	ReportSoftwareConfiguration is an <<exchange>> that represents a message associated with a use case (UC51207) providing the information required to report on the configuration of software.	S5000F Use Cases
ReportSoftwareError	Class	exchange	ReportSoftwareError is an <<exchange>> that represents a a message associated with a use case (UC51202) providing the information required to report a software bug.	S5000F Use Cases
ReportSoftwareInstallation	Class	exchange	ReportSoftwareInstallation is an <<exchange>> that represents a message associated with a use case (UC51206) providing the information required to report that a piece of software has been installed on an item.	S5000F Use Cases
ReportSparesAndPool	Class	exchange	ReportSparesAndPool is an <<exchange>> that represents a message associated with a use case (UC50603) providing the information required to report on the spares available in a warehouse or spares pool.	S5000F Use Cases
ReportStructuralDamage	Class	exchange	ReportStructuralDamage is an <<exchange>> that represents a message associated with a use case (UC50408) providing the information required to report any structural damage.	S5000F Use Cases
ReportSWDocumentationErrors	Class	exchange	ReportSWDocumentationErrors is an <<exchange>> that represents a message associated with a use case (UC50501) providing the information required to report errors in the documentation of a software item.	S5000F Use Cases
ReportTechnicalQueries	Class	exchange	ReportTechnicalQueries is an <<exchange>> that represents a message associated with a use case (UC50406) providing the information required to perform a technical query and receive a response.	S5000F Use Cases
ReportTestability	Class	exchange	ReportTestability is an <<exchange>> that represents a message associated with a use case (UC50310) providing the information required to assess the testability of an item.	S5000F Use Cases

Class name	Type	Stereotype	Definition	UoF
ReportTrendsAndFailures	Class	exchange	ReportTrendsAndFailures is an <<exchange>> that represents a message associated with a use case (UC50303) providing the information about failures in order to report failure trends.	S5000F Use Cases
ReportUsageInformation	Class	exchange	ReportUsageInformation is an <<exchange>> that represents a message associated with a use case (UC50902) providing the information about a Product usage.	S5000F Use Cases
ReportValuableItemsFromDisposal	Class	exchange	ReportValuableItemsFromDisposal is an <<exchange>> that represents a message associated with a use case (UC51604) allowing reporting on the valuable items that have been recovered during the disposal of a SerializedProductVariant.	S5000F Use Cases
ReportWasteDisposal	Class	exchange	ReportWasteDisposal is an <<exchange>> that represents a message associated with a use case (UC51608) allowing information about the disposal of waste to be reported.	S5000F Use Cases
RequestItemDisposal	Class	exchange	RequestItemDisposal is an <<exchange>> that represents a message associated with a use case (UC51605) allowing the disposal of a Product or other end item to be requested.	S5000F Use Cases
RequestResource	Class	exchange	RequestResource is an <<exchange>> that represents a message associated with a use case (UC51411) providing the required information to request the usage of a resource.	S5000F Use Cases
RequestSoftwareFeature	Class	exchange	RequestSoftwareFeature is an <<exchange>> that represents a message associated with a use case (UC51201) providing the information required to request a new software feature.	S5000F Use Cases
RequestWasteDisposal	Class	exchange	RequestWasteDisposal is an <<exchange>> that represents a message associated with a use case (UC51607) that allows the disposal of waste or hazardous material to be requested.	S5000F Use Cases
RequiredDisposalPolicy	Class	relationship	RequiredDisposalPolicy is a <<relationship>> that allows to indicate the policies to be applied when disposing of an item.	S5000F Disposal Requirement

Class name	Type	Stereotype	Definition	UoF
RequiredFleetRole	Class	relationship	RequiredFleetRole is a <<relationship>> that allows to define the OperationalRoles that a FleetRequirement must meet.	S5000F Fleet Planning and Product Assignment
RequiredPartStockLevelInPool	Class	relationship	RequiredPartStockLevelInPool is a <<relationship>> that defines the number of parts that must be stored in a Pool.	S5000F Warehouse and Spare Pool
RequiredSafetyAction	Class	class	RequiredSafetyAction is a <<class>> representing the action to be taken as part of a SpecialSafetyInstruction so as to ensure the Product safety.	S5000F Safety
RequiredSafetyActionImplementation	Interface	select	RequiredSafetyActionImplementation is a <<select>> interface that allows to provide traceability between taken a RequiredSafetyAction and the actions effectively implementing it.	S5000F Safety
Requirement	Class	class	Requirement is a documented need that has to be implemented.	S5000F Requirement
RequirementParty	Class	relationship	RequirementParty is a <<relationship>> that associates a Requirement with a Party.	S5000F Requirement
RequirementRelationship	Class	relationship	RequirementRelationship is a <<relationship>> that defines the association between two Requirements.	S5000F Requirement
ResourceItem	Interface	select	ResourceItem is a <<select>> interface representing items whose usage can be requested for a specific period of time and during which they cannot be used by somebody else.	S5000F Resource Usage Request
ResourceRealization	Class	relationship	ResourceRealization is a <<relationship>> where a ResourceSpecification relates to an instance of PartAsDesigned that fulfills the resource specification.	CDM UoF Resource Specification
ResourceSpecification	Class	class	ResourceSpecification is a <<class>> that defines a resource by its characteristics. **Note** ResourceSpecification allows for more generic resource definitions ie, a task/subtask does not need to be changed due to eg, customer specific resource preferences.	CDM UoF Resource Specification

Class name	Type	Stereotype	Definition	UoF
ResourceUsageParty	Class	relationship	ResourceUsageParty is a <<relationship>> that defines which party request which one to use a resource.	S5000F Resource Usage Request
ResourceUsageRequest	Class	class	ResourceUsageRequest is a class representing a demand from a party to use a resource belonging to a different party. **Example** – request for a simulator slot – request for usage of a ship dock	S5000F Resource Usage Request
RespondToUsageInformation	Class	exchange	RespondToUsageInformation is an <<exchange>> that represents a message associated with a use case (UC50903) providing the information required to take action after receiving usage information.	S5000F Use Cases
RetainingPerformance	Class	exchange	RetainingPerformance is an <<exchange>> that represents a message associated with a use case (UC50307) providing the information required to ensure that proper Product performance is maintained.	S5000F Use Cases
RoleCapability	Class	relationship	RoleCapability is a <<relationship>> that defines which product capabilities are provided by a specific OperationalRole.	S5000F Operational Roles
S1000DDataModule	Class	class	S1000DDataModule is a Document that is written in accordance with an S1000D schema.	CDM UoFDocument
S1000DDataModuleIssue	Class	class	S1000DDataModuleIssue is a DocumentIssue that identifies a specific issue of a data module produced in accordance with S1000D.	CDM UoF Document
S1000DPublicationModule	Class	class	S1000DPublicationModule is a Document that identifies a publication published in accordance with S1000D.	CDM UoFDocument
S1000DPublicationModuleIssue	Class	class	S1000DPublicationModuleIssue is a DocumentIssue that identifies a specific issue of a publication module published in accordance with S1000D.	CDM UoF Document
SafetyDocument	Class	class	SafetyDocument is a Document associated to the safety of an item.	S5000F Safety

Class name	Type	Stereotype	Definition	UoF
SafetyIssue	Class	class	SafetyIssue is a SafetyDocument reporting a safety issue associated to the safety of a Product, Service or Part (hardware or software) item. **Note** SafetyIssues are usually generated by a productvariant operator, typically as the result of an (operational) Event. **Note** The organization reporting the SafetyIssue, the relationship with other SafetyIssues, applicability, etc, are inherited from the Document class.	S5000F Safety
SafetyIssueEvent	Class	relationship	SafetyIssueEvent is a <<relationship>> that allows to associate a SafetyIssue to associated Events.	S5000F Safety
SafetyItem	Interface	select	SafetyItem is a <<select>> interface that allows to identify an item to which as SafetyDocument applies.	S5000F Safety
SafetyRequirement	Class	class	SafetyRequirement is a Requirement that has to be applied for safety purposes.	S5000F Requirement
SafetyRequirementsDocument	Class	class	SafetyRequirementsDocument is a SafetyDocument that defines the necessary SafetyRequirements for a specific purpose.	S5000F Safety
SafetyWarning	Class	class	SafetyWarning is a SafetyDocument that provides information about potential safety issues associated to a Product, service or hardware or software items. **Note** SafetyWarnings are usually generated by the Product manufacturer or by legal authorities. **Note** The organization generating the SafetyWarning, relationship with other SafetyIssues or SafetyWarnings, applicability, etc, are inherited from the Document class.	S5000F Safety

Class name	Type	Stereotype	Definition	UoF
`SCORMContentPackage`	Class	class	`SCORMContentPackage` is a specialization of class `Document` and represents a SCORM content package.	S5000F Document
`SecurityClass`	Class	class	`SecurityClass` is a `<<class>>` that identifies a level of confidentiality which can be used to protect something against unauthorized access.	CDM UoF Security Classification
`SecurityClassification`	Class	relationship	`SecurityClassification` is a `<<relationship>>` that associates a given `SecurityClass` with the item that must be protected against unauthorized access or distribution	CDM UoF Security Classification
`SecurityClassificationItem`	Interface	extend	`SecurityClassificationItem` is an `<<extend>>` interface that provides its associated data model to those classes that implement it.	CDM UoF Security Classification
`Sensor`	Class	class	`Sensor` is an individual `SensorType` that has a unique identity and can be used to measure values of a specific type. **Note** The unique identification of a `Sensor` can be a part number+serial number (if it is serialized) or a location identifier together with the identifier of the SerializedProduct where it is mounted.	S5000F Serialized Product Health Monitoring
`SensorSample`	Class	class	`SensorSample` is a particular reading of an individual sensor at a specific point in time.	S5000F Serialized Product Health Monitoring
`SensorType`	Class	class	`SensorType` is `HardwarePartAsDesigned` that measures physical events and provides the information to external devices. **Example** – `Accelerometer` – Pressure gauge – Strain gauge – `Tachometer` – Temperature sensor	S5000F Serialized Product Health Monitoring
`SerializedAssertItem`	Interface	select	`SerializedAssertItem` is a `<<select>>` interface that identifies classes from which an instance can be used as the `EvaluationByAssertionOfSerializedItems` assert item	CDM UoF Applicability Statement

Class name	Type	Stereotype	Definition	UoF
SerializedHardwarePart	Class	class	SerializedHardwarePart is <<class>> that represent an actual physical part which can be identified as an individual. **Note** A SerializedHardwarePart is usually referred to as "Equipment". This name has not been used in the data model so as to distinguish between the generic equipment and the individual ones. **Note** A SerializedHardwarePart can evolve due to modifications. The actual build standard at a given moment is defined through the relationship SerializedPartDesignAssociation.	S5000F Specializations
SerializedItem	Interface	extend	SerializedItem is an <<extend>> interface class representing all serialized items. **Example** – hardware part as serialized – serialized product variant	S5000F Serialized Item
SerializedItemOwner	Class	relationship	SerializedItemOwner is a <<relationship>> describing the party holding the partial or total ownership of an item implementing the SerializedItem <<interface>>.	S5000F Serialized Item
SerializedPartDesignAssociation	Class	relationship	SerializedPartDesignAssociation is a <<relationship>> that associates a SerializedHardwarePart to the HardwarePartAsDesigned that defines its functionality during a specific period of time. **Note** Several relationships can exist for different periods if the SerializedHardwarePart has been modified to adhere to a new specification. **Note** The periods of the different relationships cannot overlap - a SerializedHardwarePart can only belong to a single specification at a specific moment in time.	S5000F Part As Realized

Class name	Type	Stereotype	Definition	UoF
			Note The relationship has an effectivityPeriod so as to indicate the period during which the `SerializedHardwarePart` adhered to this specification. **Example** – Part A belongs to build standard BS1 from 2013-01-01 to 2016-08-31 – Part A belongs to build standard BS2 from 2016-08-31 onwards	
`SerializedPartsListPosition`	Class	class	`SerializedPartsListPosition` is a <<class>> that represents a position within the associated `SerializedHardwarePart`.	CDM UoF Serialized Part Configuration
`SerializedProductOperationalPeriod`	Class	relationship	`SerializedProductOperationalPeriod` is a <<relationship>> that describes the specific operational role of a `SerializedProductVariant` during a particular operational period.	S5000F Operational Period
`SerializedProductVariant`	Class	class	`SerializedProductVariant` is a <<class>> that represent an actual product variant which is identified as an individual. **Note** A `SerializedProductVariant` must be manufactured in accordance with its definition as defined by its productVariantIdentifier.	S5000F Specializations
`SerializedProductVariantAssignment`	Class	relationship	`SerializedProductVariantAssignment` is a <<relationship>> between a `FleetTask` and the vehicle that has been assigned to perform that `FleetTask`. **Note** The `SerializedProductVariant` is in this case always a vehicle.	S5000F Fleet Planning and Product Assignment
`SerializedProductVariantConfigurationConformance`	Class	relationship	`SerializedProductVariantConfigurationConformance` is a <<relationship>> that identifies the allowed product configuration to which the `SerializedProductVariant` complies with during a defined period of time.	CDM UoF Serialized Product Variant Configuration

Class name	Type	Stereotype	Definition	UoF
`SerializedProductVariantInFleet`	Class	relationship	`SerializedProductVariantInFleet` is a `<<relationship>>` that defines the association between a `SerializedProductVariant` and the `Fleet` to which it belongs.	S5000F Fleet Definition
`SerializedProductVariantOperatingBase`	Class	relationship	`SerializedProductVariantOperatingBase` is a `<<relationship>>` that establishes in which `OperatingBase` a `SerializedProductVariant` has been operating during a specific period of time.	S5000F Operating Base
`SerializedProductVariantOperator`	Class	relationship	`SerializedProductVariantOperator` is a `<<relationship>>` defining the operation of a `SerializedProductVariant` during a specific period of time.	S5000F Operator
`SerializedProductVariantZone`	Class	relationship	`SerializedProductVariantZone` is a `<<relationship>>` that allows to associate a `Damage` to a serialied ProductVariantZone.	S5000F Damage
`SerializedSupportEquipment`	Class	class	`SerializedSupportEquipment` is a SerialiedHardwarePart that is used exclusively for support purposes.	S5000F Support Equipment
`SerialNumberRange`	Class	compoundAttribute	`SerialNumberRange` is a `<<compoundAttribute>>` that identifies an interval of serialized items. **Note** The range pattern can be open-ended.	S-Series_Compound_Attributes_2-0_002-00
`Service`	Class	class	`Service` is a contract where technical or intellectual work is performed but no delivery of goods takes place.	S5000F Service Contract Management
`ServiceBulletin`	Class	class	`ServiceBulletin` is a class representing a set of documentation, material, spares and possibly other resources required to embody a change embodiment requirement into a `ProductVariant` or `SerializedProductVariant`.	S5000F Change Embodiment
`ServiceContract`	Class	relationship	`ServiceContract` is a `<<relationship>>` that allows a service being provided to be associated to a specific contract.	S5000F Service Contract Management

Class name	Type	Stereotype	Definition	UoF
`ServiceItem`	Interface	select	`ServiceItem` is a `<<select>>` interface that allows to define the items for which a service can be requested.	S5000F Service Request
`ServiceLevelAgreementClause`	Class	class	`ServiceLevelAgreementClause` is a contractual clause related to a service that determines the level of service to be provided.	S5000F Service Contract Management
`ServiceRelationship`	Class	relationship	`ServiceRelationship` is a `<<relationship>>` that allows to associate two `Services`.	S5000F Service Contract Management
`ServiceRequest`	Class	class	`ServiceRequest` is a class representing a demand from one party to another partyto provide a service.	S5000F Service Request
`ServiceRequestCancellation`	Class	class	`ServiceRequestCancellation` is a `<<class>>` that allows to cancel one or more `Services` by a `Party`.	S5000F Service Request
`ServiceRequestItem`	Class	relationship	`ServiceRequestItem` is a `<<relationship>>` that allows to associate one or several items of a same type to a `ServiceRequest`.	S5000F Service Request
`ServiceRequestLocation`	Class	relationship	`ServiceRequestLocation` is a `<<relationship>>` stating the locating where a `ServiceRequest` has to be complied with.	S5000F Service Request
`ServiceRequestParty`	Class	relationship	`ServiceRequestParty` is a `<<relationship>>` that associates a `ServiceRequest` to the party that has demanded it or has to provide it. **Note** Additional relationships can exist, eg, for a subcontractor or another `Party` that will assist to that `ServiceRequest`. **Note** At least two relationships must exist, one for the `Party` demanding the `ServiceRequest` and one for the `Party` that will fulfill it.	S5000F Service Request
`ServiceRequestRelationship`	Class	relationship	`ServiceRequestRelationship` is a `<<relationship>>` that indicates the association between two different `ServiceRequests`.	S5000F Service Request
`ShopFindings`	Class	class	`ShopFindings` is a class representing the results of a fault investigation performed on an equipment in a workshop.	S5000F Shop Findings

Class name	Type	Stereotype	Definition	UoF
ShopFindingsDeterminedBy	Class	relationship	ShopFindingsDeterminedBy is a <<relationship>> that allows ShopFindings to be associated to the DetectionMeans that allowed such findings.	S5000F Shop Findings
Skill	Class	class	Skill is a <<class>> that represents human cognitive, psychomotor, and affective abilities.	CDM UoF Competence Definition
SkillLevel	Class	class	SkillLevel is a <<class>> that represents a defined proficiency of a Trade.	CDM UoF Competence Definition
SoftwareElement	Class	class	SoftwareElement is a BreakdownElement that is realized as a SoftwarePartAsDesigned.	CDM UoF Software Element
SoftwareElementPartRealizat ion	Class	relationship	SoftwareElementPartRealization is a <<relationship>> where a SoftwareElementRevision relates to an instance of SoftwarePartAsDesigned which fulfills the SoftwareElement specification.	CDM UoF Software Element
SoftwareElementRevision	Class	class	SoftwareElementRevision is a BreakdownElementRevision representing an iteration applied to a SoftwareElement.	CDM UoF Software Element
SoftwareError	Class	class	SoftwareError is a <<class>> that represents a fault detected during the execution of a SoftwarePartAsReleased.	S5000F Software
SoftwareErrorOS	Class	relationship	SoftwareErrorOS is a <<relationship>> that indicates the operating system on which a SoftwarePartAsReleased was executing when a SoftwareError was detected.	S5000F Software
SoftwareErrorPlatform	Class	relationship	SoftwareErrorPlatform is a <<relationship>> that indicates the HardwarePartAsDesigned on which a SoftwarePartAsReleased was executing when a SoftwareError was detected.	S5000F Software
SoftwareOS	Class	relationship	SoftwareOS is a <<relationship>> that defines the operating system on which a SoftwarePartAsReleased executes.	S5000F Software

Applicable to: All

Class name	Type	Stereotype	Definition	UoF
SoftwarePartAsDesigned	Class	class	SoftwarePartAsDesigned is a PartAsDesigned that is produced as an executable software or as a data file. **Note** Non-executable software includes eg, maps.	CDM UoF Part Definition
SoftwarePartAsReleased	Class	class	SoftwarePartAsReleased is <<class>> that represents actual build of a software which is delivered.	S5000F Specializations
SoftwarePlatform	Class	relationship	SoftwarePlatform is a <<relationship>> that indicates the HardwarePartAsDesigned on which a SoftwarePartAsReleased can execute.	S5000F Software
SolveObsolescence	Class	exchange	SolveObsolescence is an <<exchange>> that represents a message associated with a use case (UC51005) providing the information required to solve an obsolescence.	S5000F Use Cases
SpecialSafetyInstruction	Class	class	SpecialSafetyInstruction is a SafetyDocument providing specific mandatory instructions to be followed in addition to those existing in the standard documentation so as that special safety issues can be addressed. **Note** SpecialSafetyInstructions are usually generated by the Product manufacturer or by legal authorities. **Note** The organization generating the SpecialSafetyInstruction and relationships with SafetyIssues, SafetyWarnings or other SpecialSafetyInstruction, applicability, etc., are inherited from the Document class.	S5000F Safety
Sphere	Class	compoundAttribute	Sphere represents a three-dimensional object where every point on its surface is equidistant from its center.	S-Series_Compound_Attributes_2-0_002-00
StoredPart	Interface	extend	StoredPart is an <<extend>> interface that provides the capability to associate a Part the Warehouse where it is stored.	S5000F Warehouse and Spare Pool

Class name	Type	Stereotype	Definition	UoF
StrainGauge	Class	class	StrainGauge is a SensorType whose resistance varies with applied force; it converts force, pressure, tension, weight, etc, into a change in electrical resistance which can then be measured.	S5000F Serialized Product Health Monitoring
StreetAddress	Class	class	StreetAddress is a <<class> that represents a locatable position along a road.	CDM UoF Location
SubjectOfPoliciesAndRegulations	Interface	select	SubjectofPoliciesAndRegulations is a <<select>> interface that allows to associate policies and regulations to the items to which they apply.	S5000F Policies and Regulations
SubstanceContainingItem	Interface	extend	SubstanceContainingItem is an <<extend>> interface that enables to identify the substances contained by an item.	S5000F Contained Substances
SubstanceDefinition	Class	class	SubstanceDefinition is a <<class>> that identifies high concern physical matter. **Example** – CAS (Chemical Abstract Substance) Registry – REACH (Registration,Evaluation,Authorisation and Restriction of Chemicals).	S5000F Specializations
SubstanceEmission	Class	relationship	SubstanceEmission is a <<relationship>> that allows to document emissions of one or several substances during a specific period of time.	S5000F Consumptions and Emissions
SubstanceEmissionPeriod	Interface	extend	SubstanceEmissionPeriod is an <<extend>> interface that allows to define the periods of time during which the associated items generate a SubstanceEmission.	S5000F Consumptions and Emissions
SubstitutePartAsDesigned	Class	relationship	SubstitutePartAsDesigned is a <<relationship>> that defines a substitute PartAsDesignedPartsListEntry which can replace the base PartAsDesignedPartsListEntry in the context of the parent PartAsDesignedPartsList.	CDM UoF Part Definition
SuppliesUsed	Class	relationship	SuppliesUsed is a <<relationship>> that describes the amount of supplies used for a MaintenanceActivity.	S5000F Maintenance Activity

Class name	Type	Stereotype	Definition	UoF
SupplyItem	Interface	select	SupplyItem is a <<select>> interface representing an item that is used for maintenance or operation.	S5000F Supply Item
SupportEquipment	Class	class	SupportEquipment is a HardwareElement used exclusively for support purposes. **Example** – Automatic Test Equipment (ATE) – borescope – hoisting device – oscilloscope – tester – tow bar	S5000F Maintenance Activity
SupportEquipmentItem	Interface	select	SupportEquipmentItem is a <<select>> interface that allows to choose between a generic SupportEquipment or a SerializedSupportEquipment.	S5000F Support Equipment
SupportEquipmentUsed	Class	relationship	SupportEquipmentUsed is a <<relationship>> that defines the equipment that has been used to perform a specific MaintenanceActivity.	S5000F Maintenance Activity
Tachometer	Class	class	Tachometer is a SensorType that measures revolutions of a rotating item.	S5000F Serialized Product Health Monitoring
Task	Class	class	Task is a <<class>> that represents the specification of work to be done or undertaken.	CDM UoF Task
TaskRequirement	Class	class	TaskRequirement is a <<class>> that represents the need for a procedure to be developed and documented. **Note** A task requirement can have more than one task being developed for different usage scenarios.	CDM UoF Task Requirement

Class name	Type	Stereotype	Definition	UoF
			Note Examples of support analysis activities which result in a set of documented task requirements are: Preventive maintenance analysis (refer to S4000P) and special event analysis. **Note** Task requirements are identified and documented prior to any detailed task analysis.	
TaskRequirementRevision	Class	class	TaskRequirementRevision is a <<class>> representing an iteration applied to a TaskRequirement.	CDM UoF Task Requirement
TaskRevision	Class	class	TaskRevision is a <<class>> representing an iteration applied to a Task.	CDM UoF Task
TechnicalOrder	Class	class	TechnicalOrder is a WorkItem raised by Maintenance Engineering to carry out a change or maintenance on a SerializedItem.	S5000F Change Embodiment
TechnicalOrderEmbodied	Class	relationship	TechnicalOrderEmbodied is a <<relationship>> that allows to report the WorkOrder that embodies a TechnicalOrder on the item on which it needs to be embodied.	S5000F Change Embodiment Reporting
TemperatureSensor	Class	class	TemperatureSensor is a SensorType that measures temperature.	S5000F Serialized Product Health Monitoring
ThreeDimensional	Class	compoundAttribute	ThreeDimensional is a <<compoundAttribute>> that represents spatial magnitudes.	S-Series_Compound_Attributes_2-0_002-00
ThresholdDefinition	Class	class	ThresholdDefinition is a <<class>> that represents the circumstance that is used as a trigger or threshold.	CDM UoF Time Limit
TimeStampedClassification	Class	compoundAttribute	TimeStampedClassification is <<compoundAttribute>> that represents a classification in conjunction with its recording time stamp.	S-Series_Compound_Attributes_2-0_002-00
TimeType	Class	compoundAttribute	TimeType is a <<compoundAttribute>> indicating the time of a day.	S-Series_Compound_Attributes_2-0_002-00

Class name	Type	Stereotype	Definition	UoF
			Example – opening time at 08:00	
`TrackablePart`	Interface	extend	`TrackablePart` is an <<extend>> interface for those items against which actions performed need to be recorded. **Example** – A serialized item or a software part, but not things like a washer.	S5000F Change Embodiment Planning
`TrackSupportEquipmentusage`	Class	exchange	`TrackSupportEquipmentusage` is an <<exchange>> that represents a message associated with a use case (UC50410) allowing to track the usage of a support equipment.	S5000F Use Cases
`Trade`	Class	class	`Trade` is a <<class>> that represents a craft or profession which requires specific skills.	CDM UoF Competence Definition
`TransportableItem`	Interface	select	`TransportableItem` is a <<select>> interface that allows to define an item that can be transported.	S5000F Transportable Item
`TransportCapability`	Class	class	`TransportCapability` is a `Capability` associated to the capacity of transporting things.	S5000F Transporting Asset
`TransportCapabilityUsage`	Class	relationship	`TransportCapabilityUsage` is a <<relationship>> that allows to associate a `TransportCapability` with the `TransportableItems` that it transports at a certain moment in time.	S5000F Transporting Asset
`TransportFeatures`	Interface	extend	`TransportFeatures` is an <<extend>> interface that allows to associate specific transport features to transportable items.	S5000F Transportable Item
`TransportingAsset`	Interface	extend	`TransportingAsset` is an <<extend>> interfaces that allows to associate a `TransportCapability` to an item.	S5000F Transporting Asset
`TransportNetwork`	Class	class	`TransportNetwork` is an `Infrastructure` used to transport items. **Example** – Airline – Railroad	S5000F Infrastructure

Class name	Type	Stereotype	Definition	UoF
`TransportPosition`	Interface	select	`TransportPosition` is a <<select>> interface that allows to identify where a `TransportableItem` is positioned during a transport.	S5000F Transporting Asset
`TransportRequirement`	Class	class	`TransportRequirement` is a `Requirement` defining the condictions under which a `TransportableItem` can be transported. **Example** – Oil reservoir must be emptied before transport. – The tires of the vehicle must be deflated for transport.	S5000F Transportable Item
`Triangle`	Class	compoundAttribute	`Triangle` is a <<class>> representing a geometrical plane figure with three straight sides and three angles.	S5000F_Compound_Attributes_002-00
`TypeOfPerson`	Class	class	`TypeOfPerson` is a <<class>> representing a neutral non-individual person that presents a set of shared common characteristics of multiple `Persons`. **Note** A `TypeOfPerson` is used mainly for planning purposes, when the exact individual(s) that are going to be associated to an activity are not yet known. **Example** – class 3 welder – electronics engineer – helicopter pilot – mechanical technician – paratrooper – truck driver	S5000F Type of Person
`UC_Facility_Budget`	Class	exchange	`UC_Facility_Budget` is an example use case to document the budget that is available for a `Facility`.	S5000F Use Case Message Definition Examples
`UC_Facility_Costs`	Class	exchange	`UC_Facility_Budget` is an example use case to document the costs that are associated to a `Facility`.	S5000F Use Case Message Definition Examples
`UC_ManagementInformation`	Class	exchange	`UC_ManagementInformation` is an example use case that combines several use cases and/or classes covering management information.	S5000F Use Case Message Definition Examples

Applicable to: All

Class name	Type	Stereotype	Definition	UoF
UnacceptableCondition	Class	class	UnacceptableCondition is a justification for the disposal of an item in case that it is no longer fit for purpose.	S5000F Unacceptable Item Condition requiring disposal
UpgradeRequirement	Class	class	UpgradeRequirement is a Requirement that must be applied during the embodiment of a change (upgrade). **Example** – The individual ProductVariant downtime for the upgrade must not exceed 3 hours. – The modification can be only embodied when the vehicle is defueled. – Upgrade to be performed during maintenance period extending for more than 3 days, so as not to impact fleet operations.	S5000F Requirement
UsableOnItem	Interface	extend	UsableOnItem is an <<extend>> interface that provides its associated data model to those classes that can have a limited effectivity with respect to its usage in one or many instances of ProductVariant.	CDM UoF Product Design Configuration
UsableOnProductVariant	Class	relationship	UsableOnProductVariant is a <<relationship>> that defines that a UsableOnItem, included in the Breakdown for the overall Product, is effective in the associated ProductVariant. **Note** UsableOnProductVariant is the equivalent of the Usable On Code in GEIA-0007.	CDM UoFProduct Design Configuration
Warehouse	Class	class	Warehouse is a Facility used to store parts.	S5000F Facility
WarrantyClaim	Class	class	WarrantyClaim is a class representing a customer's claim for repair or replacement of a defective item or non-performance of that item as established in a warranty contract.	S5000F Warranty
WarrantyClaimContact	Class	relationship	WarrantyClaimContact is a <<relationship>> that associates a WarrantyClaim to a Party.	S5000F Warranty
WarrantyClaimEvents	Class	relationship	WarrantyClaimEvents is a <<relationship>> that associates WarrantyClaims to WarrantyEvents.	S5000F Warranty

Class name	Type	Stereotype	Definition	UoF
WarrantyClaimFollowUp	Class	class	WarrantyClaimFollowUp is a class that represents any follow-up associated to a WarrantyClaim.	S5000F Warranty
WarrantyClaimResolution	Class	class	WarrantyClaimResolution is a class that represents the conclusion of the WarrantyClaim.	S5000F Warranty
WarrantyEvent	Class	class	WarrantyEvent is an Event that has as the consequence that a WarrantyClaim is raised.	S5000F Warranty
WarrantyItem	Interface	select	WarrantyItem is a <<select>> interface that allows to define the items that are subject to Warranty or on which a Warranty Event occurs.	S5000F Warranty
WasteContainer	Class	class	WasteContainer is a Container containing waste or hazardous material (HAZMAT) substances that need to be recycled or be disposed of in an acceptable manner. **Example** – oil drum – plastic bag	S5000F Container
WasteDisposalOperation	Class	class	WasteDisposalOperation is a <<class>> representing the action that has been taken in order to dispose of a waste item. **Note** The disposal of waste always refers to bulk items such as a drum of oil, or a container of discarded fasteners.	S5000F Waste Disposal Operation
WasteDisposalOperationActio n	Class	relationship	WasteDisposalOperationAction is a <<relationship>> that allows to associate a DisposalOperation with additional actions taken as a result of it. **Example** – disinfection of facility – return of waste container	S5000F Waste Disposal Operation
WasteDisposalRequirement	Class	class	WasteDisposalRequirement is a DisposalRequirement oriented towards the disposal of waste.	S5000F Disposal Requirement

Class name	Type	Stereotype	Definition	UoF
`WasteItem`	Interface	select	`WasteItem` is a `<<select>>` interface that allows to define the items that are considered waste.	S5000F Waste Disposal Requirement
`WasteRecoveredItem`	Class	relationship	`WasteRecoveredItem` is a `<<relationship>>` that allows to document the recovered material or substances from a `WasteDisposalOperation`.	S5000F Recovered Material or Substances
`WorkBreakdown`	Class	class	`WorkBreakdown` is a class used to group all the different activities associated to a particular purpose.	S5000F Work Breakdown
`WorkBreakdownContext`	Interface	extend	WorkBreakDownContext is an `<<extend>>` interface that allows to associated workBreakDowns to individual items.	S5000F Work Breakdown
`WorkBreakdownRelationship`	Class	relationship	`WorkBreakdownRelationship` is a `<<relationship>>` that allows to associate different `WorkBreakdowns`.	S5000F Work Breakdown
`WorkBreakdownRevision`	Class	class	`WorkBreakdownRevision` is an iteration that is applied to a `WorkBreakdown`.	S5000F Work Breakdown
`WorkItem`	Class	class	`WorkItem` is a generic concept defined to group individual activities for planning, costing or program management purposes. **Note** A same `WorkItem` can be associated to several `WorkBreakdownRevisions`.	S5000F Work Breakdown
`WorkItemRelationship`	Class	relationship	`WorkItemRelationship` is a `<<relationship>>` that establishes the association between two instances of `WorkItem`. The class allows to define both hierarchical associations and time-dependent associations. For hierarchical associations, it defines the pa	S5000F Work Breakdown
`WorkOrder`	Class	class	`WorkOrder` is an instruction to perform maintenance work on a `SerializedItem`.	S5000F Maintenance Activity

Class name	Type	Stereotype	Definition	UoF
ZoneElement	Class	class	ZoneElement is a BreakdownElement that represents a three-dimensional space related to a Product. **Note** A zone can also represent a work area such as a mechanical workshop onboard a ship.	CDM UoFZone Element
ZoneElementRevision	Class	class	ZoneElementRevision is a BreakdownElementRevision representing an iteration applied to a ZoneElement.	CDM UoFZone Element

3   Data element list

The full list of S5000F data elements is provided in Table 3 List of data elements

. This includes data elements from SX002D used by S5000F but defined in SX001G. Table 3 is organized alphabetically by the data element name, and contains:

- Data element name
- Data element data type (refer to Chap 24.4 on more details on data types used in S5000F)
- Data element definition contains a textual definition.
- Class name identifies the classes in the S5000F data model where the data element is used as an attribute.
- Unit of Functionality (UoF), identifies the section in Chap XX where the Class is defined. If the UoF name is preceded by "CDM", then the UoF is originally defined in SX002D.

For completeness, the data elements of the UoFs used "as is" from SX002D are also listed in this specification, The UoFs from SX002D used by this specification are listed in Chap 24.3.

A mapping of the classes and attributes required for the individual use cases can be found in Chap 28.

Table 3 List of data elements

Attribute Name	Type	Definition	Class Name	UoF
actionCloseDate	DateType	actionCloseDate is the date at which the action was closed.	Action	S5000F Event

---

Attribute Name	Type	Definition	Class Name	UoF
actionCreationDate	DateType	actionCreationDate is the date at which the action is created.	Action	S5000F Event
actionDescription	DescriptorType	actionDescription is a textual description of a taken action.	Action	S5000F Event
actionIdentifier	IdentifierType	actionIdentifier is a string of characters used to uniquely identify an Action and to differentiate it from other Actions.	Action	S5000F Event
actionPriority	ClassificationType	actionPriority is a classification that determines the urgency of an action.	Action	S5000F Event
actionScheduledDate	DateType	actionScheduledDate is the date for which the action is scheduled.	Action	S5000F Event
actionType	ClassificationType	actionType is a classification that characterizes an Action.	Action	S5000F Event
additionalAddressInformation	DescriptorType	additionalAddressInformation is a description that provides additional information to further locate an address. **Example** – Building 7 in campus – First floor, apartment 7 – Suite 204	StreetAddress	CDM UoF Location
aggregatedElementType	ClassificationType	aggregatedElementType is a classification that identifies further specialization for an AggregatedElement.	AggregatedElement	CDM UoF Aggregated Element
allowedProductConfigurationIdentifier	IdentifierType	allowedProductConfigurationIdentifier is an identifier that establishes a unique designator for a AllowedProductConfigurationByConfigurationIdentifier and to differentiate it from other instances of AllowedProductConfigurationByConfigurationIdentifier.	AllowedProductConfigurationByConfigurationIdentifier	CDM UoF Product Design Configuration

Attribute Name	Type	Definition	Class Name	UoF
allowedProductConfigurationPhysicalDataDimensions	ThreeDimensional	allowedProductConfigurationPhysicalDataDimensions are the dimensions of a ProductVariant when it is in a specific AllowedProductConfiguration.	AllowedProductConfigurationPhysicalData	S5000F Operational Roles
allowedProductConfigurationPhysicalDataParameter	PropertyType	allowedProductConfigurationPhysicalDataParameter is a parameter of a ProductVariant that varies when it is in a specific AllowedProductConfiguration. **Example** – range	AllowedProductConfigurationPhysicalData	S5000F Operational Roles
allowedProductConfigurationPhysicalDataWeight	NumericalPropertyType	allowedProductConfigurationPhysicalDataWeight is the weight of a ProductVariant when it is in a specific AllowedProductConfiguration.	AllowedProductConfigurationPhysicalData	S5000F Operational Roles
allowedRoleChangeDuration	NumericalPropertyType	allowedRoleChangeDuration is the time that it takes to change from one specific OperationalRole to a different associated OperationalRole.	AllowedRoleChange	S5000F Operational Roles
altitude	umlString	altitude is a string of characters that represents the height above or below a fixed reference point. **Example** – 34m above sea level	GlobalPosition	CDM UoF Location
anchoringPointFixed	umlBoolean	anchoringPointFixed is a <<boolean>> that indicates whether an anchoring point is permanent or can be removed.	AnchoringPoint	S5000F Transport Anchoring Point
anchoringPointIdentifier	IdentifierType	anchoringPointIdentifier is a string of text that allows to uniquely identify an AnchoringPoint and differentiate it from other AnchoringPoints.	AnchoringPoint	S5000F Transport Anchoring Point
anchoringPointMaxLoad	NumericalPropertyType	anchoringPointMaxLoad is the maximum load that can be applied to an anchoring point.	AnchoringPoint	S5000F Transport Anchoring Point

Attribute Name	Type	Definition	Class Name	UoF
applicabilitySta tementDateRange	DateRange	applicabilityStatementDateRange is a date range that defines the date interval for when the applicabillity evaluation can result in a TRUE result. **Note** If outside that date range, the ApplicabilityStatement always results in a FALSE statement.	ApplicabilitySt atement	CDM UoF Applicability Statement
applicabilitySta tementDescriptio n	DescriptorType	applicabilityStatementDescription is a description that provides a human readable expression of the defined rule.	ApplicabilitySt atement	CDM UoF Applicability Statement
applicabilitySta tementIdentifier	IdentifierType	applicabilityStatementIdentifier is an identifier that establishes a unique designator for an ApplicabilityStatement and to differentiate it from other instances of ApplicabilityStatement.	ApplicabilitySt atement	CDM UoF Applicability Statement
applicableSerial NumberRange	SerialNumberRang e	applicableSerialNumberRange is a serial number range that identifies a limited effectivity with respect to a given interval of serialized items.	EvaluationByAss ertionOfSeriali zedItems	CDM UoF Applicability Statement
			EffectiveOnProd uctConfiguratio n	CDM UoF Product Design Configuration
			UsableOnProduct Variant	CDM UoF Product Design Configuration
assembly	umlString	assembly is a string of characters that represents the unit or assembly attribute of the data module code.	S1000DDataModul e	CDM UoF Document
associatedActual EnvironmentPerio d	DateRange	associatedActualEnvironmentPeriod is the period of time during which the association between an EnvironmentItem and an ActualEnvironment is or was applicable.	AssociatedActua lEnvironment	S5000F Environment

Attribute Name	Type	Definition	Class Name	UoF
authorityToOpera teIdentifier	IdentifierType	authorityToOperateIdentifier is an identifier that establishes a unique designator for an AuthorityToOperate and to differentiate it from other instances of AuthorityToOperate.	AuthorityToOper ate	CDM UoF Product Design Configuration
authorizedLifeVa lue	PropertyType	authorizedLifeValue is a property that specifies the maximum usage limit.	AuthorizedLife	S-Series_Compound_Attributes_2-0_002-00
availabilityDate s	DateRange	availabilityDates is a period of time for which the availability of an AvailabilityItem is reported. **Note** The date range can also be open-ended (until a certain date or from a certain date onwards). This possibility should be used only with uttermost care. **Note** The date range can be one single date.	Availability	S5000F Availability
availabilityDesc ription	DescriptorType	availabilityDescription is a narrative statement clarifying the status of the Availability.	Availability	S5000F Availability
availabilityIden tifier	IdentifierType	availabilityIdentifier is a string of text that uniquely identifies an Availability entry and allows to differentiate it from other SerializedProductVariantAvailability entries.	Availability	S5000F Availability
availabilityRepo rtingDate	DateType	availabilityReportingDate is the date at which the Availability was reported.	Availability	S5000F Availability
availabilityStat us	StateType	availabilityStatus is a classification that indicates the availability of an AvailabilityItem at a specific date. **Example** – operational – performing scheduled maintenance – unavailable – use blocked	Availability	S5000F Availability

S5000F

Attribute Name	Type	Definition	Class Name	UoF
base	PropertyType	base is the longest side of a triangle.	Triangle	S5000F_Compound_Attributes_002-00
batchHardwarePartDescription	DescriptorType	batchHardwarePartDescription is a textual narrative statement that explains what the BatchHardwarePart is.	BatchHardwarePart	S5000F Specializations
batchHardwarePartLife	AuthorizedLife	batchHardwarePartLife is the AuthorizedLife for a BatchHardwarePart.	BatchHardwarePart	S5000F Specializations
batchHardwarePartManufacturingDate	DateType	batchHardwarePartManufacturingDate is a Date at which a BatchHardwarePart was manufactured.	BatchHardwarePart	S5000F Specializations
breakdownElementChildSequenceNumber	umlString	breakdownElementChildSequenceNumber is a string of characters that controls the order for the included child element. **Note** The sequence number can be used to control how child elements are presented in eg, a list.	BreakdownElementStructure	CDM UoF Breakdown Structure
breakdownElementDescription	DescriptorType	breakdownElementDescription is a description that gives more information on the BreakdownElement.	BreakdownElementRevision	CDM UoF Breakdown Structure
breakdownElementEssentiality	ClassificationType	breakdownElementEssentiality is a classification that identifies the operational importance of the BreakdownElement at the Product level. **Note** Based on the criticality as defined during the FMECA.	BreakdownElement	CDM UoF Breakdown Structure
breakdownElementIdentifier	IdentifierType	breakdownElementIdentifier is an identifier that establishes a unique designator for a BreakdownElement and to differentiate it from other instances of BreakdownElement. **Note** Can be used to establish a hierarchical structure of the technical system.	BreakdownElement	CDM UoF Breakdown Structure

Attribute Name	Type	Definition	Class Name	UoF
		Example – The combination of logistics support analysis control number and alternate logistics support analysis control number within GEIA-STD-0007. – The Standard Numbering System defined by S1000D.		
breakdownElement Name	NameType	breakdownElementName is a name by which the BreakdownElement is known and can be easily referenced.	BreakdownElemen t	CDM UoF Breakdown Structure
breakdownElement RevisionDate	DateType	breakdownElementRevisionDate is a date that specifies when the BreakdownElement was revised.	BreakdownElemen tRevision	CDM UoF Breakdown Structure
breakdownElement RevisionIdentifi er	IdentifierType	breakdownElementRevisionIdentifier is an identifier that establishes a unique designator for a BreakdownElementRevision and to differentiate it from other instances of BreakdownElementRevision.	BreakdownElemen tRevision	CDM UoF Breakdown Structure
breakdownElement RevisionRational e	DescriptorType	breakdownElementRevisionRationale is a description that gives more information on the justification for revising the BreakdownElement.	BreakdownElemen tRevision	CDM UoF Breakdown Structure
breakdownElement RevisionRelation shipType	ClassificationType	breakdownElementRevisionRelationshipType is a classification that identifies the meaning of the established relationship. **Note** The related breakdown elements do not need to be used in the same breakdown, ie, it can be used to establish the relationship between a breakdown element in a functional breakdown and a breakdown element in a physical breakdown.	BreakdownElemen tRevisionRelati onship	CDM UoF Breakdown Structure
breakdownElement RevisionStatus	StateType	breakdownElementRevisionStatus is a state that identifies the maturity of a BreakdownElementRevision.	BreakdownElemen tRevision	CDM UoF Breakdown Structure
breakdownElement UsageIdentifier	IdentifierType	breakdownElementUsageIdentifier is an identifier that establishes a unique designator for a BreakdownElementUsageInBreakdown and to differentiate it from other instances of BreakdownElementUsageInBreakdown.	BreakdownElemen tUsageInBreakdo wn	CDM UoF Breakdown Structure

Attribute Name	Type	Definition	Class Name	UoF
breakdownElementUsageQuantity	PropertyType	breakdownElementUsageQuantity is a property that specifies the amount of the BreakdownElement used in its parent BreakdownElement. **Note** If no value is given, it must be interpreted as value "1" with a unit of "each". For as required amounts, the text property is used with "As Required" or other text as appropriate.	BreakdownElementUsageInBreakdown	CDM UoF Breakdown Structure
breakdownElementUsageRelationshipType	ClassificationType	breakdownElementUsageRelationshipType is a classification that identifies the meaning of the established relationship.	BreakdownElementUsageRelationship	CDM UoF Breakdown Structure
breakdownRevisionDate	DateType	breakdownRevisionDate is a date that specifies when the Breakdown was revised.	BreakdownRevision	CDM UoF Breakdown Structure
breakdownRevisionIdentifier	IdentifierType	breakdownRevisionIdentifier is an identifier that establishes a unique designator for a BreakdownRevision and to differentiate it from other instances of BreakdownRevision.	BreakdownRevision	CDM UoF Breakdown Structure
breakdownRevisionRationale	DescriptorType	breakdownRevisionRationale is a description that gives more information on the justification for revising the Breakdown.	BreakdownRevision	CDM UoF Breakdown Structure
breakdownRevisionStatus	StateType	breakdownRevisionStatus is a state that identifies the maturity of a BreakdownRevision.	BreakdownRevision	CDM UoF Breakdown Structure
breakdownType	ClassificationType	breakdownType is a classification that identifies the perspective from which the Breakdown is defined.	Breakdown	CDM UoF Breakdown Structure
budgetApprovedDate	DateType	budgetApprovedDate is the date at which a Budget was approved.	Budget	S5000F Budget
budgetApprovedStatus	StateType	budgetApprovedStatus is the state at which a Budget proposal is.	Budget	S5000F Budget
budgetDate	DateType	budgetDateTime is the date at which the budget was released.	Budget	S5000F Budget

Attribute Name	Type	Definition	Class Name	UoF
budgetDescription	DescriptorType	budgetDescription is a textual narrative explaining the Budget.	Budget	S5000F Budget
budgetIdentifier	IdentifierType	budgetIdentifier is a string of text that uniquely identifies the Budget and allows to differentiate it from other Budgets.	Budget	S5000F Budget
budgetName	DescriptorType	budgetName is a word or phrase by which the budget is commonly known.	Budget	S5000F Budget
budgetType	ClassificationType	budgetType is a <<classification>> that allows to group similar Budgets.	Budget	S5000F Budget
budgetValidUntilDate	DateType	budgetValidUntilDate is a date until which the budget is valid.	Budget	S5000F Budget
calibrationDocumentType	ClassificationType	calibrationDocumentType is a <<classification>> that indicates the kind of relationship that is established between a Calibration and an associated Document.	CalibrationDocument	S5000F Equipment Calibration Certificate Information
calibrationIdentifier	IdentifierType	calibrationIdentifier is an identifier that establishes an unique designator for a Calibration and to differentiate it from other instances of Calibration.	Calibration	S5000F Equipment Calibration Certificate Information
calibrationMeasurementNotes	DescriptorType	calibrationMeasurementNotes is a descriptive text that provides additional information to a specific CalibrationMeasurement.	CalibrationMeasurement	S5000F Equipment Calibration Certificate Information
calibrationMeasurementPattern	NumericalPropertyType	calibrationMeasurementPattern is a <<numericPropertyType>> that provides the reference value used to calibrate or verify an instrument or measurement device.	CalibrationMeasurement	S5000F Equipment Calibration Certificate Information
calibrationMeasurementReading	NumericalPropertyType	calibrationMeasurementReading is a <<numericPropertyType>> that provides the actual value obtained during calibration or verification of an instrument or measurement device.	CalibrationMeasurement	S5000F Equipment Calibration Certificate Information

Attribute Name	Type	Definition	Class Name	UoF
`calibrationNotes`	DescriptorType	`calibrationNotes` is a textual description of noteworthy items associated to the calibration performed on a specific date.	`Calibration`	S5000F Equipment Calibration Certificate Information
`calibrationResult`	PropertyType	`calibrationResult` is a <<PropertyType>> that documents the result of the calibration.	`Calibration`	S5000F Equipment Calibration Certificate Information
`calibrationUncertainty`	PropertyType	`calibrationUncertainty` is a <<PropertyType>> that defines the uncertainty of the calibration.	`Calibration`	S5000F Equipment Calibration Certificate Information
`capabilityDefinitionCategory`	ClassificationType	`capabilityDefinitionCategory` is a classification that identifies a generalization that organize capabilities into an overarching capability taxonomy.	`CapabilityDefinition`	CDM UoF Capability Definition
`capabilityDefinitionCharacteristicDescription`	DescriptorType	`capabilityDefinitionCharacteristicDescription` is a description that gives more information on the `CapabilityDefinitionCharacteristic`.	`CapabilityDefinitionCharacteristic`	CDM UoF Capability Definition
`capabilityDefinitionCharacteristicName`	NameType	`capabilityDefinitionCharacteristicName` is a name by which the `CapabilityDefinitionCharacteristic` is known and can be easily referenced.	`CapabilityDefinitionCharacteristic`	CDM UoF Capability Definition
`capabilityDefinitionCharacteristicValue`	PropertyType	`capabilityDefinitionCharacteristicValue` is a property that represents a measurable or observable characteristic for that is significant to the `CapabilityDefinition`.	`CapabilityDefinitionCharacteristic`	CDM UoF Capability Definition
`capabilityDefinitionCharacteristicValueComparisonOperator`	ClassificationType	capabilityDefinitionCharacteristicValueComparisonOperatorr is a classification that identifies the comparison operator which is to be used in order to qualify whether an actual capability complies with the defined `CapabilityDefinition`.	`CapabilityDefinitionCharacteristic`	CDM UoF Capability Definition
`capabilityDefinitionDescription`	DescriptorType	`capabilityDefinitionDescription` is a description that gives more information on the defined capability.	`CapabilityDefinitionRevision`	CDM UoF Capability Definition
`capabilityDefinitionIdentifier`	IdentifierType	`capabilityDefinitionIdentifier` is an identifier that establishes a unique designator for a `CapabilityDefinition` and to differentiate it from other instances of `CapabilityDefinition`.	`CapabilityDefinition`	CDM UoF Capability Definition

Attribute Name	Type	Definition	Class Name	UoF
`capabilityDefini tionName`	NameType	`capabilityDefinitionName` is a name by which the `CapabilityDefinition` is known and can be easily referenced.	`CapabilityDefin itionRevision`	CDM UoF Capability Definition
`capabilityDefini tionRevisionDate`	DateType	`capabilityDefinitionRevisionDate` is a date that specifies when the `CapabilityDefinition` was revised.	`CapabilityDefin itionRevision`	CDM UoF Capability Definition
`capabilityDefini tionRevisionIden tifier`	IdentifierType	`capabilityDefinitionRevisionIdentifier` is an identifier that establishes a unique designator for a `CapabilityDefinitionRevision` and to differentiate it from other instances of `CapabilityDefinitionRevision`.	`CapabilityDefin itionRevision`	CDM UoF Capability Definition
`capabilityDefini tionRevisionRati onale`	DescriptorType	`capabilityDefinitionRevisionRationale` is a description that provides a justification for revising the `CapabilityDefinition`.	`CapabilityDefin itionRevision`	CDM UoF Capability Definition
`capabilityDefini tionRevisionStat us`	StateType	`capabilityDefinitionRevisionStatus` is a state that identifies the maturity of an `CapabilityDefinitionRevision`.	`CapabilityDefin itionRevision`	CDM UoF Capability Definition
`capabilityDescri ption`	DescriptorType	`capabilityDescription` is a narrative statement explaining the capability. **Example** – Cargo transport – Fligh refuelling – Medical evacuation	`Capability`	S5000F Capability
`capabilityIdenti fier`	IdentifierType	`capabilityIdentifier` is a string of characters that uniquely identifies a specific capability.	`Capability`	S5000F Capability
`capabilityLimita tionDescription`	DescriptorType	`capabilityLimitationDescription` is a description that provides a human readable expression of a `CapabilityLimitation`.	`CapabilityLimit ation`	S5000F Capability
`capabilityLimita tionDuration`	DateRange	`capabilityLimitationDuration` is the period of time during which a `Capability` is limited.	`CapabilityLimit ation`	S5000F Capability

Applicable to: All

Attribute Name	Type	Definition	Class Name	UoF
capabilityLimita tionIdentifier	IdentifierType	capabilityLimitationIdentifier is a <<compositeKey>> that allows with a master key to uniquely identify a CapabilityLimitation.	CapabilityLimit ation	S5000F Capability
capabilityLimita tionName	NameType	capabilityLimitationName is a name by which the CapabilityLimitation is known and can be easily referenced.	CapabilityLimit ation	S5000F Capability
capabilityLimita tionType	ClassificationType	capabilityLimitationType is a <<classification>> that allows to group similar CapabilityLimitations.	CapabilityLimit ation	S5000F Capability
capabilityLimita tionValue	PropertyType	capabilityLimitationValue is a value that measures the CapabilityLimitation.	CapabilityLimit ation	S5000F Capability
capabilityName	NameType	capabilityName is a string of characters that represents the name under which the Capability is referenced or is known.	Capability	S5000F Capability
capabilityType	ClassificationType	capabilityType is a <<classification» that allows to group different Capabilities in accordance with a same Capability purpose.	Capability	S5000F Capability
cargoItemDescrip tion	DescriptorType	cargoItemDescription is a narrative statement explaining the CargoItem.	CargoItem	S5000F Transportable Item
cargoItemIdentif ier	IdentifierType	cargoItemIdentifier is a string of text that allows to uniquely identify a CargoItem and differentiate it from other CargoItems.	CargoItem	S5000F Transportable Item
cargoItemName	TextPropertyType	cargoItemName is a text by which a CargoItem is commonly known.	CargoItem	S5000F Transportable Item
cargoItemStackab le	umlBoolean	cargoItemStackable is a boolean that indicates whether a CargoItem can be stacked.	CargoItem	S5000F Transportable Item
cargoItemUnitary Dimensions	ThreeDimensional	cargoItemUnitaryDimensions represents the dimensions (length, width and height) or each individual unit that forms part of the CargoItem.	CargoItem	S5000F Transportable Item

Attribute Name	Type	Definition	Class Name	UoF
cargoItemUnitary Weight	NumericalPropertyType	cargoItemUnitaryWeight represents the weight of each individual unit that forms the CargoItem.	CargoItem	S5000F Transportable Item
cargoItemUnits	umlInteger	cargoItemUnits is an integer that represents the number of units of a same type that a CargoItem represents.	CargoItem	S5000F Transportable Item
changeAuthorizat ionIdentifier	IdentifierType	changeAuthorizationIdentifier is an identifier that establishes a unique designator for an ChangeAuthorization and to differentiate it from other instances of ChangeAuthorization	ChangeAuthoriza tion	CDM UoF Change Information
changeEmbodiment RequirementType	ClassificationType	changeEmbodimentRequirementType is a classification that allows to group similar ChangeEmbodimentRequirements **Example** – Mandatory – Recommended	ChangeEmbodimen tRequirement	S5000F Requirement
changeNotificati onDescription	DescriptorType	changeNotificationDescription is a description providing a summary of affects made to the related item due to a ChangeAuthorization.	ChangeNotificat ion	CDM UoF Change Information
changeNotificati onType	ClassificationType	changeNotificationType is a classification that identifies a change effect as belonging to a group of change effects sharing a particular characteristic or set of characteristics.	ChangeNotificat ion	CDM UoF Change Information
changeRequestAdd edOrRemovedMater ialAmount	PropertyType	changeRequestAddedOrRemovedMaterialAmount is a property that documents the amount of material that has been added to or removed from an item as the result of a ChangeRequest.	ChangeRequestAd dedOrRemovedMat erial	S5000F Change Request Environmental Impact
changeRequestAdd edOrRemovedMater ialIdentifier	IdentifierType	changeRequestAddedOrRemovedMaterialIdentifier is a string of text that uniquely identifies a ChangeRequestAddedOrRemovedMaterial and differentiates it from other ChangeRequestAddedOrRemovedMaterial instances.	ChangeRequestAd dedOrRemovedMat erial	S5000F Change Request Environmental Impact

Attribute Name	Type	Definition	Class Name	UoF
changeRequestAddedOrRemovedSubstanceAmount	PropertyType	changeRequestAddedOrRemovedSubstanceAmount is a property that documents the amount of the substances that have been added to or removed from an item as the result of a ChangeRequest.	ChangeRequestAddedOrRemovedSubstance	S5000F Change Request Environmental Impact
changeRequestAddedOrRemovedSubstanceIdentifier	IdentifierType	changeRequestAddedOrRemovedSubstanceIdentifier is a string of text that uniquely identifies a ChangeRequestAddedOrRemovedSubstance and differentiates it from other ChangeRequestAddedOrRemovedSubstance instances.	ChangeRequestAddedOrRemovedSubstance	S5000F Change Request Environmental Impact
changeRequestCauseIdentifier	IdentifierType	changeRequestCauseIdentifier is a string of text that uniquely identifies a ChangeRequestCause and differentiates it from other ChangeRequestCauses.	ChangeRequestCause	S5000F Change Request
changeRequestConsumptionChangeAmount	PropertyType	changeRequestConsumptionChangeAmount is a property that quantifies the change in substance consumptions derived from a ChangeRequest.	ChangeRequestConsumptionChange	S5000F Change Request Environmental Impact
changeRequestEmissionChangeAmount	PropertyType	changeRequestEmissionChangeAmount is a property that quantifies the change in substance emissions derived from a ChangeRequest.	ChangeRequestEmissionChange	S5000F Change Request Environmental Impact
changeRequestName	NameType	changeRequestName is a text that summarizes the content of the ChangeRequest and provide a standard way to refer commonly to the ChangeRequest.	ChangeRequest	S5000F Specializations
circuitBreakerIdentifier	IdentifierType	circuitBreakerIdentifier is an identifier that establishes a unique designator for a CircuitBreaker and to differentiate it from other instances of CircuitBreaker.	CircuitBreaker	CDM UoF Circuit Breaker
circuitBreakerName	NameType	circuitBreakerName is a name by which the CircuitBreaker is known and can be easily referenced	CircuitBreaker	CDM UoF Circuit Breaker
circuitBreakerSettingIdentifier	IdentifierType	circuitBreakerSettingIdentifier is an identifier that establishes a unique designator for a defined circuit breaker setting, and to differentiate it from other instances of circuit breaker setting.	CircuitBreakerSetting	CDM UoF Task

Applicable to: All

Attribute Name	Type	Definition	Class Name	UoF
circuitBreakerSe ttingsIdentifier	IdentifierType	circuitBreakerSettingsIdentifier is an identifier that establishes a unique designator for a defined set of circuit breaker settings, and to differentiate it from other instances of circuit breaker settings.	CircuitBreakerS ettings	CDM UoF Task
circuitBreakerSe ttingsOrdered	umlBoolean	circuitBreakerSettingsOrdered is a boolean that defines if the individual circuit breaker setting must be performed in the specified order. **Note** True specifies that the circuit breaker settings must be accomplished in the defined order. False specifies that the circuit breaker settings can be accomplished in any order.	CircuitBreakerS ettings	CDM UoF Task
circuitBreakerSt ate	StateType	circuitBreakerState is a state that identifies the position that a given circuit breaker must be in after the accomplishment of a defined circuit breaker setting.	CircuitBreakerS etting	CDM UoF Task
circuitBreakerTy pe	ClassificationType	circuitBreakerType is a classification that defines the technical principle for the CircuitBreaker.	CircuitBreaker	CDM UoF Circuit Breaker
cityName	NameType	cityName is a name by which an incorporated municipal unit is known and can be easily referenced.	StreetAddress	CDM UoF Location
classificationDa te	DateType	classificationDate is a calendar date that identifies when the classification was recorded.	DatedClassifica tion	S-Series_Compound_Attributes_2-0_002-00
classificationDa teTime	DateTimeType	classificationDateTime is a calendar date and time that identifies when the classification was recorded.	TimeStampedClas sification	S-Series_Compound_Attributes_2-0_002-00
classifier	validValue	classifier is a word or code that represents the term used for classification.	DatedClassifica tion	S-Series_Compound_Attributes_2-0_002-00

Attribute Name	Type	Definition	Class Name	UoF
			`TimeStampedClassification`	S-Series_Compound_Attributes_2-0_002-00
`codePropertyAssignment`	ClassificationType	`codePropertyAssignment` is a classification that allows to separate assigned codes by the specification where these have been defined. **Example** – FIPS10-4 – IANA internet top-level domain code – ITU-T E.164 – S2000M	`CodeProperty`	S5000F_Compound_Attributes_002-00
`codePropertyDescription`	DescriptorType	`codePropertyDescription` is a narrative statement explaining the meaning of a code.	`CodeProperty`	S5000F_Compound_Attributes_002-00
`codePropertyValue`	TextPropertyType	`codePropertyValue` is a text indicating a code defined by a specific specification. **Example** – .es – +34 – SP	`CodeProperty`	S5000F_Compound_Attributes_002-00
`commentActionType`	ClassificationType	`commentActionType` is a <<classification>> that allows to group similar `CommentActions`.	`CommentAction`	S5000F Comment
`commentDate`	DateType	`commentDate` is the date at which a comment was raised.	`Comment`	S5000F Comment
`commentIdentifier`	IdentifierType	`commentIdentifier` is a string of characters that is used to uniquely identify a `Comment` and to differentiate it from other `Comments`.	`Comment`	S5000F Comment
`commentPartyRole`	ClassificationType	`commentPartyRole` is a classification that indicates the role of a specific `Party` in a specific `Comment`.	`CommentParty`	S5000F Comment

Attribute Name	Type	Definition	Class Name	UoF
`commentPriority`	ClassificationType	`commentPriority` is a classification that allows to define the importance of a comment and the need for an urgent response. **Example** – routine – urgent	`Comment`	S5000F Comment
`commentRelationshipType`	ClassificationType	`commentRelationshipType` is a classification that allows to identify the relationship between two comments. **Example** – clarification – response	`CommentRelationship`	S5000F Comment
`commentStatus`	ClassificationType	`commentStatus` is a classification that allows to determine whether a comment has been responded to. **Example** – Closed – Open	`Comment`	S5000F Comment
`commentText`	DescriptorType	`commentText` is a text describing the comment.	`Comment`	S5000F Comment
`commentTitle`	DescriptorType	`commentTitle` is a textual description that summarizes the comment.	`Comment`	S5000F Comment
`commentType`	ClassificationType	`commentType` is a classification that allows the grouping of similar comments.	`Comment`	S5000F Comment
`conditionInstanceDescription`	DescriptorType	`conditionInstanceDescription` is a description that gives more information on the meaning of the `ConditionInstance`.	`ConditionInstance`	CDM UoF Applicability Statement
`conditionInstanceIdentifier`	IdentifierType	`conditionInstanceIdentifier` is an identifier that establishes a unique designator for a `ConditionInstance` and to differentiate it from other instances of `ConditionInstance`.	`ConditionInstance`	CDM UoF Applicability Statement
`conditionInstanceName`	NameType	`conditionInstanceName` is a name by which the `ConditionInstance` is known and can be easily referenced.	`ConditionInstance`	CDM UoF Applicability Statement

Attribute Name	Type	Definition	Class Name	UoF
conditionTypeAssertMemberAssertValue	PropertyType	conditionTypeAssertMemberAssertValue is a numerical property that specifies values which can be used to further characterize the ConditionTypeAssertMember.	ConditionTypeAssertMember	CDM UoF Applicability Statement
conditionTypeAssertMemberAssertValueComparisonOperator	ClassificationType	conditionTypeAssertMemberAssertValueComparisonOperator is a classification that identifies a mathematical operation to be applied when testing a value against a defined conditionTypeAssertMemberAssertValue. **Example** – greater than – less than	ConditionTypeAssertMember	CDM UoF Applicability Statement
conditionTypeAssertMemberDescription	DescriptorType	conditionTypeAssertMemberDescription is a description that gives more information on meaning of the condition type assert member.	ConditionTypeAssertMember	CDM UoF Applicability Statement
conditionTypeAssertMemberName	NameType	conditionTypeAssertMemberName is a name that identifies a condition type member assert value.	ConditionTypeAssertMember	CDM UoF Applicability Statement
conditionTypeDescription	DescriptorType	conditionTypeDescription is a description that gives more information on the meaning of the condition type.	ConditionType	CDM UoF Applicability Statement
conditionTypeName	NameType	conditionTypeName is a name by which the ConditionType is known and can be easily referenced. **Example** – ashore or afloat – maintenance environment – operational environment – service bulletin	ConditionType	CDM UoF Applicability Statement
configurationConformanceEndDateTime	DateTimeType	configurationConformanceEndDateTime is a date and time that specifies the point in time when the SerializedProductVariant no longer complies with the associated product configuration.	SerializedProductVariantConfigurationConformance	CDM UoF Serialized Product Variant Configuration

Attribute Name	Type	Definition	Class Name	UoF
configurationConformanceStartDateTime	DateTimeType	configurationConformanceStartDateTime is a date and time that specifies the point in time when the SerializedProductVariant changed to the associated product configuration.	SerializedProductVariantConfigurationConformance	CDM UoF Serialized Product Variant Configuration
consequenceDescription	DescriptorType	consequenceDescription is a textual narrative statement explaining the consequence of an Event.	Consequence	S5000F Event
consequenceIdentifier	IdentifierType	consequenceIdentifier is a string of text that uniquely identifies a Consequence in the context of an Event, differentiating it from otehr Consequences.	Consequence	S5000F Event
consequenceType	ClassificationType	consequenceType is a classification that allows to group Consequences.	Consequence	S5000F Event
consumableItemDescription	DescriptorType	consumableItemDescription is a narrative statement explaining the ConsumableItem.	ConsumableItem	S5000F Supply Item
consumableItemIdentifier	IdentifierType	consumableItemIdentifier is a string of text that uniquely identifies a ConsumableItem and differentiates it from other ConsumableItems.	ConsumableItem	S5000F Supply Item
consumableItemName	TextPropertyType	consumableItemName is a text by which the ConsumableItem is commonly known.	ConsumableItem	S5000F Supply Item
consumableItemRiskDescription	DescriptorType	consumableItemRiskDescription is a narrative statement explaining the risk factor of the ConsumableItem.	ConsumableItem	S5000F Supply Item
consumableItemRiskFactor	ClassificationType	consumableItemRiskFactor is a classification that allows to define whether the ConsumableItem presents any safety issues or hazards.	ConsumableItem	S5000F Supply Item
consumableType	ClassificationType	consumableType is a classification that allows to group ConsumableItems of similar characteristics.	ConsumableItem	S5000F Supply Item

Applicable to: All

S5000F

Attribute Name	Type	Definition	Class Name	UoF
consumptionIdentifier	IdentifierType	`consumptionIdentifier` is a string that uniquely identifies a `Consumption` and differentiates it from other `Consumptions`.	Consumption	S5000F Consumptions and Emissions
consumptionType	ClassificationType	`consumptionType` is a <<classification>> that allows to differentiate between different types of `Consumptions`. **Example** – actual consumption – actual fuel loaded – expected fuel consumption – expected refuelling – jettisoned fuel	Consumption	S5000F Consumptions and Emissions
consumptionValue	NumericalPropertyType	`consumptionValue` is the amount of a `ConsumableItem` consumed by the `SerializedProductVariant` during the associated operational period, movement or movement leg. **Example** – 3000 liters – 4 tons	Consumption	S5000F Consumptions and Emissions
containerAsDesignedDescription	DescriptorType	`containerAsDesignedDescription` s a textual narrative providing further deatils about the `ContainerAsDesigned`.	ContainerAsDesigned	S5000F Container
containerAsDesignedIsReusable	umlBoolean	`containerAsDesignedIsReusable` is a `TRUE` or `FALSE` statement indicating whether the container can or not be reused.	ContainerAsDesigned	S5000F Container
containerAsDesignedMaterial	ClassificationType	`containerAsDesignedMaterial` is a classification that describes the main type of material of which the Container has been made of.	ContainerAsDesigned	S5000F Container
containerAsDesignedPayloadLimitation	PropertyType	`containerAsDesignedPayloadLimitation` is a property that defines the limitations about the amount that the container can contain. **Example** – max 400 kg weight – max. 10 bar pressure.	ContainerAsDesigned	S5000F Container

Attribute Name	Type	Definition	Class Name	UoF
containerAsDesig nedType	ClassificationType	containerAsDesignedType is a classification that indicates the kind of container. **Example** – cardboard box – drum – metallic container – plastic bag – wooden crate	ContainerAsDesi gned	S5000F Container
containerPartDur ing	DateRange	containerPartDuring is a period during which a (reusable) container contains a certain number of HardwarePartAsDesigned. **Note** This attribute is only applcable if the container is reusable and can therefore hold different parts or quantities at different moments in time.	ContainerPart	S5000F Container
containerPartIde ntifier	IdentifierType	containerPartIdentifier is a string of characters that allows to uniquely identify a ContainerPart <<relationship>> from other ones. **Note** The containerPartIdentifier is used only for reusable containers, as it allows to associate the content of a container to a spec fic transport.	ContainerPart	S5000F Container
containerPartQua ntity	PropertyType	containerPartQuantity is a property that indicates the number of HardwarePartAsDesigned that a HardwarePartContainer holds at a specific moment in time.	ContainerPart	S5000F Container
contractClauseDe scription	DescriptorType	contractClauseDescription is a phrase stating the contract clause or summarizing the content of the contract clause.	ContractClause	S5000F Contract Breakdown
contractClauseId entifier	IdentifierType	contractClauseIdentifier is a string of characters that are unique to the ContractClause and is used to designate a ContractClause and to differentiate it from other ContractClauses.	ContractClause	S5000F Contract Breakdown

Applicable to: All

Attribute Name	Type	Definition	Class Name	UoF
contractClauseRelationshipType	ClassificationType	contractClauseRelationshipType is a <<classification>> that defines how two ContractClauses are related.	ContractClauseRelationship	S5000F Contract Breakdown
contractClauseValidityPeriod	DateRange	contractClauseValidityPeriod is the period of time during which the ContractClause is in effect. **Note** The validity period of the ContractClause can be different from that of the Contract to which it belongs.	ContractClause	S5000F Contract Breakdown
contractDescription	DescriptorType	contractDescription is a description that provides a human readable expression of a Contract.	Contract	S5000F Specializations
contractEffectivityDateTimes	DateTimeRange	contractEffectivityDateTimes is the range of time during which the Contract if effective. **Example** – from 1/1/2018 12:00 until 31/12/2022 12:00	Contract	S5000F Specializations
contractItemDetailsContractQuantity	PropertyType	contractItemDetailsContractQuantity is a property that identifies the number of contract items that are included in the Contract	ContractItemDetails	CDM UoF Product and Project
contractPartyRole	ClassificationType	contractPartyRole is a classification that defines the purpose of the association between a ContractParty and the Contract. **Example** – Contractor – Customer – Escrow holder – Subcontractor – Supplier	ContractParty	CDM UoF Product and Project
contractRelationshipType	ClassificationType	contractRelationshipType is a classification that identifies the meaning of the established relationship. **Example** – associated – extends	ContractRelationship	CDM UoF Product and Project

Attribute Name	Type	Definition	Class Name	UoF
		– replaces – subcontract		
contractSignatureDate	DateType	contractSignatureDate is the date at which the Contract was signed or agreed.	Contract	S5000F Specializations
contractStatus	StateType	contractStatus is a timestampedState that indicates the state of a Contract at a specific moment in time.	Contract	S5000F Specializations
contractType	ClassificationType	contractType is a classification describing the Contract. **Example** – development contract – procurement contract – service contract	Contract	S5000F Specializations
contractValue	SingleValuePropertyType	contractValue is the amount of money that the Contract is worth.	Contract	S5000F Specializations
costBreakdownDescription	DescriptorType	costBreakdownDescription is a narrative statement explaining the CostBreakdown.	CostBreakdown	S5000F Cost Breakdown
costBreakdownIdentifier	IdentifierType	costBreakdownIdentifier is a string of text that uniquely identifies a CostBreakdown, allowing to differentiate it from all other CostBreakdowns.	CostBreakdown	S5000F Cost Breakdown
costBreakdownName	DescriptorType	costBreakdownName is a word or phrase by which the CostBreakdown is commonly known.	CostBreakdown	S5000F Cost Breakdown
costBreakdownRelationshipType	ClassificationType	costBreakdownRelationshipType is a <<classification>> that defines how two CostBreakdowns are related.	CostBreakdownRelationship	S5000F Cost Breakdown
costBreakdownRevisionDate	DateType	costBreakdownRevisionDate is a Date that indicates when the CostBreakdownRevision was created.	CostBreakdownRevision	S5000F Cost Breakdown
costBreakdownRevisionIdentifier	IdentifierType	costBreakdownRevisionIdentifier is a string of characters that uniquely identifies a CostBreakdownRevision.	CostBreakdownRevision	S5000F Cost Breakdown

Attribute Name	Type	Definition	Class Name	UoF
costBreakdownRevisionRationale	DescriptorType	costBreakdownRevisionRationale is a description that provides a human readable expression of a CostBreakdownRevision.	CostBreakdownRevision	S5000F Cost Breakdown
costBreakdownRevisionStatus	StateType	costBreakdownRevisionStatus is a state that defines the active status of a CostBreakdownRevision. **Example** – approved – cancelled – draft – under review	CostBreakdownRevision	S5000F Cost Breakdown
costEntryDate	DateType	costEntryDate is the date at which the cost entry was made or incurred.	CostEntry	S5000F Cost Breakdown
costEntryDescription	DescriptorType	costEntryDescription is a textual narrative statement explaining the nature of the CostEntry	CostEntry	S5000F Cost Breakdown
costEntryIdentifier	IdentifierType	costEntryIdentifier is a string of characters used to uniquely identify a CostEntry and differentiate it from other CostEntries.	CostEntry	S5000F Cost Breakdown
costEntryPeriod	DateRange	costEntryPeriod is the period of time during which the cost for this CostEntry was incurred.	CostEntry	S5000F Cost Breakdown
costEntryType	ClassificationType	costEntryType is a classification used to differentiate between different kinds of costs incurred. **Example** – labour – material	CostEntry	S5000F Cost Breakdown
costEntryValue	PropertyType	costEntryValue is the actual or estimated value of the cost. **Example** – $1250.55 – 1330 €	CostEntry	S5000F Cost Breakdown

Attribute Name	Type	Definition	Class Name	UoF
costItemDescript ion	DescriptorType	costItemDescription is a narrative statement explaining what the CostItem is.	CostItem	S5000F Cost Breakdown
costItemIdentifi er	IdentifierType	costItemIdentifier is a string of characters that is used to uniquely designate a CostItem and to differentiate it from other CostItems.	CostItem	S5000F Cost Breakdown
costItemRelation shipType	ClassificationType	costItemRelationshipType is a classification that defines the relationship between two CostItems. **Example** – Part of – Related to	CostItemRelatio nship	S5000F Cost Breakdown
countryCode	ClassificationType	countryCode is a string of characters used to uniquely identify a Country and to differentiate it from other instances of Country. **Note** It is advised to use ISO 3166-1 alpha-2.	Country	CDM UoF Location
countryName	NameType	countryName is a name by which the Country is known and can be easily referenced.	Country	CDM UoF Location
damageCharacteri cType	ClassificationType	damageCharactericType is a <<classification>> that defines the characteristics of a Damage.	DamageCharacter istic	S5000F Damage
damageCharacteri sticDescription	DescriptorType	damageCharacteristicDescription is a textual narrative that provides a human readable expression of a DamageCharacteristic.	DamageCharacter istic	S5000F Damage
damageCharacteri sticIdentifier	IdentifierType	damageCharacteristicIdentifier is a <<compositeKey>> that allows with a master key to uniquely identify a DamageCharacteristic.	DamageCharacter istic	S5000F Damage
damageColor	ClassificationType	damageColor is a <<classification>> that defines the color of a Damage.	Damage	S5000F Damage

Attribute Name	Type	Definition	Class Name	UoF
damageDefinition Description	DescriptorType	`damageDefinitionDescription` is a description that gives more information on the `DamageDefinition`.	`DamageDefinitio n`	CDM UoF Damage Definition
damageDefinition Family	ClassificationType	`damageDefinitionFamily` is a classification that identifies a group of damages which share the damage characteristics and often lead to the same, or similar, corrective action. **Example** – crack – dent – scratch	`DamageDefinitio n`	CDM UoF Damage Definition
damageDefinition Name	NameType	`damageDefinitionName` is a name by which the `DamageDefinition` is known and can be easily referenced.	`DamageDefinitio n`	CDM UoF Damage Definition
damageDescriptio n	DescriptorType	`damageDescription` is a textual description of the damage.	`Damage`	S5000F Damage
damageDimensions	`Dimensions`	`damageDimensions` is a set of values that define a geometrical figure that determines the extension of the damage.	`DamageCharacter istic`	S5000F Damage
damageEstimatedC ost	ValueRangePropertyTy pe	`damageEstimatedCost` is a range of possible costs associated to a specific damage.	`Damage`	S5000F Damage
damageFamily	ClassificationType	`damageFamily` is a classification that defines the type of damage. **Example** – paint damage – structural damage	`Damage`	S5000F Damage
damageIdentifier	IdentifierType	`damageIdentifier` is a string of characters used to uniquely identify a `Damage`.	`Damage`	S5000F Damage
damageRepairStat us	ClassificationType	`damageRepairStatus` is a <<classificationType>> that indicates the status of the `Damage` repair.	`Damage`	S5000F Damage
damageSeverity	ClassificationType	`damageSeverity` is a classification that defines how serious a `Damage` is.	`Damage`	S5000F Damage

Attribute Name	Type	Definition	Class Name	UoF
damageStatus	DatedClassification	damageStatus is a classification that indicates the status of the damage at a specific moment in time. **Example** – pending repair – repaired – unrepairable	Damage	S5000F Damage
dataAssociatedWithType	ClassificationType	dataAssociatedWithType is a <<classification>> that allows to define the type of relationship between a DataSetAsDesigned and a ParAsDesigned.	DataSetAssociatedWith	S5000F Data Sets
dataModuleIssueInWorkNumber	umlString	dataModuleIssueInWorkNumber is a string of characters used for monitoring and control of intermediate drafts of S1000DDataModuleIssue. **Note** A dataModuleIssueInWorkNumber must be created in accordance with the rules defined in S1000D.	S1000DDataModuleIssue	CDM UoF Document
dataModuleIssueLanguage	ClassificationType	dataModuleIssueLanguage is a classification that identifies the language used to produce the content of the S1000DDataModuleIssue. **Note** A dataModuleIssueLanguage must be created in accordance with the rules defined in S1000D.	S1000DDataModuleIssue	CDM UoF Document
dataModuleIssueLanguageCountry	ClassificationType	dataModuleIssueLanguageCountry is a classification that identifies the country where the language, identified by dataModuleIssueLanguage, is spoken **Note** A dataModuleIssueLanguageCountry must be created in accordance with the rules defined in S1000D.	S1000DDataModuleIssue	CDM UoF Document
dataModuleIssueNumber	umlString	dataModuleIssueNumber is a string of characters used to identify the release number of the S1000DDataModuleIssue	S1000DDataModuleIssue	CDM UoF Document

Applicable to: All

Attribute Name	Type	Definition	Class Name	UoF
		Note A `dataModuleIssueNumber` must be created in accordance with the rules defined in S1000D.		
`dataSetAsDesigne dDescription`	DescriptorType	`dataSetAsDesignedDescription` is a narrative description of a `DataSetAsDesigned` data structure.	`DataSetAsDesign ed`	S5000F Data Sets
`dataSetAsDesigne dType`	ClassificationType	`dataSetAsDesignedType` is a classification that allows to group different `DataSetAsDesigned` data structures according to common characteristics.	`DataSetAsDesign ed`	S5000F Data Sets
`dataSetAsRelease dNotes`	DescriptorType	`dataSetAsReleasedNotes` is a narrative description that provides additional information about a specific `DataSetAsReleased`.	`DataSetAsReleas ed`	S5000F Data Sets
`dateRangeEnd`	DateType	`dateRangeEnd` is a date that represents the conclusion of the range.	`DateRange`	S-Series_Compound_Attributes_2-0_002-00
`dateRangeStart`	DateType	`dateRangeStart` is a date that represents the beginning of the range.	`DateRange`	S-Series_Compound_Attributes_2-0_002-00
`dateTimeRangeEnd`	DateTimeType	`dateTimeRangeEnd` is a calendar date and time that represents the culmination of the range.	`DateTimeRange`	S-Series_Compound_Attributes_2-0_002-00
`dateTimeRangeSta rt`	DateTimeType	`dateTimeRangeStart` is a calendar date and time that represents the beginning of the range.	`DateTimeRange`	S-Series_Compound_Attributes_2-0_002-00
`detectionMeanCap abilityCapabilit yType`	ClassificationType	`detectionMeanCapabilityCapabilityType` is a <<classification>> that allows to group different DetectionMeanCapabilities based on their individual characteristics.	`DetectionMeanCa pability`	S5000F Failure Detection and Location
`detectionMeanCap abilityDescripti on`	DescriptorType	`detectionMeanCapabilityDescription` is a narrative statement that explains a `DetectionMeanCapability`.	`DetectionMeanCa pability`	S5000F Failure Detection and Location

Attribute Name	Type	Definition	Class Name	UoF
detectionMeanCap abilityIdentifie r	IdentifierType	detectionMeanCapabilityIdentifier is a string of text that uniquely identifies a DetectionMeanCapability and differentiates it from other DetectionMeanCapabilities.	DetectionMeanCa pability	S5000F Failure Detection and Location
detectionMechani smDescription	DescriptorType	detectionMechanismDescription is a textual narrative statement that explains a DetectionMechanism.	DetectionMechan ism	S5000F Failure Detection and Location
detectionMechani smFalseAlarmRate	PropertyType	detectionMechanismFalseAlarmRate is the frequency at which the DetectionMechanism is expected to raise a false alarm.	DetectionMechan ism	S5000F Failure Detection and Location
detectionMechani smIdentifier	IdentifierType	detectionMechanismIdentifier is a string of text that uniquely identifies a DetectionMechanism and differentiates it from other DetectionMechanisms.	DetectionMechan ism	S5000F Failure Detection and Location
detectionMechani smPresentation	DescriptorType	detectionMechanismPresentation is a textual narrative statement that indicates how the FailureMechanism is brought to the attention of the user. **Example** – buzzer – flashing display – red lamp	DetectionMechan ism	S5000F Failure Detection and Location
detectionMechani smType	ClassificationType	detectionMechanismType is a classification that allows to group similar DetectionMechanisms.	DetectionMechan ism	S5000F Failure Detection and Location
diameter	PropertyType	diameter is a property that specifies the longitudinal dimension of a circular section when measured through its center.	Circle	S5000F_Compound_Attributes_ 002-00
			Cylinder	S-Series_Compound_Attributes_2-0_002-00
			Sphere	S-Series_Compound_Attributes_2-0_002-00

Attribute Name	Type	Definition	Class Name	UoF
`digitalFileConte ntClass`	ClassificationType	`digitalFileContentClass` is a classification that determine the meaning of the information within the `DigitalFile`.	`DigitalFile`	CDM UoF Digital File
`digitalFileConte ntDescription`	DescriptorType	`digitalFileContentDescription` is a phrase that gives more details about the information contained in the `DigitalFile`	`DigitalFile`	CDM UoF Digital File
`digitalFileLocat or`	IdentifierType	`digitalFileLocator` is an identifier that establishes a unique designator for a `DigitalFile` used to locate and identify a `DigitalFile` and to differentiate it from other instances of `DigitalFile`.	`DigitalFile`	CDM UoF Digital File
`digitalFileRefer enceJustificatio n`	DescriptorType	`digitalFileReferenceJustification` is a description that provides more on information on the reason why the `DigitalFileReferencedItem` is referenced. **Example** – Crack discovered on `BreakdownElement` ABC-123	`DigitalFileRefe rence`	CDM UoF Digital File
`digitalFileRepre sentation`	umlString	`digitalFileRepresentation` is a string of characters representing the content of the `DigitalFile`. **Example** – A uuencoded ASCII umlString representing a binary source file.	`DigitalFile`	CDM UoF Digital File
`digitalFileType`	ClassificationType	`digitalFileType` is a classification that specifies the format of the data within the `DigitalFile`. **Note** Typically, the file name extension in Microsoft Windows.	`DigitalFile`	CDM UoF Digital File
`disassemblyCode`	umlString	`disassemblyCode` is a string of characters that represents the disassembly code attribute of the data module code. **Note** A `disassemblyCode` must be created in accordance with the rules defined in S1000D.	`S1000DDataModul e`	CDM Document

Attribute Name	Type	Definition	Class Name	UoF
disassemblyCodeVariant	umlString	`disassemblyCodeVariant` is a string of characters that represents the disassembly code variant attribute of the data module code. **Note** A `disassemblyCodeVariant` must be created in accordance with the rules defined in S1000D.	`S1000DDataModule`	CDM Document
disposalLocationRole	ClassificationType	`disposalLocationRole` is a classification that allows to define the role that a `Location` has in teh context of a `DisposalRequirement`.	`DisposalLocation`	S5000F Disposal Requirement
disposalRequirementDueDate	DateType	`disposalRequirementDueDate` is the date at which the disposal item or waste must be disposed of.	`DisposalRequirement`	S5000F Disposal Requirement
disposalRequirementJustification	DescriptorType	`disposalRequirementJustification` is a textual description of the reason(s) why the disposal is required.	`DisposalRequirement`	S5000F Disposal Requirement
disposalRequirementMethod	ClassificationType	`disposalRequirementMethod` is a classification that indicates the method(s) to be applied for the disposal of an item.	`DisposalRequirement`	S5000F Disposal Requirement
disposalRequirementReason	ClassificationType	`disposalRequirementReason` is a classification indicating the reason for the disposal.	`DisposalRequirement`	S5000F Disposal Requirement
documentCreationDate	DateType	`documentCreationDate` is the date at which the document was published.	`Document`	S5000F Specializations
documentDescription	DescriptorType	`documentDescription` is a textual narrative statement that explains what the document is about.	`Document`	S5000F Specializations
documentIssueReason	ClassificationType	`documentIssueReason` is a <<classification>> that allows to group `DocumentIssues` bythe different causes for their release.	`DocumentIssue`	S5000F Specializations
documentPartyRelationshipType	DatedClassification	`documentPartyRelationshipType` ia relationship identifying the type of association between a document and a `Party` at a specific date. **Example** – approved by – distributed to	`DocumentParty`	S5000F Document

Attribute Name	Type	Definition	Class Name	UoF
		– prepared by – reviewed by		
documentStatus	StateType	documentStatus is a state that indicates the status of the document. **Example** – draft – published	Document	S5000F Specializations
downTimeIdentifier	IdentifierType	downTimeIdentifier is a string of text that uniquely identifies a DownTimePeriod and differentiates it from other DownTimePeriods.	DownTimePeriod	S5000F Change Embodiment Planning
downTimePeriodReason	ClassificationType	downTimePeriodReason is a narrative text providing information about the DownTimePeriod. **Example** – overhaul – scheduled maintenance	DownTimePeriod	S5000F Change Embodiment Planning
downTimePeriodValue	DateTimeRange	downTimePeriodValue is a period of time during which the SerializedProductVariant is or will be not available.	DownTimePeriod	S5000F Change Embodiment Planning
downTimeStatus	ClassificationType	downTimeStatus is a classification allowing to determine the validity of a DownTime.	DownTimePeriod	S5000F Change Embodiment Planning
environmentCondition	NumericalPropertyType	environmentCondition is a <<NumericPropertyType>> that describes the normal quantitative values that define an Environment and differentiate it from other Environments. **Example** – air particle size – humidity – temperature	Environment	S5000F Environment
environmentDefinitionDescription	DescriptorType	environmentDefinitionDescription is a description that gives more information on the EnvironmentDefinition.	EnvironmentDefinitionRevision	CDM UoF Environment Definition

Attribute Name	Type	Definition	Class Name	UoF
environmentDefin itionIdentifier	IdentifierType	environmentDefinitionIdentifier is an identifier that establishes a unique designator for an EnvironmentDefinition and to differentiate it from other instances of EnvironmentDefinition.	EnvironmentDefi nition	CDM UoF Environment Definition
environmentDefin itionName	NameType	environmentDefinitionName is a name by which the EnvironmentDefinition is known and can be easily referenced.	EnvironmentDefi nitionRevision	CDM UoF Environment Definition
environmentDefin itionRevisionDat e	DateType	environmentDefinitionRevisionDate is a date that specifies when the EnvironmentDefinition was revised.	EnvironmentDefi nitionRevision	CDM UoF Environment Definition
environmentDefin itionRevisionIde ntifier	IdentifierType	environmentDefinitionRevisionIdentifier is an identifier that establishes a unique designator for a EnvironmentDefinitionRevision and to differentiate it from other instances of EnvironmentDefinitionRevision.	EnvironmentDefi nitionRevision	CDM UoF Environment Definition
environmentDefin itionRevisionRat ionale	DescriptorType	environmentDefinitionRevisionRationale is a description that provides a justification for revising the EnvironmentDefinition.	EnvironmentDefi nitionRevision	CDM UoF Environment Definition
environmentDefin itionRevisionSta tus	StateType	environmentDefinitionRevisionStatus is a state that identifies the maturity of an EnvironmentDefinitionRevision.	EnvironmentDefi nitionRevision	CDM UoF Environment Definition
environmentDescr iption	DescriptorType	environmentDescription is a textual description of an environment.	Environment	S5000F Environment
environmentIdent ifier	IdentifierType	environmentIdentifier is a string of characters used to uniquely identify an Environment and to differentiate it from other Environments.	Environment	S5000F Environment
environmentName	NameType	environmentName is a name by which the Environment is known and can be easily referenced.	Environment	S5000F Environment

Attribute Name	Type	Definition	Class Name	UoF
environmentRelat ionshipType	ClassificationType	environmentRelationshipType is a <<classification>> that allows to indicate the kind of relationship between two Environments.	EnvironmentRela tionship	S5000F Environment
environmentRevis ionCondition	NumericalPropertyType	environmentRevisionCondition is a <<NumericPropertyType>> that describes the quantitative conditions that define an environmentRevision and differentiate it from other environmentRevisions.	EnvironmentRevi sion	S5000F Environment
environmentRevis ionDate	DateType	environmentRevisionDate is the date at which the EnvironmentRevision was created.	EnvironmentRevi sion	S5000F Environment
environmentRevis ionIdentifier	IdentifierType	environmentRevisionIdentifier is a <<compositeKey>> that allows with a master key to uniquely identify an EnvironmentRevision.	EnvironmentRevi sion	S5000F Environment
environmentRevis ionRationale	DescriptorType	environmentRevisionRationale is a decription that provides a justification for the EnvironmentRevision.	EnvironmentRevi sion	S5000F Environment
environmentRevis ionStatus	StateType	environmentRevisionStatus is a state that identifies the maturity of an EnvironmentRevision.	EnvironmentRevi sion	S5000F Environment
environmentRevis ionType	ClassificationType	environmentRevisionType is a <<classification>> that allows to group similar EnvironmentRevisions. **Example** – environment change due to installation of air conditioning – seasonal climate change – temporary environmental change due to volcanic eruption	EnvironmentRevi sion	S5000F Environment
environmentRevis ionValidity	DateRange	environmentRevisionValidity is a DateRange during which an EnvironmentRevision is valid. **Example** – a period during which a volcano is erupting and there are volcanic ashes. – long seasonal change, such as the monsoon period.	EnvironmentRevi sion	S5000F Environment

Attribute Name	Type	Definition	Class Name	UoF
environmentType	ClassificationType	environmentType is a classification that allows to group different Environments by their characteristics. **Example** – interior environment – tropical climate	Environment	S5000F Environment
equipmentOperatingPeriod	DateRange	equipmentOperatingPeriod is the period during which the equipment is operated by a specific Party.	EquipmentOperation	S5000F Equipment
equipmentOwnershipPeriod	DateRange	equipmentOwnershipPeriod is the period during which the item was owned by a specific Party.	EquipmentOwner	S5000F Equipment
equipmentStatusPeriod	DateTimeRange	equipmentStatusPeriod is the period during which the equipment had that specific status.	EquipmentStatus	S5000F Equipment
equipmentStatusReason	ClassificationType	equipmentStatusReason is a classification indicating the reason for which an equipment has been in that status during a specific period of time. **Example** – failure – operation – scheduled maintenance – waiting for material	EquipmentStatus	S5000F Equipment
equipmentStatusType	ClassificationType	equipmentStatusType is a classification that describes the status of the equipment. **Example** – broken – operational – scrapped	EquipmentStatus	S5000F Equipment
evaluationByAssertionRole	ClassificationType	evaluationByAssertionRole is a classification that defines the context in which the EvaluationByAssertionOfClassInstance is being referenced.	EvaluationByAssertionOfClassInstance	CDM UoF Applicability Statement

Attribute Name	Type	Definition	Class Name	UoF
eventConfirmedSt atus	DatedClassificat ion	eventConfirmedStatus is a classification at a specific moment in time describing whether the event has or not been confirmed. **Example** – confirmed, 31-12-2018 13:30 GMT	Event	S5000F Event
eventDescription	DescriptorType	eventDescription is a narrative statement explaining an Event or the circumstances surrounding it.	Event	S5000F Event
eventGroup	ClassificationType	eventGroup is a classification that is used to categorize the type of Event.	Event	S5000F Event
eventIdentifier	IdentifierType	eventIdentifier is a string of characters that uniquely identifies an Event so as to differentiate it from other Events.	Event	S5000F Event
eventOcurrenceDa teTime	DateTimeType	eventOcurrenceDateTime is the date and time at which the Event occurred.	Event	S5000F Event
eventRelationshi pItemRole	ClassificationType	eventRelationshipItemRole is a <<classification>> that allows to indicate the type of relationship that an item has regarding an Event.	EventRelationsh ipItem	S5000F Event
eventRelationshi pType	ClassificationType	eventRelationshipType is a classification that indicates the type of relationship between two different Events.	EventRelationsh ip	S5000F Event
eventReporterDat eTime	DateTimeType	eventReporterDateTime is a DateTime which represents the date and time at which the EventReporter reported the Event.	EventReporter	S5000F Event
eventSeverity	ClassificationType	eventSeverity is a <<classification>> that allows to indicate the impact of the event.	Event	S5000F Event
explanatoryFacto rDescription	DescriptorType	explanatoryFactorDescription is a textual explanation of the ExplanatoryFactor.	ExplanatoryFact or	S5000F Event
explanatoryFacto rIdentifier	IdentifierType	explanatoryFactorIdentifier is an unique identifier that allows to differentiate between one ExplanatoryFactor and another one.	ExplanatoryFact or	S5000F Event

Attribute Name	Type	Definition	Class Name	UoF
explanatoryFacto rName	DescriptorType	explanatoryFactorName is a short textual description that allows to identify an explanatoryFactor. **Example** – "Human failure"	ExplanatoryFact or	S5000F Event
explanatoryFacto rOrganization	Organization	explanatoryFactorOrganization is the Organization that has defined the ExplanatoryFactor. **Example** – ECCAIRS – ICAO	ExplanatoryFact or	S5000F Event
exportControlLic enseDescription	DescriptorType	exportControlLicenseDescription is a description that provides a human readable expression of an ExportControlLicense.	ExportControlLi cense	S5000F Export Control License
exportControlLic enseIdentifier	IdentifierType	exportControlLicenseIdentifier is a string of characters that uniquely identifies an ExportControlLicense.	ExportControlLi cense	S5000F Export Control License
exportControlLic enseItemCategory	ClassificationType	exportControlLicenseItemCategory is a <<classification>> that allows to group ExportControlLicenseItems.	ExportControlLi censeItem	S5000F Export Control License
exportControlLic enseItemidentifi er	IdentifierType	exportControlLicenseItemidentifier is a string of characters that uniquely identifies an ExportControlLicenseItem.	ExportControlLi censeItem	S5000F Export Control License
exportControlLic enseItemQuantity	umlInteger	exportControlLicenseItemQuantity is a numeric value representing the amount of items covered by an ExportControlLicense.	ExportControlLi censeItem	S5000F Export Control License
exportControlLic enseItemSubCateg ory	ClassificationType	exportControlLicenseItemSubCategory is a <<classification>> that allows to further subgroup ExportControlLicenseItems.	ExportControlLi censeItem	S5000F Export Control License

Attribute Name	Type	Definition	Class Name	UoF
exportControlLicensePurpose	DescriptorType	`exportControlLicensePurpose` is a description that provides a human readable expression of the purpose of an `ExportControlLicense`.	`ExportControlLicense`	S5000F Export Control License
exportControlLicenseType	ClassificationType	`exportControlLicenseType` is a <<classification>>; that defines the type of export control license.	`ExportControlLicense`	S5000F Export Control License
exportControlPartyClearanceCode	ClassificationType	`exportControlPartyClearanceCode` is a classification that indicates the type of clearance that the exportControlParty has received to house export controlled goods.	`ExportControlParty`	S5000F Export Control License
exportControlPartyClearanceDate	DateType	`exportControlPartyClearanceDate` is a date that indicates when the exportControlParty has received the clearance to house export controlled goods.	`ExportControlParty`	S5000F Export Control License
exportControlPartyClearanceLevel	ClassificationType	`exportControlPartyClearanceLevel` is a classification that indicates the level of the clearance that the exportControlParty has received to house export controlled goods.	`ExportControlParty`	S5000F Export Control License
exportControlPartyIdentifier	IdentifierType	`exportControlPartyIdentifier` is a string of characters that uniquely identifies an `ExportControlParty`.	`ExportControlParty`	S5000F Export Control License
exportControlPartyRole	ClassificationType	`exportControlPartyRole` is a <<classification>> that defines the role of an `ExportControlParty`.	`ExportControlParty`	S5000F Export Control License
exportControlPartyType	ClassificationType	`exportControlPartyType` is a <<classification» that indicates the characteristic of the `Party` involved in the export control.	`ExportControlParty`	S5000F Export Control License
exportControlRegulationLegalCode	ClassificationType	`exportControlRegulationLegalCode` is a <<classification>> that provides the identifier for the legal export control regulation.	`ExportControlRegulation`	S5000F Export Control Requirement
exportControlRegulationtPeculiarityCode	ClassificationType	`exportControlRegulationtPeculiarityCode` is a <<classification>> that allows to use codes used by different `ExportControlRegulations`.	`ExportControlRegulation`	S5000F Export Control Requirement

Attribute Name	Type	Definition	Class Name	UoF
exportControlRequirementAppliedToCountryDescription	DescriptorType	exportControlRequirementAppliedToCountryDescription is a description that provides a human readable expression of how or why an ExportControlRequirement is applied to Country.	ExportControlRequirementAppliedToCountry	S5000F Export Control Requirement
exportControlRequirementAppliedToCountryDuring	DateRange	exportControlRequirementAppliedToCountryDuring is a DataRange during which an ExportControlRequirement is applied to a specific country.	ExportControlRequirementAppliedToCountry	S5000F Export Control Requirement
exportControlRequirementGrouping	ClassificationType	exportControlRequirementGrouping is a <<classification>> that allows to group similar ExportControlRegulations.	ExportControlRegulation	S5000F Export Control Requirement
expressionEvaluationDateRange	DateRange	expressionEvaluationDateRange is a date range that defines the date interval for when the defined evaluation can result in a TRUE result.	ExpressionEvaluation	S5000F Expression Evaluation
expressionEvaluationDescription	DescriptorType	expressionEvaluationDescription is a description that provides a human readable expression of the defined rule.	ExpressionEvaluation	S5000F Expression Evaluation
expressionEvaluationIdentifier	IdentifierType	expressionEvauationIdentifieris an identifier that establishes an unique designator for an ExpressionEvaluation and to differentiate it from other instances of ExpressionEvaluation.	ExpressionEvaluation	S5000F Expression Evaluation
extensionCode	umlString	extensionCode is a string of characters used to identify the organization receiving the customized data module. **Note** An extensionCode must be created in accordance with the rules defined in S1000D. **Note** An extensionCode must be created in accordance with the rules defined in S1000D.	S1000DDataModule S1000DPublicationModule	CDM UoF Document CDM UoF Document
extensionProducer	umlString	extensionProducer is a string of characters used to identify the organization providing the customized data module.	S1000DDataModule	CDM UoF Document

Applicable to: All

Attribute Name	Type	Definition	Class Name	UoF
		Note An `extensionProducer` must be created in accordance with the rules defined in S1000D.	`S1000DPublicationModule`	CDM UoF Document
`externalDocumentType`	ClassificationType	`externalDocumentType` is a classification that allows to group `ExternalDocuments` of a similar nature.	`ExternalDocument`	S5000F Document
`facilityCleansiness`	ClassificationType	`facilityCleansiness` is a classification that indicates the cleansiness that is required for the facility. **Example** – Dust-free clean room	`Facility`	S5000F Specializations
`facilityDimensions`	Dimensions	`facilityDimensions` are the dimensions of the `Facility`. **Note** Some facilities (eg, a parking lot or a runway) can have only two dimensions, though most of the facilities will have three.	`Facility`	S5000F Specializations
`facilityExistsDuring`	DateRange	`facilityExistsDuring` represents the period of time during which a tempoerarty `Facility` exists.	`Facility`	S5000F Specializations
`facilityLocationIdentifier`	IdentifierType	`facilityLocationIdentifier` is a string of characters that uniquely identifies a `FacilityLocation`.	`FacilityLocation`	S5000F Facility
`facilityLocationPeriod`	DateRange	`facilityLocationPeriod` is a `DateRange` during which a `Facility` is located at a specific `Location`.	`FacilityLocation`	S5000F Facility
`facilityOperatorDuring`	DateRange	`facilityOperatorDuring` is the period during which a certain `Party` operates a `Facility`.	`FacilityOperator`	S5000F Specializations
`facilityOwnedDuring`	DateRange	`facilityOwnedDuring` is the period during which a facility is or has been owned by a specific `Party`.	`FacilityOwner`	S5000F Facility
`facilityOwnershipRatio`	SingleValuePropertyType	`facilityOwnershipRatio` is the percentage of ownership that a `Party` has over the associated facility during the associated period.	`FacilityOwner`	S5000F Facility

Attribute Name	Type	Definition	Class Name	UoF
		Note This wil be 100% for the sole owner, and a fraction in case of shared property.		
facilityRelation shipType	ClassificationType	facilityRelationshipType is a classification that describes the relationship between two facilities. **Note** The relationship can be used for example to indicate that a workshop is located inside a specific building within a specific plant. **Example** – is co-located with – Is part of	FacilityRelatio nship	S5000F Facility
facilityWeight	PropertyType	facilityWeight is a property that specifies the mass for the Facility.	Facility	S5000F Specializations
failureDetection Rate	ClassificationType	failureDetectionRate is a classification that indicates the rate at which a failure can be detected.	FailureDetectio n	S5000F Failure Detection and Location
failureModeCause Description	DescriptorType	failureModeCauseDescription is a description that gives more information on the FailureModeCause.	FailureModeCaus e	CDM UoF Failure Mode
failureModeCause Identifier	IdentifierType	failureModeCauseIdentifier is an identifier that establishes a unique des gnator for a FailureModeCause and to differentiate it from other instances of FailureModeCause.	FailureModeCaus e	CDM UoF Failure Mode
failureModeCause Ratio	PropertyType	failureModeCauseRatio identifies the fraction of an individual FailureModeCause in relation to the entire population of FailureModeCauses identified for the FailureMode.	FailureModeCaus e	CDM UoF Failure Mode
failureModeCriti cality	ClassificationType	failureModeCriticality is a classification that identifies the most serious impact that the FailureMode will have on the referred item.	FailureModeEffe ct	CDM UoF Failure Mode
failureModeDescr iption	DescriptorType	failureModeDescription is a description that gives more information on the FailureMode.	FailureMode	CDM UoF Failure Mode

Attribute Name	Type	Definition	Class Name	UoF
failureModeEffectDescription	DescriptorType	`failureModeEffectDescription` is a description that gives more information on the `FailureModeEffect`.	`FailureModeEffect`	CDM UoF Failure Mode
failureModeEffectLevel	ClassificationType	`failureModeEffectLevel` is classification that identifies the higher indenture level that will be affected by the `FailureMode`.	`FailureModeEffect`	CDM UoF Failure Mode
failureModeEffectName	NameType	`failureModeEffectName` is a name by which the `FailureModeEffect` is known and can be easily referenced.	`FailureModeEffect`	CDM UoF Failure Mode
failureModeIdentifier	IdentifierType	`failureModeIdentifier` is an identifier that establishes a unique designator for a `FailureMode` and to differentiate it from other instances of `FailureMode`.	`FailureMode`	CDM UoF Failure Mode
failureModeName	NameType	`failureModeName` is a name by which the `FailureMode` is known and can be easily referenced.	`FailureMode`	CDM UoF Failure Mode
failureModeRatio	PropertyType	`failureModeRatio` identifies the fraction of an individual `FailureMode` in relation to the entire population of `FailureModes` identified for the FailureModeAnalysisItem. **Note** If the `failureModeRatio` equals '0' then the failure mode is only driven by damages.	`FailureMode`	CDM UoF Failure Mode
faultDeferredToDate	DateType	`faultDeferredToDate` is the date that indicates when resolution of a `Fault` will be solved.	`Fault`	S5000F Actual Fault Indication
faultDetectedDate	DateType	`faultDetectedDate` is the date at which the `Fault` has been detected.	`Fault`	S5000F Actual Fault Indication
faultFixedDate	DateType	`faultFixedDate` is the date at which the `Fault` was fixed.	`Fault`	S5000F Actual Fault Indication
faultIdentifier	IdentifierType	FaultIdentifier is a string of characters that is used to uniquely identify a `Fault` and to differentiate it from other `Faults`.	`Fault`	S5000F Actual Fault Indication
faultStatus	ClassificationType	`faultStatus` is a classification that indicates whether a `Fault` has been resolved or not.	`Fault`	S5000F Actual Fault Indication

Applicable to: All

Attribute Name	Type	Definition	Class Name	UoF
faultSymptomDate Time	DateTimeType	`faultSymptomDateTime` is a DateTime which represents the date and time at which the `Fault` occurred.	`FaultSymptom`	S5000F Actual Fault Indication
faultSymptomIden tifier	IdentifierType	`faultSymptomIdentifier` is a <<compositeKey>> that allows with a master key to uniquely identify a `FaultSymptom`.	`FaultSymptom`	S5000F Actual Fault Indication
fleetBasedAtDuri ng	`DateRange`	`fleetBasedAtDuring` is a `DateRange` during which a `Fleet` is based at a specific location.	`FleetBasedAt`	S5000F Fleet Definition
fleetDescription	DescriptorType	`fleetDescription` is a narrative statement explaining the `Fleet`.	`Fleet`	S5000F Fleet Definition
fleetIdentifier	IdentifierType	`fleetIdentifier` is a string of text that uniquely identifies a `Fleet` and differentiates it from other `Fleets`.	`Fleet`	S5000F Fleet Definition
fleetOperatedByD uring	`DateRange`	`fleetOperatedByDuring` is a <<`DateRange`>> that indicates the period of time during which a `Fleet` is operated by a specific `Operator`.	`FleetOperatedBy`	S5000F Fleet Definition
fleetOperatesAtL ocationDuring	`DateRange`	`fleetOperatesAtLocationDuring` is a `DateRange` during which a `Fleet` has operated at a specific location.	`FleetOperatesAt Location`	S5000F Fleet Definition
fleetPlanningDes cription	DescriptorType	`fleetPlanningDescription` is a narrative statement explaining the `FleetPlanning`.	`FleetPlanning`	S5000F Fleet Planning and Product Assignment
fleetPlanningIde ntifier	IdentifierType	`fleetPlanningIdentifier` is a string of text that uniquely identifies a `FleetPlanning` and allows to differentiate it from other `FleetPlannings`.	`FleetPlanning`	S5000F Fleet Planning and Product Assignment
fleetPlanningPer iod	`DateRange`	`fleetPlanningPeriod` is a range of dates for which the `FleetPlanning` is being performed.	`FleetPlanning`	S5000F Fleet Planning and Product Assignment
fleetPlanningSta tus	ClassificationType	`fleetPlanningStatus` is a classification that allows to define the validity of a `FleetPlanning`.	`FleetPlanning`	S5000F Fleet Planning and Product Assignment
fleetRelationshi pType	ClassificationType	`fleetRelationshipType` is a <<classification>> that defines how two `Fleets` are related.	`FleetRelationsh ip`	S5000F Fleet Definition

Applicable to: All

Attribute Name	Type	Definition	Class Name	UoF
`fleetRequirement Availability`	`SingleValuePropertyTy pe`	`fleetRequirementAvailability` is the availability that the fleet must have to comply with a specific FLeetRequirement.	`FleetRequiremen t`	S5000F Fleet Planning and Product Assignment
`fleetRequirement Date`	`DateType`	`fleetRequirementDate` is the date at which a `FleetRequirement` has been defined.	`FleetRequiremen t`	S5000F Fleet Planning and Product Assignment
`fleetRequirement MinimumFleetSize`	`umlInteger`	`fleetRequirementMinimumFleetSize` is the minimum number of vehicles that a fleet must contain so as to comply with the `FleetRequirement.`	`FleetRequiremen t`	S5000F Fleet Planning and Product Assignment
`fleetRequirement Period`	`DateRange`	`fleetRequirementPeriod` is the period of time during which a fleet must meet this requirement.	`FleetRequiremen t`	S5000F Fleet Planning and Product Assignment
`fleetRequirement Usage`	`SingleValuePropertyTy pe`	`fleetRequirementUsage` reflects the planned usage of the fleet. **Example** – 1000 hours/year – 50 times per day	`FleetRequiremen t`	S5000F Fleet Planning and Product Assignment
`fleetRequirement UsageLimitation`	`DescriptorType`	`fleetRequirementUsageLimitation` is a narrative statement explaining potential limitations of usage of the fleet.	`FleetRequiremen t`	S5000F Fleet Planning and Product Assignment
`fleetTaskCancell ationNoticeDatet ime`	`DateTimeType`	`fleetTaskCancellationNoticeDatetime` is a DateTime which represents the date and time at which the `FleetTaskCancellationNotice` took place.	`FleetTaskCancel lationNotice`	S5000F Fleet Task Cancellation
`fleetTaskCancell ationNoticeIdent ifier`	`IdentifierType`	`fleetTaskCancellationNoticeIdentifier` is a string of text that uniquely identifies a `FleetTaskCancellationNotice` and differentiates it from other `FleetTaskCancellationNotices.`	`FleetTaskCancel lationNotice`	S5000F Fleet Task Cancellation
`fleetTaskCancell ationNoticeReaso n`	`DescriptorType`	`fleetTaskCancellationNoticeReason` is a description that provides a human readable expression of why the `FleetTaskCancellationNotice` took place.	`FleetTaskCancel lationNotice`	S5000F Fleet Task Cancellation
`fleetTaskDescrip tion`	`DescriptorType`	`fleetTaskDescription` is a narrative statement explaining the `FleetTask.`	`FleetTask`	S5000F Fleet Planning and Product Assignment

Attribute Name	Type	Definition	Class Name	UoF
fleetTaskExpecte dEnd	DateTimeType	fleetTaskExpectedEnd is the date and time at which the FleetTask is expected to end.	FleetTask	S5000F Fleet Planning and Product Assignment
fleetTaskExpecte dStart	DateTimeType	fleetTaskExpectedStart is the date and time at which the FleetTask is expected to start.	FleetTask	S5000F Fleet Planning and Product Assignment
fleetTaskIdentif ier	IdentifierType	fleetTaskIdentifier is a string of text that uniquely identifies a FleetTask and differentiates it from other FleetTasks.	FleetTask	S5000F Fleet Planning and Product Assignment
fleetTaskPriorit y	ClassificationType	fleetTaskPriority is a classification that allows to define the importance of a FleetTask.	FleetTask	S5000F Fleet Planning and Product Assignment
fleetTaskRequire dFuel	SingleValuePropertyTy pe	fleetTaskRequiredFuel is the amount of fuel estimated to be required to carry out the FleetTask.	FleetTask	S5000F Fleet Planning and Product Assignment
geographicalArea Description	DescriptorType	geographicalAreaDescription is a description that provides more information about the GeographicalArea.	GeographicalAre a	CDM UoF Location
geographicalArea Name	NameType	geographicalAreaName is a name by which the GeographicalArea is known and can be easily referenced. **Example** – Central Alps – Dade county – Europe – Gobi desert – Tokyo – USA	GeographicalAre a	CDM UoF Location
geographicalArea Type	ClassificationType	geographicalAreaType is a classification that identifies the nature of the GeographicalArea.	GeographicalAre a	CDM UoF Location
geographicalCoor dinateSystem	ClassificationType	geographicalCoordinateSystem is a classification that identifies the geographical coordinate system used to determine latitude and longitude.	GlobalPosition	CDM UoF Location

Attribute Name	Type	Definition	Class Name	UoF
`hardwareElementRepairability`	ClassificationType	`hardwareElementRepairability` is a classification that indicates whether the `HardwareElement` part realization is expected to be repairable from a technical standpoint, independent of customer maintenance concepts.	`HardwareElement Revision`	CDM UoF Hardware Element
`hardwareElementReplaceability`	ClassificationType	`hardwareElementReplaceability` is a classification that identifies whether the `HardwareElement` part realization is expected to be replaceable from a technical standpoint, independent from customer maintenance concepts.	`HardwareElement Revision`	CDM UoF Hardware Element
`hardwareElementType`	ClassificationType	`hardwareElementType` is a classification that identifies further specialization for a `HardwareElement`. **Example** – Access point – Door – Electrical panel – Equipment – Panel – Slot	`HardwareElement`	CDM UoF Hardware Element
`hardwarePartContainerDescription`	DescriptorType	`hardwarePartContainerDescription` is a textual narrative that describes a `HardwarePartContainer`.	`HardwarePartContainer`	S5000F Container
`hardwarePartContainerIdentifier`	IdentifierType	`hardwarePartContainerIdentifier` is a string of characters that allows to uniquely identify a `HardwarePartContainer` and differentiate it from other ones. **Note** This identifier is not always institutionally defined by the manufacturer, but can be as informal as manually marked or drawn on the container (eg, in case of a plastic container, or cardboard box).	`HardwarePartContainer`	S5000F Container
`hardwarePartHazardousClass`	ClassificationType	`hardwarePartHazardousClass` is a classification that identifies to what extent a `HardwarePartAsDesigned` is capable of posing a significant risk to health, safety or property during transportation, handling or storage.	`HardwarePartAsDesignedDesignData`	CDM UoF Part Definition

Attribute Name	Type	Definition	Class Name	UoF
hardwarePartLogi sticsCategory	ClassificationType	hardwarePartLogisticsCategory is a classification that defines the role of the HardwarePartAsDesigned in the context of product support.	HardwarePartAsD esignedSupportD ata	CDM UoF Part Definition
hardwarePartOper ationalAuthorize dLife	AuthorizedLife	hardwarePartOperationalAuthorizedLife is an extended property that identifies the maximum usage limit for which an item can be operated, and upon reaching this limit, any further usage of the item must be re-authorized. **Example** – Calendar – Cycles – Hours – Landings	HardwarePartAsD esignedDesignDa ta	CDM UoF Part Definition
hardwarePartRepa irability	ClassificationType	hardwarePartRepairability is a classification that identifies the extent to which the HardwarePartAsDesigned is repairable from a technical perspective, independent of customer maintenance concepts.	HardwarePartAsD esignedSupportD ata	CDM UoF Part Definition
hardwarePartScra pRate	NumericalPropertyType	hardwarePartScrapRate is a property that defines the fraction of repairable units which, when removed from service, will be found to be beyond economic repair and therefore have to be scrapped.	HardwarePartAsD esignedSupportD ata	CDM UoF Part Definition
hardwarePartUnit OfIssuePrice	SingleValuePropertyTy pe	hardwarePartUnitOfIssuePrice is used to indicate the price of an item related to: – Unit of isue – Currency – Eccnomic conditions – Type of price – Price condition	PriceBreakData	S5000F Warehouse and Spare Pool
height	PropertyType	height is a property that specifies the vertical longitudinal dimension of an object.	Cuboid	S-Series_Compound_Attributes_2-0_002-00

Attribute Name	Type	Definition	Class Name	UoF
hour	umlInteger	hour is an Integer that represents the hour of a day expressed as a value between '0' and '24'.	TimeType	S-Series_Compound_Attributes_2-0_002-00
informationCode	umlString	informationCode is a string of characters that represents the information code attribute of the data module code. **Note** An informationCode must be created in accordance with the rules defined in S1000D.	S1000DDataModule	CDM UoF Document
informationCodeVariant	umlString	informationCodeVariant is a string of characters that represents the information code variant attribute of the data module code. **Note** An informationCodeVariant must be created in accordance with the rules defined in S1000D.	S1000DDataModule	CDM UoF Document
infrastructureAvailableDuring	DateRange	infrastructureAvailableDuring is a DateRange that represents the period during which an Infrastructure is or not available for an item.	InfrastructureAvailable	S5000F Infrastructure Availability
infrastructureAvailableRestriction	DescriptorType	infrastructureAvailableRestriction is a textual description explaining an infrastructure restriction during the specific period of time.	InfrastructureAvailable	S5000F Infrastructure Availability
infrastructureAvailableType	ClassificationType	infrastructureAvailableType is a <<classification>> that provides information about the type of availability that is available for an item.	InfrastructureAvailable	S5000F Infrastructure Availability
infrastructureComplianceDate	DateType	infrastructureComplianceDate is a date that defines when infrastructure compliance was declared.	InfrastructureCompliance	CDM UoF Facility
infrastructureComplianceDescription	DescriptorType	infrastructureComplianceDescription is a description that gives more information on compliance fulfillment.	InfrastructureCompliance	CDM UoF Facility

Attribute Name	Type	Definition	Class Name	UoF
infrastructureComplianceLevel	ClassificationType	infrastructureComplianceLevel is a classification that specifies the degree of compliance.	InfrastructureCompliance	CDM UoF Facility
infrastructureDescription	DescriptorType	infrastructureDescription is a description that provides a human readable expression of an Infrastructure.	Infrastructure	S5000F Infrastructure
infrastructureIdentifier	IdentifierType	infrastructureIdentifier is a string of characters that uniquely identifies an Infrastructure.	Infrastructure	S5000F Infrastructure
infrastructureName	NameType	infrastructureName is a name by which the Infrastructure is known and can be easily referenced.	Infrastructure	S5000F Infrastructure
infrastructureNodeLocatedAtDuring	DateRange	infrastructureNodeLocatedAtDuring is a DateRange during which an InfrastructureNote has been located at a specific place.	InfrastructureNodeAtLocation	S5000F Infrastructure
infrastructureOperatingPeriodDateTimeRange	DateTimeRange	infrastructureOperatingPeriodDateTimeRange is the period of time during which the associated Infrastructure has operated in a specific mode.	InfrastructureOperatingPeriod	S5000F Infrastructure Operating Period
infrastructureOperatingPeriodDescription	DescriptorType	infrastructureOperatingPeriodDescription is a textual narrative that provides further information about the InfrastructureOperatingPeriod.	InfrastructureOperatingPeriod	S5000F Infrastructure Operating Period
infrastructureOperatingPeriodIdentifier	IdentifierType	infrastructureOperatingPeriodIdentifier is a text string that uniquely identifies an instance of InfrastructureOperatingPeriod and allows to differentiate it from other instances of InfrastructureOperatingPeriod.	InfrastructureOperatingPeriod	S5000F Infrastructure Operating Period
infrastructureOperatingPeriodMode	ClassificationType	infrastructureOperatingPeriodMode is a classification indicating how the associated Infrastructure has operated during the spec fied operating period. **Example** – down for maintenance – fully operational	InfrastructureOperatingPeriod	S5000F Infrastructure Operating Period

Attribute Name	Type	Definition	Class Name	UoF
		– partially operational		
infrastructureOperatingPeriodName	NameType	infrastructureOperatingPeriodName is a name by which the InfrastructureOperatingPeriod is known and commonly referred to.	InfrastructureOperatingPeriod	S5000F Infrastructure Operating Period
infrastructurePartyRole	ClassificationType	infrastructurePartyRole is a <<classification>> that defines the role of an InfrastructureParty.	InfrastructureParty	S5000F Infrastructure
infrastructurePartyRoleDuring	DateRange	infrastructurePartyRoleDuring is a DateRange during which a Party has a specific role regarding a specific Infrastructure.	InfrastructureParty	S5000F Infrastructure
infrastructureRelationshipType	ClassificationType	infrastructureRelationshipType is a <<classification>> that defines how two Infrastructures are related.	InfrastructureRelationship	S5000F Infrastructure
infrastructureRevisionDate	DateType	infrastructureRevisionDate is the date at which the InfrastructureRevision was created.	InfrastructureRevision	S5000F Infrastructure
infrastructureRevisionIdentifier	IdentifierType	infrastructureRevisionIdentifier is a string of characters that uniquely identifies an InfrastructureRevision.	InfrastructureRevision	S5000F Infrastructure
infrastructureRevisionRationale	DescriptorType	infrastructureRevisionRationale is a description of the reason for the creation of the InfrastructureRevision.	InfrastructureRevision	S5000F Infrastructure
infrastructureRevisionStatus	StateType	infrastructureRevisionStatus is a state that identifies the maturity of an InfrastructureRevision.	InfrastructureRevision	S5000F Infrastructure
infrastructureRevisionValidity	DateRange	infrastructureRevisionValidity is a DateRange during which an InfrastructureRevision is valid.	InfrastructureRevision	S5000F Infrastructure
installationLocationIdentifier	IdentifierType	installationLocationIdentifier is an identifier that establishes a unique designator for a InstallationLocation and to differentiate it from other instances of InstallationLocation.	InstallationLocation	CDM UoF Serialized Product Variant Configuration

Applicable to: All

Attribute Name	Type	Definition	Class Name	UoF
installationLoca tionName	NameType	installationLocationName is a name by which the InstallationLocation is known and can be easily referenced.	InstallationLoc ation	CDM UoF Serialized Product Variant Configuration
installedDateTim e	DateTimeType	installedDateTime is a date and time that specifies the exact point in time when the RealizedPart was installed at the InstallationLocation.	InstalledPart	CDM UoF Serialized Product Variant Configuration
involvedDisposal OrganizationRole	ClassificationType	involvedDisposalOrganizationRole is a classification that allows to determine the role played by an organization as part of the disposal.	InvolvedDisposa lOrganization	S5000F Disposal Requirement
itemDemilitariza tionDataClass	DatedClassificat ion	itemDemilitarizationDataClass is a classification defining special measures to be taken when an item is being disposed of. **Note 1** Special measures can include to render an item useless for military purposes or destroy any indications of military purposes or performance characteristics. **Note 2** This classification usually corresponds to the partDemilitarizationClass, but can be different for the individual item due to special use or ad-hoc (and possibly undocumented) modifications to the individual item.	ItemDemilitariz ationData	S5000F Item Disposal Requirement
itemDemilitariza tionDataDescript ion	DescriptorType	itemDemilitarizationDataDescription is a textual narrative providing further information related to the demilitarization of an item.	ItemDemilitariz ationData	S5000F Item Disposal Requirement
itemDisposalOper ationActionJusti fication	DescriptorType	itemDisposalOperationActionJustification is a narrative text providing the justification for an Action derived from an ItemDisposalOperation.	ItemDisposalOpe rationAction	S5000F Item Disposal Operation
itemDisposalOper ationIdentifier	IdentifierType	itemDisposalOperationIdentifier is a text string that uniquely identifies an ItemDisposalOperation and allows to differentiate it from other ItemDisposalOperation instances.	ItemDisposalOpe ration	S5000F Item Disposal Operation

Attribute Name	Type	Definition	Class Name	UoF
itemDisposalOperationMethod	ClassificationType	itemDisposalOperationMethod is a classification that indicates the method by which the ItemDisposalOperation is performed.	ItemDisposalOperation	S5000F Item Disposal Operation
itemDisposalOperationMethodDetails	DescriptorType	itemDisposalOperationMethodDetails is a textual narrative providing further information on the itemDisposalOperationMethod.	ItemDisposalOperation	S5000F Item Disposal Operation
itemDisposalOperationOrganization	Organization	itemDisposalOperationOrganization is the organization that performs the ItemDisposalOperation.	ItemDisposalOperation	S5000F Item Disposal Operation
itemDisposalOperationPeriod	DateRange	itemDisposalOperationPeriod is the period of time during which the item was disposed of.	ItemDisposalOperation	S5000F Item Disposal Operation
itemExportControlRegulationClassification	ClassificationType	itemExportControlRegulationClassification is the classification that is associated to an export controlled item under a specific ExportControlRegulation.	ItemExportControlRegulation	S5000F Export Control Requirement
itemLocationCode	umlString	itemLocationCode is a string of characters that represents the item location code attribute of the data module code. **Note** An itemLocationCode must be created in accordance with the rules defined in S1000D.	S1000DDataModule	CDM Document
laborRate	NumericalPropertyType	laborRate is a value indicating the monetary value of an hour of a person with particular skills or competences.	LaborRates	S5000F Contract Breakdown

latitude	umlString	latitude is a string of characters that contributes to uniquely identifies a GlobalPosition.
		Example
		  – 39.5693900
		  – 39°34.1634' N
		  – 39°34'09" N
			GlobalPosition	CDM UoF Location

Attribute Name	Type	Definition	Class Name	UoF
learnCode	umlString	learnCode is a string of characters that represents the learn code attribute of the data module code. **Note** A learnCode must be created in accordance with the rules defined in S1000D.	S1000DDataModule	CDM UoF Document
learnEventCode	umlString	learnEventCode is a string of characters that represents the learn event code attribute of the data module code. **Note** A learnEventCode must be created in accordance with the rules defined in S1000D.	S1000DDataModule	CDM UoF Document
length	PropertyType	length is a property that specifies the most extended longitudinal dimension of an object.	Rectangle	S5000F_Compound_Attributes_002-00
			Cuboid	S-Series_Compound_Attributes_2-0_002-00
			Cylinder	S-Series_Compound_Attributes_2-0_002-00
lifeAuthorizingOrganization	Organization	lifeAuthorizingOrganization identifies the organization that is the authoritative source for the authorizedLifeValue.	AuthorizedLife	S-Series_Compound_Attributes_2-0_002-00
localPositionDescription	DescriptorType	localPositionDescription is a narrative text explaining the rationale for a LocalPosition.	LocalPosition	S5000F Local Position
localPositionIdentifier	IdentifierType	localPositionIdentifier is a string of text that uniquely identifies a LocalPosition and differentiates it from other LocalPositions.	LocalPosition	S5000F Local Position
localPositionName	NameType	localPositionName is a text by which a LocalPosition is commonly known.	LocalPosition	S5000F Local Position

Attribute Name	Type	Definition	Class Name	UoF
localPositionRefType	ClassificationType	localPositionRefType is a classification that determines the point in a referenced item where all LocalPosition coordinates are zero.	LocalPosition	S5000F Local Position
locationRelationshipType	ClassificationType	locationRelationshipType is a classification that identifies the meaning of the established relationship. **Example** – Located in – Located next to	LocationRelationship	CDM UoF Location
locatorDescription	DescriptorType	locatorDescription is a narrative statement about the locator.	Locator	S5000F Location and Locator
locatorIdentifier	IdentifierType	locatorIdentifier is a string of characters used to uniquely identify a Locator.	Locator	S5000F Location and Locator
locatorName	TextPropertyType	locatorName is a word or phrase by which a locator is known and can easily be referenced.	Locator	S5000F Location and Locator
logBookDescription	DescriptorType	logBookDescription is a narrative statement explaining what the LogBook is.	LogBook	S5000F Logbook
logBookEntryComment	DescriptorType	logBookEntryComment is a textual wording providing additional information to a logBookEntry.	LogBookEntry	S5000F Logbook
logBookEntryDateTime	DateTimeType	logBookEntryDateTime is the date and time at which the logbook entry was recorded.	LogBookEntry	S5000F Logbook
logBookEntryIdentifier	IdentifierType	logBookEntryIdentifier is a string of characters used to uniquely identify a LogBookEntry, thus being able to differentiate it from other LogBookEntries.	LogBookEntry	S5000F Logbook
logbookEntryMeasurementPointIdentifier	IdentifierType	logbookEntryMeasurementPointIdentifier is a string of text that uniquely identifies a LogbookEntryMeasurementPoint and differentiates it from other instances of LogbookEntryMeasurementPoint.	LogBookEntryMeasurementPoint	S5000F Logbook

Attribute Name	Type	Definition	Class Name	UoF
logbookEntryMeas urementPointNote	DescriptorType	logbookEntryMeasurementPointNote is a narrative text that provides a human readable expression of a LogBookEntryMeasurementPoint.	LogBookEntryMea surementPoint	S5000F Logbook
logbookEntryMeas urementPointType	ClassificationType	logbookEntryMeasurementPointType is a classification that allows to group similar instances of LogbookEntryMeasurementPoint.	LogBookEntryMea surementPoint	S5000F Logbook
logbookEntryMeas urementPointValu e	PropertyType	logbookEntryMeasurementPointValue is a property that represents the value that is recorded for the LogbookEntryMeasurementPoint.	LogBookEntryMea surementPoint	S5000F Logbook
logBookEntryType	ClassificationType	logBookEntryType is a classification that is valid for a specific LogBookEntry.	LogBookEntry	S5000F Logbook
logBookIdentifie r	IdentifierType	logBookIdentifier is a string of characters used to uniquely identify a LogBook, thus being able to differentiate it from other logBooks.	LogBook	S5000F Logbook
logBookType	ClassificationType	logBookType is a classification that allows to define the purpose of a logbook.	LogBook	S5000F Logbook
longitude	umlString	longitude is a string of characters that represents a geographic coordinate specifying the east–west position of a point. **Example** – 2.6502400° – 2°39.0144' E – 2°39'00" E	GlobalPosition	CDM UoF Location
looseWasteDescri ption	DescriptorType	looseWasteDescription is a narrative text explaining the nature of the LooseWaste.	LooseWaste	S5000F Waste Disposal Requirement
looseWasteIdenti fier	IdentifierType	looseWasteIdentifier is a string of characters that uniquely identifies a LooseWaste instance and differentiates it from other LooseWaste instances.	LooseWaste	S5000F Waste Disposal Requirement

Attribute Name	Type	Definition	Class Name	UoF
looseWasteName	NameType	looseWasteName is a name by which the LooseWaste is known and commonly referred to.	LooseWaste	S5000F Waste Disposal Requirement
looseWasteType	ClassificationType	looseWasteType is a classification that defines the characteristics of the LooseWaste.	LooseWaste	S5000F Waste Disposal Requirement
looseWasteVolume	ThreeDimensional	looseWasteVolume is a set of measures describing the volume of the LooseWaste.	LooseWaste	S5000F Waste Disposal Requirement
looseWasteWeight	PropertyType	looseWasteWeight is a property describing the mass of the LooseWaste.	LooseWaste	S5000F Waste Disposal Requirement
lowerBound	umlString	lowerBound is a string of characters that represents the lower limit of the range.	SerialNumberRange	S-Series_Compound_Attributes_2-0_002-00
lowerLimitSalesQuantity	umlInteger	upperLimitSalesQuantity indicates a hardwarePartUnitOfIssuePrice valid for an individual, specified range of buy quantities. **Note** The upperLimitSalesQuantity must always be presented with and read in conjunction with the lowerLimitSalesQuantity and a hardwarePartUnitOfIssuePrice. If absent, there is no upper quantity limit to which the price is applicable.	PriceBreakData	S5000F Warehouse and Spare Pool
maintenanceActivityNote	DescriptorType	maintenanceActivityNote is a narrative statement about potential issues encountered during the MaintenanceActivity.	MaintenanceActivity	S5000F Maintenance Activity
maintenanceActivityPartyRole	ClassificationType	maintenanceActivityPartyRole is a <<classification>> that defines the role of a Party in the context of a MaintenanceActivity..	MaintenanceActivityParty	S5000F Maintenance Activity
maintenanceActivityPartyTime	NumericalPropertyType	maintenanceActivityPartyTime is the period of time spent by a Party during a MaintenanceActivity on a specific role.	MaintenanceActivityParty	S5000F Maintenance Activity

Applicable to: All

S5000F

Attribute Name	Type	Definition	Class Name	UoF
maintenanceActivityPlanAccessHours	SingleValuePropertyType	maintenanceActivityPlanAccessHours is the is the expected time to be spent in gaining access for the MaintenanceActivity.	MaintenanceActivityPlan	S5000F Maintenance Activity
maintenanceActivityPlanExecutionHours	SingleValuePropertyType	maintenanceActivityPlanExecutionHours is the planned time to be spent carrying out the MaintenanceActivity.	MaintenanceActivityPlan	S5000F Maintenance Activity
maintenanceActivityPlanPeriod	DateTimeRange	maintenanceActivityPlanPeriod is the period of time during which the MaintenanceActivity is or was planned.	MaintenanceActivityPlan	S5000F Maintenance Activity
maintenanceActivityPlanPreparationHours	SingleValuePropertyType	maintenanceActivityPlanPreparationHours is the expected time to be spect on preparation for the MaintenanceActivity.	MaintenanceActivityPlan	S5000F Maintenance Activity
maintenanceActivityRecordAccessHours	SingleValuePropertyType	maintenanceActivityRecordAccessHours is the real time in hours spent in gaining access for the MaintenanceActivity.	MaintenanceActivityRecord	S5000F Maintenance Activity
maintenanceActivityRecordApprovalTime	DateTimeType	maintenanceActivityRecordApprovalTime is the date and time at which the MaintenanceActivity was approved.	MaintenanceActivityRecord	S5000F Maintenance Activity
maintenanceActivityRecordExecutionHours	SingleValuePropertyType	maintenanceActivityRecordExecutionHours is the real time in hours spent carrying out the MaintenanceActivity.	MaintenanceActivityRecord	S5000F Maintenance Activity
maintenanceActivityRecordPeriod	DateTimeRange	maintenanceActivityRecordPeriod is the period of time during which the maintenance was actually executed.	MaintenanceActivityRecord	S5000F Maintenance Activity
maintenanceActivityRecordPreparationHours	SingleValuePropertyType	maintenanceActivityRecordPreparationHours is the real time in hours spent for the preparation of the MaintenanceActivity.	MaintenanceActivityRecord	S5000F Maintenance Activity

Attribute Name	Type	Definition	Class Name	UoF
maintenanceActivityRecordWorkDone	TextPropertyType	maintenanceActivityRecordWorkDone is a text that briefly describes the work that has been done as part of a MaintenanceActivity.	MaintenanceActivityRecord	S5000F Maintenance Activity
maintenanceActivitySequence	umlInteger	maintenanceActivitySequence is an integer that indicates the sequence number of the MaintenanceActivity in a set of MaintenanceActivities that are part of a WorkOrder.	MaintenanceActivity	S5000F Maintenance Activity
maintenanceEventCategoryType	ClassificationType	maintenanceEventCategoryType is a classification that indicates a characteristic of a MaintenanceEvent.	MaintenanceEvent	S5000F Maintenance Activity
maintenanceFacilityShifts	umlInteger	maintenanceFacilityShifts is the number of staff shifts in a MaintenanceFacility.	MaintenanceFacility	S5000F Facility
maintenanceFacilitySlotDescription	DescriptorType	maintenanceFacilitySlotDescription is a textual explanation of the characteristics of a MaintenanceFacilitySlot.	MaintenanceFacilitySlot	S5000F Maintenance Facility Planning
maintenanceFacilitySlotIdentifier	IdentifierType	maintenanceFacilitySlotIdentifier is a string of characters that allows to uniquely identify a MaintenanceFacilitySlot and differentiate it from other MaintenanceFacilitySlots.	MaintenanceFacilitySlot	S5000F Maintenance Facility Planning
maintenanceFacilitySlotPlannedUsagePeriod	DateRange	maintenanceFacilitySlotPlannedUsagePeriod is a period of time in which a specific MaintenanceFacilitySlot has been allocated to a specific SerializedProductVariant.	MaintenanceFacilitySlotPlannedUsage	S5000F Maintenance Facility Planning
maintenanceFacilitySlotType	ClassificationType	maintenanceFacilitySlotType is a classification that allows to group MaintenanceFacilitySlots.	MaintenanceFacilitySlot	S5000F Maintenance Facility Planning
maintenanceFacilityType	ClassificationType	maintenanceFacilityType is a classification that identifies further specialization for a MaintenanceFacility.	MaintenanceFacility	S5000F Facility
maintenanceLevelCapabilityDescription	DescriptorType	maintenanceLevelCapabilityDescription is a description that gives more information on the ability to perform maintenance based on availability of support resources and environmental conditions.	MaintenanceLevel	CDM UoF Product Usage Context

Applicable to: All

Attribute Name	Type	Definition	Class Name	UoF
		Note 1 The defined abilities are the basis for determining the functions to be accomplished at the defined maintenance level. **Note 2** Support resources include eg, personnel and skills, special facilities and support equipment, etc.		
maintenanceLevel Identifier	IdentifierType	maintenanceLevelIdentifier is an identifier that establishes a unique designator for a MaintenanceLevel and to differentiate it from other instances of MaintenanceLevel.	MaintenanceLeve l	CDM UoF Product Usage Context
maintenanceLevel Name	NameType	maintenanceLevelName is a name by which the MaintenanceLevel is known and can be easily referenced.	MaintenanceLeve l	CDM UoF Product Usage Context
maintenanceLicen ceIdentifier	IdentifierType	maintenanceLicenceIdentifier is a string of characters that allows to uniquely identify a MaintenanceLicense and differentiate it from other MaintenanceLicenses.	MaintenanceLice nse	S5000F Maintenance Personnel
maintenanceLicen ceName	DescriptorType	maintenanceLicenceName is a name or short phrase by which a MaintenanceLicense is usually known.	MaintenanceLice nse	S5000F Maintenance Personnel
maintenanceLicen ceType	DatedClassificat ion	maintenanceLicenceType is a DatedClassification that defines the kind of MaintenanceLicence that has been granted.	MaintenanceLice nse	S5000F Maintenance Personnel
maintenanceLicen ceValidity	DateRange	maintenanceLicenceValidity is the standard duration for which a maintenance license is granted.	MaintenanceLice nse	S5000F Maintenance Personnel
maintenanceOrgan izationApprovalD uring	DateRange	maintenanceOrganizationApprovalDuring is a period during which a specific MaintenanceOrganizationApproval is in effect.	MaintenanceOrga nizationApprova l	S5000F Maintenance Organization
maintenanceOrgan izationApprovalT ype	ClassificationType	maintenanceOrganizationApprovalType is a classification that defines the kind of MaintenanceOrganizationApproval that has been granted. **Example** – EASA AR100	MaintenanceOrga nizationApprova l	S5000F Maintenance Organization

Attribute Name	Type	Definition	Class Name	UoF
		– FAA Part 145 – ISO 9000		
maintenancePerso nApprovedProduct Period	DateRange	maintenancePersonApprovedProductPeriod is a period of time during which a MaintenancePerson has been approved to work on a specific ProductVariant.	MaintenancePers onApprovedProdu ct	S5000F Maintenance Personnel
maintenancePerso nFacilityPeriod	DateRange	maintenancePersonFacilityPeriod is the time period during which a MaintenancePerson has worked at a specific MaintenanceFacility.	MaintenancePers onFacility	S5000F Maintenance Personnel
maintenancePerso nJobType	ClassificationType	maintenancePersonJobType is a classification that identifies the kind of maintenance job that a MaintenancePerson has. **Example** – electrician – mechanic – painter	MaintenancePers on	S5000F Maintenance Personnel
maintenancePerso nRemarks	DescriptorType	maintenancePersonRemarks is a textual statement related to a person.	MaintenancePers on	S5000F Maintenance Personnel
maintenanceProgr amRevisionDescri ption	DescriptorType	maintenanceProgramRevisionDescription is a narrative statement explaining the MaintenanceProgramRevision and/or the changes that have been made to the MaintenanceProgram.	MaintenanceProg ramRevision	S5000F Maintenance Program
maintenanceProgr amRevisionIdenti fier	IdentifierType	maintenanceProgramRevisionIdentifier is a string of text that uniquely identifies a MaintenanceProgramRevision and allows to differentiate it from other MaintenanceProgramRevisions.	MaintenanceProg ramRevision	S5000F Maintenance Program
maintenanceProgr amRevisionStatus	StateType	maintenanceProgramRevisionStatus is a state that identifies the maturity of a MaintenanceProgramRevision	MaintenanceProg ramRevision	S5000F Maintenance Program
maintenanceProgr amType	ClassificationType	maintenanceProgramType is a classification that allows to group different types of Maintenance Programs.	MaintenanceProg ram	S5000F Maintenance Program

Attribute Name	Type	Definition	Class Name	UoF
maintenanceSigni ficantOrRelevant	ClassificationType	maintenanceSignificantOrRelevant is a classfication that identifies whether a BreakdownElement requires maintenance activities or not. **Note 1** A maintenance relevant item is an item which can be repaired or replaced as a result of failure or damage. **Note 2** A maintenance significant item is an item which was identified by any selection process coming from a scheduled maintenance analysis like MSG-3 or S4000P. For this type of item, a scheduled maintenance task will be documented.	BreakdownElemen tRevision	CDM UoF Breakdown Structure
managedFleetDuri ng	DateRange	managedFleetDuring is a <<DateRange>> that represents the period during which a FleetManager manages a specific Fleet.	ManagedFleet	S5000F Fleet Definition
materialCharacte risticsRecording Date	DateType	materialCharacteristicsRecordingDate is the date at which the Material information was last recorded or updated.	Material	S5000F Supply Item
materialDescript ion	DescriptorType	materialDescription is a narrative statement explaining the Material.	Material	S5000F Supply Item
materialIdentifi er	IdentifierType	materialIdentifier is a string of text that uniquely identifies a Material and differentiates it from other materials.	Material	S5000F Supply Item
materialItemCate goryCode	umlString	materialItemCategoryCode is a string of characters that represents the material item category code attribute of the data module code. **Note** A materialItemCategoryCode must be created in accordance with the rules defined in S1000D.	S1000DDataModul e	CDM Document
materialName	TextPropertyType	materialName is a text under which the Material is commonly known.	Material	S5000F Supply Item

Attribute Name	Type	Definition	Class Name	UoF
materialRiskDesc ription	DescriptorType	materialRiskDescription is a narrative statement explaining the Material risk.	Material	S5000F Supply Item
materialRiskFact or	DatedClassificat ion	materialRiskFactor is a classification that allows to determine whether the Material presents some safety or hazard risk.	Material	S5000F Supply Item
materialSubstanc eUsageCategory	ClassificationType	materialSubstanceUsageCategory is a classification that defines the purpose for which the Material is used.	Material	S5000F Supply Item
measurementPoint Identifier	IdentifierType	measurementPointIdentifier is an identifier that establishes a unique designator for a MeasurementPoint and to differentiate it from other instances of MeasurementPoint.	MeasurementPoin t	CDM UoF Measurement Point
measurementPoint Value	PropertyType	measurementPointValue is a property that represents the value that is recorded for the MeasurementPoint.	MeasurementPoin t	CDM UoF Measurement Point
messageContentSt atus	StateType	messageContentStatus is a state that identifies the quality assurance status of the message content.	Message	CDM UoF Message
messageContentTy pe	ClassificationType	messageContentType is a classification that characterizes the information included in the message content.	Message	CDM UoF Message
messageCreationD ateTime	DateTimeType	messageCreationDateTime is a date and time that defines when the Message was generated.	Message	CDM UoF Message
messageIdentifie r	IdentifierType	messageIdentifier is an identifier that establishes a unique designator for a Message and allows it to be differentiated from other instances of Messages.	Message	CDM UoF Message
messageLanguage	ClassificationType	messageLanguage is a classification that identifies the language of the information in the message content.	Message	CDM UoF Message
messagePartyType	ClassificationType	messagePartyType is a classification that identifies the role of the associated Party. **Example** – Receiver	MessageParty	CDM UoF Message

Attribute Name	Type	Definition	Class Name	UoF
		– Sender		
messageRelations hipType	ClassificationType	messageRelationshipType is a classification that characterizes the relationship that is established between two Messages.	MessageRelation ship	CDM UoF Message
minimumSalesQuan tity	umlInteger	minimumSalesQuantity identifies the minimum quantity that can be purchased at the quoted hardwarePartUnitOfIssuePrice.	HardwarePartAsD esignedCommerce Data	S5000F Warehouse and Spare Pool
minute	umlInteger	minute is an Integer that represents the minute within an hour expressed as a value between '0' and '59'.	TimeType	S5000F_Compound_Attributes_ 002-00
modelIdentificat ionCode	umlString	modelIdentificationCode is a string of characters that represents the model identification code attribute of the data module code. **Note 1** A modelIdentificationCode must be created in accordance with the rules defined in S1000D. **Note 2** A modelIdentificationCode must be created in accordance with the rules defined in S1000D.	S1000DDataModul e S1000DPublicati onModule	CDM UoF Document CDM UoF Document
movementIdentifi er	IdentifierType	movementIdentifier is a string of characters that uniquely defines a Movement and allows to differentiate it from other Movements.	Movement	S5000F Operational Period
movementLegDelay Cause	DescriptorType	movementLegDelayCause is a textual narrative describing the reason for the delay.	MovementLegDela y	S5000F Operational Period
movementLegDelay Date	DateType	movementLegDelayDate is the date at which the delay took place.	MovementLegDela y	S5000F Operational Period
movementLegDelay Duration	SingleValuePropertyTy pe	movementLegDelayDuration represents the duration of the travel leg delay.	MovementLegDela y	S5000F Operational Period

Attribute Name	Type	Definition	Class Name	UoF
movementLegDelay Identifier	IdentifierType	`movementLegDelayIdentifier` is a string of text that allows to uniquely identify a `MovementLegDelay` and differentiate it from other `MovementLegDelays`.	`MovementLegDelay`	S5000F Operational Period
movementLegDelay Type	ClassificationType	`movementLegDelayType` is a classification that permits to group the `MovementLegDelays`. **Example** – malfunction or failure – strike – weather	`MovementLegDelay`	S5000F Operational Period
movementLegGeoLo cationTime	DateTimeType	`movementLegGeoLocationTime` is the time at which a serialized product variant was at a specific geo-location during a movement leg.	`MovementLegPosition`	S5000F Operational Period
movementLegIdent ifier	IdentifierType	`movementLegIdentifier` s a string of characters used to uniquely identify a `MovementLeg` and differentiate it from other `MovementLegs`.	`MovementLeg`	S5000F Operational Period
movementLegPerio d	DateTimeRange	`movementLegPeriod` is the period during which the product is performing a travel leg (is in transit).	`MovementLeg`	S5000F Operational Period
movementLegResul t	ClassificationType	`movementLegResult` is a classification that allows to group different movement legs based on the result of the `MovementLeg`. **Example** – cancelled – diverted – OK	`MovementLeg`	S5000F Operational Period
movementLegSeque nce	umlInteger	`movementLegSequence` is an integer that indicates the sequence in which the travel leg has been performed during a specific product movement.	`MovementLeg`	S5000F Operational Period
movementResult	ClassificationType	`movementResult` is a classification that allows to group different movement legs based on the result of the `Movement`.	`Movement`	S5000F Operational Period

Attribute Name	Type	Definition	Class Name	UoF
		Example – aborted – delayed – OK		
`movementTransit`	`DateTimeRange`	`movementTransit` is the period during which the product has been in movement from its start location until its end location, considering both the individual travel legs and intermediate times that can have taken place between different travel legs. **Example** – Overnight stay	`Movement`	S5000F Operational Period
`movementType`	ClassificationType	`movementType` is a classification of the movement of the product. (eg, ferry, transport, etc)	`Movement`	S5000F Operational Period
`nonAvailabilityCauseDescription`	DescriptorType	`nonAvailabilityCauseDescription` is a description that provides a human readable expression of a `NonAvailabilityCause`.	`NonAvailability Cause`	S5000F Availability
`nonAvailabilityCauseIdentifier`	IdentifierType	`nonAvailabilityCauseIdentifier` is a string of characters that uniquely identifies a `NonAvailabilityCause`.	`NonAvailability Cause`	S5000F Availability
`nonAvailabilityCauseType`	ClassificationType	`nonAvailabilityCauseType` is a <<classification>> that allows to group similar `NonAvailabilityCauses`.	`NonAvailability Cause`	S5000F Availability
`nonConformanceDescription`	DescriptorType	`nonConformanceDescription` is a description that gives more information on how the `EffectiveOnProductConfigurationItem` does not comply with its requirements.	`NonConformanceD ata`	CDM Product Design Configuration
`nonConformanceRestriction`	DescriptorType	`nonConformanceRestriction` is a description that gives more information on how the use of the related `EffectiveOnProductConfigurationItem` restricts the specified capabilities of the `AllowedProductConfiguration` in which it is contained.	`NonConformanceD ata`	CDM Product Design Configuration

Attribute Name	Type	Definition	Class Name	UoF
nonConformanceType	ClassificationType	nonConformanceType is a classification that identifies in which way the EffectiveOnProductConfigurationItem does not comply with its requirements.	NonConformanceData	CDM Product Design Configuration
obsolescenceParameterDescription	DescriptorType	obsolescenceParameterDescription is a narrative statement describing the ObsolescenceParameter.	ObsolescenceParameter	S5000F Obsolescence Management Candidates
obsolescenceParameterIdentifier	IdentifierType	obsolescenceParameterIdentifier is a string of text that uniquely identifies an ObsolescenceParameter and differentiates it from other ObsolescenceParameters.	ObsolescenceParameter	S5000F Obsolescence Management Candidates
obsolescenceParameterName	DescriptorType	obsolescenceParameterName is a text that represents an identifier by which an ObsolescenceParamenter is commonly known.	ObsolescenceParameter	S5000F Obsolescence Management Candidates
obsolescenceParameterType	ClassificationType	obsolescenceParameterType is a classification that describes the type of parameter (eg,. obsolescence parameter, order, reliability, etc)	ObsolescenceParameter	S5000F Obsolescence Management Candidates
obsolescenceParameterValue	PropertyType	obsolescenceParameterValue is a property that represents the value of the ObsolescenceParameter that indicates that an item is obsolete.	ObsolescenceParameter	S5000F Obsolescence Management Candidates
openingTimeDay	ClassificationType	openingTimeDay is a <<classification>> that indicates at which day(s) of the week the opening times apply.	OpeningTimes	S5000FLocation and Locator
openingTimeFrom	TimeType	openingTimeFrom is the time of the day at which a certain address opens.	OpeningTimes	S5000FLocation and Locator
openingTimeTo	TimeType	openingTimeTo is the time of the day at which a certain address closes to the public.	OpeningTimes	S5000FLocation and Locator
operatingBaseCapacityIdentifier	IdentifierType	operatingBaseCapacityIdentifier is a string that uniquely identifies an OperatingBaseCapacity and allows to differentiate it from other OperatingBaseCapacities.	OperatingBaseCapacity	S5000F Operating Base

Attribute Name	Type	Definition	Class Name	UoF
operatingBaseProductVariantCapacity	umlInteger	operatingBaseProductVariantCapacity is the number of ProductVariants that can operate simultaneously at a specific OperatingBase.	OperatingBaseCapacity	S5000F Operating Base
operatingBaseType	ClassificationType	operatingBaseType is a classification that identifies further specialization for a OperatingBase.	OperatingBase	S5000F Operating Base
operatingLocationTypeDescription	DescriptorType	operatingLocationTypeDescription is a description that gives more information on the OperatingLocationType, including the environmental conditions to be expected.	OperatingLocationType	CDM Product Usage Context
operatingLocationTypeIdentifier	IdentifierType	operatingLocationTypeIdentifier is an identifier that establishes a unique designator for an OperatingLocationType and to differentiate it from other instances of OperatingLocationType.	OperatingLocationType	CDM UoF Product Usage Context
operatingLocationTypeName	NameType	operatingLocationTypeName is a name by which the OperatingLocationType is known and can be easily referenced.	OperatingLocationType	CDM UoF Product Usage Context
operationalApprovalIdentifier	IdentifierType	operationalApprovalIdentifier is a string that allows to uniquely identify an OperationalApproval and differentiate it from other OperationalApprovals.	OperationalApproval	S5000F Operational Period
operationalApprovalType	DatedClassification	operationalApprovalType is a dated classification that describes the type of operational approval that is approved for use.	OperationalApproval	S5000F Operational Period
operationalEventCategoryType	ClassificationType	operationalEventCategoryType is a classification that indicates a characteristic of an OperationalEvent. **Note** An OperationalEvent can have multiple classifications associated to it. **Example** – safety-critical incident	OperationalEvent	S5000F Operational Event

Attribute Name	Type	Definition	Class Name	UoF
operationalEvent MaintenanceDown	ClassificationType	operationalEventMaintenanceDown is a classification indicating that the OperationalEvent caused a maintenance down time to the SerializedProductVariant.	OperationalEvent	S5000F Operational Event
operationalEvent MaintenanceNotif icationDateTime	DateTimeType	operationalEventMaintenanceNotificationDateTime is the date and time where the maintenance organization has been notified that maintenance was required due to the OperationalEvent.	OperationalEvent	S5000F Operational Event
operationalEvent MaintenanceRelea sedDateTime	DateTimeType	operationalEventMaintenanceReleasedDateTime is the date and time at which the maintenance organization released the serialized product from maintenance after solving the issues caused by the operational event.	OperationalEvent	S5000F Operational Event
operationalEvent MessageIdentifie r	IdentifierType	operationalEventMessageIdentifier is a string of characters used to uniquely identify an OperationalEventMessage and to differentiate it from other operationalEventMessages.	OperationalEventMessage	S5000F Operational Event
operationalEvent MessageSequence	umlInteger	operationalEventMessageSequence is an integer stating the sequence in which a particular OperationalEventMessage was made.	OperationalEventMessage	S5000F Operational Event
operationalEvent MessageText	DescriptorType	operationalEventMessageText is a text that appears during or as a consequence of an OperationalEvent (eg, on an operator display or maintenance panel).	OperationalEventMessage	S5000F Operational Event
operationalEvent MessageType	ClassificationType	operationalEventMessageType is a classification of the operationalEventMessage. **Example** – acoustic – text – visual	OperationalEventMessage	S5000F Operational Event
operationalEvent OperationalMode	ClassificationType	operationalEventOperationalMode is a classification indicating the specific operational mode during which the operationalEvent occurred.	OperationalEvent	S5000F Operational Event

Attribute Name	Type	Definition	Class Name	UoF
		Example – flying – immersed – orbiting		
operationalEvent ReportedDate	DateType	operationalEventReportedDate is the date at which the operational event was reported.	OperationalEven t	S5000F Operational Event
operationalEvent Symptom	ClassificationType	operationalEventSymptom is a classification of the symptom that the product presents during the OperationalEvent.	OperationalEven t	S5000F Operational Event
operationalModeC lassification	ClassificationType	operationalModeClassification is a classification that allows to assign an OperationalMode to a specific category or place the operationalModeIdentifier in context. **Example** – ICAO	OperationalMode	S5000F Operational Period
operationalModeD escription	DescriptorType	operationalModeDescription is a textual explanation of an OperationalMode.	OperationalMode	S5000F Operational Period
operationalModeI dentifier	IdentifierType	operationalModeIdentifier is an unique identifier that allows to distinguish one OperationalMode from a different one. **Note** For example, ICAO ADREP 2000 code	OperationalMode	S5000F Operational Period
operationalModeN ame	TextPropertyType	operationalModeName is a text that identifies an OperationalMode in an understandable way. **Example** – cruise – immersion – start – take-off	OperationalMode	S5000F Operational Period
operationalModeS tatusType	ClassificationType	operationalModeStatusType is a classification of the operational mode.	OperationalMode Status	S5000F Logbook

Attribute Name	Type	Definition	Class Name	UoF
operationalModeStatusUsed	PropertyType	operationalModeStatusUsed is an indicator of whether the operationModeType was or not used, and how.	OperationalModeStatus	S5000F Logbook
operationalPeriodActual	DateTimeRange	operationalPeriodActual is the period of time during which the OperationalPeriod took effectively place.	OperationalPeriod	S5000F Operational Period
operationalPeriodIdentifier	IdentifierType	operationalPeriodIdentifier is a string of characters used to uniquely identify an OperationalPeriod of an individual Product instance.	OperationalPeriod	S5000F Operational Period
operationalPeriodName	TextPropertyType	operationalPeriodName is a word or phrase by which an Operational Period is commonly known and can be easily referenced.	OperationalPeriod	S5000F Operational Period
operationalPeriodPhase	ClassificationType	operationalPeriodPhase is a classification that allows to classify an OperationalPeriod.	OperationalPeriod	S5000F Operational Period
operationalPeriodRelationshipType	ClassificationType	operationalPeriodRelationshipType is a classification that defines the association between two individual operational periods. **Example** – at the same time as – before	OperationalPeriodRelationship	S5000F Operational Period
operationalPeriodResult	ClassificationType	operationalPeriodResult is a classification that defines the result of the OperationalPeriod. **Example** – abort – partial success – sucess	OperationalPeriod	S5000F Operational Period
operationalPeriodScheduled	DateTimeRange	operationalPeriodScheduled is the period of time during which it was forseen that the OperationalPeriod would take place.	OperationalPeriod	S5000F Operational Period
operationalRequirementPeriod	DateRange	operationalRequirementPeriod is a period of time during which an OperationalRequirement is in effect.	OperationalRequirement	S5000F Fleet Planning and Product Assignment

Attribute Name	Type	Definition	Class Name	UoF
operationalRoleD elta	ValueWithTolerancesPr opertyType	operationalRcleDelta is a value that describes the delta regarding the baseline configuration of the OperationalRole for a specific ProductVariant. **Example** – additional weight – range reduction	OperationalRole	S5000F Operational Roles
operationalRoleD escription	DescriptorType	operationalRoleDescription is a narrative statement of what a specific OperationalRole is.	OperationalRole	S5000F Operational Roles
operationalRolei dentifier	IdentifierType	operationalRoleIdentifier is a string of characters that uniquely identifies an OperationalRole.	OperationalRole	S5000F Operational Roles
operationalRoleT ime	PropertyType	operationalRoleTime is a period of time associated to the OperationalRole. **Example** – pre-flight time – start-up time – turn-around time	OperationalRole	S5000F Operational Roles
operationalRoleT ype	ClassificationType	operationalRoleType is a classification that allows to group different OperationalRoles.	OperationalRole	S5000F Operational Roles
operationalTimeT ype	ClassificationType	operationalTimeType is a <<classificationType>> that determines the type of operationalTime that is being measured. **Example** – preparation – shutdown – startup – turn-around-time	OperationalTime	S5000F Operational Times
operationalTimeV alue	NumericalPropertyType	operationalTimeValue is a time that defines the duration of a specific operationalTime.	OperationalTime	S5000F Operational Times

Attribute Name	Type	Definition	Class Name	UoF
oppositeAngle	PropertyType	oppositeAngle is the angle between the two sides opposite of the base of a triangle.	Triangle	S5000F_Compound_Attributes_002-00
organizationalBreakdownStructureRevisionDate	DateType	organizationalBreakdownStructureRevisionDate is the date at which the OrganizationalBreakdownStructureRevision was created.	OrganizationalBreakdownStructureRevision	S5000F Organizational Breakdown Structure
organizationalBreakdownStructureRevisionIdentifier	IdentifierType	organizationalBreakdownStructureRevisionIdentifier is a string of characters that allow to uniquely identify an OrganizationalBreakdownStructureRevision and differentiate it from other OrganizationalBreakdownStructureRevisions.	OrganizationalBreakdownStructureRevision	S5000F Organizational Breakdown Structure
organizationalBreakdownStructureRevisionPeriod	DateRange	organizationalBreakdownStructureRevisionPeriod is the period of time during which an OrganizationalBreakdownStructureRevision is or has been in effect.	OrganizationalBreakdownStructureRevision	S5000F Organizational Breakdown Structure
organizationalBreakdownStructureRevisionRationale	DescriptorType	organizationalBreakdownStructureRevisionRationale is a description that indicates the reason for this OrganizationalBreakdownStructureRevision.	OrganizationalBreakdownStructureRevision	S5000F Organizational Breakdown Structure
organizationalBreakdownStructureRevisionStatus	StateType	organizationalBreakdownStructureRevisionStatus is a state that identifies the maturity of an OrganizationalBreakdownStructureRevision.	OrganizationalBreakdownStructureRevision	S5000F Organizational Breakdown Structure
organizationalRoleDescription	DescriptorType	organizationalRoleDescription is a textual narrative statement describing an OrganizationalRole	OrganizationalRole	S5000F Organizational Breakdown Structure
organizationalRoleType	ClassificationType	organizationalRoleType is a classification that allows to group similar OrganisationalRoles.	OrganizationalRole	S5000F Organizational Breakdown Structure
organizationDates	DateRange	organizationDates is a period of time during which the organization exists.	Organization	S5000F Specializations

Attribute Name	Type	Definition	Class Name	UoF
organizationDesc ription	DescriptorType	organizationDescription is a textual narrative statement that explains what the Organization is.	Organization	S5000F Specializations
organizationOper ationsApprovalDu ring	DateRange	organizationOperationsApprovalDuring is the period of time during which the approval of an OperatorOrganization to operate during a specific product variant is in effect.	OrganizationOpe rationsApproval	S5000F Operator
organizationType	ClassificationType	organizationType is a classification that allows to define groups of organizations.	Organization	S5000F Specializations
otherFacilityTyp e	ClassificationType	otherFacilityType is a classification that allows to differentiate between different classes of OtherFacilities.	OtherFacility	S5000F Facility
parkingFacilityT ype	ClassificationType	parkingFacilityType is a classification that allows to differentiate between different classes of ParkingFacilities.	ParkingFacility	S5000F Facility
partActionCause	ClassificationType	partActionCause is a classification describing the cause for a specific PartAction. **Example** – failure – scheduled maintenance or overhaul	PartAction	S5000F Equipment
partActionCauseD escription	DescriptorType	partActionCauseDescription is a narrative text describing the underlying cause for a PartAction. **Example** – 4C check	PartAction	S5000F Equipment
partActionDate	DateTimeType	partActionDate is the date at which a specific PartAction was performed.	PartAction	S5000F Equipment
partActionIdenti fier	IdentifierType	partActionIdentifier is a string that uniquely identifies a PartAction and differentiates it from other PartActions.	PartAction	S5000F Equipment
partActionTimeSi nceNew	SingleValuePropertyTy pe	partActionTimeSinceNew is the elapsed time since the part was put into service at the moment of the PartAction.	PartAction	S5000F Equipment

Attribute Name	Type	Definition	Class Name	UoF
partActionTimeSinceOverhaul	SingleValuePropertyType	`partActionTimeSinceOverhaul` is the elapsed time since the part was overhauled for the last time at the moment that the `PartAction` took place.	`PartAction`	S5000F Equipment
partActionType	ClassificationType	`partActionType` is a classification describing the `PartAction` that has been performed on a part. **Example** – Install	`PartAction`	S5000F Equipment
partAsDesignedPartsListRelationshipType	ClassificationType	`partAsDesignedPartsListRelationshipType` is a classification that identifies the meaning of the established relationship.	`PartAsDesignedPartsListRelationship`	CDM UoF Part Definition
partDescription	DescriptorType	`partDescription` is a textual narrative statement that explains what the `HardwarePartAsDesigned` is.	`HardwarePartAsDesigned`	S5000F Specializations
partExportControl	ClassificationType	`partExportControl` is a classification that indicates whether the part is subject to export control restrictions.	`HardwarePartAsDesigned`	S5000F Specializations
partIdentifier	IdentifierType	`partIdentifier` is an identifier that establishes a unique designator for a `PartAsDesigned` and to differentiate it from other instances of `PartAsDesigned`. **Note** Part identification includes drawing, model, type or source controlling numbers. **Example** – "12345-501"	`PartAsDesigned`	CDM UoF Part Definition
partInPoolPeriod	`DateRange`	`partInPoolPeriod` is a range of dates representing the period during which a HardwarePart belonged to a specific `Pool` of parts.	`PartInPool`	S5000F Warehouse and Spare Pool
partInPoolQuantityDuringPeriod	SingleValuePropertyType	`partInPoolQuantityDuringPeriod` is a value representing the quantity of HardwareParts stocked in a `Pool` during the specified period of time.	`PartInPool`	S5000F Warehouse and Spare Pool

Attribute Name	Type	Definition	Class Name	UoF
partInWarehouseP eriod	DateRange	partInWarehousePeriod is the period of time that a part is stored in a specific warehouse.	PartInWarehouse	S5000F Warehouse and Spare Pool
partInWarehouseQ uantityDuringPer iod	SingleValuePropertyTy pe	partInWarehouseQuantityDuringPeriod is a value representing the quantity of HardwareParts stocked in a warehouse during the specified period.	PartInWarehouse	S5000F Warehouse and Spare Pool
partMajorCompone nt	umlBoolean	partMajorCcmponent is a classification that indicates that a part needs separate tracking because it can be considered a major SerializedProductVariant by its own right. **Note** Used for engines, landing gears, etc.	HardwarePartAsD esigned	S5000F Specializations
partName	NameType	partName is a name by which the PartAsDesigned is known and can be easily referenced.	PartAsDesigned	CDM UoF Part Definition
partOwnerIdentif ier	IdentifierType	partOwnerIdentifier is a string of text that uniquely identifies a PartOwner <<relationshp>> and allows to differentiate it from other ones.	PartOwner	S5000F Part As Realized
partOwnerPeriod	DateRange	partOwnerPeriod is a date range that defined the period of time during which a SerializedHardwarePart is owned by a specific Party.	PartOwner	S5000F Part As Realized
partsListEntryId entifier	IdentifierType	partsListEntryIdentifier is an identifier that establishes a unique designator for a PartAsDesignedPartsListEntry and to differentiate it from other instances of PartAsDesignedPartsListEntry.	PartAsDesignedP artsListEntry	CDM UoF Part Definition
partsListEntryQu antity	PropertyType	partsListEntryQuantity is a property that specifies the amount of the PartAsDesigned used in its parent PartAsDesignedPartsListRevision.	PartAsDesignedP artsListEntry	CDM UoF Part Definition

Attribute Name	Type	Definition	Class Name	UoF
partsListRevisionDate	DateType	`partsListRevisionDate` is a date that specifies when the `PartAsDesignedPartsList` was revised.	`PartAsDesignedPartsListRevision`	CDM UoF Part Definition
partsListRevisionIdentifier	IdentifierType	`partsListRevisionIdentifier` is an identifier that establishes a unique designator for a `PartAsDesignedPartsListRevision` and to differentiate it from other instances of `PartAsDesignedPartsListRevision` for the same `partsListType`.	`PartAsDesignedPartsListRevision`	CDM UoF Part Definition
partsListRevisionRationale	DescriptorType	`partsListRevisionRationale` is a description that gives more information on the justification for revising the `PartAsDesignedPartsList`.	`PartAsDesignedPartsListRevision`	CDM UoF Part Definition
partsListRevisionStatus	StateType	`partsListRevisionStatus` is a state that identifies the maturity of a `PartAsDesignedPartsListRevision`.	`PartAsDesignedPartsListRevision`	CDM UoF Part Definition
partsListType	ClassificationType	`partsListType` is a classification that identifies the context and intended use of the `PartAsDesignedPartsList`.	`PartAsDesignedPartsList`	CDM UoF Part Definition
partyAddressDuration	DateRange	`partyAddressDuration` is the period of time during which the address of a `Party` is valid.	`PartyAddress`	S5000F Party
partyAddressType	ClassificationType	`partyAddressType` is a <<classification>> describing the type of relationship between a `Party` and an Address.	`PartyAddress`	S5000F Party
partyContactDataDetails	TextPropertyType	`partyContactDataDetails` is a description that provides further details on the contact data of a `Party`.	`PartyContactData`	S5000F Party
partyContactDataType	ClassificationType	`partyContactDataType` is a <<classification>> that allows to qualify the `PartyContactData`.	`PartyContactData`	S5000F Party
partyRelationshipDescription	DescriptorType	`partyRelationshipDescription` is a textual narrative statement explaining the association between two Parties.	`PartyRelationship`	S5000F Party

Attribute Name	Type	Definition	Class Name	UoF
partyRelationshi pDuration	DateRange	partyRelationshipDuration is the range of dates during which the association between two parties exists.	PartyRelationsh ip	S5000F Party
partyRelationshi pType	ClassificationType	partyRelationshipType is a relationship describing how two Parties are associated. **Example** – is associated with – is department of – is legal succcessor of – is subsidiary of – works for	PartyRelationsh ip	S5000F Party
penaltyAmount	SingleValuePropertyTy pe	penaltyAmount is a number that represents the amount corresponding to a Penalty.	Penalty	S5000F Service Contract Penalty
penaltyDate	DateType	penaltyDate is a Date at which a Penalty was established.	Penalty	S5000F Service Contract Penalty
penaltyDescripti on	DescriptorType	penaltyDescription is a description that provides a human readable expression of a Penalty.	Penalty	S5000F Service Contract Penalty
penaltyIdentifie r	IdentifierType	penaltyIdentifier is a string of characters that uniquely identifies a Penalty.	Penalty	S5000F Service Contract Penalty
penaltySettledAt	DateType	penaltySettledAt is a Date at which a Penalty was settled.	Penalty	S5000F Service Contract Penalty
performanceParam eterCalculationM ethod	DescriptorType	performanceParameterCalculationMethod is a description that gives more information on the method by which the performanceParameterValue has been derived.	PerformancePara meterValueGroup	CDM UoF Performance Parameter
performanceParam eterRevisionDate	DateType	performanceParameterRevisionDate is a date that defines when a PerformanceParameterRevision was defined.	PerformancePara meterRevision	CDM UoF Performance Parameter

Attribute Name	Type	Definition	Class Name	UoF
performanceParameterRevisionIdentifier	IdentifierType	performanceParameterRevisionIdentifier is an identifier that establishes a unique designator for a PerformanceParameterRevision and to differentiate it from other instances of PerformanceParameterRevision.	PerformanceParameterRevision	CDM UoF Performance Parameter
performanceParameterRevisionRationale	DescriptorType	performanceParameterRevisionRationale is a description that gives more information on the justification for revising the defined PerformanceParameter and its values.	PerformanceParameterRevision	CDM UoF Performance Parameter
performanceParameterRevisionStatus	StateType	performanceParameterRevisionStatus is a state that identifies the maturity of a PerformanceParameterRevision.	PerformanceParameterRevision	CDM UoF Performance Parameter
performanceParameterType	ClassificationType	performanceParameterType is a classification that identifies the type of PerformanceParameter being exchanged.	PerformanceParameter	CDM UoF Performance Parameter
performanceParameterValue	PropertyType	performanceParameterValue is a property that represents a value which is determined for the PerformanceParameter.	PerformanceParameterValueGroup	CDM UoF Performance Parameter
performanceParameterValueFraction	PropertyType	performanceParameterValueFraction is a property that represents the fraction of all occurrences related to a specified PerformanceParameter that must be within the limit of the defined performanceParameterValue. **Example** – A customer requirement is that 98% of all replacement tasks must be performed below a specified value of two hours (= maximum replacement time)	PerformanceParameterValueGroup	CDM UoF Performance Parameter
performanceParameterValueLimitQualifier	ClassificationType	performanceParameterValueLimitQualifier is a classification that specifies a directed limit to be applied when testing a value against the defined PerformanceParameter.	PerformanceParameter	CDM UoF Performance Parameter
personCompetenceAcquired	DateType	personCompetenceAcquired is a Date at which a PersonCompetence was acquired.	PersonCompetence	S5000F Person Competences and Labor Rates

Attribute Name	Type	Definition	Class Name	UoF
personDates	DateRange	personDates are the dates during which a Person exists. **Example** – birth and death dates – employment dates	Person	S5000F Party
personFamilyName	TextPropertyType	PersonFamilyName is a text that indicates the family name of a Person.	Person	S5000F Party
personIdentifier	IdentifierType	personIdentifier is an unique identifier that differentiates a Person from any other Person.	Person	S5000F Party
personMiddleName	TextPropertyType	personMiddleName is a text that indicates the middle name of a person.	Person	S5000F Party
personName	TextPropertyType	personName is a textual description used normally to identify a Person	Person	S5000F Party
personOperations ApprovalDuring	DateRange	personOperationsApprovalDuring is the period of time during which the approval of an OperatorPerson to operate during a specific product variant is in effect.	PersonOperation sApproval	S5000F Operator
personPrefixTitl e	ClassificationType	personPrefixTitle is a classification indicating a title that is used before a Person's name. **Example** – Dr. – Mrs.	Person	S5000F Party
personSuffixTitl e	ClassificationType	personSuffixTitle is a classification indicating a title that is added after a Person name.	Person	S5000F Party
plannedItemUpgra deIdentifier	IdentifierType	plannedItemUpgradeIdentifier is a string of text that uniquely identifies a PlannedItemUpgrade and differentiates it from all othe rplanned PlannedItemUpgrades.	PlannedItemUpgr ade	S5000F Change Embodiment Strategy

Attribute Name	Type	Definition	Class Name	UoF
`plannedItemUpgradePriority`	ClassificationType	`plannedItemUpgradePriority` is a string of characters that uniquely identifies a PlannedProductUpgrade, differentiating it from all other PlannedProductUpgrades.	`PlannedItemUpgrade`	S5000F Change Embodiment Strategy
`plannedItemUpgradeReason`	ClassificationType	`plannedItemUpgradeReason` is a <<classification>> that allows to group different `PlannedItemUpgrades` by the root causes for such upgrade.	`PlannedItemUpgrade`	S5000F Change Embodiment Strategy
`plannedUpgradePeriod`	DateTimeRange	`plannedUpgradePeriod` is the range of time during which the product update has been planned.	`PlannedUpgradeTimescales`	S5000F Change Embodiment Planning
`plannedUpgradeTimescaleIdentifier`	IdentifierType	`plannedUpgradeTimescaleIdentifier` is a string of text that uniquely identifies a PlannedProductUpgrade and differentiates it from the other PlannedProductUpgrades.	`PlannedUpgradeTimescales`	S5000F Change Embodiment Planning
`plannedUpgradeTimescaleVersion`	IdentifierType	`plannedUpgradeTimescaleVersion` is a string of text that allows to differentiate a different version for a same PlannedProductUpgrade. **Note** Used for replanning.	`PlannedUpgradeTimescales`	S5000F Change Embodiment Planning
`policiesAndRegulationsEffectivity`	DateRange	`policiesAndRegulationsEffectivity` is the period of time during which a policy or regulation is in effect.	`PoliciesAndRegulations`	S5000F Policies and Regulations
`poolDescription`	DescriptorType	`poolDescription` is textual narrative statement explaining the purpose of a `Pool`.	`Pool`	S5000F Warehouse and Spare Pool
`poolIdentifier`	IdentifierType	`poolIdentifier` is string of characters that allows to uniquely identify a specific `Pool` among other `Pools`.	`Pool`	S5000F Warehouse and Spare Pool
`poolName`	TextPropertyType	`poolName` is a word or phrase under which the `Pool` is commonly known and to which it can be referred.	`Pool`	S5000F Warehouse and Spare Pool
`poolOwnershipDuring`	DateRange	`poolOwnershipDuring` defines the period of time during which the ownership of a `Pool` by a specific Part is valid.	`PoolOwner`	S5000F Warehouse and Spare Pool

Attribute Name	Type	Definition	Class Name	UoF
poolOwnershipRat io	SingleValuePropertyTy pe	poolOwnershipRatio is the percentage of ownership of a Pool by a specific Party during a specific period of time.	PoolOwner	S5000F Warehouse and Spare Pool
poolStockedInWar eHouseDuring	DateRange	poolStockedInWareHouseDuring is a range of dates indicating the period during which a Pool of parts was stocked at a defined Warehouse.	PoolStockedInWa reHouse	S5000F Warehouse and Spare Pool
poolType	ClassificationType	poolType is a classification that allows to determine the kind of Pool. **Example** – contractual – customer consignment stock – multi-customer stock, contractor-owned	Pool	S5000F Warehouse and Spare Pool
poolUsageDescrip tion	DescriptorType	poolUsageDescription is a textual narrative statement explaining the usage of a Pool by a specific Party.	PoolUser	S5000F Warehouse and Spare Pool
poolUsageDuring	DateRange	poolUsageDuring is the period during which a Party can have a certain type of access to a spares Pool.	PoolUser	S5000F Warehouse and Spare Pool
poolUsageType	ClassificationType	poolUsageType is a classification that defines the kind of usage that a Party can have on a specific spares Pool.	PoolUser	S5000F Warehouse and Spare Pool
postalCode	umlString	postalcode is a string of characters that represents a short code used by the postal service to identify a geographical area.	StreetAddress	CDM UoF Location
productDescripti on	DescriptorType	productDescription is a textual narrative statement that explains what the Product is.	Product	S5000F Specializations
productLife	DateRange	productLife is a date range that indicates the expected or actual life of a Product.	Product	S5000F Specializations
productParameter AtOperationalEve ntName	DescriptorType	productParameterAtOperationalEventName is a word or phrase by which the productParameter that occurred at an OperationalEvent is known. **Example** – operating hours	ProductParamete rAtOperationalE vent	S5000F Operational Event

Attribute Name	Type	Definition	Class Name	UoF
`productParameterAtOperationalEventValue`	PropertyType	`productParameterAtOperationalEventValue` is the value of the productParametersAtOperationalEvent.	`ProductParameterAtOperationalEvent`	S5000F Operational Event
`productParametersAtOperationalEventIdentifier`	IdentifierType	`productParametersAtOperationalEventIdentifier` is a string of text that uniquely identifies a `ProductParameterAtOperationalEvent` and allows to differentiate it from other `ProductParameterAtOperationalEvent`.	`ProductParameterAtOperationalEvent`	S5000F Operational Event
`productUsagePhaseDescription`	DescriptorType	`productUsagePhaseDescription` is a textual narrative statement explaining a `ProductUsagePhase`.	`ProductUsagePhase`	S5000F Product Usage Phase
`productUsagePhaseDuration`	PropertyType	`productUsagePhaseDuration` is a property indicating the period of time during which the `ProductUsagePhase` extends. **Example** – 5% – 7 hours – While under water	`ProductUsagePhase`	S5000F Product Usage Phase
`productUsagePhaseIdentifier`	IdentifierType	`productUsagePhaseIdentifier` is a string that uniquely identifies a `ProductUsagePhase` and differentiates it from other `ProductUsagePhases`.	`ProductUsagePhase`	S5000F Product Usage Phase
`productUsagePhaseRelationshipIdentifier`	IdentifierType	`productUsagePhaseRelationshipIdentifier` is a string of characters that uniquely identifies a `ProductUsagePhaseRelationship`.	`ProductUsagePhaseRelationship`	S5000F Product Usage Phase
`productUsagePhaseRelationshipType`	ClassificationType	`productUsagePhaseRelationshipType` is a <<classification>> that defines how two `ProductUsagePhases` are related.	`ProductUsagePhaseRelationship`	S5000F Product Usage Phase
`productVariantDescription`	DescriptorType	`productVariantDescription` is a narrative text explaining a `ProductVariant`.	`ProductVariant`	S5000F Specializations

Applicable to: All

Attribute Name	Type	Definition	Class Name	UoF
productVariantDimensions	ThreeDimensional	productVariantDimensions are the ThreeDimensional characteristics of a ProductVariant,	ProductVariant	S5000F Specializations
productVariantEntryIntoServiceDate	DateType	productVariantEntryIntoServiceDate is the date at which the first item or product of a specific ProductVariant entered service.	ProductVariant	S5000F Specializations
productVariantLastBuyDate	DateType	productVariantLastBuyDate is the last date at which a ProductVariant can be purchased.	ProductVariant	S5000F Specializations
productVariantMaintenancePeriod	DateRange	productVariantMaintenancePeriod is a DateRange during which a ProductVariantMaintenance takes place.	ProductVariantMaintenance	S5000F Maintenance Organization
productVariantProductionDates	DateRange	productVariantProductionDates is the period of time during which a ProductVariant is in production.	ProductVariant	S5000F Specializations
productVariantSupportedByPoolDuring	DateRange	productVariantSupportedByPoolDuring is a range of dates indicating the period of time during which a ProductVariant is supported by a defined parts Pool.	ProductVariantSupportedByPool	S5000F Warehouse and Spare Pool
productVariantWeight	NumericalPropertyType	productVariantWeight is a number that represents the weight of a ProductVariant.	ProductVariant	S5000F Specializations
projectIdentifier	IdentifierType	projectIdentifier is an identifier that establishes a unique designator for a Project and to differentiate it from other instances of Project.	Project	CDM UoF Product and Project
projectName	NameType	projectName is a name by which the Project is known and can be easily referenced.	Project	CDM UoF Product and Project
projectRelationshipType	ClassificationType	projectRelationshipType is a classification that defines the type of relationship between two Projects.	ProjectRelationship	S5000F Project and Contract
publicationModuleIssueInWorkNumber	umlString	publicationModuleIssueInWorkNumber is a string of characters used for monitoring and control of intermediate drafts of S1000DPublicationModuleIssue.	S1000DPublicationModuleIssue	CDM UoF Document

Attribute Name	Type	Definition	Class Name	UoF
		Note A `publicationModuleIssueInWorkNumber` must be created in accordance with the rules defined in S1000D.		
`publicationModuleIssueLanguage`	ClassificationType	`publicationModuleIssueLanguage` is a classification that identifies the language used to produce the content of the `S1000DPublicationModuleIssue`. **Note** A `publicationModuleIssueLanguage` must be created in accordance with the rules defined in S1000D.	`S1000DPublicationModuleIssue`	CDM UoF Document
`publicationModuleIssueLanguageCountry`	ClassificationType	`publicationModuleIssueLanguageCountry` is a classification that identifies the country where the language, identified by `publicationModuleIssueLanguage`, is spoken **Note** A `publicationModuleIssueLanguageCountry` must be created in accordance with the rules defined in S1000D.	`S1000DPublicationModuleIssue`	CDM UoF Document
`publicationModuleIssueNumber`	umlString	`publicationModuleIssueNumber` is a string of characters used to identify the release number of the `S1000DPublicationModuleIssue`. **Note** A `publicationModuleIssueNumber` must be created in accordance with the rules defined in S1000D.	`S1000DPublicationModuleIssue`	CDM UoF Document
`publicationModuleIssuer`	umlString	`publicationModuleIssuer` is a string of characters that represents the issuing authority attribute of the publication module code. **Note** A `publicationModuleIssuer` must be created in accordance with the rules defined in S1000D.	`S1000DPublicationModule`	CDM UoF Document
`publicationModuleNumber`	umlString	`publicationModuleNumber` is a string of characters that represents the number of the publication module attribute of the publication module code.	`S1000DPublicationModule`	CDM UoF Document

Attribute Name	Type	Definition	Class Name	UoF
		Note A `publicationModuleNumber` must be created in accordance with the rules defined in S1000D.		
`publicationModuleVolume`	umlString	`publicationModuleVolume` is a string of characters that represents the volume of the publication attribute of the publication module code. **Note** A `publicationModuleVolume` must be created in accordance with the rules defined in S1000D.	`S1000DPublicationModule`	CDM UoF Document
`quantityOfContainedMaterial`	PropertyType	`quantityOfContainedMaterial` is a property that identifies the amount of material included in an item..	`ContainedMaterial`	S5000F Contained Materials
`quantityOfContainedSubstance`	PropertyType	`quantityOfContainedSubstance` is a property that identifies the amount of the substance included in the `HardwarePartAsDesigned`.	`ContainedSubstance`	CDM UoF Part Definition
`reasonForShopSubmission`	ClassificationType	`reasonForShopSubmission` is a classification that provides the justification for the submission of an equipment to a workshop.	`ShopFindings`	S5000F Shop Findings
`recoveredItemStatus`	ClassificationType	`recoveredItemStatus` is a classification that allows to identify whether a recovered item is fit for service or requires further actions in order to make it useable.	`RecoveredItem`	S5000F Recovered Item
`recoveredItemValue`	PropertyType	`recoveredItemValue` is a property that documents the monetary value of a recovered item.	`RecoveredItem`	S5000F Recovered Item
`referencedDigitalFileJustification`	DescriptorType	`referencedDigitalFileJustification` is a phrase that provides more on information on the reason why the `DigitalFile` is referenced. **Example** – A video showing the task execution.	`ReferencedDigitalFile`	CDM UoF Digital File

Attribute Name	Type	Definition	Class Name	UoF
referencedDocumentPortion	DescriptorType	referencedDocumentPortion is a description that provides a reference to the portion of a document which is of interest in a specific usage.	ReferencedDocument	CDM UoF Document
referencedDocumentRole	ClassificationType	referencedDocumentRole is a classification that identifies the function of the established relationship. **Example** – design document reference – directive – document reference – drawing reference – source – verification	ReferencedDocument	CDM UoF Document
referenceDesignator	IdentifierType	referenceDesignator is an identifier that establishes a unique designator for a location within the overall Product, and to differentiate it from other locations. **Note** Reference designators serve as a cross reference between parts contained in wiring diagrams, hydraulic systems etc. and eg, the Illustrated Parts Data (IPD).	BreakdownElementUsageInBreakdown PartAsDesignedPartsListEntry	CDM UoF Breakdown Structure CDM UoF Part Definition
releasedDataSetAssociatedWithType	ClassificationType	releasedDataSetAssociatedWithType is a classification that allows to establish the type of relationship with which a DataSetAsReleased is associated with another item.	ReleasedDataSetAssociatedWith	S5000F Data Sets
remarkText	DescriptorType	remarkText is a description that provides the text of the additional information.	Remark	CDM UoF Remark
remarkType	ClassificationType	remarkType is a classification that defines the purpose of the remark. **Example** – internal note – technical fact	Remark	CDM UoF Remark

Attribute Name	Type	Definition	Class Name	UoF
removedDateTime	DateTimeType	removedDateTime is a date and time that specifies the exact point in time when the RealizedPart was uninstalled from the InstallationLocation.	InstalledPart	CDM UoF Serialized Product Variant Configuration
reportableActivityIdentifier	IdentifierType	reportableActivityIdentifier is a string of characters that is used to uniquely identify a ReportableActivity and to differentiate it from other ReportableActivities.	ReportableActivity	S5000F Reportable Activity
reportableActivityPeriod	DateRange	reportableActivityPeriod is the period of time on which the reporting is performed.	ReportableActivity	S5000F Reportable Activity
reportableActivityReportingDate	DateType	reportableActivityReportingDate is the date at which the reporting is performed.	ReportableActivity	S5000F Reportable Activity
reportableMetricDescription	DescriptorType	reportableMetricDescription is a textual narrative explaining the reportableMetric details.	ReportableMetric	S5000F Reportable Metric
reportableMetricIdentifier	IdentifierType	reportableMetricIdentifier is an unique identifier that allows to uniquely identify a ReportableMetric from any other one.	ReportableMetric	S5000F Reportable Metric
reportableMetricPeriod	DateTimeRange	reportableMetricPeriod is the period of time over which the metric was collected.	ReportableMetric	S5000F Reportable Metric
reportableMetricType	ClassificationType	reportableMetricType is a classification that allows to group ReportabaleMetrics by its characteristics.	ReportableMetric	S5000F Reportable Metric
reportableMetricValue	PropertyType	reportableMetricValue is a PropertyType providing the measurable value that a ReportableMetric has during a specific reporting period.	ReportableMetric	S5000F Reportable Metric
reportPartyRole	ClassificationType	reportPartyRole is a <<classification>> that allows to define the role of a Party in relationship with a Report.	ReportParty	S5000F Report
reportPeriod	DateRange	reportPeriod is the period of time on which a report is providing information.	Report	S5000F Report

Applicable to: All

S5000F

Attribute Name	Type	Definition	Class Name	UoF
		Example – 1-31 January 2018		
requiredDisposal PolicyMandate	ClassificationType	requiredDisposalPolicyMandate is a classification that indicates how the disposal policy has to be applied.	RequiredDisposa lPolicy	S5000F Disposal Requirement
requiredFleetRol eAvailability	SingleValuePropertyTy pe	requiredFleetRoleAvailability defines the necessary availability in a specific OperationalRole to be able to comply with a FleetRequirement.	RequiredFleetRo le	S5000F Fleet Planning and Product Assignment
requiredPartStoc kLevelValue	PropertyType	requiredPartStockLevelValue is a value indicating the required number of parts that have to be stocked for a specific spare pool.	RequiredPartSto ckLevelInPool	S5000F Warehouse and Spare Pool
requirementDate	DateType	requirementDate is the date at which a Requirement was defined.	Requirement	S5000F Requirement
requirementDescr iption	DescriptorType	requirementDescription is a narrative statement that explains what the requirement is.	Requirement	S5000F Requirement
requirementIdent ifier	IdentifierType	requirementIdentifier is a string of text that allows to uniquely identify a Requirement and differentiate it from other Requirements.	Requirement	S5000F Requirement
requirementName	TextPropertyType	requirementName is a text that provides an identifier by which a Requirement is commonly known.	Requirement	S5000F Requirement
requirementParty Role	ClassificationType	requirementPartyRole is a <<classification>> that defines the role of a Party with regard to a Requirement.	RequirementPart y	S5000F Requirement
requirementRaise dBy	Organization	requirementRaisedBy represents the organization that has raised a requirement.	Requirement	S5000F Requirement
requirementRelat ionshipType	ClassificationType	requirementRelationshipType is a <<classification>> that defines how two Requirements are related.	RequirementRela tionship	S5000F Requirement

Attribute Name	Type	Definition	Class Name	UoF
requirementStatus	StateType	requirementStatus is a state that identifies the status of the Requirement.	Requirement	S5000F Requirement
requirementType	ClassificationType	requirementType is a classification that allows to group Requirements of a same kind.	Requirement	S5000F Requirement
resourceSpecificationIdentifier	IdentifierType	resourceSpecificationIdentifier is an identifier that establishes a unique designator for a ResourceSpecification and to differentiate it from other instances of ResourceSpecification.	ResourceSpecification	CDM UoF Resource Specification
resourceSpecificationType	ClassificationType	resourceSpecificationType is a classification that identifies further specialization for a ResourceSpecification.	ResourceSpecification	CDM UoF Resource Specification
resourceUsagePartyRole	ClassificationType	resourceUsagePartyRole is the role that the party is performing for a specific ResourceUsageRequest.	ResourceUsageParty	S5000F Resource Usage Request
resourceUsageRequestDate	DateType	resourceUsageRequestDate is the date at which a ResourceUsageRequest was perfromed.	ResourceUsageRequest	S5000F Resource Usage Request
resourceUsageRequestDescription	DescriptorType	resourceUsageRequestDescription is a textual narrative explaining the ResourceUsageRequest.	ResourceUsageRequest	S5000F Resource Usage Request
resourceUsageRequestIdentifier	IdentifierType	resourceUsageRequestIdentifier is a text that uniquely identifies a ResourceUsageRequest and differentiates it from other ResourceUsageRequests.	ResourceUsageRequest	S5000F Resource Usage Request
resourceUsageRequestName	DescriptorType	resourceUsageRequestName is a string of text that summarizes the ResourceUsageRequest and can be used to easily reference it in common speech.	ResourceUsageRequest	S5000F Resource Usage Request
resourceUsageRequestPeriod	DateRange	resourceUsageRequestPeriod is the period of time during which a Resource is requested.	ResourceUsageRequest	S5000F Resource Usage Request
resourceUsageRequestStatus	StateType	resourceUsageRequestStatus is a state indicating what the current status of a ResourceUsageRequest is.	ResourceUsageRequest	S5000F Resource Usage Request

Attribute Name	Type	Definition	Class Name	UoF
roleCapabilityLevel	ClassificationType	roleCapabilityLevel is a <<classification>> that allows to define the level of a RoleCapability.	RoleCapability	S5000F Operational Roles
safetyDocumentCriticality	ClassificationType	safetyDocumentCriticality is a classification on the criticality of a safety issue addressed in a SafetyDocument.	SafetyDocument	S5000F Safety
safetyIssueAssessmentBy	Organization	safetyIssueAssessmentBy is the Orgamization that has to assess the safety issue.	SafetyIssue	S5000F Safety
safetyIssueFirstIdentificationDateTime	DateTimeType	safetyIssueFirstIdentificationDateTime is the date and time at which the SafetyIssue was first identified.	SafetyIssue	S5000F Safety
safetyIssueReportingDateTime	DateTimeType	safetyIssueReportingDateTime is the date and time at which the SafetyIssue was reported.	SafetyIssue	S5000F Safety
safetyWarningAplicabilityDates	DateRange	safetyWarningAplicabilityDates is the period of time during which a SafetyWarning is applicable.	SafetyWarning	S5000F Safety
safetyWarningPriority	ClassificationType	safetyWarningPriority is a <<classification>> that allows to group SafetyWarnings by their priority.	SafetyWarning	S5000F Safety
second	umlInteger	second is an Integer that represents the second within a minute expressed as a value between '0' and '59'.	TimeType	S5000F_Compound_Attributes_002-00
securityClassificationAuthority	Organization	securityClassificationAuthority identifies the Organization that is the authoritative source for the defined SecurityClassification.	SecurityClassification	CDM UoF Security Classification
securityClassificationDate	DateType	securityClassificationDate is a date when the security classification is declared.	SecurityClassification	CDM UoF Security Classification
securityClassValue	NameType	securityClassValue is a name that defines the level of confidentiality. **Example** – Company confidential	SecurityClass	CDM UoF Security Classification

Attribute Name	Type	Definition	Class Name	UoF
		– Confidential – Restricted – Secret – Top secret – Unclassified		
sensorDetectionR ange	ValueRangePropertyTy pe	sensorDetectionRange is the range of values measured by the SensorType.	SensorType	S5000F Serialized Product Health Monitoring
sensorIdentifier	IdentifierType	sensorIdentifier is a string of text that uniquely identifies a Sensor and differentiates it from any other Sensor.	Sensor	S5000F Serialized Product Health Monitoring
sensorName	TextPropertyType	sensorName is a string of text that is used to commonly refer to a sensor of a specific type.	Sensor	S5000F Serialized Product Health Monitoring
sensorSamplingMo de	ClassificationType	sensorSamplingMode is a classification of the type of sensor sampling if it can provide multiple samples or error codes.	SensorSample	S5000F Serialized Product Health Monitoring
sensorSamplingRa te	ValueRangePropertyTy pe	sensorSamplingRate is the frequency by which a SensorType measures values.	SensorType	S5000F Serialized Product Health Monitoring
sensorSensitivit y	ValueRangePropertyTy pe	sensorSensitivity is the range of values that a SensorType can measure.	SensorType	S5000F Serialized Product Health Monitoring
serializedHardwa rePartAuthorized Life	AuthorizedLife	serializedHardwarePartAuthorizedLife is the AuthorizedLife for a SerializedHardwarePart	SerializedHardw arePart	S5000F Specializations
serializedHardwa rePartDescriptio n	DescriptorType	serializedHardwarePartDescription is a textual narrative statement that explains what the SerializedHardwarePart is and/or why it is different from other serializedHardwareParts.	SerializedHardw arePart	S5000F Specializations
serializedHardwa rePartDimensions	ThreeDimensional	serializedHardwarePartDimensions are the ThreeDimensional characteristics of a SerializedHardwarePart.	SerializedHardw arePart	S5000F Specializations

Applicable to: All

Attribute Name	Type	Definition	Class Name	UoF
serializedHardwarePartInServicePeriod	DateRange	serializedHardwarePartInServicePeriod is a date range during which the serialized hardware part was in service.	SerializedHardwarePart	S5000F Specializations
serializedHardwarePartManufacturingDate	DateType	serializedHardwarePartManufacturingDate is the date when the item was manufactured.	SerializedHardwarePart	S5000F Specializations
serializedHardwarePartWeight	NumericalPropertyType	serializedHardwarePartWeight is is a property that specifies the mass for a SerializedHardwarePart.	SerializedHardwarePart	S5000F Specializations
serializedItemOwnerDuring	DateRange	serializedItemOwnerDuring is a date range that indicates during which time a SerializedItemOwner held ownership of a serialized item.	SerializedItemOwner	S5000F Serialized Item
serializedItemOwnerRatio	SingleValuePropertyType	serializedItemOwnerRatio is the percentage of ownership of the serialized item by the owner during the period of time defined for that ownership period. **Example** – 25%	SerializedItemOwner	S5000F Serialized Item
serializedItemWarrantyPeriod	DateRange	serializedItemWarrantyPeriod is the period of time during which the warranty for a SerializedItem is in effect.	ItemWarranty	S5000F Warranty
serializedItemWarrantyType	ClassificationType	serializedItemWarrantyType is a classification that allows to categorize a SerielizedItem warranty.	ItemWarranty	S5000F Warranty
serializedPartEffectivityPeriod	DateRange	serializedPartEffectivityPeriod is the period of time during which a serializedHardwarePart has complied with the specification that defines it.	SerializedPartDesignAssociation	S5000F Part As Realized
serializedPartsListPositionIdentifier	IdentifierType	serializedPartsListPositionIdentifier is an identifier that establishes a unique designator for a SerializedPartsListPosition and to differentiate it from other instances of SerializedPartsListPosition.	SerializedPartsListPosition	CDM UoF Serialized Part Configuration

Attribute Name	Type	Definition	Class Name	UoF
serializedPartsL istPositionName	NameType	serializedPartsListPositionName is a name by which the SerializedPartsListPosition is known and can be easily referenced.	SerializedParts ListPosition	CDM UoF Serialized Part Configuration
serializedProduc tVariantAssignme ntDate	DateType	serializedProductVariantAssignmentDate is the date at which a specific serializedProductVariant was assigned to perform a specific OperationalRole.	SerializedProdu ctVariantAssign ment	S5000F Fleet Planning and Product Assignment
serializedProduc tVariantAssignme ntIdentifier	IdentifierType	serializedProductVariantAssignmentIdentifier is an unique identifier that unambiguously allows to identify different OperationalRole assignments to individual serializedProductVariants as specific moments in time ("tasking").	SerializedProdu ctVariantAssign ment	S5000F Fleet Planning and Product Assignment
serializedProduc tVariantAssignme ntStatus	ClassificationType	serializedProductVariantAssignmentStatus is a classification that allows to determine the status of an assignment of a serializedProductVariant to carry out a specific OperationalRole.	SerializedProdu ctVariantAssign ment	S5000F Fleet Planning and Product Assignment
serializedProduc tVariantAssignme ntType	ClassificationType	serializedProductVariantAssignmentType is a classification that allows to define the type of assignment of a specific serializedProductVariant to an OperationalRole.	SerializedProdu ctVariantAssign ment	S5000F Fleet Planning and Product Assignment
serializedProduc tVariantDescript ion	DescriptorType	serializedProductVariantDescriptionis a textual narrative statement that explains what the SerializedProductVariant is and/or why it is different from other SerializedProductVariants.	SerializedProdu ctVariant	S5000F Specializations
serializedProduc tVariantDimensio ns	ThreeDimensional	serializedProductVariantDimensions are the ThreeDimensional characteristics of a SerializedProductVariant.	SerializedProdu ctVariant	S5000F Specializations
serializedProduc tVariantEndOfSer viceDate	DateType	serializedProductVariantEndOfServiceDate is the date at which the serialized product variant was retired from service.	SerializedProdu ctVariant	S5000F Specializations
serializedProduc tVariantEntryInt oServiceDate	DateType	serializedProductVariantEntryIntoServiceDate is the date at which the serialized product variant entered into service.	SerializedProdu ctVariant	S5000F Specializations

Attribute Name	Type	Definition	Class Name	UoF
serializedProductVariantInFleetDuring	DateRange	serializedProductVariantInFleetDuring is a range of dates that indicate the period of time during which a SerializedProductVariant belongs to a specific fleet.	SerializedProductVariantInFleet	S5000F Fleet Definition
serializedProductVariantManufacturer	Organization	serializedProductVariantManufacturer is the organization which has manufactured a SerializedProductVariant.	SerializedProductVariant	S5000F Specializations
serializedProductVariantManufacturingDate	DateType	serializedProductVariantManufacturingDate is the date at which the manufacturing of a SerializedProductVariant was finished.	SerializedProductVariant	S5000F Specializations
serializedProductVariantOperatingBasePeriod	DateRange	serializedProductVariantOperatingBasePeriod is a range of dates during which a SerializedProductVariant was operating at a specific OperatingBase.	SerializedProductVariantOperatingBase	S5000F Operating Base
serializedProductVariantOperatorDuring	DateRange	serializedProductVariantOperatorDuring is the period of time during which the SerializedProductVariant was operated by a specific operator.	SerializedProductVariantOperator	S5000F Operator
serializedProductVariantWeight	NumericalPropertyType	serializedProductVariantWeight is a number that represents the weight of a SerializedProductVariantWeight.	SerializedProductVariant	S5000F Specializations
serviceBulletinCost	SingleValuePropertyType	serviceBulletinCost is the monetary cost of a ServiceBulletin.	ServiceBulletin	S5000F Change Embodiment
serviceBulletinEmbodimentLimit	DateType	serviceBulletinEmbodimentLimit is a Date by which a ServiceBulletin must be mandatorily embodied.	ServiceBulletin	S5000F Change Embodiment
serviceBulletinPriority	ClassificationType	serviceBulletinPriority is a classification that determines the urgency with which a ServiceBulletin should be embodied.	ServiceBulletin	S5000F Change Embodiment
serviceBulletinType	ClassificationType	serviceBulletinType is classification that allows to group different types of ServiceBulletins.	ServiceBulletin	S5000F Change Embodiment

Attribute Name	Type	Definition	Class Name	UoF
		Example – authority requirement (such as airworthiness directive implementation)		
serviceContractPeriod	DateRange	serviceContractPeriod is the period of time during which a Service is associated to a Contract.	ServiceContract	S5000F Service Contract Management
serviceDescription	DescriptorType	serviceDescription is a narrative statement explaining a Service.	Service	S5000F Service Contract Management
serviceIdentifier	IdentifierType	serviceIdentifier is an unique identifier that allows to uniquely identify a Service from any other one.	Service	S5000F Service Contract Management
serviceLevelAgreementClauseDescription	DescriptorType	serviceLevelAgreementClauseDescription is a narrative statement of the meaning of serviceLevelAgreementClause.	ServiceLevelAgreementClause	S5000F Service Contract Management
serviceRelationshipType	ClassificationType	serviceRelationshipType is a <<classification>> that defines how two Services are related.	ServiceRelationship	S5000F Service Contract Management
serviceRequestCancellationDetails	DescriptorType	serviceRequestCancellationDetails is a description that provides a human readable expression of ServiceRequestCancellation.	ServiceRequestCancellation	S5000F Service Request
serviceRequestCancellationIdentifier	IdentifierType	serviceRequestCancellationIdentifier is a string of characters that uniquely identifies a ServiceRequestCancellation	ServiceRequestCancellation	S5000F Service Request
serviceRequestCancellationReason	ClassificationType	serviceRequestCancellationReason is a <<classification>> that defines the reason for a ServiceRequestCancellation.	ServiceRequestCancellation	S5000F Service Request
serviceRequestDateTime	DateTimeType	serviceRequestDateTime is teh date and time at which a ServiceRequest has been made.	ServiceRequest	S5000F Service Request
serviceRequestDescription	DescriptorType	serviceRequestDescription is a narrative statement explaining the ServiceRequest.	ServiceRequest	S5000F Service Request

Attribute Name	Type	Definition	Class Name	UoF
serviceRequestId entifier	IdentifierType	serviceRequestIdentifier is a string of text that uniquely identifies a ServiceRequest and differentiates it from other ServiceRequests.	ServiceRequest	S5000F Service Request
serviceRequestIt emQuantity	SingleValuePropertyTy pe	serviceRequestItemQuantity is a the number of ServiceItems that are requested as part of a ServiceRequest.	ServiceRequestI tem	S5000F Service Request
serviceRequestLo cationDuring	DateRange	serviceRequestLocationDuring is the period during which the service is requested at a specific location.	ServiceRequestL ocation	S5000F Service Request
serviceRequestLo cationNotes	DescriptorType	serviceRequestLocationNotes is a textual narrative providing clarifications about when the location where the service has t be provided.	ServiceRequestL ocation	S5000F Service Request
serviceRequestNa me	DescriptorType	serviceRequestName is a string of characters by which a ServiceRequest is commonly known.	ServiceRequest	S5000F Service Request
serviceRequestPa rtyRole	ClassificationType	serviceRequestPartyRole is a classification that allows to determine the role of a Party regarding a ServiceRequest.	ServiceRequestP arty	S5000F Service Request
serviceRequestPr iority	ClassificationType	serviceRequestPriority is a classification that allows to determine how urgent a ServiceRequest is.	ServiceRequest	S5000F Service Request
serviceRequestRe lationshipType	ClassificationType	serviceRequestRelationshipType is a classification that defines the type of relationship between two ServiceRequests.	ServiceRequestR elationship	S5000F Service Request
serviceRequestTy pe	ClassificationType	serviceRequestType is a classification that allows to group different types of ServiceRequests.	ServiceRequest	S5000F Service Request
shopFindingsDesc ription	DescriptorType	shopFindingsDescription is a narrative text explaining the ShopFindings.	ShopFindings	S5000F Shop Findings
shopFindingsFaul tCode	ClassificationType	shopFindingsFaultCode is a classification that represents a fault code that the equipment under test has provided during the problem investigation.	ShopFindings	S5000F Shop Findings

Attribute Name	Type	Definition	Class Name	UoF
shopFindingsFaul tConfirmed	ClassificationType	shopFindingsFaultConfirmed is a classification of the fault that has been confirmed as part of the shop findings.	ShopFindings	S5000F Shop Findings
shopFindingsIden tifier	IdentifierType	shopFindingsIdentifier is a string of characters that uniquely identifies a ShopFinding and differentiates it from other ShopFindings.	ShopFindings	S5000F Shop Findings
shopReceivedDate	DateType	shopReceivedDate is the Date at which an equipment was received at a workshop for diagnostics.	ShopFindings	S5000F Shop Findings
skillCode	IdentifierType	skillCode is an identifier that establishes a unique designator for a Skill and to differentiate it from other instances of Skill.	Skill	CDM UoF Competence Definition
skillLevelDescri ption	DescriptorType	skillLevelDescription is a description that gives more information on a proficiency.	SkillLevel	CDM UoF Competence Definition
skillLevelName	NameType	skillLevelName is a name that uniquely establishes a proficiency.	SkillLevel	CDM UoF Competence Definition
softwareElementM odificationFrequ ency	PropertyType	softwareElementModificationFrequency is a property that defines the expected frequency with which the SoftwarePartAsDesigned which realizes this SoftwareElementRevision will be modified. **Example** – 3 months – 5 years	SoftwareElement Revision	CDM Software Element
softwareElementS ize	PropertyType	softwareElementSize is a property that defines the size of the SoftwarePartAsDesigned which realizes this SoftwareElementRevision. **Example** – 10.000 lines of code - estimated – 23.5 Mbytes - executable – 800 Kbytes - contracted	SoftwareElement Revision	CDM Software Element

Attribute Name	Type	Definition	Class Name	UoF
softwareElementType	ClassificationType	softwareElementType is a classification that identifies further specialization for a SoftwareElement.	SoftwareElement	CDM Software Element
softwareErrorDateTime	DateTimeType	softwareErrorDateTime is the date and time at which a SoftwareError occurred.	SoftwareError	S5000F Software
softwareErrorDescription	DescriptorType	softwareErrorDescription is a description that provides a human readable expression of a SoftwareError.	SoftwareError	S5000F Software
softwareErrorFixPriority	ClassificationType	softwareErrorFixPriority is a classification that allows to determnie the urgency to fix a SoftwareError	SoftwareError	S5000F Software
softwareErrorIdentifier	IdentifierType	softwareErrorIdentifier is a string of characters that uniquely identifies a SoftwareError.	SoftwareError	S5000F Software
softwareErrorName	NameType	softwareErrorName is a name by which the SoftwareError is known and can be easily referenced.	SoftwareError	S5000F Software
softwareErrorReproducibility	ClassificationType	softwareErrorReproducibility is a <<classification>> that allows to qualify the reproducibility of a SoftwareError.	SoftwareError	S5000F Software
softwareErrorSeverity	ClassificationType	softwareErrorSeverity is a <<classification>> about how severe a SoftwareError is.	SoftwareError	S5000F Software
softwareErrorStepsToReproduce	DescriptorType	softwareErrorStepsToReproduce is a description that provides a human readable expression of the steps required to reproduce a SoftwareError.	SoftwareError	S5000F Software
softwarePartAsReleasedChecksum	TextPropertyType	softwarePartAsReleasedChecksum is a string of text used verify that the code of a SoftwarePartAsReleased has not been corrupted or tampered with.	SoftwarePartAsReleased	S5000F Specializations
softwarePartAsReleasedDateTime	DateTimeType	softwarePartAsReleasedDateTime is the date and time at which a software part was released for service.	SoftwarePartAsReleased	S5000F Specializations

Attribute Name	Type	Definition	Class Name	UoF
softwarePartAsReleasedDescription	DescriptorType	softwarePartAsReleasedDescription is a textual narrative statement that explains what the softwarePartAsReleased is.	SoftwarePartAsReleased	S5000F Specializations
softwarePartAsReleasedSize	SingleValuePropertyType	softwarePartAsReleasedSize is a value representing the actual size of the delivered code of a software part. **Example** – 2.5 Mbytes	SoftwarePartAsReleased	S5000F Specializations
specialSafetyInstructionApplicabilityDates	DateRange	specialSafetyInstructionApplicabilityDates is the period during which the SpecialSafetyInstruction must be applied.	SpecialSafetyInstruction	S5000F Safety
specialSafetyInstructionPriority	ClassificationType	specialSafetyInstructionPriority is a classification that defines the urgency of a SpecialSafetyInstruction.	SpecialSafetyInstruction	S5000F Safety
strainGaugeFactor	SingleValuePropertyType	strainGaugeFactor is the gauge factor (also called strain factor) of a StrainGauge.	StrainGauge	S5000F Serialized Product Health Monitoring
streetName	NameType	streetName is the name by which a road is officially known and can be easily referenced. **Example** – E-2561 Road – Main Street	StreetAddress	CDM UoF Location
streetNumber	umlString	streetNumber is a string of characters that represents the position along a street **Example** – Km 35.5 – 4	StreetAddress	CDM UoF Location
substanceDefinitionDescription	DescriptorType	substanceDefinitionDescription is a textual narrative statement that explains what the Substance is.	SubstanceDefinition	S5000F Specializations

Attribute Name	Type	Definition	Class Name	UoF
substanceDefinit ionExceptedQuant ities	ClassificationType	`substanceDefinitionExceptedQuantities` is a classification that can be referenced to determine the maximum quantity per inner and outer packaging.	`SubstanceDefini tion`	S5000F Specializations
substanceDefinit ionHazardousClas s	ClassificationType	`substanceDefinitionHazardousClass` is a classification that identifies to what extent a substance is capable of posing a significant risk to health, safety or property during transportation, handling or storage.	`SubstanceDefini tion`	S5000F Specializations
substanceDefinit ionLimitedQuanti ty	PropertyType	`substanceDefinitionLimitedQuantity` identifies the maximum quantity per inner packaging for dangerous goods transported in limited quantities.	`SubstanceDefini tion`	S5000F Specializations
substanceDefinit ionPackingGroup	ClassificationType	`substanceDefinitionPackingGroup` is a classification about which kind of packing is allowed for this substance. **Note** The `substanceDefinitionPackingGroup` is often determined by the `substanceDefinitionHazardousClass`.	`SubstanceDefini tion`	S5000F Specializations
substanceDefinit ionSpecialProvis ions	ClassificationType	`substanceDefinitionSpecialProvisions` is a classification that indicates special actions to be taken in relationship with this item for handling, storage or disposal.	`SubstanceDefini tion`	S5000F Specializations
substanceDefinit ionState	ClassificationType	`substanceDefinitionState` is a classification indicating the state or phase in which is substance is. **Note** Different states can be associated at the same time, but then these must be associated to an `ApplicabilityStatement`. **Example** – water is gaseous above 100 degrees Celsius – water is liquid between 0 and 100 degrees celsius – water is solid (ice) below 0 degrees Celsius	`SubstanceDefini tion`	S5000F Specializations
substanceEmissio nValue	PropertyType	`substanceEmissionValue` is a property that defines the amount of substance emitted during a specific period of time.	`SubstanceEmissi on`	S5000F Consumptions and Emissions

Attribute Name	Type	Definition	Class Name	UoF
subSubSystem	umlString	subSubSystem is a string of characters that represents the sub-subsystem attribute of the data module code. **Note** A subSubSystem must be created in accordance with the rules defined in S1000D.	S1000DDataModule	CDM Document
subSystem	umlString	subSystem is a string of characters that represents the subsystem attribute of the data module code. **Note** A subSystem must be created in accordance with the rules defined in S1000D.	S1000DDataModule	CDM Document
suppliesUsedAmount	SingleValuePropertyType	suppliesUsedAmount is the amount of supply items used for a MaintenanceActivity. **Example** – 2 pounds – 3.5 meters – 8 units	SuppliesUsed	S5000F Maintenance Activity
supportEquipmentCalibrationRequired	ClassificationType	supportEquipmentCalibrationRequired is a classification that indicates whether a support equipment requires calibration.	SupportEquipment	S5000F Maintenance Activity
supportEquipmentPower	PropertyType	supportEquipmentPower indicates the type of power that a support equipment requires. **Example** – 400 VAC – 5 psi air	SupportEquipment	S5000F Maintenance Activity
supportEquipmentType	ClassificationType	supportEquipmentType is a classification that allows to group different types of support equipment. **Example** – Automatic Test Equipment – Hand Tool	SupportEquipment	S5000F Maintenance Activity

Attribute Name	Type	Definition	Class Name	UoF
supportEquipment UsedAmount	umlInteger	supportEquipmentUsedAmount is the number of a specific SupportEquipment that has been used in a MaintenanceActivity.	SupportEquipmen tUsed	S5000F Maintenance Activity
supportEquipment UsedDuration	SingleValuePropertyTy pe	supportEquipmentUsedDuration is the time that the SupportEquiment is used during a MaintenanceActivity.	SupportEquipmen tUsed	S5000F Maintenance Activity
system	umlString	system is a string of characters that represents the system attribute of the data module code. **Note** A system must be created in accordance with the rules defined in S1000D.	S1000DDataModul e	CDM Document
systemDifference Code	umlString	systemDifferenceCode is a string of characters that represents the system difference code attribute of the data module code. **Note** A systemDifferenceCode must be created in accordance with the rules defined in S1000D.	S1000DDataModul e	CDM Document
taskDuration	PropertyType	taskDuration is a property that specifies the average time required for the performance of a Task, regardless of the number of personnel working simultaneously . **Note 1** taskDuration does not include time spent awaiting spares, support equipment, facilities or personnel (logistics delay time). **Note 2** taskDuration could be calculated from the subtask durations.	TaskRevision	CDM UoF Task
taskIdentifier	IdentifierType	taskIdentifier is an identifier that establishes a unique designator for a Task and to differentiate it from other instances of Task.	Task	CDM UoF Task
taskInformationC ode	ClassificationType	taskInformationCode is a classification that identifies the main purpose for the Task.	TaskRevision	CDM UoF Task

Attribute Name	Type	Definition	Class Name	UoF
		Note Valid classifications are defined in the ASD ILS Specification S1000D, Technical Publications using a Common Source Database.		
taskName	NameType	taskName is a name by which the Task is known and can be easily referenced.	TaskRevision	CDM UoF Task
taskRequirementDescription	DescriptorType	taskRequirementDescription is a description that summarizes the procedure that needs to be performed based on the outcome of a support analysis activity.	TaskRequirement Revision	CDM UoF Task Requirement
taskRequirementIdentifier	IdentifierType	taskRequirementIdentifier is an identifier that establishes a unique designator for a TaskRequirement and to differentiate it from other instances of TaskRequirement.	TaskRequirement	CDM UoF Task Requirement
taskRequirementInformationCode	ClassificationType	taskRequirementInformationCode is a classification that identifies the main purpose for the TaskRequirement. **Note** Valid classifications are defined in the ASD ILS Specification S1000D, Technical Publications using a Common Source Database.	TaskRequirement Revision	CDM UoF Task Requirement
taskRequirementRevisionChangeDescription	DescriptorType	taskRequirementRevisionChangeDescription is description that gives more information on content that has been altered between two revisions of a TaskRequirement.	TaskRequirement Revision	CDM UoF Task Requirement
taskRequirementRevisionDate	DateType	taskRequirementRevisionDate is a date that specifies when a TaskRequirementRevision was defined.	TaskRequirement Revision	CDM UoF Task Requirement
taskRequirementRevisionIdentifier	IdentifierType	taskRequirementRevisionIdentifier is an identifier that establishes a unique designator for a TaskRequirementRevision and to differentiate it from other instances of TaskRequirementRevision.	TaskRequirement Revision	CDM UoF Task Requirement
taskRequirementRevisionRationale	DescriptorType	taskRequirementRevisionRationale is a description that gives more information on the justification for revising the TaskRequirement.	TaskRequirement Revision	CDM UoF Task Requirement

Attribute Name	Type	Definition	Class Name	UoF
taskRequirementRevisionStatus	StateType	taskRequirementRevisionStatus is a state that identifies the maturity of a TaskRequirementRevision.	TaskRequirementRevision	CDM UoF Task Requirement
taskRequirementSpecialResourceRequirement	DescriptorType	taskRequirementSpecialResourceRequirement is a description that gives more information on unusual resources which are needed for the performance of the required Task.	TaskRequirementRevision	CDM UoF Task Requirement
taskRevisionChangeDescription	DescriptorType	taskRevisionChangeDescription is a description that gives more information on content that has been altered between two revisions of a Task.	TaskRevision	CDM UoF Task
taskRevisionDate	DateType	taskRevisionDate is a date that specifies when the Task was revised.	TaskRevision	CDM UoF Task
taskRevisionIdentifier	IdentifierType	taskRevisionIdentifier is an identifier that establishes a unique designator for a TaskRevision and to differentiate it from other instances of TaskRevision.	TaskRevision	CDM UoF Task
taskRevisionRationale	DescriptorType	taskRevisionRationale is a description that gives more information on the justification for revising the Task.	TaskRevision	CDM UoF Task
taskRevisionStatus	StateType	taskRevisionStatus is a state that identifies the progress on the development of a TaskRevision.	TaskRevision	CDM UoF Task
taskTotalLaborTime	PropertyType	taskTotalLaborTime is a property that specifies the total time to be expended during a task. **Note** taskTotalLaborTime includes the labor time for all required personnel resources.	TaskRevision	CDM UoF Task
technicalOrderEmbodimentDate	DateType	technicalOrderEmbodimentDate is a Date at which a TechnicalOrder was embodied.	TechnicalOrderEmbodied	S5000F Change Embodiment Reporting
technicalOrderIdentifier	IdentifierType	technicalOrderIdentifier is a string of text that allows to uinquely identify a TechnicalOrder and differentiate it from otehr TechnicalOrders.	TechnicalOrder	S5000F Change Embodiment

Attribute Name	Type	Definition	Class Name	UoF
technicalOrderPriority	ClassificationType	technicalOrderPriority is a classification that indicates the urgency with which an TechnicalOrder must be implemented.	TechnicalOrder	S5000F Change Embodiment
technicalOrderRequiredImplementationDate	DateType	technicalOrderRequiredImplementationDate is the mandatory date by which the TechnicalOrder must be executed.	TechnicalOrder	S5000F Change Embodiment
tradeName	NameType	tradeName is a name that uniquely establishes a craft or profession.	Trade	CDM UoF Competence Definition
transportCapabilityDimensions	ThreeDimensional	transportCapabilityDimensions are the ThreeDimensional characteristics of a ThreeDimensional.	TransportCapability	S5000F Transporting Asset
transportCapabilityQuantity	NumericalPropertyType	transportCapabilityQuantity is a number that defines how many items of a specific type can be transported as part of a TransportCapability.	TransportCapability	S5000F Transporting Asset
transportCapabilityRange	NumericalPropertyType	transportCapabilityRange is a number that represents the distance to which a TransportCapability can transport items.	TransportCapability	S5000F Transporting Asset
transportCapabilityUsageDescription	DescriptorType	transportCapabilityUsageDescription is a textual narrative that provides a human readable expression of a TransportCapabilityUsage.	TransportCapabilityUsage	S5000F Transporting Asset
transportCapabilityUsageIdentifier	IdentifierType	transportCapabilityUsageIdentifier is a string of text that allows to uniquely identify a TransportCapabilityUsage and differentiate it from a different TransportCapabilityUsage instance.	TransportCapabilityUsage	S5000F Transporting Asset
transportCapabilityUsagePeriod	DateTimeRange	transportCapabilityUsagePeriod is a DateTimeRange representing the period of time during which a TransportCapability is used.	TransportCapabilityUsage	S5000F Transporting Asset
typeOfPersonDescription	DescriptorType	typeOfPersonDescription is a textual narrative statement explaining a TypeOfPerson	TypeOfPerson	S5000F Type of Person

Attribute Name	Type	Definition	Class Name	UoF
typeOfPersonIdentifier	IdentifierType	typeOfPersonIdentifier is a string of characters that uniquely defines a TypeOfPerson and allows to differentiate it from other TypeOfPersons.	TypeOfPerson	S5000F Type of Person
typeOfPersonName	NameType	typeOfPersonName is a text by which a TypeOfPerson is commonly known.	TypeOfPerson	S5000F Type of Person
typeOfPersonSize	ThreeDimensional	typeOfPersonSize is the average size of Persons of the TypeOfPerson.	TypeOfPerson	S5000F Type of Person
typeOfPersonType	ClassificationType	typeOfPersonType is a <<classification>> that allows to group different Persons that sahre the same characteristics.	TypeOfPerson	S5000F Type of Person
typeOfPersonWeight	NumericalPropertyType	typeOfPersonWeight is the average weight of Persons of the TypeOfPerson.	TypeOfPerson	S5000F Type of Person
typeOfPrice	ClassificationType	typeOfPrice is a classification that defines the type of a provided price.	HardwarePartAsDesignedCommerceData	S5000F Warehouse and Spare Pool
unacceptableConditionDescription	DescriptorType	unacceptableConditionDescription is a narrative text providing the justification for an UnacceptableCondition.	UnacceptableCondition	S5000F Unacceptable Item Condition requiring disposal
unacceptableConditionIdentifier	IdentifierType	unacceptableConditionIdentifier is a string of text that uniquely identifies an UnacceptableCondition and differentiates it from other ones.	UnacceptableCondition	S5000F Unacceptable Item Condition requiring disposal
unacceptableConditionReason	ClassificationType	unacceptableConditionReason is a classification that determines the reason that underlies an UnacceptableCondition.	UnacceptableCondition	S5000F Unacceptable Item Condition requiring disposal
upperBound	umlString	upperBound is a string of characters that represents the upper limit of the range.	SerialNumberRange	S-Series_Compound_Attributes_2-0_002-00

Attribute Name	Type	Definition	Class Name	UoF
upperLimitSalesQuantity	umlInteger	upperLimitSalesQuantity indicates a hardwarePartUnitOfIssuePrice valid for an individual, specified range of buy quantities. **Note** The upperLimitSalesQuantity must always be presented with and read in conjunction with the lowerLimitSalesQuantity and a hardwarePartUnitOfIssuePrice. If absent, there is no upper quantity limit to which the price is applicable.	PriceBreakData	S5000F Warehouse and Spare Pool
warehouseType	ClassificationType	warehouseType is a classification that allows to differentiate between different classes of Warehouses.	Warehouse	S5000F Facility
warrantyClaimCommunicationMeans	ClassificationType	warrantyClaimCommunicationMeans is a classification that defines the means by which a WarrantyClaim was raised.	WarrantyClaim	S5000F Warranty
warrantyClaimContactType	ClassificationType	warrantyClaimContactType is a classification that allows to group different types of WarrantyClaimContacts.	WarrantyClaimContact	S5000F Warranty
warrantyClaimFilingDate	DateType	warrantyClaimFilingDate is the date at which the Warranty Claim has been sent.	WarrantyClaim	S5000F Warranty
warrantyClaimFollowUpDate	DateType	warrantyClaimFollowUpDate is a date at which the WarrantyFollowUp took place.	WarrantyClaimFollowUp	S5000F Warranty
warrantyClaimFollowUpNotes	DescriptorType	warrantyClaimFollowUpNotes is a narrative text describing the follow-up of a WarrantyClaim.	WarrantyClaimFollowUp	S5000F Warranty
warrantyClaimIdentifier	IdentifierType	warrantyClaimIdentifier is a string of text that uniquely identifies a WarrantyClaim and differentiates it from other WarrantyClaims.	WarrantyClaim	S5000F Warranty
warrantyClaimOccurrenceDate	DateType	warrantyClaimOccurrenceDate is the date at which the event that generated the claim occurred.	WarrantyClaim	S5000F Warranty

Attribute Name	Type	Definition	Class Name	UoF
`warrantyClaimResolutionDate`	DateType	`warrantyClaimResolutionDate` is a classification that indicates the kind of resolution that was taken.	`WarrantyClaimResolution`	S5000F Warranty
`warrantyClaimResolutionDescription`	DescriptorType	`warrantyClaimResolutionDescription` is a narrative text explaining the `WarrantyClaimResolution`.	`WarrantyClaimResolution`	S5000F Warranty
`warrantyClaimResolutionIdentifier`	IdentifierType	`warrantyClaimResolutionIdentifier` is a string that allows to uniquely identify a `WarrantyClaimResolution` and differentiate it from other `WarrantyClaimResolutions`.	`WarrantyClaimResolution`	S5000F Warranty
`warrantyClaimResolutionType`	ClassificationType	`warrantyClaimResolutionType` is a <<classification>> that allows to group the `WarrantyClaimResolutions` by different criteria.	`WarrantyClaimResolution`	S5000F Warranty
`warrantyClaimSettlementDate`	DateType	`warrantyClaimSettlementDate` is the date at which the `WarrantyClaim` has been settled.	`WarrantyClaim`	S5000F Warranty
`warrantyClaimType`	ClassificationType	`warrantyClaimType` is a classification that permits to group different types of `WarrantyClaims`.	`WarrantyClaim`	S5000F Warranty
`warrantyEventPeriod`	DateRange	`warrantyEventPeriod` is the period of time during which the `WarrantyEvent` extended. **Example** – downtime period	`WarrantyEvent`	S5000F Warranty
`warrantyEventReason`	ClassificationType	`warrantyEventReason` is a classification that describes the type of `WarrantyEvent`.	`WarrantyEvent`	S5000F Warranty
`wasteContainerIdentifier`	IdentifierType	`wasteContainerIdentifier` is a string of characters that allows to uniquely identify a `WasteContainer` and differentiate it from other ones.	`WasteContainer`	S5000F Container
`wasteDisposalOperationActionJustification`	DescriptorType	`wasteDisposalOperationActionJustification` is a descriptive text that allows to document why a certain `Action` has been taken after a DisposalOperation.	`WasteDisposalOperationAction`	S5000F Waste Disposal Operation

S5000F

Attribute Name	Type	Definition	Class Name	UoF
wasteDisposalOpe rationDate	DateType	wasteDisposalOperationDate is the date at which the WasteDisposalOperation was performed.	WasteDisposalOp eration	S5000F Waste Disposal Operation
wasteDisposalOpe rationIdentifier	IdentifierType	wasteDisposalOperationIdentifier is a text string that uniquely identifies a WasteDisposalOperation and allows to differentiate it from other WasteDisposalOperation instances.	WasteDisposalOp eration	S5000F Waste Disposal Operation
wasteDisposalOpe rationMethod	ClassificationType	wasteDisposalOperationMethod is a classificatio that allows to define the method of disposal used during a WasteDisposalOperation.	WasteDisposalOp eration	S5000F Waste Disposal Operation
wasteDisposalOpe rationMethodDeta ils	DescriptorType	wasteDisposalOperationMethodDetails is a textual description providing further details on the disposal operation.	WasteDisposalOp eration	S5000F Waste Disposal Operation
wasteDisposalOpe rationOrganizati on	Organization	wasteDisposalOperationOrganization is the organization that carries out the wasteDisposal.	WasteDisposalOp eration	S5000F Waste Disposal Operation
wasteRecoveredIt emQuality	ClassificationType	wasteRecoveredItemQuality is a classification that allows to define the quality of the material or substance recovered as the result of a WasteDisposalOperation,	WasteRecoveredI tem	S5000F Recovered Material or Substances
wasteRecoveredIt emQuantity	PropertyType	wasteRecoveredItemQuantity is a property that defines the amount of material or substance recovered as the result of a WasteDisposalOperation,	WasteRecoveredI tem	S5000F Recovered Material or Substances
wasteRecoveredIt emValue	PropertyType	wasteRecoveredItemValue is a property that documents the value of the material or substance recovered as the result of a WasteDisposalOperation,	WasteRecoveredI tem	S5000F Recovered Material or Substances
width	PropertyType		Rectangle	S5000F_Compound_Attributes_ 002-00

Attribute Name	Type	Definition	Class Name	UoF
		`width` is a property that specifies the less extended longitudinal dimension of an object.	`Cuboid`	S-Series_Compound_Attributes_2-0_002-00
`workBreakdownDescription`	DescriptorType	`workBreakdownDescription` is a narrative statement explaining the `WorkBreakdown`.	`WorkBreakdown`	S5000F Work Breakdown
`workBreakdownIdentifier`	IdentifierType	`workBreakdownIdentifier` is a string of text that uniquely identifies a `WorkBreakdown`, allowing to differentiate it from all other `WorkBreakdowns`.	`WorkBreakdown`	S5000F Work Breakdown
`workBreakdownName`	DescriptorType	`workBreakdownName` is a word or phrase by which the `WorkBreakdown` is commonly known.	`WorkBreakdown`	S5000F Work Breakdown
`workBreakdownRelationshipType`	ClassificationType	`workBreakdownRelationshipType` is a <<classification>> that defines how two `WorkBreakdowns` are related.	`WorkBreakdownRelationship`	S5000F Work Breakdown
`workBreakdownRevisionDate`	DateType	`workBreakdownRevisionDate` is a date that indicates when a WorkBreadownRevision was created.	`WorkBreakdownRevision`	S5000F Work Breakdown
`workBreakdownRevisionIdentifier`	IdentifierType	`workBreakdownRevisionIdentifier` is a string of characters which uniquely identifies a `WorkBreakdownRevision`.	`WorkBreakdownRevision`	S5000F Work Breakdown
`workBreakdownRevisionRationale`	DescriptorType	`workBreakdownRevisionRationale` is a description of why the revision for the `WorkBreakdown` was created.	`WorkBreakdownRevision`	S5000F Work Breakdown
`workBreakdownRevisionStatus`	StateType	`workBreakdownRevisionStatus` is a state that identifies the maturity of a `WorkBreakdownRevision`.	`WorkBreakdownRevision`	S5000F Work Breakdown
`workItemDescription`	DescriptorType	`workItemDescription` is a narrative statement explaining what the `WorkItem` is.	`WorkItem`	S5000F Work Breakdown
`workItemIdentifier`	IdentifierType	`workItemIdentifier` is a string of characters that uniquely identifies a `WorkItem`.	`WorkItem`	S5000F Work Breakdown

Attribute Name	Type	Definition	Class Name	UoF
workItemPeriod	DateRange	workItemPeriod is the period during which a WorkItem has to take place.	WorkItem	S5000F Work Breakdown
workItemRelationshipType	ClassificationType	workItemRelationshipType is a classification indicating the relationship type between two WorkItems.	WorkItemRelationship	S5000F Work Breakdown
workItemStatus	ClassificationType	workItemStatus is a classification that defines the situation of a WorkItem.	WorkItem	S5000F Work Breakdown
workItemTimelineEvent	ClassificationType	workItemTimelineEvent is a classification which identifies the starting point for the WorkItem under consideration in relation to the start or end point of the WorkItem playing the role of its predecessor, if any.	WorkItemRelationship	S5000F Work Breakdown
workItemTimelineLag	PropertyType	workItemTimelineLag is the time between the related WorkItem timeline event (start/end) and the start for the WorkItem under consideration.	WorkItemRelationship	S5000F Work Breakdown
workItemType	ClassificationType	workItemType is a classification that allows to define different categories of work for a WorkItems.	WorkItem	S5000F Work Breakdown
workOrderDateRaised	DateType	workOrderDateRaised is the date at which the work order was raised.	WorkOrder	S5000F Maintenance Activity
workOrderDescription	DescriptorType	workOrderDescription is a narrative statement explaining the WorkOrder.	WorkOrder	S5000F Maintenance Activity
workOrderExecutionPeriod	DateTimeRange	workOrderExecutionPeriod is the period of time during which the work order must be carried out.	WorkOrder	S5000F Maintenance Activity
workOrderIdentifier	IdentifierType	workOrderIdentifier is a string of text that uniquely identifies a WorkOrder and allows to distinguish it from other WorkOrders.	WorkOrder	S5000F Maintenance Activity
workOrderImplementationTimeLimit	DateTimeType	workOrderImplementationTimeLimit is a DateTime which represents the date and time at which the WorkOrder was implemented.	WorkOrder	S5000F Maintenance Activity

Applicable to: All

Attribute Name	Type	Definition	Class Name	UoF
workOrderPriority	ClassificationType	workOrderPriority is a <<classification>> that allows to define the priority of a WorkOrder.	WorkOrder	S5000F Maintenance Activity
workOrderStatus	StateType	workOrderStatus is a state describing the current status of the WorkOrder.	WorkOrder	S5000F Maintenance Activity
workOrderType	ClassificationType	workOrderType is a classification that allows to group different WorkOrders of similar characteristics.	WorkOrder	S5000F Maintenance Activity
xCoordinate	NumericalPropertyType	xCoordinate is a numerical value representing the longitudinal coordinate of a position within the referenced area.	LocalPosition	S5000F Local Position
yCoordinate	NumericalPropertyType	yCoordinate is a numerical value representing the tramnsversal coordinate of a position within the referenced area.	LocalPosition	S5000F Local Position
zCoordinate	NumericalPropertyType	zCoordinate is a numerical value representing the height coordinate of a position within the referenced area.	LocalPosition	S5000F Local Position
zoneElementType	ClassificationType	zoneElementType is a classification that identifies further specialization for a ZoneElement.	ZoneElement	CDM Zone Element

4   Data element valid values

The full list of S5000F attribute valid values is provided in Table 4. This includes valid values from SX002D used by S5000F but defined in SX001G. Note that the specification does not yet define valid values for all classification types and identifiers that can require one. Similarly, it should be highlighted that the valid values are recommended values and not mandatory. Refer to Chap 27 for the tailoring of the valid values.

Note

In addition to the values below, all classification attributes include the following values:

- "N/A" (Not applicable value)
- "/EMPTY" (Non-shared value)
- "/NULL" (Currently unknown value)

Table 4 List of valid values

Attribute name	Valid value	Valid value name
`actionIdentifier`	AU	SX001G:automaticallyAssignedID
	MA	SX001G:manuallyAssignedID
`actionPriority`	C	SX001G:criticalAction
	R	SX001G:routineAction
	U	SX001G:urgentAction
`actionType`	ANA	SX001G:analyzeAction
	APP	SX001G:approveAction
	BLK	SX001G:blockAction
	CHG	SX001G:changeAction
	DIS	SX001G:discardAction
	HLD	SX001G:putOnHoldAction
	INS	SX001G:inspectAction
	RED	SX001G:redesignAction
	REJ	SX001G:rejectAction
	REP	SX001G:repairAction
	RPL	SX001G:replaceAction
	RPT	SX001G:reportAction
	WDR	SX001G:withdrawAction
`aggregatedElementType`	FA	SX001G:familyBreakdownElement
	FU	SX001G:functionBreakdownElement
	GR	SX001G:groupBreakdownElement
	SY	SX001G:systemBreakdownElement
`allowedProductConfigurationIdentifier`	ID	SX001G:allowedProductConfigurationIdentifier

Attribute name	Valid value	Valid value name
anchoringPointIdentifier	OEM	SX001G:originalEquipmentManufacturer
applicabilityStatementIdentifier	ID	SX001G:applicabilityStatementIdentifier
authorityToOperateIdentifier	ID	SX001G:authorityToOperateIdentifier
availabilityIdentifier	ID	SX001G:availabilityIdentifier
availabilityStatus	A	SX001G:available
	L	SX001G:locked
	N	SX001G:notAvailable
breakdownElementEssentiality	1	SX001G:criticalBreakdownElement
	2	SX001G:partialCriticalBreakdownElement
	3	SX001G:nonCriticalBreakdownElement
breakdownElementIdentifier	ASD	SX001G:asdSystemHardwareIdentificationCode
	CSN	SX001G:figureItemIdentifier
	ID	SX001G:breakdownElementIdentifier
	LCN	SX001G:fullLogisticsSupportAnalysisControlNumber
	SNS	SX001G:standardNumberingSystemIdentifier
breakdownElementRevisionIdentifier	ID	SX001G:breakdownElementRevisionIdentifier
breakdownElementRevisionRelationshipType	ALT	SX001G:alternateToBreakdownElement
	AP	SX001G:breakdownElementAccessPoint
	FUPH	SX001G:functionalToPhysicalBreakdownElementRelationship
breakdownElementRevisionStatus		Refer to revisionStatusCode valid value library, Para 5
breakdownElementUsageIdentifier	ID	SX001G:breakdownElementUsageIdentifier
breakdownElementUsageRelationshipType	AND	SX001G:mutualBreakdownElementInclusion
	XOR	SX001G:mutualBreakdownElementExclusion
breakdownRevisionIdentifier	ID	SX001G:breakdownRevisionIdentifier
breakdownRevisionStatus		Refer to revisionStatusCode valid value library, Para 5
breakdownType	ASD	SX001G:asdSystemHardwareBreakdown
	FAM	SX001G:familyBreakdown
	FU	SX001G:functionalBreakdown
	HY	SX001G:hybridBreakdown
	PH	SX001G:physicalBreakdown

Attribute name	Valid value	Valid value name
	PR	SX001G:provisioningBreakdown
	SY	SX001G:systemBreakdown
	ZONE	SX001G:zonalBreakdown
budgetApprovedStatus	A	SX001G:approved
	C	SX001G:cancelled
	D	SX001G:draft
	E	SX001G:expired
	P	SX001G:pendingApproval
budgetIdentifier	BI	SX001G:budgetIdentifierCode
budgetType	C	SX001G:cashFlowBudget
	F	SX001G:financialBudget
	M	SX001G:masterBudget
	O	SX001G:operationalBudget
	P	SX001G:provisionalBudget
	S	SX001G:staticBudget
calibrationDocumentType	CER	SX001G:calibrationCertificate
	PR	SX001G:calibrationProcedure
	SP	SX001G:calibrationSpecification
calibrationIdentifier	CAL	SX001G:calibratingOrganisation
capabilityDefinitionCategory	MI	SX001G:MissionCapability
	OP	SX001G:operationalCapability
	SU	SX001G:supportCapability
capabilityDefinitionCharacter isticValueComparisonOperator		Refer to comparisonOperatorCode valid value library, Para 5
capabilityDefinitionIdentifie r	ID	SX001G:capabilityDefinitionIdentifier
capabilityDefinitionRevisionI dentifier	ID	SX001G:capabilityDefinitionRevisionIdentifier
capabilityDefinitionRevisionS tatus		Refer to revisionStatusCode valid value library, Para 5
capabilityIdentifier	OEM	SX001G:originalEquipmentManufacturer
	OP	SX001G:operator
capabilityLimitationIdentifie r	OEM	SX001G:originalEquipmentManufacturer
	OP	SX001G:operator
	ALT	SX001G:altitudeCapabilityLimitation

Attribute name	Valid value	Valid value name
capabilityLimitationType	DEP	SX001G:depthCapabilityLimitation
	DIS	SX001G:distanceCapabilityLimitation
	HGT	SX001G:heightCapabilityLimitation
	LEN	SX001G:lengthCapabilityLimitation
	NUM	SX001G:numericUnitCapabilityLimitation
	PERF	SX001G:performanceCapabilityLimitation
	VOL	SX001G:volumeCapabilityLimitation
	WGT	SX001G:weightCapabilityLimitation
	WID	SX001G:widthCapabilityLimitation
capabilityType	MAN	SX001G:manufacturingCapabilit
	RE	SX001G:repairCapability
	ST	SX001G:storageCapability
	TR	SX001G:transportCapability
cargoItemIdentifier	OPER	SX001G:operator
changeAuthorizationIdentifier	AMN	SX001G:changeAmendmentNumber
	CAN	SX001G:changeAuthorizationNumber
	ID	SX001G:changeAuthorizationIdentifier
changeEmbodimentRequirementType	M	SX001G:mandatoryEmbodiment
	O	SX001G:optionalEmbodiment
	R	SX001G:recommendedEmbodiment
changeNotificationType	A	SX001G:applicabilityChangeNotification
	E	SX001G:editorialChangeNotification
	M	SX001G:markupChangeNotification
	T	SX001G:technicalChangeNotification
changeRequestAddedOrRemovedMaterialIdentifier	ID	SX001G:changeRequestAddedOrRemovedMaterialIdentifier
changeRequestAddedOrRemovedSubstanceIdentifier	ID	SX001G:changeRequestAddedOrRemovedSubstanceIdentifier
changeRequestCauseIdentifier	ID	SX001G:changeRequestCauseIdentifier
circuitBreakerIdentifier	ID	SX001G:circuitBreakerIdentifier
circuitBreakerSettingIdentifier	ID	SX001G:circuitBreakerSettingIdentifier
circuitBreakerSettingsIdentifier	ID	SX001G:circuitBreakerSettingsIdentifier
	C	SX001G:closedCircuitBreakerState

Attribute name	Valid value	Valid value name
circuitBreakerState	O	SX001G:openedCircuitBreakerState
	VC	SX001G:verifyCloseCircuitBreakerState
	VO	SX001G:verifyOpenCircuitBreakerState
circuitBreakerType	CLIP	SX001G:dummyCircuitBreaker
	ELMEC	SX001G:electroMechanicCircuitBreaker
	ELTRO	SX001G:electronicCircuitBreaker
classifier	-	No valid values defined for this attribute in current specification issue.
codePropertyAssignment	S1000D	SX001G:codeFromS1000D
	S2000M	SX001G:codeFromS2000M
	S3000L	SX001G:codeFromS3000L
	S4000P	SX001G:codeFromS4000P
	S5000F	SX001G:codeFromS5000F
commentActionType	AP	SX001G:commentApproved
	CLA	SX001G:commentClarificationRequested
	CLO	SX001G:commentClosed
	CR	SX001G:commentRaised
	RJ	SX001G:commentRejected
	RP	SX001G:commentResponded
	UI	SX001G:commentUnderInvestigation
commentIdentifier	C	SX001G:commentId
commentPartyRole	A	SX001G:analyst
	C	SX001G:commenter
	R	SX001G:responder
commentPriority	C	SX001G:critical
	L	SX001G:low
	N	SX001G:normal
	U	SX001G:urgent
commentRelationshipType	A	SX001G:associatedTo
	C	SX001G:clarifiesOrComplements
	R	SX001G:respondsTo
commentStatus	A	SX001G:answered
	C	SX001G:closed
	O	SX001G:open

Attribute name	Valid value	Valid value name
	R	SX001G:reopened
commentType	F	SX001G:failure
	G	SX001G:generalComment
	P	SX001G:problemReport
	Q	SX001G:questionOrQuery
	R	SX001G:recommendation
conditionInstanceIdentifier	ID	SX001G:conditionInstanceIdentifier
	SB	SX001G:serviceBulletinIdentifier
conditionTypeAssertMemberAssertValueComparisonOperator		Refer to comparisonOperatorCode valid value library, Para 5
consequenceIdentifier	AUTH	SX001G:authorities
	OEM	SX001G:originalEquipmentManufacturer
	OPER	SX001G:operator
consequenceType	DEA	SX001G:death
	DEL	SX001G:delay
	DES	SX001G:productDestruction
	INJ	SX001G:injuries
	LOSS	SX001G:economicLoss
	MAT	SX001G:MaterialDamage
	NONE	SX001G:noConsequences
consumableItemIdentifier	M	SX001G:manufacturer
consumableItemRiskFactor	R10	SX001G:flammable
	R20	SX001G:harmfulByInhalation
	R21	SX001G:harmfulInContactWithSkin
	R22	SX001G:harmfulIfSwallowed
	R23	SX001G:toxicByInhalation
	R24	SX001G:toxicInContactWith Skin
	R25	SX001G:ToxicIfSwallowed
	R34	SX001G:causes Burns
	R35	SX001G:causesSevereBurns
	R36	SX001G:irritatingToEyes
	R37	SX001G:irritatingToRespiratorySystem
	R38	SX001G:irritatingToSkin
	R5	SX001G:heatingMayCauseAnExplosion

Attribute name	Valid value	Valid value name
consumableType	BOLT	SX001G:bolt
	FUEL	SX001G:fuel
	GRE	SX001G:grease
	OIL	SX001G:oil
	SCRW	SX001G:screw
	WIRE	SX001G:wire
consumptionIdentifier	S	SX001G:sensor
consumptionType	-	No valid values defined for this attribute in current specification issue.
containerAsDesignedMaterial	C	SX001G:cardboardContainerMaterial
	F	SX001G:foamContainerMaterial
	G	SX001G:glassContainerMaterial
	M	SX001G:metalContainerMaterial
	O	SX001G:otherContainerMaterial
	P	SX001G:plasticContainerMaterial
	W	SX001G:woodContainerMaterial
containerAsDesignedType	-	No valid values defined for this attribute in current specification issue.
containerPartIdentifier	ID	SX001G:containerPartIdentifier
contractClauseIdentifier	C	SX001G:contract
contractClauseRelationshipType	BE	SX001G:belongsTo
	CL	SX001G:clarifies
	RE	SX001G:replaces
	SU	SX001G:subordinateTo
contractPartyRole	AGNT	SX001G:contractAgent
	CTR	SX001G:contractor
	CUS	SX001G:customer
	ESCR	SX001G:escrowHolder
	SUB	SX001G:subContractor
	USER	SX001G:user
contractRelationshipType	EXTC	SX001G:extendsContract
	RELC	SX001G:relatedContract
	REPC	SX001G:replacesContract
	SUBC	SX001G:subContractOf

Attribute name	Valid value	Valid value name
contractStatus	A	SX001G:contractAgreedButNotSigned
	C	SX001G:contractCancelled
	D	SX001G:contractInDraft
	E	SX001G:contractExtended
	N	SX001G:contractUnderNegotiation
	P	SX001G:contractInPrincipleAgreed
	S	SX001G:contractSigned
contractType	CI	SX001G:costIncentivesContract
	CO	SX001G:costContract
	CON	SX001G:consultingContract
	CPIF	SX001G:costPlusIncentiveFeeContract
	CR	SX001G:costReimbursementContract
	CS	SX001G:costSharingContract
	DEV	SX001G:developmentContract
	DI	SX001G:deliveryIncentivesContract
	EIS	SX001G:entryIntoServiceContract
	FCP	SX001G:fixedCeilingPriceContract
	FCPP	SX001G:fixedPriceProspectivePriceRedetermination Contract
	FCPR	SX001G:fixedCeilingPriceRetroactivePriceRedeterminationContract
	FFP	SX001G:firmFixedPriceContract
	FFPL	SX001G:firmFixedPriceLevelOfEffortTermContract
	FPA	SX001G:fixedPriceEconomicPriceAdjustmentContract
	FPI	SX001G:fixedPriceIncentiveContract
	LAB	SX001G:laborHoursContract
	MAN	SX001G:manufacturing contract
	MI	SX001G:multipleIncentivesContract
	MOD	SX001G:modificationContract
	PI	SX001G:performanceIncentivesContract
	PRO	SX001G:procurementContract
	RES	SX001G:researchContract
	SERV	SX001G:serviceContract
	SUP	SX001G:supplyContract

Attribute name	Valid value	Valid value name
	TAM	SX001G:timeAndMaterialsContract
	THRU	SX001G:troughLifeContract
costBreakdownIdentifier	CBS	SX001G:costBreakdownStructure
costBreakdownRelationshipType	AS	SX001G:associatedTo
	IN	SX001G:includes
	RE	SX001G:replaces
	SI	SX001G:similarTo
costBreakdownRevisionIdentifier	CBSRID	SX001G:costBreakdownStructureRevisionId
costBreakdownRevisionStatus	A	SX001G:approved
	C	SX001G:cancelled
	D	SX001G:draft
	R	SX001G:underReview
costEntryIdentifier	C	SX001G:contract
	O	SX001G:organization
	P	SX001G:project
costEntryType	EXP	SX001G:expenses
	HR	SX001G:hours
	INT	SX001G:interest
	LAB	SX001G:labour
	MAT	SX001G:material
	PEN	SX001G:penalty
	PRO	SX001G:procurement
	SRV	SX001G:services
	TAX	SX001G:taxes
costItemIdentifier	CI	SX001G:costIdentifier
costItemRelationshipType	IN	SX001G:includes
	PA	SX001G:isPartOf
	RE	SX001G:relatedTo
countryCode		Refer to countryCodeValues valid value library, Para 5
damageCharactericType	AB	SX001G:abrasion
	BE	SX001G:bend
	BL	SX001G:blisters

Attribute name	Valid value	Valid value name
	BR	SX001G:brinelling
	BU	SX001G:burn
	CK	SX001G:crack
	CN	SX001G:contamination
	CO	SX001G:corrosion
	CP	SX001G:creep
	CR	SX001G:crease
	DB	SX001G:debonding
	DL	SX001G:delamination
	DN	SX001G:dent
	DS	SX001G:distortion
	FI	SX001G:fireDamage
	FR	SX001G:fretting
	GO	SX001G:gouge
	GR	SX001G:grinding
	HO	SX001G:hole
	LK	SX001G:leakage
	ME	SX001G:melting
	MK	SX001G:mark
	MS	SX001G:misalignment
	NK	SX001G:nick
	RB	SX001G:rubbing
	RU	SX001G:rupture
	SC	SX001G:scratch
	SH	SX001G:shortcircuit
	SO	SX001G:soaked
	SR	SX001G:shear
	SZ	SX001G:seizure
	TO	SX001G:torn
	WA	SX001G:waterDamage
	WE	SX001G:wear
`damageCharacteristicIdentifier`	ID	SX001G:`damageCharacteristicIdentifier`
	BE	SX001G:blue

Attribute name	Valid value	Valid value name
damageColor	BK	SX001G:black
	BR	SX001G:brown
	CY	SX001G:cyan
	GN	SX001G:green
	GY	SX001G:grey
	OR	SX001G:orange
	PU	SX001G:purple
	RE	SX001G:red
	VI	SX001G:violet
	WH	SX001G:white
	YE	SX001G:yellow
damageDefinitionFamily	CRK	SX001G:crackDamageDefinition
	DNT	SX001G:dentDamageDefinition
	SCR	SX001G:scratchDamageDefinition
damageFamily	A	SX001G:aestheticDamage
	C	SX001G:corrosionDamage
	E	SX001G:electromagneticalDamager
	F	SX001G:fireDamage
	M	SX001G:mechanicalDamage
	O	SX001G:opticalDamage
	P	SX001G:personalInjuries
	S	SX001G:structuralDamage
	U	SX001G:unclassifiedDamage
	W	SX001G:waterDamage
damageIdentifier	MAIN	SX001G:maintainer
	OEM	SX001G:originalEquipmentManufacturer
	OPER	SX001G:operator
	OWN	SX001G:owner
	THIRD	SX001G:thirdParty
damageRepairStatus	P	SX001G:pendingRepair
	R	SX001G:repaired
	U	SX001G:unrepairable
	M	SX001G:minorDamage

Attribute name	Valid value	Valid value name
damageSeverity	N	SX001G:negligibleDamage
	R	SX001G:repairableDamage
	S	SX001G:severeDamage
	U	SX001G:unknownDamageSeverity
	UR	SX001G:unrepairableDamage
damageStatus	C	SX001G:confirmed
	P	SX001G:preliminary
	U	SX001G:unconfirmed
dataAssociatedWithType	C	SX001G:dataSetConfigures
	G	SX001G:dataSetGeneratedBy
	I	SX001G:datasetIncompatibleWith
	L	SX001G:dataSetLoadedInto
	R	SX001G:dataSetRequiredBy
dataModuleIssueLanguage		Refer to languageCodeValues valid value library, Para 5
dataModuleIssueLanguageCountry		Refer to countryCodeValues valid value library, Para 5
dataSetAsDesignedType	B	SX001G:builtInTestData
	C	SX001G:configurationData
	CL	SX001G:calibrationData
	D	SX001G:diagnosticData
	M	SX001G:missionData
	MP	SX001G:measurementPointData
	N	SX001G:navigationData
	T	SX001G:testData
detectionMeanCapabilityCapabilityType	HU	SX001G:human
	HW	SX001G:hardware
	SW	SX001G:software
detectionMeanCapabilityIdentifier	OEM	SX001G:originalEquipmentManufacturer
detectionMechanismIdentifier	OEM	SX001G:originalEquipmentManufacturer
detectionMechanismType	BIT	SX001G:builtInTest
	CUE	SX001G:visualOrAudioCue
	INS	SX001G:inspection
	MAL	SX001G:malfunction

Attribute name	Valid value	Valid value name
	SND	SX001G:sound
	TRB	SX001G:troubleshooting
	TST	SX001G:test
	VIS	SX001G:visualInspection
	WRN	SX001G:warning
digitalFileContentClass	3D	SX001G:3dModelFileContent
	AUD	SX001G:audioFileContent
	BIT	SX001G:builtInTestFileContent
	CSW	SX001G:coursewareFileContent
	DRW	SX001G:drawingFileContent
	HUM	SX001G:healthAndUsageDataFileContent
	INS	SX001G:instructionsFileContent
	INV	SX001G:invoiceFileContent
	MAN	SX001G:manualFileContent
	MOV	SX001G:movieFileContent
	OTH	SX001G:otherFileContent
	PHO	SX001G:photographFileContent
	PRB	SX001G:problemReportFileContent
	PUB	SX001G:publicationFileContent
	REP	SX001G:reportFileContent
	SCH	SX001G:schematicsFileContent
	SOU	SX001G:soundFileContent
	TST	SX001G:testResultsFileContent
	VID	SX001G:videoFileContent
	WIR	SX001G:wiringFileContent
digitalFileLocator	ID	SX001G:digitalFileLocator
digitalFileType	ASF	SX001G:advanceSystemsFormatFileType
	AVI	SX001G:audioVideoInterleavedFileType
	BIN	SX001G:binaryFileType
	CGM	SX001G:computerGraphicsMetafileFileType
	DAT	SX001G:dataFormatFileType
	DOC	SX001G:microsoftWordFormatFileType
	DOCX	SX001G:microsoftWordFormatFileType

Attribute name	Valid value	Valid value name
	EDF	SX001G:europeanDataFormatSigalFileType
	HTM	SX001G:hyperTextMarkupLanguageFileType
	JPEG	SX001G:jointPhotographicExpertsGroupFileType
	MOV	SX001G:quickTimeMovieFileType
	MP3	SX001G:mp3AudioFileType
	MPEG	SX001G:motionPictureExpertsGroupMovieFileType
	ODS	SX001G:openDocumentSpreadsheetFileType
	ODT	SX001G:openDocumentTextFileType
	OTH	SX001G:otherFileType
	PDF	SX001G:portableDocumentFormatFileType
	PNG	SX001G:portableNetworkGraphicsFileType
	RAW	SX001G:rawSampleAudioFileType
	TIFF	SX001G:taggedImageFileFormatFileType
	TXT	SX001G:textFileType
	UNK	SX001G:unknownFileType
	WAV	SX001G:waveformAudioFileType
	XLS	SX001G:microsoftExcelFormatFileType
	XLSX	SX001G:microsoftExcelFormatFileType
	XSD	SX001G:xmlSchemaDefinitionFileType
disposalLocationRole	D	SX001G:finalDisposalLocation
	I	SX001G:IntermediateStorageOfDisposableItem
	O	SX001G:originOfDisposalableItem
disposalRequirementMethod	D	SX001G:disposalByDestruction
	F	SX001G:disposalByRefittingRepairOrOverhaul
	L	SX001G:disposalByLandFill
	O	SX001G:disposalByOtherMeans
	R	SX001G:disposalByRecycling
disposalRequirementReason	B	SX001G:beyondEconomicRepairDisposal
	E	SX001G:endOfLifeDisposal
	F	SX001G:notFitForPurposeDisposal
	N	SX001G:noLongerNecessaryDisposal
	O	SX001G:otherReasonForDisposal
	U	SX001G:unacceptableProductConditionDisposal

Attribute name	Valid value	Valid value name
`documentIssueReason`	E	SX001G:editorialChange
	N	SX001G:newDocument
	T	SX001G:technicalChange
`documentPartyRelationshipType`	AP	SX001G:approver
	AU	SX001G:author
	CO	SX001G:consumer
	RE	SX001G:reviewer
`documentStatus`	A	SX001G:approved
	C	SX001G:cancelled
	D	SX001G:draft
	I	SX001G:issued
	R	SX001G:underReview
	S	SX001G:superseded
`downTimeIdentifier`	OPER	SX001G:operator
`downTimePeriodReason`	D	SX001G:investigatingDamage
	F	SX001G:investigatingFailure
	OV	SX001G:undergoingOverhaul
	PM	SX001G:undergoingPreventiveMaintenance
	SB	SX001G:serviceBulletinEmbodiment
	SF	SX001G:blockedOrImpoundedForSafetyReasons
	SM	SX001G:undergoingScheduledMaintenance
	SR	SX001G:sentForRepairOrOverhaul
	WA	SX001G:waitingForAuthorization
	WC	SX001G:waitingForCalibration
	WE	SX001G:waitingForEquipment
	WI	SX001G:waitingForInvestigation
	WM	SX001G:waitingForMaterial
	WP	SX001G:waitingForPersonnel
	WS	SX001G:waitingForSpares
`downTimeStatus`	D	SX001G:down
	OP	SX001G:operational
	SF	SX001G:equipmentNotAvalableDueToSafetyRestriction

Attribute name	Valid value	Valid value name
environmentDefinitionIdentifier	ID	SX001G:environmentDefinitionIdentifier
environmentDefinitionRevisionIdentifier	ID	SX001G:environmentDefinitionRevisionIdentifier
environmentDefinitionRevisionStatus		Refer to revisionStatusCode valid value library, Para 5
environmentIdentifier	OEM	SX001G:originalEquipmentManufacturer
	OPER	SX001G:operator
environmentRelationshipType	CAN	SX001G:cancels
	REF	SX001G:refinementOf
	STA	SX001G:stationalVersionOf
	TEM	SX001G:temporaryVersionOf
environmentRevisionIdentifier	OEM	SX001G:originalEquipmentManufacturer
	OPER	SX001G:operator
environmentRevisionStatus	A	SX001G:approved
	C	SX001G:canceled
	D	SX001G:draft
	R	SX001G:underReview
environmentRevisionType	CLI	SX001G:climateChange
	SEA	SX001G:seasonalChange
	TEM	SX001G:temporaryChange
environmentType	ART	SX001G:artic
	CON	SX001G:continental
	DES	SX001G:desertic
	MAR	SX001G:maritime
	TRO	SX001G:tropical
	VOL	SX001G:volcanic
equipmentStatusReason	D	SX001G:damage
	F	SX001G:failure
	OK	SX001G:equipmentOK
	OP	SX001G:currentlyUnderOperation
	SF	SX001G:blockedOrImpoundedForSafetyReasons
	SR	SX001G:sentForRepair
	WA	SX001G:waitingForAuthorization

Attribute name	Valid value	Valid value name
	WC	SX001G:waitingForCalibration
	WE	SX001G:waitingForEquipment
	WI	SX001G:waitingForInvestigation
	WM	SX001G:waitingForMaterial
	WP	SX001G:waitingForPersonnel
	WS	SX001G:waitingForSpares
equipmentStatusType	FL	SX001G:equipmentFailed
	OP	SX001G:equipmentOperational
	SC	SX001G:equipmentScrapped
	SF	SX001G:equipmentNotAvailableDueToSafetyRestriction
evaluationByAssertionRole	CUS	SX001G:customer
	OP	SX001G:operator
eventConfirmedStatus	C	SX001G:confirmed
	U	SX001G:unconfirmed
eventGroup	C	SX001G:contractual
	M	SX001G:maintenance
	O	SX001G:operational
	T	SX001G:technical
eventIdentifier	M	SX001G:maintainer
	O	SX001G:operator
	R	SX001G:reporter
eventRelationshipItemRole	A	SX001G:eventAffects
	C	SX001G:eventCausedBy
	O	SX001G:eventOccursOn
eventRelationshipType	AFT	SX001G:after
	BEF	SX001G:before
	CAU	SX001G:causeFor
	CON	SX001G:consequenceOf
	DUR	SX001G:during
	INP	SX001G:inParallelTo
	REL	SX001G:relatedTo
eventSeverity	C	SX001G:critical
	M	SX001G:minor

Attribute name	Valid value	Valid value name
	R	SX001G:routine
	S	SX001G:serious
explanatoryFactorIdentifier	AUTH	SX001G:authorities
	OEM	SX001G:originalEquipmentManufacturer
	OPER	SX001G:operator
exportControlLicenseIdentifier	ID	SX001G:exportControlLicenseIdentifier
exportControlLicenseItemCategory	-	No valid values defined for this attribute in current specification issue.
exportControlLicenseItemidentifier	ID	SX001G:exportControlLicenseItemidentifier
exportControlLicenseItemSubCategory	-	No valid values defined for this attribute in current specification issue.
exportControlLicenseType	PRM	SX001G:permanent
	TMP	SX001G:temporary
exportControlPartyClearanceCode	-	No valid values defined for this attribute in current specification issue.
exportControlPartyClearanceLevel	-	No valid values defined for this attribute in current specification issue.
exportControlPartyIdentifier	ID	SX001G:exportControlPartyIdentifier
exportControlPartyRole	CON	SX001G:consignor
	FRE	SX001G:freightForwarder
	MAN	SX001G:manufacturer
	SEL	SX001G:seller
	SRC	SX001G:source
	USR	SX001G:endUser
exportControlPartyType	G	SX001G:government
	I	SX001G:industry
exportControlRegulationLegalCode	AWV	SX001G:AWV
	AWV9	SX001G:AWV9
	EAR	SX001G:EAR
	EG	SX001G:EG
	ESA11	SX001G:ESA11
	ESA12	SX001G:ESA12
	ESA22	SX001G:ESA22

Attribute name	Valid value	Valid value name
	ESA31	SX001G:ESA31
	FRMTG	SX001G:FRMTG
	FRNAT	SX001G:FRNAT
	ITAR	SX001G:ITAR
	KWKG	SX001G:KWKG
	UKMIL	SX001G:UKMIL
exportControlRegulationtPeculiarityCode	-	No valid values defined for this attribute in current specification issue.
exportControlRequirementGrouping	-	No valid values defined for this attribute in current specification issue.
expressionEvaluationIdentifier	ID	SX001G:expressionEvaluationIdentifier
externalDocumentType	O	SX001G:other
facilityCleansiness	C	SX001G:cleanRoom
	N	SX001G:normal
	S	SX001G:substandard
facilityLocationIdentifier	OPER	SX001G:operator
	OWN	SX001G:owner
facilityRelationshipType	ALT	SX001G:isAlternateFor
	COL	SX001G:colocatedWith
	INC	SX001G:includes
	ISP	SX001G:isPartOf
	SUB	SX001G:isSubsidiaryOf
failureDetectionRate	C	SX001G:continuously
	I	SX001G:intermitently
	O	SX001G:occasionally
failureModeCauseIdentifier	ID	SX001G:failureModeCauseIdentifier
failureModeCriticality	I	SX001G:catastrophicFailureModeConsequence
	II	SX001G:criticalFailureModeConsequence
	III	SX001G:marginalFailureModeConsequence
	IV	SX001G:negligibleFailureModeConsequence
failureModeEffectLevel	E	SX001G:systemEndItemFailureModeEffect
	H	SX001G:higherFailureModeEffect
	L	SX001G:localFailureModeEffect

Attribute name	Valid value	Valid value name
	N	SX001G:nextHigherFailureModeEffect
failureModeIdentifier	ID	SX001G:failureModeIdentifier
faultIdentifier	MAIN	SX001G:maintainer
	OPER	SX001G:operator
faultStatus	D	SX001G:deferredRepair
	P	SX001G:pendingRepair
	R	SX001G:repaired
faultSymptomIdentifier	ID	SX001G:faultSymptomIdentifier
fleetIdentifier	OEM	SX001G:originalEquipmentManufacturer
	OPER	SX001G:operator
fleetPlanningIdentifier	OPER	SX001G:operator
fleetPlanningStatus	A	SX001G:approved
	C	SX001G:cancelled
	D	SX001G:draft
fleetRelationshipType	AS	SX001G:associatedWith
	IN	SX001G:includes
	RE	SX001G:replaces
fleetTaskCancellationNoticeIdentifier	OP	SX001G:operator
	OWN	SX001G:owner
fleetTaskIdentifier	OPER	SX001G:operator
	SERV	SX001G:serviceProvider
fleetTaskPriority	C	SX001G:criticalPriority
	H	SX001G:highPriority
	L	SX001G:lowPriority
	R	SX001G:routinePriority
geographicalAreaType	ADM	SX001G:administrativeRegion
	CITY	SX001G:city
	CON	SX001G:continent
	CTYG	SX001G:countryGroup
	DES	SX001G:desert
	ISL	SX001G:island
	LAN	SX001G:landmass
	LND	SX001G:landmark

Attribute name	Valid value	Valid value name
	MOU	SX001G:mountainRange
	MUL	SX001G:multiGeographicalArea
	OCE	SX001G:ocean
	REG	SX001G:geographicalRegion
	SEA	SX001G:sea
geographicalCoordinateSystem	DD	SX001G:decimalDegreeGeographicalCoordinateSystem
	DMS	SX001G:degreeMinutesSecondsGeographicalCoordinateSystem
hardwareElementRepairability	N	SX001G:nonRepairableHardwareElement
	P	SX001G:partialRepairableHardwareElement
	R	SX001G:repairableHardwareElement
hardwareElementReplaceability	N	SX001G:nonReplaceableHardwareElement
	R	SX001G:replaceableHardwareElement
hardwareElementType	EQP	SX001G:equipmentHardwareElement
	OPN	SX001G:openingHardwareElement
	PNL	SX001G:panelHardwareElement
hardwarePartContainerIdentifier	ID	SX001G:hardwarePartContainerIdentifier
hardwarePartHazardousClass		Refer to hardwarePartHazardousClassCode valid value library, Para 5
hardwarePartLogisticsCategory	C	SX001G:consumablePart
	D	SX001G:disposablePart
	E	SX001G:expendableSparePart
	EP	SX001G:expendablePersonalProtectionPart
	HT	SX001G:standardHandTool
	IT	SX001G:informationTechnologyPart
	M	SX001G:rawMaterial
	PA	SX001G:packagingPart
	PE	SX001G:personalProtectionPart
	PR	SX001G:productProtectionPart
	R	SX001G:repairableSparePart
	S	SX001G:sparePart
	SE	SX001G:supportEquipment
	N	SX001G:nonRepairablePart

Attribute name	Valid value	Valid value name
hardwarePartRepairability	P	SX001G:partialRepairablePart
	R	SX001G:repairablePart
infrastructureAvailableType	F	SX001G:fullyAvailable
	N	SX001G:notAvailable
	P	SX001G:partiallyAvailable
	R	SX001G:availableWithRestrictions
	S	SX001G:availableOnSharedBasis
infrastructureComplianceLevel	F	SX001G:fullInfrastructureCompliance
	N	SX001G:nonInfrastructureCompliance
	P	SX001G:partialInfrastructureCompliance
infrastructureIdentifier	OPER	SX001G:operator
	OWN	SX001G:owner
infrastructureOperatingPeriodIdentifier	ID	SX001G:infrastructureOperatingPeriodIdentifier
infrastructureOperatingPeriodMode	F	SX001G:infrastructureFullyOperational
	M	SX001G:infrastructureDownForScheduledMaintenance
	N	SX001G:infrastructureNotOperational
	P	SX001G:infrastructurePartiallyOperational
infrastructurePartyRole	OP	SX001G:infrastructureOperator
	OW	SX001G:infrastructureOwner
	USR	SX001G:infrastructureUser
infrastructureRelationshipType	CO	SX001G:competitorOf
	CP	SX001G:complements
	P	SX001G:isPartOf
	RE	SX001G:relatedWith
	RP	SX001G:replacementOf
infrastructureRevisionIdentifier	OPER	SX001G:operator
	OWN	SX001G:owner
infrastructureRevisionStatus	A	SX001G:approved
	C	SX001G:cancelled
	D	SX001G:draft
installationLocationIdentifier	ID	SX001G:installationLocationIdentifier
	D	SX001G:disposalItemDisposingOrganization

Attribute name	Valid value	Valid value name
involvedDisposalOrganizationRole	O	SX001G:disposalItemOwner
	T	SX001G:disposalItemTransportingOrganization
itemDemilitarizationDataClass	A	SX001G:demilitarizationNotRequiredPart
	B	SX001G:tradeSecurityControlAtDisposalPart
	C	SX001G:keyPointsDemilitarizationPart
	D	SX001G:mutilationDemilitarizationPart
	E	SX001G:nationalFurnishedDemilitarizationPart
	F	SX001G:managerFurnishedDemilitarizationPart
	G	SX001G:demilitarizationPriorToTransferPart
	R	SX001G:specificInstructionsDemilitarizationPart
	Y	SX001G:specificInstructionsDemilitarizationCryptoMaterial
itemDisposalOperationIdentifier	ID	Sx001G:itemDisposalOperationIdentifier
itemDisposalOperationMethod	D	SX001G:disposalByDestruction
	F	SX001G:disposalByRefittingRepairOrOverhaul
	L	SX001G:disposalByLandFill
	O	SX001G:disposalByOtherMeans
	R	SX001G:disposalByRecycling
itemExportControlRegulationClassification	-	No valid values defined for this attribute in current specification issue.
localPositionIdentifier	OEM	SX001G:originalEquipmentManufacturer
localPositionRefType	COG	SX001G:centerOfGravity
	GC	SX001G:geometricalCenter
locationRelationshipType	IN	SX001G:locationLocatedIn
	NXT	SX001G:locationLocatedNextTo
locatorIdentifier	LCRID	SX001G:locatorIdentifier
logBookEntryIdentifier	MAIN	SX001G:maintainer
	OPER	SX001G:operator
	PROD	SX001G:productGenerated
logbookEntryMeasurementPointIdentifier	ID	SX001G:logbookEntryMeasurementPointIdentifier
logbookEntryMeasurementPointType	EQ	SX001G:equipmentCounter
	OP	SX001G:operatingHourCounter
	OTH	SX001G:otherCounterType

Attribute name	Valid value	Valid value name
	PR	SX001G:productCounter
	TO	SX001G:timeSinceOverHaulCounter
logBookEntryType	ACC	SX001G:accident
	BIT	SX001G:builtInTest
	CHK	SX001G:check
	FAIL	SX001G:failure
	HUM	SX001G:healthAndUsageMonitrong
	INC	SX001G:incident
	INS	SX001G:install
	OPEV	SX001G:operationalEvent
	UNI	SX001G:uninstall
logBookIdentifier	AUTO	SX001G:automaticGeneration
	OEM	SX001G:originalEquipmentManufacturer
	OPER	SX001G:operator
logBookType	MAIN	SX001G:maintenance
	OPER	SX001G:operational
looseWasteIdentifier	ID	SX001G:looseWasteIdentifier
looseWasteType	HE	SX001G:electronicWaste
	HI	SX001G:hazardousIndustrialWaste
	HM	SX001G:hazardousMedicalWaste
	HO	SX001G:hazardousOrganicWaste
	HR	SX001G:hazardousRadioactiveWaste
	HS	SX001G:otherHazardousSolidWaste
	HW	SX001G:otherHazardousWaste
	ME	SX001G:metallicWaste
	NI	SX001G:nonHazardousIndustrialWaste
	NO	SX001G:nonHazardousOrganicWaste
	NP	SX001G:nonHazardousPackagingWaste
	NS	SX001G:otherNonHazardousSolidWaste
maintenanceActivityPartyRole	AP	SX001G:approvesMaintenance
	EX	SX001G:executesMaintenance
	IN	SX001G:inspectsMaintenance
	AC	SX001G:accident

Attribute name	Valid value	Valid value name
maintenanceEventCategoryType	AS	SX001G:assembly
	CL	SX001G:cleaning
	DI	SX001G:disassembly
	IN	SX001G:inspection
	OT	SX001G:other
maintenanceFacilitySlotIdentifier	OPER	SX001G:operator
	OWN	SX001G:owner
maintenanceFacilitySlotType	D	SX001G:dock
	H	SX001G:hangar
	O	SX001G:other
	R	SX001G:repairStation
maintenanceFacilityType	BAT	SX001G:batteryShop
	CAL	SX001G:calibrationFacility
	HAN	SX001G:hangar
	HYD	SX001G:hydraulicShop
	REP	SX001G:repairShop
	SHOP	SX001G:generalShop
maintenanceLevelIdentifier	ID	SX001G:maintenanceLevelIdentifier
maintenanceLicenceIdentifier	MLID	SX001G:maintenanceLicenseID
maintenanceLicenceType	A1	SX001G:easa66CatA1
	A2	SX001G:easa66CatA2
	A3	SX001G:easa66CatA3
	B1.1	SX001G:easa66CatB1.1
	B1.2	SX001G:easa66CatB1.2
	B1.3	SX001G:easa66CatB1.3
	B1.4	SX001G:easa66CatB1.4
	B2	SX001G:easa66CatB2
	B3	SX001G:easa66CatB3
	C	SX001G:easa66CatC
maintenanceOrganizationApprovalType	145	SX001G:aviationPart145
	147	SX001G:aviationPart147
	21	SX001G:aviationPart21
	571	SX001G:aviationCAR571

Attribute name	Valid value	Valid value name
	573	SX001G:aviationCAR573
	66	SX001G:aviationPart66
	A823	SX001G:AviationBcarA8-23
	A824	SX001G:AviationBcarA8-24
	A825	SX001G:AviationBcarA8-25
	AMC	SX001G:AMC
	ARC	SX001G:aviationPartMSubpartGARC
	M	SX001G:aviationPartM
	MF	SX001G:aviationPartMSubpartF
	MG	SX001G:aviationPartMSubpartG
maintenancePersonJobType	E	SX001G:electrician
	M	SX001G:mechanic
maintenanceProgramRevisionIdentifier	OEM	SX001G:originalEquipmentManufacturer
maintenanceProgramRevisionStatus	A	SX001G:approved
	C	SX001G:cancelled
	D	SX001G:draft
	R	SX001G:underReview
maintenanceProgramType	DEP	SX001G:deploymentSpecific
	ENV	SX001G:environmentSpecific
	OEM	SX001G:originalEquipmentManufacturer
	OPE	SX001G:operatorSpecific
maintenanceSignificantOrRelevant	N	SX001G:nonMaintenanceSignificantOrRelevantBreakdownElement
	R	SX001G:maintenanceRelevantBreakdownElement
	S	SX001G:maintenanceSignificantBreakdownElement
materialIdentifier	M	SX001G:manufacturer
materialRiskFactor	A	SX001G:authorizedSubstance
	AL	SX001G:authorizedWithLimitationSubstance
	F	SX001G:forbiddenSubstance
materialSubstanceUsageCategory	CAS	SX001G:chemicalAbstractsServiceNumber
	EINECS	SX001G:europeanInventoryOfExistingChemicalSubstancesNumber
	SI	SX001G:substanceIdentifier
measurementPointIdentifier	ID	SX001G:measurementPointIdentifier

Attribute name	Valid value	Valid value name
messageContentStatus	D	SX001G:draftMessageContent
	F	SX001G:finalMessageContent
	P	SX001G:preliminaryMessageContent
messageContentType	B	SX001G:baselineMessage
	U	SX001G:netChangeMessage
messageIdentifier	ID	SX001G:messageIdentifier
messageLanguage		Refer to languageCodeValues valid value library, Para 5
messagePartyType	F	SX001G:messageForwarder
	R	SX001G:messageReceiver
	S	SX001G:messageSender
messageRelationshipType	A	SX001G:acknowledgementOfMessage
	O	SX001G:observationOnMessage
	R	SX001G:replyToMessage
	U	SX001G:updateToMessage
movementIdentifier	OPER	SX001G:operator
movementLegDelayIdentifier	OPER	SX001G:operator
movementLegDelayType	AUTH	SX001G:delayDueToLackOfAuthorization
	CAR	SX001G:delayDueToCargo
	FAIL	SX001G:delayDueToEquipmentFailure
	FUEL	SX001G:delayDueToFuel
	OTH	SX001G:delayDueToOtherReasons
	WEA	SX001G:delayDueToWeather
movementLegIdentifier	OPER	SX001G:operator
movementLegResult	AB	SX001G:movementLegAborted
	CA	SX001G:movementLegCancelled
	DE	SX001G:movementLegDelayed
	DI	SX001G:movementLegDiverted
	OK	SX001G:movementLegOK
movementResult	AB	SX001G:movementAborted
	CA	SX001G:movementCancelled
	DE	SX001G:movementDelayed
	DI	SX001G:movementDiverted
	OK	SX001G:movementOK

Attribute name	Valid value	Valid value name
movementType	DEP	SX001G:deployment
	FE	SX001G:ferry
	MIS	SX001G:mission
	TR	SX001G:transport
	TRN	SX001G:training
nonAvailabilityCauseIdentifier	ID	SX001G:nonAvailabilityCauseIdentifier
nonAvailabilityCauseType	CUS	SX001G:customerRelated
	OTH	SX001G:other
	SB	SX001G:serviceBulletin
	SCH	SX001G:scheduledMaintenance
	UNSR	SX001G:unserviceable
	USCH	SX001G:unscheduledMaintenance
nonConformanceType	C	SX001G:concession
	W	SX001G:waiver
obsolescenceParameterIdentifier	ID	SX001G:obsolescenceParameterIdentifier
obsolescenceParameterType	AGE	SX001G:obsolescenceDueToAge
	ALL	SX001G:obsolescenceDueToAllocation
	CHG	SX001G:obsolescenceDueToMarketChange
	ENV	SX001G:obsolescenceDueToEnvironmentalRestrictions
	PLA	SX001G:plannedObsolescence
	PRO	SX001G:obsolescenceDueToProcurementLastBuy
	TEC	SX001G:tecnologicalObsolescence
openingTimeDay	ALL	SX001G:openingAllDays
	FRI	SX001G:openingOnFriday
	MON	SX001G:openingOnMonday
	SAT	SX001G:openingOnSaturday
	SUN	SX001G:openingOnSunday
	THU	SX001G:openingOnThursday
	TUE	SX001G:openingOnTuesday
	WED	SX001G:openingOnWednesday
operatingBaseCapacityIdentifier	OPER	SX001G:operator
	OWN	SX001G:owner

Attribute name	Valid value	Valid value name
operatingBaseType	AIR	SX001G:airport
	BUS	SX001G:busStation
	CAR	SX001G:carPark
	CIV	SX001G:civilianBase
	CONS	SX001G:constructionSite
	DEPLOY	SX001G:deployedBase
	MIL	SX001G:militaryBase
	PORT	SX001G:port
	TRAIN	SX001G:trainStation
operatingLocationTypeIdentifier	ID	SX001G:operatingLocationTypeIdentifier
operationalApprovalIdentifier	AUTH	SX001G:legalAuthority
	OEM	SX001G:originalEquipmentManufacturer
operationalApprovalType	C	SX001G:cargoTransportOnly
	E	SX001G:extendedOperations
	F	SX001G:fullOperationalApproval
	L	SX001G:operationalApprovalWithLimitations
	P	SX001G:passengerTransportOnly
	X	SX001G:experimentalOrProtypeUseOnly
operationalEventCategoryType	A	SX001G:accident
	I	SX001G:incident
	N	SX001G:normalOperation
	S	SX001G:safetyCriticalIncident
operationalEventMaintenanceDown	D	SX001G:eventAllowsDeferredMaintenance
	M	SX001G:eventRequiresMandatoryMaintenance
	N	SX001G:eventRequiresNoMaintenance
operationalEventMessageIdentifier	MID	SX001G:messageIdentifier
	MSN	SX001G:messageSequenceNumber
operationalEventMessageType	AW	SX001G:audibleWarning
	MP	SX001G:maintenancePanel
	OP	SX001G:operatorConsole
	VW	SX001G:visualWarning
operationalEventOperationalMode	AIR	SX001G:flying
	CR	SX001G:cruising

Attribute name	Valid value	Valid value name
	GR	SX001G:onGround
	ORB	SX001G:orbiting
	STA	SX001G:stationaryPosition
	SUB	SX001G:immersed
	SUR	SX001G:onSurface
operationalEventSymptom	AN	SX001G:anomalousBehaviour
	FI	SX001G:fire
	HT	SX001G:abnormalHeating
	IF	SX001G:intermintentFailure
	MA	SX001G:malfunction
	NO	SX001G:noise
	SC	SX001G:shortcircuit
	SH	SX001G:shutdown
	TF	SX001G:totalFailure
	VI	SX001G:vibration
operationalModeClassification	CG	SX001G:cargoTransport
	CO	SX001G:combat
	ME	SX001G:medicalEvacuation
	MT	SX001G:mixedModeTransport
	PT	SX001G:passengerTransport
	RE	SX001G:reconnaissance
	TR	SX001G:productTransfer
operationalModeIdentifier	OEM	SX001G:originalEquipmentManufacturer
	OPER	SX001G:operator
operationalModeStatusType	E	SX001G:ETOPS
	F	SX001G:fullPower
	H	SX001G:halfPower
	I	SX001G:idle
	Q	SX001G:quarterPower
	S	SX001G:stopped
operationalPeriodIdentifier	OPER	SX001G:operator
operationalPeriodPhase	ASC	SX001G:ascending
	CRU	SX001G:cruise

Attribute name	Valid value	Valid value name
	DES	SX001G:descending
	IDL	SX001G:idle
	IMM	SX001G:immersed
	LAN	SX001G:landing
	RUN	SX001G:running
	STA	SX001G:starting
	STP	SX001G:stopped
	SUR	SX001G:surface
	TAG	SX001G:touchAndGo
	TOF	SX001G:takeOff
operationalPeriodRelationship Type	A	SX001G:after
	B	SX001G:before
	IF	SX001G:includes
	O	SX001G:overlapping
	P	SX001G:inParallelTo
operationalPeriodResult	CAN	SX001G:operationaPeriodCancellation
	DEL	SX001G:operationaPeriodDelay
	OK	SX001G:operationaPeriodOK
	PAR	SX001G:operationalPeriodPartialSuccess
operationalRoleidentifier	OEM	SX001G:originalEquipmentManufacturer
	OPER	SX001G:operator
operationalRoleType	R	SX001G:routine
	S	SX001G:special
	T	SX001G:training
operationalTimeType	POS	SX001G:postOperationTime
	PRE	SX001G:preparationTime
	STA	SX001G:startupTime
	STP	SX001G:shutdownTime
	TAT	SX001G:turnAroundTime
organizationalBreakdownStructureRevisionIdentifier	C	SX001G:contract
	P	SX001G:project
organizationalBreakdownStructureRevisionStatus	A	SX001G:approved
	C	SX001G:cancelled

Attribute name	Valid value	Valid value name
	D	SX001G:draft
	R	SX001G:underReview
organizationalRoleType	CM	SX001G:configurationManager
	DM	SX001G:dataManager
	PJ	SX001G:projectManager
	PR	SX001G:productManager
	SM	SX001G:securityManager
	WP	SX001G:workPackageManager
organizationType	BRA	SX001G:companyBranch
	DEF	SX001G:defenseOrganization
	DEP	SX001G:department
	DIV	SX001G:companyDivision
	GOV	SX001G:government
	JV	SX001G:jointVenture
	MUL	SX001G:multinationalOrganization
	NGO	SX001G:nonGovernmentOrganization
	PAR	SX001G:paramilitaryOrPolice
	PRIV	SX001G:privateCompany
	PROJ	SX001G:projectOrganization
	PUB	SX001G:publicSector
	STAN	SX001G:standardizationOrganization
otherFacilityType	BLD	SX001G:generalBuilding
	COM	SX001G:computingCenter
	MFG	SX001G:manufacturingSite
	OFF	SX001G:office
	PWR	SX001G:powerStation
	RAIL	SX001G:railStation
parkingFacilityType	APR	SX001G:apron
	CAR	SX001G:carPark
	DOCK	SX001G:dock
	GAR	SX001G:garage
	HAN	SX001G:hangar
	PAR	SX001G:generalParking

Attribute name	Valid value	Valid value name
	STA	SX001G:station
partActionCause	F	SX001G:failure
	O	SX001G:other
	R	SX001G:rob
	S	SX001G:scheduledMaintenance
	U	SX001G:unrob
partActionIdentifier	AU	SX001G:automaticallyAssignedID
	MA	SX001G:manuallyAssignedID
partActionType	C	SX001G:checkOrInspect
	I	SX001G:install
	S	SX001G:service
	U	SX001G:uninstall
partAsDesignedPartsListRelationshipType	C	SX001G:correspondsToPartsList
	D	SX001G:derivedFromPartsList
	E	SX001G:extendsPartsList
partExportControl	EAR99	SX001G:NotInCommerceControlList
partIdentifier	ID	SX001G:partIdentifier
	OEM	SX001G:originalEquipmentManufacturerPartNumber
	REF	SX001G:partReferenceNumber
	STD	SX001G:standardsReferenceDesignator
	SUP	SX001G:supplierPartNumber
partOwnerIdentifier	ID	SX001G:partOwnerIdentifier
partsListEntryIdentifier	ID	SX001G:partsListEntryIdentifier
	LN	SX001G:partsListLineNumber
partsListRevisionIdentifier	ID	SX001G:partsListRevisionIdentifier
partsListRevisionStatus		Refer to revisionStatusCode valid value library, Para 5
partsListType	EBOM	SX001G:engineeringPartsList
	MBOM	SX001G:manufacturingPartsList
	PBOM	SX001G:provisioningPartsList
	SBOM	SX001G:supportPartsList
partyAddressType	A	SX001G:alternateAddress
	M	SX001G:mainAddress

Attribute name	Valid value	Valid value name
partyContactDataType	E	SX001G:eMail
	F	SX001G:fax
	P	SX001G:phone
partyRelationshipType	ASC	SX001G:isAssociatedWith
	BEL	SX001G:belongsTo
	CUS	SX001G:isCustomerOf
	OWN	SX001G:owns
	SUB	SX001G:isSubcontractorOf
	SUP	SX001G:isSupplierOf
	WOR	SX001G:worksFor
penaltyIdentifier	CON	SX001G:contractualPenaltyIdentifier
performanceParameterRevisionIdentifier	ID	SX001G:performanceParameterRevisionIdentifier
performanceParameterRevisionStatus		Refer to revisionStatusCode valid value library, Para 5
performanceParameterType	AF	SX001G:maintenanceFacilityAvailabilityPerformanceParameter
	AM	SX001G:materialAvailabilityPerformanceParameter
	AO	SX001G:operationalAvailabilityPerformanceParameter
	AP	SX001G:personnelAvailabilityPerformanceParameter
	AS	SX001G:sparesIAvailabilityPerformanceParameter
	ASE	SX001G:supportEquipmentAvailabilityPerformanceParameter
	CWT	SX001G:customerWaitTimePerformanceParameter
	DMC	SX001G:directMaintenanceCostPerformanceParameter
	FOH	SX001G:failuresPerOperatingHourPerformanceParameter
	FR	SX001G:failureRatePerformanceParameter
	LCC	SX001G:lifeCycleCostPerformanceParameter
	MC	SX001G:missionCapableRatePerformanceParameter
	MDT	SX001G:meanDownTimePerformanceParameter
	MFOP	SX001G:maintenanceFreeOperatingPeriodPerformanceParameter
	MISR	SX001G:missionReliabilityPerformanceParameter

Attribute name	Valid value	Valid value name
	MMHOH	SX001G:maintenanceManHoursPerOperatingHourPerformanceParameter
	MR	SX001G:materialReadinessPerformanceParameter
	MTBF	SX001G:meanTimeBetweenFailurePerformanceParameter
	MTBUR	SX001G:meanTimeBetweenUnscheduledRemovalPerformanceParameter
	MTTF	SX001G:meanTimeToFailurePerformanceParameter
	MTTR	SX001G:meanTimeToRepairPerformanceParameter
	NMC	SX001G:nonlMissionCapableRatePerformanceParameter
	OEE	SX001G:overallEquipmentEffectivenessPerformanceParameter
	OSC	SX001G:operatingAndSupportCostPerformanceParameter
	PMC	SX001G:partialMissionCapableRatePerformanceParameter
	PME	SX001G:preventiveMaintenanceEffectivenessPerformanceParameter
	PMP	SX001G:plannedMaintenancePercentagePerformanceParameter
	PSL	SX001G:productServiceLifePerformanceParameter
	RT	SX001G:replacementTimePerformanceParameter
	SE	SX001G:supplyEffectivenesssPerformanceParameter
	SMI	SX001G:scheduledMaintenanceIntervalPerformanceParameter
	SPT	SX001G:shopProcessingTimePerformanceParameter
	TE	SX001G:trainingEffectivenessPerformanceParameter
	TSHIP	SX001G:shippingTimePerformanceParameter
performanceParameterValueLimitQualifier	MAX	SX001G:maximumValueLimitQualifier
	MIN	SX001G:minimumValueLimitQualifier
personIdentifier	A	SX001G:anonymizingIdentifier
	E	SX001G:employeeNumber
	I	SX001G:identificationCard
	P	SX001G:passportNumber
	S	SX001G:socialSecurityNumber

Attribute name	Valid value	Valid value name
personPrefixTitle	Dr.	SX001G:doctor
	Mr.	SX001G:mister
	Mrs.	SX001G:Mrs
	Ms.	SX001G:miss
	Prof.	SX001G:professor
personSuffixTitle	Jr.	SX001G:junior
	Sr.	SX001G:senior
plannedItemUpgradeIdentifier	ID	SX001G:plannedItemUpgradeIdentifier
plannedItemUpgradePriority	C	SX001G:critical
	L	SX001G:low
	N	SX001G:normal
	U	SX001G:urgent
plannedItemUpgradeReason	A	SX001G:aesthetic
	F	SX001G:functional
	I	SX001G:improvement
	O	SX001G:obsolescence
	S	SX001G:safety
plannedUpgradeTimescaleIdentifier	ID	SX001G:plannedUpgradeTimescaleIdentifier
plannedUpgradeTimescaleVersion	-	No valid values defined for this attribute in current specification issue.
poolIdentifier	OWN	SX001G:owner
poolType	COM	SX001G:commitedForSpecificPurpose
	CON	SX001G:contractorOwned
	CSHA	SX001G:CustomerSharedContractorOwned
	CUS	SX001G:customerOwned
	OEM	SX001G:originalEquipmentManufacturerOwned
	REG	SX001G:regionalPool
	SHAC	SX001G:sharedCustomerOwned
poolUsageType	EXT	SX001G:externalRequestUsage
	INT	SX001G:internalUsage
	PAR	SX001G:partialAccessAlowed
	UNL	SX001G:unlimitedUse

Attribute name	Valid value	Valid value name
productParametersAtOperationalEventIdentifier	P	SX001G:product
productUsagePhaseIdentifier	OEM	SX001G:originalEquipmentManufacturer
productUsagePhaseRelationshipIdentifier	ID	SX001G:productUsagePhaseRelationshipIdentifier
productUsagePhaseRelationshipType	A	SX001G:after
	B	SX001G:before
	D	SX001G:during
projectIdentifier	ID	SX001G:projectIdentifier
	MOI	SX001G:modelIdentificationCode
projectRelationshipType	C	SX001G:contributingTo
	R	SX001G:relatedTo
	S	SX001G:subproject
publicationModuleIssueLanguage		Refer to languageCodeValues valid value library, Para 5
publicationModuleIssueLanguageCountry		Refer to countryCodeValues valid value library, Para 5
reasonForShopSubmission	F	SX001G:fault investigation
	O	SX001G:other
	R	SX001G:repair
recoveredItemStatus	O	SX001G:recoveredItemToBeOverhauled
	R	SX001G:recoveredItemToBeRepaired
	S	SX001G:recoveredItemIsServiceable
referencedDocumentRole	DES	SX001G:designDocumentReference
	DIR	SX001G:directiveDocumentReference
	DRW	SX001G:drawingDocumentReference
	REF	SX001G:generalDocumentReference
	REQ	SX001G:requirementsDocumentReference
	RES	SX001G:resultDocumentReference
	SRC	SX001G:sourceDocumentReference
	VAL	SX001G:validationDocumentReference
	VER	SX001G:verificationDocumentReference
referenceDesignator	RFD	SX001G:referenceDesignator
	RFD	SX001G:referenceDesignator
	C	SX001G:dataSetConfigures

Attribute name	Valid value	Valid value name
releasedDataSetAssociatedWith Type	G	SX001G:dataSetGeneratedBy
	I	SX001G:dataSetIncompatibleWith
	L	SX001G:dataSetLoadedInto
	R	SX001G:dataSetRequiredBy
remarkType	INT	SX001G:internalRemark
	PUB	SX001G:publicRemark
	RSP	SX001G:responseToRemark
reportableActivityIdentifier	AU	SX001G:automaticallyAssignedID
	MA	SX001G:manuallyAssignedID
reportableMetricIdentifier	KPI	SX001G:keyPerformanceIndicator
reportableMetricType	A	SX001G:availability
	C	SX001G:cost
	M	SX001G:milestone achievement
	O	SX001G:operational
	OT	SX001G:other
	P	SX001G:performance
	R	SX001G:reliability
reportPartyRole	A	SX001G:addressee
	R	SX001G:reporter
requiredDisposalPolicyMandate	M	SX001G:mandatoryPolicy
	R	SX001G:recommendedPolicy
requirementIdentifier	ID	SX001G:requirementIdentifier
requirementPartyRole	ORG	SX001G:originator
	OWN	SX001G:owner
	STK	SX001G:stakeholder
requirementRelationshipType	A	SX001G:associatedWith
	C	SX001G:complementaryTo
	P	SX001G:isPartOf
requirementStatus	A	SX001G:requirementStatusApproved
	C	SX001G:requirementCancelled
	D	SX001G:requirementStatusDraft
	R	SX001G:requirementStatusUnderReview
	FU	SX001G:functional

Attribute name	Valid value	Valid value name
requirementType	OB	SX001G:obsolescence
	OP	SX001G:operational
	PH	SX001G:physical
	SF	SX001G:safety
	TE	SX001G:technical
	TR	SX001G:training
resourceSpecificationIdentifier	ID	SX001G:resourceSpecificationIdentifier
	STD	SX001G:standardsReferenceDesignator
resourceSpecificationType	C	SX001G:consumablePart
	CNWK	SX001G:communicationNetworkInfrastructureResource
	COMP	SX001G:computerInfrastructureResource
	DOCK	SX001G:dockInfrastructureResource
	DRYD	SX001G:dryDockInfrastructureResource
	E	SX001G:expendableSparePart
	EP	SX001G:expendablePersonalProtectionPart
	GAR	SX001G:garageInfrastructureResource
	HNG	SX001G:hangarInfrastructureResource
	HT	SX001G:standardHandTool
	INF	SX001G:infrastructureResource
	IT	SX001G:informationTechnologyPart
	M	SX001G:rawMaterial
	PA	SX001G:packagingPart
	PE	SX001G:personalProtectionPart
	POW	SX001G:powerInfrastructureResource
	PR	SX001G:productProtectionPart
	R	SX001G:repairableSparePart
	S	SX001G:sparePart
	SE	SX001G:supportEquipment
	SSE	SX001G:safetyRelatedSupportEquipment
	TNWK	SX001G:transportNetworkInfrastructureResource
resourceUsagePartyRole	O	SX001G:resourceOwner
	R	SX001G:resourceRequester
	O	SX001G:owner

Attribute name	Valid value	Valid value name
resourceUsageRequestIdentifier	R	SX001G:requester
resourceUsageRequestStatus	A	SX001G:accepted
	C	SX001G:cancelled
	D	SX001G:denied
	H	SX001G:onHoldByGrantor
	N	SX001G:underNegotiation
	R	SX001G:raised
	S	SX001G:suspendedByRequester
roleCapabilityLevel	F	SX001G:full
	P	SX001G:partial
safetyDocumentCriticality	C	SX001G:critical
	L	SX001G:low
	R	SX001G:routine
	T	SX001G:lifeThreatening
	U	SX001G:urgent
safetyWarningPriority	C	SX001G:critical
	R	SX001G:routine
	U	SX001G:urgent
sensorIdentifier	OEM	SX001G:originalEquipmentManufacturer
sensorSamplingMode	C	SX001G:continuous
	E	SX001G:on event
	P	SX001G:periodic
	T	SX001G:on threshold
serializedItemWarrantyType	E	SX001G:extended warranty
	L	SX001G:life warranty
	M	SX001G:manufacturing defect
serializedPartsListPositionIdentifier	ID	SX001G:serializedPartsListPositionIdentifier
serializedProductVariantAssignmentIdentifier	OPER	SX001G:operator
	PLAN	SX001G:planner
	SERV	SX001G:serviceProvider
serializedProductVariantAssignmentStatus	KO	SX001G:assigmentStatusNotReady
	OK	SX001G:assigmentStatusReady

Attribute name	Valid value	Valid value name
	PL	SX001G:assigmentStatusPlanned
serializedProductVariantAssignmentType	A	SX001G:assigned
	B	SX001G:assignedAsBackup
	P	SX001G:potentialAssignment
serviceBulletinPriority	C	SX001G:critical
	L	SX001G:low
	N	SX001G:normal
	U	SX001G:urgent
serviceBulletinType	A	SX001G:authorityRequirement
	C	SX001G:critical
	F	SX001G:functional
	M	SX001G:mandatory
	O	SX001G:operationalImprovement
	R	SX001G:reliabilityImprovement
	S	SX001G:safetyRelated
serviceIdentifier	S	SX001G:serviceProvider
serviceRelationshipType	AS	SX001G:associatedTo
	CO	SX001G:complements
	EX	SX001G:extensionOf
	IN	SX001G:incompatibleWith
	PO	SX001G:partOf
	RE	SX001G:replaces
	SI	SX001G:similarTo
serviceRequestCancellationIdentifier	OPER	SX001G:operator
serviceRequestCancellationReason	C	SX001G:customerCancellation
	N	SX001G:serviceRequestItemNotAvailable
serviceRequestIdentifier	R	SX001G:serviceRequester
	S	SX001G:serviceProvider
serviceRequestPartyRole	AG	SX001G:agent
	CUS	SX001G:customer
	INT	SX001G:internalStaff
	MAN	SX001G:mantainer
	OP	SX001G:operator

Attribute name	Valid value	Valid value name
	SRV	SX001G:serviceProvider
	SUP	SX001G:supplier
serviceRequestPriority	C	SX001G:critical
	L	SX001G:low
	R	SX001G:routine
	U	SX001G:urgent
serviceRequestRelationshipType	CAN	SX001G:cancels
	REL	SX001G:relatedTo
serviceRequestType	CAL	SX001G:calibrate
	LOAN	SX001G:loan
	OVR	SX001G:overhaul
	REP	SX001G:replace
	SND	SX001G:send
	TRN	SX001G:train
	USE	SX001G:use
shopFindingsFaultCode	C	SX001G:corrosion
	D	SX001G:damage
	E	SX001G:electricalFailure
	F	SX001G:fire
	H	SX001G:hardwareFailure
	O	SX001G:other
	S	SX001G:softwareFault
	X	SX001G:explosion
shopFindingsFaultConfirmed	C	SX001G:confirmed
	N	SX001G:noFaultFound
shopFindingsIdentifier	S	SX001G:shop
skillCode	ID	SX001G:skillCode
softwareElementType	D	SX001G:distributedSoftwareElement
	E	SX001G:embeddedSofwareElement
	L	SX001G:loadableSofwareElement
softwareErrorFixPriority	H	SX001G:highPriority
	N	SX001G:normalPriority
	U	SX001G:urgentPriority

Attribute name	Valid value	Valid value name
softwareErrorIdentifier	ID	SX001G:softwareErrorIdentifier
softwareErrorReproducibility	A	SX001G:swErrorAlwaysReproducible
	I	SX001G:swErrorIntermitentlyReproduceable
	N	SX001G:swErrorNotReproduceable
softwareErrorSeverity	B	SX001G:blockingSoftwareError
	C	SX001G:criticalSoftwareError
	F	SX001G:featureSoftwareError
	K	SX001G:tweakSoftwareError
	M	SX001G:majorSoftwareError
	R	SX001G:minorSoftwareError
	T	SX001G:trivialSoftwareError
	X	SX001G:textSoftwareError
specialSafetyInstructionPriority	C	SX001G:critical
	R	SX001G:routine
	U	SX001G:urgent
substanceDefinitionExceptedQuantities	-	No valid values defined for this attribute in current specification issue.
substanceDefinitionHazardousClass		Refer to hardwarePartHazardousClassCode valid value library, Para 5
substanceDefinitionPackingGroup	-	No valid values defined for this attribute in current specification issue.
substanceDefinitionSpecialProvisions	-	No valid values defined for this attribute in current specification issue.
substanceDefinitionState	A	SX001G:aerosolSubstance
	G	SX001G:gaseousSubstance
	L	SX001G:liquidSubstance
	S	SX001G:solidSubstance
supportEquipmentCalibrationRequired	A	SX001G:asRequired
	D	SX001G:daily
	M	SX001G:monthly
	N	SX001G:none
	W	SX001G:weekly
	Y	SX001G:yearly
supportEquipmentType	ATE	SX001G:automaticTestEquipment
	CA	SX001G:calibrationTool

Attribute name	Valid value	Valid value name
	HO	SX001G:hoistingTool
	HT	SX001G:handTool
	OTH	SX001G:other
	ST	SX001G:supportingTool
	TST	SX001G:testTool
	VE	SX001G:vehicle
`taskIdentifier`	ID	SX001G:taskIdentifier
`taskInformationCode`		Refer to taskInformationCodeValues valid value library, Para 5
`taskRequirementIdentifier`	ID	SX001G:taskRequirementIdentifier
`taskRequirementInformationCode`		Refer to taskInformationCodeValues valid value library, Para 5
`taskRequirementRevisionIdentifier`	ID	SX001G:taskRequirementRevisionIdentifier
`taskRequirementRevisionStatus`		Refer to revisionStatusCode valid value library, Para 5
`taskRevisionIdentifier`	ID	SX001G:taskRevisionIdentifier
`taskRevisionStatus`		Refer to revisionStatusCode valid value library, Para 5
`technicalOrderIdentifier`	OEM	SX001G:originalEquipmentManufacturer
`technicalOrderPriority`	C	SX001G:critical
	L	SX001G:low
	R	SX001G:routine
	U	SX001G:urgent
`transportCapabilityUsageIdentifier`	OPER	SX001G:operator
`typeOfPersonIdentifier`	ID	SX001G:typeOfPersonIdentifier
`typeOfPersonType`	-	No valid values defined for this attribute in current specification issue.
`typeOfPrice`	ACTU	SX001G:Actual
	ASKK	SX001G:Ask
	AUCT	SX001G:Auction
	AVER	SX001G:Average
	AVOV	SX001G:AverageOverride
	BIDE	SX001G:Bid
	CALC	SX001G:Calculated

Attribute name	Valid value	Valid value name
	CANC	SX001G:Cancellation
	CLEN	SX001G:Clean
	COMB	SX001G:Combined
	CREA	SX001G:Creation
	DDVR	SX001G:DailyDividendRate
	DIRT	SX001G:Dirty
	DRAW	SX001G:Draw
	EGAV	SX001G:EstimatedGAV
	ENAV	SX001G:EstimatedNAV
	FAVA	SX001G:FairValue
	GAVL	SX001G:GrossAssetValue
	GREX	SX001G:GrossOfAll
	GUAR	SX001G:Guaranteed
	INDC	SX001G:Indicative
	INPA	SX001G:IndicativePaid
	INTE	SX001G:Interim
	KASA	SX001G:Kassa
	LIMI	SX001G:Limit
	MIDD	SX001G:Mid
	MRKT	SX001G:Market
	NAUP	SX001G:NonAdjustedUnpublished
	NAVL	SX001G:NetAssetValue
	NAVS	SX001G:SidePocketNAV
	NDIS	SX001G:NetDisclosed
	NET1	SX001G:NetOfAll
	NET2	SX001G:Net
	NOGR	SX001G:NotionalGross
	NUND	SX001G:NetUndisclosed
	OFFR	SX001G:Offer
	OTHR	SX001G:Other
	PAID	SX001G:Paid
	PARV	SX001G:ParValue
	RDAV	SX001G:RoundedAverage

Attribute name	Valid value	Valid value name
	REDN	SX001G:RedemptionNAV
	RINV	SX001G:Reinvestment
	SETM	SX001G:Settlement
	SPRE	SX001G:Spread
	STOP	SX001G:Stop
	SUBN	SX001G:SubscriptionNAV
	SWIC	SX001G:Switch
	SWNG	SX001G:Swing
	TAXE	SX001G:Tax
	TISC	SX001G:TaxableIncomePerShareCalculated
unacceptableConditionIdentifier	ID	SX001G:unacceptableConditionIdentifier
unacceptableConditionReason	C	SX001G:unacceptableCosts
	O	SX001G:otherUnacceptableCharacteristics
	P	SX001G:unacceptablePerformance
	R	SX001G:unacceptableReliability
	S	SX001G:unacceptableSafety
warehouseType	PHY	SX001G:physical
	VIR	SX001G:virtual
warrantyClaimCommunicationMeans	E	SX001G:eMail
	F	SX001G:fax
	M	SX001G:mail
	P	SX001G:phone
	T	SX001G:telex
warrantyClaimContactType	A	SX001G:agent
	C	SX001G:customer/warranty holder
	F	SX001G:finance
	L	SX001G:legal
	R	SX001G:warranty reporter
	W	SX001G:warrantor
warrantyClaimIdentifier	OEM	SX001G:originalEquipmentManufacturer
warrantyClaimResolutionIdentifier	OEM	SX001G:originalEquipmentManufacturer
	A	SX001G:approved

Attribute name	Valid value	Valid value name
warrantyClaimResolutionType	C	SX001G:closed
	D	SX001G:draft
	DF	SX001G:deferred
	P	SX001G:partiallyApproved
	R	SX001G:rejected
	S	SX001G:settled
warrantyClaimType	DAM	SX001G:damage
	EXP	SX001G:expenses
	EXT	SX001G:extended
	HRS	SX001G:laborHours
	INS	SX001G:inspection
	MAT	SX001G:material
	REC	SX001G:recall
	RES	SX001G:restore
	REV	SX001G:lostRevenue
	STD	SX001G:standard
	TRA	SX001G:transport
	UPD	SX001G:productUpdate
warrantyEventReason	D	SX001G:manufacturingDefect
	DE	SX001G:delay
	DT	SX001G:downTime
	F	SX001G:failure
	O	SX001G:other
wasteContainerIdentifier	ID	SX001G:wasteContainerIdentifier
wasteDisposalOperationIdentifier	ID	SX001G:wasteDisposalOperationIdentifier
wasteDisposalOperationMethod	D	SX001G:disposalByDestruction
	L	SX001G:disposalByLandFill
	O	SX001G:disposalByOtherMeans
	R	SX001G:disposalByRecycling
wasteRecoveredItemQuality	E	SX001G:exceptionalRecoveredSubstanceOrMaterialQuality
	H	SX001G:highRecoveredSubstanceOrMaterialQuality
	L	SX001G:lowRecoveredSubstanceOrMaterialQuality

Attribute name	Valid value	Valid value name
	N	SX001G:normalRecoveredSubstanceOrMaterialQuality
	U	SX001G:unusableRecoveredSubstanceOrMaterialQuality
workBreakdownIdentifier	C	SX001G:contract
workBreakdownRelationshipType	IN	SX001G:includes
	RE	SX001G:relatedTo
	RP	SX001G:replaces
workBreakdownRevisionIdentifier	WBSRID	SX001G:workBreakdownStructureRevisionId
workBreakdownRevisionStatus	A	SX001G:approved
	C	SX001G:cancelled
	D	SX001G:draft
	R	SX001G:underReview
workItemIdentifier	WIID	SX001G:workItemIdentifier
workItemRelationshipType	A	SX001G:startsAfter
	AS	SX001G:endsAtSameTimeAs
	B	SX001G:before
	C	SX001G:isChildOf
	CS	SX001G:cannotStartBefore
	P	SX001G:isParentOf
	R	SX001G:relatedTo
	S	SX001G:simultaneousTo
workItemStatus	A	SX001G:approved
	C	SX001G:contracted
	D	SX001G:draft
	F	SX001G:finished
	S	SX001G:started
workItemTimelineEvent	M	SX001G:milestone
	T	SX001G:task
workItemType	C	SX001G:common
	D	SX001G:development
	I	SX001G:internal
	M	SX001G:manufacturing
	P	SX001G:projectManagement

Attribute name	Valid value	Valid value name
	R	SX001G:research
	S	SX001G:subcontracted
	T	SX001G:training
workOrderIdentifier	MAIN	SX001G:maintainer
workOrderPriority	H	SX001G:highPriority
	L	SX001G:lowPriority
	R	SX001G:routinePriority
workOrderStatus	C	SX001G:closed
	D	SX001G:deferred
	E	SX001G:execution
	O	SX001G:open
workOrderType	COR	SX001G:correctiveWorkOrder
	INS	SX001G:inspectWorkOrder
	MOD	SX001G:modificationWorkOrder
	PRE	SX001G:predictiveWorkOrder
	PRV	SX001G:preventiveWorkOrder
	TST	SX001G:testWorkOrder
zoneElementType	W	SX001G:productWorkArea
	Z	SX001G:productZone

5 Valid value libraries

The list of valid value libraries used by S5000F is provided in Table 5. These libraries include codes from international specifications. Refer to these specifications for a full list of valid value codes.

Table 5 List of valid value libraries

Library name	Valid value	Source/Valid value name
comparisonOperatorCode	EQ	SX001G:equalToComparisonOperator
	GE	SX001G:greaterThanOrEqualToComparisonOperator
	GT	SX001G:greaterThanComparisonOperator
	IN	SX001G:withinRangeComparisonOperator
	LE	SX001G:lessThanOrEqualToComparisonOperator
	LT	SX001G:lessThanComparisonOperator

Library name	Valid value	Source/Valid value name
	NE	SX001G:notEqualToComparisonOperator
	OUT	SX001G:outsideRangeComparisonOperator
countryCodeValues	-	**Note** The country codes valid value XML schema for S5000F issue 3.0 lists 193 county codes from ISO 3166-1
hardwarePartHazardousClassCode	-	**Note** The hazardous class code valid value XML schema does not include any predefined valid values
languageCodeValues	-	**Note** The language codes valid value XML schema for S5000F issue 3.0 lists 136 language codes from ISO 639:1988
revisionStatusCode	A	SX001G:approvedStatus
	C	SX001:cancelledStatus
	D	SX001G:draftStatus
	IW	SX001G:inWorkStatus
	R	SX001G:reviewedStatus
taskInformationCodeValues	-	**Note** The task information codes valid value XML schema for S5000F issue 3.0 lists 41 information codes from S1000D

Chapter 27

Tailoring and contracting against S5000F

Table of contents

Page

Tailoring and contracting against S5000F 1

References 2

1	General	2
1.1	Introduction	2
1.2	Scope	2
2	Tailoring	2
3	Basic contracting process	3
3.1	Contracting principles	3
3.2	Contracting steps	3
3.2.1	Activity contracting	3
3.2.2	Shared activities	3
3.2.3	Special activities	3
3.2.4	Reporting	4
4	Contract details	4
4.1	Guidance conference	4
4.1.1	Agree implementation timescales	5
4.1.2	Define organizational aspects	5
4.1.3	Define the exchange mechanism	5
4.1.4	Confirm the data delivery responsibilities	5
4.1.5	Define data security and access	5
4.1.6	Define the data exchange frequency	6
4.1.7	Refine the agreed data exchange	6
4.1.8	Define project-specific values and data	6
4.1.9	Define master data and primary data sources	6
4.1.10	Define specific business rules	7
4.1.11	Define data analysis guidelines	7
4.1.12	Data quality and data feedback reporting	7
4.2	Additional technical meetings	8
4.3	Technical data exchange document	8
4.4	Stepwise implementation	9
5	Practical tailoring example	9
5.1	Contractual requirement	9
5.2	Identifying the UoFs of the contractual requirement	9
5.3	Removing unnecessary classes from the UoF	10
5.4	Tailoring of data elements	12
5.5	Tailoring of valid values	12

List of tables

1	References	2

List of figures

1	Example top-level data feedback report	8
2	Reduction of UoF Safey to the essential information for SpecialSafetyInstruction	11
3	Reduced UoF Safety	12

References

Table 1 References

Chap No./Document No.	Title
Chap 1	Introduction
Chap 5	Feedback of safety data
Chap 23	Feedback of non-predefined information
Chap 24	Data model
Chap 24.5	Mapping of use cases to individual UoFs
Chap 26	Data element list
Chap 28	Data required for the different use cases
SX000i	International guide for the use of the S-Series Integrated Logistics Support (IPS) specifications
SX001G	Glossary for the S-Series IPS Specifications
SX005G	S-Series IPS specifications XML schema implementation guidance

1 General

1.1 Introduction

The purpose of this chapter is to define the general rules to be followed when tailoring or contracting against this specification, thus providing a contractual framework that can be invoked between two parties.

1.2 Scope

The scope only extends to tailoring and contractual aspects, and does not cover the data model itself, the data to be exchanged or the mechanism of exchange, only the means to agree to the exchange.

2 Tailoring

Tailoring of the specification is the adaptation of it for a specific purpose and is therefore not different from the contracting steps listed below, as the tailoring is usually part of the contract or technical negotiations.

S5000F is very large, containing over a 1000 data elements (attributes). However, it is not intended to be used in its entirety, but rather designed to be tailored. Tailoring, in this context, means using just the information that is required for a particular purpose, usually for the activities to be carried out in the context of a contract. Depending on the contract complexity and required information, the necessary data elements to implement S5000F can range from a few hundred to less than a dozen.

The smallest known S5000F implementation includes just four data elements apart from the message information itself.

In order to tailor the specification for internal purposes without a contract, proceed with the steps listed in Para 3, Para 4.1 and Para 4.2. In this case, replace the word Contract by

Agreement between involved organizations. In this particular case, <u>Para 4.3</u> is not necessary, but its use is recommended. An example is provided in <u>Para 5</u>.

3 Basic contracting process

3.1 Contracting principles

As every contracting process is different due to different contractual environments and applicable laws, S5000F provides a simple mechanism for contracting. All data are directly associated to the use of such data (use cases), and hence the contracting mechanism is not associated to the data itself, but to the activity that is carried out, which requires such data. That is, a contract will define the use cases (activities) to be carried out by the contractor and customer, and the data required for that particular use case will be delivered by the customer or contractor, as applicable, depending on who will carry out the activity.

S5000F does not indicate the direction of the data flow, because the same activities can be performed by different actors, depending on the contract. The receiver of the data will always be the party carrying out the activity for which the data is required.

However, there can be the need for data that are not directly associated to an activity. This information can be necessary from a legal or controlling point of view, or on specific customer request. This is a special case that has also been considered in the contracting process.

3.2 Contracting steps

The contracting process can be defined as follows:

3.2.1 Activity contracting

The customer and the contractor must agree on the activities to be carried out by the contractor and the customer. It is recommended that all activities are defined so that each of them maps exactly to one single use case as defined in S5000F.

The associated use cases for each activity will be identified in the different chapters. If no equivalent use case is found for a certain activity, proceed as indicated in <u>Para 3.2.3</u>.

The contract must also define the basic data delivery intervals required to perform each activity in a reasonable manner.

Note

Different activities can require different data delivery intervals, ranging from real-time delivery to a monthly delivery.

These activities and their required information must be included in the work breakdown structure.

The basic contractual data to be delivered for each work item (activity) are those that correspond to the associated use case in S5000F. For that purpose, the tables provided in <u>Chap 28</u> and the use cases of each chapter are the only normative portion of S5000F and must be called upon in the contract for the definition of the data to be provided. The rest of the specification must be treated as informative.

3.2.2 Shared activities

In case an activity is shared by several parties, it must be documented who will provide the data for the activity to be carried out and who is responsible for providing the resulting data from the activity. This is particularly important for reporting purposes. Normally, the party that must provide the resulting data for a specific activity is the party that is accountable for such activity.

3.2.3 Special activities

If an activity to be carried out contractually is not defined as a use case in S5000F, the recommended way to contract such an activity as follows:

1. Identify the Units of Functionality (UoF) that provide the necessary information to carry out that activity, in a similar way as that in Chap 24.5.

2. Within each UoF, identify the classes that provide the necessary data, including the intermediate classes that provide the required relationships between the data.

3. Create a table similar to those listed in Chap 28 and include it in the contract and/or work breakdown structure document, associated to that particular activity, together with the exchange frequency. Alternatively, the technical data exchange document defined in Para 4.3 can be used for this purpose.

It is recommended that, should special activities be encountered, a comment is raised against S5000F (refer to Chap 1) defining the activity and required UoFs/classes, so as to include it in a future S5000F issue as a new use case.

3.2.4 Reporting

Each individual program will have different reporting requirements. S5000F provides a mechanism for providing reports in a structured way that can be automatically processed. S5000F however does not mandate explicit reporting information, as this will be usually specific to each program.

To define the reporting in a contractual manner, the contract must define the information that needs to be exchanged for reporting purposes and its periodicity. This will usually be in the form of Key Performance Indicators (KPIs), activity reporting and textual information. The UoF Reporting, UoF Reportable Activity, UoF Cost Entries and UoF Service Contract Management will cover probably most of the reporting requirements.

4 Contract details

No matter how descriptive a contract is, there are always technical details that can escape the global negotiation or that are left for later agreement in order to speed up the contractual negotiations. For this purpose, it is recommended to have a guidance conference to establish the main exchange agreements/framework and a technical exchange document defining the detailed exchange parameters. Both the guidance conference and the technical data exchange document must be called upon in the contract.

The guidance conference must be held after a global IPS guidance conference has been held as required by SX000i, and ideally after the guidance conference of the individual IPS elements that are affected by this data exchange, so as to ensure that their data feedback requirements are properly covered.

4.1 Guidance conference

It is recommended to hold a guidance conference between all parties affected by S5000F exchange so as to:

- agree implementation timescales
- define organizational aspects
- define the exchange mechanism
- confirm the data delivery responsibilities
- define data security and access
- define the data exchange frequency
- refine the agreed data exchange
- define project-specific values and data
- define master data sources
- define specific business rules
- define data analysis guidelines
- data quality and data feedback reporting
- any other aspect that can require agreement regarding the data exchange

The results of the agreements of this guidance conference must be documented in a technical data exchange document. Refer to Para 4.1.1 through Para 4.1.12.

4.1.1 Agree implementation timescales

Normally, an IT system needs to be put in place to carry out the exchange. Even though the contract will define a specific data for the exchange system to be in place, it is necessary to test it before going live, and an agreement is required between both sides about when such testing will be performed, as both will have to commit resources for this purpose.

4.1.2 Define organizational aspects

It is necessary to identify on both sides the organizations that are involved in the exchange, including technical focal points for IT problems or data quality issues, so that potential problems can be solved quickly.

4.1.3 Define the exchange mechanism

This can be either pull (ie, the receiving party extracts the data) or push (ie, the data is sent by the data originating party). The usual mechanism is push, because the party sending the data is usually the one that knows when the data is ready. Similarly, the exchange can be synchronous or asynchronous. The exchange method can also be by means of FTP, http, web services or similar, and needs to be agreed. It is necessary to agree on the data exchange handshake, and to ensure that this handshake effectively occurs, including error recovery. Finally, it is necessary to define whether the data will be sent in full or only the modified (delta) data will be exchanged.

As part of the exchange mechanism definition it can also be necessary to define the message file naming conventions if the S5000F data are exchanged by means of files (eg, if using FTP). This allows for automatic validation and processing of the files by the receiver.

S5000F does not require a specific naming convention, but it is recommended to use something along the lines recommended by SX005G:

S5000F_2-0_isfdataset_uc27_contract1_001-02.xml

Where:

- S5000F_2-0_isfdataset indicates the specification and its version
- uc27 indicates the use case for which data is sent
- contract1 indicates the contract for which the data is sent
- 001 indicates the message sequence, and
- 02 indicates that it has been re-sent twice (eg, due to transmission errors)

4.1.4 Confirm the data delivery responsibilities

Normally, the responsibility for delivering a data set for a specific activity will be already established in the contract. However, lower-level data exchanges can sometimes not have been covered. The guidance conference must in that case ensure that all data exchanges have a responsible assigned for such data delivery, including the responsibility for data quality. It is recommended that the data exchanges are defined at use case level. The responsibility for defining master data should also be established at the guidance conference.

4.1.5 Define data security and access

If not contractually specified, it is necessary to agree on the security classification of the data, the security of the networks and encryption mechanisms for the data exchange. Whether there are restrictions on the access to the data that is being provided, and whether it can be mixed or not with data from other customers or a physical or functional segregation is required, must be defined.

Part of the data access agreements can include read/write rights by individual organizations. If not already contractually established, these agreements can also cover the intellectual property of the created data, and the processed data (analysis results).

Note

> Such restrictions can have an impact on other contractual aspects. (eg, if data cannot be consolidated, a comparison analysis of customer fleet behavior in respect to the overall fleet behavior, across all customers, cannot be performed and this can mask potential fleet problems.)

4.1.6   **Define the data exchange frequency**

This frequency will usually be established based on the activity for which the data is required. An activity that is performed once a month (eg, reliability analysis) does not require a daily data exchange. Other activities (eg, fleet management) can require data to be exchanged in (near) real time. Typical exchange rates will be quarterly, monthly, weekly or daily. In special cases, hourly or real-time exchange can be required. Depending on the activity, specific dates can also be required for the data delivery (eg, one week before the activity is due to start, due to data processing requirements).

There can also be restrictions on the times at which the data can be exchanged (eg, only at certain hours or on certain days) due to infrastructure issues or security constraints.

4.1.7   **Refine the agreed data exchange**

The tables provided in Chap 23 provide an overview of what data is required for each use case/ contractual activity. However, in some cases, there can be issues because some data can be unavailable for one or several Products or because the effort to collect the data does not justify the benefit of receiving that information. In some cases, the tables in Chap 28 will require modification or reduction by mutual agreement. Para 5 provides a practical example about how such tables can be adapted to the peculiarities of a program.

4.1.8   **Define project-specific values and data**

If not already identified in the contract, it will be necessary to agree on project-specific values (eg, a special data classification for a particular attribute), so that the project-specific values can be included in the XML file. The standard S5000F allowed values, supplemented by the project-specific values, are commonly referred to as reference data. Reference data (eg, country codes, units of measure or project codes) typically does not change over the lifetime of a project, thought it can require periodic revisions.

Note

> The list of valid values listed in the XSD ValidValues file for the individual attributes is recommended and not mandatory. It is permitted by the specification to remove unwanted values or add necessary values to a specific attribute in the XSD ValidValues file. When adding new values, it is recommended not to use one of the recommended codes but rather add a new one, in order to maintain the compatibility with other projects that can share a same S5000F database, refer to Para 5.5. If it is determined that a code is necessary across multiple projects, then a change request should be submitted to the specification.

Similarly, there can be a need for a specific project data set that is not covered in the standard S5000F data elements set. S5000F provides the means to include project-specific data, but it is necessary to define such data, as well as its data types. Refer to Chap 26. Para 5 also provides a practical example about how to add such project-specific information.

4.1.9   **Define master data and primary data sources**

It is essential that define standard business objects that need to be referred to across the project and across all involved systems (eg, organizations, locations, etc) are defined. This information, commonly referred to as master data, must be managed by a single entity, in order to ensure data consistency. Given that master data tends to change over the lifetime of a project, the guidance conference needs to nominate a single entity that is responsible for the maintenance of the master data, and the process to update the master data to ensure that all the involved actors are aware of a necessary change.

In some cases, specifying which data sources will be used as the primary data for the delivery of the information can be required. This is especially true if certain data can come from several systems and can be subject to transformation and/or different validation rules within those systems. In these cases, it is essential that all parties reference the same data from the same source. For example, flight hours can be extracted by electronic operators, an aircraft/helicopter logbook or by a ground station. The usage of different primary data sources by the different parties involved in a project will inevitably lead to data quality issues.

4.1.10 Define specific business rules

S5000F provides a mechanism for data exchange. It does not, however, mandate specific business rules for data validation, which must be defined by a project. Such rules can, for example, require that part identifiers are based on a NATO Stock Number (NSN), have a specific part number range or adhere to a project-specific codification. Refer to Chap 24.

4.1.11 Define data analysis guidelines

If data analysis is required, the rules for the analysis must be agreed, including potential analysis extensions, such as root cause analysis, for anomalies detected during the analysis.

4.1.12 Data quality and data feedback reporting

A specific reporting of the data feedback itself can be agreed, so that the adequacy of the data feedback is ensured. Specifically, it is important to ensure that this data feedback report is used to continuously improve data quality at the data source systems when systematic data quality problems are detected, and to correct potentially incorrect source data.

Note

This data feedback reporting can also be performed using S5000F constructs. An example of data feedback reporting is provided at Fig 1. S5000F does not mandate any specific data feedback report.

Typically, the entity responsible for the data quality is the producer of such data, refer to Para 4.1.4. However, it is convenient that one single entity controls all the data quality and data exchange at project level, and reports this information to all involved stakeholders, so that a unified view of all data exchange issues is ensured. It is recommended that data quality is either a fixed point of the agenda in the periodic project review meetings, or an ad-hoc data quality working group is established between all the involved parties.

<table>
<tr><td colspan="3" align="center">Data feedback report</td></tr>
<tr><td>Project: XYZ Manufacturing robot line</td><td>Product: HiTech Rob-32</td><td>Reported by: Robot-X Associates</td></tr>
<tr><td>Reporting date: 2016-09-01</td><td>Reporting period: 2016-08</td><td>Days: 31</td></tr>
<tr><td>Messages received: 3765
Total data transfer: 1.7 Gbytes
Message rejection rate: 0.61%
Total data objects: 647581</td><td>Messages rejected: 23
Average message size: 459 kbytes
Message repetition rate: 0.16%
Average data objects/message: 172</td><td>Messages repeated: 11
Average messages/day: 121.5
Transfer availability: 99.97%
Non-predefined info files: 134</td></tr>
</table>

Messages rejected:
334, 476, 544, 545, 612, 752, 1033, 1489, 2131, 2541, 2917, 3002, 3047, 2541
Causes for message rejection:
- Wrong sender/wrong recipient: 544, 545
- Invalid XML schema: 334, 2131, 2541, 3002 -
Not S5000D data: 1033
- Business rule #12: 476, 3047
- Business rule #15: 752
- Corrupted information: 2917
- Other: 612, 1489

Messages repeated: **Main reasons for message repetition:**
734 (3x), 1095 (2x), 2376 (1x), 2917 (5x)   Timeout, data corruption

Data quality errors:

Average data object errors: 2.6%	Dubious data object information: 0.7%
Business rule violations: 1026	Average business rule violations: 0.16%
Master data violations: 1720	Average master data violations: 2.54%
Reference data violations: 955	Average reference data violations: 0.15%

Top 5 BR violations: BR32, BR17, BR52, BR78, BR5
Top 5 MASTERDATA violations: Contract, Organization, Location, Facility, Fleet
Top 5 REFDATA violations: unit, partsListType, securityClass, zoneElementType, amountCurrency

Refer to Annex for detailed data quality report.

ICN-B6865-S5000F18001-001-00

Fig 1 Example top-level data feedback report

4.2   Additional technical meetings

It can be necessary to have additional technical meetings to refine the agreements of the guidance conference (eg, to discuss specific points between specialists). Additional technical meetings can also be required to reflect potential contract amendments, based on the updated technical requirements.

These meetings must be properly recorded in meeting minutes, all agreements be properly documented, and such agreements must be included in the technical data exchange document.

4.3   Technical data exchange document

Not to be confused with an interface control document (ICD), which defines a technical interface between computer systems, the technical data exchange document provides a detailed description of the data exchange, including but not limited to:

– responsible organizations and points of contact at both sides (for IT and data quality)
– planning/implementation timescales (including testing)
– infrastructure details (eg, IP addresses)

- help desk
- reporting on exchange issues
- security requirements (eg, https, ftps, encryption mechanisms, etc)
- responsible entity for the maintenance of the master data and change process for such data
- responsible entity for delivery of each individual data set and delivery frequency
- exchange mechanisms
- exact data to be exchanged (copying the tables from Chap 28 as necessary, including changes agreed at the guidance conference and any additional technical meetings)
- XML schema for project-specific values
- business rules for data validation
- Service Level Agreement (SLA), exchange times (if synchronous)

The technical data exchange document will be an official delivery and must be considered as being contractual. This document will contain all technical aspects agreed at the guidance conference and possible ad-hoc additional technical meetings. It must be approved by both parties involved in the exchange and its modifications must be properly approved by authorized personnel.

4.4 Stepwise implementation

It should be noted that S5000F does not require that all required data sets are implemented at the same time, as different activities can start to be performed at different times. Therefore, it is possible to implement S5000F in a step-by-step manner, (eg, initially exchanging only the program-level information, then later extending the exchange to include maintenance, then later, RAMCT or fleet management).

Contractual changes implying new activities after the original contract was developed are also feasible. Refer to Para 4. The data exchange should in no way be affected by these contractual changes, except for the need to send (and process) additional data that can be required by the new contract.

5 Practical tailoring example

This example shows how the data exchange can be reduced to its essential aspects.

5.1 Contractual requirement

In this example, the contract states:

> *The Contractor shall provide safety instructions on how to proceed in case of a safety issue.*

In this case, the mapping to the contractual requirement is trivial, as this corresponds to Use Case 3 of Chap 5. Other contractual requirements can be more complex, and can correspond to several use cases, or even to a new use case.

Note

This particular contractual requirement (and Use Case) assumes that the safety issue has already been sent.

5.2 Identifying the UoFs of the contractual requirement

Checking the required UoFs in Chap 24.5 for this particular use case, the following UoFs are obtained:

- CDM UoF Remark. This UoF provides the capability to attach remarks to an item. It is not essential to this example, so it can be discarded.
- S5000F UoF Applicability Assignment Item. This UoF provides the capability to manage an item's applicability. In this example, however only the document that identifies the safety

issue related to the item is required. Since the applicability of the safety issue is the same as that of the safety recommendation, this UoF can be discarded.
- S5000F UoF Comment. This UoF provides the capability to raise comments against an item. It is not essential to this example, so it can be discarded.
- S5000F UoF Document. This UoF provides the capability to establish relationships between documents. Since only the relationship to the safety issue is required, which is covered by the UoF Safety, this UoF can be discarded.
- S5000F UoF Safety. This UoF will include the required instructions.

5.3 Removing unnecessary classes from the UoF

S5000F UoF Safety includes 12 classes, but, in this example, not all are needed.

For example, since applicabilities are not required, the class `ApplicabilityStatementitem` can be removed. Also, the implementation of the required safety action corresponds to the customer, therefore the classes `RequiredSafetyActionImplementation`, *Action* and *PartAction* can also be removed. The class `SafetyWarning` is not required since it is a warning that a safety issue exists and not the instruction. Similarly, the relationship of the `SafetyIssue` with the Event that caused it is not required because this is not related to the `SpecialSafetyInstruction` itself.

Sending the `SafetyIssue` again is not required, but a reference to it should be included.

The tailoring so far results in the schema at Fig 2.

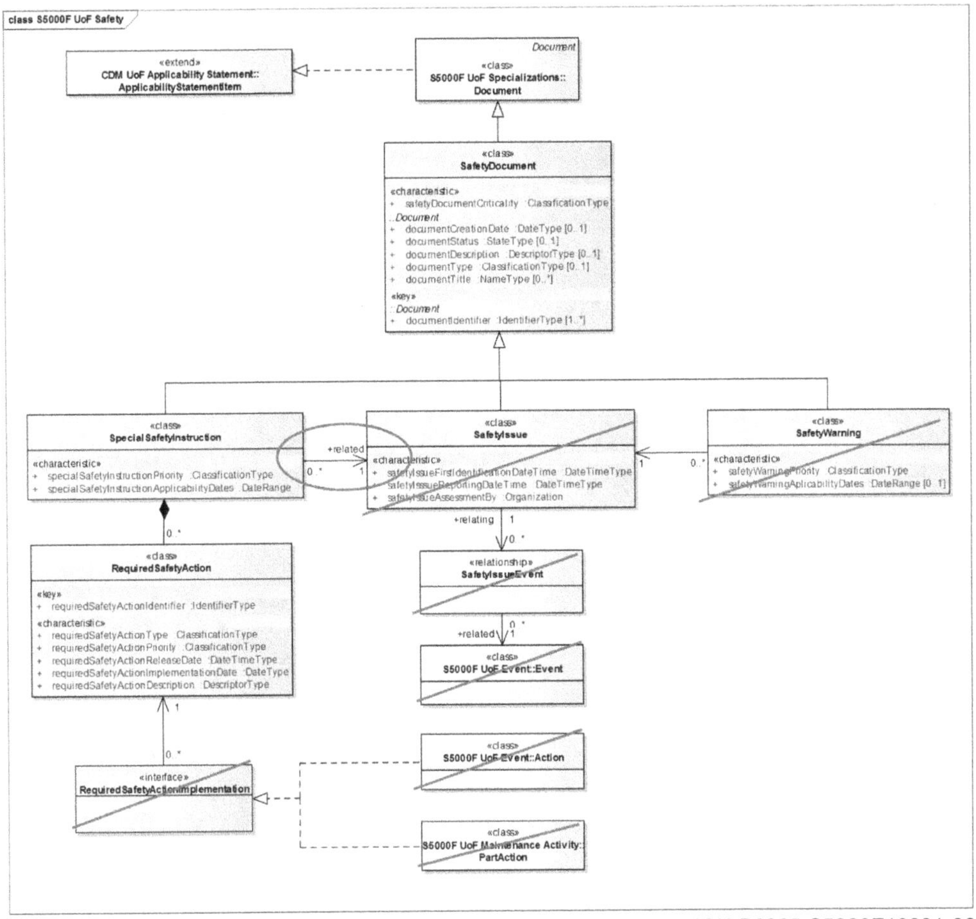

class S5000F UoF Safety

«extend»
CDM UoF Applicability Statement::
ApplicabilityStatementItem

Document
«class»
S5000F UoF Specializations::
Document

«class»
SafetyDocument

«characteristic»
+ safetyDocumentCriticality : ClassificationType
..Document
+ documentCreationDate : DateType [0..1]
+ documentStatus : StateType [0..1]
+ documentDescription : DescriptorType [0..1]
+ documentType : ClassificationType [0..1]
+ documentTitle : NameType [0..*]
«key»
Document
+ documentIdentifier : IdentifierType [1..*]

«class»
SpecialSafetyInstruction

«characteristic»
+ specialSafetyInstructionPriority : ClassificationType
+ specialSafetyInstructionApplicabilityDates : DateRange

+related   0..*   1

«class»
SafetyIssue

«characteristic»
+ safetyIssueFirstIdentificationDateTime : DateTimeType
+ safetyIssueReportingDateTime : DateTimeType
+ safetyIssueAssessmentBy : Organization

1   0..*

«class»
SafetyWarning

«characteristic»
+ safetyWarningPriority : ClassificationType
+ safetyWarningApplicabilityDates : DateRange [0..1]

0..*

«class»
RequiredSafetyAction

«key»
+ requiredSafetyActionIdentifier : IdentifierType
«characteristic»
+ requiredSafetyActionType : ClassificationType
+ requiredSafetyActionPriority : ClassificationType
+ requiredSafetyActionReleaseDate : DateTimeType
+ requiredSafetyActionImplementationDate : DateType
+ requiredSafetyActionDescription : DescriptorType

+relating   1   0..*

«relationship»
SafetyIssueEvent

+related   0..*   1

«class»
S5000F UoF Event::Event

«interface»
RequiredSafetyActionImplementation

«class»
S5000F UoF Event::Action

«class»
S5000F UoF Maintenance Activity::
PartAction

ICN-B6865-S5000F19001-001-00

Fig 2 Reduction of UoF Safey to the essential information for SpecialSafetyInstruction

However, the classes `Document` and `SafetyDocument` are parent classes of the class *SpecialSafetyInstruction*, so, as the class `SpecialSafetyInstruction` inherits the properties of its parents, the UoF Safety is reduced to that shown in Fig 3. This example has shown how five UoFs and their classes have been reduced to one UoF with two classes and one reference to the `SafetyIssue` to which it is related. Though the UoFs show all the relationships between the information, it is not necessary to send again information that has already been submitted.

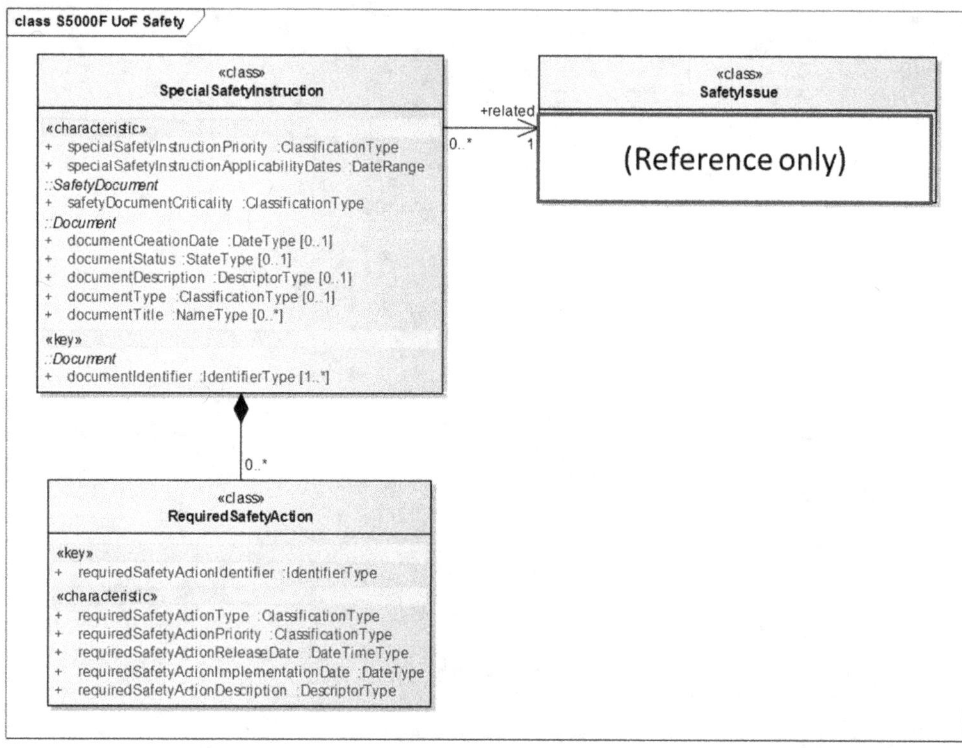

ICN-B6865-S5000F19001-001-00

Fig 3 Reduced UoF Safety

5.4 Tailoring of data elements

The data elements that are required for this use case are the attributes (data elements) listed in
Fig 3.

Note

> Some inherited attributes are optional (ie, those that have "[0..1]" or "[0..*]" after their
> name). Strictly speaking, the whole use case could therefore be implemented with just 10
> attributes (ie, those that are mandatory) and one reference.

Similarly, the tailoring described in Para 4.1.7 can include one or several additional optional
data elements, and/or some additional project-specific information. Refer to Chap 26.

5.5 Tailoring of valid values

Para 4.1.8 states that the valid values listed in the S5000F XSD file are the recommended
values to be used. They are not mandatory and can be removed or complemented as
necessary. For example, an `ashoreOrAfloadCondition` value would be applicable for
a ship, but not for a ground vehicle, aircraft, factory robot or other machinery. In this case, this
value should be removed from the valid values file.

Project-specific values for existing attributes are also allowed. For example, the attribute
`requiredSafetyActionType` could have a project specific value of "recallFleet", or
similar. This project specific value would be agreed (refer to Para 4.1.8) and included in the
valid values file of the XML Schema.

It is recommended that additional values have:

- a value that is <u>not</u> the same as a value defined in SX001G
- the associated *source* annotation uses the end item acronym code (EIAC) of the applicable project for its namespace definition. This will prevent using the wrong values on the wrong project if data from multiple projects is stored in a same database.

<u>Note</u>

Replacing an existing valid value by a different code will make it non-compliant with this specification if the SX001G source annotation is not changed!

Example of deletion and addition of code values:

```
<xsd:simpleType  name="zoneElementTypeCodeValues">
    <xsd:restriction base="xsd:string">
        <xsd:enumeration value="WA"> <xsd:annotation>
            <xsd:appinfo>
                <source>SX001G:workArea</source> </xsd:appinfo>
        </xsd:annotation> </xsd:enumeration>
        <xsd:enumeration value="Z"> <xsd:annotation>
            <xsd:appinfo>
                <source>SX001G:zone</source> </xsd:appinfo>
        </xsd:annotation> </xsd:enumeration>
    </xsd:restriction>
    <xsd:restriction base="xsd:string"> <xsd:enumeration value="X">
        <xsd:annotation> <xsd:appinfo>
                <source>ProjXXX:underwaterSpace</source>
            </xsd:appinfo>
        </xsd:annotation> </xsd:enumeration>
</xsd:simpleType>
```

In the example above, the value "WA" has been deleted because it is not applicable, and a new value "X" has been defined that is only applicable to project XXX.

Page intentionally blank.

Chapter 28

Data required for the different use cases

Table of contents

Page

Data required for the different use cases 1

References 2

1   General 2
2   Mapping of use cases against data model classes 2
2.1   Classes for reliability, availability, maintainability, capability and testability 3
2.2   Classes for maintenance analysis 17
2.3   Classes for safety analysis 26
2.4   Classes for supply support 34
2.5   Classes for life cycle cost analysis 40
2.6   Classes for warranty analysis 47
2.7   Classes for product health and usage monitoring 55
2.8   Classes for obsolescence management 59
2.9   Classes for integrated fleet management 67
2.10   Classes for software support cases 74
2.11   Classes for configuration management 80
2.12   Classes used for in-service contract management 88
2.13   Classes for in-service environment data 97
2.14   Classes for Product environmental impact and disposal data 102
2.15   Classes used for non-predefined information 109
3   Mapping of data elements against chapter use cases 112

List of tables

1   References 2
2   Classes used for RAMCT use cases 4
3   Classes used for maintenance analysis use cases 17
4   Classes used for safety analysis use cases 27
5   Classes used for supply support use cases 35
6   Classes used for LCC use cases 40
7   Classes used for warranty analysis use cases 47
8   Classes used for product health and usage monitoring use cases 55
9   Classes used for obsolescence management use cases 59
10   Classes used for integrated fleet management use cases 67
11   Classes used for software support use cases 74
12   Classes used for configuration management use cases 81
13   Classes used for in-service contract management use cases 88
14   Classes used for in-service environment data use cases 97
15   Classes used for in-service environment data use cases 103
16   Classes used for non-predefined information use cases 109

References

Table 1 References

Chap No./Document No.	Title
Chap 3	Feedback data for the purpose of reliability, availability, maintainability, capability and testability analysis
Chap 4	Feedback of data for maintenance analysis
Chap 5	Feedback of safety data
Chap 6	Feedback of data for supply support
Chap 7	Feedback for Life Cycle Cost analysis
Chap 8	Feedback of data for warranty analysis
Chap 9	Feedback data for the purpose of product health and usage monitoring
Chap 10	Feedback of data to support obsolescence management
Chap 11	Feedback of integrated fleet management data
Chap 12	Feedback of data for software support
Chap 13	Feedback of data for configuration management
Chap 14	Feedback of data to support the management of in-service contracts
Chap 15	Feedback of in-service environment data
Chap 16	Feedback of environmental impact and disposal data
Chap 23	Feedback of non-predefined information
Chap 24	Data model
Chap 27	Tailoring and contracting against S5000F
Chap 29	Implementation example

1 General

This chapter provides a mapping of the classes and data elements (attributes) as defined in the data model described in Chap 24 against the individual use cases described in the different chapters. The purpose of this mapping is to enable a quick determination of what information is required to carry out the activities for a specific use case. This also facilitates tailoring and contracting for the data as described in Chap 27.

2 Mapping of use cases against data model classes

The current section provides a detailed mapping of all data model classes to the use cases of each individual chapter, for easy cross-referencing.

Note

It is important to observe that the mapping provided in this chapter is not mandatory and is just a guidance provided to assist the users in identifying the information that they could require for a specific use case.

Note

It is an acceptable practice to remove unnecessary classes from a specific use case, in the same way that it is acceptable to add related classes to it, provided that the data model is not modified. Refer to Chap 27.

The following tables describe the classes that are used for each individual use case, using the following codes:

- "X" - mandatory
- "O" - optional/recommended
- (blank) - not used

Note

This mapping is a recommendation and can be tailored for each specific project. "Mandatory", in this context, must be understood as "required to maintain the data model consistency". If a class is not used, then it cannot be mandatory. For example, if during an operational phase (use case UC50703) there is no movement because the product is stationary (eg, a machine in a permanent location), then the classes *Movement* and *MovementLeg* should not be mandatory. On the other hand, it two classes are used, and a relationship between the two classes exists, then this relationship must be maintained.

2.1 Classes for reliability, availability, maintainability, capability and testability

The classes used for each Reliability, Availability, Maintainability, Capability and Testability (RAMCT) use case as defined in Chap 3 are listed in Table 2.The use cases are numbered:

Reliability use cases:

1   UC50301: Monitor the performance of equipment

2   UC50302: Influencing future designs

3   UC50303: Trends, failures, root cause analysis, and issue warnings

Availability use cases:

4   UC50304: Operations and deployment support, through-life support and equipment availability

5   UC50305: Maintenance management and contracting for availability

Maintainability use cases:

6   UC50306: Maintenance activities, effectiveness of repairs, specified maintenance, predict maintenance periods, Product status

7   UC50307: Retaining performance, support manuals and support infrastructure

Capability use cases:

8   UC50308: Mission capable, capability shortfalls

9   UC50309: Efficiency, performance against specification **Testability** use cases:

10   UC50310: Can product be tested

11   UC50311: Fault diagnosis, fault identification

Table 2 Classes used for RAMCT use cases

Class name	UC50301	UC50302	UC50303	UC50304	UC50305	UC50306	UC50307	UC50308	UC50309	UC50310	UC50311
Accelerometer			X								X
Action	X	X	X	X	O	X	X	X	X	X	X
ActualEnvironment	X	X	X	X		X	X	X	X	X	X
AllocatedTaskLocation	X	X	X								
AllowedProductConfiguration	X	X	X	X	O	X	X	X	X	X	X
AllowedProductConfigurationByConfigurationIdentifier	X	X	X	O	O	X		X	X	X	X
AllowedProductConfigurationHardwarePartAsDesigned	X	X	X	O	O	X		X	X	X	X
AllowedProductConfigurationItem	X	X	X	O	O	X	X	X	X	X	X
AllowedProductConfigurationPhysicalData	X	X	X	X	X		X	X	X		
AllowedProductConfigurationRole	X	X	X	X	O	X	X	X	X	X	X
AllowedProductOperationalConfigurationItem		X	X	O	O	X	X	X			X
AllowedRoleChange	X	X	X	X	X		X	X	X		
AlternatePartAsDesigned	X	X	X	O	X	X	X	O	X	X	X
ApplicabilityStatement	X	X	X								
ApplicabilityStatementItem	X										
AssociatedActualEnvironment	X	X	X	X		X	X	X	X	X	X
AuthorityRequirement		X	X		X					X	
AuthorityToOperate	X	X	X	O	O	X		X	X	X	X
Availability	X	X	X	X	X	X	X			X	X
AvailabilityItem	X	X	X	X	X	X	X	X	X	X	X
BatchHardwarePart	X	X	X	O	O	X	X	X	X	X	X
Breakdown	X	X	X	O	X	X	X	O	X	X	X
BreakdownElement	X	X	X	X	X	X	X	X	X	X	X
BreakdownElementInZone	X	X	X	X						X	X
BreakdownElementRevision	X	X	X	X	X	X	X	O	X	X	X
BreakdownElementRevisionRelationship	X	X	X	X	X	X	X	O	X	X	X
BreakdownElementRevisionRelationshipItem	X	X	X	O	X	X	X	O	X	X	X
BreakdownElementStructure	X	X	X	O	X	X	X	O	X	X	X

Class name	UC50301	UC50302	UC50303	UC50304	UC50305	UC50306	UC50307	UC50308	UC50309	UC50310	UC50311
BreakdownElementUsageInBreakdown	X	X	X	X	X	X	X	X	X	X	X
BreakdownElementUsageRelationship	X	X	X	X	X	X	X	O	X	X	X
BreakdownItem	X	X	X	O	X	X	X	O	X	X	X
BreakdownRevision	X	X	X	O	X	X	X	O	X	X	X
BreakdownRevisionRelationship	X										
Budget	O	O	O	O	O	O	O	O	O	O	O
Calibration										X	X
CalibrationDocument										X	X
CalibrationMeasurement										X	X
Capability	X	X	X	X	X		X	X	X		
CapabilityDefinitionCharacteristic								X	X		
CapabilityDefinitionRevision								X	X		
CapabilityItem	X	X	X	X	X		X	X	X		
CapabilityLimitation								X	X		
CargoItem	O	O	O	O	O	O	O	X	O	O	O
ChangeAuthorization	X	X	X								
ChangeEmbodimentRequirement		X	O	O	O	O	O		O		
ChangeRequest	X	X	X	X	O	O	O	O	O	X	X
CircuitBreaker	X	X	X	X						X	X
CircuitBreakerSetting	X	X	X	X						X	X
CircuitBreakerSettings	X	X	X	X						X	X
ClassInstanceAssertItem	X	X	X								
CloudInfrastructure				O			X	O			
Comment	O	O	O	O	O	O	O	O	O	O	O
CommentAction	O	O	O	O	O	O	O	O	O	O	O
CommentItem	O	O	O	O	O	O	O	O	O	O	O
CommentParty	O	O	O	O	O	O	O	O	O	O	O
CommentRelationship	O	O	O	O	O	O	O	O	O	O	O
CommunicationsNetwork				O			X	O			
CompliesWith		X									

Class name	UC50301	UC50302	UC50303	UC50304	UC50305	UC50306	UC50307	UC50308	UC50309	UC50310	UC50311
ComputerNetwork				O			X	O			
ConditionDefinitionItem	X	X	X		X						
ConditionInstance	X	X	X		X						
ConditionType	X	X	X		X						
ConditionTypeAssertMember	X	X	X		X						
Consequence	X	X	X	X	O	X	X	X	X	X	X
ConsumableItem				X	X						
Consumption				X	X						
ConsumptionPeriod				X	X						
Contract	X	X	X	X	X	X	X	O	O	X	X
ContractClause		X			X						
ContractClauseRelationship					X						
ContractItem					X						
ContractItemDetails					X						
ContractParty					X						
ContractRelationship					X						
CostBreakdownContext					X						
CostEntry	O	X	O	O	O	X	O	O	O	O	X
CostEntryItem	O	X	O	O	O	X	O	O		O	X
CostItem	O	O	O	O	O	O	O	O	O	O	O
Country			O								
Damage	X	X	X	X	O	X	X	X	X	X	X
DataSetAsReleased		X									
DetectionMean			X							X	
DetectionMeanCapability			X							X	
DetectionMechanism			X							X	
Detector			X							X	X
DigitalFile	O	O	O	O	O	O	O	O	O	O	O
DisposalRequirement		X									
Document	X	X	X	X	X	X	X	O	X	X	X

Class name	UC50301	UC50302	UC50303	UC50304	UC50305	UC50306	UC50307	UC50308	UC50309	UC50310	UC50311
DocumentCharacteristicItem	O	O	O	O	X	X		O			
DocumentIssue	O	O	X	O	X	X		O	X		
DocumentItem	O									X	X
DocumentParty	O	O	O	O	X	X		O			
DocumentReferencingItem	O										
DownTimePeriod	X	X	X	X	X	X	X	X	X	X	X
EffectiveOnProductConfiguration	X	X	X	O	O	X		X	X	X	X
EffectiveOnProductConfigurationItem	X	X	X	O	O	X		X	X	X	X
Environment	O	O	O	O	O	X	O	O	O	O	X
EnvironmentDefinition			O								
EnvironmentDefinitionRevision			O								
EnvironmentItem	X	X	X	X		X	X	X	X	X	X
EnvironmentRelationship			O								
EnvironmentRevision			O							X	X
EquipmentOperation	X	X	X		O	X	X	O	X	X	X
EquipmentOwner	X	X	X		O	X	X	O	X	X	X
EquipmentStatus	X	X	X		O	X	X	O	X	X	X
EvaluationByAssertionOfClassInstance	X	X	X								
EvaluationByAssertionOfCondition	X	X	X		X						
EvaluationByAssertionOfSerializedItems	X	X	X								
EvaluationByNestedApplicabilityStatement	X	X	X								
EvaluationByNestedExpression					X						
EvaluationCriteria	X	X	X		X						
Event	X	X	X	X	X	X	X	X	X	X	X
EventAffectedBreakdownElement	X	X	X	X	O	X	X	X	X	X	X
EventExplanation	X	X	X	X	O	X	X	X	X	X	X
EventItem	X	X	X	X	O	X	X	X	X	X	X
EventRelationship	X	X	X	X	O	X	X	X	X	X	X
EventRelationshipItem	X	X	X	X	O	X	X	X	X	X	X
EventReporter	X	X	X	X	O	X	X	X	X	X	X

Class name	UC50301	UC50302	UC50303	UC50304	UC50305	UC50306	UC50307	UC50308	UC50309	UC50310	UC50311
ExplanatoryFactor	X	X	X	X	O	X	X	X	X	X	X
ExportControlLicense	O	O	O	O	O	O	O	O	O	O	O
ExportControlRegulation		X									
ExpressionEvaluation					X						
ExternalDocument	O	O	O	O	X	X		O			
Facility	X	X	X	X	X	X	X	X	X	X	X
FacilityLocation				O	X	X	O		O	X	
FacilityOperator	X	X	X	X	X	X	O		X	X	
FacilityOperatorItem				O	X	X	O		O	X	
FacilityOwner				O	X	X	O		O	X	
FacilityRelationship				O	X	X	O		O	X	
Failure		X								X	X
FailureDetection		X								X	
FailureMode		X								X	X
FailureModeCause		X								X	X
FailureModeEffect		X								X	
Fault		X								X	
FaultCause		X								X	
Fleet	X	X	X	X	X	X	X	X	X	X	X
FleetManager								X			
FleetPlanning								X			
FleetRequirement		X						X			
FleetTask				X	X			X			
FleetTaskCancellationNotice	O	O	O	O	X	X		O			
FleetTaskCargo								X			
FleetTaskList								X			
GeographicalArea	X	X	X								
GlobalPosition			X								
HardwareElement	X	X	X	X	X	X	X	X	X	X	X
HardwareElementPartRealization	X	X	X	X	X	X	X	X	X	X	X

Class name	UC50301	UC50302	UC50303	UC50304	UC50305	UC50306	UC50307	UC50308	UC50309	UC50310	UC50311
HardwareElementRevision	X	X	X	X	X	X	X	O	X	X	X
HardwarePartAsDesigned	X	X	X	X	X	X	X	X	X	X	X
HardwarePartAsDesignedDesignData	X	X	X	O	X	X	X	O	X	X	X
HardwarePartAsDesignedSupportData	X	X	X	O	X	X	X	O	X	X	X
IdentifiedTaskRequirement	X	X	X								
Infrastructure	X	X	X	X	X	X	X	X	X	X	X
InfrastructureAvailable				X			X	O			
InfrastructureCompliance				O			X	O			
InfrastructureCompliantItem				X		X	X	O		O	X
InfrastructureItem				O			X	O			
InfrastructureNode				O			X	O			
InfrastructureNodeAtLocation				O			X	O			
InfrastructureParty				O			X	O			
InfrastructureRelationship				O			X	O			
InfrastructureRequiringItem				X			X	O			
InfrastructureRevision	X	X	O	X	O	O	X	O	O	O	O
InstallationLocation	X	X	X	O	O	X	X	X	X	X	X
InstallationLocationDefinitionItem	X	X	X	O	O	X	X	X	X	X	X
InstalledPart	X	X	X	O	O	X	X	X	X	X	X
InstalledPartItem	X	X	X	O	O	X	X	X	X	X	X
InventoryActivity	O	O	O	O	X					X	
ItemDisposalOperation		X	O	O	O	O	O		O		
ItemWarranty		X									
LaborRateItem					X						
LaborRates					X						
LegalParty					X						
LocationItem			O	X	X	X	X	O		O	X
Locator	O	O	O	O	X	X		O			
LogBook	X	X	X	X	X	X	X	X	X	X	X
LogBookEntry	X	X	X	X	O	X	X	X	X	X	X

Class name	UC50301	UC50302	UC50303	UC50304	UC50305	UC50306	UC50307	UC50308	UC50309	UC50310	UC50311
LogBookEntryMeasurementPoint	X	X	X	X	O	X		X	X	X	X
LogicalAND	X	X	X		X						
LogicalNOT	X	X	X		X						
LogicalOR	X	X	X		X						
LogicalXOR	X	X	X		X						
MaintenanceActivity	X	X	O	X	X	X			X	X	X
MaintenanceActivityDocument	X	X	X	X	X			X	X	X	
MaintenanceActivityParty	X	X	X	X	X			X	X	X	
MaintenanceActivityPlan	X	X	X	X	X			X	X	X	
MaintenanceActivityRecord	X	X	X	X	X			X	X	X	
MaintenanceEvent	X	X	X	X	X	X	X	X	X	X	X
MaintenanceFacility	X	X	X	X	X	X	X	X	X	X	X
MaintenanceFacilityLevel				X	X	X	X		O	O	
MaintenanceFacilitySlot				X	X	X	X		O	O	
MaintenanceFacilitySlotAccomodation				X	X	X	X		O	O	
MaintenanceFacilitySlotPlannedUsage				X	X	X	X		O	O	
MaintenanceItem	X	X	X	X	X	X	O	O	X	X	X
MaintenanceLevel	X	X	X	X	X		X	X	X	O	O
MaintenanceLicense			X	O	X	X	X			O	O
MaintenanceOrganization					X		X				
MaintenanceOrganizationApproval					X		X				
MaintenancePerson	X	X	X	X	X	X	X		X	X	X
MaintenancePersonApprovedProduct			X	O	X	X	X			O	O
MaintenancePersonFacility			X	O	X	X	X			O	O
MaintenanceProgram	X	X	X	X	X	X		O	X	X	
MaintenanceProgramItem			X		X					X	
MaintenanceProgramRevision			X		X					X	
MaintenanceRequirement		X									
MaintenanceWorkOrderSource	X	X	X	X	X	X			X	X	X
MajorComponent	X		X	O	X	O	O	X	X	O	X

Class name	UC50301	UC50302	UC50303	UC50304	UC50305	UC50306	UC50307	UC50308	UC50309	UC50310	UC50311
Material		X	O	O	O	O	O		O		
MeasurementPoint	X	X	X	X	X	X	X	X	X	X	X
MeasurementPointItem	X	X	X	X	X	X	X	X	X	X	X
Message	O	O	O	O	O	O	O	O	O	O	O
Movement	O	X	X	X	X	O	O	O	O	O	O
MovementLeg	O	X	X	X	X	O	O	O	O	O	O
MovementLegDelay			O	X	X						
MovementLegPosition			O	X	X						
MRONetwork				O			X	O			
NestedAllowedProductConfiguration	X	X	X	O	O	X		X	X	X	X
NestedProductVariant	X	X	X	O	O	X		X	X	X	X
NestedSerializedProductVariant	X		X	O	X	O	O	X	X	O	X
NonAvailabilityAttribution	X	X	X	X	X	X	X			X	X
NonAvailabilityCause	X	X	X	X	X	X	X			X	X
NonAvailabilityCauseItem	X	X	X	X	X	X	X			X	X
NonConformanceData	X	X	X	O	O	X		X	X	X	X
ObsolescenceRequirement		X									
OperatingBase	X	X	X	X	X	X	X	X	X	O	X
OperatingLocationType	X	X	X					X	X		
OperationalActivity	O	O	O	O	X					X	
OperationalApproval		X	X	X				X	X	O	X
OperationalEvent	X	X	X	X	O	X	X	X	X	X	X
OperationalEventMessage	X	X	X	X		X	X	X	X	X	X
OperationalEventOperator	X	X	X	X		X	X	X	X	X	X
OperationalMode			O	X	X						
OperationalModeStatus	X	X	X	X	O	X	X	X	X	X	X
OperationalMoment	X	X	X	X	O	X		X	X	X	X
OperationalMomentItem	X	X	X	X	O	X		X	X	X	X
OperationalPeriod			X	X	X						
OperationalPeriodOperator			O	X	X						

Class name	UC50301	UC50302	UC50303	UC50304	UC50305	UC50306	UC50307	UC50308	UC50309	UC50310	UC50311
OperationalPeriodRelationship			O	X	X						
OperationalRequirement		X						X			
OperationalRequirementsPlanning								X			
OperationalRole	X	X	X	X	X	X	X	X	X	X	X
OperationalTime		X	X	X				X		O	
OperationalTimeItem		X	X	X				X		O	
Operator	X	X	X	X	X	X	X	X	X	X	X
Organization	X	X	X	X	X	X	X	O	O	X	X
OrganizationalBreakdownStructureRevision	O	O	O	O	O	O	O	O	O	O	O
OtherFacility				O	X	X	O		O	X	
ParkingFacility				O	X	X	O		O	X	
PartAction	X	X	X	X	X	X	X	X	X	X	X
PartAsDesigned	X	X	X	O	X	X	X	X	X	X	X
PartAsDesignedPartsList	X	X	X	O	X	X	X	O	X	X	X
PartAsDesignedPartsListEntry	X	X	X	O	X	X	X	X	X	X	X
PartAsDesignedPartsListRelationship	X	X	X	O	X	X	X	O	X	X	X
PartAsDesignedPartsListRevision	X	X	X	O	X	X	X	X	X	X	X
PartOwner		X									
Party	X	X	X	X	X	X	X	X	X	X	X
Penalty	O	X	O	O	O	O	O	O	O	O	O
Person	X	X	X	X	X	X	X	O	O	X	X
PoliciesAndRegulations		X									
PoliciesAndRegulationsCompliantItem		X									
Pool	O	O	O	O	O	X	O	O	O	O	X
Port				O			X	O			
PowerGrid				O			X	O			
PressureSensor		X									X
Product	X	X	X	X	X	X	X	X	X	O	X
ProductParameterAtOperationalEvent	X	X	X	X		X	X	X	X	X	X
ProductUsagePhase	X	X	X	X	O	X	X	X	X	X	X

Class name	UC50301	UC50302	UC50303	UC50304	UC50305	UC50306	UC50307	UC50308	UC50309	UC50310	UC50311
ProductUsagePhaseHierarchicalRelationship		X									
ProductUsagePhaseItem		X									
ProductUsagePhaseRelationship		X									
ProductUsagePhaseSequentialRelationship		X									
ProductVariant	X	X	X	X	X	X	X	X	X	X	X
ProductVariantMaintenance					X		X				
Project	X	X	X	X	X	X	O	O	O	X	X
ProjectContract					X						
ProjectRelationship					X						
RealizedPart	X	X	X	O	O	X	X	X	X	X	X
ReferencedDocument	X	X	X	X						X	X
Remark	O	O	O	O	O	O	O	O	O	O	O
RemarkItem	O	O	O	O	O	O	O	O	O	O	O
Report	O	O	O	O	X	X	X	X	O		X
ReportableActivity	O	X	O	O	O	X	O	O		O	X
ReportableItem	O	O	O	O	O	X					X
ReportableMetric	O	O	O	O	X	X	O	O	O	O	X
ReportableMetricItem	O	O		X							
ReportContext	O	O	O	O	X					X	
ReportContextItem	O	O	O	O	X					X	
ReportingParty	O	O	O	O	X					X	
ReportParty	O	O	O	O	X					X	
RequiredFleetRole								X			
RequiredSafetyAction	X	X	X	X						X	X
RequiredSafetyActionImplementation	X	X	X	X						X	X
Requirement	X	X	X	X	O	O	O	O	O	X	X
RequirementParty		X									
RequirementRelationship		X									
ResourceRealization	X	X	X								
ResourceSpecification				O			X	O			

Class name	UC50301	UC50302	UC50303	UC50304	UC50305	UC50306	UC50307	UC50308	UC50309	UC50310	UC50311
ResourceUsageRequest		X	O	O	O	O	O		O		
RoleCapability	X	X	X	X	X		X	X	X		
S1000DDataModule	O										
S1000DDataModuleIssue	O										
S1000DPublicationModule	O										
S1000DPublicationModuleIssue	O										
SafetyDocument	X	X	X	X	X	X		O	X	X	
SafetyIssue	X	X	X	X						X	X
SafetyIssueEvent	X	X	X	X						X	X
SafetyItem	X	X	X	X						X	X
SafetyRequirement	X	X	X	X						X	X
SafetyRequirementsDocument	X	X	X	X						X	X
SafetyWarning	X	X	X	X						X	X
SCORMContentPackage	O	O	O	O	X	X		O			
SecurityClass	O	O	O	O	O	O	O	O	O	O	O
SecurityClassification	X	X	X	O	O	O	O	O	O	O	O
SecurityClassificationItem	O	O	O	O	O	O	O	O	O	O	O
Sensor			X								X
SensorSample			X								X
SensorType			X								X
SerializedAssertItem	X	X	X								
SerializedHardwarePart	X	X	X	X	X	X	X	X	X	X	X
SerializedItem	X	X	X	X	X	X	X	X	X	X	X
SerializedItemOwner	X	X	X	X	X	O	O	O	O	X	X
SerializedPartDesignAssociation			X								
SerializedProductOperationalPeriod			O	X	X						
SerializedProductVariant	X	X	X	X	X	X	X	X	X	X	X
SerializedProductVariantAssignment				X	X			X			
SerializedProductVariantConfigurationConformance	X	X	X	O	O	X	X	X	X	X	X
SerializedProductVariantInFleet	X	X	X	X	X	O	O	X	X	O	X

Class name	UC50301	UC50302	UC50303	UC50304	UC50305	UC50306	UC50307	UC50308	UC50309	UC50310	UC50311
SerializedProductVariantOperatingBase	X	X	X	X	X	O	O	X	X	O	X
SerializedProductVariantOperator	X	X	X	X	X	O	O	X	X	O	X
Service	X	X	X	X	X	X	X	O	O	X	X
ServiceBulletin	X	X	X	X	X	X	X	O	O	X	X
ServiceLevelAgreementClause	O	O			X						
ServiceRequest		X	O	O	O	O	O		O		
ShopFindings											X
ShopFindingsDeterminedBy											X
SoftwareElement	X	X	X	O	X	X	X	X	X	X	X
SoftwareElementPartRealization	X	X	X	X	X	X	X	X	X	X	X
SoftwareElementRevision	X	X	O	O	X	X		X			
SoftwarePartAsDesigned	X	X	X	O	X	X	X	O	X	X	X
SoftwarePartAsReleased	X	X	X	X	X	X	X	X	X	X	X
SpecialSafetyInstruction	X	X	X	X						X	X
StrainGauge				X							X
SubjectOfPoliciesAndRegulations		X									
SubstanceContainingItem	X	X	X	O	X	X	X	O	X	X	X
SubstitutePartAsDesigned	X	X	X	O	X	X	X	O	X	X	X
SubtaskInZone	X	X	X								
SubtaskTimeline	X	X	X								
SubtaskWarningCautionNote	X	X	X								
SuppliesUsed	X	X	X	X	X			X	X	X	
SupplyItem	X	X	X	X	X			X	X	X	
SupportEquipment				O		X	X	O		O	X
SupportEquipmentItem	X	X	X	X	X			X	X	X	
SupportEquipmentUsed	X	X	X	X	X			X	X	X	
Tachometer			X								X
Task	O	O	O	O	O	O	O	O	O	O	O
TaskPersonnelResourceCompetence	X	X	X								
TaskRequirement	O	O	O	O	O	O	O	O	O	O	O

Class name	UC50301	UC50302	UC50303	UC50304	UC50305	UC50306	UC50307	UC50308	UC50309	UC50310	UC50311
TaskResource	X	X	X								
TaskRevision	X	X	X	X	X	X			X	X	X
TaskRevisionWarningCautionNote	X	X	X								
TaskUsage	X	X	X								
TechnicalOrder			X								
TemperatureSensor			X								X
ThresholdDefinition	X	X	X	X						X	X
TrackablePart	X	X	X		O	X	X	O	X	X	X
TransportCapability								X	X		
TransportNetwork				O			X	O			
TransportRequirement		X									
UpgradeRequirement		X									
UsableOnItem	X	X	X	O	O	X		X	X	X	X
UsableOnProductVariant	X	X	X	O	O	X		X	X	X	X
Warehouse				O	X	X	O		O	X	
WarrantyClaim		X									
WarrantyClaimContact		X									
WarrantyClaimEvents		X									
WarrantyClaimFollowUp		X									
WarrantyClaimResolution		X	O	O	O	O	O		O		
WarrantyEvent	X	X	X	X	O	X	X	X	X	X	X
WarrantyItem		X									
WasteDisposalOperation		X	O	O	O	O	O		O		
WorkBreakdown	O	O	O	O	O	O	O	O	O	O	O
WorkBreakdownContext					X						
WorkItem	O	O	O	O	O	X	O	O	O	O	X
WorkOrder	X	X	X	X	X	X	O	O	X	X	X
ZoneElement	X	X	X	X	X			X	X	X	

2.2 Classes for maintenance analysis

The classes used for each maintenance analysis use case as defined in Chap 4 are listed in Table 3. The use cases are numbered:

1 UC50401: Manufacturer maintenance schedule

2 UC50402: Product user maintenance program

3 UC50403: Maintenance performed

4 UC50404: Product performance

5 UC50405: New modifications for in-service products

6 UC50406: Technical queries

7 UC50407: Component Shop Findings

8 UC50408: Structural Damages

9 UC50409: Equipment calibration certificate

10 UC50410 Track support equipment usage

Table 3 Classes used for maintenance analysis use cases

Class name	UC50401	UC50402	UC50403	UC50404	UC50405	UC50406	UC50407	UC50408	UC50409	UC50410
Action	O	O	X	O	X	X	O	X	O	O
ActualEnvironment				X		X		X		
AllowedProductConfiguration				X		X				
AllowedProductConfigurationPhysicalData				X		X				
AllowedProductConfigurationRole				X		X				
AllowedRoleChange				X		X				
AlternatePartAsDesigned					X			X		
AnchoringPoint							O			
AssociatedActualEnvironment				X		X		X		
AuthorityRequirement	X	X								
Availability				X						
AvailabilityItem				X						
BatchHardwarePart					X	X				
BreakdownElement	O	O	X	O	O	X	O	X	O	O
BreakdownElementInZone						X				
BreakdownElementRevision			O		X		O			
BreakdownElementRevisionRelationship						X				

Class name	UC50401	UC50402	UC50403	UC50404	UC50405	UC50406	UC50407	UC50408	UC50409	UC50410
BreakdownElementUsageInBreakdown					X	X				
BreakdownElementUsageRelationship						X				
BreakdownRevision					X					
Budget	O	O	O	O	O	O	O	O	O	O
Calibration			X						X	X
CalibrationDocument			O						X	X
CalibrationMeasurement			O						X	X
Capability				X		X				
CapabilityItem				X		X				
CargoItem	O	O	O	O	O	X	O	O	O	O
ChangeAuthorization					X					
ChangeControlledItem					X					
ChangedItemAvailabilityRequirement					X					
ChangeEmbodimentRequirement					X		X	O		
ChangeNotification					X					
ChangeRequest	O	O	O	O	X	X	X	O	O	O
ChangeRequestCause					X					
ChangeRequestItem					X					
ChangeRequestReasonItem					X					
CircuitBreaker						X				
CircuitBreakerSetting						X				
CircuitBreakerSettings						X				
Comment	O	O	O	O	O	X	O	O	O	O
CommentAction	O	O	O	O	O	X	O	O	O	O
CommentItem	O	O	O	O	O	X	O	O	O	O
CommentParty	O	O	O	O	O	X	O	O	O	O
CommentRelationship	O	O	O	O	O	X	O	O	O	O
Consequence			X			X		X		
Contract	O	O	X	X	X	X	X	O	O	O
ContractClause					X					

Class name	UC50401	UC50402	UC50403	UC50404	UC50405	UC50406	UC50407	UC50408	UC50409	UC50410
CostEntry	O	O	O	O	O	O	X	O	O	O
CostEntryItem							X	O		
CostItem	O	O	O	O	O	O	O	O	O	O
Country						X				
Damage			X			X	X	X		
DamageAnalysis			X					X		
DamageAnalysisRevision			X					X		
DamageCharacteristic			X					X		
DamageDefinition			X					X		
DamagedItem			X					X		
DetectionMean			O				O			
DetectionMeanCapability			O				O			
DetectionMechanism			O				O			
Detector			X				X			
DigitalFile	O	O	O	O	O	X	O	O	O	O
DigitalFileReference						X				
DigitalFileReferencedItem						X				
DigitalFileReferencingItem						X				
Document	X	X	X	O	O	X	O	O	O	X
DocumentCharacteristicItem	O	O	O		O	X		O	O	
DocumentIssue	X	X	O		X	X		O	O	
DocumentItem			O			X			X	X
DocumentParty	O	O	O		O	X		O	O	
DocumentReferencingItem						X				
DownTimePeriod			X	X	X	X		X		
EffectiveOnProductConfiguration					X					
Environment	O	O	O	O	O	X	O	O	O	O
EnvironmentItem				X		X		X		
EnvironmentRevision			O						X	X
EquipmentOperation			X							

Class name	UC50401	UC50402	UC50403	UC50404	UC50405	UC50406	UC50407	UC50408	UC50409	UC50410
EquipmentOwner			X							
EquipmentStatus			X							
Event	O	O	X	X	X	X	O	X	O	O
EventAffectedBreakdownElement			X			X		X		
EventExplanation			X			X		X		
EventItem			X			X		X		
EventRelationship			X			X		X		
EventRelationshipItem			X			X		X		
EventReporter			X			X		X		
ExplanatoryFactor			X			X		X		
ExportControlLicense	O	O	O	O	O	O	O	O	O	O
ExternalDocument	O	O	O		O	X		O	O	
Facility	X	X	X	X	X	X	X	O	O	O
FacilityOperator						X				
Failure			X				X			
FailureDetection			O				O			
FailureMode			X				X			
FailureModeCause			X				X			
FailureModeEffect			O				O			
Fault	O	O	X				O			
FaultCause			O				O			
Fleet	O	O	O	X	X	X	X	O	O	O
FleetTaskCancellationNotice	O	O	O		O	X		O	O	
GeographicalArea						X				
GlobalPosition						X				
HardwareElement					X					
HardwareElementPartRealization					X	X				
HardwarePartAsDesigned	X	X	X		X	X	X	O	X	X
HardwarePartAsDesignedDesignData									X	
HardwarePartAsDesignedSupportData									X	

Applicable to: All

Class name	UC50401	UC50402	UC50403	UC50404	UC50405	UC50406	UC50407	UC50408	UC50409	UC50410
Infrastructure	X	X	X	X	X	X	X	O	O	O
InfrastructureRevision	O	O	O	O	X	O	O	O	O	O
InstallationLocation			X			X				
InstallationLocationDefinitionItem			X							
InstalledPart					X					
ItemDamage			X					X		
ItemDisposalOperation							X	O		
LocalPosition			X					X		
LocationItem				X		O				
Locator	O	O	O		O	X		O	O	
LogBook			X							
LogBookEntry			X	X		X		X		
MaintenanceActivity			X		X					X
MaintenanceActivityDocument			X							X
MaintenanceActivityParty			X							X
MaintenanceActivityPlan			X							X
MaintenanceActivityRecord			X							X
MaintenanceEvent			X			X		X		X
MaintenanceFacility	X	X	X							X
MaintenanceFacilityLevel	O	O	X							
MaintenanceFacilitySlot	O	O	X							
MaintenanceFacilitySlotAccomodation	O	O	X							
MaintenanceFacilitySlotPlannedUsage	O	O	X							
MaintenanceItem			X							X
MaintenanceLevel	O	O	X							
MaintenanceLicense	O	O	X							
MaintenanceOrganization	X	X	X						O	
MaintenanceOrganizationApproval	X	X	X							
MaintenancePerson	O	O	X						O	X
MaintenancePersonApprovedProduct	O	O	X							

Class name	UC50401	UC50402	UC50403	UC50404	UC50405	UC50406	UC50407	UC50408	UC50409	UC50410
MaintenancePersonFacility	O	O	X							
MaintenanceProgram	X	X	X		O	X		O	O	
MaintenanceProgramItem	X	X								
MaintenanceProgramRevision	X	X								
MaintenanceWorkOrderSource	O	O	X		X					X
Material							X	O		
MeasurementPoint					X	X				
MeasurementPointItem					X	X				
Message	O	O	O	O	O	O	O	O	O	O
Movement	O	O	O	X	O	O	X	O	O	O
MovementLeg	O	O	O	X	O	O	X	O	O	O
MovementLegDelay				X		O				
MovementLegPosition				X		O				
NonAvailabilityAttribution				X						
NonAvailabilityCause				X						
NonAvailabilityCauseItem				X						
OperatingBase				X	X	X				
OperatingBaseCapacity				X						
OperationalApproval				X		X				
OperationalEvent			X	X		X		X		
OperationalEventMessage				X		X		X		
OperationalEventOperator				X		X		X		
OperationalMode				X		O				
OperationalModeStatus				X		X		X		
OperationalPeriod				X	X	O				
OperationalPeriodOperator				X		O				
OperationalPeriodRelationship				X		O				
OperationalRole				X		X				
Operator				X		X		X		
OperatorOrganization				X					O	

Class name	UC50401	UC50402	UC50403	UC50404	UC50405	UC50406	UC50407	UC50408	UC50409	UC50410
OperatorPerson				X					O	
Organization	X	X	X	X	O	X	X	O	X	X
OrganizationalBreakdownStructureRevision	O	O	O	O	O	O	O	O	O	O
OrganizationOperationsApproval				X						
PartAction				X	X	X				X
PartAsDesigned	O	O	O	O	X	X	O	O	X	O
PartAsDesignedPartsList									X	
PartAsDesignedPartsListEntry					X				X	
PartAsDesignedPartsListRelationship									X	
PartAsDesignedPartsListRevision					X				X	
PartOwner					X	X				
Party	O	O	X	X	X	X	O	X	O	X
PartyAddress									O	
PartyContactData									O	
PartyItem									O	
PartyRelationship									O	
Penalty	O	O	O	O	O	O	X	O	O	O
Person	O	O	X	X	O	X	X	O	X	X
PersonOperationsApproval				X						
PlannedItemUpgrade					X					
PlannedPartInstallationLocation					X					
PlannedUpgradeTimescales					X					
Pool	O	O	O	O	O	X	O	O	O	O
PositionReferencingItem			X					X		
Product	O	O	O	O	X	X	X	O	O	O
ProductParameterAtOperationalEvent				X		X		X		
ProductUsagePhase			X			X		X		
ProductVariant	X	X	X	X	X	X	X	O	O	O
ProductVariantMaintenance	X	X	X							

Class name	UC50401	UC50402	UC50403	UC50404	UC50405	UC50406	UC50407	UC50408	UC50409	UC50410
Project	O	O	O	O	O	X	O	O	O	O
ReferencedDigitalFile						X				
ReferencedDocument						X				
ReferencedPositionItem								O		
Remark	O	O	O	O	O	O	O	O	O	O
RemarkItem	O	O	O	O	O	O	O	O	O	O
Report	O	O	O		O	X		O	O	
ReportableActivity							X	O		
ReportableMetric	O	O	O	O	O	O	O	O	O	O
RequiredSafetyAction						X				
RequiredSafetyActionImplementation						X				
Requirement	O	O	X	O	X	X	O	O	O	O
ResourceSpecification						X				
ResourceUsageRequest							X	O		
RoleCapability				X		X				
S1000DDataModule						X				
S1000DDataModuleIssue						X				
S1000DPublicationModule						X				
S1000DPublicationModuleIssue						X				
SafetyDocument	O	O	O		O	X		O	O	
SafetyIssue					X	X				
SafetyIssueEvent						X				
SafetyItem						X				
SafetyRequirement						X				
SafetyRequirementsDocument						X				
SafetyWarning						X				
SCORMContentPackage	O	O	O		O	X		O	O	
SecurityClass	O	O	O	O	O	O	O	O	O	O
SecurityClassification	O	O	O	O	O	X	O	O	O	O
SecurityClassificationItem	O	O	O	O	O	O	O	O	O	O

Class name	UC50401	UC50402	UC50403	UC50404	UC50405	UC50406	UC50407	UC50408	UC50409	UC50410
SerializedHardwarePart	X	X	X	X	X	X	X	X	X	X
SerializedHardwarePart					X	X				
SerializedItem			X		X	X				
SerializedItemOwner			X							
SerializedPartDesignAssociation					X	X				
SerializedPartsListPosition					X					
SerializedProductOperationalPeriod				X		O				
SerializedProductVariant	X	X	X	X	X	X	X	X	O	O
SerializedProductVariantInFleet					X		X			
SerializedProductVariantOperatingBase					X	X	X			
SerializedProductVariantOperator					X		X			
SerializedProductVariantZone				X				X		
SerializedSupportEquipment				X					X	X
Service	O	O	O	O	X	X	X	O	O	O
ServiceBulletin	O	O	O	X	X	X	X	O	O	
ServiceRequest							X	O		
ShopFindings				X				X		
ShopFindingsDeterminedBy				X				X		
SoftwareElement					X					
SoftwareElementPartRealization					X	X				
SoftwarePartAsDesigned					X	X			X	
SoftwarePartAsReleased				X	X	X	X	O		
SpecialSafetyInstruction						X				
StreetAddress						X			O	
SubstanceContainingItem									X	
SubstanceDefinition						X				
SubstitutePartAsDesigned									X	
SuppliesUsed				X						X
SupplyItem				X						X
SupportEquipment				X					X	X

Class name	UC50401	UC50402	UC50403	UC50404	UC50405	UC50406	UC50407	UC50408	UC50409	UC50410
SupportEquipmentItem			X						X	X
SupportEquipmentUsed			X							X
Task	O	O	O	O	O	X	O	O	O	O
TaskRequirement	O	O	O	O	O	O	O	O	O	O
TaskRequirementRevision					X					
TaskRevision	X	X	X		X					X
TechnicalOrder	O	O	X		X					
TechnicalOrderEmbodied					X					
ThresholdDefinition						X				
TrackablePart			X		X					
UpgradeRequirement					X					
UsableOnProductVariant					X					
WarrantyClaim						X				
WarrantyClaimResolution							X	O		
WarrantyEvent			X			X		X		
WasteDisposalOperation							X	O		
WorkBreakdown	O	O	O	O	O	O	O	O	O	O
WorkItem	O	O	O	O	X	O	O	O	O	O
WorkOrder	O	O	X		X		X	O		X
ZoneElement			X					O		X
ZoneElementRevision			X			X		X		

2.3 Classes for safety analysis

The classes used for each safety analysis use case as defined in Chap 5 are listed in Table 4. The use cases are numbered:

1 UC50501: Report safety issue

2 UC50502: Provide operational limitations due to safety issue

3 UC50503: Provide special safety instructions

Table 4 Classes used for safety analysis use cases

Class name	UC50501	UC50502	UC50503
Action	X	X	X
ActualEnvironment	X		
AllocatedTaskLocation	O	X	X
AllowedProductConfiguration	X	X	X
AllowedProductConfigurationByConfigurationIdentifier	X	X	X
AllowedProductConfigurationHardwarePartAsDesigned	X	X	X
AllowedProductConfigurationItem	X	X	X
AllowedProductConfigurationRole	X	X	
AllowedProductOperationalConfigurationItem	X	X	
ApplicabilityStatement	O	X	X
AssociatedActualEnvironment	X		
AuthorityRequirement		X	X
AuthorityToOperate	X	X	X
Availability	X	X	
BatchHardwarePart	X	X	X
BreakdownElement	X	X	X
BreakdownElementInZone	X	X	X
BreakdownElementRevision		X	X
BreakdownElementRevisionRelationship	X	X	X
BreakdownElementUsageInBreakdown	X	X	X
BreakdownElementUsageRelationship	X	X	X
Budget	O	O	O
CargoItem	O	O	O
ChangeAuthorization	O	X	X
ChangeEmbodimentRequirement		X	X
ChangeRequest	X	X	X
CircuitBreaker	X	X	X
CircuitBreakerSetting	X	X	X
CircuitBreakerSettings	X	X	X

Class name	UC50501	UC50502	UC50503
ClassInstanceAssertItem	O	X	X
Comment	O	O	O
CommentAction	O	O	O
CommentItem	O	O	O
CommentParty	O	O	O
CommentRelationship	O	O	O
ConditionDefinitionItem	O	X	X
ConditionInstance	O	X	X
ConditionType	O	X	X
ConditionTypeAssertMember	O	X	X
Consequence	X		
Contract	O	X	X
CostEntry	X	X	O
CostItem	O	O	O
Damage	X		
DigitalFile	O	O	O
DisposalRequirement		X	X
Document	X	X	X
DocumentCharacteristicItem	O	O	O
DocumentIssue	O	O	O
DocumentItem	O	O	O
DocumentParty	O	O	O
DocumentReferencingItem	O	O	O
DownTimePeriod	X		
EffectiveOnProductConfiguration	X	X	X
EffectiveOnProductConfigurationItem	X	X	X
Environment	X	O	O
EnvironmentItem	X		
EvaluationByAssertionOfClassInstance	O	X	X
EvaluationByAssertionOfCondition	O	X	X

Class name	UC50501	UC50502	UC50503
EvaluationByAssertionOfSerializedItems	O	X	X
EvaluationByNestedApplicabilityStatement	O	X	X
EvaluationCriteria	O	X	X
Event	X	X	X
EventAffectedBreakdownElement	X		
EventExplanation	X		
EventItem	X		
EventRelationship	X		
EventRelationshipItem	X		
EventReporter	X		
ExplanatoryFactor	X		
ExportControlLicense	O	O	O
ExternalDocument	O	O	O
Facility	X	X	X
FacilityOperator	X	X	X
Fleet	X	X	X
FleetRequirement		X	X
FleetTaskCancellationNotice	O	O	O
GeographicalArea	O	X	X
HardwareElement	O		
HardwareElementPartRealization	X	X	X
HardwarePartAsDesigned	X	X	X
HardwarePartAsDesigned	X	X	X
IdentifiedTaskRequirement	O	X	X
Infrastructure	X	X	X
InfrastructureRevision	O	O	O
InstallationLocation	O		
InstallationLocationDefinitionItem	O		
InstalledPart	O		
InstalledPartItem	O		

Class name	UC50501	UC50502	UC50503
LocationItem	X		
Locator	O	O	O
LogBook	X		
LogBookEntry	X		
LogBookEntryMeasurementPoint	X		
LogicalAND	O	X	X
LogicalNOT	O	X	X
LogicalOR	O	X	X
LogicalXOR	O	X	X
MaintenanceEvent	X		
MaintenanceLevel	O	X	X
MaintenanceOrganization	X	X	X
MaintenancePerson	X	X	X
MaintenanceProgram	X	X	X
MaintenanceRequirement		X	X
MeasurementPoint	X	X	X
MeasurementPointItem	X	X	X
Message	O	O	O
Movement	X	O	O
MovementLeg	X	O	O
MovementLegDelay	X		
MovementLegPosition	X		
NestedAllowedProductConfiguration	X	X	X
NestedProductVariant	X	X	X
NonConformanceData	X	X	X
ObsolescenceRequirement		X	X
OperatingBase	X		
OperatingLocationType	O	X	X
OperationalApproval	X		
OperationalEvent	X	X	

Class name	UC50501	UC50502	UC50503
OperationalEventMessage	O		
OperationalEventOperator	O		
OperationalMode	X		
OperationalModeStatus	X		
OperationalMoment	X		
OperationalMomentItem	X		
OperationalPeriod	X		
OperationalPeriodOperator	X		
OperationalPeriodRelationship	X		
OperationalRequirement		X	X
OperationalRole	X	X	
Operator	X		
OperatorOrganization	X	X	X
OperatorPerson	X	X	X
Organization	X	X	X
OrganizationalBreakdownStructureRevision	O	O	O
PartAction	X	X	X
PartAsDesigned	X	X	X
PartAsDesignedPartsListEntry	X	X	X
PartAsDesignedPartsListRevision	X	X	X
PartOwner	X	X	X
Party	X	X	X
PartyAddress	X	X	X
PartyContactData	X	X	X
PartyItem	X	X	X
PartyRelationship	X	X	X
Penalty	O	O	O
Person	X	X	X
PoliciesAndRegulationsCompliantItem		X	X
Pool	X	O	O

Class name	UC50501	UC50502	UC50503
Product	X	X	X
ProductParameterAtOperationalEvent	O		
ProductUsagePhase	X		
ProductVariant	X	X	X
ProductVariant	X	X	X
Project	X	X	X
RealizedPart	O		
ReferencedDocument	X	X	X
Remark	O	O	O
RemarkItem	O	O	O
Report	X	X	O
ReportableActivity	X	X	
ReportableItem	X	X	
ReportableMetric	X	X	O
ReportContext	X	X	
ReportContextItem	X	X	
ReportingParty	X	X	
ReportParty	X	X	
RequiredSafetyAction	X	X	X
RequiredSafetyActionImplementation	X	X	X
Requirement	X	X	X
RequirementParty		X	X
RequirementRelationship		X	X
ResourceRealization	O	X	X
S1000DDataModule	O	O	O
S1000DDataModuleIssue	O	O	O
S1000DPublicationModule	O	O	O
S1000DPublicationModuleIssue	O	O	O
SafetyDocument	X	X	X
SafetyIssue	X	X	X

Class name	UC50501	UC50502	UC50503
SafetyIssueEvent	X	X	X
SafetyItem	X	X	X
SafetyRequirement	X	X	X
SafetyRequirementsDocument	X	X	X
SafetyWarning	X	X	X
SCORMContentPackage	O	O	O
SecurityClass	O	O	O
SecurityClassification	O	X	X
SecurityClassificationItem	O	O	O
SerializedAssertItem	O	X	X
SerializedHardwarePart	X	X	X
SerializedHardwarePart	X	X	X
SerializedItem	X	X	X
SerializedPartDesignAssociation	X	X	X
SerializedProductOperationalPeriod	X		
SerializedProductVariant	X	X	X
SerializedProductVariant	O	X	X
SerializedProductVariantConfigurationConformance	O		
SerializedProductVariantInFleet	X		
SerializedProductVariantOperatingBase	X		
SerializedProductVariantOperator	X		
Service	X	X	X
ServiceBulletin	O	O	O
SoftwareElement	O	X	X
SoftwareElementPartRealization	X	X	X
SoftwareElementRevision		X	X
SoftwarePartAsDesigned	X	X	X
SoftwarePartAsReleased	X	X	X
SpecialSafetyInstruction	X	X	X
StreetAddress	X	X	X

Class name	UC50501	UC50502	UC50503
SubjectOfPoliciesAndRegulations		X	X
SubtaskInZone	O	X	X
SubtaskTimeline	O	X	X
SubtaskWarningCautionNote	O	X	X
Task	O	O	O
TaskPersonnelResourceCompetence	O	X	X
TaskRequirement	O	O	O
TaskResource	O	X	X
TaskRevisionWarningCautionNote	O	X	X
TaskUsage	O	X	X
ThresholdDefinition	X	X	X
TransportRequirement		X	X
UpgradeRequirement		X	X
UsableOnItem	X	X	X
UsableOnProductVariant	X	X	X
WarrantyEvent	X		
WorkBreakdown	O	O	O
WorkItem	O	O	O
WorkOrder	X	X	

2.4 Classes for supply support

The classes used for each supply support use case as defined in Chap 6 are listed in Table 5. The use cases are numbered:

1. UC50601: Inventory management

2. UC50602: Shelf life management

3. UC50603: Spares and support equipment pool management

4. UC50604: Logistic response time

5. UC50605: Facilities management and maintenance

6. UC50606: Plan for transport

Table 5 Classes used for supply support use cases

Class name	UC50601	UC50602	UC50603	UC50604	UC50605	UC50606
Action	O	O	O	O	O	O
ActualEnvironment	O		X		X	
AlternatePartAsDesigned		X				
AnchoringPoint						X
AssociatedActualEnvironment	O		X		X	
Availability	X			X	X	
BatchHardwarePart	X	X	X	X		
BreakdownElement	O	O	O	O	O	O
Budget	O	O	O	O	O	O
Capability						X
CapabilityLimitation						X
CargoItem	O	O	O	O	O	X
ChangeRequest	O	O	O	O	O	O
CloudInfrastructure					X	
Comment	O	O	O	O	O	O
CommentAction	O	O	O	O	O	O
CommentItem	O	O	O	O	O	O
CommentParty	O	O	O	O	O	O
CommentRelationship	O	O	O	O	O	O
CommunicationsNetwork					X	
ComputerNetwork					X	
ContainerAsDesigned						X
Contract	X	X	X	X	X	
CostEntry	X	O	O	X	X	O
CostEntryItem	X			X		
CostItem	O	O	O	O	O	O
Detector	X					
DigitalFile	O	O	O	O	O	O
Document	X	O	O	X	X	O

Class name	UC50601	UC50602	UC50603	UC50604	UC50605	UC50606
DownTimePeriod						X
Environment	O	O	O	X	X	O
EnvironmentItem	O		X		X	
Event	O	O	O	X	X	O
ExportControlLicense	O	O	O	O	O	O
Facility	X	O	X	X	X	X
FacilityLocation	O		X		X	
FacilityOperator	O		X		X	
FacilityOperatorItem	O		X		X	
FacilityOwner	O		X		X	
FacilityRelationship	O		X		X	
Failure	X					
FailureMode	X					
FailureModeCause	X					
Fleet	O	O	O	X	X	X
HardwareElement					X	
HardwarePartAsDesigned	X	X	X	X	X	X
HardwarePartAsDesignedCommerceData	X	X	X	X		
HardwarePartAsDesignedDesignData		X				
HardwarePartContainer						X
Infrastructure	O	O	X	X	X	O
InfrastructureAvailable					X	
InfrastructureCompliance					X	
InfrastructureCompliantItem	O		X		X	
InfrastructureItem					X	
InfrastructureNode					X	
InfrastructureNodeAtLocation					X	
InfrastructureParty					X	
InfrastructureRelationship					X	
InfrastructureRequiringItem					X	

Class name	UC50601	UC50602	UC50603	UC50604	UC50605	UC50606
InfrastructureRevision	O	O	O	O	X	O
InventoryActivity	X			X		
LocalPosition						X
LocationItem	O		X		X	X
MaintenanceActivity	X			X		
MaintenanceFacility	O		X		X	
MeasurementPoint		X	X			
MeasurementPointItem		X	X			
Message	O	O	O	O	O	O
Movement	O	O	O	O	O	X
MovementLeg	O	O	O	O	O	X
MovementLegDelay						X
MovementLegPosition						X
MRONetwork					X	
OperatingBase	O		X		X	
OperationalActivity	X			X		
OperationalEvent	X			X	X	
OperationalMode						X
OperationalMomentItem						X
OperationalPeriod						X
OperationalPeriodOperator						X
OperationalPeriodRelationship						X
OperationalRole						X
Operator						X
Organization	X	O	X	X	X	O
OrganizationalBreakdownStructureRevision	O	O	O	O	O	O
OtherFacility	O		X		X	
ParkingFacility	O		X		X	
PartAsDesigned	O	X	X	O	O	O
PartAsDesignedPartsList		X				

Class name	UC50601	UC50602	UC50603	UC50604	UC50605	UC50606
PartAsDesignedPartsListEntry		X				
PartAsDesignedPartsListRelationship		X				
PartAsDesignedPartsListRevision		X				
PartInPool	X	X	X	X		
PartInWarehouse	X	X	X	X		
PartOwner		X	X			
Party	X	X	X	X	X	O
Penalty	O	O	O	O	O	O
Person	X	O	O	X	X	X
Pool	X	X	X	X	X	O
PoolItem	X	X	X	X		
PoolOwner	X	X	X	X		
PoolStockedInWareHouse	X	X	X	X		
PoolUser	X	X	X	X		
Port					X	
PositionReferencingItem						X
PowerGrid					X	
PriceBreakData	X	X	X	X		
Product	O	O	O	X	X	O
ProductVariant	X	X	X	X	X	X
ProductVariantSupportedByPool	X	X	X	X		
Project	O	O	O	X	X	O
Remark	O	O	O	O	O	O
RemarkItem	O	O	O	O	O	O
Report	X			X	X	
ReportableActivity	X			X	X	
ReportableItem	X			X	X	
ReportableMetric	X	O	O	X	X	O
ReportableMetricItem				X	X	
ReportContext	X			X	X	

Class name	UC50601	UC50602	UC50603	UC50604	UC50605	UC50606
ReportContextItem	X			X	X	
ReportingParty	X			X	X	
ReportParty	X			X	X	
RequiredPartStockLevelInPool	X	X	X	X		
Requirement	O	O	O	O	O	O
ResourceSpecification					X	
SecurityClass	O	O	O	O	O	O
SecurityClassification	O	O	O	O	O	O
SecurityClassificationItem	O	O	O	O	O	O
SerializedHardwarePart	X	X	X	X	X	X
SerializedItem		X	X			
SerializedPartDesignAssociation		X	X			
SerializedProductOperationalPeriod						X
SerializedProductVariant	O	O	O	X	X	X
Service	O	O	O	X	X	O
ServiceLevelAgreementClause				X	X	
ShopFindings	X					
ShopFindingsDeterminedBy	X					
SoftwareElement					X	
SoftwarePartAsDesigned	X	X	X	X	X	
SoftwarePartAsReleased	X	X	X	X	X	
StoredPart	X	X	X	X		
SubstanceContainingItem		X				
SubstitutePartAsDesigned		X				
SupportEquipment	O		X		X	
Task	O	O	O	O	O	O
TaskRequirement	O	O	O	O	O	O
TransportableItem						X
TransportCapability						X
TransportCapabilityUsage						X

Class name	UC50601	UC50602	UC50603	UC50604	UC50605	UC50606
TransportFeatures						X
TransportingAsset						X
TransportNetwork					X	X
TransportPosition						X
TransportRequirement						X
TypeOfPerson						X
Warehouse	X	X	X	X	X	
WorkBreakdown	O	O	O	O	O	O
WorkItem	X	O	O	X	O	O
WorkOrder	X			X	X	
ZoneElementRevision						X

2.5 Classes for life cycle cost analysis

The classes used for each LCC use case as defined in Chap 7 are listed in Table 6. The use cases are numbered:

1 UC50701: Provide cost breakdown structure

2 UC50702: Estimate maintenance costs

3 UC50703: Costs due to operational requirements

4 UC50704: Cost of modifications or upgrades

5 UC50705: Costs of in-service support

Table 6 Classes used for LCC use cases

Class name	UC50701	UC50702	UC50703	UC50704	UC50705
Action	O	O	O	X	O
AlternatePartAsDesigned				O	
AuthorityRequirement			X		
Availability		X	X	X	X
BatchHardwarePart					X
BreakdownElement	X	X	X	X	X
BreakdownElementRevision				O	

Class name	UC50701	UC50702	UC50703	UC50704	UC50705
BreakdownElementUsageInBreakdown				O	
BreakdownRevision				O	
Budget	X	X	X	X	X
Capability					X
CargoItem	O	O	X	O	O
ChangeAuthorization				O	
ChangeControlledItem				O	
ChangedItemAvailabilityRequirement				O	
ChangeEmbodimentRequirement	X	X	X	X	X
ChangeNotification				O	
ChangeRequest	X	X	X	X	X
ChangeRequestCause				X	
ChangeRequestItem				X	
ChangeRequestReasonItem				X	
Comment	O	O	O	O	O
CommentAction	O	O	O	O	O
CommentItem	O	O	O	O	O
CommentParty	O	O	O	O	O
CommentRelationship	O	O	O	O	O
ConsumableItem			X		
Consumption			X		
ConsumptionPeriod			X		
Contract	X	X	X	X	X
ContractClause	X	X	X	X	X
ContractClauseRelationship			X	X	
ContractItem	O			O	X
ContractItemDetails	O			O	X
ContractParty	O			O	X
ContractRelationship	O		X	X	X
CostBreakdown	X	X	X	X	X

Class name	UC50701	UC50702	UC50703	UC50704	UC50705
CostBreakdownContext	X	X	X	X	X
CostBreakdownRelationship	X	X	X	X	X
CostBreakdownRevision	X	X	X	X	X
CostEntry	X	X	X	X	X
CostEntryItem	X	X	X	X	X
CostItem	X	X	X	X	X
CostItemRelationship	X	X	X	X	X
Damage	X	X	X	X	X
DigitalFile	O	O	O	O	O
DisposalRequirement	X	X	X	X	X
Document	O	X	X	X	X
DocumentCharacteristicItem				X	
DocumentIssue				X	
DocumentItem				O	X
DocumentParty				X	
DocumentReferencingItem				O	
DownTimePeriod			X		
EffectiveOnProductConfiguration				O	
Environment	O	X	X	X	X
Event	O	X	X	X	X
ExportControlLicense	O	O	O	O	O
ExternalDocument				X	
Facility	X	X	X	X	X
Fleet	X	X	X	X	X
FleetManager			X		
FleetPlanning			X		
FleetRequirement			X		
FleetTask			X		
FleetTaskCancellationNotice				X	
FleetTaskCargo			X		

Class name	UC50701	UC50702	UC50703	UC50704	UC50705
FleetTaskList			X		
HardwareElement				X	
HardwareElementPartRealization				O	
HardwarePartAsDesigned	X	X	X	X	X
Infrastructure	X	X	X	X	X
InfrastructureRevision	O	O	O	X	O
InstalledPart				O	
InventoryActivity		X	X	X	X
ItemDisposalOperation	X	X	X	X	X
LaborRateItem				X	X
LaborRates				X	X
LegalParty	O			O	X
LocationItem				X		X
Locator				X	
MaintenanceActivity		X	X	X	X
MaintenanceProgram				X	
MaintenanceRequirement			X		
MaintenanceWorkOrderSource				X	
Material	X	X	X	X	X
MeasurementPoint			X		
MeasurementPointItem			X		
Message	O	O	O	O	O
Movement	X	X	X	X	X
MovementLeg	X	X	X	X	X
MovementLegDelay			X		
MovementLegPosition			X		
ObsolescenceRequirement			X		
OperationalActivity		X	X	X	X
OperationalEvent		X	X	X	X
OperationalMode			X		

Class name	UC50701	UC50702	UC50703	UC50704	UC50705
OperationalPeriod			X	X	
OperationalPeriodOperator			X		
OperationalPeriodRelationship			X		
OperationalRequirement			X		
OperationalRequirementsPlanning			X		
OperationalRole			X		
OperationalTime			X		
OperationalTimeItem			X		
Operator			X		
Organization	X	X	X	X	X
Organization	O			O	X
OrganizationalBreakdownStructureRevision	O	O	O	O	O
PartAsDesigned	X	X	X	X	X
PartAsDesignedPartsListEntry				O	
PartAsDesignedPartsListRevision				O	
Party	X	X	X	X	X
Penalty	X	X	X	X	X
PerformanceParameter					X
PerformanceParameterItem					X
PerformanceParameterRevision					X
Person	X	X	X	X	X
PlannedItemUpgrade				O	
PlannedUpgradeTimescales				O	
PoliciesAndRegulationsCompliantItem			X		
Pool	O	X	X	X	X
Product	X	X	X	X	X
ProductVariant	X	X	X	X	X
Project	X	X	X	X	X
ProjectContract	O			O	X
ProjectRelationship	O			O	X

Class name	UC50701	UC50702	UC50703	UC50704	UC50705
ReferencedDocument				O	
Remark	O	O	O	O	O
RemarkItem	O	O	O	O	O
Report		X	X	X	X
ReportableActivity	X	X	X	X	X
ReportableItem		X	X	X	X
ReportableMetric	O	X	X	X	X
ReportContext		X	X	X	X
ReportContextItem		X	X	X	X
ReportingParty		X	X	X	X
ReportParty		X	X	X	X
RequiredFleetRole			X		
Requirement	O	O	X	O	X
RequirementParty			X		
RequirementRelationship			X		
ResourceUsageRequest	X	X	X	X	X
S1000DDataModule				O	
S1000DDataModuleIssue				O	
S1000DPublicationModule				O	
S1000DPublicationModuleIssue				O	
SafetyDocument				X	
SafetyIssue				X	
SafetyRequirement			X		
SCORMContentPackage				X	
SecurityClass	O	O	O	O	O
SecurityClassification	O	O	O	O	O
SecurityClassificationItem	O	O	O	O	O
SerializedHardwarePart	X	X	X	X	X
SerializedPartsListPosition				O	
SerializedProductOperationalPeriod			X		

Class name	UC50701	UC50702	UC50703	UC50704	UC50705
SerializedProductVariant	X	X	X	X	X
SerializedProductVariantAssignment			X		
SerializedProductVariantInFleet			X		
Service	X	X	X	X	X
ServiceBulletin	X	X	X	X	X
ServiceContract					X
ServiceItem					X
ServiceLevelAgreementClause			X	X	X
ServiceRelationship					X
ServiceRequest	X	X	X	X	X
ServiceRequestCancellation					X
ServiceRequestItem					X
ServiceRequestLocation					X
ServiceRequestParty					X
ServiceRequestRelationship					X
SoftwareElement				X	
SoftwareElementPartRealization				O	
SoftwarePartAsDesigned	O	X	X	X	X
SoftwarePartAsReleased	X	X	X	X	X
SubjectOfPoliciesAndRegulations			X		
Task	O	O	O	O	O
TaskRequirement	O	O	O	O	O
TaskRequirementRevision				O	
TaskRevision				O	
TechnicalOrder				X	
TechnicalOrderEmbodied				X	
TransportRequirement			X		
UpgradeRequirement			X	O	
UsableOnProductVariant				O	
WarrantyClaimResolution	X	X	X	X	X

Class name	UC50701	UC50702	UC50703	UC50704	UC50705
WasteDisposalOperation	X	X	X	X	X
WorkBreakdown	O	O	O	O	O
WorkBreakdownContext			X	X	
WorkItem	O	X	X	X	X
WorkOrder	X	X	X	X	X

2.6 Classes for warranty analysis

The classes used for each warranty analyis use case as defined in <u>Chap 8</u> are listed in <u>Table 7</u>. The use cases are numbered:

1. UC50801: Evaluate maintenance actions

2. UC50802: Collect warranty costs

3. UC50803: Determine misuse of warranty

4. UC50804: Identify items causing risk to warranty program

5. UC50805: Improve standard warranty rules and process

Table 7 Classes used for warranty analysis use cases

Class name	UC50801	UC50802	UC50803	UC50804	UC50805
Action	X	X	X	X	X
ActualEnvironment	X		X	X	X
AllowedProductConfiguration	X			X	X
AllowedProductConfigurationByConfigurationIdentifier	X			X	X
AllowedProductConfigurationHardwarePartAsDesigned	X			X	X
AllowedProductConfigurationItem	X	O	O	X	X
AssociatedActualEnvironment	X		X	X	X
AuthorityRequirement	X				
AuthorityToOperate	X			X	X
Availability		X	X		
BatchHardwarePart	O	O	X	X	X
BreakdownElement	O	O	O	X	O
BreakdownElementRevision	O				

Class name	UC50801	UC50802	UC50803	UC50804	UC50805
BreakdownElementUsageInBreakdown	X	O	O	X	X
Budget	O	O	O	O	O
Calibration				X	X
CalibrationDocument				X	X
CalibrationMeasurement				X	X
CargoItem	O	O	O	O	O
ChangeEmbodimentRequirement		X			
ChangeRequest	O	X	O	O	O
ChangeRequestItem					X
Comment	O	O	O	O	O
CommentAction	O	O	O	O	O
CommentItem	O	O	O	O	O
CommentParty	O	O	O	O	O
CommentRelationship	O	O	O	O	O
Consequence				X	
Contract	X	X	X	X	X
ContractClause	X	X	X	X	X
ContractClauseRelationship		X	X		O
ContractItem		O	X		O
ContractItemDetails		O	X		O
ContractParty		O	X		O
ContractRelationship		X	X		O
CostBreakdown		O			
CostBreakdownContext		X	X		O
CostBreakdownRelationship		O			
CostBreakdownRevision		O			
CostEntry	O	X	X	O	O
CostEntryItem		X	X		
CostItem	O	O	O	O	O
CostItemRelationship		O			

Class name	UC50801	UC50802	UC50803	UC50804	UC50805
Damage	X	X	X	X	X
DamageAnalysis	X	X	X	X	X
DamageAnalysisRevision	X	X	X	X	X
DamageCharacteristic	X	X	X	X	X
DamageDefinition	X	X	X	X	X
DamagedItem	X	X	X	X	X
DetectionMean	O				
DetectionMeanCapability	O				
DetectionMechanism	O				
Detector	X		X	X	X
DigitalFile	O	O	O	O	O
Document	X	X	X	O	O
DocumentIssue	X				
DocumentItem				X	X
DownTimePeriod				X	
EffectiveOnProductConfiguration	X			X	X
EffectiveOnProductConfigurationItem	X			X	X
Environment	O	X	O	O	O
EnvironmentItem	X		X	X	X
EnvironmentRevision				X	X
EquipmentOperation	X	X		X	X
EquipmentOwner	X	X		X	X
EquipmentStatus	X	X		X	X
Event	X	X	X	X	X
EventAffectedBreakdownElement				X	
EventExplanation				X	
EventItem				X	
EventRelationship				X	
EventRelationshipItem				X	
EventReporter				X	

Class name	UC50801	UC50802	UC50803	UC50804	UC50805
ExplanatoryFactor				X	
ExportControlLicense	O	O	O	O	O
Facility	X	X	X	X	X
Failure	X		X	X	X
FailureDetection	O				
FailureMode	X		X	X	X
FailureModeCause	X		X	X	X
FailureModeEffect	O				
Fault	O				
FaultCause	O				
Fleet	O	X	X	X	X
HardwareElement		O	O	O	X
HardwareElementPartRealization	X			X	X
HardwarePartAsDesigned	X	X	X	X	X
HardwarePartAsDesignedCommerceData				X	
Infrastructure	X	X	X	X	X
InfrastructureRevision	O	O	O	O	O
InstallationLocation	X	X	O	X	X
InstallationLocationDefinitionItem	X	X	O	X	X
InstalledPart		O	O	O	X
InstalledPartItem		O	O	O	X
InventoryActivity		X	X		
ItemDamage	X	X	X	X	X
ItemDisposalOperation		X			
ItemWarranty	X	X	X	X	X
LaborRateItem		X	X		O
LaborRates		X	X		O
LegalParty		O	X		O
LocalPosition	X	X	X	X	X

Class name	UC50801	UC50802	UC50803	UC50804	UC50805
LogBook	X	X		X	X
LogBookEntry	X	X	X	X	X
MaintenanceActivity	X	X	X		
MaintenanceActivityDocument	X				
MaintenanceActivityParty	X				
MaintenanceActivityPlan	X				
MaintenanceActivityRecord	X				
MaintenanceEvent	X			X	
MaintenanceFacility	X				
MaintenanceItem	X				
MaintenancePerson	X				
MaintenanceProgram	X				
MaintenanceProgramItem	X				
MaintenanceProgramRevision	X				
MaintenanceWorkOrderSource	X				X
Material		X			
MeasurementPoint	O	O	X	X	X
MeasurementPointItem	O	O	X	X	X
Message	O	O	O	O	O
Movement	O	X	O	O	O
MovementLeg	O	X	O	O	O
NestedAllowedProductConfiguration	X			X	X
NestedProductVariant	X			X	X
NonConformanceData	X			X	X
OperatingBase			X	X	X
OperationalActivity		X	X		
OperationalApproval			X	X	X
OperationalEvent	X	X	X	X	
OperationalEventMessage	X		X		
OperationalEventOperator	X		X		

Class name	UC50801	UC50802	UC50803	UC50804	UC50805
OperationalModeStatus	X		X		
OperationalTime			X		
OperationalTimeItem			X		
Operator	X		X		
Organization	X	X	X	X	X
Organization		O	X		O
OrganizationalBreakdownStructureRevision	O	O	O	O	O
PartAction	X	X		X	X
PartAsDesigned	O	O	X	X	X
PartAsDesignedPartsListEntry	X			X	X
PartAsDesignedPartsListRevision	X			X	X
PartInPool				X	
PartInWarehouse				X	
PartOwner	O		X	X	X
Party	X	X	X	X	X
Penalty	O	X	O	O	O
Person	O	X	X	X	X
Pool	O	X	O	X	O
PoolItem				X	
PoolOwner				X	
PoolStockedInWareHouse				X	
PoolUser				X	
PositionReferencingItem	X	X	X	X	X
PriceBreakData				X	
Product	O	X	X	O	O
ProductParameterAtOperationalEvent	X		X		
ProductUsagePhase				X	
ProductVariant	X	X	X	X	
ProductVariant	X	O	X	X	X
ProductVariantSupportedByPool				X	

Class name	UC50801	UC50802	UC50803	UC50804	UC50805
Project	O	X	X	O	O
ProjectContract		O	X		O
ProjectRelationship		O	X		O
RealizedPart		O	O	O	X
Remark	O	O	O	O	O
RemarkItem	O	O	O	O	O
Report		X	X		
ReportableActivity		X	X		
ReportableItem		X	X		
ReportableMetric	O	X	X	O	O
ReportableMetricItem		O	O		
ReportContext		X	X		
ReportContextItem		X	X		
ReportingParty		X	X		
ReportParty		X	X		
RequiredPartStockLevelInPool				X	
Requirement	O	O	O	O	O
ResourceUsageRequest		X			
SecurityClass	O	O	O	O	O
SecurityClassification	O	O	O	O	O
SecurityClassificationItem	O	O	O	O	O
SerializedHardwarePart	X	X	X	X	X
SerializedHardwarePart	O	O	X	X	X
SerializedItem	X	X	X	X	X
SerializedPartDesignAssociation	O		X	X	X
SerializedProductVariant	X	X	X	X	X
SerializedProductVariant	X	X	O	X	X
SerializedProductVariantConfigurationConformance		O	O	O	X
SerializedProductVariantInFleet			X	X	X

Class name	UC50801	UC50802	UC50803	UC50804	UC50805
SerializedProductVariantOperatingBase			X	X	X
SerializedProductVariantOperator			X	X	X
SerializedProductVariantZone	X	X	X	X	X
Service	X	X	X	X	X
ServiceBulletin	X	X	X	X	X
ServiceLevelAgreementClause		X	X		O
ServiceRequest		X			
ShopFindings	X		X	X	X
ShopFindingsDeterminedBy	X		X	X	X
SoftwareElement		O	O	O	X
SoftwareElementPartRealization	X			X	X
SoftwarePartAsDesigned	O	X	X	X	X
SoftwarePartAsReleased	X	X	X	X	X
SoftwarePartAsReleased		O	O	O	X
StoredPart				X	
SuppliesUsed	X				
SupplyItem	X				
SupportEquipmentItem	X			X	X
SupportEquipmentUsed	X				
Task	O	O	O	O	O
TaskRequirement	O	O	O	O	O
TaskRevision	X				
TechnicalOrder					X
TechnicalOrderEmbodied					X
TrackablePart	X	X		X	X
UsableOnItem	X			X	X
UsableOnProductVariant	X			X	X
Warehouse				X	
WarrantyClaim	X	X	X	X	X
WarrantyClaimContact	X	X	X	X	X

Class name	UC50801	UC50802	UC50803	UC50804	UC50805
WarrantyClaimEvents	X	X	X	X	X
WarrantyClaimFollowUp	X	X	X	X	X
WarrantyClaimResolution	X	X	X	X	X
WarrantyEvent	X	X	X	X	X
WarrantyItem	X	X	X	X	X
WasteDisposalOperation		X			
WorkBreakdown	O	O	O	O	O
WorkBreakdownContext		X	X		O
WorkItem	O	X	X	O	O
WorkOrder	X	X	X		X
ZoneElement		X			
ZoneElementRevision	X	X	X	X	X

2.7 Classes for product health and usage monitoring

The classes used for each poduct health and usage monitoring use case as defined in <u>Chap 9</u> are listed in <u>Table 8</u>. The use cases are numbered:

1 UC50901: Record usage and health data

2 UC50902: Report usage information

3 UC50903: Respond to usage information

Table 8 Classes used for product health and usage monitoring use cases

Class name	UC50901	UC50902	UC50903
Accelerometer	X	X	X
Action	O	O	O
AllowedProductConfiguration			X
AllowedProductConfigurationRole			X
AllowedProductOperationalConfigurationItem			X
BatchHardwarePart	X	X	
BreakdownElement	O	O	O
BreakdownElementUsageInBreakdown			X

Class name	UC50901	UC50902	UC50903
Budget	O	O	O
CargoItem	X	X	X
ChangeRequest	X	X	O
CircuitBreaker	X	X	
Comment	O	O	O
CommentAction	O	O	O
CommentItem	O	O	O
CommentParty	O	O	O
CommentRelationship	O	O	O
Contract	X	X	O
CostEntry	O	O	O
CostItem	O	O	O
Country	X	X	
DigitalFile	X	X	O
DigitalFileReference	X	X	
DigitalFileReferencedItem	X	X	
DigitalFileReferencingItem	X	X	
Document	X	X	O
DocumentIssue	X	X	
DownTimePeriod	X	X	X
Environment	X	X	O
Event	X	X	X
ExportControlLicense	O	O	O
Facility	X	X	O
Fleet	X	X	X
FleetManager			X
FleetPlanning			X
FleetRequirement			X
FleetTask			X
FleetTaskCargo			X

Class name	UC50901	UC50902	UC50903
FleetTaskList			X
GeographicalArea	X	X	
GlobalPosition	X	X	
HardwarePartAsDesigned	X	X	X
Infrastructure	X	X	O
InfrastructureRevision	O	O	O
InstallationLocation	X	X	
LocationItem	X	X	
Locator	X	X	
LogBook	X	X	X
LogBookEntry	X	X	X
LogBookEntryMeasurementPoint	X	X	X
MaintenanceLevel			X
MeasurementPoint	X	X	X
Message	O	O	O
Movement	X	X	O
MovementLeg	X	X	O
MovementLegDelay	X	X	
MovementLegPosition	X	X	
OperatingLocationType			X
OperationalMode	X	X	
OperationalModeStatus	X	X	X
OperationalMoment	X	X	X
OperationalMomentItem	X	X	X
OperationalPeriod	X	X	
OperationalPeriodOperator	X	X	
OperationalPeriodRelationship	X	X	
OperationalRequirement			X
OperationalRequirementsPlanning			X
OperationalRole	X	X	X

Class name	UC50901	UC50902	UC50903
Operator	X	X	
Organization	X	X	O
OrganizationalBreakdownStructureRevision	O	O	O
PartAction	X	X	X
PartAsDesigned	X	X	O
Party	O	O	O
Penalty	O	O	O
Person	O	O	O
Pool	X	X	O
PressureSensor	X	X	X
Product	X	X	O
ProductUsagePhase		X	X
ProductUsagePhaseHierarchicalRelationship		X	X
ProductUsagePhaseItem		X	X
ProductUsagePhaseRelationship		X	X
ProductUsagePhaseSequentialRelationship		X	X
ProductVariant	X	X	X
Project	O	O	O
ReferencedDigitalFile	X	X	
Remark	O	O	O
RemarkItem	O	O	O
Report			X
ReportableMetric	O	O	O
RequiredFleetRole			X
Requirement	O	O	O
ResourceSpecification	X	X	
SecurityClass	O	O	O
SecurityClassification	X	X	O
SecurityClassificationItem	O	O	O
Sensor	X	X	X

Class name	UC50901	UC50902	UC50903
SensorSample	X	X	X
SensorType	X	X	X
SerializedHardwarePart	X	X	O
SerializedItem	X	X	X
SerializedProductOperationalPeriod	X	X	
SerializedProductVariant	X	X	X
SerializedProductVariant	X	X	
SerializedProductVariantAssignment			X
SerializedProductVariantInFleet			X
Service	X	X	O
SoftwarePartAsReleased			X

2.8 Classes for obsolescence management

The classes used for each obsolescence management use case as defined in Chap 10 are listed in Table 9. The use cases are numbered:

1. UC51001: Create basis for obsolescence management planning

2. UC51002: Determine obsolescence candidates /perform risk assessment

3. UC51003: Determine obsolescence strategy

4. UC51004: Obsolescence monitoring

5. UC51005: Solutions /proposals to solve obsolescence

6. UC51006: Provide obsolescence alert

Table 9 Classes used for obsolescence management use cases

Class name	UC51001	UC51002	UC51003	UC51004	UC51005	UC51006
Action	O	O	O	O	O	O
AllowedProductConfiguration	X					
AllowedProductConfigurationByConfigurationIdentifier	X					
AllowedProductConfigurationHardwarePartAsDesigned	X					
AllowedProductConfigurationItem	X	X				
AuthorityRequirement		X	X			X

Class name	UC51001	UC51002	UC51003	UC51004	UC51005	UC51006
AuthorityToOperate	X					
Availability				X		X
BatchHardwarePart	X	X	X	X		O
BreakdownElement	X	O	O	O	O	O
BreakdownElementRevision	X					
BreakdownElementUsageInBreakdown	X	X				
Budget	O	O	O	O	O	O
CargoItem	O	O	X	O	O	O
ChangeAuthorization					X	
ChangeControlledItem		X	X		X	X
ChangedItemAvailabilityRequirement					X	
ChangeEmbodimentRequirement		X	X		X	X
ChangeNotification					X	
ChangeRequest	O	O	O	O	O	O
ChangeRequestItem				X		X
Comment	O	O	O	O	O	O
CommentAction	O	O	O	O	O	O
CommentItem	O	O	O	O	O	O
CommentParty	O	O	O	O	O	O
CommentRelationship	O	O	O	O	O	O
Contract	O	X	X	X	O	X
ContractClause						O
ContractClauseRelationship						O
ContractRelationship						O
CostBreakdownContext						O
CostEntry	O	O	O	X	O	X
CostEntryItem				X		X
CostItem	O	O	O	O	O	O
Detector				X		O
DigitalFile	O	O	O	O	O	O

Class name	UC51001	UC51002	UC51003	UC51004	UC51005	UC51006
DisposalRequirement		X	X			X
Document	O	X	X	X	O	X
DocumentCharacteristicItem		O				O
DocumentIssue		O				O
DocumentItem		O				
DocumentParty		O				O
DocumentReferencingItem		O				
DownTimePeriod		X	X		X	
EffectiveOnProductConfiguration	X					
EffectiveOnProductConfigurationItem	X					
Environment	O	O	O	O	O	O
EquipmentOperation			X			
EquipmentOwner			X			
EquipmentStatus			X			
Event	O	X	X	X	O	O
ExportControlLicense	O	O	O	O	O	O
ExternalDocument		O				O
Facility	O	X	O	X	O	X
Failure				X		O
FailureMode				X		O
FailureModeCause				X		O
Fleet	O	O	X	O	O	O
FleetManager			X			
FleetPlanning			X			
FleetRequirement		X	X			X
FleetTask			X			
FleetTaskCancellationNotice		O				O
FleetTaskCargo			X			
FleetTaskList			X			
HardwareElement	X	X				

Class name	UC51001	UC51002	UC51003	UC51004	UC51005	UC51006
HardwareElementPartRealization	X					
HardwarePartAsDesigned	X	X	X	X		X
HardwarePartAsDesignedCommerceData		X	X	X		O
Infrastructure	O	X	O	O	O	X
InfrastructureRevision	O	O	O	O	O	O
InstallationLocation	X	X	X			
InstallationLocationDefinitionItem	X	X	X			
InstalledPart	X	X				
InstalledPartItem	X	X				
InventoryActivity				X		X
LaborRateItem						O
LaborRates						O
LocationItem		X				
Locator		O				O
LogBook		X	X	X		
LogBookEntry		X	X	X		
LogBookEntryMeasurementPoint		X	X	X		
MaintenanceActivity		X		X		X
MaintenanceActivityDocument		X				
MaintenanceActivityParty		X				
MaintenanceActivityPlan		X				
MaintenanceActivityRecord		X				
MaintenanceEvent		X				
MaintenanceFacility		X				
MaintenanceItem		X				
MaintenanceLevel	X					
MaintenancePerson		X				
MaintenanceProgram		O				O
MaintenanceRequirement		X	X			X
MaintenanceWorkOrderSource		X		X		X

Class name	UC51001	UC51002	UC51003	UC51004	UC51005	UC51006
MeasurementPoint	X	X				O
MeasurementPointItem	X	X				O
Message	O	O	O	O	O	O
Movement	O	X	O	O	O	O
MovementLeg	O	X	O	O	O	O
MovementLegDelay		X				
MovementLegPosition		X				
NestedAllowedProductConfiguration	X					
NestedProductVariant	X					
NonConformanceData	X					
ObsolescenceItem		X				X
ObsolescenceParameter		X				X
ObsolescenceRequirement		X	X			X
OperatingBase				X	X	
OperatingLocationType	X					
OperationalActivity				X		X
OperationalEvent				X		X
OperationalMode		X				
OperationalModeStatus		X	X	X		
OperationalMoment		X	X	X		
OperationalMomentItem		X	X	X		
OperationalPeriod		X				
OperationalPeriodOperator		X				
OperationalPeriodRelationship		X				
OperationalRequirement		X	X			X
OperationalRequirementsPlanning			X			
OperationalRole		X	X			
Operator		X				
Organization	O	O	O	X	O	X
OrganizationalBreakdownStructureRevision	O	O	O	O	O	O

Class name	UC51001	UC51002	UC51003	UC51004	UC51005	UC51006
PartAction		X	X	X	X	
PartAsDesigned	X	X	O	O	O	O
PartAsDesignedPartsListEntry	X					
PartAsDesignedPartsListRevision	X					
PartInPool		X	X	X		O
PartInWarehouse		X	X	X		O
PartOwner	X					O
Party	X	X	X	X	O	X
Penalty	O	O	O	O	O	O
Person	O	O	O	X	O	X
PlannedItemUpgrade					X	
PlannedPartInstallationLocation			X		X	
PlannedUpgradeTimescales			X		X	
PoliciesAndRegulationsCompliantItem		X	X			X
Pool	O	X	X	X	O	O
PoolItem		X	X	X		O
PoolOwner		X	X	X		O
PoolStockedInWareHouse		X	X	X		O
PoolUser		X	X	X		O
PriceBreakData		X	X	X		O
Product	O	X	O	O	O	X
ProductVariant	X	X	X	X	O	X
ProductVariantSupportedByPool		X	X	X		O
Project	O	O	O	O	O	O
RealizedPart	X	X				
ReferencedDocument		O				
Remark	O	O	O	O	O	O
RemarkItem	O	O	O	O	O	O
Report		O	X	X		X
ReportableActivity				X		X

Class name	UC51001	UC51002	UC51003	UC51004	UC51005	UC51006
ReportableItem				X		X
ReportableMetric	O	O	O	X	O	X
ReportableMetricItem						X
ReportContext				X		X
ReportContextItem				X		X
ReportingParty				X		X
ReportParty				X		X
RequiredFleetRole			X			
RequiredPartStockLevelInPool		X	X	X		O
Requirement	O	X	X	O	O	X
RequirementParty		X	X			X
RequirementRelationship		X	X			X
S1000DDataModule		O				
S1000DDataModuleIssue		O				
S1000DPublicationModule		O				
S1000DPublicationModuleIssue		O				
SafetyDocument		O				O
SafetyRequirement		X	X			X
SCORMContentPackage		O				O
SecurityClass	O	O	O	O	O	O
SecurityClassification	O	O	O	O	O	O
SecurityClassificationItem	O	O	O	O	O	O
SerializedHardwarePart	X	X	X	X	X	X
SerializedItem	X	X	X	X		O
SerializedPartDesignAssociation	X					O
SerializedProductOperationalPeriod		X				
SerializedProductVariant	X	X	X	O	X	X
SerializedProductVariantAssignment			X			
SerializedProductVariantConfigurationConformance	X	X				
SerializedProductVariantInFleet			X			

Class name	UC51001	UC51002	UC51003	UC51004	UC51005	UC51006
SerializedProductVariantOperatingBase			X		X	
Service	O	O	O	O	O	O
ServiceBulletin		O		X		X
ServiceLevelAgreementClause						X
ShopFindings				X		O
ShopFindingsDeterminedBy				X		O
SoftwareElement	X	X				
SoftwareElementPartRealization	X					
SoftwareElementRevision	X					
SoftwarePartAsDesigned	X			X		X
SoftwarePartAsReleased	X	X	X	X	X	X
StoredPart		X	X	X		O
SubjectOfPoliciesAndRegulations		X	X			X
SuppliesUsed		X				
SupplyItem		X				
SupportEquipmentItem		X				
SupportEquipmentUsed		X				
Task	O	O	O	O	O	O
TaskRequirement	O	O	O	O	O	O
TaskRevision		X				
TechnicalOrder				X		X
TechnicalOrderEmbodied				X		X
TrackablePart			X		X	
TransportRequirement		X	X			X
UpgradeRequirement		X	X		X	X
UsableOnItem	X					
UsableOnProductVariant	X					
Warehouse		X	X	X		O
WorkBreakdown	O	O	O	O	O	O

Class name	UC51001	UC51002	UC51003	UC51004	UC51005	UC51006
WorkBreakdownContext						O
WorkItem	O	O	O	X	O	X
WorkOrder		X		X		X
ZoneElement		X				

2.9 Classes for integrated fleet management

The classes used for each integrated fleet management use case as defined in <u>Chap 11</u> are listed in <u>Table 10</u>. The use cases are numbered:

1. UC51101: Assignment proposal elaboration
2. UC51102: Fleet task cancellation
3. UC51103: Fleet task modification
4. UC51104: Fleet availability plan elaboration
5. UC51105: Fleet task evaluation
6. UC51106: Product preparation for fleet task
7. UC51107: Product recovery after fleet task

Table 10 Classes used for integrated fleet management use cases

Class name	UC51101	UC51102	UC51103	UC51104	UC51105	UC51106	UC51107	UC51108
Action	O	O	O	O	O	O	O	O
ActualEnvironment	X		X	X	X	X	X	
AllowedProductConfiguration	X					X	X	
AllowedProductConfigurationItem						X	X	
AllowedProductConfigurationPhysicalData	X					X	X	
AllowedProductConfigurationRole	X					X	X	
AllowedProductOperationalConfigurationItem	X							
AllowedRoleChange	X					X	X	
AssociatedActualEnvironment	X		X	X	X	X	X	
Availability				X	X			X
AvailabilityItem				X	X			X
BatchHardwarePart					O	X	X	

Class name	UC51101	UC51102	UC51103	UC51104	UC51105	UC51106	UC51107	UC51108
BreakdownElement	O	O	O	O	O	O	O	O
BreakdownElementUsageInBreakdown	X					X	X	
Budget	O	O	O	O	O	O	O	O
Capability	X				X	X	X	
CapabilityItem	X					X	X	
CargoItem	X	X	X	X	X	X	X	O
ChangeRequest	O	O	O	O	O	O	O	O
CloudInfrastructure	O			X				
Comment	O	O	O	O	O	O	O	O
CommentAction	O	O	O	O	O	O	O	O
CommentItem	O	O	O	O	O	O	O	O
CommentParty	O	O	O	O	O	O	O	O
CommentRelationship	O	O	O	O	O	O	O	O
CommunicationsNetwork	O			X				
CompliesWith				X				
ComputerNetwork	O			X				
ConsumableItem	X				X		X	
Consumption	X				X		X	
ConsumptionPeriod	X				X		X	
Contract	X	O	O	X	X	O	O	X
ContractClause	X				X			
CostEntry	O	O	O	O	O	O	O	O
CostItem	O	O	O	O	O	O	O	O
Country	X							
DataSetAsReleased				X				
DigitalFile	O	O	O	O	O	O	O	O
Document	O	O	X	X	O	O	O	O
DocumentCharacteristicItem		O	O	X			O	
DocumentIssue	O	O	X	X			O	O
DocumentItem	O	O	X	X			O	O

Applicable to: All

Class name	UC51101	UC51102	UC51103	UC51104	UC51105	UC51106	UC51107	UC51108
DocumentParty		O	O	X			O	
DocumentReferencingItem	O	O	X	X			O	O
DownTimePeriod	X	X	X	X	X	X	X	
Environment	O	O	O	O	O	O	O	O
EnvironmentItem	X		X	X	X	X	X	
Event	O	O	O	X	X	O	X	X
ExportControlLicense	O	O	O	O	O	O	O	O
ExportControlRegulation				X				
ExternalDocument		O	O	X			O	
Facility	X	O	X	X	X	X	X	X
Fleet	X	X	X	X	X	X	X	X
FleetBasedAt	X		X	X	X			X
FleetManager	X	X	X	X	X	X	X	X
FleetOperatedBy	X		X	X	X			X
FleetOperatesAtLocation	X		X	X	X			X
FleetOperator	X		X	X	X			X
FleetPlanning	X	X	X	X	X	X	X	
FleetRelationship	X		X	X	X			X
FleetRequirement	X	X	X	X	X	X	X	
FleetTask	X	X	X	X	X	X	X	
FleetTaskCancellationNotice		X	O	X			O	
FleetTaskCargo	X	X	X	X	X	X	X	
FleetTaskList	X	X	X	X	X	X	X	
GeographicalArea	X							
GlobalPosition	X							
HardwareElement	O			X		X	X	
HardwarePartAsDesigned	X				O			
Infrastructure	O	O	X	X	X	O	O	X
InfrastructureAvailable	O		X	X				
InfrastructureCompliance	O			X				

Class name	UC51101	UC51102	UC51103	UC51104	UC51105	UC51106	UC51107	UC51108
InfrastructureCompliantItem	O		X	X				
InfrastructureItem	O			X				
InfrastructureNode	O			X				
InfrastructureNodeAtLocation	O			X				
InfrastructureParty	O			X				
InfrastructureRelationship	O			X				
InfrastructureRequiringItem	O		X	X				
InfrastructureRevision	O	O	X	X	O	O	O	O
InstallationLocation						X	X	
InstallationLocationDefinitionItem						X	X	
InstalledPart						X	X	
InstalledPartItem						X	X	
ItemDisposalOperation				X				
Location	X							
LocationItem	X			X	O		O	
LocationRelationship	X							
Locator	X	O	O	X			O	
LogBook					X			
LogBookEntry					X		X	
LogBookEntryMeasurementPoint					X			
MaintenanceProgram		O	O	X			O	
ManagedFleet	X		X	X	X			X
MeasurementPoint	X				X	X	X	
MeasurementPointItem	X				X	X	X	
Message	O	O	O	O	O	O	O	O
Movement	X	O	O	O	X	O	X	O
MovementLeg	X	O	O	O	X	O	X	O
MovementLegDelay	X				X		X	
MovementLegPosition							O	
MRONetwork	O			X				

Class name	UC51101	UC51102	UC51103	UC51104	UC51105	UC51106	UC51107	UC51108
NonAvailabilityAttribution				X	X			X
NonAvailabilityCause				X	X			X
NonAvailabilityCauseItem				X	X			X
OpeningTimes	X							
OperatingBase	X		X	X	X	X	X	X
OperatingBaseCapacity	X		X	X	X	X	X	
OperatingLocationType	X		X	X	X			X
OperationalApproval				X	X		X	
OperationalEvent							X	
OperationalEventMessage							X	
OperationalEventOperator							X	
OperationalMode							O	
OperationalModeStatus					X		X	
OperationalMoment					X			
OperationalMomentItem					X			
OperationalPeriod	X				X		X	
OperationalPeriodOperator							O	
OperationalPeriodRelationship							O	
OperationalRequirement	X	X	X	X	X	X	X	
OperationalRequirementsPlanning	X	X	X	X	X	X	X	
OperationalRole	X	X	X	X	X	X	X	
Operator							X	
OperatorOrganization	X		X	X	X			X
OperatorPerson	X		X	X	X			X
Organization	O	O	O	X	X	O	O	X
OrganizationalBreakdownStructureRevision	O	O	O	O	O	O	O	O
PartAction					X			
PartAsDesigned	O	O	O	X	O	X	X	O
Party	O	O	O	X	X	O	O	X
Penalty	O	O	O	O	O	O	O	O

Class name	UC51101	UC51102	UC51103	UC51104	UC51105	UC51106	UC51107	UC51108
PerformanceParameter	X				X			
PerformanceParameterItem	X				X			
Person	O	O	O	X	X	O	O	X
PoliciesAndRegulations				X				
PoliciesAndRegulationsCompliantItem				X				
Pool	O	O	O	O	O	O	O	O
Port	O			X				
PowerGrid	O			X				
Product	O	O	X	X	O	O	O	O
ProductParameterAtOperationalEvent							X	
ProductVariant	X	O	X	X	X	X	X	O
Project	O	O	O	X	O	O	O	O
RealizedPart						X	X	
ReferencedDocument	O	O	X	X			O	O
Remark	O	O	O	O	O	O	O	O
RemarkItem	O	O	O	O	O	O	O	O
Report	X	X	X	X	X	X	X	
ReportableActivity					O			
ReportableMetric	O	O	O	O	O	O	O	O
RequiredFleetRole	X	X	X	X	X	X	X	
Requirement	O	O	O	X	O	O	O	O
ResourceSpecification	O			X				
RoleCapability	X					X	X	
S1000DDataModule	O	O	X	X			O	O
S1000DDataModuleIssue	O	O	X	X			O	O
S1000DPublicationModule	O	O	X	X			O	O
S1000DPublicationModuleIssue	O	O	X	X			O	O
SafetyDocument		O	O	X			O	
SCORMContentPackage		O	O	X			O	

Class name	UC51101	UC51102	UC51103	UC51104	UC51105	UC51106	UC51107	UC51108
SecurityClass	O	O	O	O	O	O	O	O
SecurityClassification	O	O	O	O	O	O	O	O
SecurityClassificationItem	O	O	O	O	O	O	O	O
SerializedHardwarePart	O	O	O	X	X	X	X	X
SerializedItem					X			
SerializedProductOperationalPeriod	X				X		X	
SerializedProductVariant	X	X	X	X	X	X	X	X
SerializedProductVariantAssignment	X	X	X	X	X	X	X	
SerializedProductVariantConfigurationConformance						X	X	
SerializedProductVariantInFleet	X	X	X	X	X	X	X	X
SerializedProductVariantOperatingBase	X		X	X	X	X	X	
SerializedProductVariantOperator			X	X		X		
Service	X	O	X	X	X	O	O	O
ServiceBulletin		O	O	X	X		O	X
ServiceContract	X				X			
ServiceItem					O			
ServiceLevelAgreementClause	X				X			
ServiceRelationship	X				X			
ServiceRequest					O			
ServiceRequestCancellation					O			
ServiceRequestItem					O			
ServiceRequestLocation					O			
ServiceRequestParty					O			
ServiceRequestRelationship					O			
SoftwareElement	O			X		X	X	
SoftwarePartAsReleased	X			X	X	X	X	X
StreetAddress	X							
SubjectOfPoliciesAndRegulations				X				
Task	O	O	O	O	O	O	O	O

Class name	UC51101	UC51102	UC51103	UC51104	UC51105	UC51106	UC51107	UC51108
TaskRequirement	O	O	O	O	O	O	O	O
TransportNetwork	O			X				
WasteDisposalOperation				X				
WorkBreakdown	O	O	O	O	O	O	O	O
WorkItem	O	O	O	O	O	O	O	O

2.10 Classes for software support cases

The classes used for the different software support use cases, as defined in Chap 12, are those listed in Table 11. The use cases are numbered:

1 UC51201: Request S/W feature

2 UC51202: Report S/W error

3 UC51203: Report S/W usability

4 UC51204: Report S/W documentation errors

5 UC51205: Report Software and hardware interoperability

6 UC51206: Report S/W installation/unloading/erasure

7 UC51207: Report S/W configuration

8 UC51208: Report S/W maturity

9 UC51209: Report help desk tickets

10 UC51210: Report S/W delivery, deployment and servicing

11 UC51211: Report Data loading for software operations

Table 11 Classes used for software support use cases

Class name	UC51201	UC51203	UC51204	UC51205	UC51206	UC51207	UC51208	UC51209	UC51210	UC51211
Action	X	O	O	O	O	O	O	O	X	O
AllowedProductConfiguration							O			
AllowedProductConfigurationByConfigurationIdentifier							O			
AllowedProductConfigurationHardwarePartAsDesigned							O			
AllowedProductConfigurationItem							O			
AlternatePartAsDesigned		O			X		X			

Class name	UC51201	UC51203	UC51204	UC51205	UC51206	UC51207	UC51208	UC51209	UC51210	UC51211
AuthorityRequirement	X									
AuthorityToOperate							O			
Availability			X	O		O		X		X
BatchHardwarePart					X				O	
BreakdownElement	X	X	X	O	X	O	X	X	X	X
BreakdownElementRevision	X	X	X		X		X	X	X	X
BreakdownElementUsageInBreakdown							O			
Budget	O	O	O	O	O	O	O	O	O	O
CargoItem	O	O	O	O	O	O	O	O	O	O
ChangeEmbodimentRequirement	X									
ChangeRequest	X	O	O	O	O	O	O	O	O	O
ChangeRequestCause	X									
ChangeRequestItem	X									
ChangeRequestReasonItem	X									
CircuitBreaker									O	
Comment	O	O	O	O	O	O	O	O	X	O
CommentAction	O	O	O	O	O	O	O	O	X	O
CommentItem	O	O	O	O	O	O	O	O	X	O
CommentParty	O	O	O	O	O	O	O	O	X	O
CommentRelationship	O	O	O	O	O	O	O	O	X	O
ConsumableItem										X
Contract	X	O	X	O	O	O	O	X	O	X
ContractClause	X									
CostEntry	O	O	X	O	O	X	O	X	O	X
CostEntryItem						X				X
CostItem	O	O	O	O	O	O	O	O	O	O
Country									O	
DataSetAsDesigned										
DataSetAsReleased										
DataSetAssociatedWith										

Class name	UC51201	UC51203	UC51204	UC51205	UC51206	UC51207	UC51208	UC51209	UC51210	UC51211
Detector					O					
DigitalFile	O	O	O	O	O	O	O	O	O	O
DigitalFileReference									O	
DigitalFileReferencedItem									O	
DigitalFileReferencingItem									O	
DisposalRequirement	X									
Document	X	O	X	O	O	O	O	X	X	X
DocumentCharacteristicItem	O			O	O	O	O		O	
DocumentIssue	X			O	O	O	O		X	
DocumentItem	X			O	O	O	O		X	
DocumentParty	O			O	O	O	O		O	
DocumentReferencingItem	X			O	O	O	O		X	
EffectiveOnProductConfiguration							O			
EffectiveOnProductConfigurationItem							O			
Environment	O	O	X	O	O	O	O	X	O	X
Event	X	O	X	O	O	O	O	X	O	X
ExportControlLicense	O	O	O	O	O	O	O	O	O	O
ExternalDocument	O			O	O	O	O		O	
Facility	X	O	X	O	O	O	O	X	O	X
Failure					O					
FailureMode					O					
FailureModeCause					O					
Fleet	X	O	X	O	O	O	O	X	O	X
FleetRequirement	X									
FleetTaskCancellationNotice	O			O	O	O	O		O	
GeographicalArea									O	
GlobalPosition									O	
HardwareElement	X				X		X		X	
HardwareElementPartRealization					X		X		X	
HardwareElementRevision					X		X		X	

Class name	UC51201	UC51203	UC51204	UC51205	UC51206	UC51207	UC51208	UC51209	UC51210	UC51211
HardwarePartAsDesigned	X	X	X	O	X	X	X	X	X	X
HardwarePartAsDesignedDesignData		O			X		X			
HardwarePartAsDesignedSupportData		O			X		X			
Infrastructure	X	O	X	O	O	O	O	X	O	X
InfrastructureRevision	X	O	O	O	O	O	O	O	O	O
InstallationLocation									O	
InventoryActivity						X				X
Locator	O			O	O	O	O		O	
MaintenanceActivity	X					X				X
MaintenanceOrganization		O								
MaintenancePerson		O								
MaintenanceProgram	O			O	O	O	O		O	
MaintenanceRequirement	X									
Material										X
MeasurementPoint					X				O	
MeasurementPointItem					X					
Message	O	O	O	O	O	O	O	O	O	O
Movement	O	O	O	O	O	O	O	O	O	O
MovementLeg	O	O	O	O	O	O	O	O	O	O
NestedAllowedProductConfiguration							O			
NestedProductVariant							O			
NonConformanceData							O			
ObsolescenceRequirement	X									
OperationalActivity						X				X
OperationalEvent			X	O		O		X		X
OperationalPeriod	X									
OperationalRequirement	X									
OperatorOrganization		O								
OperatorPerson		O								
Organization	O	O	X	O	O	O	O	X	O	X

Class name	UC51201	UC51203	UC51204	UC51205	UC51206	UC51207	UC51208	UC51209	UC51210	UC51211
OrganizationalBreakdownStructureRevision	O	O	O	O	O	O	O	O	O	O
PartAsDesigned	O	O	O	O	X	O	X	O	O	O
PartAsDesignedPartsList		O			X		X			
PartAsDesignedPartsListEntry		O			X		X			
PartAsDesignedPartsListRelationship		O			X		X			
PartAsDesignedPartsListRevision		O			X		X			
PartOwner					X					
Party	X	X	X	O	X	X	X	X	X	X
PartyAddress		O								
PartyContactData		O								
PartyItem		O								
PartyRelationship		O								
Penalty	O	O	O	O	O	O	O	O	O	O
Person	O	O	X	O	O	O	O	X	O	X
PoliciesAndRegulationsCompliantItem	X									
Pool	O	O	X	O	O	O	O	X	O	X
Product	X	O	X	O	O	O	O	X	O	X
ProductParameterAtOperationalEvent										
ProductVariant	X	O	X	O	O	O	O	X	O	X
Project	O	O	X	O	O	O	O	X	O	X
ReferencedDigitalFile									O	
ReferencedDocument	X			O	O	O	O		X	
ReleasedDataSetAssociatedWith										
ReleasedDataSetItem Remark										
	O	O	O	O	O	O	O	O	O	O
RemarkItem	O	O	O	O	O	O	O	O	O	O
Report	O		X	O	O	O	O	X	O	X
ReportableActivity			X	O		X		X		X
ReportableItem			X	O		X		X		X

Class name	UC51201	UC51203	UC51204	UC51205	UC51206	UC51207	UC51208	UC51209	UC51210	UC51211
ReportableMetric	O	O	X	O	O	O	O	X	O	X
ReportableMetricItem			X					X		
ReportContext			X	O		O		X		X
ReportContextItem			X	O		O		X		X
ReportingParty			X	O		O		X		X
ReportParty			X	O		O		X		X
Requirement	X	O	O	O	O	O	O	O	O	O
RequirementParty	X									
RequirementRelationship	X									
ResourceSpecification									O	
S1000DDataModule	X			O	O	O	O	X		
S1000DDataModuleIssue	X			O	O	O	O	X		
S1000DPublicationModule	X			O	O	O	O	X		
S1000DPublicationModuleIssue	X			O	O	O	O	X		
SafetyDocument	O			O	O	O	O		O	
SafetyIssue	X									
SafetyRequirement	X									
SCORMContentPackage	O			O	O	O	O		O	
SecurityClass	O	O	O	O	O	O	O	O	O	O
SecurityClassification	O	O	O	O	O	O	O	O	O	O
SecurityClassificationItem	O	O	O	O	O	O	O	O	O	O
SerializedHardwarePart	X	O	X	O	X	O	O	X	O	X
SerializedItem					X					
SerializedPartDesignAssociation					X					
SerializedProductVariant	X	O	X	O	O	O	O	X	O	X
Service	X	O	X	O	O	O	O	X	O	X
ServiceBulletin	O			O	O	O	O		O	
ServiceLevelAgreementClause			X					X		
ShopFindings					O					
ShopFindingsDeterminedBy					O					

Class name	UC51201	UC51203	UC51204	UC51205	UC51206	UC51207	UC51208	UC51209	UC51210	UC51211
SoftwareElement	X	X	X		X		X	X	X	X
SoftwareElementPartRealization	X	X	X		X		X	X	X	X
SoftwareElementRevision	X	X	X		X		X	X	X	X
SoftwareError	X	X	X		X	X	X	X		X
SoftwareErrorOS	X	X	X		X	X	X	X		X
SoftwareErrorPlatform	X	X	X		X	X	X	X		X
SoftwareOS	X	X	X		X	X	X	X		X
SoftwarePartAsDesigned	X	X	X	O	X	X	X	X	X	X
SoftwarePartAsReleased	X	X	X	O	X	X	X	X		X
SoftwarePlatform	X	X	X		X	X	X	X		X
StreetAddress		O							O	
SubjectOfPoliciesAndRegulations	X									
SubstanceContainingItem		O			X		X			
SubstanceDefinition									O	X
SubstitutePartAsDesigned		O			X		X			
SupplyItem										X
Task	O	O	O	O	O	O	O	O	O	O
TaskRequirement	O	O	O	O	O	O	O	O	O	O
TransportRequirement	X									
UpgradeRequirement	X									
UsableOnItem								O		
UsableOnProductVariant								O		
WarrantyClaim									O	
WorkBreakdown	O	O	O	O	O	O	O	O	O	O
WorkItem	O	O	O	O	O	X	O	O	O	X
WorkOrder			X	O		O		X		X
ZoneElementRevision									O	

2.11 Classes for configuration management

The classes used for each configuration management use case as defined in Chap 13 are listed in Table 12. The use cases are numbered:

1   UC51301: Provide as-delivered configuration

2   UC51302: Provide as-allowed configuration

3   UC51303: Provide operational configuration

4   UC51304: Provide customer modification

5   UC51305: Provide as-desired configuration

Table 12   Classes used for configuration management use cases

Class name	UC51301	UC51302	UC51303	UC51304	UC51305
Action	O	O	O	X	O
AllocatedTaskLocation	X	X	X	X	X
AllowedProductConfiguration	X	X	X		X
AllowedProductConfigurationByConfigurationIdentifier	X	X	X	X	X
AllowedProductConfigurationHardwarePartAsDesigned	X	X			
AllowedProductConfigurationItem	X	X	X		X
AllowedProductConfigurationPhysicalData			X		
AllowedProductConfigurationRole	X		X		X
AllowedProductOperationalConfigurationItem			X		
AllowedRoleChange			X		
AlternatePartAsDesigned	X	X		X	
ApplicabilityStatement	X	X	X	X	X
AuthorityToOperate	X	X			X
BatchHardwarePart	X		X	X	
Breakdown	X	X			
BreakdownElement	X	X	X	X	X
BreakdownElementInZone	X	X	X	X	X
BreakdownElementRevision	X	X		X	
BreakdownElementRevisionRelationship	X	X	X	X	X
BreakdownElementRevisionRelationshipItem	X	X			
BreakdownElementStructure	X	X			
BreakdownElementUsageInBreakdown	X	X	X	X	X
BreakdownElementUsageRelationship	X	X	X	X	X
BreakdownItem	X	X			

Class name	UC51301	UC51302	UC51303	UC51304	UC51305
BreakdownRevision	X	X		X	
Budget	O	O	O	O	O
Capability			X		
CapabilityItem			X		
CargoItem	O	O	O	O	O
ChangeAuthorization	X	X	X	X	X
ChangeControlledItem	X			X	
ChangedItemAvailabilityRequirement				O	
ChangeEmbodimentRequirement				O	
ChangeNotification	X			X	
ChangeRequest	X	X	X	X	X
ChangeRequestCause				X	
ChangeRequestItem				X	
ChangeRequestReasonItem				X	
CircuitBreaker	X	X	X	X	X
CircuitBreakerSetting	X	X	X	X	X
CircuitBreakerSettings	X	X	X	X	X
ClassInstanceAssertItem	X	X	X	X	X
Comment	O	O	O	O	O
CommentAction	O	O	O	O	O
CommentItem	O	O	O	O	O
CommentParty	O	O	O	O	O
CommentRelationship	O	O	O	O	O
ConditionDefinitionItem	X	X	X	X	X
ConditionInstance	X	X	X	X	X
ConditionType	X	X	X	X	X
ConditionTypeAssertMember	X	X	X	X	X
Contract	X	X	X	X	X
ContractClause				X	
CostEntry	O	O	O	O	O

Class name	UC51301	UC51302	UC51303	UC51304	UC51305
CostItem	O	O	O	O	O
Country	O				
DigitalFile	O	O	O	O	O
DigitalFileReference	O				
DigitalFileReferencedItem	O				
DigitalFileReferencingItem	O				
Document	O	O	O	O	O
DocumentCharacteristicItem	O				O
DocumentIssue	X			X	O
DocumentItem	O				O
DocumentParty	O				O
DocumentReferencingItem	O				O
DownTimePeriod				O	
EffectiveOnProductConfiguration	X	X		X	
EffectiveOnProductConfigurationItem	X	X			
Environment	O	O	O	O	O
EvaluationByAssertionOfClassInstance	X	X	X	X	X
EvaluationByAssertionOfCondition	X	X	X	X	X
EvaluationByAssertionOfSerializedItems	X	X	X	X	X
EvaluationByNestedApplicabilityStatement	X	X	X	X	X
EvaluationCriteria	X	X	X	X	X
Event	X	O	X	X	O
ExportControlLicense	O	O	O	O	O
ExternalDocument	O				O
Facility	X	X	X	X	X
FacilityOperator	X	X	X	X	X
Fleet	X	X	X	X	X
FleetTask	X				X
FleetTaskCancellationNotice	O				O
GeographicalArea	X	X	X	X	X

Class name	UC51301	UC51302	UC51303	UC51304	UC51305
GlobalPosition	O				
HardwareElement	X	X	X	X	
HardwareElementPartRealization	X	X	X	X	X
HardwareElementRevision	X	X		O	
HardwarePartAsDesigned	X	X	X	X	
HardwarePartAsDesignedDesignData	X	X		O	
HardwarePartAsDesignedSupportData	X	X		O	
IdentifiedTaskRequirement	X	X	X	X	X
Infrastructure	X	X	X	X	X
InfrastructureRevision	X	O	O	X	O
InstallationLocation	X		X		
InstallationLocationDefinitionItem	X		X		
InstalledPart	X		X	X	
InstalledPartItem	X		X		
Locator	O				O
LogBook	X		X		
LogBookEntry	X		X		
LogBookEntryMeasurementPoint	X		X		
LogicalAND	X	X	X	X	X
LogicalNOT	X	X	X	X	X
LogicalOR	X	X	X	X	X
LogicalXOR	X	X	X	X	X
MaintenanceActivity				X	
MaintenanceLevel	X	X	X	X	X
MaintenanceProgram	O				O
MaintenanceWorkOrderSource				O	
MeasurementPoint	X		X	X	
MeasurementPointItem	X		X	X	
Message	O	O	O	O	O

Class name	UC51301	UC51302	UC51303	UC51304	UC51305
Movement	O	O	O	O	O
MovementLeg	O	O	O	O	O
NestedAllowedProductConfiguration	X	X			X
NestedProductVariant	X	X			
NonConformanceData	X	X			
OperatingBase				O	
OperatingLocationType	X	X	X	X	X
OperationalModeStatus	X		X		
OperationalMoment	X		X		
OperationalMomentItem	X		X		
OperationalPeriod				X	
OperationalRole	X		X		X
Organization	X	X	X	X	X
OrganizationalBreakdownStructureRevision	O	O	O	O	O
PartAction	X		X	O	
PartAsDesigned	X	X	X	X	X
PartAsDesignedPartsList	X	X		O	
PartAsDesignedPartsListEntry	X	X		X	
PartAsDesignedPartsListRelationship	X	X		O	
PartAsDesignedPartsListRevision	X	X		X	
PartOwner	X		X	X	
Party	X	O	X	X	O
Penalty	O	O	O	O	O
Person	O	O	O	O	O
PlannedItemUpgrade				O	
PlannedPartInstallationLocation				O	
PlannedUpgradeTimescales				O	
Pool	O	O	O	O	O
Product	X	X	X	X	X
ProductVariant	X	X	X	X	X

Class name	UC51301	UC51302	UC51303	UC51304	UC51305
Project	X	X	X	X	X
RealizedPart	X		X		
ReferencedDigitalFile	O				
ReferencedDocument	X	X	X	X	X
Remark	O	O	O	O	O
RemarkItem	O	O	O	O	O
Report	O				O
ReportableMetric	O	O	O	O	O
Requirement	X	X	X	X	X
ResourceRealization	X	X	X	X	X
ResourceSpecification	O				
RoleCapability			X		
S1000DDataModule	O				O
S1000DDataModuleIssue	O				O
S1000DPublicationModule	O				O
S1000DPublicationModuleIssue	O				O
SafetyDocument	O				O
SafetyIssue				X	
SCORMContentPackage	O				O
SecurityClass	O	O	O	O	O
SecurityClassification	X	X	X	X	X
SecurityClassificationItem	O	O	O	O	O
SerializedAssertItem	X	X	X	X	X
SerializedHardwarePart	X	X	X	X	X
SerializedItem	X		X	X	
SerializedPartDesignAssociation	X		X	X	
SerializedPartsListPosition	X			X	
SerializedProductVariant	X	X	X	X	X
SerializedProductVariantAssignment	X				X
SerializedProductVariantConfigurationConformance	X		X		X

Class name	UC51301	UC51302	UC51303	UC51304	UC51305
SerializedProductVariantOperatingBase				O	
Service	X	X	X	X	X
ServiceBulletin	O			O	O
SoftwareElement	X	X	X	X	
SoftwareElementPartRealization	X	X	X	X	X
SoftwareElementRevision	X	X		O	
SoftwarePartAsDesigned	X	X	X	X	
SoftwarePartAsReleased	X	X	X	X	X
StreetAddress	O				
SubstanceContainingItem	X	X		O	
SubstanceDefinition	O				
SubstitutePartAsDesigned	X	X		O	
SubtaskInZone	X	X	X	X	X
SubtaskTimeline	X	X	X	X	X
SubtaskWarningCautionNote	X	X	X	X	X
Task	O	O	O	O	O
TaskPersonnelResourceCompetence	X	X	X	X	X
TaskRequirement	O	O	O	O	O
TaskRequirementRevision	X			X	
TaskResource	X	X	X	X	X
TaskRevision	X			X	
TaskRevisionWarningCautionNote	X	X	X	X	X
TaskUsage	X	X	X	X	X
TechnicalOrder				O	
TechnicalOrderEmbodied				O	
ThresholdDefinition	X	X	X	X	X
TrackablePart				O	
UpgradeRequirement				O	
UsableOnItem	X	X			
UsableOnProductVariant	X	X		X	

Class name	UC51301	UC51302	UC51303	UC51304	UC51305
WarrantyClaim	O				
WorkBreakdown	O	O	O	O	O
WorkItem	O	O	O	O	O
WorkOrder				O	
ZoneElementRevision	O				

2.12 Classes used for in-service contract management

The classes used for each in-service contract management use case as defined in Chap 14 are listed in Table 13. The use cases are numbered:

1. UC51401: Provide contractual information
2. UC51402: Provide Work Breakdown Structure (WBS)
3. UC51403: Provide Cost Breakdown Structure (CBS)
4. UC51404: Provide Organisational Breakdown Structure (OBS)
5. UC51405: Provide /update activity planning
6. UC51406: Report Service Level Agreement (SLA) compliance
7. UC51407: Provide contract incurred costs
8. UC51408: Provide status report
9. UC51409: Replaced by UC51503. Refer to Para 2.13.
10. UC51410: Manage service request
11. UC51411: Request/grant/deny usage of resource
12. UC51412: Assign security classification
13. UC51413: Provide exchange export control information
14. UC51414: Provide labour rates
15. UC51415: Provide documentation traceability

Table 13 Classes used for in-service contract management use cases

Class name	UC51401	UC51402	UC51403	UC51404	UC51405	UC51406	UC51407	UC51408	UC51410	UC51411	UC51412	UC51413	UC51414	UC51415
Action	O	O	O	O	O	O	O	O	O	O	O	O	O	O
ActualEnvironment	O													

Class name	UC51401	UC51402	UC51403	UC51404	UC51405	UC51406	UC51407	UC51408	UC51410	UC51411	UC51412	UC51413	UC51414	UC51415
AssociatedActualEnvironment	O													
AuthorityRequirement									O					
Availability					X	X		X						
BatchHardwarePart	X								X					O
BreakdownElement	O	X	X	O	X	O	X	O	O	O	X	O	O	X
Budget	X	O	X	O	O	O	X	O	X	X	X	O	O	X
BudgetingItem			O				O		O	O				
Capability	X					X			O	O				
CargoItem	O	O	O	O	X	O	O	O	O	O	X	O	O	X
ChangeEmbodimentRequirement			X				X		O	O				
ChangeRequest	O	O	X	O	O	O	X	O	O	O	X	O	O	X
CircuitBreaker														O
CloudInfrastructure	O													
Comment	O	O	O	O	O	O	O	O	O	O	X	O	O	X
CommentAction	O	O	O	O	O	O	O	O	O	O	O	O	O	O
CommentItem	O	O	O	O	O	O	O	O	O	O	O	O	O	O
CommentParty	O	O	O	O	O	O	O	O	O	O	O	O	O	O
CommentRelationship	O	O	O	O	O	O	O	O	O	O	O	O	O	O
CommunicationsNetwork	O													
CompetenceDefinitionItem													X	
CompliesWith	X					O			X			X		
ComputerNetwork	O													
ConditionDefinitionItem	X					X			O					
ConditionInstance	X					X			O					
ConditionType	X					X			O					
ConditionTypeAssertMember	X					X			O					
Contract	X	X	X	X	X	X	X	X	X	X	X	X	X	X
ContractClause	X	X	X		X	X	X	O	O	O			X	

Class name	UC51401	UC51402	UC51403	UC51404	UC51405	UC51406	UC51407	UC51408	UC51410	UC51411	UC51412	UC51413	UC51414	UC51415
ContractClauseRelationship	X		O			X	X	O		O			X	
ContractItem	X	O		O			X		O					O
ContractItemDetails	X	O		O			X		O					O
ContractParty	X	O		O			X		O					O
ContractRelationship	X	O	O	O		X	X	O	O	O			X	O
CostBreakdown	O		X				X			O				
CostBreakdownContext	X		X			X	X	O		O			X	
CostBreakdownRelationship	O		X				X			O				
CostBreakdownRevision	O		X				X			O				
CostEntry	O	O	X	O	X	X	X	X	O	O	X	O	O	X
CostEntryItem	O		X		X	O	X	X		O				
CostItem	O	X	X	O	X	O	X	O	O	X	X	O	O	X
CostItemRelationship	O		X				X			O				
Country	O								O			X		X
Damage			X				X			O				
DataSetAsReleased	X					O		X			X			
DigitalFile	O	O	O	O	O	O	O	O	O	O	X	O	O	X
DigitalFileReference														O
DigitalFileReferencedItem														O
DigitalFileReferencingItem														O
DisposalRequirement			X				X		O	O				
Document	X	O	O	O	X	X	O	X	X	O	X	X	O	X
DocumentCharacteristicItem	O	O	O	O	O		O	O			O	O		X
DocumentIssue	O	O	O	O	O		O	O	O		O	X		X
DocumentItem	X	O	O	O	O	X	O	O	O		O	O		
DocumentParty	O	O	O	O	O		O	O			O	O		X
DocumentReferencingItem	O	O	O	O	O		O	O			O	O		
DownTimePeriod				X										
Environment	O	O	O	O	X	O	O	X	O	O	X	O	O	X
EnvironmentItem	O													

Class name	UC51401	UC51402	UC51403	UC51404	UC51405	UC51406	UC51407	UC51408	UC51410	UC51411	UC51412	UC51413	UC51414	UC51415
EvaluationByAssertionOfCondition	X					X			O					
EvaluationByNestedExpression	X					X			O					
EvaluationCriteria	X					X			O					
Event	O	O	O	O	X	O	O	X	O	O	X	O	O	X
ExportControlledItem	O								O			X		X
ExportControlLicense	O	O	O	O	O	O	O	O	O	O	X	X	O	X
ExportControlLicenseItem	O								O			X		X
ExportControlParty	O								O			X		X
ExportControlRegulation	X					O			X			X		X
ExportControlRequirementAppliedToCountry	O								O			X		X
ExpressionEvaluation	X					X			O					
ExternalDocument	O	O	O	O	O		O	O			O	O		X
Facility	X	X	X	O	X	X	X	X	X	X	X	X	O	X
FacilityLocation	O													
FacilityOperator	O													
FacilityOperatorItem	O													
FacilityOwner	O													
FacilityRelationship	O													
Fleet	X	O	X	O	X	O	X	X	X	X	X	O	O	X
FleetManager					X									
FleetPlanning					X									
FleetRequirement					X				O					
FleetTask	X													
FleetTaskCancellationNotice	O	O	O	O	O		O	O			O	O		X
FleetTaskCargo					X									
FleetTaskList					X									
GeographicalArea														O

Class name	UC51401	UC51402	UC51403	UC51404	UC51405	UC51406	UC51407	UC51408	UC51410	UC51411	UC51412	UC51413	UC51414	UC51415
GlobalPosition														O
HardwareElement	O													
HardwarePartAsDesigned	X	O	X	O	X		X	X	X	X		X		X
Infrastructure	X	X	X	O	X	X	X	X	X	X	X	X	O	X
InfrastructureCompliance	O													
InfrastructureCompliantItem	O													
InfrastructureItem	O													
InfrastructureNode	O													
InfrastructureNodeAtLocation	O													
InfrastructureParty	O													
InfrastructureRelationship	O													
InfrastructureRevision	O	X	O	O	X	O	O	O	O	O	X	O	O	X
InstallationLocation														O
InventoryActivity					X	O		X						
ItemDisposalOperation	X		X			O	X		X	O		X		
ItemExportControlRegulation	O								O			X		X
ItemUnderExportControl	O								O			X		X
LaborRateItem	X		O		X	X	O			O			X	
LaborRates	X		O		X	X	O			O			X	
LegalParty	X	O		O			X		O					O
LocationItem	X								X					
Locator	O	O	O	O	O		O	O			O	O		X
LogicalAND	X					X			O					
LogicalNOT	X					X			O					
LogicalOR	X					X			O					
LogicalXOR	X					X			O					
MaintenanceActivity					X	O		X						
MaintenanceFacility	O				X									
MaintenanceFacilityLevel					X									
MaintenanceFacilitySlot					X									

Class name	UC51401	UC51402	UC51403	UC51404	UC51405	UC51406	UC51407	UC51408	UC51410	UC51411	UC51412	UC51413	UC51414	UC51415
MaintenanceFacilitySlotAccomodation					X									
MaintenanceFacilitySlotPlannedUsage					X									
MaintenanceLevel					X									
MaintenanceOrganization	X	X		X				O		O				O
MaintenancePerson	X	X		X				O		O				O
MaintenanceProgram	O	O	O	O	O		O	O			O	O		X
MaintenanceRequirement									O					
Material			X				X			O				
MeasurementPoint														O
Message	O	O	O	O	O	O	O	O	O	O	X	O	O	X
Movement	O	O	X	O	O	O	X	O	O	O	X	O	O	X
MovementLeg	O	O	X	O	O	O	X	O	O	O	X	O	O	X
MRONetwork	O													
ObsolescenceRequirement								O						
OperatingBase	O													
OperationalActivity					X	O		X						
OperationalEvent					X	X		X						
OperationalRequirement					X				O					
OperationalRequirementsPlanning					X									
OperationalRole					X									
OperatorOrganization	X	X		X				O		O				O
OperatorPerson	X	X		X				O		O				O
Organization	X	X	X	X	X	X	X	X	X	O	X	X	O	X
OrganizationalBreakdownStructure	O			X	O									
OrganizationalBreakdownStructureRevision	O	O	O	X	O	O	O	O	O	O	X	O	O	X
OrganizationalRole	O			X	O									
OtherFacility	O													

Class name	UC51401	UC51402	UC51403	UC51404	UC51405	UC51406	UC51407	UC51408	UC51410	UC51411	UC51412	UC51413	UC51414	UC51415
ParkingFacility	O													
PartAsDesigned	X	X	X	O	X	O	X	O	X	O	X	X	O	X
Party	X	X	X	X	X	O	X	X	X	X	O	X	O	X
PartyAddress	X	X		X				O		O				O
PartyContactData	X	X		X				O		O				O
PartyItem	X	X		X				O		O				O
PartyRelationship	X	X		X	O			O		O				O
Penalty	X	O	X	O	O	X	X	O	O	O	X	O	O	X
PerformanceParameter	X					X			O	O				
PerformanceParameterItem	X					X			O	O				
PerformanceParameterRevision	X					X			O					
Person	X	X	X	X	X	X	X	X	O	X	X	O	X	X
PersonCompetence													X	
PersonCompetenceItem													X	
PoliciesAndRegulations	X					O			X			X		X
PoliciesAndRegulationsCompliantItem	X					O			X			X		
Pool	O	O	O	O	X	O	O	X	O	O	X	O	O	X
Port	O													
PowerGrid	O													
Product	X	X	X	O	X	O	X	X	X	O	X	X	O	X
ProductVariant	X	X	X	O	X	X	X	X	X	X	X	X	O	X
Project	X	X	X	X	X	O	X	X	X	O	X	X	O	X
ProjectContract	X	O		O			X		O					O
ProjectRelationship	X	O		O			X		O					O
ReferencedDigitalFile														O
ReferencedDocument	O	O	O	O	O		O	O			O	O		
Remark	O	O	O	O	O	O	O	O	O	O	O	O	O	O
RemarkItem	O	O	O	O	O	O	O	O	O	O	O	O	O	O

Class name	UC51401	UC51402	UC51403	UC51404	UC51405	UC51406	UC51407	UC51408	UC51410	UC51411	UC51412	UC51413	UC51414	UC51415
Report	O	O	O	O	X	X	O	X			O	O		X
ReportableActivity	X	X	X		X	X	X	X	X	O				
ReportableItem					X	X		X						
ReportableMetric	X	O	O	O	X	X	O	X	O	O	X	O	O	X
ReportableMetricItem					X			X						
ReportContext					X	X		X						
ReportContextItem					X	X		X						
ReportingParty					X	X		X						
ReportParty					X	X		X						
RequiredFleetRole					X									
Requirement	X	O	O	O	O	O	O	O	X	O	X	X	O	X
RequirementParty									O					
RequirementRelationship									O					
ResourceItem										X				
ResourceSpecification	O													O
ResourceUsageParty										X				
ResourceUsageRequest			X				X			X				
S1000DDataModule	O	O	O	O	O		O	O			O	O		
S1000DDataModuleIssue	O	O	O	O	O		O	O			O	O		
S1000DPublicationModule	O	O	O	O	O		O	O			O	O		
S1000DPublicationModuleIssue	O	O	O	O	O		O	O			O	O		
SafetyDocument	O	O	O	O	O		O	O			O	O		X
SafetyRequirement									O					
SCORMContentPackage	O	O	O	O	O		O	O			O	O		X
SecurityClass	O	O	O	O	O	O	O	O	O	O	X	O	O	X
SecurityClassification	O	O	O	O	O	O	O	O	O	O	X	O	O	X
SecurityClassificationItem	O	O	O	O	O	O	O	O	O	O	X	O	O	X
SerializedHardwarePart	X	X	X	O	X	O	X	X	X	X	X	X	O	X
SerializedProductVariant	X	X	X	O	X	X	X	X	X	X	X	X	O	X

Class name	UC51401	UC51402	UC51403	UC51404	UC51405	UC51406	UC51407	UC51408	UC51410	UC51411	UC51412	UC51413	UC51414	UC51415
SerializedProductVariantAssignment					X									
SerializedProductVariantInFleet					X									
Service	X	X	X	O	X	X	X	X	X	O	X	X	O	X
ServiceBulletin	O	O	X	O	O		X	O		O	O	O		X
ServiceContract	X					X			O	O				
ServiceItem	X								X					
ServiceLevelAgreementClause	X		O			X	X	X	O	O			X	
ServiceRelationship	X					X			O	O				
ServiceRequest	X		X				X		X	O				
ServiceRequestCancellation	X								X					
ServiceRequestItem	X								X					
ServiceRequestLocation	X								X					
ServiceRequestParty	X								X					
ServiceRequestRelationship	X								X					
Skill													X	
SkillLevel													X	
SoftwareElement	O													
SoftwarePartAsDesigned	X	O		O	X	X	X	X	O			X		X
SoftwarePartAsReleased	X	X	X	O	X	X	X	X	O	O		X		X
StreetAddress	X	X		X				O		O				O
SubjectOfPoliciesAndRegulations	X					O			X			X		
SubstanceDefinition														O
SupportEquipment	O													
Task	O	O	O	O	O	O	O	O	O	O	X	O	O	X
TaskRequirement	O	O	O	O	O	O	O	O	O	O	X	O	O	X
Trade													X	
TransportNetwork	O													

Class name	UC51401	UC51402	UC51403	UC51404	UC51405	UC51406	UC51407	UC51408	UC51410	UC51411	UC51412	UC51413	UC51414	UC51415
TransportRequirement									O					
TypeOfPerson													X	
UpgradeRequirement									O					
Warehouse	O													
WarrantyClaim														O
WarrantyClaimResolution			X						X			O		
WasteDisposalOperation	X		X		O	X		X	O			X		
WorkBreakdown	O	X	O	O	X	O	O	O	O	O	X	O	O	X
WorkBreakdownContext	X	X	O		X	X	X	O		O			X	
WorkBreakdownRelationship	O	X			X		O	O						
WorkBreakdownRevision	O	X			X		O	O						
WorkItem	O	X	O	O	X	O	O	X	O	O	X	O	O	X
WorkItemRelationship	O	X			X		O	O						
WorkOrder			X		X	X	X	X		O				
ZoneElementRevision														O

2.13   Classes for in-service environment data

The classes used for each in-service environment data use case as defined in Chap 15 are listed in Table 14. The use cases are numbered:

1. UC51501: Replaced by UC52301. Refer to Para 2.15.

2. UC51502: Replaced by UC52302. Refer to Para 2.15.

3. UC51503: Location information

4. UC51504: Infrastructure availability

5. UC51505: Environment definition of update

6. UC51506: Reallocation of fleet or product

Table 14 Classes used for in-service environment data use cases

Class name	UC51503	UC51504	UC51505	UC51506
Action	O	O	O	O
ActualEnvironment	X		X	X

Class name	UC51503	UC51504	UC51505	UC51506
AssociatedActualEnvironment	X		X	X
Availability		X		
AvailabilityItem		X		X
BreakdownElement	O	O	O	O
Budget	O	O	O	O
CargoItem	O	O	O	O
ChangeRequest	O	O	O	O
CloudInfrastructure	X	X		
Comment	O	O	O	O
CommentAction	O	O	O	O
CommentItem	O	O	O	O
CommentParty	O	O	O	O
CommentRelationship	O	O	O	O
CommunicationsNetwork	X	X		
ComputerNetwork	X	X		
Contract	O	X	O	O
CostEntry	O	O	O	O
CostItem	O	O	O	O
Country	X		X	
DigitalFile	O	O	O	O
Document	O	O	O	O
Environment	O	O	X	O
EnvironmentDefinition		X		
EnvironmentDefinitionRevision		X		
EnvironmentItem	X		X	X
EnvironmentRelationship		X		
EnvironmentRevision		X		
Event	O	X	X	O
ExportControlLicense	O	O	O	O
Facility	X	X	X	X

Class name	UC51503	UC51504	UC51505	UC51506
FacilityLocation	X			
FacilityOperator	X			
FacilityOperatorItem	X			
FacilityOwner	X			
FacilityRelationship	X			
Fleet	O	X	O	X
FleetBasedAt				X
FleetManager				X
FleetOperatedBy				X
FleetOperatesAtLocation				X
FleetOperator				X
FleetRelationship				X
GeographicalArea	X		X	
GlobalPosition	X		X	
HardwareElement	X	X		
Infrastructure	X	X	O	O
InfrastructureAvailable		X		
InfrastructureCompliance	X	X		
InfrastructureCompliantItem	X	X		
InfrastructureItem	X	X		
InfrastructureNode	X	X		
InfrastructureNodeAtLocation	X	X		
InfrastructureParty	X	X		
InfrastructureRelationship	X	X		
InfrastructureRequiringItem		X		
InfrastructureRevision	X	X	O	O
Location	X			
LocationItem	X	X		
LocationRelationship	X			
Locator	X			

Class name	UC51503	UC51504	UC51505	UC51506
LogBook				O
MaintenanceFacility	X			
MaintenanceItem				O
MaintenanceLevel	X			
MajorComponent				X
ManagedFleet				X
MeasurementPoint				X
MeasurementPointItem				X
Message	O	O	O	O
Movement	O	O	X	O
MovementLeg	O	O	X	O
MRONetwork	X	X		
NestedSerializedProductVariant				X
NonAvailabilityAttribution		X		
NonAvailabilityCause		X		
NonAvailabilityCauseItem		X		
OpeningTimes	X			
OperatingBase	X		O	X
OperatingBaseCapacity				X
OperatingLocationType	X			X
OperationalApproval			O	
OperationalPeriod			X	
Operator				X
OperatorOrganization				X
OperatorPerson				X
Organization	X	X	O	O
OrganizationalBreakdownStructureRevision	O	O	O	O
OrganizationOperationsApproval				O
OtherFacility	X			
ParkingFacility	X			

Applicable to: All

Class name	UC51503	UC51504	UC51505	UC51506
PartAsDesigned	O	O	O	O
Party	X	X	O	O
Penalty	O	O	O	O
Person	O	X	O	O
PersonOperationsApproval				O
Pool	O	O	O	O
Port	X	X		
PowerGrid	X	X		
Product	O	X	O	O
ProductVariant	X	X	O	X
Project	O	O	O	O
Remark	O	O	O	O
RemarkItem	O	O	O	O
ReportableMetric	O	O	O	O
Requirement	O	O	O	O
ResourceSpecification	X	X		
SecurityClass	O	O	O	O
SecurityClassification	O	O	O	O
SecurityClassificationItem	O	O	O	O
SerializedHardwarePart	X	X	O	X
SerializedItem				O
SerializedItemOwner				O
SerializedProductVariant	X	X	X	X
SerializedProductVariantInFleet			O	X
SerializedProductVariantOperatingBase			O	X
SerializedProductVariantOperator			O	X
Service	O	X	O	O
ServiceBulletin		X		
SoftwareElement	X	X		
SoftwarePartAsReleased	X	X		

Class name	UC51503	UC51504	UC51505	UC51506
StreetAddress	X			
SupportEquipment	X			
Task	O	O	O	O
TaskRequirement	O	O	O	O
TransportNetwork	X	X		
Warehouse	X			
WorkBreakdown	O	O	O	O
WorkItem	O	O	O	O

2.14 Classes for Product environmental impact and disposal data

The classes used for each for Product environmental impact and disposal data use case as defined in Chap 16 are listed in UC51601: Exchange environmental data

7 UC51602: Environmental data for authorities

8 UC51603: Impact of modification on environment or disposal

9 UC51604: Valuable items recovered from disposal

10 UC51605: Request disposal of item

11 UC51606: Product disposal information

12 UC51607: Request waste disposal

13 UC51608: Waste disposal information

14 UC51609: Disposal costs

15 UC51610: Notification of disposal due to unacceptable condition

Table 15. The use cases are numbered:

16 UC51601: Exchange environmental data

17 UC51602: Environmental data for authorities

18 UC51603: Impact of modification on environment or disposal

19 UC51604: Valuable items recovered from disposal

20 UC51605: Request disposal of item

21 UC51606: Product disposal information

22 UC51607: Request waste disposal

23 UC51608: Waste disposal information

24 UC51609: Disposal costs

25   UC51610: Notification of disposal due to unacceptable condition

Table 15 Classes used for in-service environment data use cases

Class name	UC51601	UC51602	UC51603	UC51604	UC51605	UC51606	UC51607	UC51608	UC51609	UC51610
Action	O	X	O	X	O	X	O	X	O	O
AllowedProductConfiguration					X					O
AllowedProductConfigurationByConfigurationIdentifier					X					O
AllowedProductConfigurationHardwarePartAsDesigned					X					O
AllowedProductConfigurationItem				X	X					X
AuthorityToOperate					X					O
BatchHardwarePart	X	X	X	X	X	X	X	X		
BreakdownElement	O	O	O	O	O	O	O	O	X	O
BreakdownElementUsageInBreakdown				X	X					O
Budget	O	O	O	O	O	O	O	O	X	O
CargoItem	O	O	O	O	O	O	O	O	O	O
ChangeAuthorization				X						
ChangeControlledItem				X						
ChangeEmbodimentRequirement				X		X		X		
ChangeNotification				X						
ChangeRequest	O	O	X	O	O	X	O	O	X	O
ChangeRequestAddedOrRemovedMaterial				X						
ChangeRequestAddedOrRemovedSubstance				X						
ChangeRequestConsumptionChange				X						
ChangeRequestEmissionChange				X						
ChangeRequestEnvironmentallyImpactedItem				X						
Comment	O	O	O	O	O	O	O	O	O	O
CommentAction	O	O	O	O	O	O	O	O	O	O
CommentItem	O	O	O	O	O	O	O	O	O	O
CommentParty	O	O	O	O	O	O	O	O	O	O
CommentRelationship	O	O	O	O	O	O	O	O	O	O
CompliesWith					O	O	O			
ConsumableItem	X	X	X							

Class name	UC51601	UC51602	UC51603	UC51604	UC51605	UC51606	UC51607	UC51608	UC51609	UC51610
Consumption	X	X								
ConsumptionPeriod	X	X								
ContainedMaterial	X	X	X		X					
ContainedSubstance	X	X	X				X	O		
ContainerAsDesigned							X			
ContainerPart							X			
Contract	O	O	O	X	X	X	X	X	X	O
ContractClause				X	X	X	X	X	X	O
CostBreakdown								X		
CostBreakdownContext								X		
CostBreakdownRelationship								X		
CostBreakdownRevision								X		
CostEntry	O	O	O	O	O	X	O	O	X	O
CostEntryItem							X		X	
CostItem	O	O	O	O	O	O	O	O	X	O
CostItemRelationship									X	
Country				X	X	X	X	X		
Damage							X		X	
DataSetAsReleased					O	O	O			
DerivedChangeRequestRequirement			X							
DigitalFile	O	O	O	O	O	O	O	O	O	O
DisposalItem				X	X	X				
DisposalLocation				X	X	X	X	X	X	O
DisposalRequirement		X		X	X	X	X	X	X	X
DisposalRequirementContext				X	X	X	X	X	X	O
DisposalRequiringItem				X	X	X				
DisposalSite		X		X	X	X	X	X	X	O
DisposalTransportRequirement				X	X	X	X	X	X	O
Document	O	O	O	X	O	X	O	O	O	O
DocumentIssue	O	O	O	X	O	X	O	O	O	O

Class name	UC51601	UC51602	UC51603	UC51604	UC51605	UC51606	UC51607	UC51608	UC51609	UC51610
DocumentItem	O	O	O	X	O	X	O	O	O	O
DocumentReferencingItem	O	O	O	X	O	X	O	O	O	O
DownTimePeriod	X	X								
EffectiveOnProductConfiguration					X					X
EffectiveOnProductConfigurationItem					X					X
Environment	O	O	O	O	O	O	O	O	O	O
Event	O	O	O	O	O	O	O	O	O	O
ExportControlLicense	O	O	O	O	O	O	O	O	O	O
ExportControlRegulation				O	O	O				
Facility	X	X	X	X	X	X	X	X	X	O
Fleet	O	O	X	O	O	X	O	O	X	O
GeographicalArea				X	X	X	X	X		
GlobalPosition				X	X	X	X	X		
HardwareElement				X	X	X				
HardwareElementPartRealization					X					O
HardwarePartAsDesigned	X	X	X		X	X	X	O	X	O
HardwarePartContainer	X	X	X		X		X	O		
Infrastructure	X	X	X	X	X	X	O	O	X	O
InfrastructureCompliantItem	X	X								
InfrastructureOperatingPeriod	X	X								
InfrastructureRevision	X	X	X	O	O	O	O	O	O	O
InstallationLocation				X	X					
InstallationLocationDefinitionItem				X	X					
InstalledPart				X	X					
InstalledPartItem				X	X					
InvolvedDisposalOrganization					X	X	X	X	X	X	O
ItemDemilitarizationData					X	X	X			
ItemDisposalOperation					X	O	X			X	
ItemDisposalOperationAction					X		X			
ItemDisposalRequirement					X	X	X	X	X	X	O

Class name	UC51601	UC51602	UC51603	UC51604	UC51605	UC51606	UC51607	UC51608	UC51609	UC51610
ItemWarranty										O
LocationItem	X	X								
LooseWaste	X	X	X				X	O		
Material	X	X	X	X	X	X		X	X	
MaterialContainingItem	X	X	X		X					
MeasurementPoint					X	X				
MeasurementPointItem					X	X				
Message	O	O	O	O	O	O	O	O	O	O
Movement	X	X	O	O	O	X	O	O	X	O
MovementLeg	X	X	O	O	O	X	O	O	X	O
MovementLegDelay	X	X								
MovementLegPosition	X	X								
NestedAllowedProductConfiguration					X					O
NestedProductVariant					X					O
NonConformanceData					X					X
OperationalMode	X	X								
OperationalMoment	X	X								
OperationalMomentItem	X	X								
OperationalPeriod	X	X								
OperationalPeriodOperator	X	X								
OperationalPeriodRelationship	X	X								
OperationalRole	X	X								
Operator	X	X								
Organization	O	O	O	X	X	X	X	X	X	O
OrganizationalBreakdownStructureRevision	O	O	O	O	O	O	O	O	O	O
PartAsDesigned	O	O	O	X	X	X	O	X	X	O
PartAsDesignedPartsListEntry					X					O
PartAsDesignedPartsListRevision					X					O
Party	O	O	O	O	O	O	O	O	X	O
Penalty	O	O	O	O	O	X	O	O	X	O

Class name	UC51601	UC51602	UC51603	UC51604	UC51605	UC51606	UC51607	UC51608	UC51609	UC51610
Person	O	O	O	O	O	X	O	O	X	O
PlannedItemUpgrade			X							
PlannedUpgradeTimescales			X							
PoliciesAndRegulations				X	X	X	X	X	X	O
PoliciesAndRegulationsCompliantItem		X		X	X	X	X	X	X	O
Pool	O	O	O	O	O	O	O	O	O	O
Product	O	O	X	O	O	X	O	O	X	O
ProductVariant	X	X	X	O	X	X	O	O	X	O
Project	O	O	O	O	O	O	O	O	X	O
RealizedPart				X	X					
RecoveredItem				X		X				
RecoveredMaterialOrSubstances				X		X		X		
ReferencedDocument	O	O	O	X	O	X	O	O	O	O
Remark	O	O	O	O	O	O	O	O	O	O
RemarkItem	O	O	O	O	O	O	O	O	O	O
ReportableActivity							X		X	
ReportableMetric	O	O	O	O	O	O	O	O	O	O
RequiredDisposalPolicy				X	X	X	X	X	X	O
Requirement	O	O	X	X	X	X	X	X	X	O
ResourceUsageRequest							X		X	
S1000DDataModule	O	O	O	X	O	X	O	O	O	O
S1000DDataModuleIssue	O	O	O	X	O	X	O	O	O	O
S1000DPublicationModule	O	O	O	X	O	X	O	O	O	O
S1000DPublicationModuleIssue	O	O	O	X	O	X	O	O	O	O
SafetyIssue			X							
SecurityClass	O	O	O	O	O	O	O	O	O	O
SecurityClassification	O	O	O	O	O	O	O	O	O	O
SecurityClassificationItem	O	O	O	O	O	O	O	O	O	O
SerializedHardwarePart	X	X	X	X	X	X	X	O	X	O
SerializedProductOperationalPeriod	X	X								

Class name	UC51601	UC51602	UC51603	UC51604	UC51605	UC51606	UC51607	UC51608	UC51609	UC51610
SerializedProductVariant	X	X	X	X	X	X	X	O	X	O
SerializedProductVariantConfigurationConformance				X	X					
Service	O	O	O	O	O	X	O	O	X	O
ServiceBulletin			X			X			X	O
ServiceRequest						X			X	
SoftwareElement			X	X	X					
SoftwareElementPartRealization						X				O
SoftwarePartAsReleased				X	X	X			X	O
StreetAddress				X	X	X	X	X		
SubjectOfPoliciesAndRegulations				X	X	X	X	X	X	O
SubstanceContainingItem	X	X	X				X	O		
SubstanceDefinition	X	X	X	X		X	X	X		
SubstanceEmission	X	X								
SubstanceEmissionPeriod	X	X								
Task	O	O	O	O	O	O	O	O	O	O
TaskRequirement	O	O	O	O	O	O	O	O	O	O
TechnicalOrder			X							
TransportRequirement				X	X	X	X	X	X	O
UnacceptableCondition										X
UsableOnItem					X					O
UsableOnProductVariant					X					O
WarrantyClaim										X
WarrantyClaimContact										O
WarrantyClaimEvents										O
WarrantyClaimFollowUp										O
WarrantyClaimResolution							X		X	O
WarrantyEvent										O
WarrantyItem										O
WasteContainer	X	X	X				X	O		
WasteDisposalOperation		X		X	O	X		X	X	

Class name	UC51601	UC51602	UC51603	UC51604	UC51605	UC51606	UC51607	UC51608	UC51609	UC51610
WasteDisposalOperationAction		X						X		
WasteDisposalRequirement		X		X	X	X	X	X	X	O
WasteItem		X		X		X	X	X		
WasteRecoveredItem				X		X		X		
WorkBreakdown	O	O	O	O	O	O	O	O	O	O
WorkItem	O	O	X	X	X	X	X	X	X	O
WorkOrder							X		X	

2.15 Classes used for non-predefined information

The classes used for each non-predefined information use case as defined in Chap 23 are listed in Table 16. The use cases are numbered:

1 UC52301: Provide project-specific values (former UC51501)

2 UC52302: Provide non-predefined information (former UC51502)

Table 16 Classes used for non-predefined information use cases

Class name	UC52301	UC52302
Action	O	O
BatchHardwarePart		X
BreakdownElement	O	O
Budget	O	O
CargoItem	O	X
ChangeRequest	O	X
CircuitBreaker		X
Comment	O	O
CommentAction	O	O
CommentItem	O	O
CommentParty	O	O
CommentRelationship	O	O
Contract	O	X
CostEntry	O	O

Class name	UC52301	UC52302
CostItem	O	O
Country		X
DigitalFile	O	X
DigitalFileReference		X
DigitalFileReferencedItem		X
DigitalFileReferencingItem		X
Document	O	X
DocumentCharacteristicItem	O	
DocumentIssue	O	X
DocumentParty	O	
Environment	O	X
Event	O	X
ExportControlLicense	O	O
ExternalDocument	O	
Facility	O	X
Fleet	O	X
FleetTaskCancellationNotice	O	
GeographicalArea		X
GlobalPosition		X
Infrastructure	O	X
InfrastructureRevision	O	O
InstallationLocation		X
Locator	O	X
MaintenanceProgram	O	
MeasurementPoint		X
Message	O	O
Movement	O	O
MovementLeg	O	O
Organization	O	X
OrganizationalBreakdownStructureRevision	O	O

Class name	UC52301	UC52302
PartAsDesigned	O	X
Party	O	O
Penalty	O	O
Person	O	O
Pool	O	X
Product	O	X
ProductVariant	O	X
Project	O	O
ReferencedDigitalFile		X
Remark	O	O
RemarkItem	O	O
Report	O	
ReportableMetric	O	O
Requirement	O	O
ResourceSpecification		X
SafetyDocument	O	
SCORMContentPackage	O	
SecurityClass	O	O
SecurityClassification	O	X
SecurityClassificationItem	O	O
SerializedHardwarePart	O	X
SerializedProductVariant	O	X
Service	O	X
ServiceBulletin	O	
StreetAddress		X
SubstanceDefinition		X
Task	O	X
TaskRequirement	O	O
WarrantyClaim		X
WorkBreakdown	O	O

Class name	UC52301	UC52302
WorkItem	O	O
ZoneElementRevision		X

3   Mapping of data elements against chapter use cases

Issue 1.0 of S5000F included a mapping of the individual data elements against chapter use cases. This has been found to be counter-productive, as projects tried to implement the specification by selecting individual data elements for the different use cases, without consideration of the classes including them, hence that this part has been removed.

It must be highlighted that the individual data elements cannot exist without the classes for which they form the attributes. Thus, an `operationalPeriodResult` data element cannot exist if the `OperationalPeriod` class is not implemented. This is because of grouping, and the relationships between different elements being defined at the class level and not at the data element level. Therefore, the relationship between the data element `operationalPeriodResult` and the `SerializedProductVariant` that performed that `OperationalPeriod` cannot be established if only this data element was selected. It is not possible to choose the individual data elements, ignoring their classes, based on some arbitrary criteria while aiming to keep a consistent data model.

The process for defining the data elements required for each individual use case is:

– Select the UoFs required for your specific use case
– Identify the classes in those UoFs that you do require for the use case
– Ensure that all necessary relationships are included in the list (eg, if the association of an *OperationalPeriod* to a *SerializedProductVariant* is desired, then the << relationship>> *SerializedProductOperationalPeriod*) is required)
– For each selected class, identify the attributes (data elements) that are mandatory. These must be included for a proper data exchange
– Attributes whose multiplicity starts with zero (0 ..1, 0 ..*, or similar) are optional. Decide which of those attributes are required for your particular use case.

Practical tailoring examples are provided in Chap 27 and Chap 29.

Chapter 29

Implementation example

Table of contents

Page

Implementation example 1
References 2
1 General 2
1.1 Introduction 2
1.2 Scope.. 2
1.3 Chapter organization 2
2 Description of example 'Fleet availability' 3
3 Modeling of process use case.. 4
3.1 Introduction 4
3.2 UML Sequence diagram 5
4 Tailoring of S5000F UML model 5
5 Tailoring the S5000F XML Schema 14
5.1 Introduction 14
5.2 Tailoring the XML Schema Definition 14
5.3 Tailoring message structure 15
5.3.1 Introduction 15
5.3.2 Example 15
5.4 Tailoring valid values 17
5.4.1 Introduction 17
5.4.2 Example of a project specific non Availability Cause type 18
6 XML messages 19
6.1 Message for the Fleet_Availability use case 19
6.1.1 Comments on the message fleet_Availability 21
6.2 Acknowledgment message 22
6.3 Observation message 24
6.4 Localization of xml information 24

List of tables

1 References 2
2 Message envelope objects 12
3 Message content objects 13
4 S5000F XML Schema Definition files 14

List of figures

1 Example of PDF form to collect fleet availability data 4
2 Example use case - UML sequence diagram 5
3 S5000F UoF Message - tailored to project 6
4 S5000F UoF Message Content - tailored to project 7
5 S5000F UoF Security Classification - tailored to project 7
6 S5000F UoF Serialized Product Variant - tailored to project 8
7 S5000F UoF Availability - tailored to project 9
8 S5000F UoF Non-Availability Cause Item - tailored to project 9

9   S5000F UoF Facility - tailored to project 10
10   UoF Fleet Availability overview diagram 11
11   Overview smart representation 12
12   XML Schema - Customization for message envelope 16
13   XML Schema - Customization for message content 17
14   Customized "Non Availability Cause Type Code" valid values 18
15   Example of message fleet availability 20
16   setBy example 22
17   Example of acknowledgment message 23
18   Example of observation message 24
19   Information location using X-Path 25

References

Table 1 References

Chap No./Document No.	Title
Chap 11	Integrated fleet management
Chap 27	Tailoring and contracting against S5000F
SX001G	Glossary for the S-Series IPS specifications
XPath	XML Path Language - W3C Recommendation 21 March 2017

1 General

1.1 Introduction

This chapter explains how S5000F can be tailored to define a data exchange protocol for a specific purpose. The successive phases of this tailoring process are described (ie, objectives, methods, results, etc) and demonstrated on an example.

As this chapter provides guidelines, it must be considered as informative and not mandatory.

1.2 Scope

Tailoring a specification is basically adapting it for a specific purpose or project. This tailoring is usually part of the contractual and technical negotiation.

The scope of this chapter only extends to technical aspects of tailoring. It does not cover contractual aspects, which are addressed in Chap 27.

1.3 Chapter organization

Para 2 proposes a business example which serves as a thread all along tailoring process phases.

This business example is modeled in Unified Modeling Language (UML) with a sequence diagram for identifying data exchanges to be implemented. Refer to Para 3.

Then S5000F UML model is tailored to represent the selected data exchanges, Refer to Para 4.

The S5000F XML Schema Definition (XSD), associated to previously tailored S5000F UML model, is identified and customized to allow a strict parsing of exchanged messages. Refer to Para 5.

S5000F-A-00-00-0000-00A-009A-A   Applicable to: All

As a conclusion, some XML instances are created and commented to highlight the result of this customization process. Refer to Para 6.

2 Description of example 'Fleet availability'

Parties that operate helicopters are managing and monitoring their fleet with Maintenance Information Systems (MIS). Each of these MIS contains the status for each helicopter and duration of every flight.

To create a common operators-industry fleet availability indicator, operators agree to periodically transfer to the manufacturer the status of their helicopters and the amount of flown flight hours. As the objective is to build a monthly indicator, exchanged information allows manufacturer to get a full understanding of detailed operational activities, is not a requirement.

After processing the collected data, the manufacturer issues a monthly fleet availability report that allows operators to compare their fleet availability with that of other parties.

Note

This use case is based on a real implementation and operators are periodically sending information (helicopters status, flown flight hours) to the manufacturer. Unfortunately these exchanges use proprietary formats (eg, MS™ Excel files, XML forms, etc) and involve manual processes (eg, typing, extraction, email, etc) which depend on the individual operators. The data in this example have been anonymized and changed so as not to provide any real information. The operating base, though a real airport, is not the one from the real report on which the example is based.

To have a realistic use case, the example will be based on operators which are manually filling PDF form (refer to Fig 1) and weekly email it to the manufacturer. The text highlighted on this PDF form will serve to populate message example. Refer to Para 6.

The objective of the project is to define an exchange protocol which allows all operators to efficiently feedback fleet availability information to manufacturer. The implementation of an exchange protocol is an investment which is justified by the workload decrease, improvement of data quality, on-time data delivery and security of exchanges.

| Issued by : | | | WEEKLY REPORT FRANCE
Based on Daily forms | | | | Week / Year
36 / 2016
(05/09/2016 - 11/09/2016) | | |
| Operator
Dummy operator | | | NH90 version/config
NFH / MOC - FOC | | | | Operating Base
NAS Hyères, NAS Lanvéoc | | |

FLEET STATUS

Serial	H/C	Registration	Type	Total FH in CW	Total FH Since Deliv	Total FH Since New	X	S	U	B	M	R	C	O
1251														
1252														
1278														
1300														
1301														
1302														
1303														
1304														
1339	NFRN009	F-XHFQ	FOC	6h58 (6.97)	35h06 (35.1)	68h51 (68.85)			6	1				
Total H/C in the fleet														
Total incl. inactive H/C														

X = serviceable ; S = scheduled maintenance ; U = unscheduled maintenance ; B = service bulletin ; M = missing spare part ; R = retrofit ; C = Customer related ; O = others

SUPPORT STATUS

Category	H/C	Technical subject	Target date (CW)
(S)cheduled maintenance		1200 FH	
		900 FH	
		600 FH	
		Other scheduled maintenance	
(B)ulletin	1339 / NFRN009	SBP-JA-A-25-12-03-02A-A-A-001	
(C)ustomer related reason			

Edited on 26/09/2016 07:34:26   NFFT Weekly Report Version 1.16   Page 1 of 1

ICN-B6865-5000F24001-001-01

Fig 1 Example of PDF form to collect fleet availability data

3 Modeling of process use case

3.1 Introduction

Starting from process description this phase identifies actors and processes on operators and manufacturer sides. This end-to-end modeling allows to identify data exchanges with their associated source/target processes.

Identification of actors/positions is also crucial since it is recommended to involve some of their representatives as project stakeholders all along project phases.

3.2 UML Sequence diagram

The process description (refer to Para 2) is represented as an UML sequence diagram (refer to Fig 2), which identifies actors, systems and data exchanges between operator and manufacturer systems.

It is good practice to have this UML diagram hosted in the same software package as the S5000F UML model to ensure its consistency.

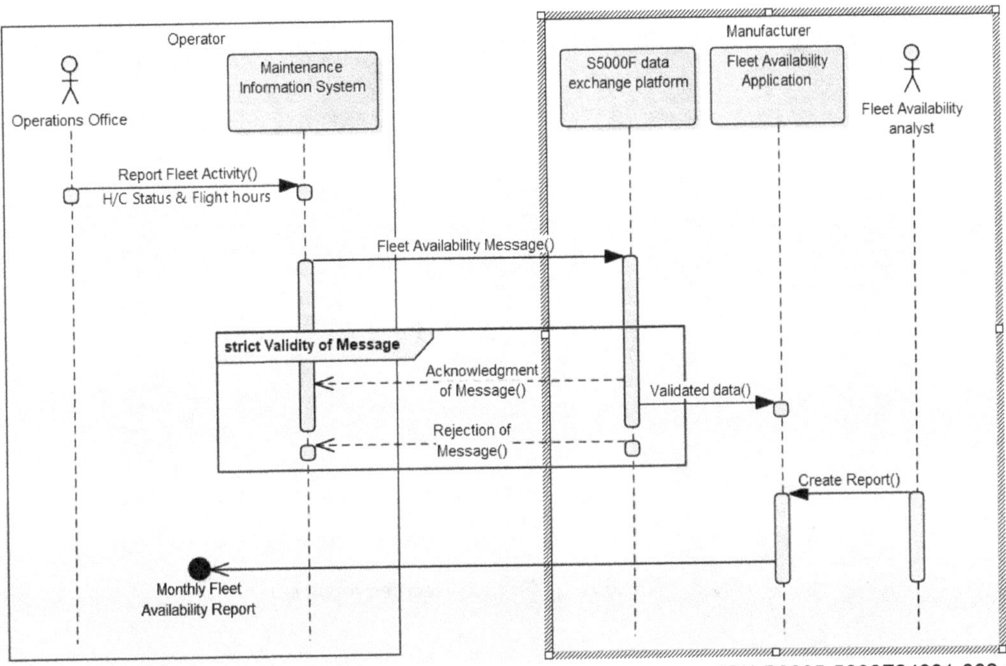

Fig 2 Example use case - UML sequence diagram

4 Tailoring of S5000F UML model

S5000F provides an UML data model for the in-service data feedback and related business processes. It is a very large model which contains around 450 classes distributed into over one hundred UoF.

Model tailoring, for limiting model to the project scope, is therefore a mandatory phase. This process is done by selecting UoF which cover functional scope and then selecting in these UoF, the classes which are necessary to represent exchanged data.

For modelling the message header and trailer, the selected UoF are:

- S5000F UoF Message (refer to Fig 3)
- S5000F UoF Message Content (refer to Fig 4)
- S5000F UoF Security Classification (refer to Fig 5)

For modelling the message content, the selected UoF are:

- S5000F UoF Serialized Product Variant (refer to Fig 6)

- S5000F UoF Availability (refer to Fig 7)
- S5000F UoF Non Availability Cause Item (refer to Fig 8)
- S5000F UoF Facility (refer to Fig 9)

On these class diagrams, those objects (ie, classes, relations, interfaces, etc) which are not retained for the data exchange are grayed out. It is good practice to let them in the background for future activation if the project scope is extended.

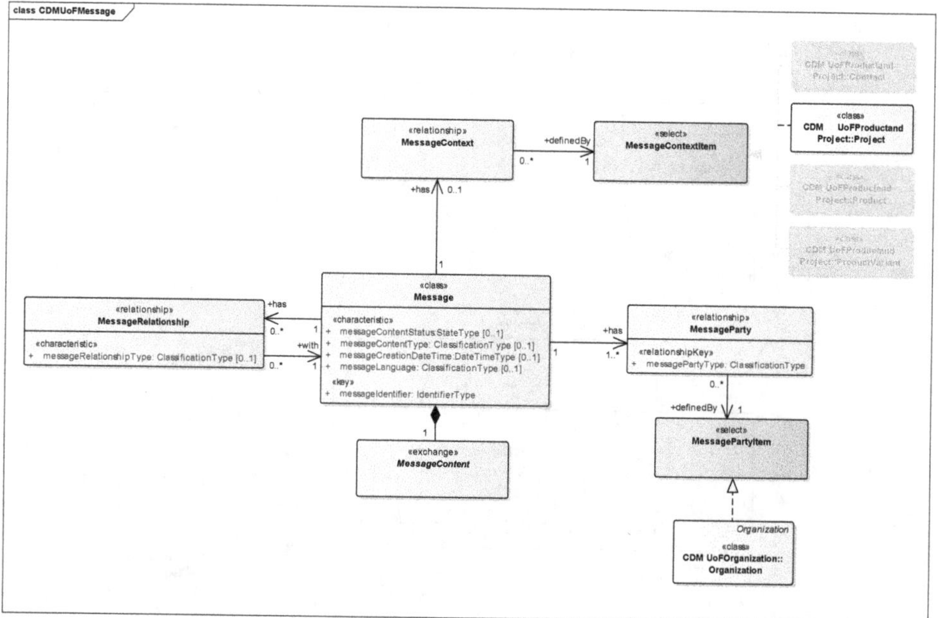

ICN-B6865-5000F24003-001-01

Fig 3 S5000F UoF Message - tailored to project

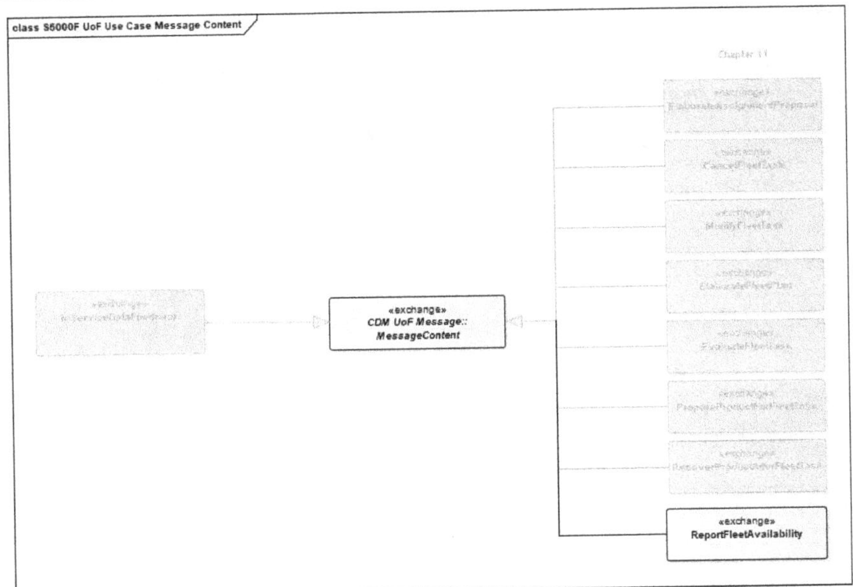

ICN-B6865-5000F24001-004-01

Fig 4 S5000F UoF Message Content - tailored to project

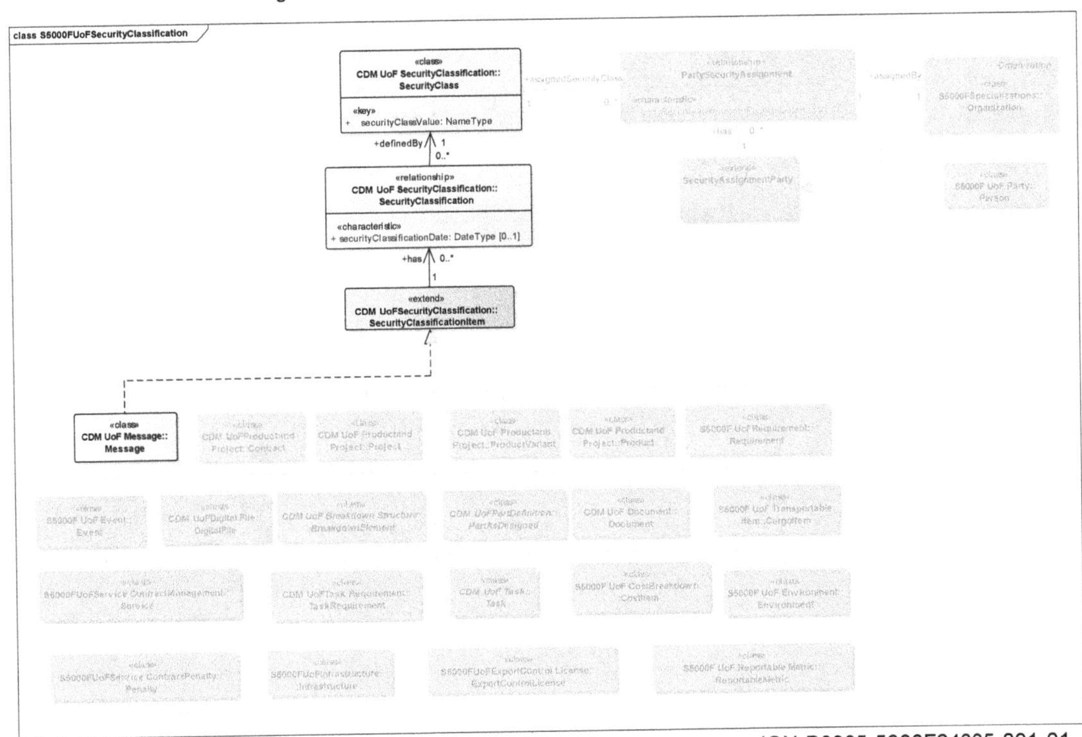

ICN-B6865-5000F24005-001-01

Fig 5 S5000F UoF Security Classification - tailored to project

Note

UoF Security Classification (refer to Fig 5) is defined in S5000F as an extension of Common Data Model (CDM) Security Classification which contains data elements common to two or more one of the S-Series IPS specification.

Note

Some classes appear in different Units of Functionality. Their selection depends on the UoF. For example, the class Project is selected in S5000F UoF Message (refer to Fig 3) and not selected in UoF Security Classification. (Refer to Fig 5).

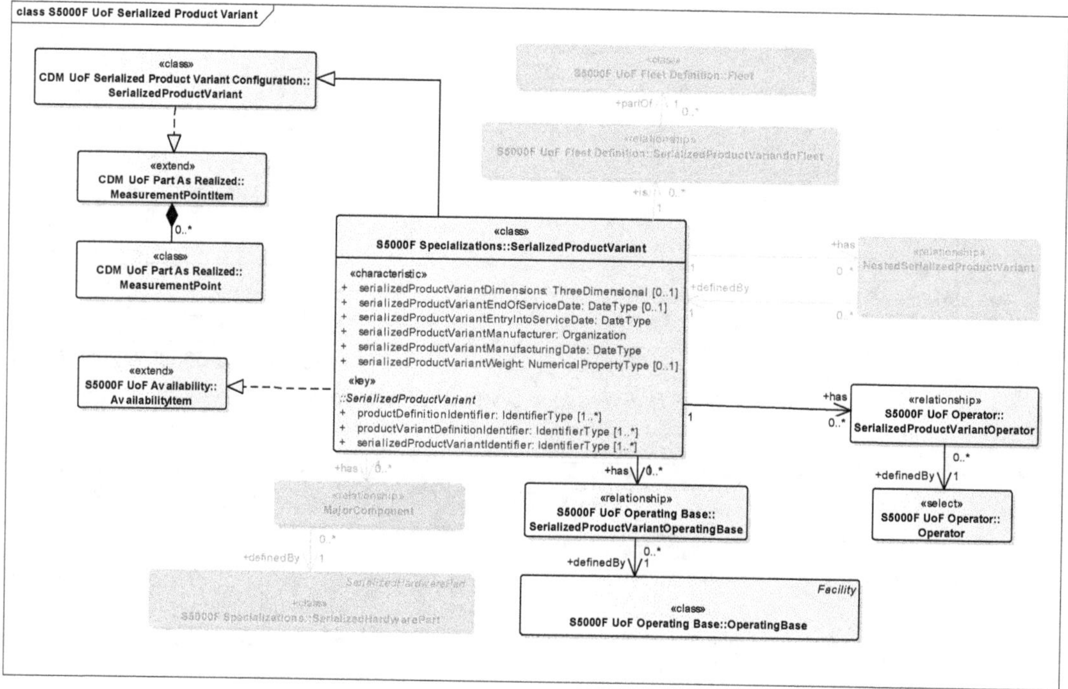

ICN-B6865-5000F24001-006-01

Fig 6 S5000F UoF Serialized Product Variant - tailored to project

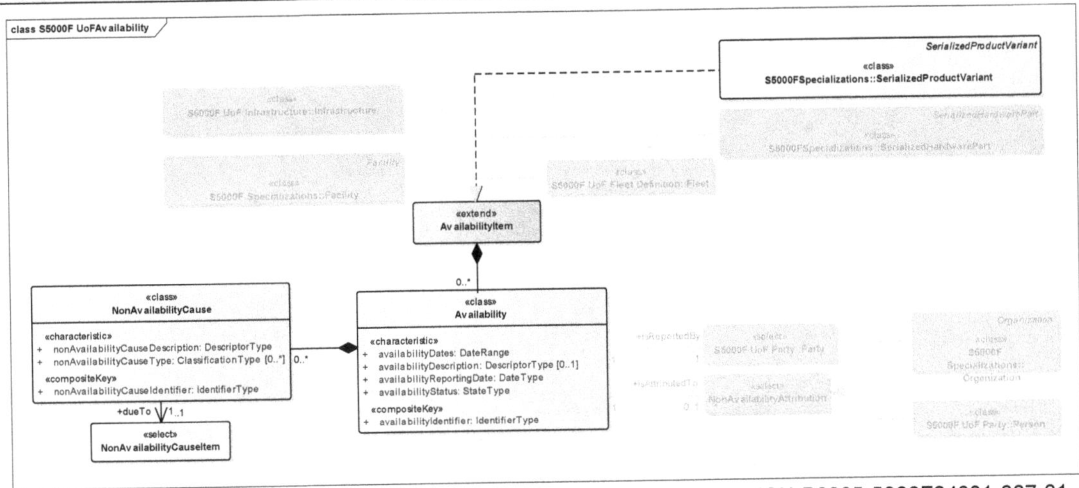

ICN-B6865-5000F24001-007-01

Fig 7 S5000F UoF Availability - tailored to project

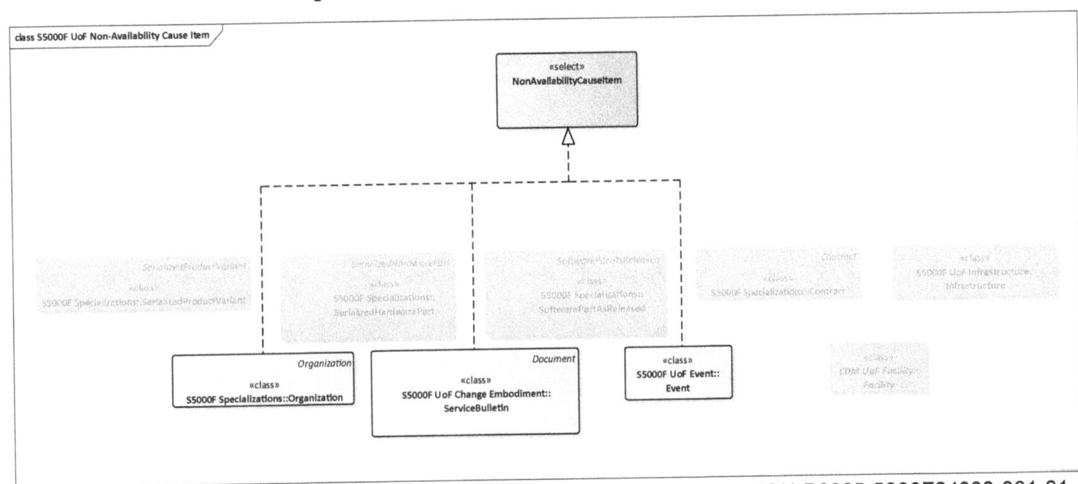

ICN-B6865-5000F24008-001-01

Fig 8 S5000F UoF Non-Availability Cause Item - tailored to project

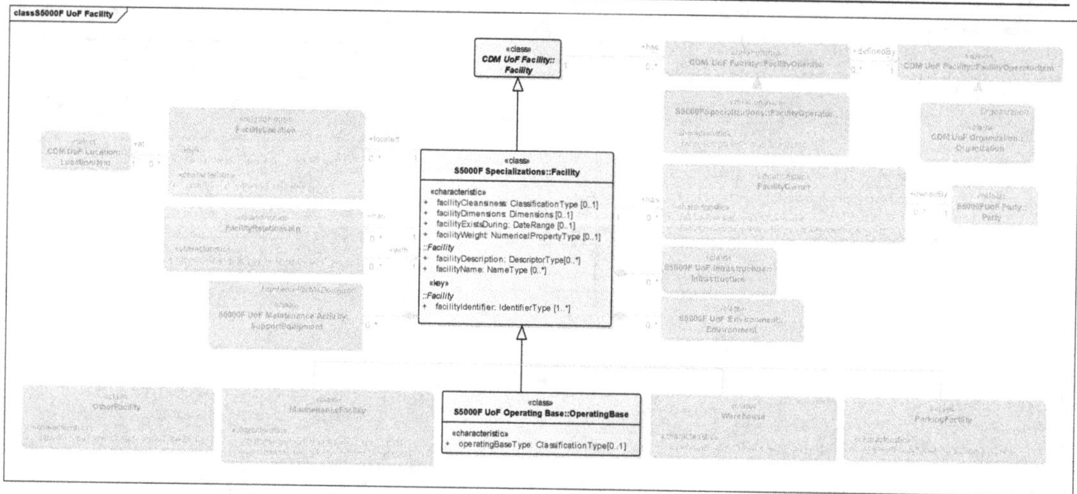

ICN-B6865-5000F24001-009-01

Fig 9 S5000F UoF Facility - tailored to project

The class diagram UoF Fleet Availability (refer to Fig 10) gathers all classes which are retained to model the project-dedicated message content.

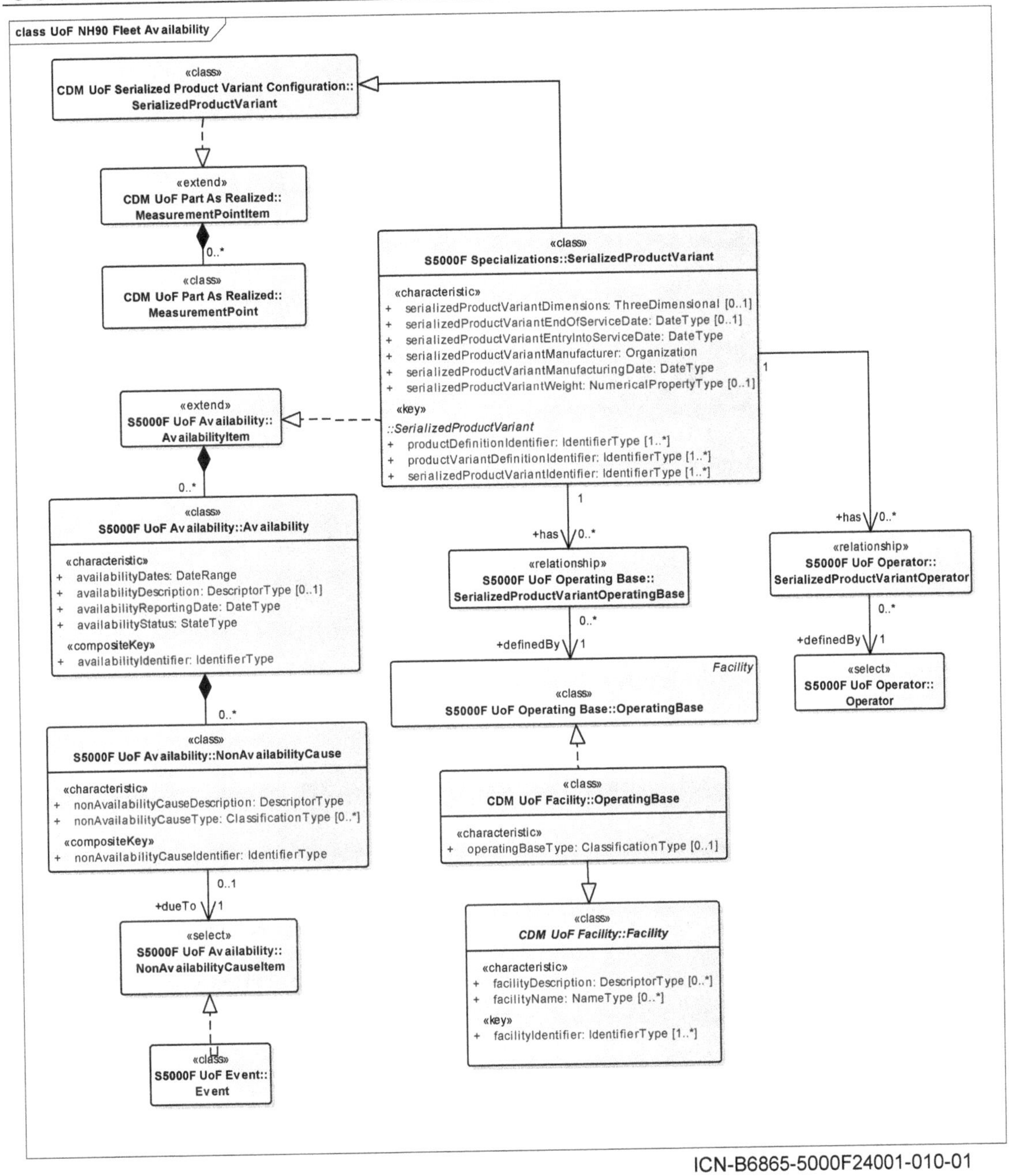

ICN-B6865-5000F24001-010-01

Fig 10 UoF Fleet Availability overview diagram

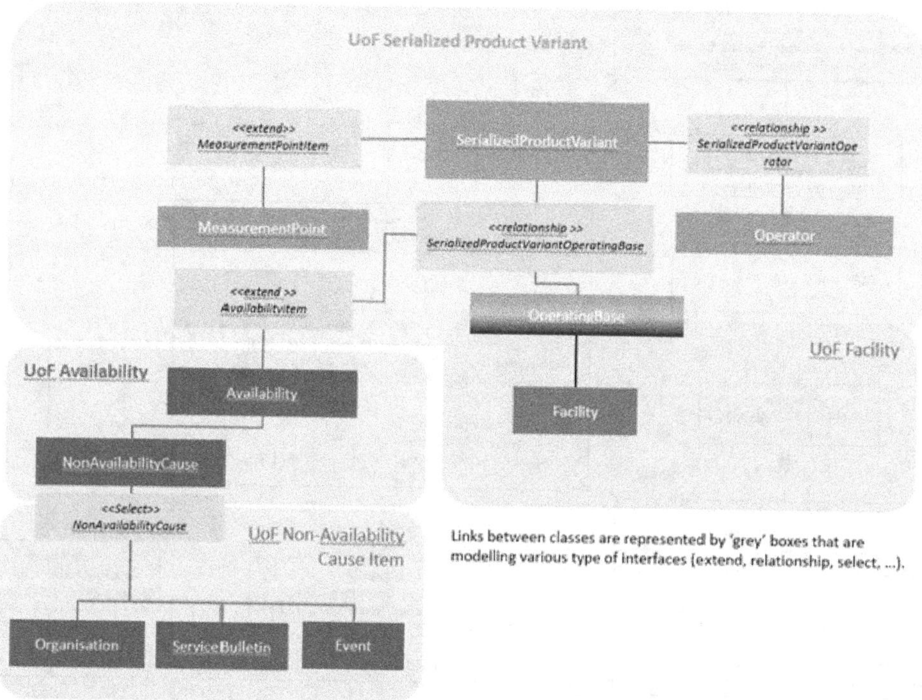

ICN-B6865-5000F24001-011-01

Fig 11 Overview smart representation

From these UML class diagrams, a list of selected UML objects (ie, classes, interfaces, etc) are extracted and loaded into tables. These tables link UML and XSD model by giving oblects xmlName.

Table 2 lists objects which represent message metadata that are stored in message envelope.

Table 3 lists objects which represent fleet availability information that is stored in message content.

Note

In these tables, there are duplicate rows since a class can occur in many unit of functionality: (eg, class Message occurs in S5000F UoF Message and S5000F UoF Security Classification). (Refer to Table 2).

Table 2 Message envelope objects

Unit of Functionality	Name	Type	xmlName
S5000F UoF Message	Message	Class	msg
S5000F UoF Message	MessageContent	Class	msgContent
S5000F UoF Message	MessageContext	Class	msgContext
S5000F UoF Message	MessageParty	Class	msgPty
S5000F UoF Message	MessageRelationship	Class	relatedMsg

Unit of Functionality	Name	Type	xmlName
S5000F UoF Message	Organization	Class	org
S5000F UoF Message	MessageContextItem	Interface	context
S5000F UoF Message	MessagePartyItem	Interface	party
S5000F UoF Message Context Item	Project	Class	proj
S5000F UoF Message Context Item	MessageContextItem	Interface	context
S5000F UoF Security Classification	Message	Class	msg
S5000F UoF Security Classification	SecurityClass	Class	secClassDef
S5000F UoF Security Classification	SecurityClassification	Class	sec
S5000F UoF Security Classification	SecurityClassificationItem	Interface	secs

Table 3 Message content objects

Unit of Functionality	Name	Type	xmlName
S5000F UoF Message Content	InServiceDataFeedback	Class	uc50000
S5000F UoF Message Content	MessageContent	Class	msgContent
S5000F UoF Serialized Product Variant	MeasurementPoint	Class	mPoint
S5000F UoF Serialized Product Variant	OperatingBase	Class	opBase
S5000F UoF Serialized Product Variant	SerializedProductVariant	Class	serialPV
S5000F UoF Serialized Product Variant	SerializedProductVariant	Class	serialPV
S5000F UoF Serialized Product Variant	SerializedProductVariantOperatingBase	Class	spvob
S5000F UoF Serialized Product Variant	SerializedProductVariantOperator	Class	spvoper
S5000F UoF Serialized Product Variant	AvailabilityItem	Interface	flta
S5000F UoF Serialized Product Variant	MeasurementPointItem	Interface	mpoints
S5000F UoF Serialized Product Variant	Operator	Interface	oper
S5000F UoF Availability	Availability	Class	avail
S5000F UoF Availability	NonAvailabilityCause	Class	navcau
S5000F UoF Availability	Organization	Class	org
S5000F UoF Availability	AvailabilityItem	Interface	flta
S5000F UoF Availability	NonAvailabilityCauseItem	Interface	navCause
S5000F UoF NonAvailability Cause Item	Event	Class	ev
S5000F UoF NonAvailability Cause Item	Organization	Class	org
S5000F UoF NonAvailability Cause Item	ServiceBulletin	Class	servBu
S5000F UoF NonAvailability Cause Item	NonAvailabilityCauseItem	Interface	navCause

Unit of Functionality	Name	Type	xmlName
S5000F UoF MeasurementPoint	MeasurementPoint	Class	mPoint
S5000F UoF MeasurementPoint	SerializedProductVariant	Class	serialPV
S5000F UoF MeasurementPoint	MeasurementPointItem	Interface	mpoints
S5000F UoF Facility	Facility	Class	facility
S5000F UoF Facility	OperatingBase	Class	opBase

5 Tailoring the S5000F XML Schema

5.1 Introduction

S5000F includes an XML Schema Definition (XSD) (refer to <u>Table 4</u>) which formally describes constraints that an S5000F XML message must fulfill.

XML parser checks validity of XML instances against constraints which are defined in XSD. These constraints are on the structure of elements and attributes, on relationship between elements and on authorized values.

The parsing phase is essential because it ensures a secure and organized data exchange.

Parties agree on data exchange rules. These rules are encoded into the XSD, so the XML parser can formally checks that XML instance is conform to agreed rules.

After success of this preliminary phase, message data can be securely processed by external applications.

Table 4 S5000F XML Schema Definition files

N°	Filename	Content
1	s5000f_2-0_isfDataset.xsd	Define structures (elements, attributes, types, …)
2	S5000F_2-0_valid_values.xsd	Valid values defined in S-series glossary
3	s5000f_2-0_valid_values_libraries.xsd	Valid values for country, currency and language defined by ISO
4	s5000f_2-0_valid_values_project_extensions.xsd	Valid values for project specific attribute names
5	s5000f_2-0_valid_values_sets.xsd	
6	s5000f_2-0_valid_values_units.xsd	Valid values for unit of measure

5.2 Tailoring the XML Schema Definition

The scope of a project is often less than that of S5000F. The project imposes constraints on the use of the S5000F, which implies that the XSD must be tailored to align with the project requirements. Parsing against this customized XSD ensures that message is fully compliant with the project business rules.

However, this tailored XSD must be compliant with the S5000F XSD, therefore, all XML instances, which are valid against this tailored XSD, are also valid against the S5000F XSD, but not the other way round.

5.3 Tailoring message structure

5.3.1 Introduction

Message structure is defined in the file s5000f_2-0_isfDataset.xsd (refer to Table 4).

The lists of classes, resulting from UML tailoring, which are necessary to model exchanged messages (refer to Table 2 and Table 3). In these lists, some classes can be considered as first-level classes, because they contain, or refer to other classes.

In the example, Message, OperatingBase and SerializedProductVariant will be considered as first-level classes because they contain all classes that have been selected in the project scope.

Class Message is represented in XSD by the element `<isfDataset>`. This element has child elements that store message metadata (eg, sender, receiver, issue date, etc) and a child element `<uc51108>` that stores data for use case ReportFleetAvailability. Refer to Chap 11 and Fig 4.

Use case classes are described to encompass all data which are relevant in that use case. There is also a general use case, `<uc50000>`, which contains over 100 elements containing all S5000F classes.

The element `<uc51108>`, which is dedicated to the ReportFleetAvailability use case, contains child elements that the project does not need to use, so the parties must agree on the business rules to exchange this data. To ensure that the data that is not required, is not included in the exchanged message, a business rule for the use of the project-specific element `<uc51108_NH90FleetAvail>`, is created. This is achieved by restricting the cardinality of the message elements.

This project specific tailoring of the element `<uc51108_NH90FleetAvail>` is agreed by all parties. However, the message is compliant with the element `<uc51108>`. Refer to Para 5.2.

In the example, the first-level class elements `<opBase>` and `<serialPV>` are retained. The element `<serialPV>` contains all project specific child elements of the element `<opBase>`.

Elements that are not used or permissible changes to cardinality must not reduce the required minimum number of occurrences or extend the permitted maximum number of occurrences of an element. Thus,

- 0..1 can become 1..1 or 0..0 (but not, for example, 1..2)
- 0..n can become 0..1, 1..m, 1..n, m..n, or 0..0 (where m<n)
- 1..n can become 1..1, m..n, or 1..m (where m<n)
- 1..1 cannot be changed

5.3.2 Example

Fig 12 shows the project specific structure of the XSD for a message envelope, the content of which is held within the element `<uc51108_NH90FleetAvail>`. Refer to Fig 13.

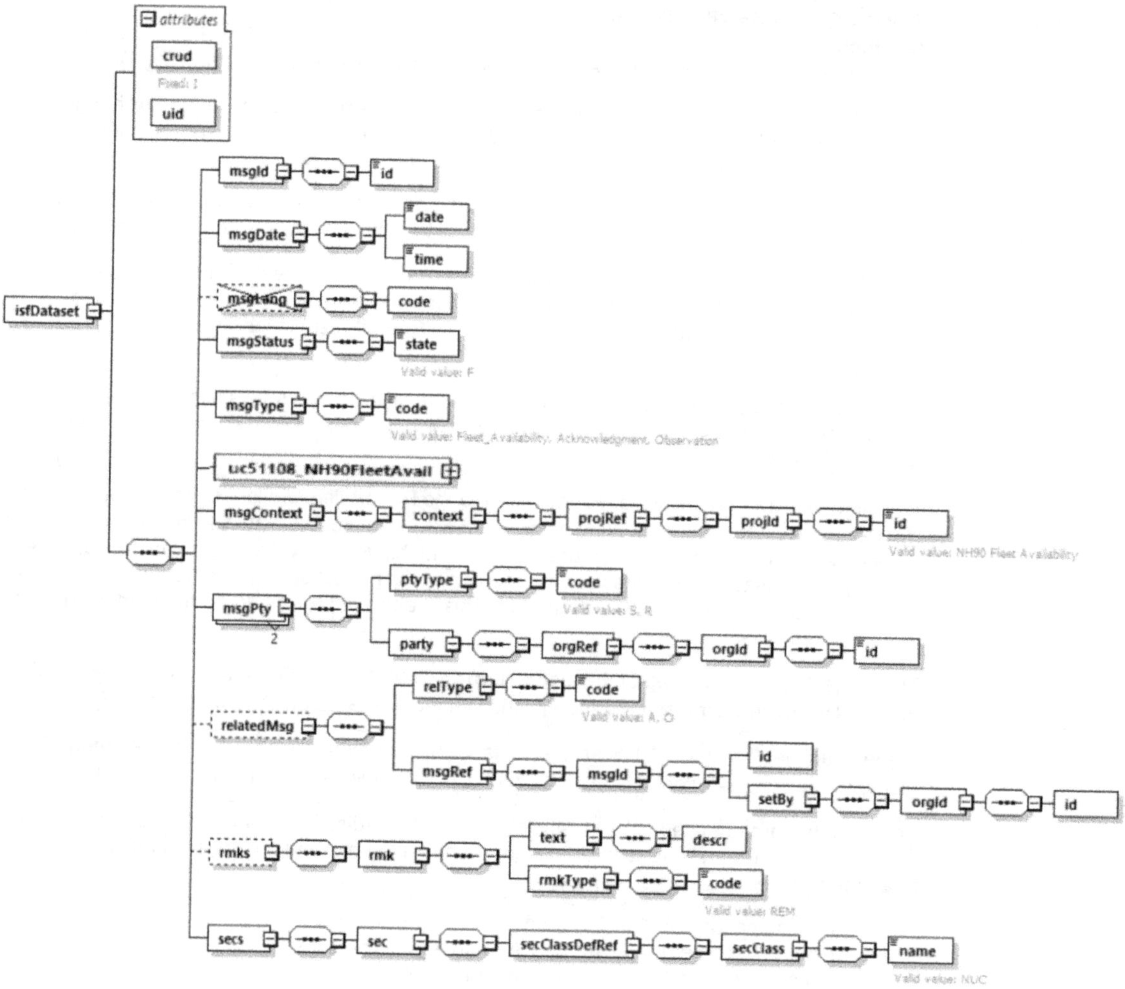

ICN-B6865-5000F24001-012-01

Fig 12 XML Schema - Customization for message envelope

The cardinality of the project specific XSD elements have been modified in a way that:

- most child of element `<uc51108_NH90FleetAvail>` have now a cardinality 1..1
- the element `<msgLang>` is removed by its cardinality 0..0 but is shown in Fig 12 for information
- the elements `<relatedMsg>` and `<rmks>` have a cardinality 0..1 because they are not used in message Fleet_Availability and used in message Acknowledgment and message Observation
- the element `<msgPty>` has a cardinality 2..2 because we require a message sender and a message receiver

Applicable to: All

DMC-S5000F-A-29-00-0000-00A-040A-A_001-00_EN-US

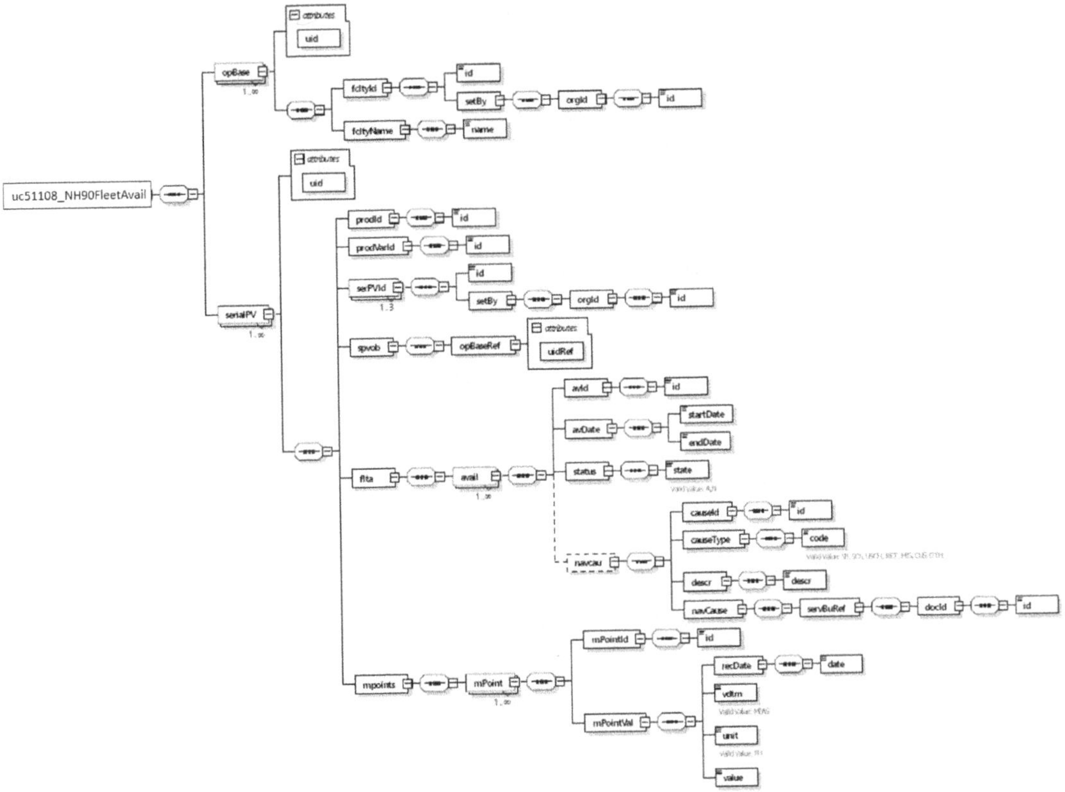

ICN-B6865-5000F24001-013-01

Fig 13 XML Schema - Customization for message content

In element `<uc51108_NH90FleetAvail>`, all elements of `<uc51108>` not necessary for message content have been tailored so that opBase (operating base) and serialPV (serialized product variant) are kept.

The cardinality of opBase and serialPV being 1..∞, message content can hold many operating bases and many serialized product variants.

SerializedProductVariant (class or complex type in xml):
- starts with helicopter product, variant, and serial number
- refers to an operating base (element `<spvob>`)
- contains availability information for different period of time (element `<flta>`)
- ends with measurement structure to hold flown flight hours (`<mpoints>`)

The cardinality of elements provide a tailored structure that can host information about one or many helicopters, during one or many periods of time with many types of measurement points.

5.4 Tailoring valid values

5.4.1 Introduction

The valid values which are listed in file S5000F_2-0_valid_values.xsd (refer to Table 4) are those defined in SX001G.

These valid values are considered as recommended and not mandatory. To adapt these values to project scope, it recommended that:

- use the valid values are applied as they are defined without any modification of value, meaning or documentation
- the valid values that are not used be removed by commenting them (no deletion to keep track of changes)
- extending existing types by adding new valid values which are required for the project
- values are identified with a documented project name
- If necessary, create new types to hold valid values which are specific to the project in S5000F_2-0_valid_values_project_extensions.xsd are created, Refer to Table 4.

Note

The addition of new valid values can make the project specific XSD not compliant with S5000F XSD. It is therefore necessary to add such new valid values in the proper format as defined by S5000F. Note that though the specification allows to introduce such new values, these values will only be valid in the context of the current project (ie, they are considered to be project-specific and cannot be exchanged with other projects).

5.4.2 **Example of** a project specific non Availability Cause **type**
S5000F XSD proposes CUS, OTH, SB, SCH, USCH and UNSR as valid values for the nonAvailability Cause type code. (Refer to SX001G).

On PDF form currently use to collect information (refer to Para 2) values for helicopter status are X (serviceable), S (scheduled maintenance), U (unscheduled maintenance), B (service bulletin), M (Missing spare), R (Retrofit), C (Customer related) and O (Others).

The nonAvailabilityCauseTypeCodeValues tailoring implies therefore that:
- valid values CUS, OTH, SB, SCH, and USCH as they are defined are kept with form values being replaced by S5000F values (eg, C becomes CUS)
- values SER and UNSR are commented out because these are not retained for the project
- values RET and SPA are inserted and documented as new valid values for the project

Fig 14 shows the tailoring of the simpleType for nonAvailabilityCauseTypeCodeValues.

```xml
<xsd:simpleType name="nonAvailabilityCauseTypeCodeValues">
    <xsd:restriction base="xsd:string">
        <xsd:enumeration value="CUS">
            <xsd:annotation><xsd:appinfo><source>SX001G:customerRelated</source></xsd:appinfo></xsd:annotation></xsd:enumeration>
        <xsd:enumeration value="OTH">
            <xsd:annotation><xsd:appinfo><source>SX001G:other</source></xsd:appinfo></xsd:annotation></xsd:enumeration>
        <xsd:enumeration value="SB">
            <xsd:annotation><xsd:appinfo><source>SX001G:serviceBulletin</source></xsd:appinfo></xsd:annotation></xsd:enumeration>
        <xsd:enumeration value="SCH">
            <xsd:annotation><xsd:appinfo><source>SX001G:scheduledMaintenance</source></xsd:appinfo></xsd:annotation></xsd:enumeration>
        <xsd:enumeration value="USCH">
            <xsd:annotation><xsd:appinfo><source>SX001G:unscheduledMaintenance</source></xsd:appinfo></xsd:annotation></xsd:enumeration>
        <xsd:enumeration value="RET">
            <xsd:annotation><xsd:appinfo><source>NH90:retrofit</source></xsd:appinfo></xsd:annotation></xsd:enumeration>
        <xsd:enumeration value="SPA">
            <xsd:annotation><xsd:appinfo><source>NH90:missingSpare</source></xsd:appinfo></xsd:annotation></xsd:enumeration>
        <!--<xsd:enumeration value="SER">
            <xsd:annotation><xsd:appinfo><source>NH90:serviceable</source></xsd:appinfo></xsd:annotation></xsd:enumeration>-->
        <!--<xsd:enumeration value="UNSR">
            <xsd:annotation><xsd:appinfo><source>SX001G:unserviceable</source></xsd:appinfo></xsd:annotation></xsd:enumeration>-->
    </xsd:restriction>
</xsd:simpleType>
```

ICN-B6865-5000F24001-014-01

Fig 14 Customized "Non Availability Cause Type Code" valid values

In Fig 12, annotations show valid values which have been tailored in the message envelope to enforce project rules so that:

- in the project, there are only three types of messages therefore msgType/code valid values are Fleet_Availability, Acknowledgment and Observation
- the status of all message is Final and therefore the msgStatus/state valid value is F
- all message are issued in the same project, and therefore the msgContext/context/projRefer to /projId/id valid value is NH90 Fleet Availability

- there is a message sender and a message receiver but no forwarder, and therefore the msgPty/ptyType/codes are S, R but not F
- all messages are NATO Unclassified, and therefore the valid value for secs/sec/secClassDefRefer to /secClass/name is NUC

The annotations in Fig 13 show valid values which have been tailored in the message content to enforce project rules:

- the helicopter is available or non-available, and therefore the valid value uc51108_NH90FleetAvail/serialPV/flta/avail/status/state are A (available) or N (non-available)
- the helicopter non availability causes are CUS, OTH, SB, SCH, USCH, RET, MIS, which are valid values for /n1:isfDataset/ uc51108_NH90FleetAvail /serialPV/flta/avail/navcau/ causeType/code
- the flown flight hours are measured, and therefore the uc51108_NH90FleetAvail / serialPV/mpoints/mPoint/mPointVal/vdtm valid value is MEAS in hour, and therefore the uc51108_NH90FleetAvail/serialPV/mpoints/mPoint/mPointVal/unit valid value is FH

Note:
XPath is used to precisely locate elements for which valid value are defined. Refer to Para 6.4.

6 XML messages

An example of, using XML messages is:

- the message Fleet_Availability sent by operator to manufacturer
- the message Acknowledgment sent by manufacturer to operator
- the message Observation sent by manufacturer to operator

All these messages are built with data displayed in PDF form described at Para 2.

Note:
In real project, data exchanged is already existing in information system. Therefores, it is possible to extract relevant data in an ad-hoc format (eg, MS™ Excel, csv, text, etc) and transform it to populate an XML message. Doing this Extraction, Transformation Loading (ETL) on a significant amount of data validates the data exchange protocol (ie, XML structure, business rules, etc) before entering into development of an industrial solution.

6.1 Message for the Fleet_Availability use case

Fig 15 shows a message Fleet_Availabilty, which is used by an operator to communicate feedback about helicopter status and flown flight hours.

This message gives information for one helicopter during a week. The same message structure can hold information for a fleet of helicopters and a different time period (eg, days, months, years.).

```
<n1:isfDataset xmlns:n1="http://www.asd-europe.org/s-series/s5000f"
        xmlns:xsi="http://www.w3.org/2001/XMLSchema-instance"
        crud="I"
        uid="msg670252383139096503"
        xsi:schemaLocation="http://www.asd-europe.org/s-series/s5000f">

    <!-- ********************************************** Message header ********************************************** -->
    <msgId><id>NH90 availability and flight hours feedback</id></msgId>
    <msgDate><date>2020-11-15</date><time>14:27:00</time></msgDate>
    <msgStatus><state>F</state></msgStatus>
    <msgType><code>Fleet_Availability</code></msgType>

    <!-- ********************************************** Message content ********************************************** -->
    <uc50000>
        <!-- Operating bases -->
        <opBase uid="facility7142199206638069214">
            <fcltyId><id>LFTH</id><setBy><orgId><id>OACI</id></orgId></setBy></fcltyId>
            <fcltyName><name>Toulon-Le Palyvestre/Hyeres International</name></fcltyName></opBase>
        <opBase uid="facility1341478319740026895">
            <fcltyId><id>LFRL</id><setBy><orgId><id>OACI</id></orgId></setBy></fcltyId>
            <fcltyName><name>Lanveoc Poulmic Airport</name></fcltyName></opBase>
        <!-- SerialProductVariant -->
        <serialPV uid="serialPV1093">
            <prodId><id>NH90</id></prodId>
            <prodVarId><id>NFRN</id></prodVarId>
            <serPVId><id>1093</id><setBy><orgId><id>FA2A5</id></orgId></setBy></serPVId>
            <serPVId><id>NH-0055</id><setBy><orgId><id>F7973</id></orgId></setBy></serPVId>
            <!-- Helicopter's operating base -->
            <spvob><opBaseRef uidRef="facility1341478319740026895"/></spvob>
            <!-- AvailabilityItem -->
            <flta>
                <avail>
                    <avId><id>STATUS-1093-2016-CW36</id></avId>
                    <avDate><startDate>2016-09-05</startDate><endDate>2016-09-10</endDate></avDate>
                    <status><state>A</state></status></avail>
                <avail>
                    <avId><id>STATUS-1093-2016-CW36</id></avId>
                    <avDate><startDate>2016-09-11</startDate><endDate>2016-09-11</endDate></avDate>
                    <status><state>N</state></status>
                    <navcau>
                        <causeId><id>SERVICE BULLETIN</id></causeId>
                        <causeType><code>SB</code></causeType>
                        <descr><descr>Applicaion of Service Bulletin</descr></descr>
                        <navCause>
                            <servBuRef><docId><id>SBP-JA-A25-12-03-02A-A-A-001</id></docId></servBuRef></navCause>
                            </navcau></avail></flta>
        <!-- MeasurementPoint -->
        <mpoints>
            <mPoint>
                <mPointId><id>TotalFH-CW36</id></mPointId>
                <mPointVal>
                    <recDate><date>2016-09-11</date></recDate>
                    <vdtm>MEAS</vdtm>
                    <unit>FH</unit>
                    <value>6.58</value></mPointVal></mPoint></mpoints></serialPV></uc50000>

    <!-- ********************************************** Message trailer ********************************************** -->
    <msgContext>
        <context><projRef><projId><id>NH90 Fleet Availability</id></projId></projRef></context></msgContext>
    <msgPty>
        <ptyType><code>S</code></ptyType>
        <party><orgRef><orgId><id>FAJ24</id></orgId></orgRef></party></msgPty>
    <msgPty>
        <ptyType><code>R</code></ptyType>
        <party><orgRef><orgId><id>FA2A5</id></orgId></orgRef></party></msgPty>
    <secs>
        <sec><secClassDefRef><secClass><name>NUC</name></secClass></secClassDefRef></sec></secs>
</n1:isfDataset>
```

ICN-B6865-5000F24001-015-01

Fig 15 Example of message fleet availability

6.1.1 Comments on the message fleet_Availability

6.1.1.1 Element id

S5000F XSD identifies information with identifier element. This identifier element has a mandatory child element `<id>` which contains text. It is recommended that a clear explanation of the information is contained in the element `<id>`.

For example, in `<avail><avId><id>STATUS-1093-2016-CW36</id></avId>`, the element `<avId>` is an availability identifier with a child element `<id>`. The text of the element `<id>` declares that the element `<avail>` is a record of the status of helicopter 1093 during 36th week in 2016.

XSD does not enforce that text in this `<id>` element is unique within the xml instance. For example, in the example there are two identical occurrences of the element `<id>STATUS-1093-2016-CW36</id>`.

Business rules must be agreed to ensure that meaningful text is stored in the element `<id>`. In some case, it is possible to use domain specific usage.

For example, International Civil Aviation Organization (ICAO) allocates a three or four-letter alphabetic identifier to airport facilities, in this case, LFTH in `<id>LFTH</id>` is clearly identifying Lanveoc airport.

Similarly, all entities involved with military aircraft are identified with a five-character Commercial and Government Entity (CAGE) code. In the example, the message sender and receiver are unambiguously identified by this code by `<orgId><id>FA2A5</id></orgId>`.

6.1.1.2 Attribute uid

In XSD there are ID and IDREFER TO types to manage references within an xml instances. The attribute having an ID type, uniquely identifies its element within a document. The attribute type IDREFER TO indicates that the attribute can contain only a value that matches an ID value within the same document.

The S5000F attribute, `uid` has an ID type, and the `uidRef` has an IDREFER TO type. In addition, the values in the attributes `uid` and `uidRef` must be compliant with a pattern given for each type of element.

In the example message `<opBase uid="facility7142199206638069214">`, the operating base is uniquely defined within the message by its `uid` value which is compliant with pattern `"facility[1-9][0-9]*"` as required by the S5000F XSD.

The XML parser will check that:

- the `uid` value is unique within the XML document, and no different elements have the same `uid`
- the `uidRef` refers to a `uid` which is existing in the XML document, and there is no broken link

If an XML document is successfully parsed, it means that this document is self-contained (all references are pointing to uniquely-defined internal element).

Note 1

The agreed business rule defines the element `<id>`. This `<id>` can feed a hash function to get a number. By concatenating this number with required pattern, a unique `uid` is obtained (unless there is a collision in the hashing function):

Hash `(LFTH)` = 7142199206638069214 to get facility 7142199206638069214

This solution allows to translate an agreed business rule into an 'understandable' identifier (the `<id>` element) and an 'information system' identifier (the attribute `<uid>`).

Note 2

An XML parser can control ID/IDREFER TO only within an XML instance, the reference across messages cannot be based on ID/IDREFER TO mechanism.

An example of a message and its acknowledgment message is:

— Fleet Availability message is uniquely identified within sender organization by a `uid` in its root element `<n1:isfdataset uid="msg6702523831390096503">`.

— Acknowledgment message Refers to Fleet Availability message by an `<id>` element (not its `uidRef` attribute). To ensure an unambiguous reference, a `<setBy>` element identifies the organization which has created the `uid`.

```
<relatedMsg>
   <relType><code>A</code></relType> <msgRefer to >
     <msgId>
        <id>msg6702523831390096503</id>
        <setBy><orgId><id>FAJ24</id></orgId></setBy> </msgId>
   </msgRefer to >
 </relatedMsg>
```

— If the attribute `uidRef` is used, parsing of the acknowledgment message fails because the corresponding attribute, `uid` is not in the message.

6.1.1.3 Element setBy

The element `<setBy>` specifies who has assigned the identifier and thus allows synonyms to coexist. For example, a manufacturer allocates a serial number to helicopters but operators create their own different identifiers. Using the element `<setBy>` both identifiers are used, and so any ambiguity with a limited increase of exchanged data is avoided. Refer to Fig 16.

```
<!-- SerialProductVariant -->
<serialPV uid="serialPV1093">
    <prodId><id>NH90</id></prodId>
    <prodVarId><id>NFRN</id></prodVarId>
    <serPVId><id>1093</id><setBy><orgId><id>FA2A5</id></orgId></setBy></serPVId>
    <serPVId><id>NH-0055</id><setBy><orgId><id>F7973</id></orgId></setBy></serPVId>
```

ICN-B6865-5000F24001-016-01

Fig 16 setBy example

6.2 Acknowledgment message

Fig 17 shows an acknowledgment message for answering a message Fleet_Availabilty. (refer to Fig 15. According to this business use case (refer to Fig 2), the manufacturer issues this message to inform the operator that his message was successfully parsed and information about helicopter status and flown flight hours will be processed.

Fig 18 shows an observation message informs the operator that his message cannot be processed because it infringes business rules for the element `<rmks>`.

```
<?xml version="1.0" encoding="UTF-8"?>
<n1:isfDataset xmlns:n1="http://www.asd-europe.org/s-series/s5000f"
               xmlns:xsi="http://www.w3.org/2001/XMLSchema-instance"
               crud="I"
               uid="msg8806989794578433218"
               xsi:schemaLocation="http://www.asd-europe.org/s-series/s5000f">
<!-- ********************************* Message header ************************** -->
<msgId><id>Acknowledgment of FleetAvailability</id></msgId>
<msgDate><date>2020-11-15</date><time>15:27:00</time></msgDate>
<msgStatus><state>F</state></msgStatus>
<msgType><code>Acknowledgment</code></msgType>
<!-- ********************************* Message content ************************** -->
<uc50000/>
<!-- ********************************* Message trailer ************************** -->
<msgContext>
    <context><projRef><projId><id>NH90 Fleet Availability</id></projId></projRef></context></msgContext>
<msgPty>
    <ptyType><code>S</code></ptyType>
    <party><orgRef><orgId><id>FA2A5</id><class>CAGE</class></orgId></orgRef></party></msgPty>
<msgPty>
    <ptyType><code>R</code></ptyType>
    <party><orgRef><orgId><id>FAJ24</id><class>CAGE</class></orgId></orgRef></party></msgPty>
<relatedMsg>
    <relType><code>A</code></relType>
    <msgRef>
        <msgId><id>msg6702523831390096503</id>
        <setBy><orgId><id>FAJ24</id></orgId></setBy></msgId></msgRef></relatedMsg>
<secs>
    <sec><secClassDefRef><secClass><name>NUC</name></secClass></secClassDefRef></sec></secs>
</n1:isfDataset>
```

ICN-B6865-5000F24001-017-01

Fig 17 Example of acknowledgment message

6.3   Observation message

```xml
<?xml version="1.0" encoding="UTF-8"?>
<n1:isfDataset xmlns:n1="http://www.asd-europe.org/s-series/s5000f"
 xmlns:xsi="http://www.w3.org/2001/XMLSchema-instance"
 crud="I" uid="msg7336027408551221798"
 xsi:schemaLocation="http://www.asd-europe.org/s-series/s5000f">
    <!-- ******************************** Message header ************************** -->
    <msgId><id>Observation about Fleet_Availability</id></msgId>
    <msgDate><date>2020-11-15</date><time>15:27:00</time></msgDate>
    <msgStatus><state>F</state></msgStatus>
    <msgType><code>Observation</code></msgType>
    <!-- ******************************** Message content ************************** -->
    <uc50000/>
    <!-- ******************************** Message trailer ************************** -->
    <msgContext>
        <context><projRef><projId><id>NH90 Fleet Availability</id></projId></projRef></context></msgContext>
    <msgPty>
        <ptyType><code>S</code></ptyType>
        <party><orgRef><orgId><id>FA2A5</id><class>CAGE</class></orgId></orgRef></party></msgPty>
    <msgPty>
        <ptyType><code>R</code></ptyType>
        <party><orgRef><orgId><id>FAJ24</id><class>CAGE</class></orgId></orgRef></party></msgPty>
    <relatedMsg>
        <relType><code>O</code></relType>
        <msgRef>
            <msgId><id>msg6702523831390096503</id>
            <setBy><orgId><id>FAJ24</id></orgId></setBy></msgId></msgRef></relatedMsg>
    <rmks>
        <rmk><text><descr>Business rule BR-011 infringement</descr></text></rmk>
        <rmk><text><descr>Business rule BR-053 infringement</descr></text></rmk></rmks>
    <secs>
        <sec><secClassDefRef><secClass><name>NUC</name></secClass></secClassDefRef></sec></secs>
</n1:isfDataset>
```

ICN-B6865-5000F24001-018-01

Fig 18 Example of observation message

6.4   Localization of xml information

The XML Path Language (refer to Table 1), can be used to precisely locate information within an XML instance. In Fig 19, the column Pathname contains an XPath expression which precisely locates the value in the example message Fleet_Availability.

This representation can be useful to precisely identify information within document, to extract data from an XML instance or to create an XML instance from other data formats.

Pathname	Value
/n1:isfDataset/@uid	msg670252383139096503
/n1:isfDataset/msgId/id	NH90 availability and flight hours feedback
/n1:isfDataset/msgDate/date	15/11/2020
/n1:isfDataset/msgDate/time	14:27:00
/n1:isfDataset/msgStatus/state	F
/n1:isfDataset/msgType/code	Fleet_Availability
/n1:isfDataset/uc50000/opBase[1]/@uid	facility7142199206638069214
/n1:isfDataset/uc50000/opBase[1]/fcltyId/id	LFTH
/n1:isfDataset/uc50000/opBase[1]/fcltyId/setBy/orgId/id	OACI
/n1:isfDataset/uc50000/opBase[1]/fcltyName/name	Toulon-Le Palyvestre/Hyeres International
/n1:isfDataset/uc50000/opBase[2]/@uid	facility1341478319740026895
/n1:isfDataset/uc50000/opBase[2]/fcltyId/id	LFRL
/n1:isfDataset/uc50000/opBase[2]/fcltyId/setBy/orgId/id	OACI
/n1:isfDataset/uc50000/opBase[2]/fcltyName/name	Lanveoc Poulmic Airport
/n1:isfDataset/uc50000/serialPV/@uid	serialPV1093
/n1:isfDataset/uc50000/serialPV/prodId/id	NH90
/n1:isfDataset/uc50000/serialPV/prodVarId/id	NFRN
/n1:isfDataset/uc50000/serialPV/serPVId[1]/id	1093
/n1:isfDataset/uc50000/serialPV/serPVId[1]/setBy/orgId/id	FA2A5
/n1:isfDataset/uc50000/serialPV/serPVId[2]/id	NH-0055
/n1:isfDataset/uc50000/serialPV/serPVId[2]/setBy/orgId/id	F7973
/n1:isfDataset/uc50000/serialPV/spvob/opBaseRef/@uidRef	facility1341478319740026895
/n1:isfDataset/uc50000/serialPV/flta/avail[1]/avId/id	STATUS-1093-2016-CW36
/n1:isfDataset/uc50000/serialPV/flta/avail[1]/avDate/startDate	2016-09-05
/n1:isfDataset/uc50000/serialPV/flta/avail[1]/avDate/endDate	2016-09-10
/n1:isfDataset/uc50000/serialPV/flta/avail[1]/status/state	A
/n1:isfDataset/uc50000/serialPV/flta/avail[2]/avId/id	STATUS-1093-2016-CW36
/n1:isfDataset/uc50000/serialPV/flta/avail[2]/avDate/startDate	2016-09-11
/n1:isfDataset/uc50000/serialPV/flta/avail[2]/avDate/endDate	2016-09-11
/n1:isfDataset/uc50000/serialPV/flta/avail[2]/status/state	N
/n1:isfDataset/uc50000/serialPV/flta/avail[2]/navcau/causeId/id	SERVICE BULLETIN
/n1:isfDataset/uc50000/serialPV/flta/avail[2]/navcau/causeType/code	SB
/n1:isfDataset/uc50000/serialPV/flta/avail[2]/navcau/descr/descr	Application of Service Bulletin
/n1:isfDataset/uc50000/serialPV/flta/avail[2]/navcau/navCause/servBuRef/docId	SBP-JA-A25-12-03-02A-A-A-001
/n1:isfDataset/uc50000/serialPV/mpoints/mPoint/mPointId/id	TotalFH-CW36
/n1:isfDataset/uc50000/serialPV/mpoints/mPoint/mPointVal/recDate/date	2016-09-11
/n1:isfDataset/uc50000/serialPV/mpoints/mPoint/mPointVal/vdtm	MEAS
/n1:isfDataset/uc50000/serialPV/mpoints/mPoint/mPointVal/unit	FH
/n1:isfDataset/uc50000/serialPV/mpoints/mPoint/mPointVal/value	6.58
/n1:isfDataset/msgContext/context/projRef/projId/id	NH90 Fleet Availability
/n1:isfDataset/msgPty[1]/ptyType/code	S
/n1:isfDataset/msgPty[1]/party/orgRef/orgId/id	FAJ24
/n1:isfDataset/msgPty[2]/ptyType/code	R
/n1:isfDataset/msgPty[2]/party/orgRef/orgId/id	FA2A5
/n1:isfDataset/secs/sec/secClassDefRef/secClass/name	NUC

ICN-B6865-5000F24019-001-01

Fig 19 Information location using X-Path

Page intentionally blank.

Chapter 30

Terms, abbreviations and acronyms

Table of contents

Page

Terms, abbreviations and acronyms 1

References 1

1   Introduction 2

2   Scope 2

3   Terms 2

4   Abbreviations and acronyms 17

4.1   General 17

4.2   Word combination - Acronym 17

4.3   Abbreviation and acronym list 17

List of tables

1 References 1

2 Terms 2

3 Abbreviations and acronyms 17

References

Table 1 References

Chap No./Document No.	Title
S3000L	International procedure specification for Logistics Support Analysis (LSA)
S4000P	International specification for developing and continuously improving preventive maintenance
SX000i	International specification for Integrated Product Support (IPS)
SX001G	Glossary for the S-Series IPS specifications
ARMP-7	NATO R&M terminology applicable to ARMPs
DEF STAN 00-42	Reliability & Maintainability (R&M) Assurance Guide
DEF STAN 00-56	Safety Management Requirements for Defence Systems
IEC 60050-191	International Electrotechnical Vocabulary. Chapter 191: Dependability and quality of service
ISO 10303-239	Industrial automation systems and integration -- Product data representation and exchange -- Part 239: Application protocol: Product life cycle support
MIL-HDBK-61A	Military Handbook Configuration Management Guide
RTCA DO-178B	Software Considerations in Airborne Systems and Equipment Certification

1 Introduction

It is necessary to be precise in the usage of terms across the whole specification and clarify the use of acronyms and abbreviations across this document.

2 Scope

This chapter includes a comprehensive terminology dictionary for the terms used throughout this specification in Para 3. A complete list of abbreviations and acronyms used throughout this specification is included in Para 4. Both the definitions of the terms and the abbreviations and acronyms are consolidated with those of the other S-Series IPS specifications in SX001G.

3 Terms

The terms defined in Table 2 have been taken as far as feasible from S3000L or other S-Series IPS specifications. When no definition for a term could be found, an alternative was sought referencing other international specifications; a new definition was created only when no alternative could be found.

Table 2   Terms

Term	Definition
Administrative delay time	Administrative time for which maintenance action cannot proceed due to administrative reasons (eg, awaiting approval to start maintenance, budget limitations, coordination requirements). Refer to IEC 60050-191.
Allowed configurations	The different configuration statuses authorized by the Product OEM Engineering, or design authority, in which a Product can be at a given moment during actual operation (Refer to SX000i).
As delivered configuration	The actual configuration (including serial numbers) that the Product has at the moment of the handover from the OEM to the Customer for the entry into service.
As desired configuration	The specified allowed configuration baseline that must be achieved at a certain moment (eg, to return a Product to service or to perform a specific mission).
As-is configuration	As-is configuration is the product configuration (including serial numbers) that exists at a given moment during the in-service (Refer to SX000i).
As maintained configuration	Refer to As-is configuration.
Availability	When the mission or operation is called for at an unknown time, availability measures the extent to which an item is in an operable and ready-for-use state at the start of a mission or operation. Refer to S3000L.
Availability Instantaneous (Point Availability)	Probability that an item is in a state to perform as required at a given instant. Refer to IEC 60050-191.
Availability, Intrinsic (inherent)	Availability value determined when maintenance and operational conditions are assumed to be ideal. Refer to IEC 60050-191.

Term	Definition
Availability, Operational	The probability than an equipment/ system at any instant in the required operating time will operate satisfactorily under stated conditions where the time considered includes operating, corrective and preventative maintenance administrative delay time and logistic delay time. Refer to ARMP-7.
Aviation Critical Safety Item	A part, an assembly, installation equipment, launch equipment, recovery equipment, or support equipment for an aircraft or aviation weapon system if the part, assembly, or equipment contains a characteristic any failure, malfunction, or absence of which could cause a catastrophic or critical failure resulting in the loss of or serious damage to the aircraft or weapon system, an unacceptable risk of personal injury or loss of life, or an non-commanded engine shutdown that jeopardizes safety. (Refer to Public law 108-136, sec 802.
Baseline Configuration	A basic allowed configuration from which by means of equipment exchange all other allowed configurations can be achieved without having to embody a modification.
Built -In Test	Built in tests (BIT) are implemented on items to enable them to carry out some self-testing up to a given degree. Usually three types of built in test are implemented: (a) power-on built-in tests (P-BIT) executed at start-up of the item (b) continuous built-in tests (C-BIT), periodically and automatically executed during the operation of the item, without any intervention from the operating crew (c) initiated built-in tests (I-BIT), executed upon order from the operator or from the maintenance team. Each of these types of tests detects specific categories of failures. Refer to S3000L.
Capability (of an item)	The ability to meet a service demand of given quantitative characteristics under given conditions. Refer to IEC 60050-191.
Cataloguing	The process of accounting for items and arranging them systematically with descriptive details to include naming, describing, classifying and assigning a unique combination of letters and numerals, or both, for easy retrieval of the item information.
Cause, external	A cause is said to be external when an event independent of Product usage occurs, eg, a bird-strike.

Term	Definition
Certification	Legal recognition by the certification authority that a Product, service, organization or person complies with the requirements. Such certification comprises the activity of technically checking the Product, service, organization or person and the formal recognition of compliance with the applicable requirements by issue of a certificate, license, approval or other documents as required by national laws and procedures. Specifically, certification of a Product involves:
	(a) the process of assessing the design of a Product to ensure that it complies with a set of standards applicable to that type of Product to demonstrate an acceptable level of safety
	(b) the process of assessing an individual Product to ensure that it conforms with the certified type design
	(c) the issuance of a certificate required by national laws to declare that compliance or conformity has been found with standards in accordance with items (a) or (b) above. Refer to RTCA DO-178B.
Certification Authority	The organization or person responsible within the state or country concerned with the certification of compliance with the requirements. Refer to RTCA DO-178B.
Combat Capability	The potential ability to do combat work, perform a combat function or combat mission, achieve a combat objective or provide a combat service
Commercial Off- The-Shelf	Software or hardware that is ready-made and available for sale, lease, or license to the public. This term is typically used in reference to technology products. Refer to S3000L.
Common Cause	Some failures can lead to several malfunctions. For instance, the failure of a power supply leads to a malfunction of all its supplied items. This type of failure with multiple impacts is called a common cause. Refer to S3000L.
Concession	Concession is an authorization granted before execution to depart from a particular performance of the contract, specification or reference document.
Condition Based Maintenance	Maintenance initiated as a result of knowledge of the condition of an item of equipment gained from routine or continuous monitoring. Refer to JSP 817.
Condition monitoring	Obtaining information about physical state or operational parameters. Refer to IEC 60050-191.
Configuration control	1) The establishment of an agreed build standard for an item and the procedure for controlling change to that standard, in order that it can be defined at any time. Refer to ARMP-7.
	2) A systematic process that ensures that changes to released configuration documentation are properly identified, documented, evaluated for impact, approved by an appropriate level of authority, incorporated, and verified. Refer to MIL-HDBK-61A.

Term	Definition
Configuration identification	(1) The process of designating the configuration items in a system and recording their characteristic. Refer to RTCA DO-178B.
	(2) The approved documentation that defines a configuration item Refer to RTCA DO-178B.
	(3) The systematic process of selecting the system attributes, organizing associated information about the attributes, and stating the attributes. Refer to MIL-HDBK-61A.
Configuration item	An element or set of elements, being hardware, software or a combination of both, or any of its discrete parts, which performs a final function, and which is decided to be subject to configuration control. This is an element that forms part of the configuration tree.
Configuration Item	A hardware, software, or combination of both that satisfies an end user function and is designed for separate configuration management. Refer to MIL-HDBK-61A.
Configuration management	(1) The process of identifying and defining the configuration items of a system, controlling the release and change of these items throughout the software life cycle, recording and reporting the status of configuration items and change requests and verifying the completeness and correctness of configuration items.
	(2) A discipline applying technical and administrative direction and surveillance to:
	(a) identify and record the functional and physical characteristics of a configuration item
	(b) control changes to those characteristics
	(c) record and report change control processing and implementation status. Refer to RTCA DO-178B.
	(3) A management process for establishing and maintaining consistency of a system's performance, functional, and physical attributes with its requirements, design and operational information throughout its life. Refer to MIL-HDBK-61A.
Configuration slot	Specific position within the Product configuration tree that can be occupied by a configuration item. A configuration item is identified by the configuration item identifier and the position it occupies. For less complex Products (eg, equipment) where the position is irrelevant, the configuration item can be identified exclusively by its identifier.
Configuration status accounting	The recording and reporting of the information necessary to manage a configuration effectively, including a listing of the approved configuration identification, the status of proposed changes to the configuration and the implementation status of approved changes. Refer to RTCA DO-178B.
Configuration tree	The representation of the Product baseline configuration, formed by blocks and structured hierarchically.
Damage	A loss or reduction of functionality, excluding inherent failure (intrinsic reliabilities). Normally a maintenance task will be required. Damages can be grouped into damage families, eg, concerning structures; typical damage can be identified like scratches, dents or cracks. These damage families are typical candidates for a standard repair procedure. Refer to S3000L.

Term	Definition
Damage, accidental	Physical deterioration of an item caused by contact or impact with an object or influence which is not part of the Product, or by human error during manufacturing, operation of the Product, or maintenance practices. Refer to S4000P.
Data	Recorded information of any nature (including administrative, managerial, financial, and technical) regardless of medium or characteristics. Refer to MIL-HDBK-61A. Reinterpretable representation of information in a formalized manner suitable for communication, interpretation, or processing. Refer to IEC 2382-1 101-12-03.
Data cluster	Family of data related to a single concept.
Data element	1) a value contained in a single message field 2) atomic unit of data
Data element list (DEL)	A list of selected data elements, generally given by the output of a data element tailoring process. This list contains all the data elements required for a project, and is not necessarily limited to data elements pre-defined by any particular information standard. Refer to S3000L.
Data Item	A document or collection of documents that must be submitted by the performing activity to the procuring or tasking activity to fulfill a contract or tasking directive requirement for the delivery of information. Refer to MIL-HDBK-61A.
Data sub-cluster	Subset of a data cluster focused on a specific type of data. As an example, Flight Fault Reports is a sub-cluster of Technical Information. Organizational Level removals is a sub-cluster of Organizational Level Events. Depot Level Events is a sub-cluster of Shop Events. Applicable configuration is a sub-cluster of Reference Data. The sub-cluster concept has only been created to ease the analysis of data elements required to implement feedback processes. It is a first-tier breakdown of data clusters.
Decommissioning	Decommissioning is the process of retiring, disassembling and dismantling a Product.
Defect	Any nonconformity of an item to its specified requirements. A defect does not necessarily result in a failure of the item. Refer to S3000L.
Deviation	The authorization to deviate from a particular requirement of an approved Product/equipment configuration for a specified period. Deviations allow the acceptance of a Product/equipment that does not fully meet a particular requirement, but is considered suitable for use either as-is, after repair, or after modification by an approved method. Refer to S3000L.
Dependability	The collective term used to describe the availability performance and its influencing factors: reliability performance, maintainability performance and maintenance support performance. Refer to IEC 60050-191.
Diagnostic test	Test procedure carried out in order to make a diagnosis. Refer to IEC 60050-191.

Term	Definition
Dispatch Interruption Rate	Ratio of the number of delays and cancellations, whose imputation is technical and intrinsic to the Product, on the number of scheduled sorties (%)
Document	A self-contained body of information or data that can be packaged for delivery on a single medium. (eg, drawings, reports, standards, databases, application software, engineering designs, virtual part-models, etc). Refer to MIL-HDBK-61A.
Down time (maximum)	The acceptable (maximum) down time (MDT), where MDT is the time where an item is non-operational.
Durability	Ability to perform as required under given conditions of use and maintenance until a limiting state is reached. Refer to IEC 60050-191.
Engineering Change Proposal	The documentation by which a proposed engineering change is described, justified, and submitted to: (a) the current document change authority for approval or disapproval of the design change in the documentation (b) to the procuring activity for approval or disapproval of implementing the design change in units to be delivered or retrofit into assets already delivered. Refer to MIL-HDBK-61A.
Environment	Environment refers to the surroundings or conditions in which a Product is maintained or in which it operates. **Examples** – Desert conditions – Artic conditions – Closed (un)heated building – High altitude – High salty air humidity
environmental	Environmental refers to the natural world and the impact of human activity on its condition. **Examples** – Pollution due to Product operation – Contamination due to the disposal of chemical products
Event	An important happening or occurrence at a specific point in time that needs to be documented or recorded.
Event description	Description of the failure event or special event that can cause a related failure mode.
Event record	Record which describes the action performed on a Product, and its results
Failure	A failure occurs when an item does not perform to the level required by its performance specification under normal use and prevents further use of the item. Refer to S3000L.
Failure cause	Any circumstance leading to a particular failure that occurred during Product design, manufacture or use. Refer to S3000L.

Term	Definition
Failure condition	Failure condition is the effect on the Product and its occupants, both direct and consequential, caused or contributed to by one or more failures, considering relevant adverse operational or environmental conditions. Refer to S4000P.
Failure criteria	Failure criteria are predefined conditions or limits to be accepted as conclusive evidence of failure. Refer to IEC 60050-191 Ed 2.0.
Failure effect	Failure effect is the consequence of a failure in terms of operation function or status of the item and higher system levels. Refer to IEC 60050-191 Ed 2.0.
Failure mechanism	Failure mechanism is the process that leads to failure. Refer to IEC 60050-191 Ed 2.0.
Failure mode	Failure mode is the manner in which the failure occurs and can be defined by the function lost or the state transition that occurred. Refer to IEC 60050-191 Ed 2.0. The end result of a predicted or observed physical, mechanical, thermal or other process whose end result can or has led to a failure. The failure mode is stated relative to the operating conditions at the time of the failure. Refer to S3000L.
Failure mode probability	Defines how often a specific event (failure, damage or special event) results in a specific failure mode.
Failure rate	Failure rate is the number of failures of an item per unit of measure, expressed in hours cycles, kilometers as applicable to the item. Refer to IEC 60050-191. The probability of a failure occurring. It is expressed in failures per unit of operating time. Refer to S3000L.
Failure, critical	Critical failure is a failure that could result in injury to persons or that prevents an item from performing an essential mission. Refer to IEC 60050-191.
Failure, primary	Primary failure is a failure not caused either directly or indirectly by a failure or fault of another item Refer to IEC 60050-191.
Fault	Fault is a state characterized by an inability to perform as required. Refer to IEC 60050-191 Ed 2.0. Fault is an identifiable condition in which one element of a redundant system has failed (no longer available) without impact on the required function output of the system (MSI). At the system level, a fault is not considered a functional failure. Refer to S4000P.
Fault found, Primary	Primary fault found is a failure not caused either directly or indirectly by a failure or fault of another item. Refer to IEC 60050-191.
Fault found, Secondary	Secondary fault found are all failures which are not originally caused by the equipment itself. Refer to IEC 60050-191.
Fault, software	Software fault is a condition of a software item (software bug) that can prevent it from performing as required. Refer to IEC 60050-191.
Fault Diagnosis	Fault diagnosis is an action to identify and characterize the fault. Refer to IEC 60050-191.

Term	Definition
Feedback	Feedback is any data transfer process between different stakeholders during the in-service of a Product.
Field loadable software	Software that can be installed into one or several pieces of equipment of a Product, without the need to remove the equipment from its installed location. Refer to S3000L.
Firmware	Software that can be loaded into a Line Replaceable Unit or Shop Replaceable Unit, but requires the host component to be removed from its installation location on the operational system and subsequently replaced. Refer to S3000L.
Fleet	A group of Products operated under unified control (eg, ships, aircraft, trucks, buses, robots, sensors, computers, etc).
Function	The normal characteristic actions of an item. Refer to S4000P.
Functional characteristics	Quantitative performance parameters and design constraints, including operational and logistic parameters and their respective tolerances. Functional characteristics include all performance parameters, such as range, speed, lethality, reliability, maintainability, and safety. Refer to MIL-HDBK-61A.
Functional check	A quantitative check to determine if one or more functions of an item or a system perform within specified limits. The task must be able to detect degradation, eg, wear, leakage, etc, and not just the complete failure. Refer to S4000P.
Functional configuration audit	The formal examination of functional characteristics of a configuration item, or system to verify that the item has achieved the requirements specified in its functional and/or allocated configuration documentation. Refer to MIL-HDBK-61A.
Functional failure	Failure of an item or system to perform its intended function within specified limits. Refer to S4000P.
Functional symptom	Refer to symptom.
Functions required	A characteristic or combination of characteristics considered necessary to complete a mission or tasks. Refer to IEC 60050-191.
Hardware part material class	Identifies articles or substances which are capable of posing a significant risk to health, safety or property during transportation, handling or storage.
Integrated Logistics Support (ILS)	Refer to Integrated Product Support (IPS).
Integrated Product Support (IPS)	Integrated Product Support is Product support that ensures that all support elements are considered and harmonized. Refer to SX001G. **Note** Integrated Product Support (IPS) replaces the legacy term Integrated Logistics Support (ILS)
Internal cause	A cause due to an event that results from normal Product usage, (eg, excessive vibration. Refer to S3000L.

Term	Definition
Item	Item is a thing of attention, concern, or interest. Refer to SX001G. **Note** An item can be physical as well as non-physical. **Note** Thing in this context is synonymous with something and anything.
Labor time	The accumulated time of personnel working on an entire task or an individual subtask. If the persons involved are of different competencies, the labor time is reported separately for each area of competency. Refer to S3000L.
Life Cycle Cost (LCC)	All direct costs plus any indirect-variable costs associated with the procurement, operations, support and disposal of the Product, Refer to S3000L.
Line Replaceable Unit (LRU)	Any item or component that is designed to be removed from the Product at its operating location.
Localization (failure)	An indication of which item or group of items has failed. This localization is generally a complement to failure detection. Refer to S3000L.
Logistic delay time	Accumulative time excluding administrative taken to provide resources needed for maintenance to proceed. Refer to IEC 60050-191.
Logistics Support Analysis (LSA)	A structured approach to increasing maintenance efficiency and reducing the cost of providing support by planning all aspects of IPS as far in advance as possible.. Refer to S3000L.
Maintainability	The measure of the ability of an item to be retained in or restored to a specified condition, when maintenance is performed by personnel having specified skill levels, using prescribed procedures and resources, at each prescribed level of maintenance and repair. Refer to S3000L.
Maintenance	Maintenance is an activity that retains or restores a physical item to a specified condition or level of performance. Refer to SX001G.
Maintenance Concept	A strategy for providing maintenance support to ensure that a Product meets its mission performance requirements. Refer to S3000L.
Maintenance free operating period	The acceptable (minimum) maintenance free operating period, where maintenance free operating period is the interval in which no maintenance actions occur.
Maintenance level type name	The name by which a maintenance level type is known
Maintenance Man hours	Sum of the individual personnel times taken to carry out a maintenance action. Refer to IEC 60050-191.
Maintenance significant item	Item that fails often and therefore requires many maintenance actions or that has a significant cost and its maintenance needs therefore to be assessed with special care.
Maintenance time	Time interval for which maintenance is performed including time attributed to maintenance actions and technical and logistic delays. Refer to IEC 60050-191.

Term	Definition
Maintenance Time, Active	That part of the overall maintenance time taken to physically perform a maintenance action and therefore includes fault isolation diagnosis of failure and subsequent testing. Logistic delays are excluded. Refer to IEC 60050-191.
Maintenance, Corrective	All maintenance activities which are carried out to reset a faulty item to full functionality. Refer to S3000L.
Maintenance, Preventive	Maintenance activities for preventing critical failures or damage in conjunction with safety, economical or ecological considerations. The term "preventive maintenance" also includes activities performed after special events, even though the occurrence of these events, chronological intervals between them, and other typical thresholds cannot be defined. Refer to S3000L.
Maintenance, Scheduled	Maintenance activities that prevent the occurrence of critical failures or damages in conjunction with safety, economical or ecological aspects. These maintenance tasks have a corresponding interval or threshold (eg, after a certain amount of elapsed time, cycles completed, rounds expended, or distance traveled). Scheduled maintenance is a subset of preventive maintenance. Refer to S3000L.
Maritime Critical Safety Item	A maritime critical safety item means any ship part, assembly, or support equipment containing a characteristic the failure, malfunction, or absence of which could cause: (1) A catastrophic or critical failure resulting in loss of or serious damage to the ship (2) An unacceptable risk of personal injury or loss of life Refer to 48 CFR 209.270.
Master data	Master data represents the business objects which are agreed on and shared across an enterprise or a project. Master data is a single source of common business data used across multiple systems, applications, and/or processes. Examples of master data are organizations, part numbers, parties, locations, etc.
Mean Active Corrective Maintenance Time	The sum of the average active scheduled/ corrective maintenance times respectively factored by their frequency of repair. Refer to IEC 60050-191.
Mean Time Between Failures (MTBF)	MTBF is the predicted elapsed time between inherent failures of a system during operation. It is calculated as the arithmetic mean (average) time between failures of a system. The MTBF is typically part of a model that assumes the failed system is immediately repaired (zero elapsed time) as a part of a renewal process. In contrast, the Mean Time To Failure (MTTF) measures the average time between failures with the modeling assumption that the failed system is not repaired. Refer to S3000L.
Mean time to First failure	Expected value of the operating time to first failure. Refer to IEC 60050-191.
Mean Variant Between failures (MVBF)	Similar to MTBF but any other variants than time or distance should use MVBF where the variant as appropriate should be defined separately. Refer to IEC 60050-191.

Term	Definition
Mission Capability	Material condition of a Product indicating it can perform at least one and potentially all its designated missions or assigned tasks.
Mission Profile	A time phased description of the events and environments an item experiences from initiation to completion of a specified mission. It identifies the tasks events durations operating conditions and environments for each phase of a mission. Refer to ARMP-7.
Model Identifier	The Model Identifier is a code, which uniquely identifies the Product variant. It is recommended to use the model identifier in conjunction with other identifiers within the entire IPS process.
No Fault Found	When the item is sent for repair with a report of failure but subsequently it is not possible to reproduce or detect the reported failure and the item meets its requirements for return to service.
Non repairable item	Any part or assembly for which user-maintenance is limited to replenishment of consumables and replacement of the part or assembly upon failure or malfunction. Refer to MIL-HDBK-61A.
Obsolescence	Obsolescence is the state of an item that is no longer needed because something newer or more efficient has been invented or its components are no longer available and it can therefore no longer be maintained or operated.
Operating requirement	Value of the (annual) operating requirement per operating location type and contracted Product.
Operating Time	The time when the system or equipment is turned on and/or actively performing at least one of its functions.
Operating Time, essential	The time period during a mission when it is essential that the item is required to be in an operating state. Refer to IEC 60050-191.
Operational check	An operational check is a task to determine that an item is fulfilling its intended purpose. Does not require quantitative tolerances. This is a failure finding task. Refer to S4000P.
Operational Readiness	The capability of a Product to perform the missions or functions for which it is organized or designed. Can be used in a general sense or to express a level or degree of readiness.
Part Number	A set of numbers, letters or other characters used to identify an item.
Party	Party is a term that identifies one side involved in a formal agreement or activity. Refer to SX001G. Note A party can be an agent, a person or an organization. Examples – Buyer – Seller – Manufacturer – Contractor
Person	Person is a living human being. Refer to SX001G.

Term	Definition
Physical breakdown	A top-down representation of hardware and software of a Product based on the engineering design model/drawings. Refer to S3000L.
Physical Configuration Audit (PCA)	The formal examination of the as-built configuration of a configuration item against its technical documentation to establish or verify the configuration item's system baseline. Refer to MIL-HDBK-61A.
Physical symptom	Refer to symptom.
Preventative maintenance	Maintenance carried out to reduce the probability of failure or degradation. Refer to IEC 60050-191.
Product	A final combination of systems, subsystems, component parts/materials, etc, such as an aircraft, a ship, vehicle, or a complex technical system. The Product always represents the top level of any hierarchical breakdown. The S3000L definition is: Any platform, system, or equipment (air, sea, land vehicle, equipment, or facility, civil or military).
Product service life	Product service life is the number of years that the Product is expected to be in service.
Product support	Product support is an activity that develops, enables, executes and maintains a sustainment strategy for the Product.
Prognostics	The process of using one or more parameters to predict the condition of an item at a defined point in its future operation and when it will no longer be able to perform its intended function.
R&M case	A reasoned auditable argument created to support the condition that a defined system will satisfy the Reliability & Maintainability requirements. Refer to DEF STAN 00-42 part 3.
Record	Two or more values or variables stored in consecutive memory positions or database entries.
Recoverability	The ability to achieve restoration (with or without repair) following a failure. Refer to IEC 60050-191.
Rectifying Task	A rectifying task is any support activity that resolves an issue, such as failures, damages, special events, or threshold. Refer to S3000L.
Reference data	The set of permissible values to be used by other (master or transaction) data fields. Typical examples of reference data are units of measure, country codes, fixed conversion rates (eg, weight, temperature or length).
Reliability	The duration or probability of failure-free performance of a Product under stated conditions, or the probability that an item can perform its intended function for a specified period under stated condition. Refer to S3000L.
Reliability Centered Maintenance	A disciplined logic or methodology used to identify scheduled maintenance tasks to maintain the inherent reliability of equipment at a minimum expenditure of resources. Refer to S3000L.
Reliability growth tests	Iterative process to improve reliability through testing until failure analysis implementing corrective action and continuing the test. Refer to IEC 60050-191.

Term	Definition
Reliability, Basic	The ability of an item to perform its required functions without failure or defect for the duration of its life profile. Refer to ARMP-7.
Reliability, Mission	The probability that an item will perform its required functions for the duration of a specified mission profile. Refer to ARMP-7.
Repair	(1) See rectifying task (2) A procedure which reduces, but does not completely eliminate, a nonconformance. Repair is distinguished from rework in that the characteristic after repair still does not completely conform to the applicable drawings, specifications, or contract requirements. Refer to MIL-HDBK-61A.
Repair Time	The part of maintenance time taken to conduct the repair action comprising of fault localization, fault correction and functional check but excludes technical administration and logistic delay. Refer to IEC 60050-191.
Repairable item	Any part or assembly which, upon failure or malfunction, is intended to be repaired or reworked. Refer to MIL-HDBK-61A.
Replacement item	One which is interchangeable with another item, but which differs physically from the original item in that the installation of the replacement item requires operations such as drilling, reaming, cutting, filing, shimming, etc, in addition to the normal application and methods of attachment. Refer to MIL-HDBK-61A.
Required time	The time interval for which the user requires the item to be in an up state (available). Refer to IEC 60050-191.
Routine inspection	Line maintenance of a Product. eg, on an aircraft: Daily- pre-flight, turnaround-/transit-, post-flight inspections. Refer to S4000P.
Safety case	A safety case is a reasoned and supported argument, one way of documenting and providing assurance to the stakeholders that a system is acceptably safe. A safety case generally consists of the argument, usually based upon following a particular safety standard, and the supporting evidence, such as is summarized in or referenced by the hazard log. Refer to DEF STAN 00-56.
Safety Case	A safety case is a structured argument, supported by a body of evidence, that provides a compelling, comprehensible and valid case that a system is safe for a given application in a given environment. Refer to DEF STAN 00-56.
Scheduled maintenance interval	The (minimum) number of operational units (eg, rounds, miles, hours, etc) between scheduled maintenance
Self-diagnose	The ability to detect, react to and highlight an anomaly; where the anomaly could lead to a failure or a failure to perform as defined.
Self-checking	Built-in capability for detecting errors in its own function. Refer to IEC 60050-191.
Self-testing	Built-in test capability for assessing internal system status. Refer to IEC 60050-191.

Term	Definition
Serial number	An identifying number consisting of alpha numeric characters which is assigned sequentially in the order of manufacture or final test and which, in conjunction with a manufacturer's identifying CAGE code, uniquely identifies a single item within a group of similar items identified by a common system-tracking base-identifier. Refer to MIL-HDBK-61A.
Serialized item	Item that has been allocated an individual identifier by the OEM and/or end user so as to be able to track its individual life, status, condition and location.
Service	Service is an activity where technical, physical or intellectual work is performed for another party to fulfill a need or demand. Refer to SX001G.

Note

Does not cover activities that deliver a physical product.

Examples

- Equipment repair
- Availability study
- Car wash
- Facility (re)painting

Term	Definition
Service Level Agreement (SLA)	A contract for the provision of a service that establishes a defined measure of the response time or level of service expected from the service provider.
Servicing	Any act of lubricating or any other servicing tasks like eg, washing, replenishment of consumables, etc, for the purpose of maintaining inherent design capabilities. Refer to S4000P.
Sharable Content Object Reference Model (SCORM)	SCORM is a standard format that different authoring applications use to format content in such a way that the content can easily be imported into a learning management system.
Shop Loadable Software	Software that can be loaded into an LRU but requires the target LRU to be dismounted from where in the system it is located. Refer to S3000L.
Software	Computer programs and, possibly, associated documentation and data pertaining to the operation of a computer system. Refer to RTCA DO-178B.
Standby time	The time interval for which a standby (non-operating time) exists. Refer to IEC 60050-191.
Status record	A record which describes an item at a given moment in time.
Support equipment	Equipment and computer software required to maintain, test, or operate a system or facility in its intended environment. Refer to MIL-HDBK-61A.
Symptom	Evidence of an abnormality directly or indirectly related to the presence of a fault. Refer to S3000L.

- A functional symptom may be observed during a functional check and/or by observing the failure of an item associated with the function.
- A physical symptom may be observed by visual inspection, measurement of a wear-out parameter, material degradation or by other means. It is detectable and/or measurable regardless of the state of operation of the system.

Term	Definition
System Configuration Documentation	A CI's detail design documentation including those verifications necessary for accepting system deliveries (first article and acceptance inspections.) Based on program production/ procurement strategies, the design information contained in the system configuration documentation can be as simple as identifying a specific part number or as complex as full design disclosure. Refer to MIL-HDBK-61A.
System Effectiveness	The probability that the system can successfully meet an operational demand within a given time when operated under specific conditions. Refer to IEC 60050-191.
Task personnel resource labor time	Time expended within a task/subtask per required human resource.
Task total labor time	Total time expended within a task. Includes the labor time for all required personnel resources.
Technical data	Technical data is recorded information (regardless of the form or method of recording) of a scientific or technical nature (including computer software documentation.) Refer to MIL-HDBK-61A.
Technical data package (TDP)	A technical description of an item adequate for supporting an acquisition strategy, production, engineering, and logistics support. The description defines the required design configuration and procedures required to ensure adequacy of item performance. It consists of all applicable technical data such as drawings and associated lists, specifications, standards, performance requirements, quality assurance provisions, and packaging details. Refer to MIL-HDBK-61A.
Technical delay	Accumulative time necessary to perform auxiliary technical actions associated with but not part of the maintenance action. Refer to IEC 60050-191.
Test	Procedure carried out to determine or verify one or more characteristics. Refer to IEC 60050-191.
Testability	Degree to which an item facilitates the establishment of test criteria and the performance of tests. Refer to IEC 60050-191.
Total Ownership Cost (TOC)	All elements that are part of LCC plus the indirect, fixed, linked costs. These latter can include items such as common support equipment, common facilities, personnel required for unit command, administration, supervision, operations planning and control, fuel and munitions handling. (NATO)
Training equipment	Items used in the support of training, such as trainers, operational equipment, and other associated hardware. Refer to MIL-HDBK-61A.
Troubleshooting	Troubleshooting consists of localizing failed replaceable units when this is not obvious or localized by other means such as through a built-in test. Troubleshooting is carried out after a failure has been detected. Refer to S3000L.
Unexpected behavior	System behavior which is neither desired by the system designer nor by the system user, but which however cannot be qualified as non-compliant.

Term	Definition
Use Case	A description of a system's behavior as it responds to a request that originates from outside of that system. In other words, a use case describes who can do what with the system in question. The use case technique is used to capture a system's behavioral requirements by detailing scenario-driven threads through the functional requirements.
Useful Life	Under given conditions, the time interval beginning at a given instant of time and ending when the failure intensity becomes unacceptable or when the item is considered un-repairable as a result of a fault. Refer to IEC 60050-191.
Waiver	Waiver is an authorization granted after execution to depart from a particular performance of the contract, specification or reference document. Refer to SX001G.
Warranty	A warranty is an expressed or implied promise from the seller that certain facts about the items or services being sold are true and that a compensation will be provided if this proves to be not correct.
Whole Life Cost (WLC)	All elements that are part of TOC plus indirect, fixed, non-linked costs. These latter can include items such as family housing, medical services, ceremonial units, basic training, headquarters and staff, academies, recruiters. In WLC all costs or expenses that are made by the organization are attributed to the systems or Products they produce. (NATO)

4 Abbreviations and acronyms

4.1 General

When an abbreviation or an acronym is used in this specification, it is written in full the first time it is used in a chapter.

The abbreviations used in this guide are defined in Table 3.

4.2 Word combination - Acronym

When an acronym combines multiple words, it is always presented the same way in this guide.

Single abbreviations can be combined where necessary, when there is no abbreviation listed for the combination.

4.3 Abbreviation and acronym list

Table 3 Abbreviations and acronyms

Abbreviation	Definition
A/C	Aircraft
AD	Airworthiness Directive
ADR	Alternative Dispute Resolution
AFRA	Aircraft Fleet Recycling Association
AIA	Aerospace Industries Association
AOG	Aircraft On Ground

Abbreviation	Definition
ARMP	Allied Reliability and Maintainability Publication
ASD	AeroSpace and Defence Industries Association of Europe
ATA	Air Transport Association
ATE	Automatic Test Equipment
BEI	Breakdown Element Identifier
BIT	Built-In Test
BITE	Built-In Test Equipment
BOM	Business Object Model
CAA	Civil Aviation Authority (UK)
CAD	Computer-Aided Design
CAMO	Continuous Airworthiness Management Organization
CAS	Chemical Abstracts Service
CAS RN	Chemical Abstracts Service (CAS) Registry Number
C-BIT	Continuous Built-In Test
CBS	Cost Breakdown Structure
CDM	Common Data Model
CHAP	Chapter
CI	Configuration Item
COTS	Commercial Of The Shelf
CRM	Customer Relationship Management
D/L	Depot Level – also called ML3
DB	Database
DEX	Data EXchange specification
DGAC-F	French Direction Générale de l'Aviation Civile
DIN	Deutsches Institut für Normung e.V.
DIR	Dispatch Interruption Rate
DMC	Direct Maintenance Cost
DMEWG	Data Modelling and Exchange Working Group
DOD	Department Of Defense (USA)
EASA	European Aviation Safety Agency
EBS	Equipment Breakdown Structure
ECCAIRS	European Co-ordination Centre for Accident and Incident Reporting Systems

Abbreviation	Definition
EOSL	End Of Service Life
EN	European Norm
ERC	Engineering Record Card
ESG	Elektoniksystem- und Logistik-GmbH
ETOPS	Extended-range Twin-engine Operational Performance Standards
FAA	Federal Aviation Authority (USA)
FFR	Flight Fault Report
FMECA	Failure Mode Effect Criticality Analysis
GCBS	Generic Cost Breakdown Structure
GFF	Government Furnished Facilities
GFI	Government Furnished Information
HAZMAT	Hazardous Material
HMD	Health Monitoring Data
HSE	Health, Safety and Environment
HUMS	Health and Usage Monitoring System
HW	Hardware
I/L	Intermediate Level – also called ML2
I-BIT	Initiated Built-In Test
IATA	International Air Transport Association
ICD	Interface Control Document
ICOR	Input, Control, Output, Resource
IEC	International Electrotechnical Commission
IEEE	Institute of Electrical and Electronics Engineers
IETP	Interactive Electronic Technical Publication
IFM	Integrated Fleet Management
ILS	Integrated Logistics Support
IPS	Integrated Product Support
ISMO	In-Service Maintenance Optimization
ISO	International Standards Organization
KPI	Key Progress Indicator
LCC	Life Cycle Cost
LRI	Liner Replaceable Item

Abbreviation	Definition
LRU	Line Replaceable Unit
LSA	Logistics Support Analysis
LSAR	Logistics Support Analysis Report
LTB	Last Time Buy
MC	Maintenance Cost
MDT	Mean Down Time
ML	Maintenance Level
ML2	Intermediate Level – also called I/L
ML3	Depot Level – also called D/L
MMH	Mean Man-Hours
MMS	Maintenance Management System
MoD	Ministry of Defence (UK)
MRBR	Maintenance Review Board Report
MRO	Maintenance, Repair and Overhaul
MRT	Mean Repair Time
MTA	Maintenance Task Analysis
MTBF	Mean Time Between Failures
MTBUR	Mean Time Between Unscheduled Removal
MTTR	Mean Time To Repair
NATO	North Atlantic Treaty Organization
NFF	No Fault Found
NSN	National Stock Number / NATO Stock Number
O/L	Organizational Level - also called ML1
OASIS	Organization for the Advancement of Structured Information Standards
OBS	Organizational Breakdown Structure
OCM	Original Component Manufacturer
OEM	Original Equipment Manufacturer
OMP	Obsolescence Management Plan
P/N	Part Number
PARA	Paragraph
P-BIT	Power-on Built-In Test
PBL	Performance-Based Logistics

Abbreviation	Definition
PCA	Physical Configuration Audit
PDF	Portable Document Format
PDF	Product Disposal File
PDM	Product Data Management
PHST	Packaging, Handling, Storage and Transportation
PIREP	Pilot Report
PLCS	Product Life-Cycle Support Refer to ISO 10303-239.
PLM	Product Life-cycle Management
PM	Product Manufacturer
PMA	Product Maintainer
POL	Petroleum, Oil and Lubricants
PSM	Platform Specific Model
RAMCT	Reliability, Availability, Maintainability, Capability and Testability
RBS	Readiness Based Sparing
REACH	Registration, Evaluation, Authorisation and Restriction of Chemicals
ROM	Raw Order of Magnitude
RMT	Reliability, Availability and Maintainability
RNAV	Area Navigation, Random navigation
RTCA	Radio Technical Commission for Aeronautics
S/N	Serial Number
SB	Service Bulletin
SCM	Supply Chain Management
SCORM	Sharable Content Object Reference Model
SE	Support Equipment
SHM	Structural Health Monitoring
SLA	Service Level Agreement
SM	Specific Means
SMR	Source, Maintenance and Recoverability
SMS	Safety Management System
SRU	Shop Replaceable Unit
SSG	Symbolic Stream Generator
STANAG	Standardization Agreement

Abbreviation	Definition
STEP	STandard for the Exchange of Product model data
SW	Software
TAT	Turn Around Time
TDP	Technical Data Package
TIR	Technical Investigation Report
TOC	Total Ownership Cost
UK	United Kingdom
UML	Unified Modeling Language
UOF	Unit Of Functionality
WBS	Work Breakdown Structure
WLC	Whole Life Cost
XML	EXtended Mark-up Language

Check out the different specifications in print:

SX000H, *Handbook for the S-Series Integrated Product Support (IPS) Specifications*, Issue 1.0,
ISBN 978-84-19125-18-7

SX000i, *International specification for integrated product support (IPS)*, Issue 3.0, ISBN 978-84-19125-19-4

S1000D, *International specification for technical publications using a common source database*, Issue 5.0,
(3 volumes), ISBN 978-84-19125-31-6, 978-84-19125-32-3 and 978-84-19125-33-0

S2000M, *International specification for material management - Integrated data processing* Issue 7.0,
ISBN 978-84-19125-29-3

S3000L, *International specification for Logistics Support Analysis – LSA*, Issue 2.0,
ISBN 978-84-19125-20-0

S4000P, *International specification for developing and continuously improving preventive maintenance*,
Issue 2.1, ISBN 978-84-19125-21-7

S5000F, *International specification for in-service data feedback*, Issue 3.0 (2 volumes),
ISBNs 978-84-19125-27-9 and 978-84-19125-28-6

S6000T, *International specification for training analysis and design*, Issue 2.0, ISBN 978-84-19125-22-4

SX001G, *Glossary for the S-Series IPS specifications*, Issue 3.0, ISBN 978-84-19125-23-1

SX002D, *Common data model for the S-Series IPS specifications*, Issue 2.1, ISBN 978-84-19125-24-8

SX004G, *UML model reader's guide*, Issue 2.0, ISBN 978-84-19125-25-5

SX005G, *S-Series IPS specifications XML schema implementation guide*, Issue 2.0,
ISBN 978-84-19125-26-2

Other books on the S-Series:

Overview of the S-Series IPS specifications, Issue 6.0, by ASD, ISBN 978-84-19125-02-6

Further books on the S-Series to be published by Editorial Dragon:

An introduction to the S-Series IPS specifications by Ramón Somoza, ISBN 978-84-19125-16-3

S-Series data models and XML schemas by Ramón Somoza, ISBN 978-84-19125-17-0